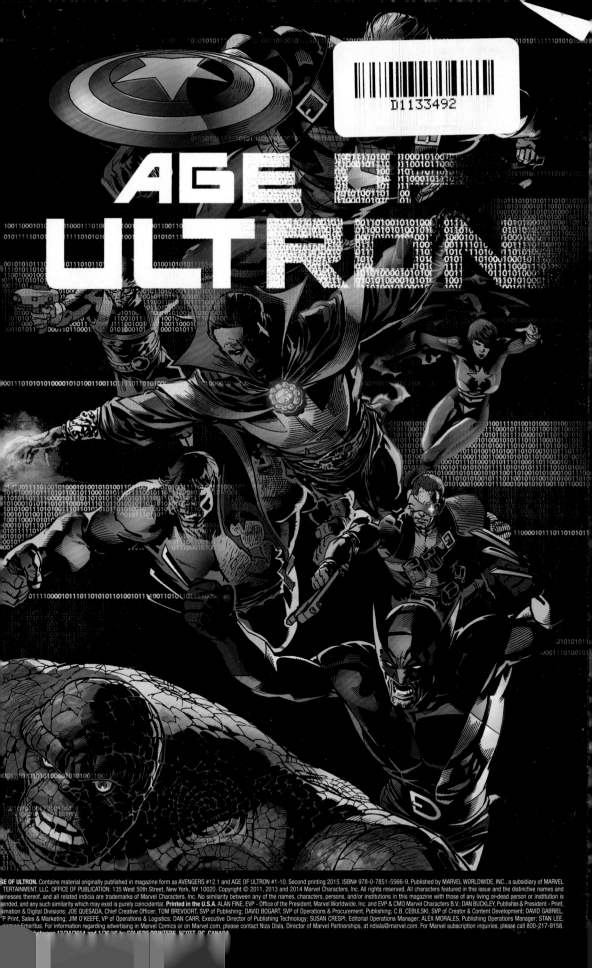

AGE OF ULTRON

GE OF ULTRON. Contains material originally published in magazine form as AVENGERS #12.1 and AGE OF ULTRON #1-10. Second printing 2015. ISBN# 978-0-7851-5566-9. Published by MARVEL WORLDWIDE, INC., a subsidiary of MARVEL
TERTAINMENT, LLC. OFFICE OF PUBLICATION: 135 West 50th Street, New York, NY 10020. Copyright © 2011, 2013 and 2014 Marvel Characters, Inc. All rights reserved. All characters featured in this issue and the distinctive names and
enesses thereof, and all related indicia are trademarks of Marvel Characters, Inc. No similarity between any of the names, characters, persons, and/or institutions in this magazine with those of any living or-dead person or institution is
ended, and any such similarity which may exist is purely coincidental. **Printed in the U.S.A.** ALAN FINE, EVP - Office of the President, Marvel Worldwide, Inc. and EVP & CMO Marvel Characters B.V.; DAN BUCKLEY, Publisher & President - Print,
mation & Digital Divisions; JOE QUESADA, Chief Creative Officer; TOM BREVOORT, SVP of Publishing; DAVID BOGART, SVP of Operations & Procurement, Publishing; C.B. CEBULSKI, SVP of Creator & Content Development; DAVID GABRIEL,
P Print, Sales & Marketing; JIM O'KEEFE, VP of Operations & Logistics; DAN CARR, Executive Director of Publishing Technology; SUSAN CRESPI, Editorial Operations Manager; ALEX MORALES, Publishing Operations Manager; STAN LEE,
airman Emeritus. For information regarding advertising in Marvel Comics or on Marvel.com, please contact Niza Disla, Director of Marvel Partnerships, at ndisla@marvel.com. For Marvel subscription inquiries, please call 800-217-9158.
between 12/24/2014 and 1/26/ by SOLISCO PRINTERS, SCOTT, QC, CANADA.

AGE OF ULTRON

WRITER:
BRIAN MICHAEL BENDIS

ISSUES #1-5 & AVENGERS #12.1
PENCILER: **BRYAN HITCH** INKER: **PAUL NEARY**
COLOR ARTIST: **PAUL MOUNTS**
COVER ART: **BRYAN HITCH, PAUL NEARY** & **PAUL MOUNTS**

ISSUES #6-9
PRESENT/FUTURE, ARTIST: **BRANDON PETERSON**
PRESENT/FUTURE, COLOR ARTIST: **PAUL MOUNTS**
PAST, PENCILER: **CARLOS PACHECO**
PAST, INKER: **ROGER BONET**
PAST, COLOR ARTIST: **JOSE VILLARRUBIA**
COVER ART: **BRANDON PETERSON** (#6-8) WITH **PAUL MOUNTS** (#6)
AND **CARLOS PACHECO** & **JOSE VILLARRUBIA** (#9)

ISSUE #10
ARTISTS: **ALEX MALEEV;**
BRYAN HITCH & **PAUL NEARY;**
BUTCH GUICE; BRANDON PETERSON;
CARLOS PACHECO & **ROGER BONET**
WITH **TOM PALMER; DAVID MARQUEZ;** AND **JOE QUESADA**
COLOR ARTISTS: **PAUL MOUNTS** & **RICHARD ISANOVE**
COVER ART: **BRANDON PETERSON**

LETTERER: **VC'S CORY PETIT**
ASSISTANT EDITORS: **JAKE THOMAS** & **JOHN DENNING**
EDITORS: **TOM BREVOORT** WITH **LAUREN SANKOVITCH**

COLLECTION EDITOR: **JENNIFER GRÜNWALD**
ASSISTANT EDITOR: **SARAH BRUNSTAD**   ASSOCIATE MANAGING EDITOR: **ALEX STARBUCK**
EDITOR, SPECIAL PROJECTS: **MARK D. BEAZLEY**   SENIOR EDITOR, SPECIAL PROJECTS: **JEFF YOUNGQUIST**
SVP PRINT, SALES & MARKETING: **DAVID GABRIEL**   BOOK DESIGNER: **RODOLFO MURAGUCHI**

EDITOR IN CHIEF: **AXEL ALONSO**   CHIEF CREATIVE OFFICER: **JOE QUESADA**
PUBLISHER: **DAN BUCKLEY**   EXECUTIVE PRODUCER: **ALAN FINE**

RAPH
ENDIS

AVENGERS #12.1

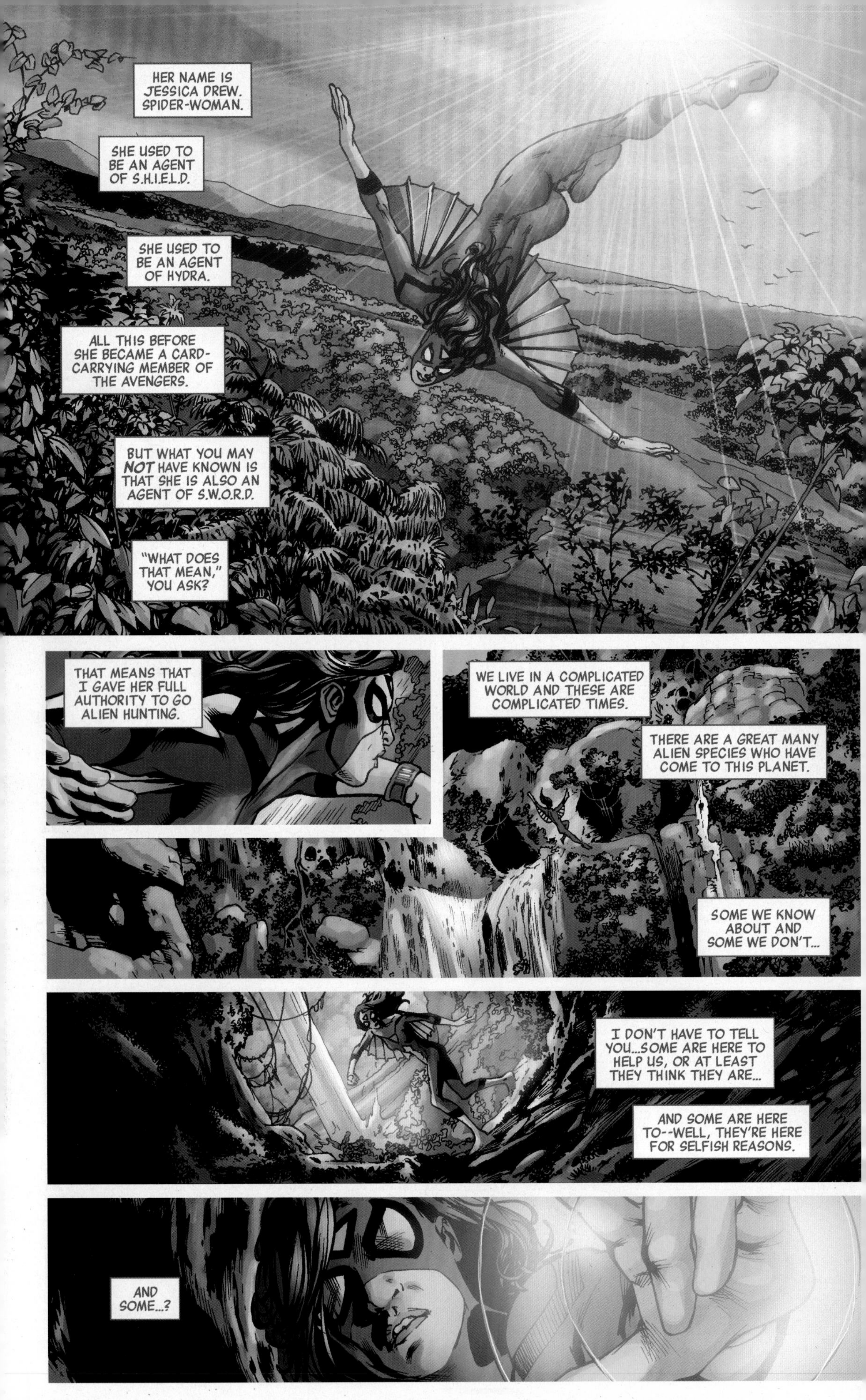
HER NAME IS JESSICA DREW. SPIDER-WOMAN.
SHE USED TO BE AN AGENT OF S.H.I.E.L.D.
SHE USED TO BE AN AGENT OF HYDRA.
ALL THIS BEFORE SHE BECAME A CARD-CARRYING MEMBER OF THE AVENGERS.
BUT WHAT YOU MAY *NOT* HAVE KNOWN IS THAT SHE IS ALSO AN AGENT OF S.W.O.R.D.
"WHAT DOES THAT MEAN," YOU ASK?
THAT MEANS THAT I GAVE HER FULL AUTHORITY TO GO ALIEN HUNTING.
WE LIVE IN A COMPLICATED WORLD AND THESE ARE COMPLICATED TIMES.
THERE ARE A GREAT MANY ALIEN SPECIES WHO HAVE COME TO THIS PLANET.
SOME WE KNOW ABOUT AND SOME WE DON'T...
I DON'T HAVE TO TELL YOU...SOME ARE HERE TO HELP US, OR AT LEAST THEY THINK THEY ARE...
AND SOME ARE HERE TO--WELL, THEY'RE HERE FOR SELFISH REASONS.
AND SOME...?

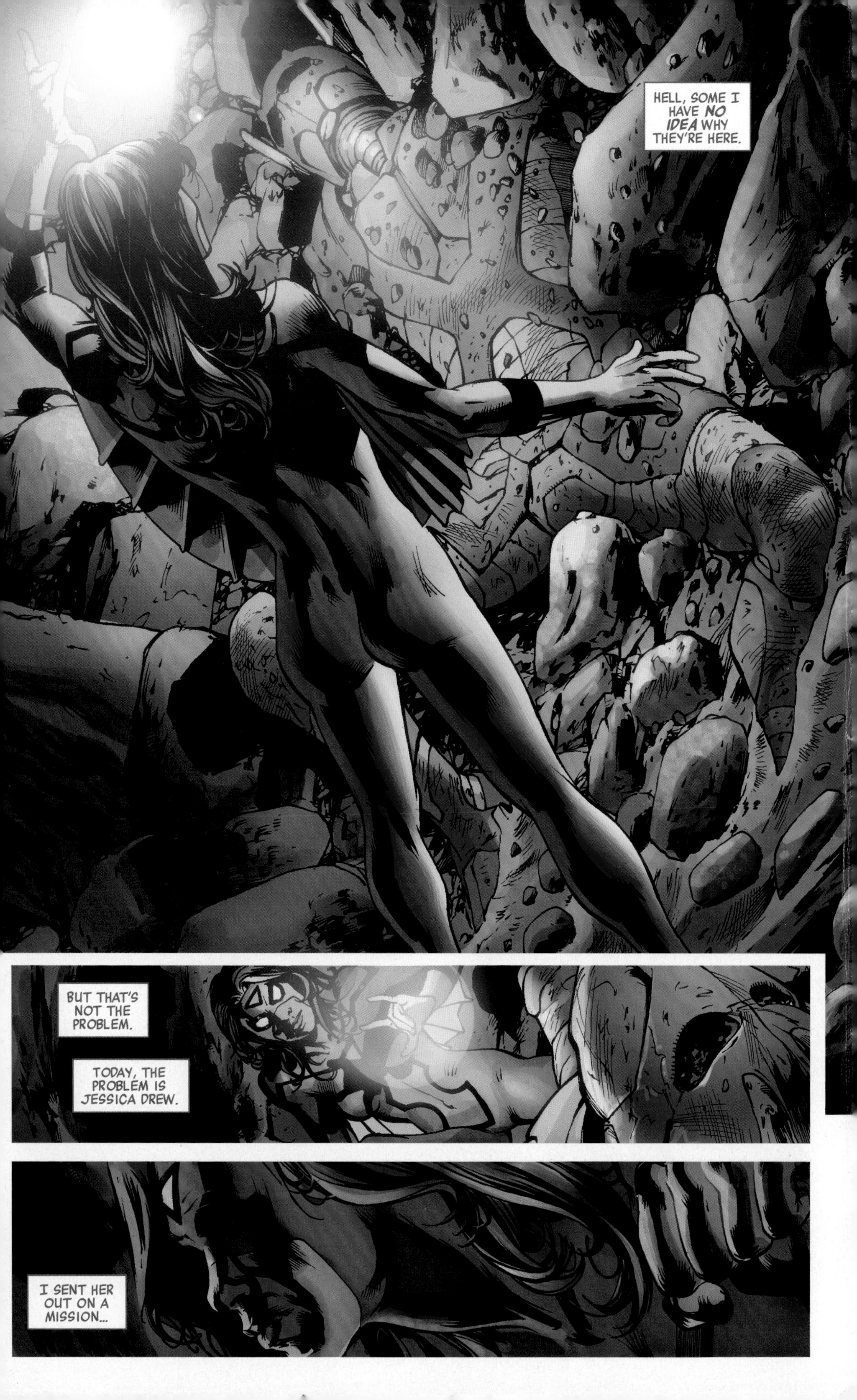
HELL, SOME I HAVE NO IDEA WHY THEY'RE HERE.
BUT THAT'S NOT THE PROBLEM.
TODAY, THE PROBLEM IS JESSICA DREW.
I SENT HER OUT ON A MISSION...

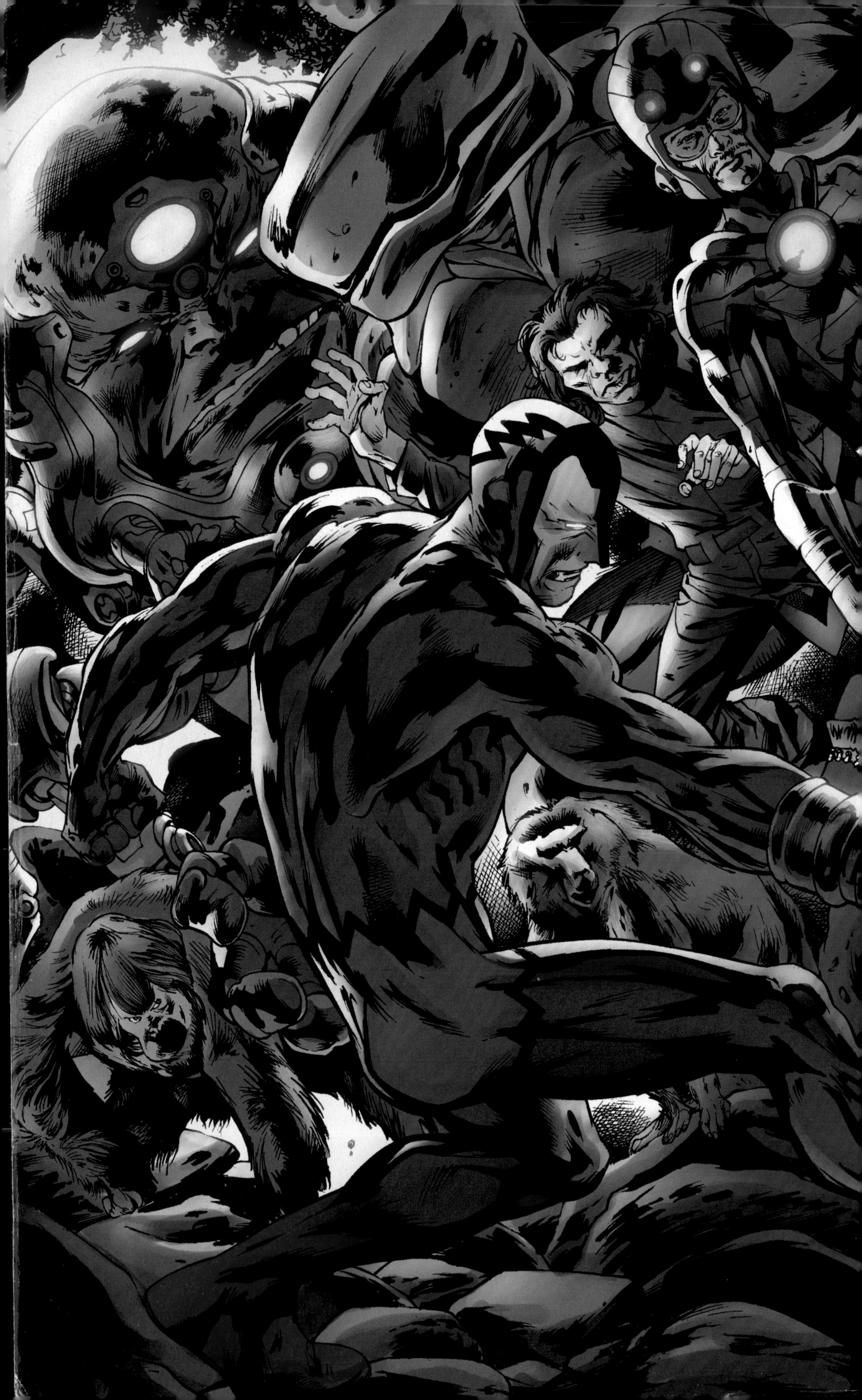

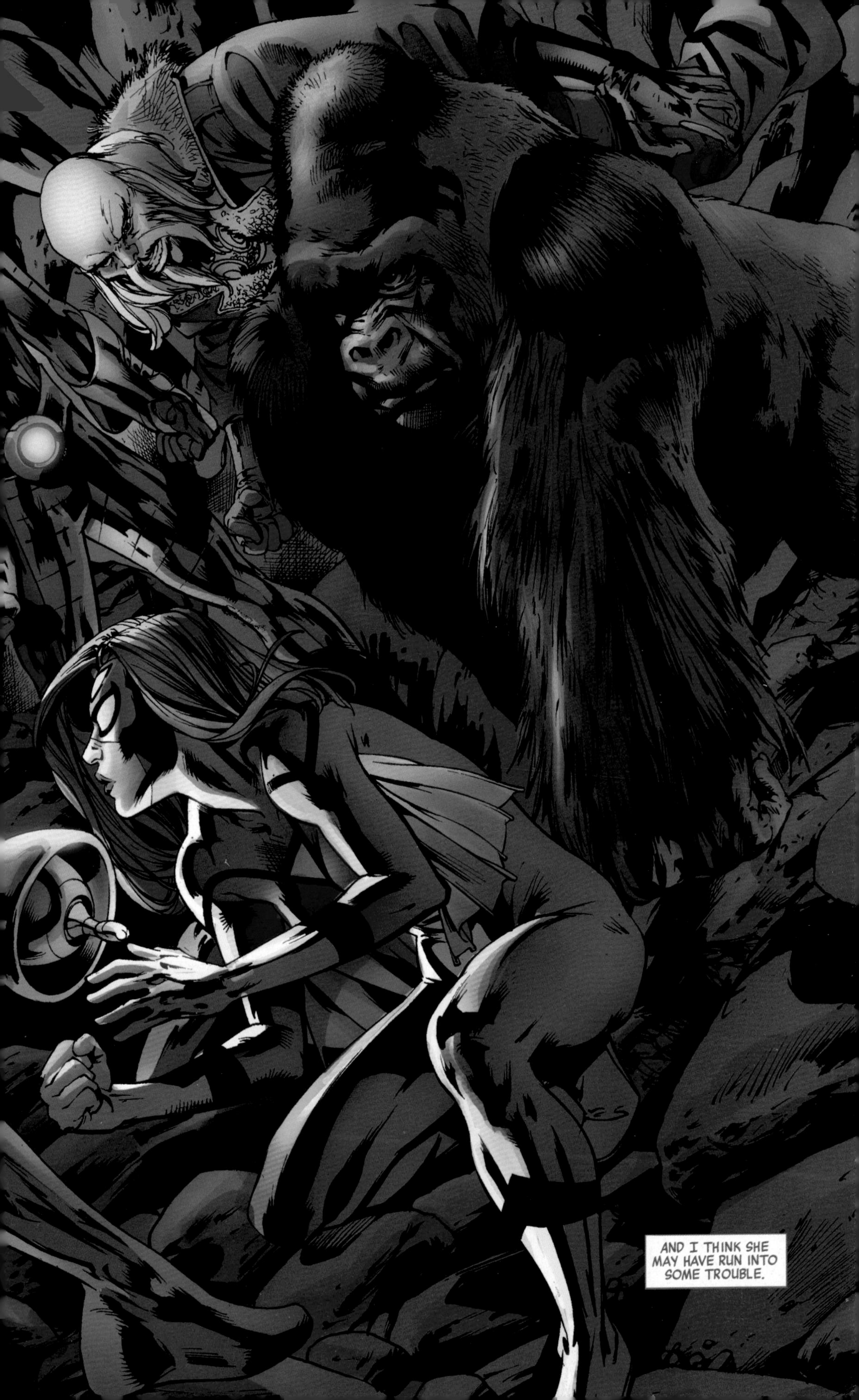
AND I THINK SHE MAY HAVE RUN INTO SOME TROUBLE.

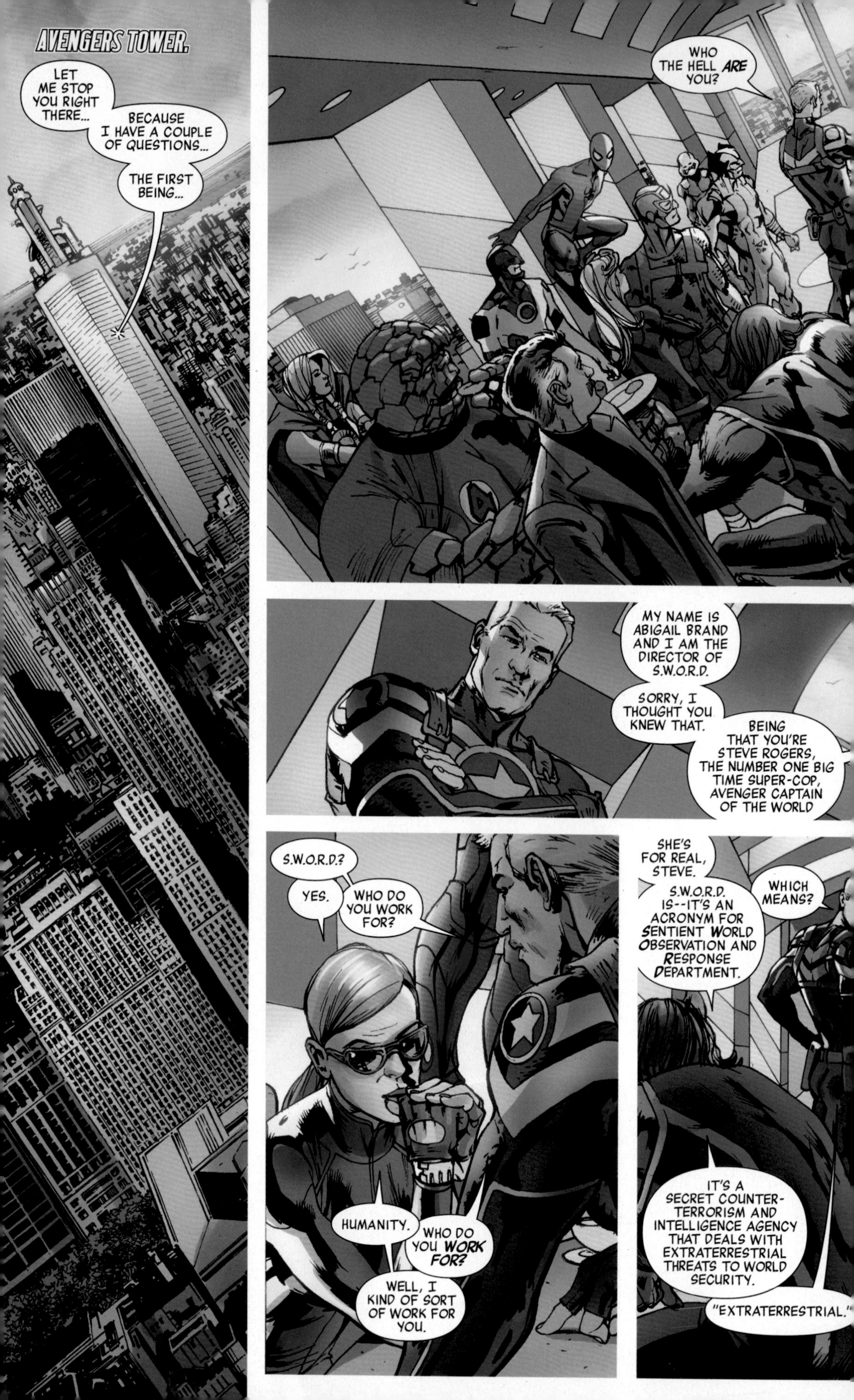
AVENGERS TOWER.
LET ME STOP YOU RIGHT THERE...
BECAUSE I HAVE A COUPLE OF QUESTIONS...
THE FIRST BEING...
WHO THE HELL ARE YOU?
MY NAME IS ABIGAIL BRAND AND I AM THE DIRECTOR OF S.W.O.R.D.
SORRY, I THOUGHT YOU KNEW THAT.
BEING THAT YOU'RE STEVE ROGERS, THE NUMBER ONE BIG TIME SUPER-COP, AVENGER CAPTAIN OF THE WORLD
S.W.O.R.D.?
YES.
WHO DO YOU WORK FOR?
HUMANITY.
WHO DO YOU WORK FOR?
WELL, I KIND OF SORT OF WORK FOR YOU.
SHE'S FOR REAL, STEVE.
S.W.O.R.D. IS--IT'S AN ACRONYM FOR SENTIENT WORLD OBSERVATION AND RESPONSE DEPARTMENT.
WHICH MEANS?
IT'S A SECRET COUNTER-TERRORISM AND INTELLIGENCE AGENCY THAT DEALS WITH EXTRATERRESTRIAL THREATS TO WORLD SECURITY.
"EXTRATERRESTRIAL."

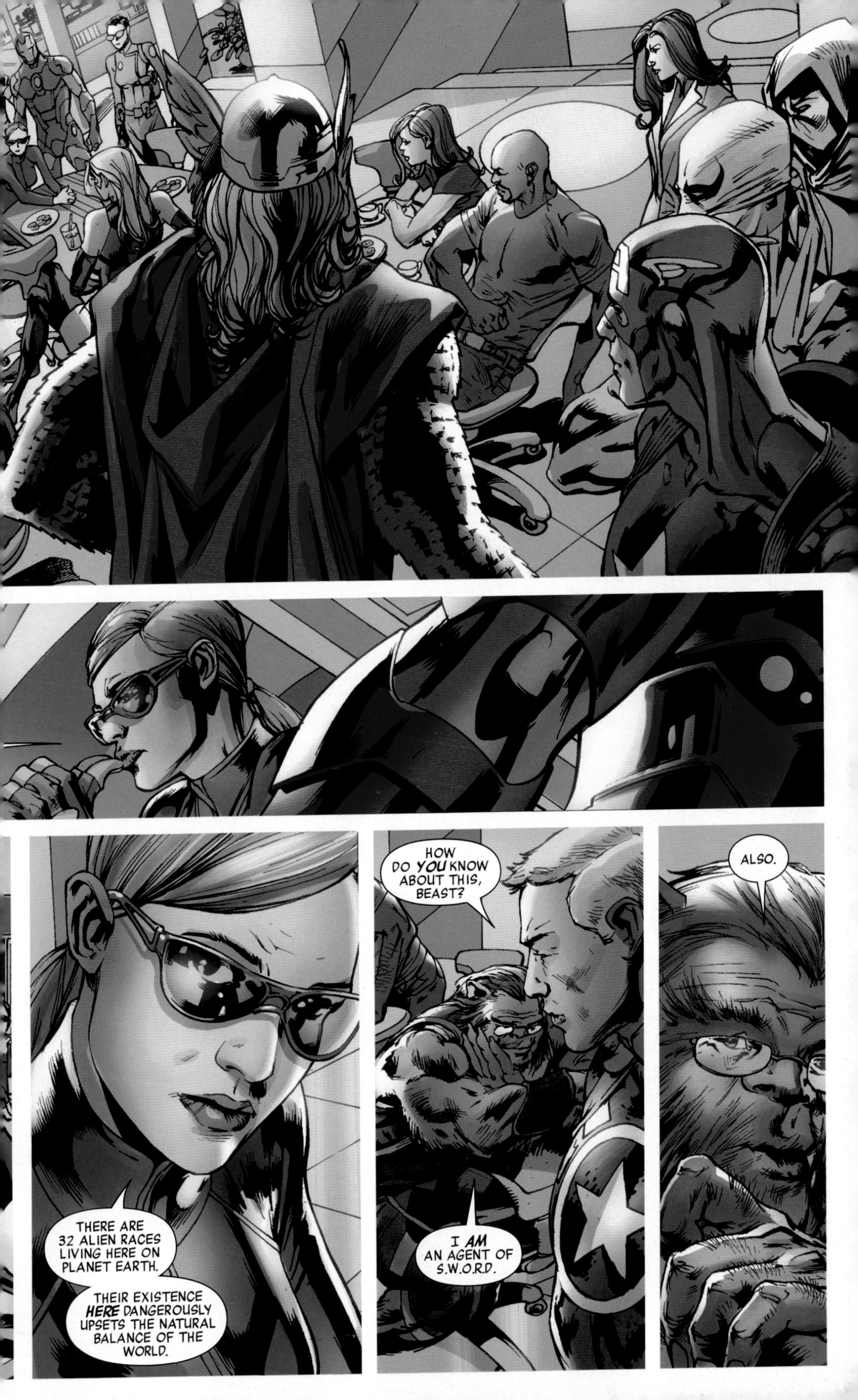
THERE ARE 32 ALIEN RACES LIVING HERE ON PLANET EARTH.
THEIR EXISTENCE HERE DANGEROUSLY UPSETS THE NATURAL BALANCE OF THE WORLD.
HOW DO YOU KNOW ABOUT THIS, BEAST?
I AM AN AGENT OF S.W.O.R.D.
ALSO.

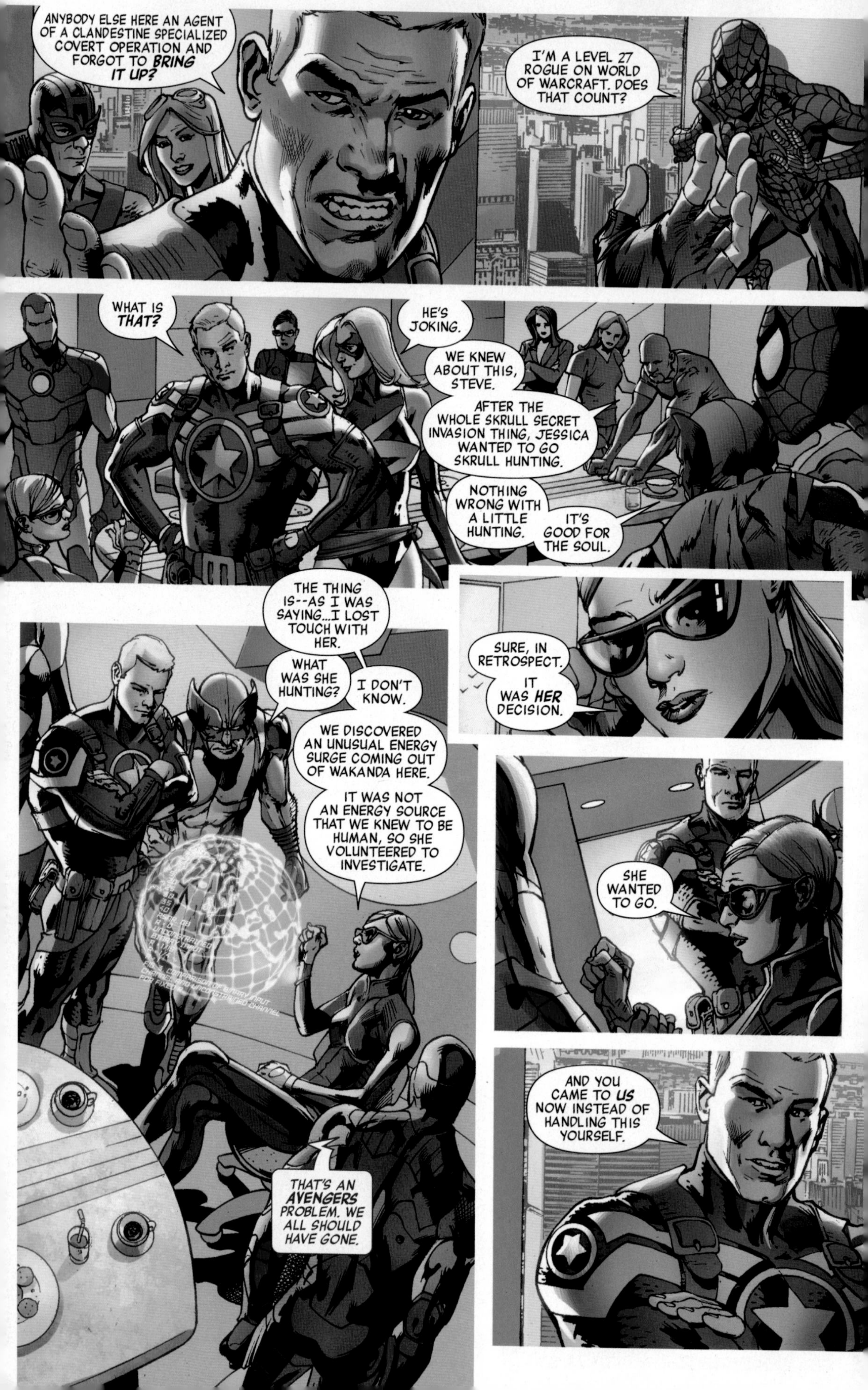

ANYBODY ELSE HERE AN AGENT OF A CLANDESTINE SPECIALIZED COVERT OPERATION AND FORGOT TO *BRING IT UP?*
I'M A LEVEL 27 ROGUE ON WORLD OF WARCRAFT. DOES THAT COUNT?
WHAT IS *THAT?*
HE'S JOKING.
WE KNEW ABOUT THIS, STEVE.
AFTER THE WHOLE SKRULL SECRET INVASION THING, JESSICA WANTED TO GO SKRULL HUNTING.
NOTHING WRONG WITH A LITTLE HUNTING.
IT'S GOOD FOR THE SOUL.
THE THING IS--AS I WAS SAYING...I LOST TOUCH WITH HER.
WHAT WAS SHE HUNTING?
I DON'T KNOW.
WE DISCOVERED AN UNUSUAL ENERGY SURGE COMING OUT OF WAKANDA HERE.
IT WAS NOT AN ENERGY SOURCE THAT WE KNEW TO BE HUMAN, SO SHE VOLUNTEERED TO INVESTIGATE.
SURE, IN RETROSPECT.
IT WAS *HER* DECISION.
SHE WANTED TO GO.
THAT'S AN AVENGERS PROBLEM. WE ALL SHOULD HAVE GONE.
AND YOU CAME TO *US* NOW INSTEAD OF HANDLING THIS YOURSELF.

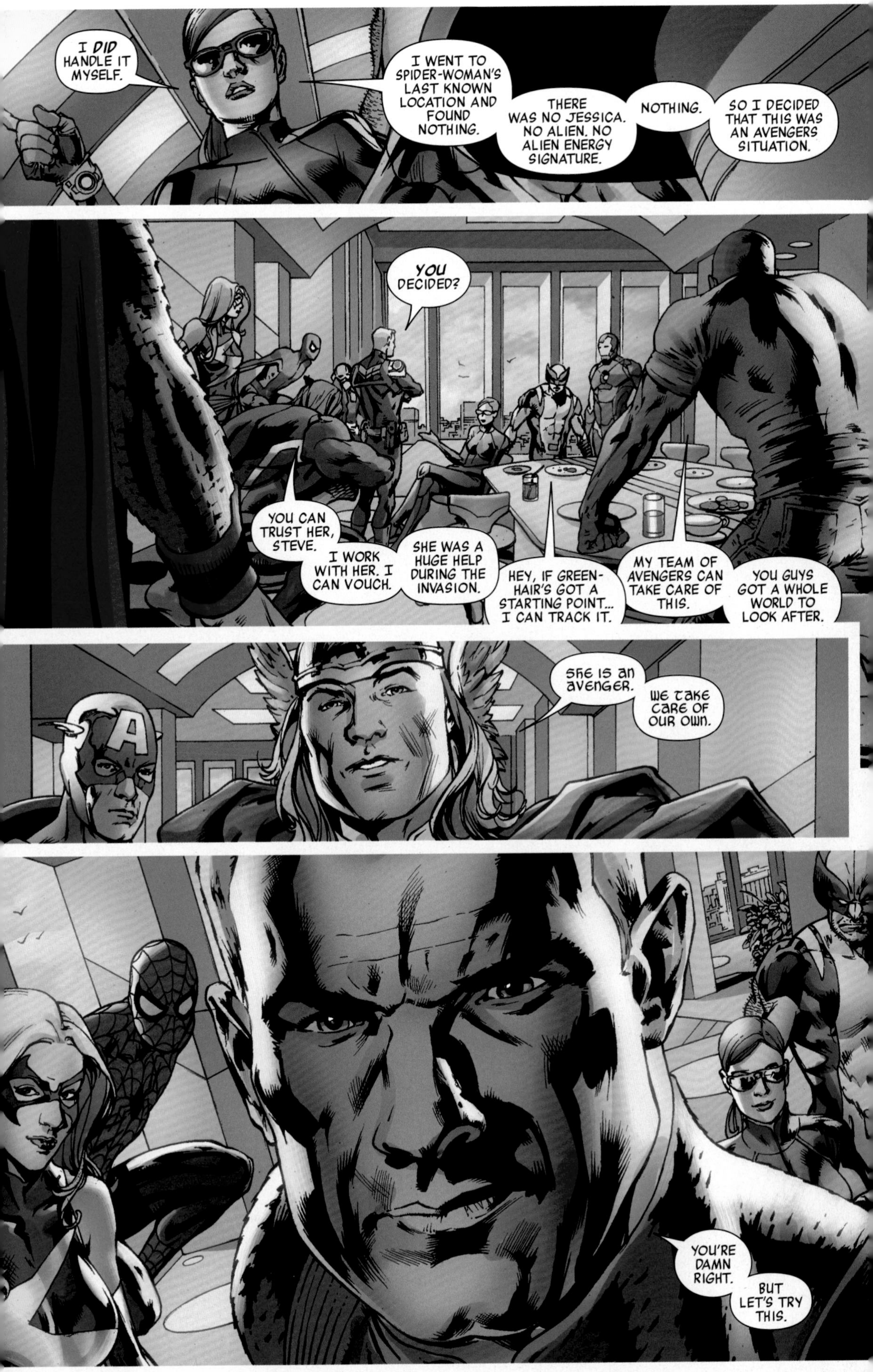

I *DID* HANDLE IT MYSELF.
I WENT TO SPIDER-WOMAN'S LAST KNOWN LOCATION AND FOUND NOTHING.
THERE WAS NO JESSICA. NO ALIEN. NO ALIEN ENERGY SIGNATURE.
NOTHING.
SO I DECIDED THAT THIS WAS AN AVENGERS SITUATION.
YOU DECIDED?
YOU CAN TRUST HER, STEVE.
I WORK WITH HER. I CAN VOUCH.
SHE WAS A HUGE HELP DURING THE INVASION.
HEY, IF GREEN-HAIR'S GOT A STARTING POINT... I CAN TRACK IT.
MY TEAM OF AVENGERS CAN TAKE CARE OF THIS.
YOU GUYS GOT A WHOLE WORLD TO LOOK AFTER.
SHE IS AN AVENGER.
WE TAKE CARE OF OUR OWN.
YOU'RE DAMN RIGHT.
BUT LET'S TRY THIS.

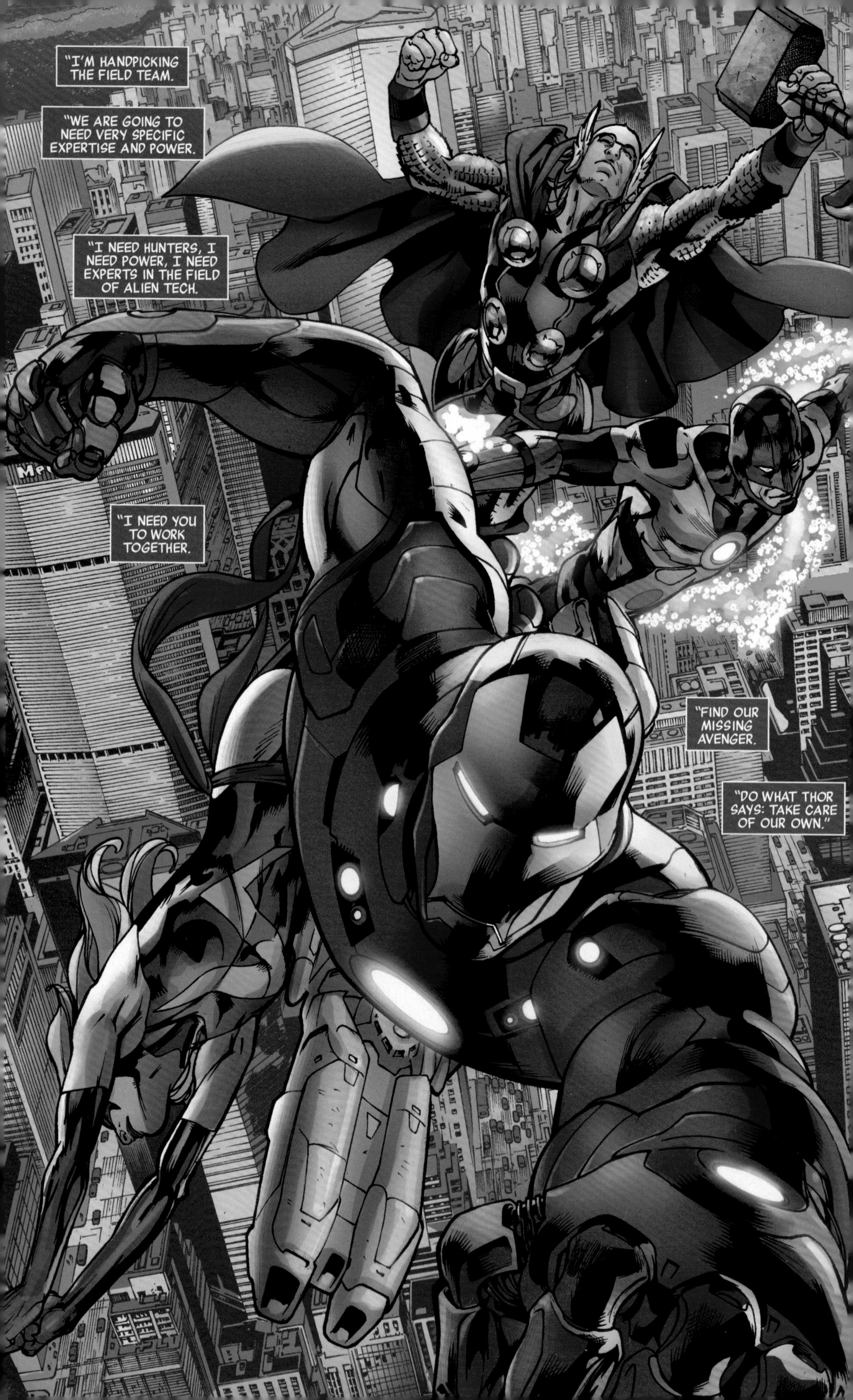
"I'M HANDPICKING THE FIELD TEAM.
"WE ARE GOING TO NEED VERY SPECIFIC EXPERTISE AND POWER.
"I NEED HUNTERS, I NEED POWER, I NEED EXPERTS IN THE FIELD OF ALIEN TECH.
"I NEED YOU TO WORK TOGETHER.
"FIND OUR MISSING AVENGER.
"DO WHAT THOR SAYS: TAKE CARE OF OUR OWN."

-SNFF-

WHAT ARE YOU DOING?

HE'S PICKING UP A SCENT.

LET HIM DO HIS THING.

I HAVE SOME READINGS.

I HAVE SOMETHING TOO.

ENVIRONMENTAL SCAN UNDERWAY.

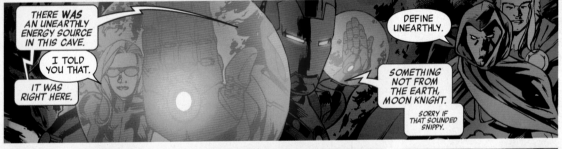

THERE WAS AN UNEARTHLY ENERGY SOURCE IN THIS CAVE.

I TOLD YOU THAT.

IT WAS RIGHT HERE.

DEFINE UNEARTHLY.

SOMETHING NOT FROM THE EARTH, MOON KNIGHT.

SORRY IF THAT SOUNDED SNIPPY.

SHE WAS RIGHT HERE.

CROUCHED DOWN.

SHE TURNED ON HER FOOT.

SEE THE MARKINGS IN THE DIRT?

NO.

SHE TURNED RIGHT HERE.

SOMEONE CAME UP BEHIND HER.

THERE...

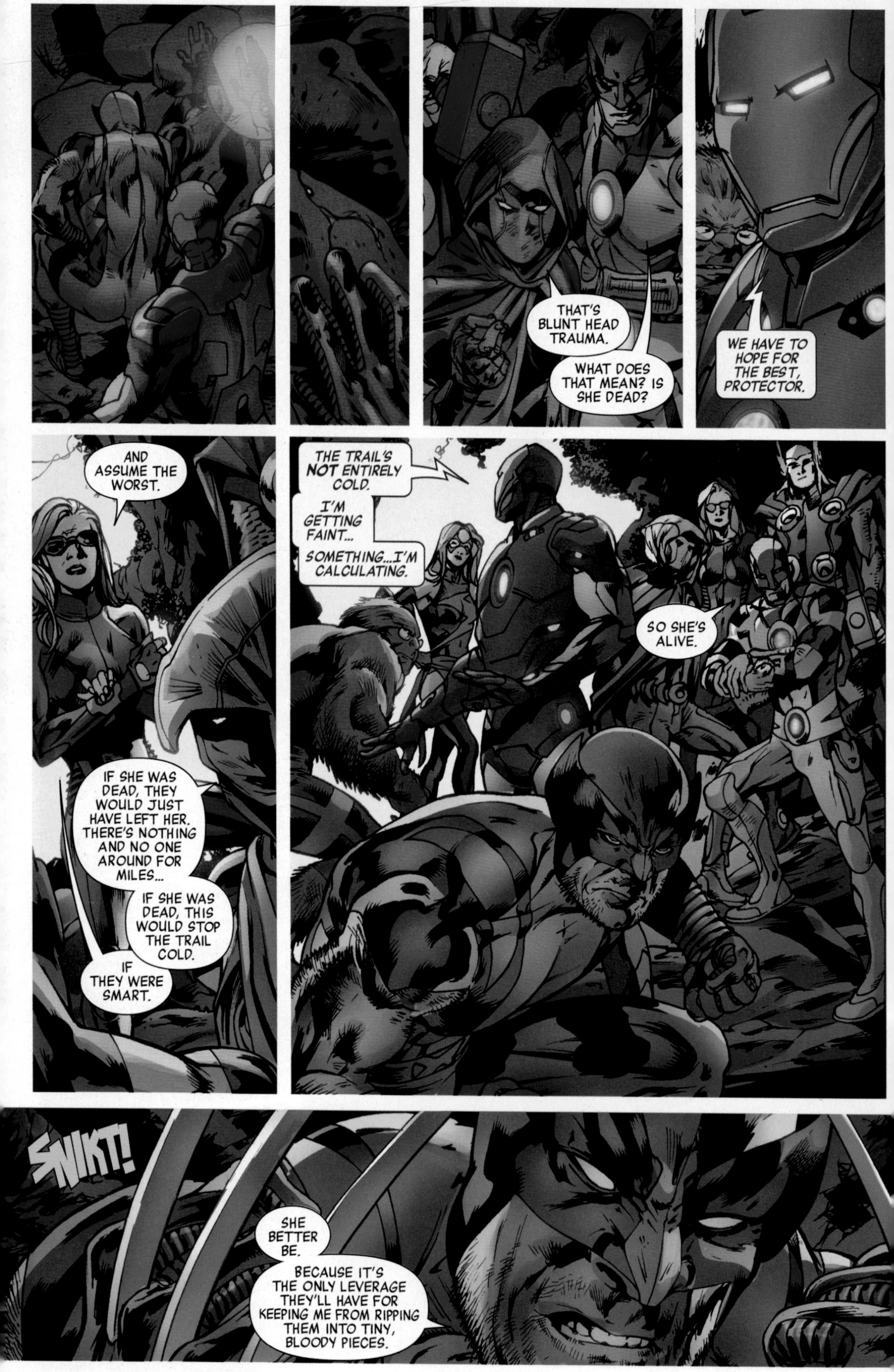

THAT'S BLUNT HEAD TRAUMA.
WHAT DOES THAT MEAN? IS SHE DEAD?
WE HAVE TO HOPE FOR THE BEST, PROTECTOR.
AND ASSUME THE WORST.
IF SHE WAS DEAD, THEY WOULD JUST HAVE LEFT HER. THERE'S NOTHING AND NO ONE AROUND FOR MILES...
IF SHE WAS DEAD, THIS WOULD STOP THE TRAIL COLD.
IF THEY WERE SMART.
THE TRAIL'S NOT ENTIRELY COLD.
I'M GETTING FAINT...
SOMETHING...I'M CALCULATING.
SO SHE'S ALIVE.
SNIKT!
SHE BETTER BE.
BECAUSE IT'S THE ONLY LEVERAGE THEY'LL HAVE FOR KEEPING ME FROM RIPPING THEM INTO TINY, BLOODY PIECES.

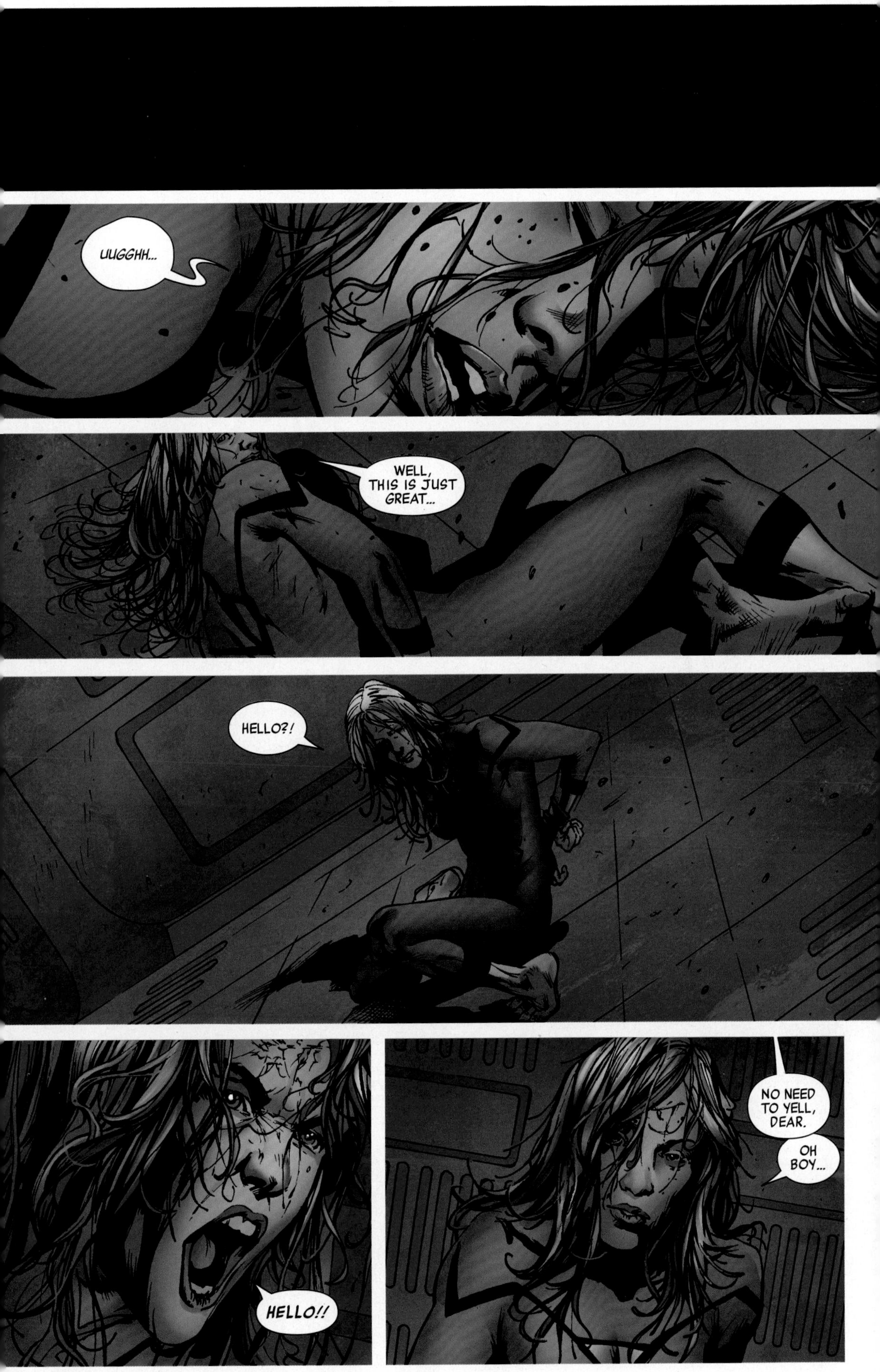
UUGGHH...
WELL, THIS IS JUST GREAT...
HELLO?!
HELLO!!
NO NEED TO YELL, DEAR.
OH BOY...

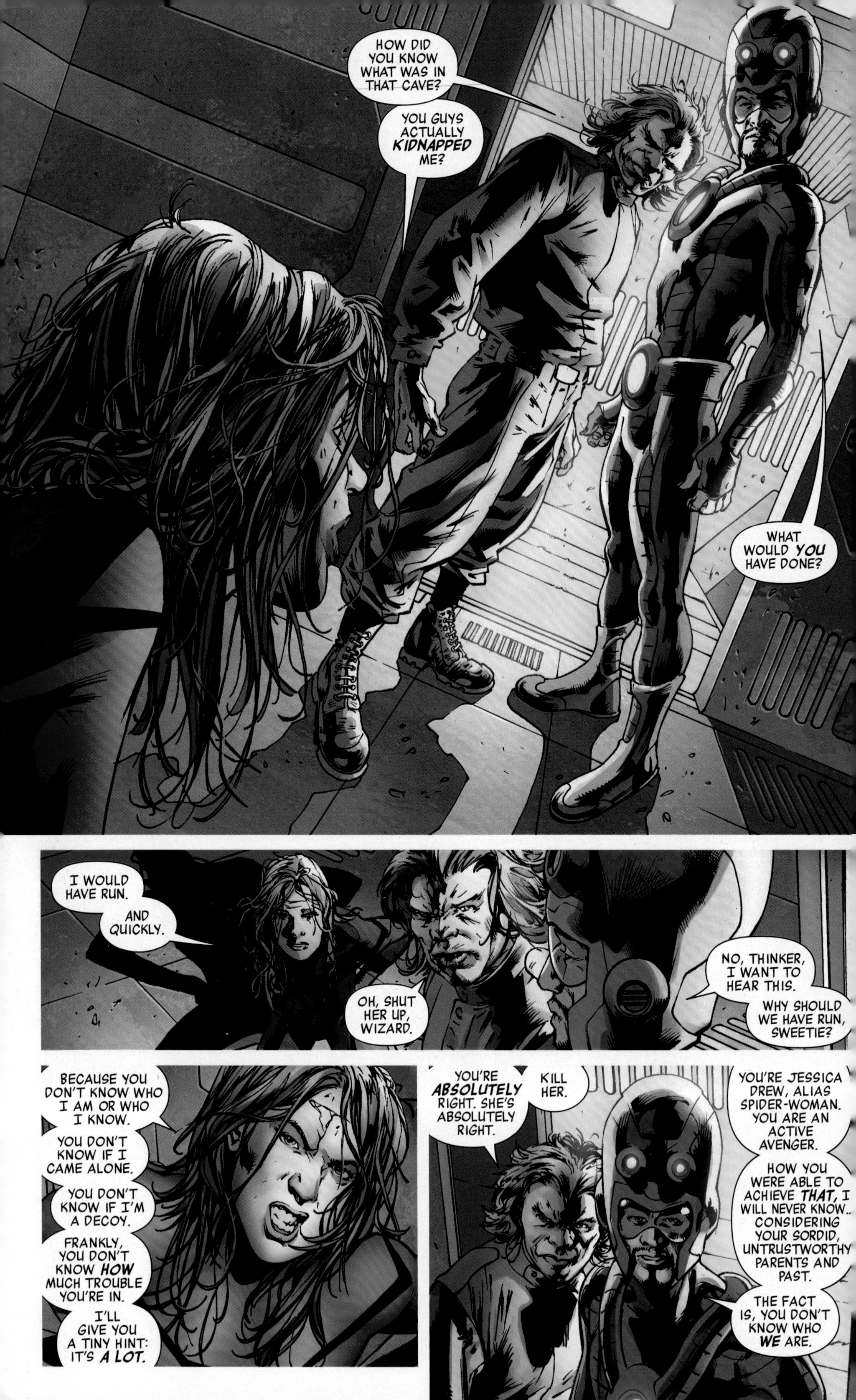
HOW DID YOU KNOW WHAT WAS IN THAT CAVE?
YOU GUYS ACTUALLY KIDNAPPED ME?
WHAT WOULD YOU HAVE DONE?
I WOULD HAVE RUN.
AND QUICKLY.
OH, SHUT HER UP, WIZARD.
NO, THINKER, I WANT TO HEAR THIS.
WHY SHOULD WE HAVE RUN, SWEETIE?
BECAUSE YOU DON'T KNOW WHO I AM OR WHO I KNOW.
YOU DON'T KNOW IF I CAME ALONE.
YOU DON'T KNOW IF I'M A DECOY.
FRANKLY, YOU DON'T KNOW HOW MUCH TROUBLE YOU'RE IN.
I'LL GIVE YOU A TINY HINT: IT'S A LOT.
YOU'RE ABSOLUTELY RIGHT. SHE'S ABSOLUTELY RIGHT.
KILL HER.
YOU'RE JESSICA DREW, ALIAS SPIDER-WOMAN. YOU ARE AN ACTIVE AVENGER.
HOW YOU WERE ABLE TO ACHIEVE THAT, I WILL NEVER KNOW... CONSIDERING YOUR SORDID, UNTRUSTWORTHY PARENTS AND PAST.
THE FACT IS, YOU DON'T KNOW WHO WE ARE.

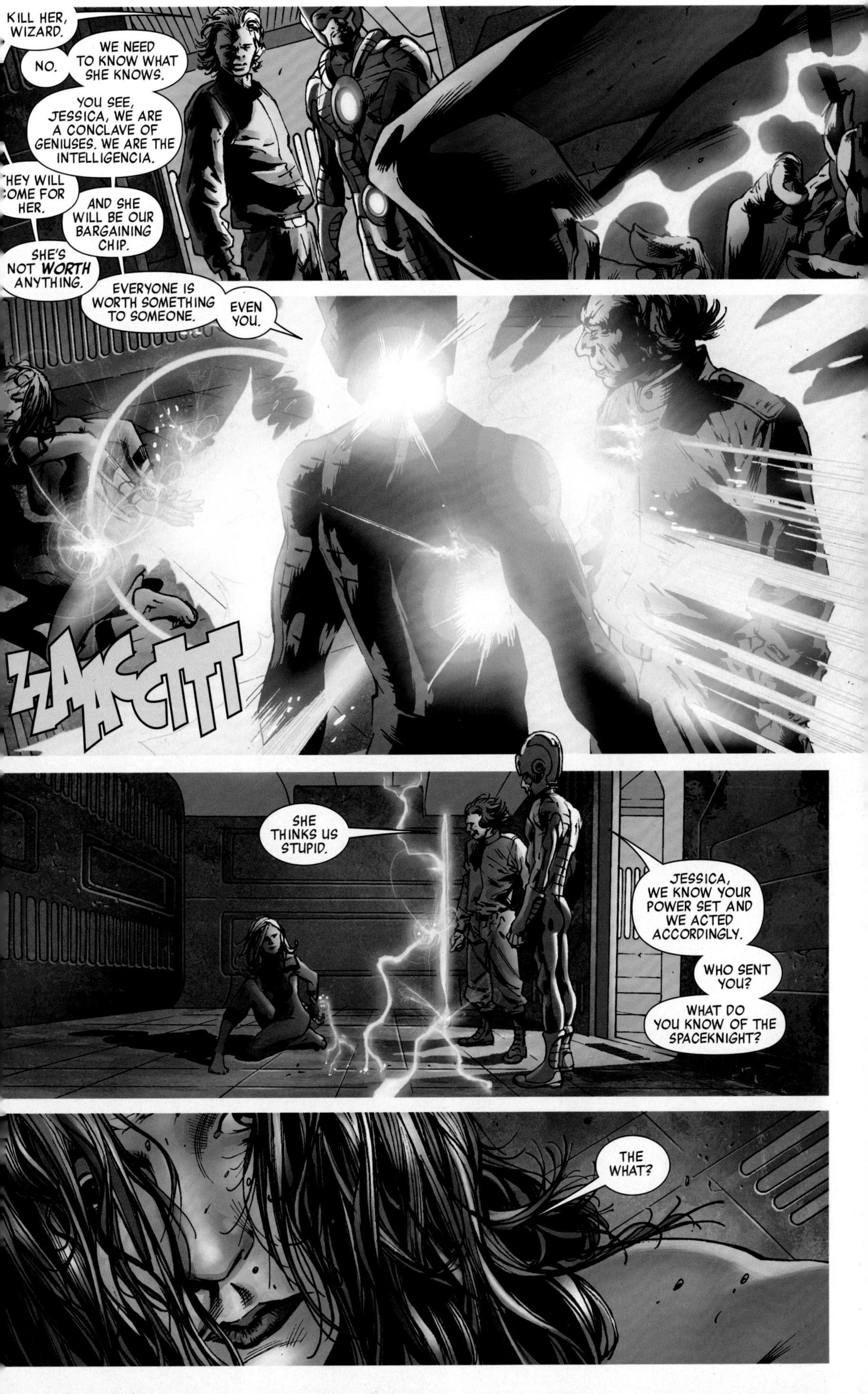

KILL HER, WIZARD.
NO.
WE NEED TO KNOW WHAT SHE KNOWS.
YOU SEE, JESSICA, WE ARE A CONCLAVE OF GENIUSES. WE ARE THE INTELLIGENCIA.
THEY WILL COME FOR HER.
AND SHE WILL BE OUR BARGAINING CHIP.
SHE'S NOT WORTH ANYTHING.
EVERYONE IS WORTH SOMETHING TO SOMEONE.
EVEN YOU.
ZZAACTTT
SHE THINKS US STUPID.
JESSICA, WE KNOW YOUR POWER SET AND WE ACTED ACCORDINGLY.
WHO SENT YOU?
WHAT DO YOU KNOW OF THE SPACEKNIGHT?
THE WHAT?

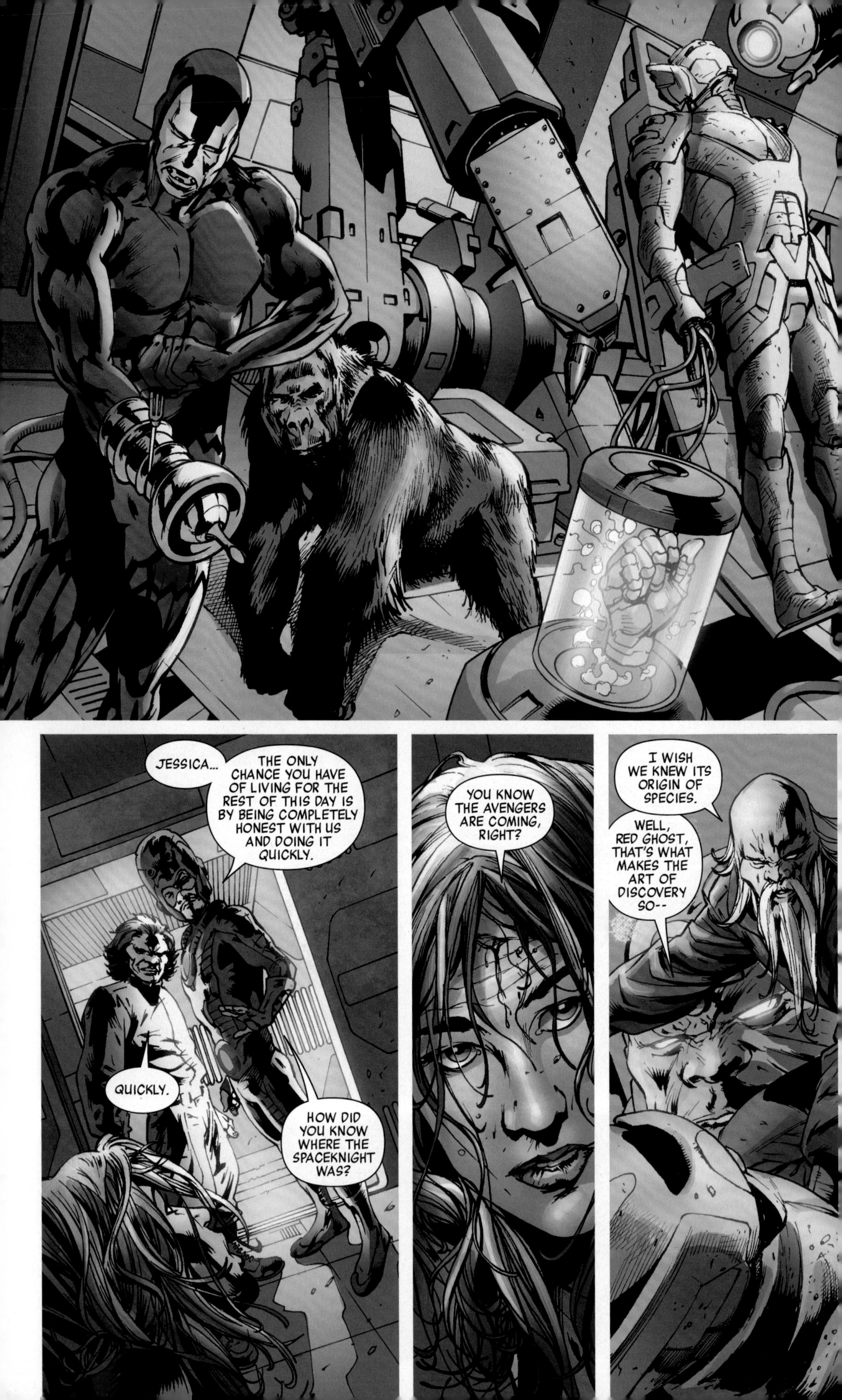
JESSICA...
THE ONLY CHANCE YOU HAVE OF LIVING FOR THE REST OF THIS DAY IS BY BEING COMPLETELY HONEST WITH US AND DOING IT QUICKLY.
QUICKLY.
HOW DID YOU KNOW WHERE THE SPACEKNIGHT WAS?
YOU KNOW THE AVENGERS ARE COMING, RIGHT?
I WISH WE KNEW ITS ORIGIN OF SPECIES.
WELL, RED GHOST, THAT'S WHAT MAKES THE ART OF DISCOVERY SO--

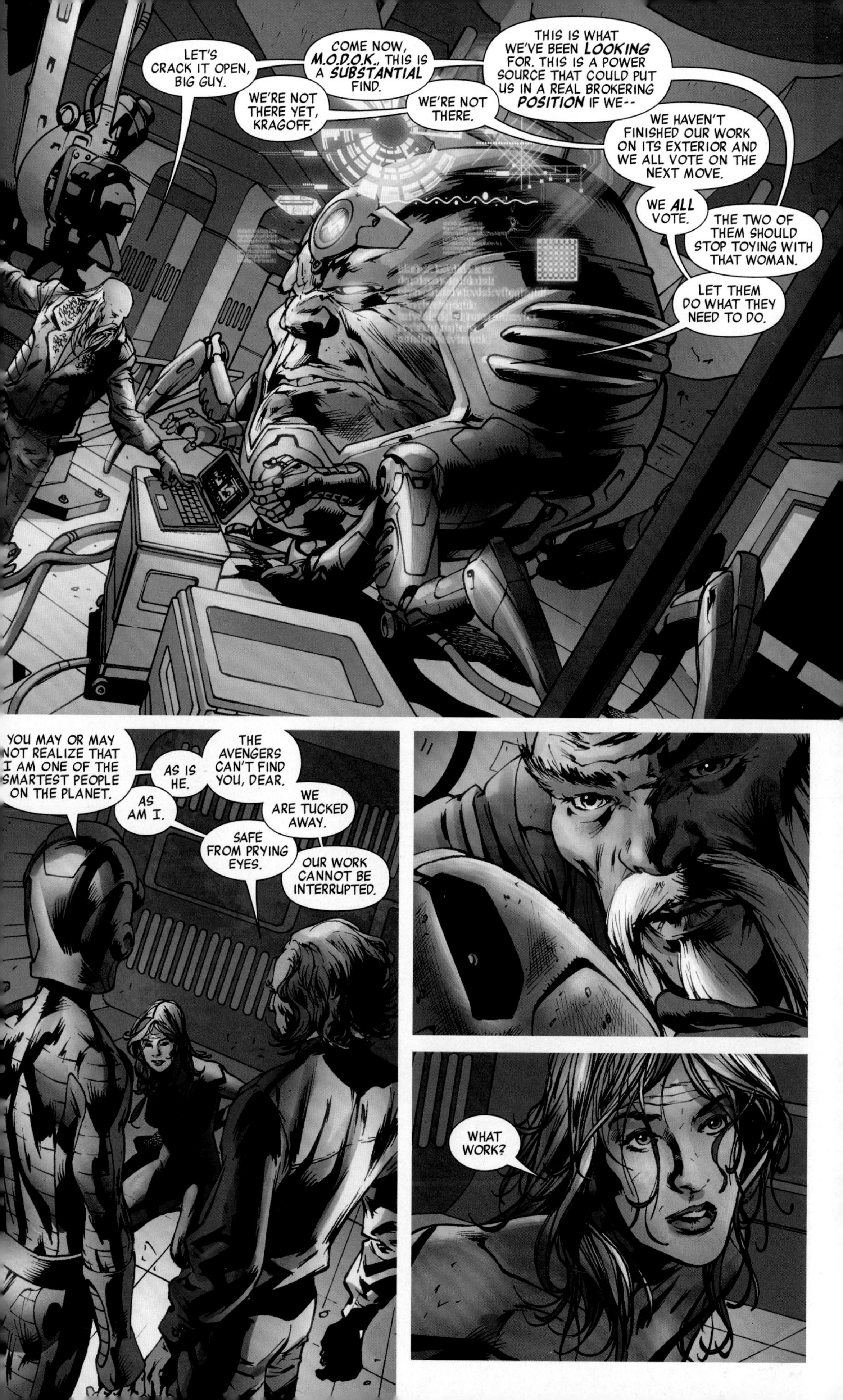

LET'S CRACK IT OPEN, BIG GUY.
COME NOW, M.O.D.O.K., THIS IS A SUBSTANTIAL FIND.
THIS IS WHAT WE'VE BEEN LOOKING FOR. THIS IS A POWER SOURCE THAT COULD PUT US IN A REAL BROKERING POSITION IF WE--
WE'RE NOT THERE YET, KRAGOFF.
WE'RE NOT THERE.
WE HAVEN'T FINISHED OUR WORK ON ITS EXTERIOR AND WE ALL VOTE ON THE NEXT MOVE.
WE ALL VOTE.
THE TWO OF THEM SHOULD STOP TOYING WITH THAT WOMAN.
LET THEM DO WHAT THEY NEED TO DO.
YOU MAY OR MAY NOT REALIZE THAT I AM ONE OF THE SMARTEST PEOPLE ON THE PLANET.
AS IS HE.
AS AM I.
THE AVENGERS CAN'T FIND YOU, DEAR.
WE ARE TUCKED AWAY.
SAFE FROM PRYING EYES.
OUR WORK CANNOT BE INTERRUPTED.
WHAT WORK?

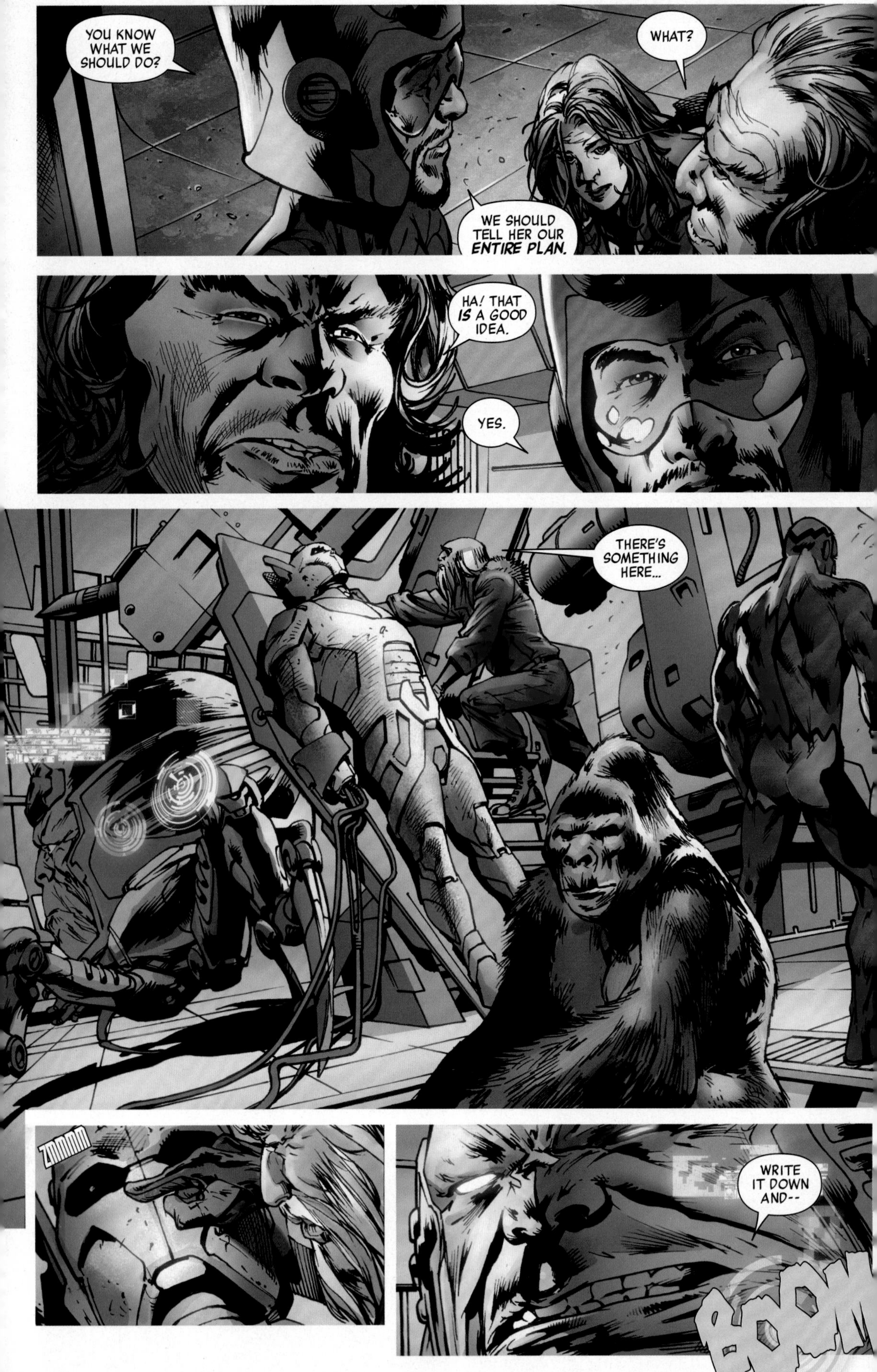
YOU KNOW WHAT WE SHOULD DO?
WHAT?
WE SHOULD TELL HER OUR ENTIRE PLAN.
HA! THAT IS A GOOD IDEA.
YES.
THERE'S SOMETHING HERE...
ZMMMM
WRITE IT DOWN AND--
BOOM

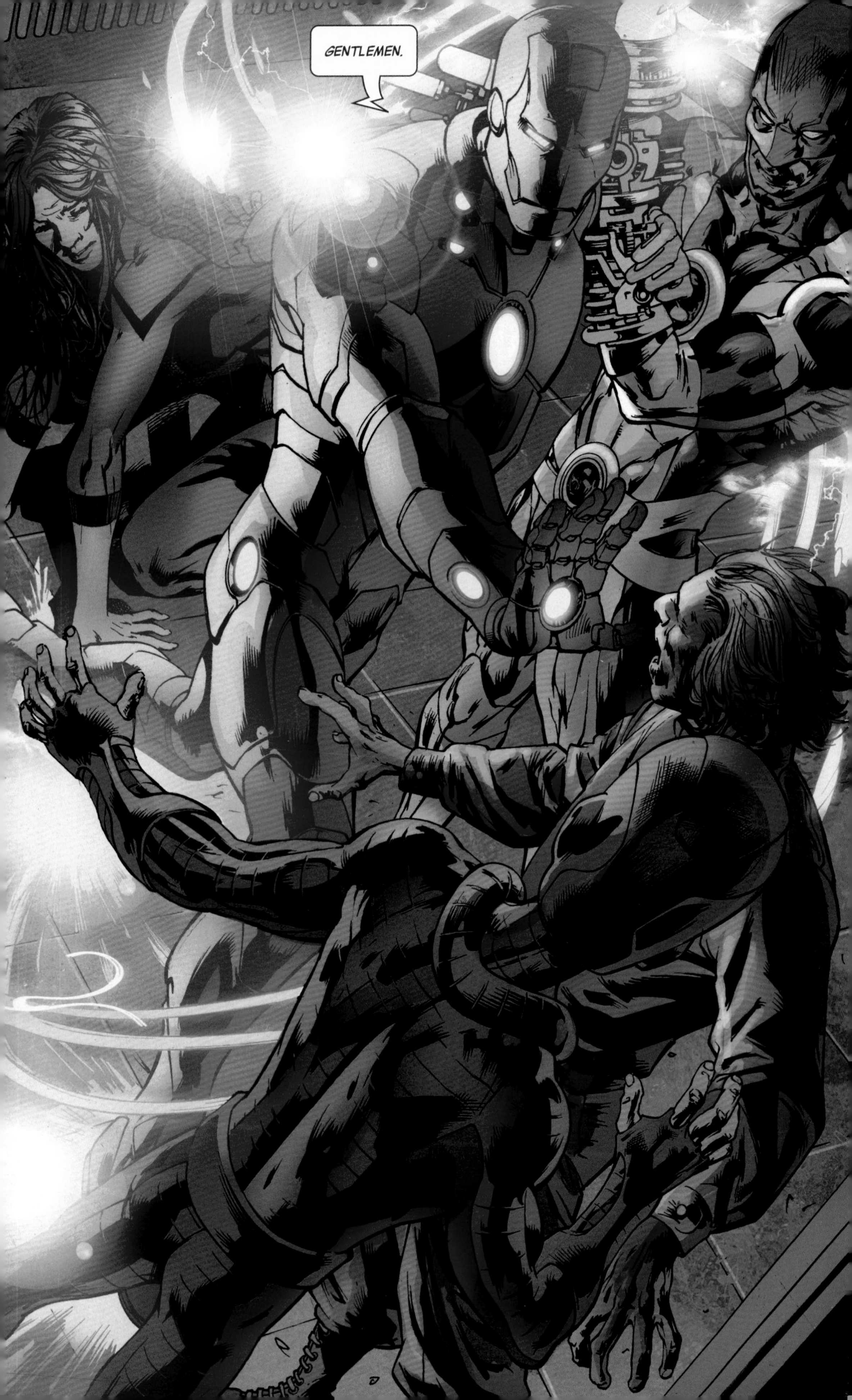
GENTLEMEN.

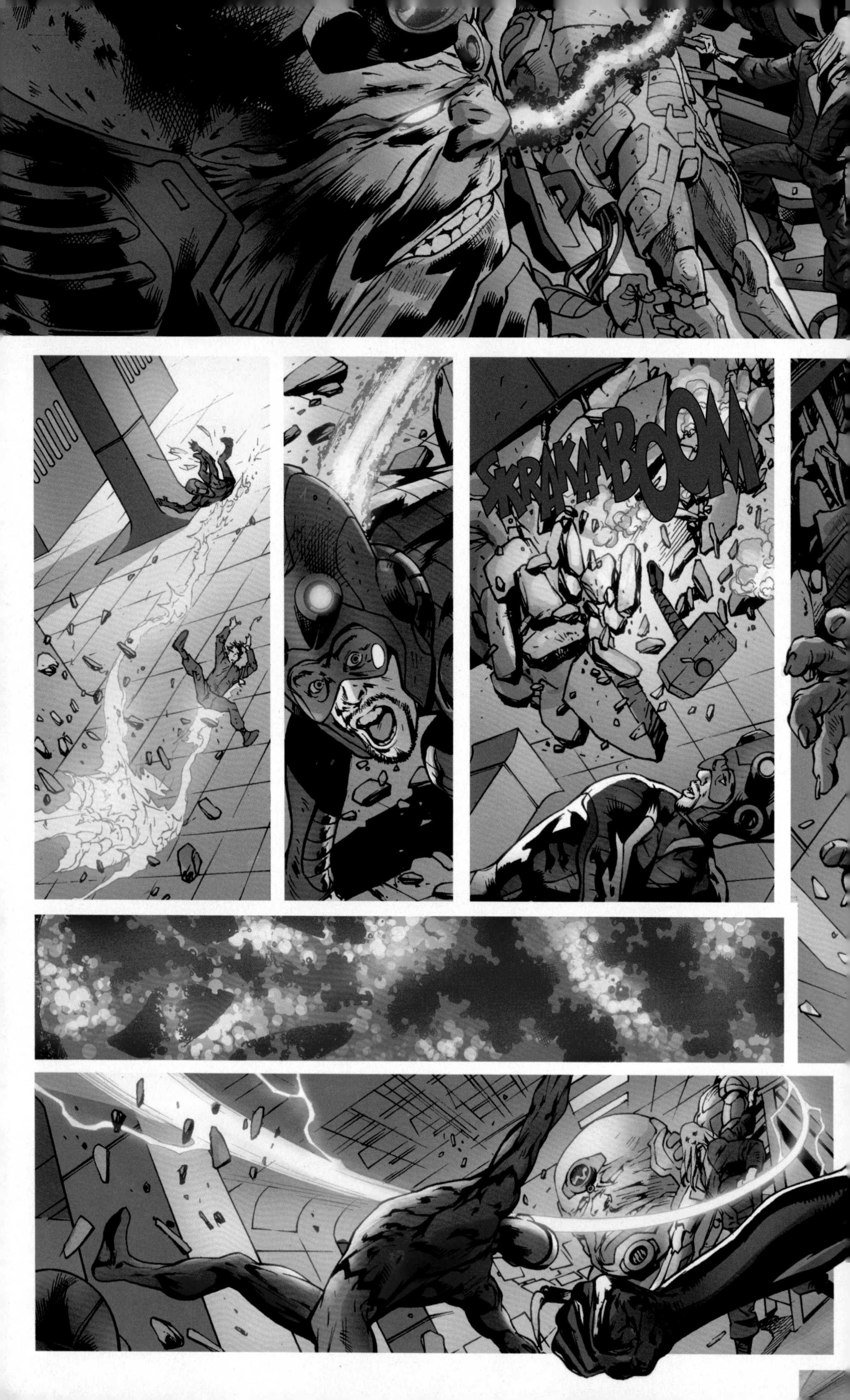
SKRAKAKBOOM

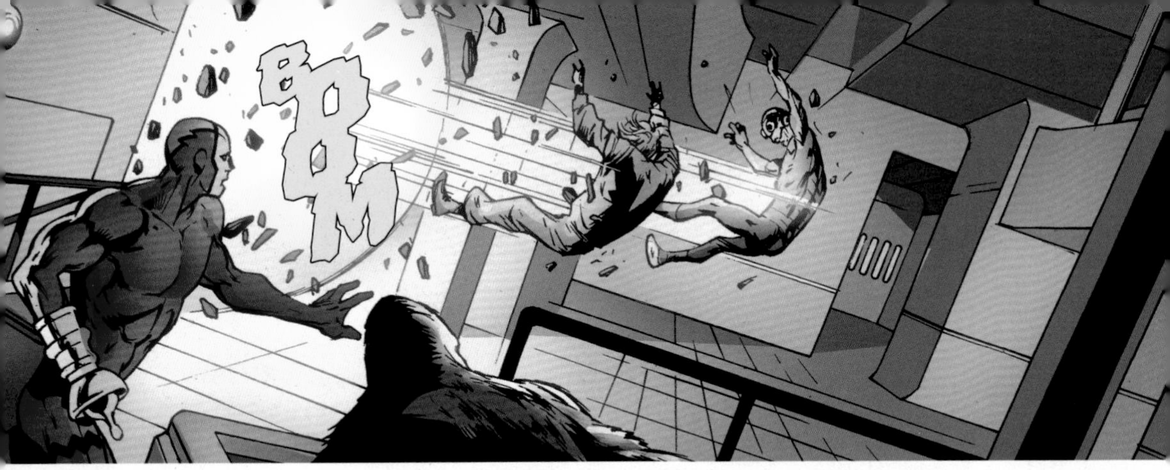
BOOM

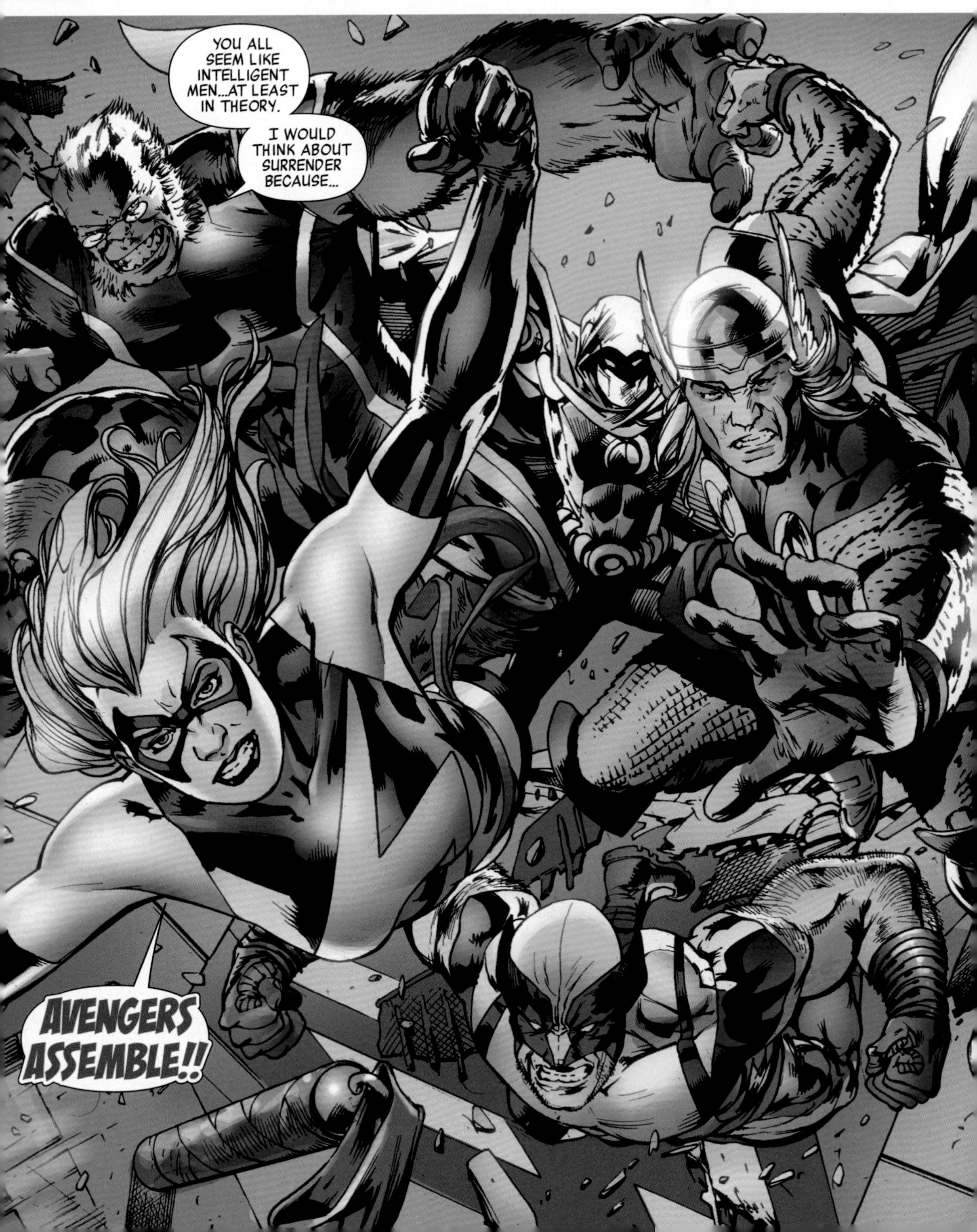
YOU ALL SEEM LIKE INTELLIGENT MEN...AT LEAST IN THEORY.
I WOULD THINK ABOUT SURRENDER BECAUSE...
AVENGERS ASSEMBLE!!

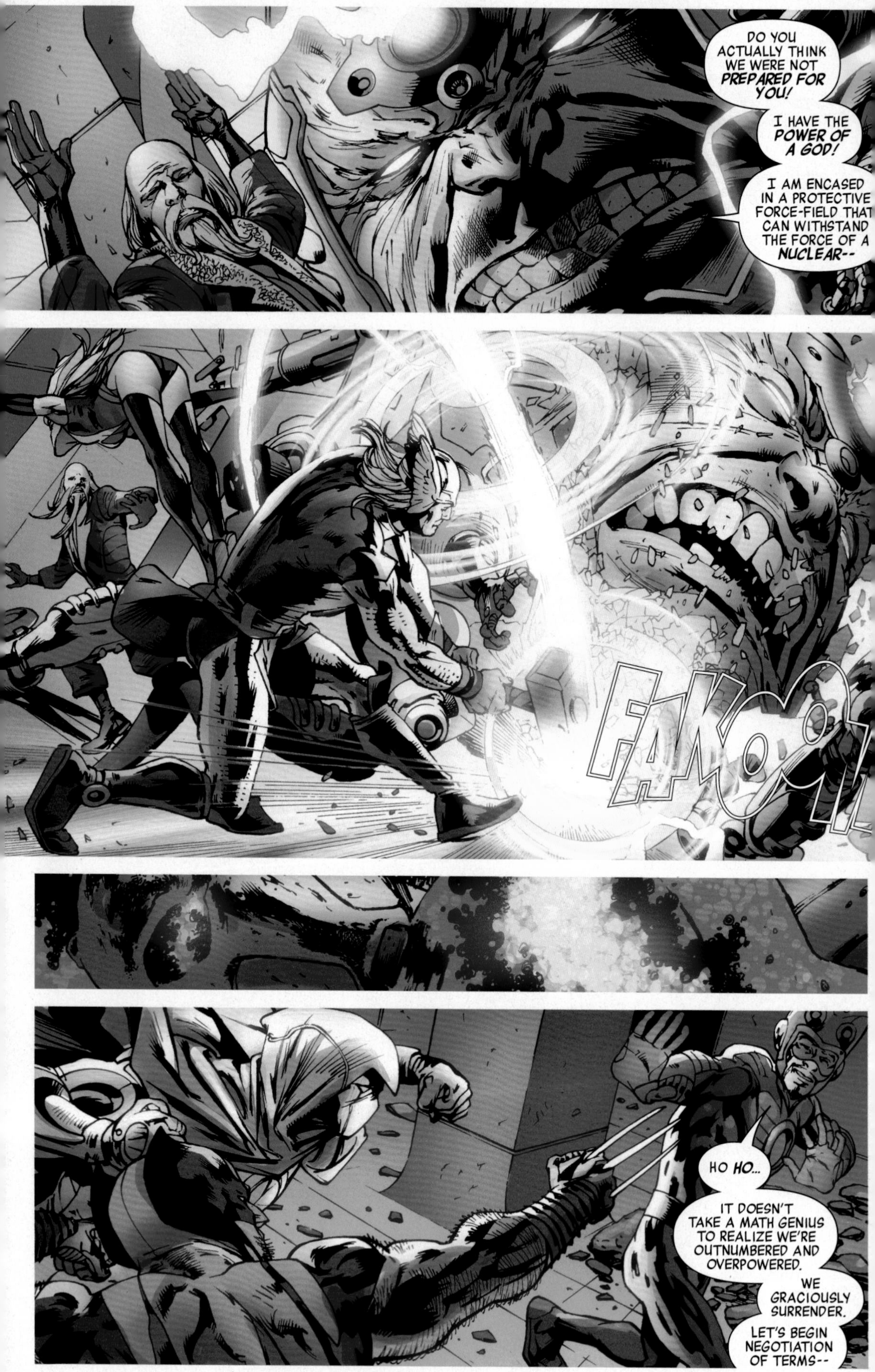

DO YOU ACTUALLY THINK WE WERE NOT PREPARED FOR YOU!
I HAVE THE POWER OF A GOD!
I AM ENCASED IN A PROTECTIVE FORCE-FIELD THAT CAN WITHSTAND THE FORCE OF A NUCLEAR--
FAKOOM!
HO HO...
IT DOESN'T TAKE A MATH GENIUS TO REALIZE WE'RE OUTNUMBERED AND OVERPOWERED.
WE GRACIOUSLY SURRENDER.
LET'S BEGIN NEGOTIATION OF TERMS--

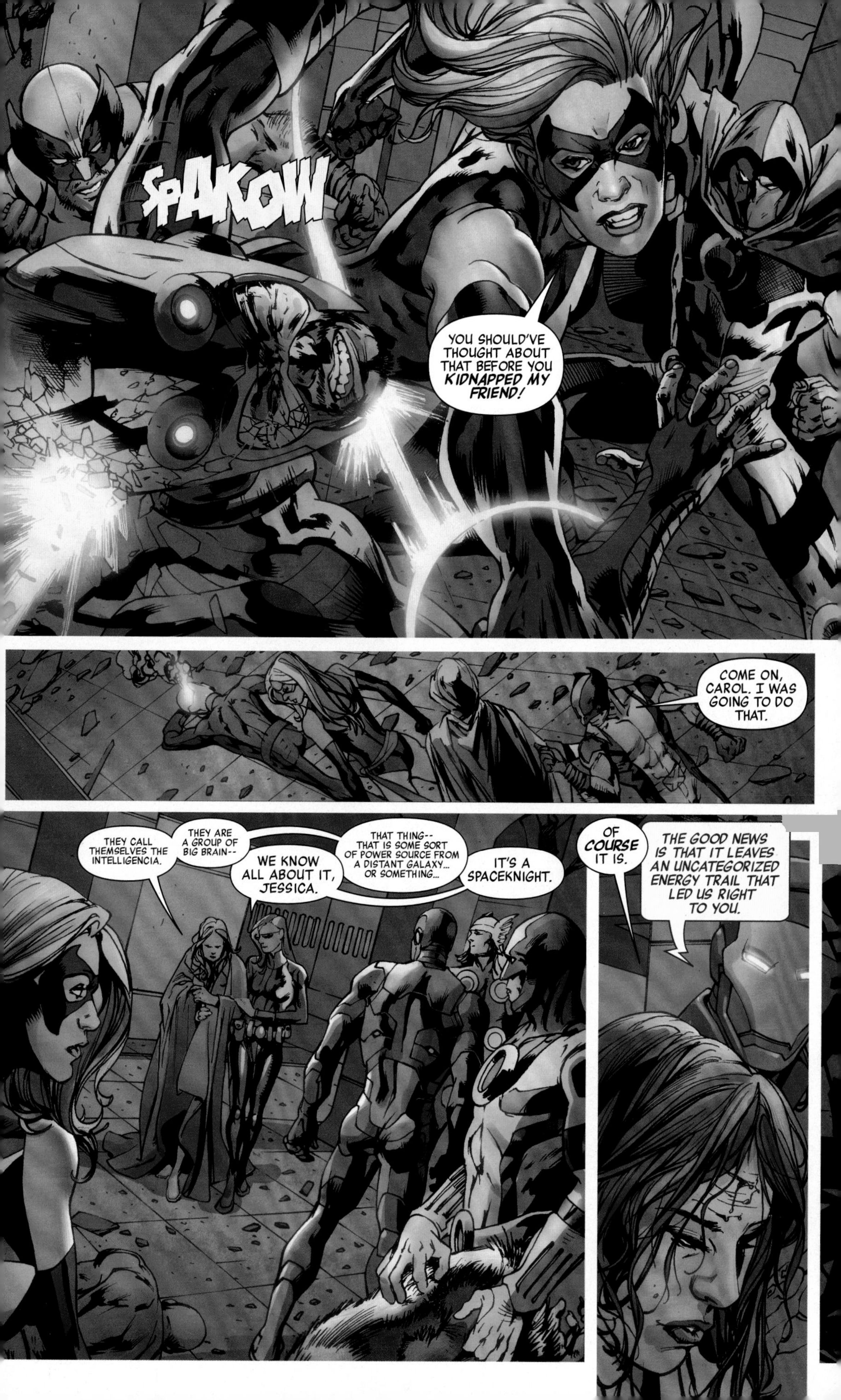
SPAKOW
YOU SHOULD'VE THOUGHT ABOUT THAT BEFORE YOU KIDNAPPED MY FRIEND!
COME ON, CAROL. I WAS GOING TO DO THAT.
THEY CALL THEMSELVES THE INTELLIGENCIA.
THEY ARE A GROUP OF BIG BRAIN--
WE KNOW ALL ABOUT IT, JESSICA.
THAT THING-- THAT IS SOME SORT OF POWER SOURCE FROM A DISTANT GALAXY... OR SOMETHING...
IT'S A SPACEKNIGHT.
OF COURSE IT IS.
THE GOOD NEWS IS THAT IT LEAVES AN UNCATEGORIZED ENERGY TRAIL THAT LED US RIGHT TO YOU.

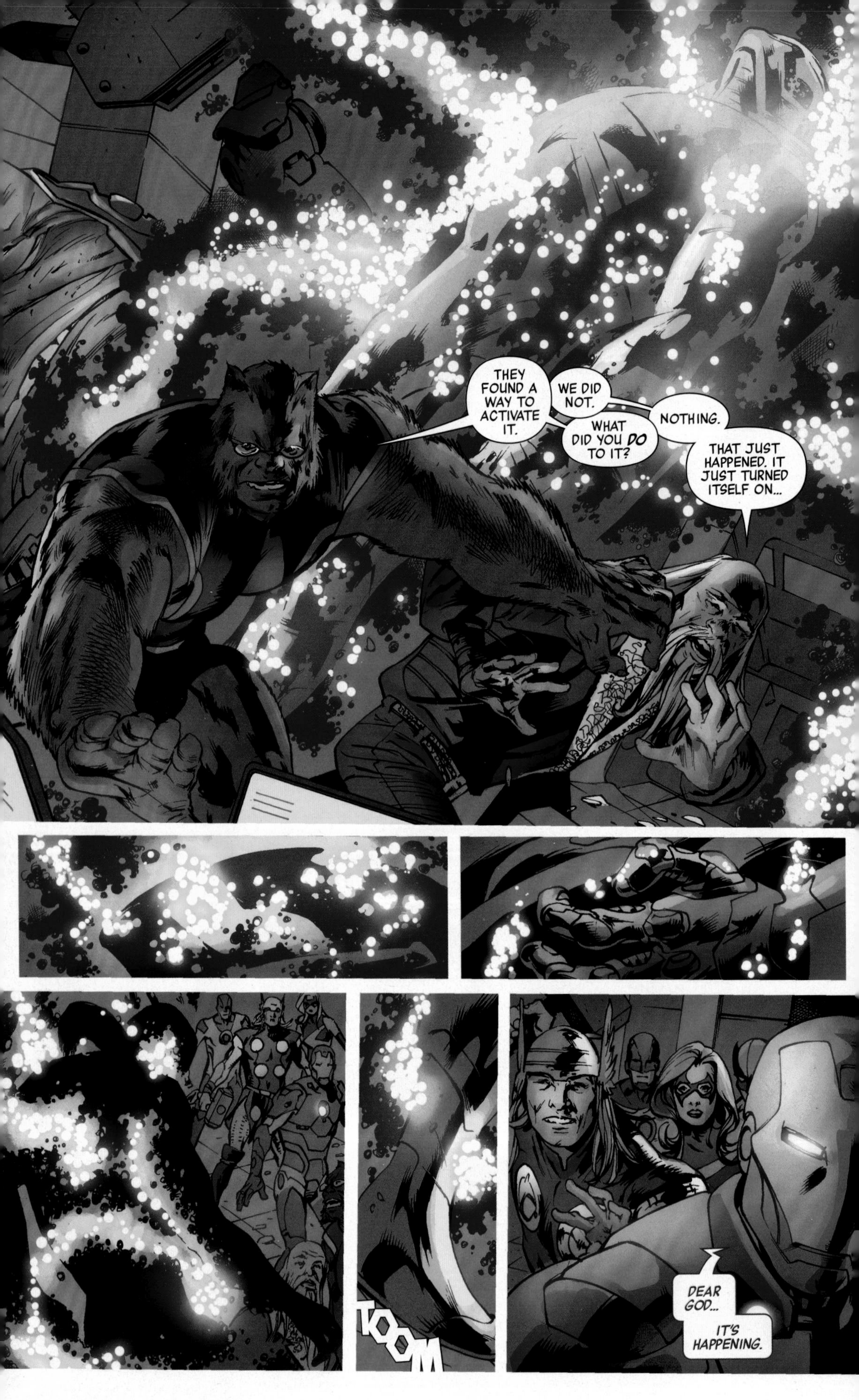
THEY FOUND A WAY TO ACTIVATE IT.
WE DID NOT.
WHAT DID YOU *DO* TO IT?
NOTHING.
THAT JUST HAPPENED. IT JUST TURNED ITSELF ON...
TOOM
DEAR GOD...
IT'S HAPPENING.

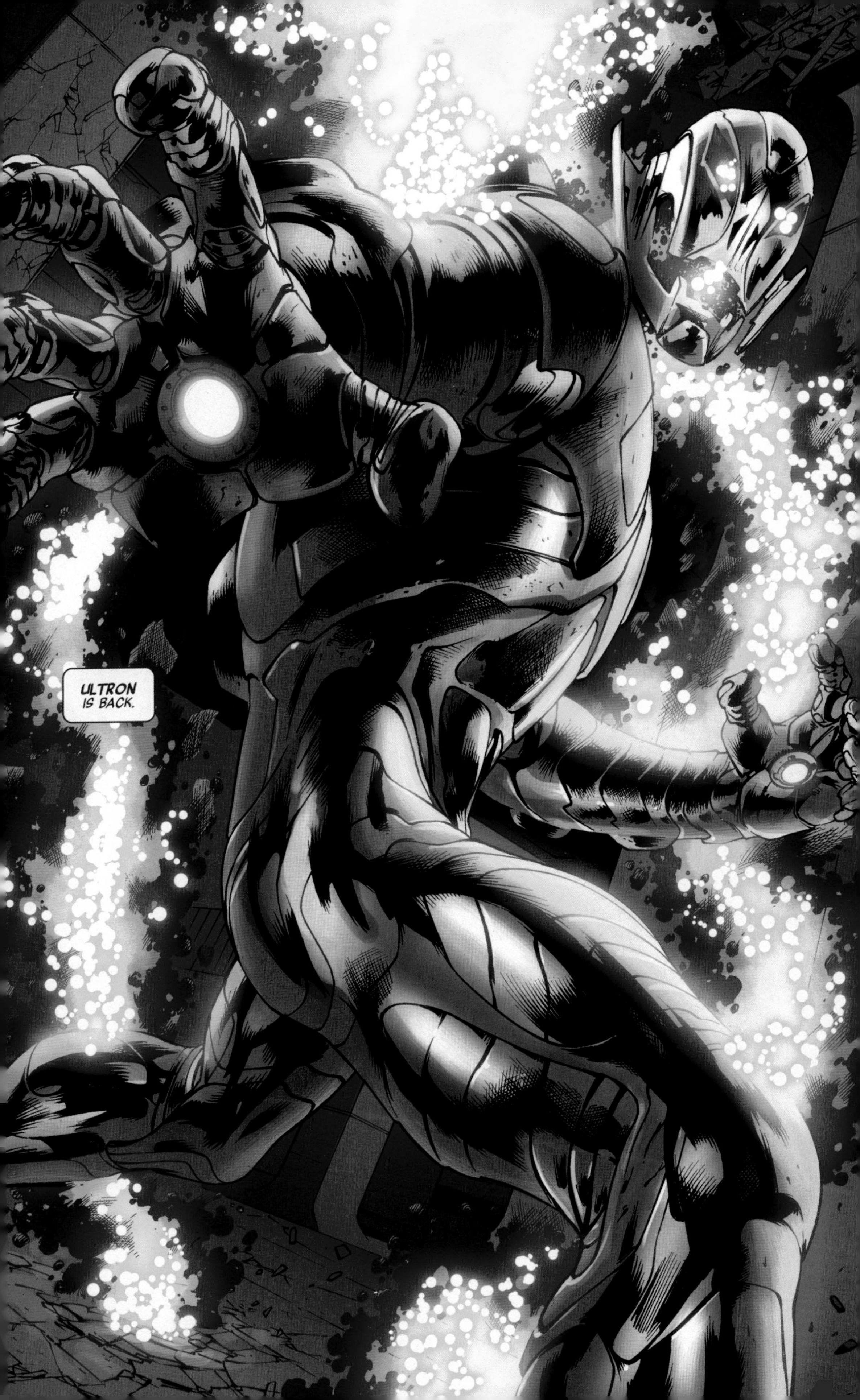
ULTRON IS BACK.

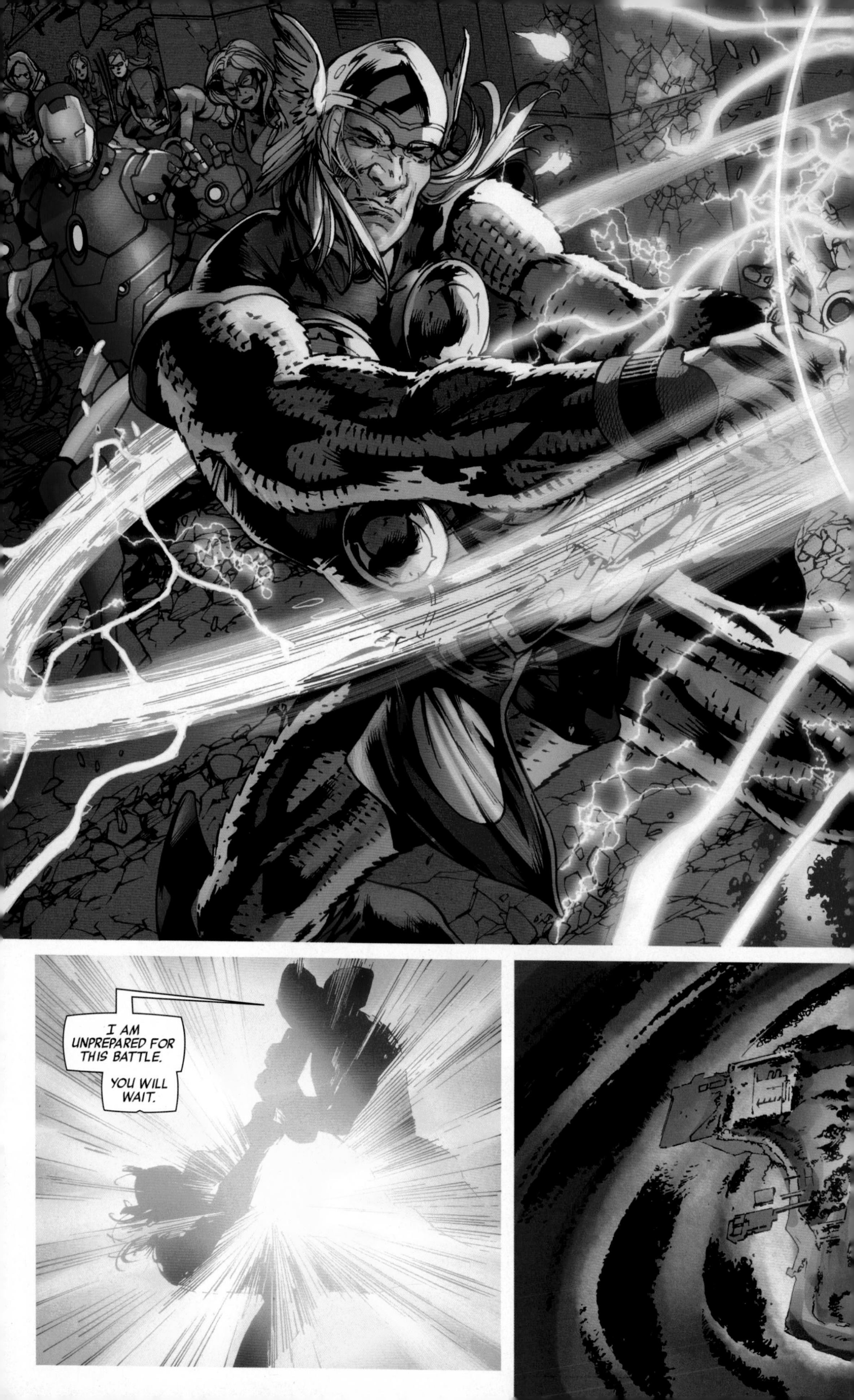
I AM UNPREPARED FOR THIS BATTLE.
YOU WILL WAIT.

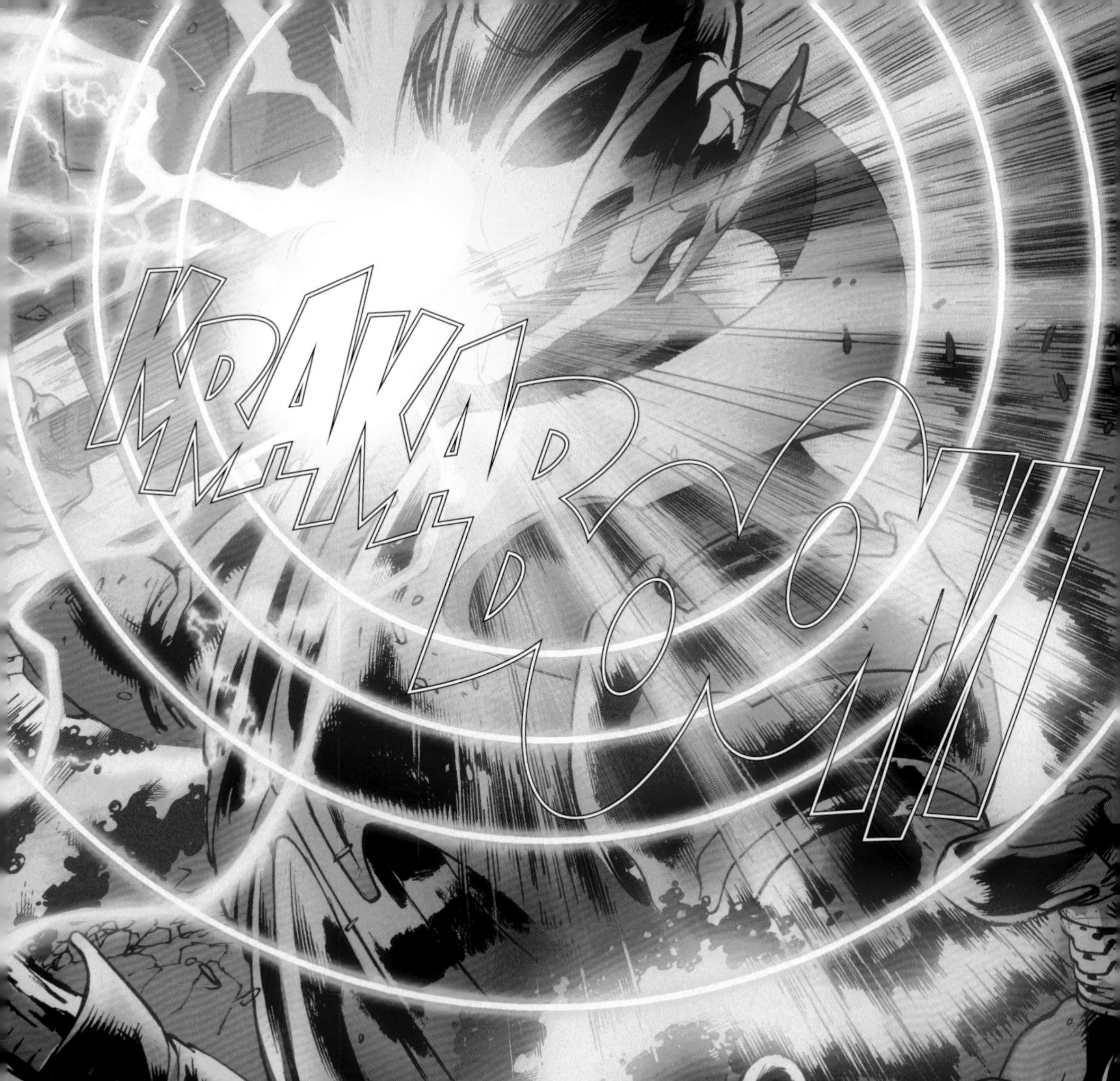
KRAKAROOOM!!

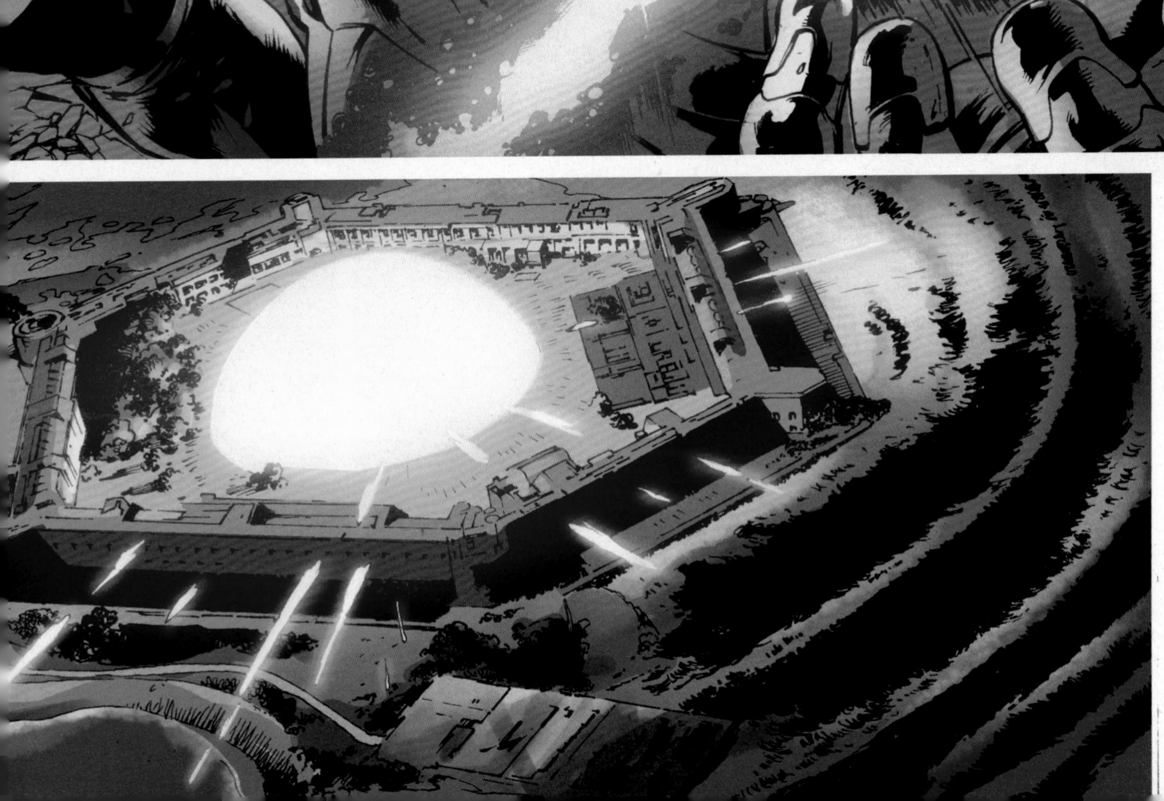

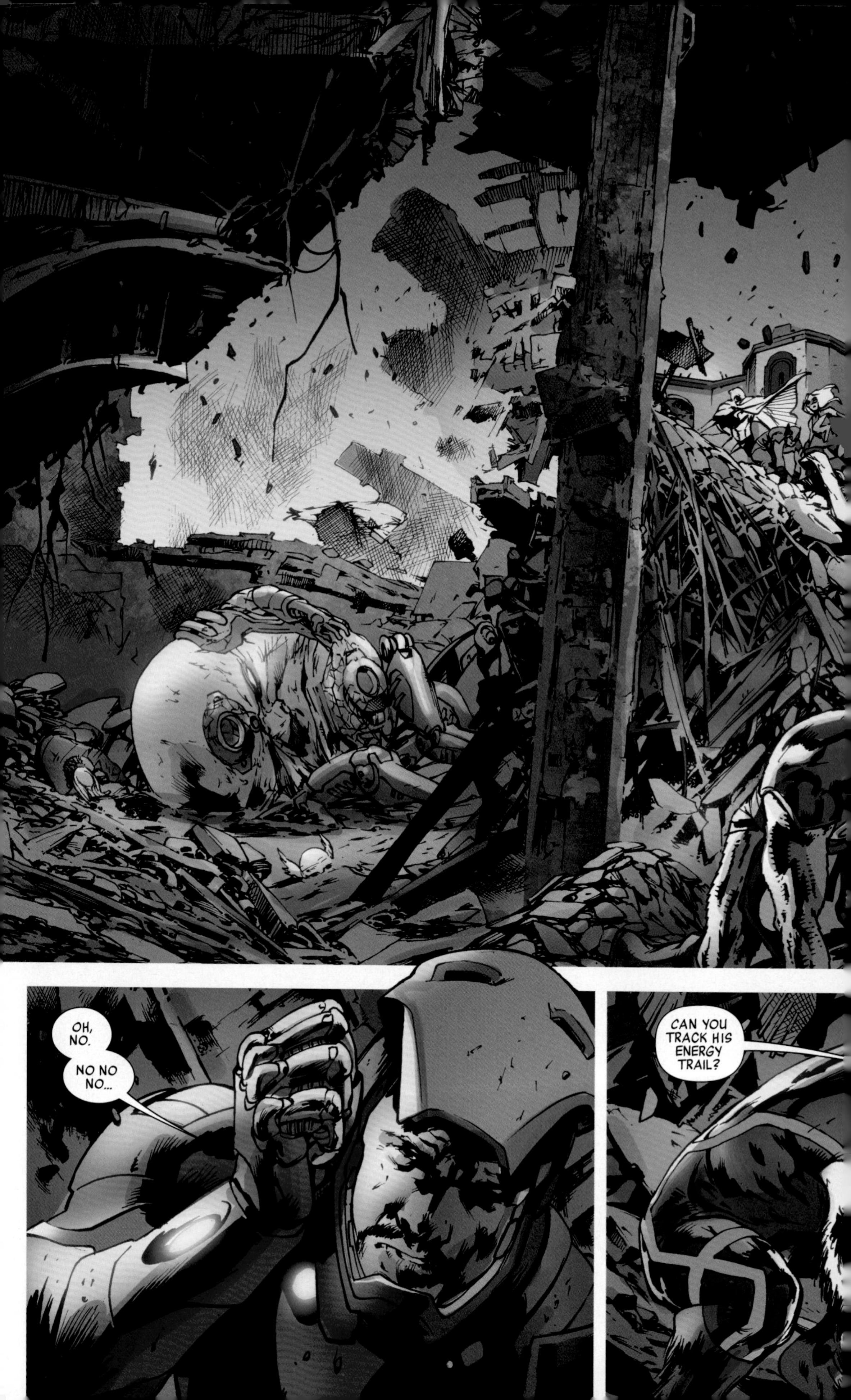
OH, NO.
NO NO NO...
CAN YOU TRACK HIS ENERGY TRAIL?

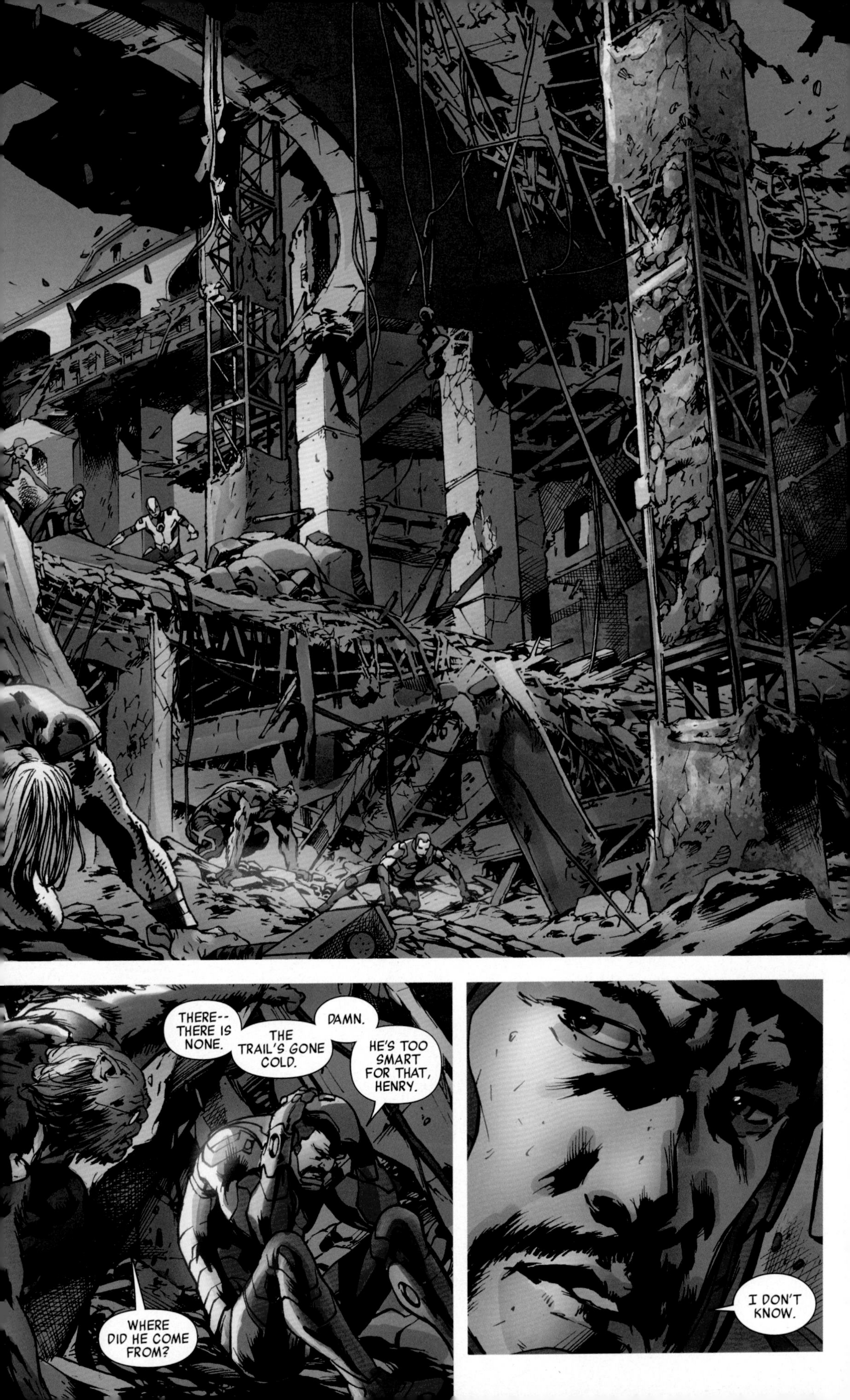
THERE-- THERE IS NONE.
THE TRAIL'S GONE COLD.
DAMN.
HE'S TOO SMART FOR THAT, HENRY.
WHERE DID HE COME FROM?
I DON'T KNOW.

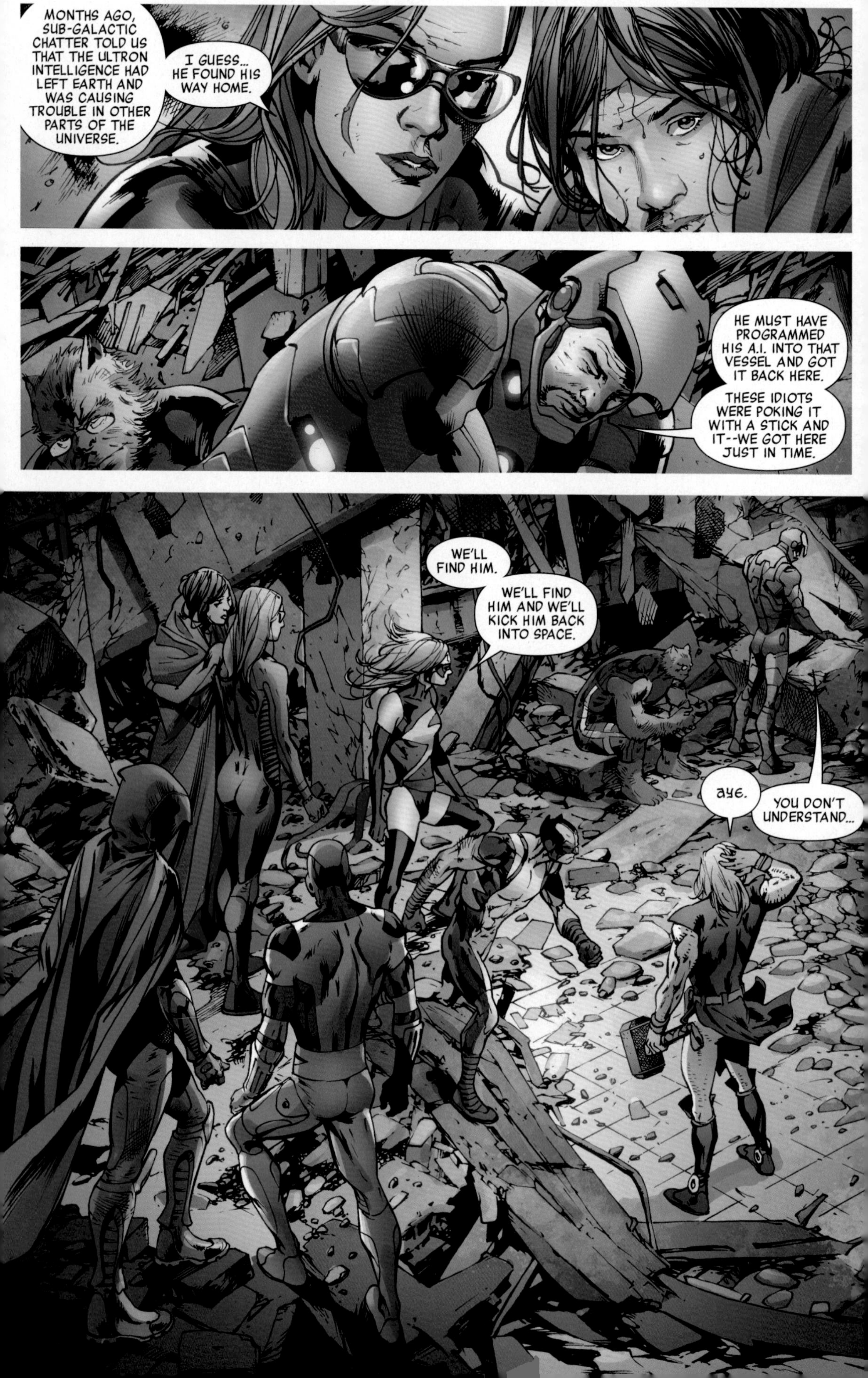
MONTHS AGO, SUB-GALACTIC CHATTER TOLD US THAT THE ULTRON INTELLIGENCE HAD LEFT EARTH AND WAS CAUSING TROUBLE IN OTHER PARTS OF THE UNIVERSE.
I GUESS... HE FOUND HIS WAY HOME.
HE MUST HAVE PROGRAMMED HIS A.I. INTO THAT VESSEL AND GOT IT BACK HERE.
THESE IDIOTS WERE POKING IT WITH A STICK AND IT--WE GOT HERE JUST IN TIME.
WE'LL FIND HIM.
WE'LL FIND HIM AND WE'LL KICK HIM BACK INTO SPACE.
aye.
YOU DON'T UNDERSTAND...

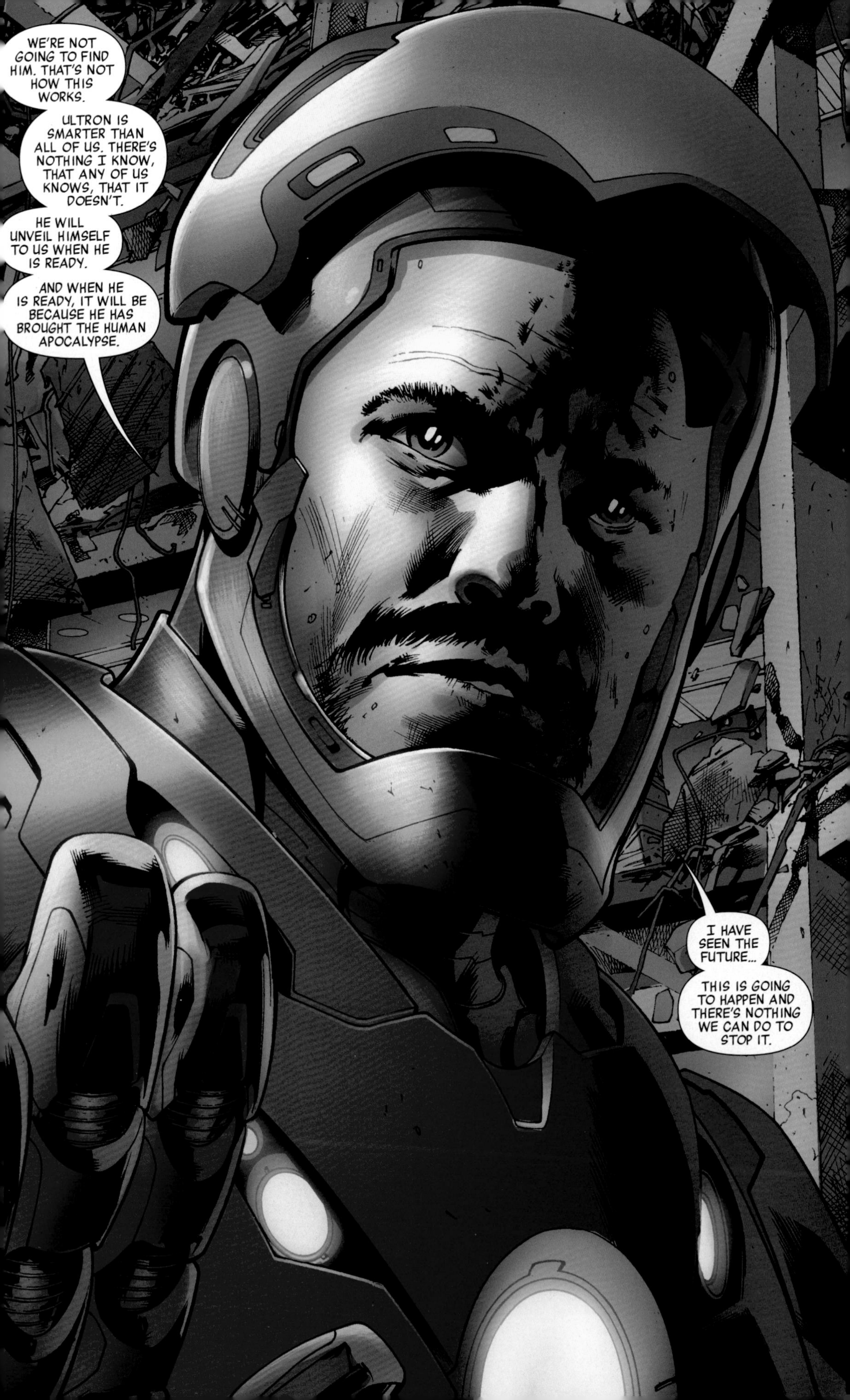
WE'RE NOT GOING TO FIND HIM. THAT'S NOT HOW THIS WORKS.
ULTRON IS SMARTER THAN ALL OF US. THERE'S NOTHING I KNOW, THAT ANY OF US KNOWS, THAT IT DOESN'T.
HE WILL UNVEIL HIMSELF TO US WHEN HE IS READY.
AND WHEN HE IS READY, IT WILL BE BECAUSE HE HAS BROUGHT THE HUMAN APOCALYPSE.
I HAVE SEEN THE FUTURE...
THIS IS GOING TO HAPPEN AND THERE'S NOTHING WE CAN DO TO STOP IT.

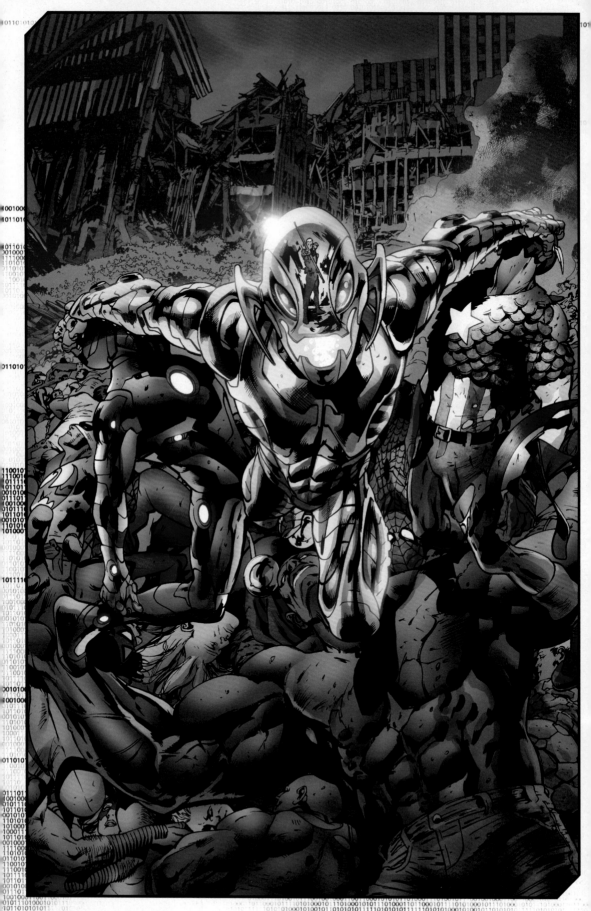

AGE OF ULTRON #1

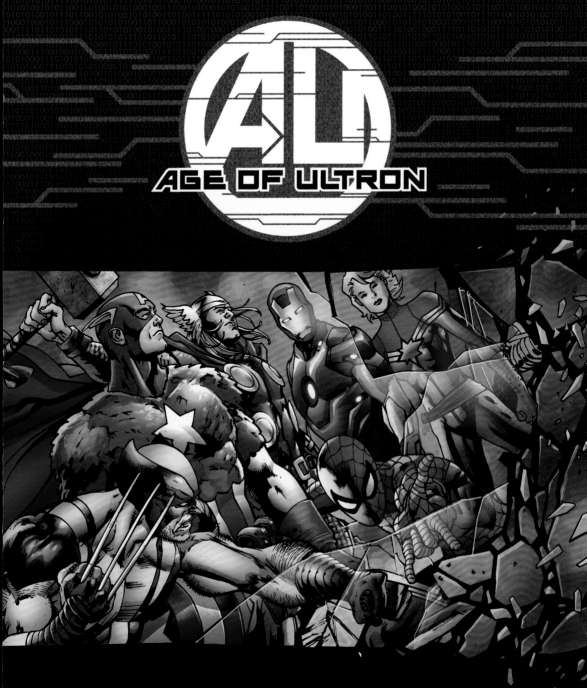

AGE OF ULTRON

HANK PYM OF THE AVENGERS CREATED THE ARTIFICIAL INTELLIGENCE KNOWN AS ULTRON.

IT HATES HUMANITY...AND IT HAS RETURNED...

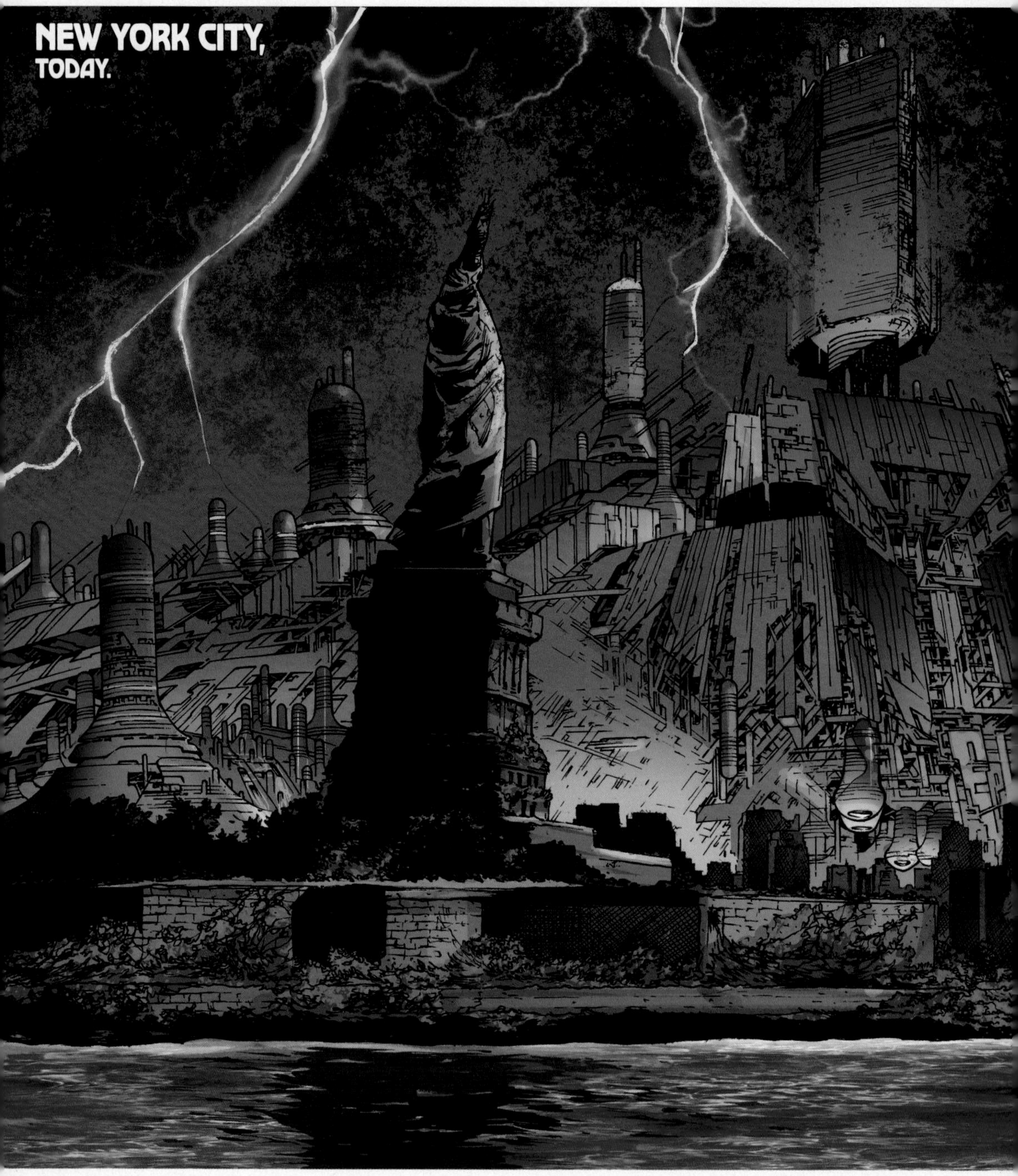
NEW YORK CITY,
TODAY.

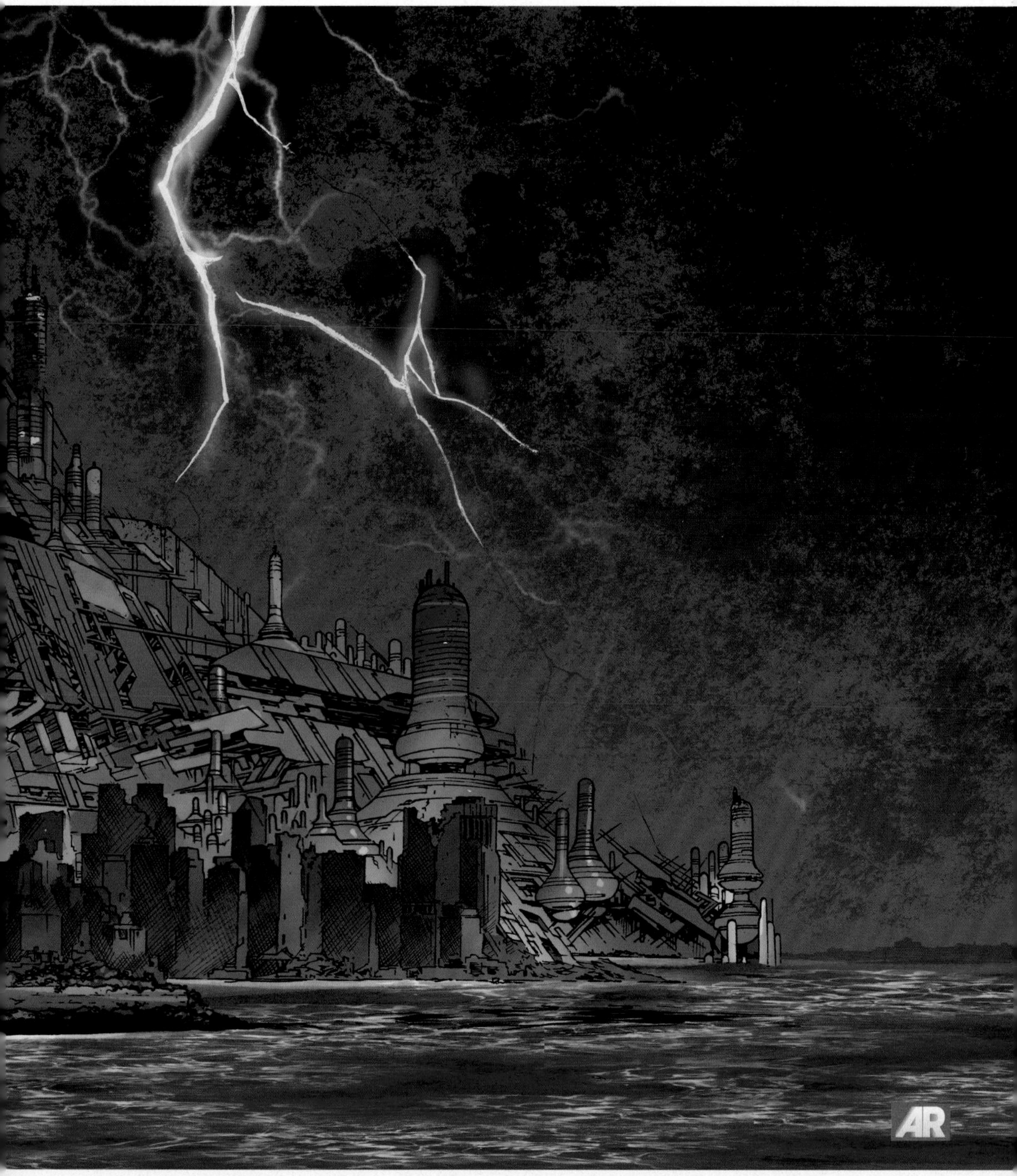

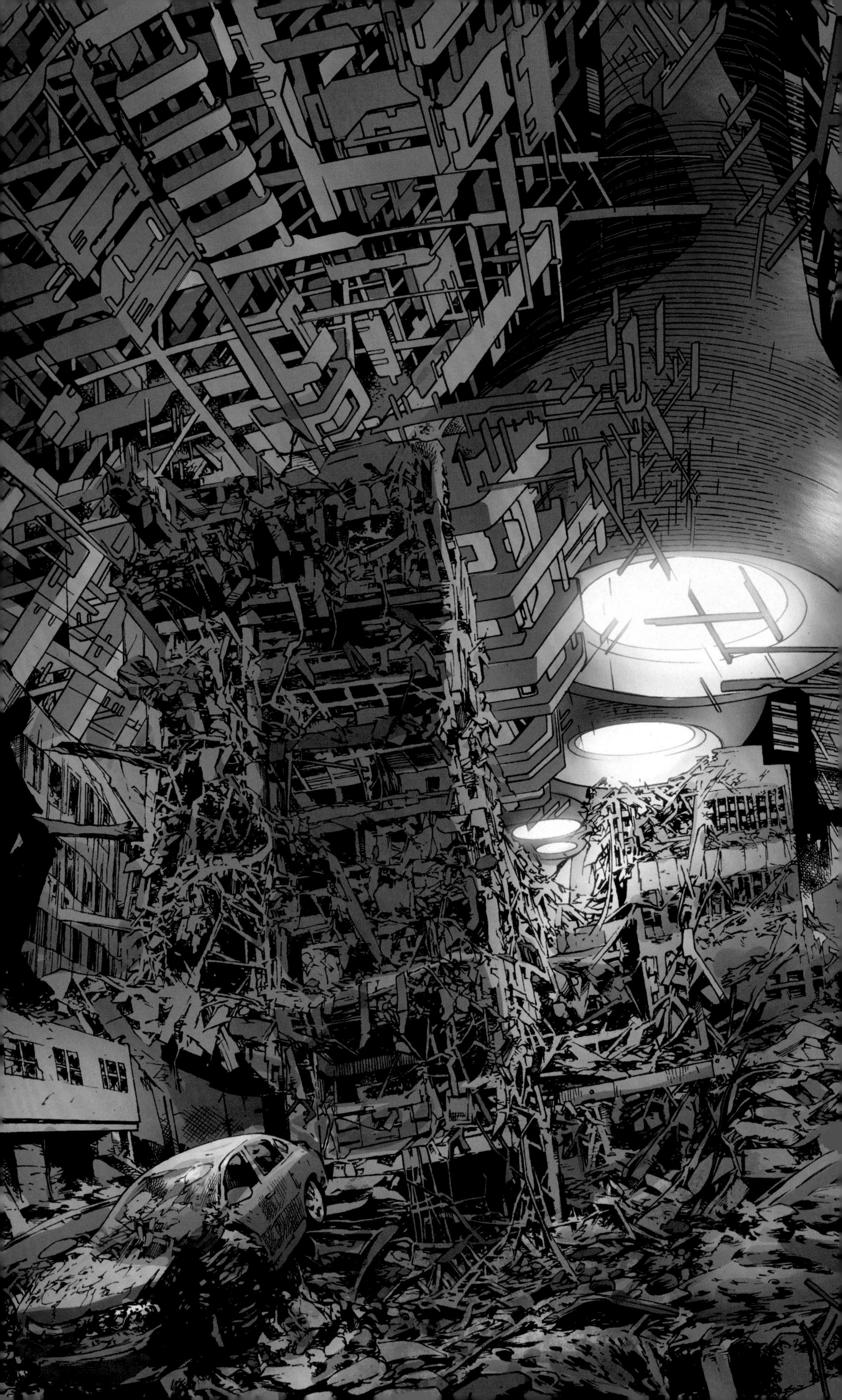

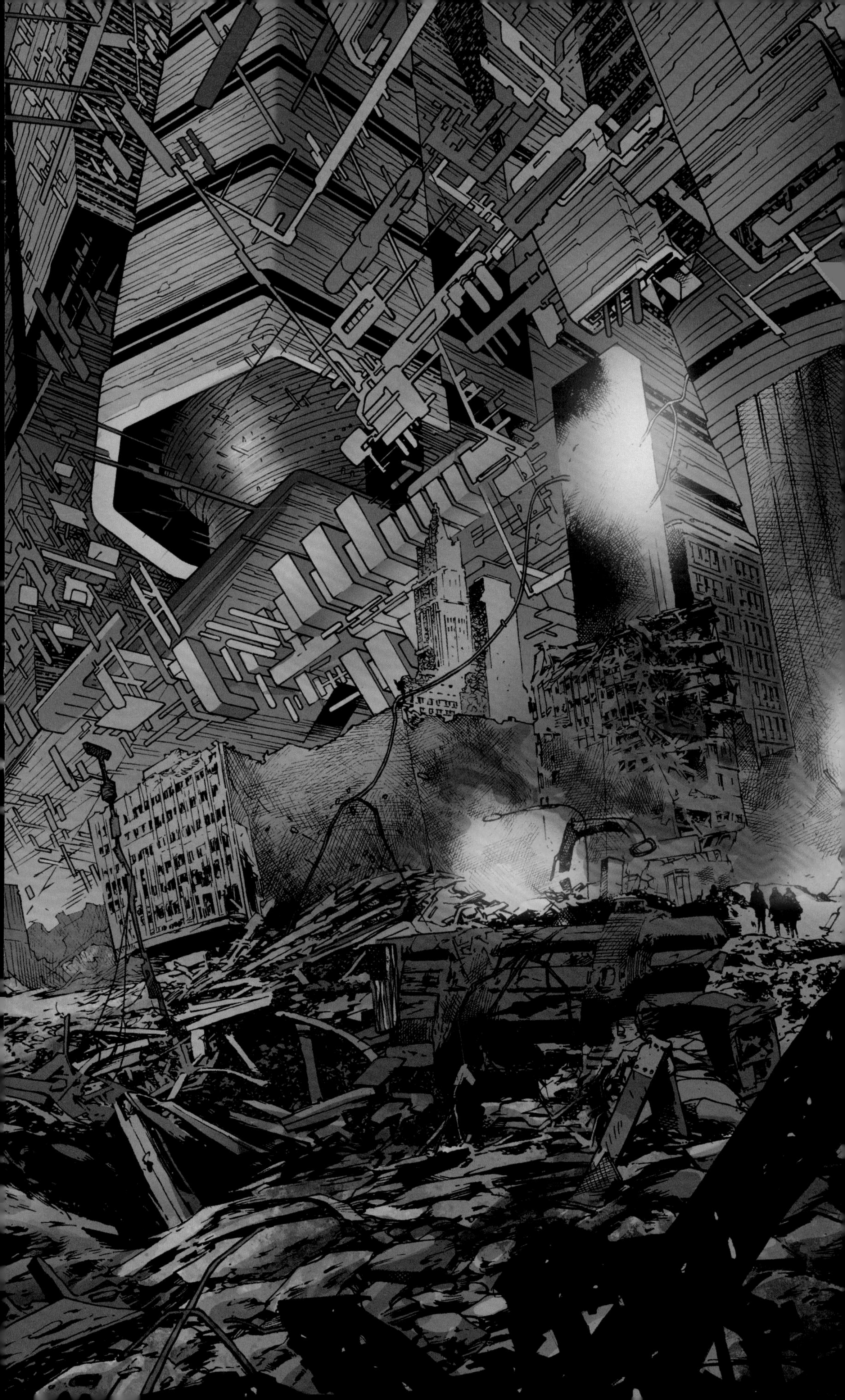

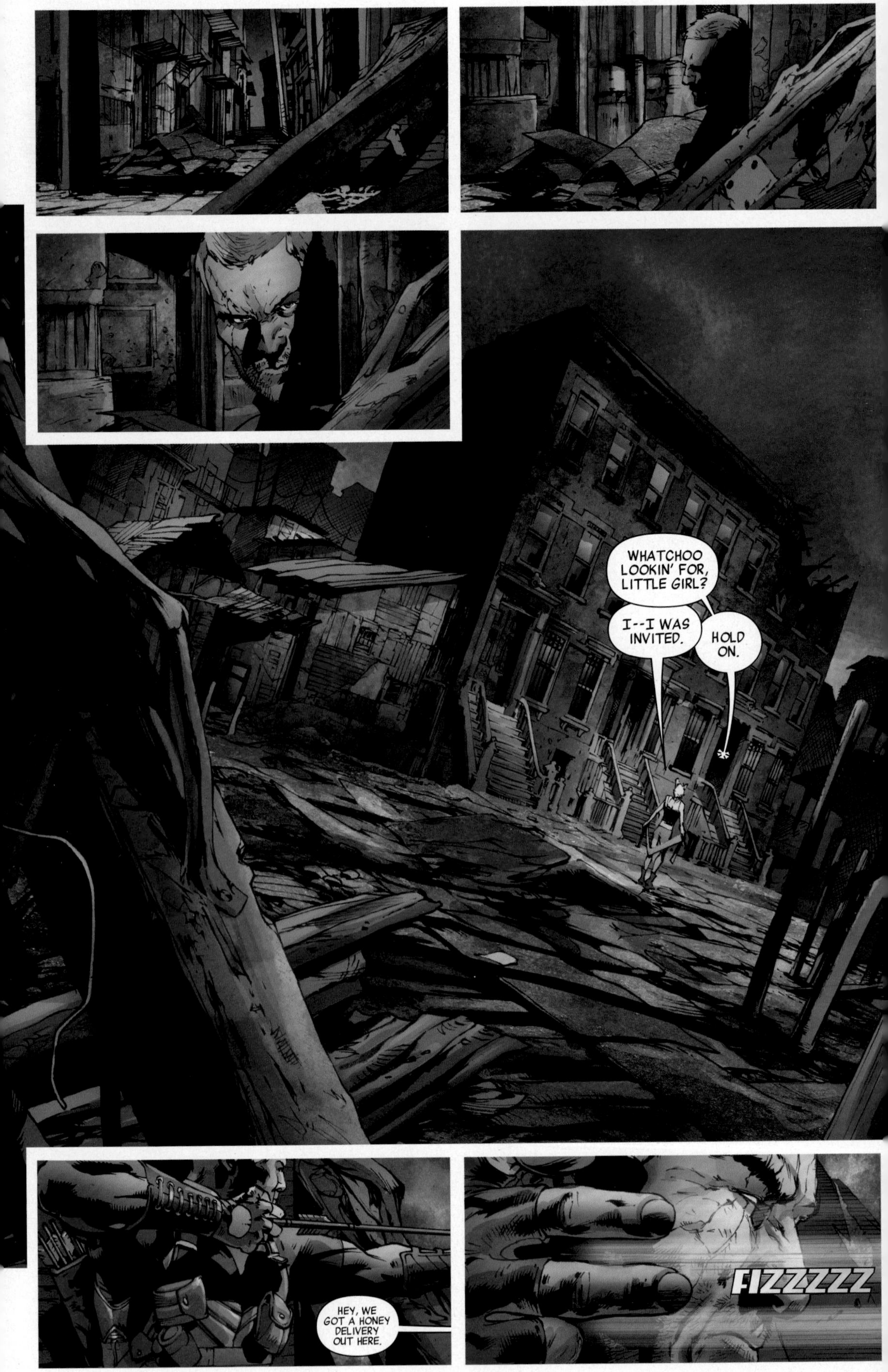
WHATCHOO LOOKIN' FOR, LITTLE GIRL?
I--I WAS INVITED.
HOLD ON.
HEY, WE GOT A HONEY DELIVERY OUT HERE.
FIZZZZZ

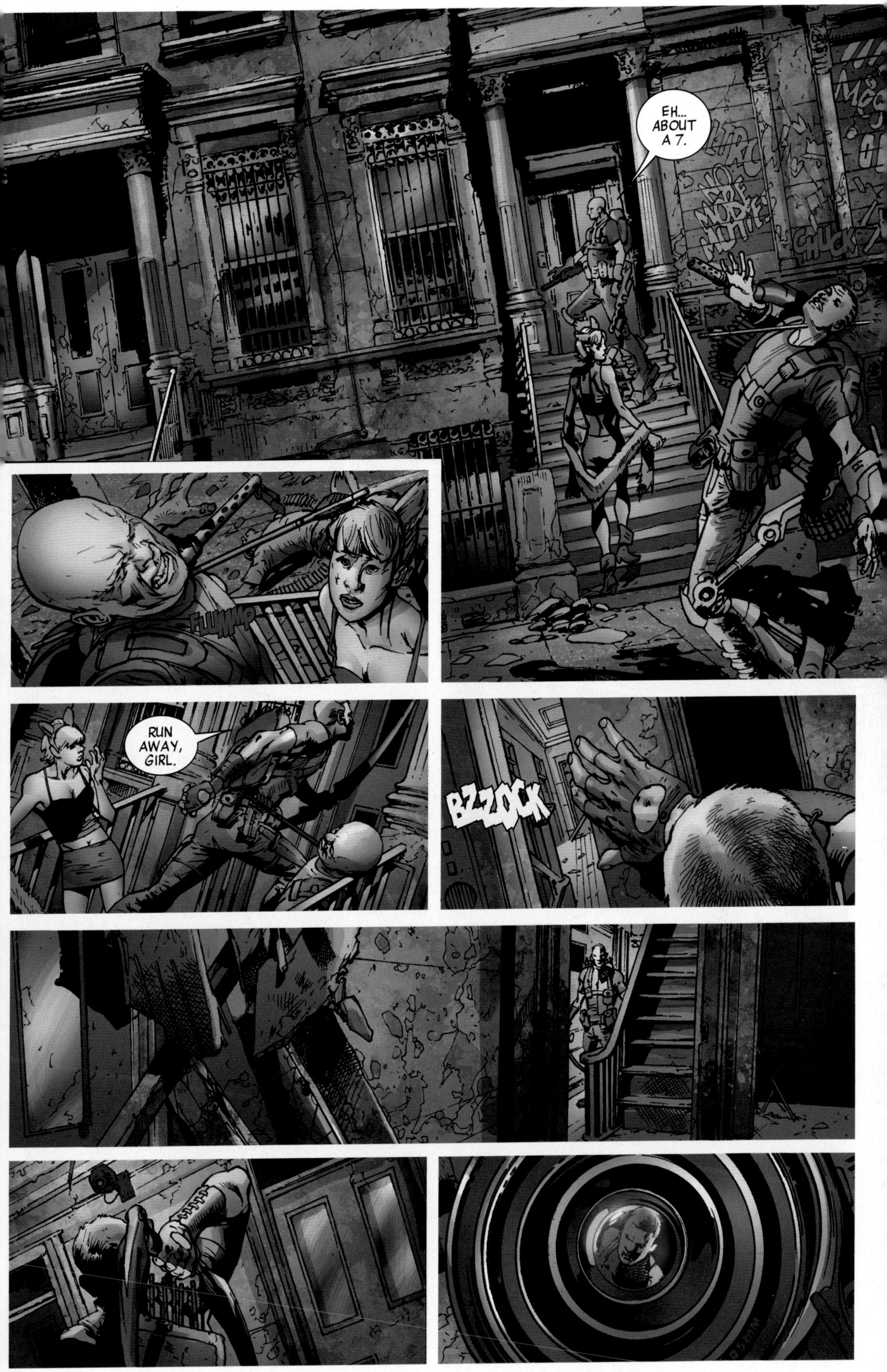

EH... ABOUT A 7.
FLUMP
RUN AWAY, GIRL.
BZZOCK

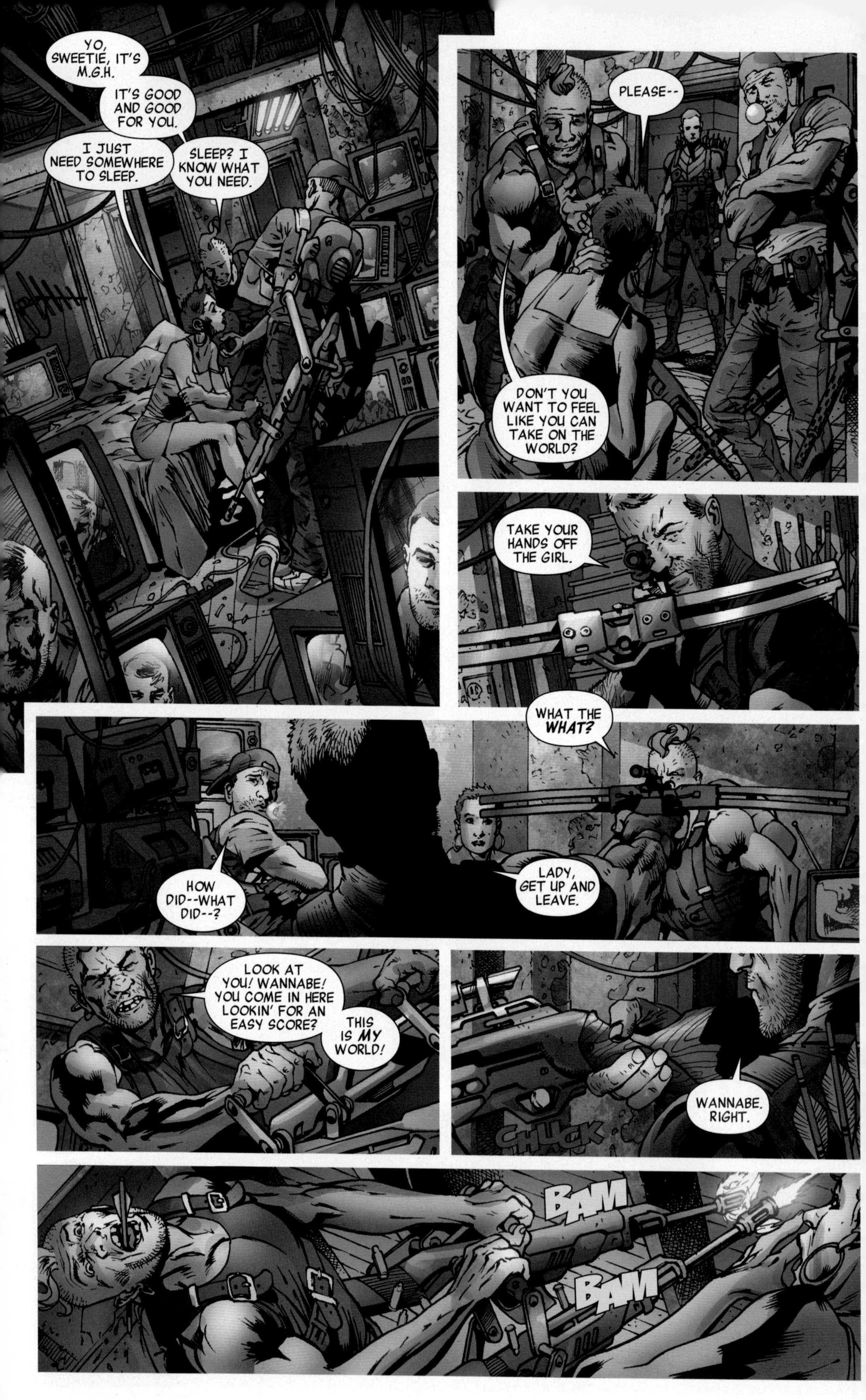

YO, SWEETIE, IT'S M.G.H.
IT'S GOOD AND GOOD FOR YOU.
I JUST NEED SOMEWHERE TO SLEEP.
SLEEP? I KNOW WHAT YOU NEED.
PLEASE--
DON'T YOU WANT TO FEEL LIKE YOU CAN TAKE ON THE WORLD?
TAKE YOUR HANDS OFF THE GIRL.
WHAT THE *WHAT?*
HOW DID--WHAT DID--?
LADY, GET UP AND LEAVE.
LOOK AT YOU! WANNABE! YOU COME IN HERE LOOKIN' FOR AN EASY SCORE?
THIS IS *MY* WORLD!
CHUCK
WANNABE. RIGHT.
BAM
BAM

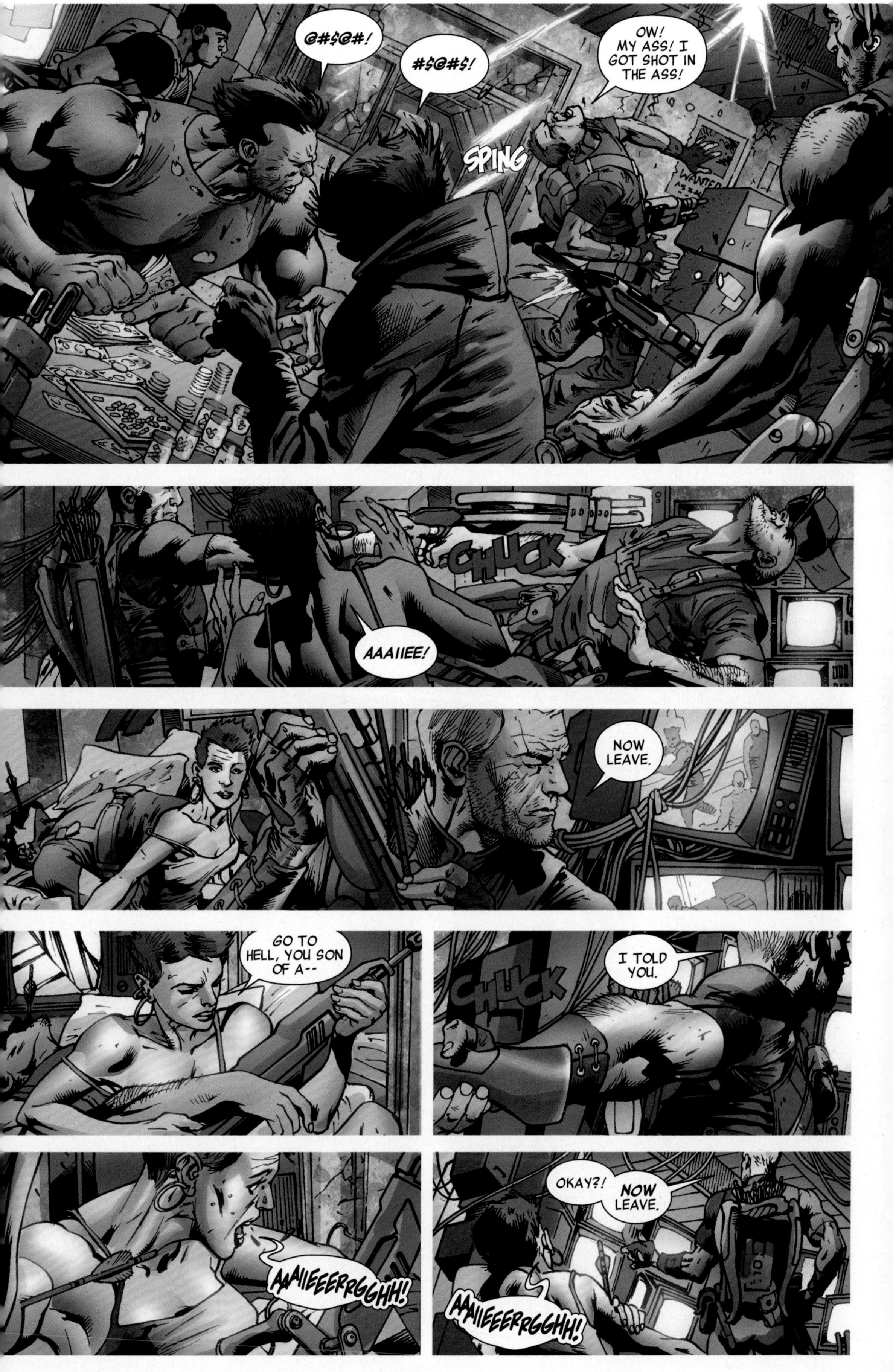
@#$@#!
#$@#$!
SPING
OW! MY ASS! I GOT SHOT IN THE ASS!
CHUCK
AAAIIEE!
NOW LEAVE.
GO TO HELL, YOU SON OF A--
CHUCK
I TOLD YOU.
AAAIIEEERRGGHH!
OKAY?!
NOW LEAVE.
AAAIIEEERRGGHH!

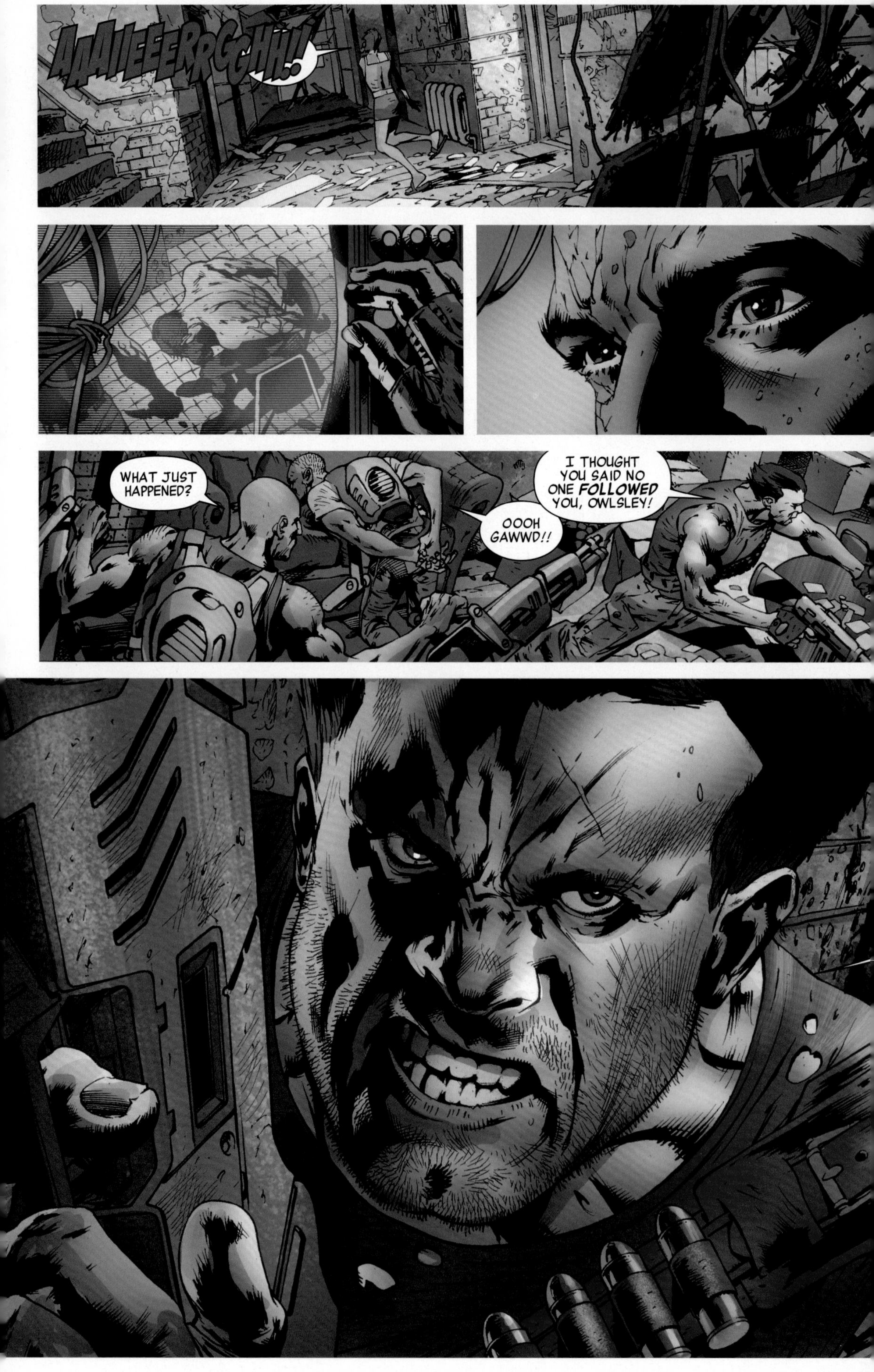
AAAIIEEERRGGHH!!
WHAT JUST HAPPENED?
OOOH GAWWD!!
I THOUGHT YOU SAID NO ONE FOLLOWED YOU, OWLSLEY!

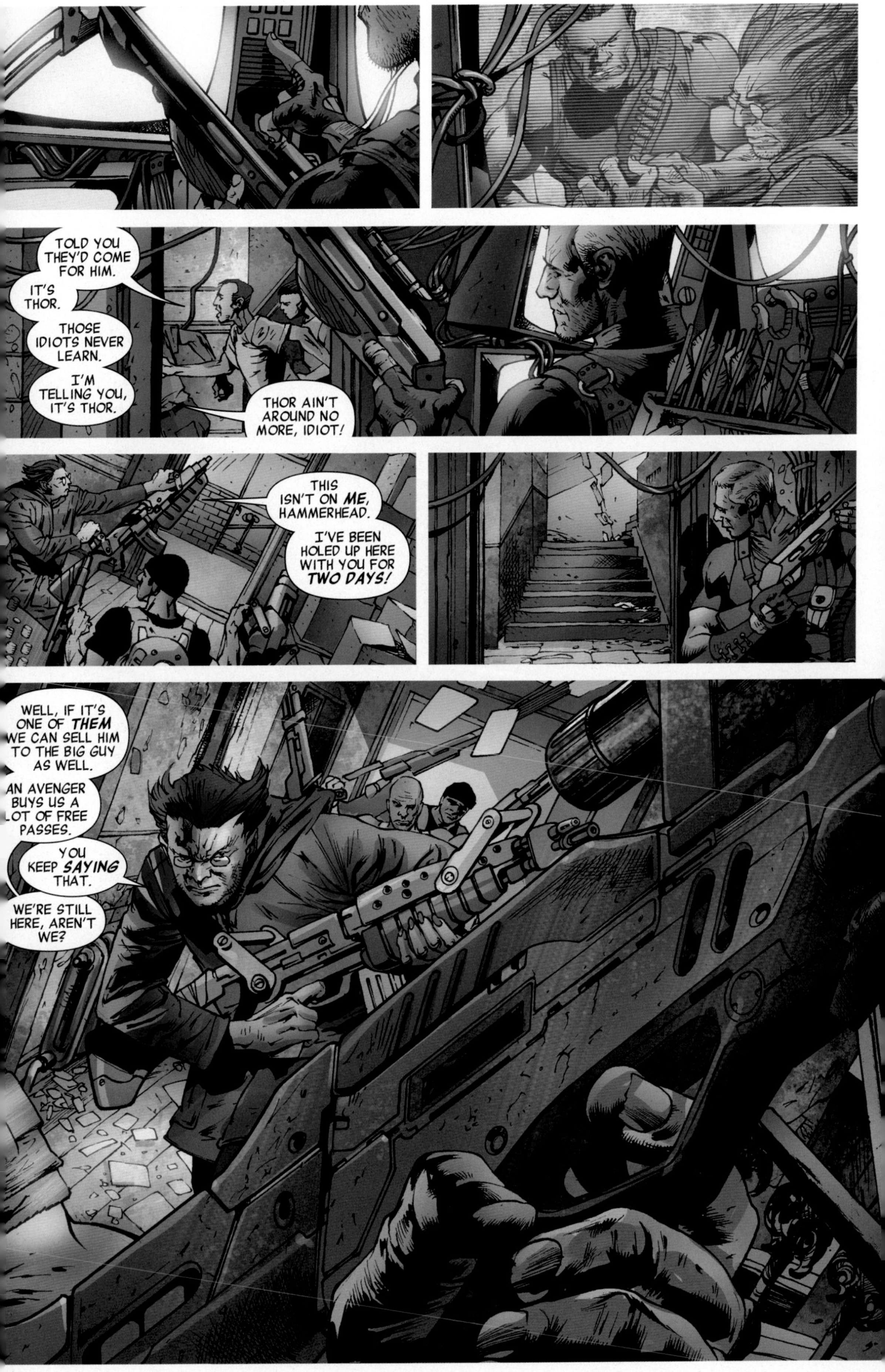
TOLD YOU THEY'D COME FOR HIM.
IT'S THOR.
THOSE IDIOTS NEVER LEARN.
I'M TELLING YOU, IT'S THOR.
THOR AIN'T AROUND NO MORE, IDIOT!
THIS ISN'T ON ME, HAMMERHEAD.
I'VE BEEN HOLED UP HERE WITH YOU FOR TWO DAYS!
WELL, IF IT'S ONE OF THEM WE CAN SELL HIM TO THE BIG GUY AS WELL.
AN AVENGER BUYS US A LOT OF FREE PASSES.
YOU KEEP SAYING THAT.
WE'RE STILL HERE, AREN'T WE?

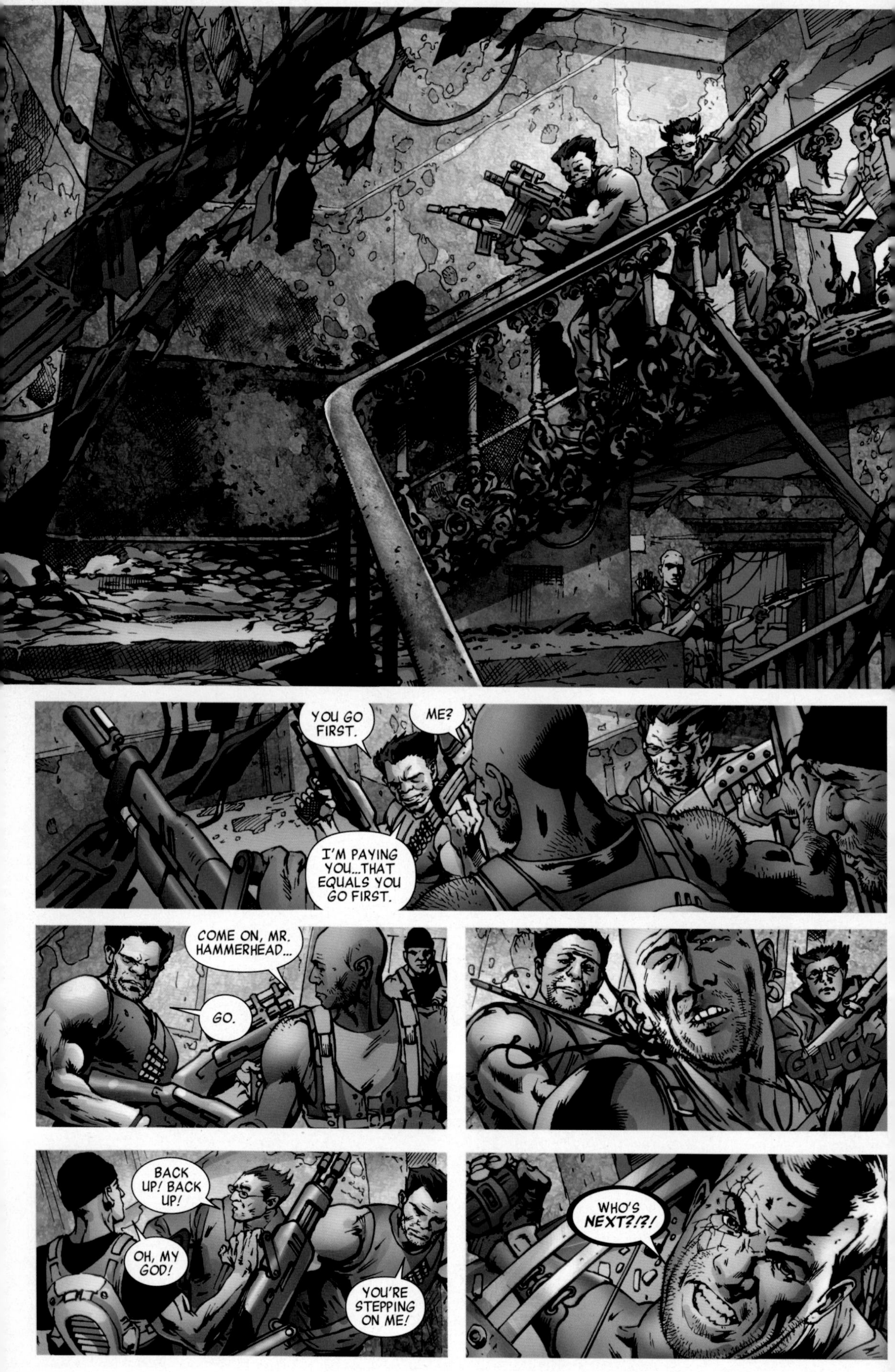
YOU GO FIRST.
ME?
I'M PAYING YOU...THAT EQUALS YOU GO FIRST.
COME ON, MR. HAMMERHEAD...
GO.
CHUCK
BACK UP! BACK UP!
OH, MY GOD!
YOU'RE STEPPING ON ME!
WHO'S NEXT?!?!

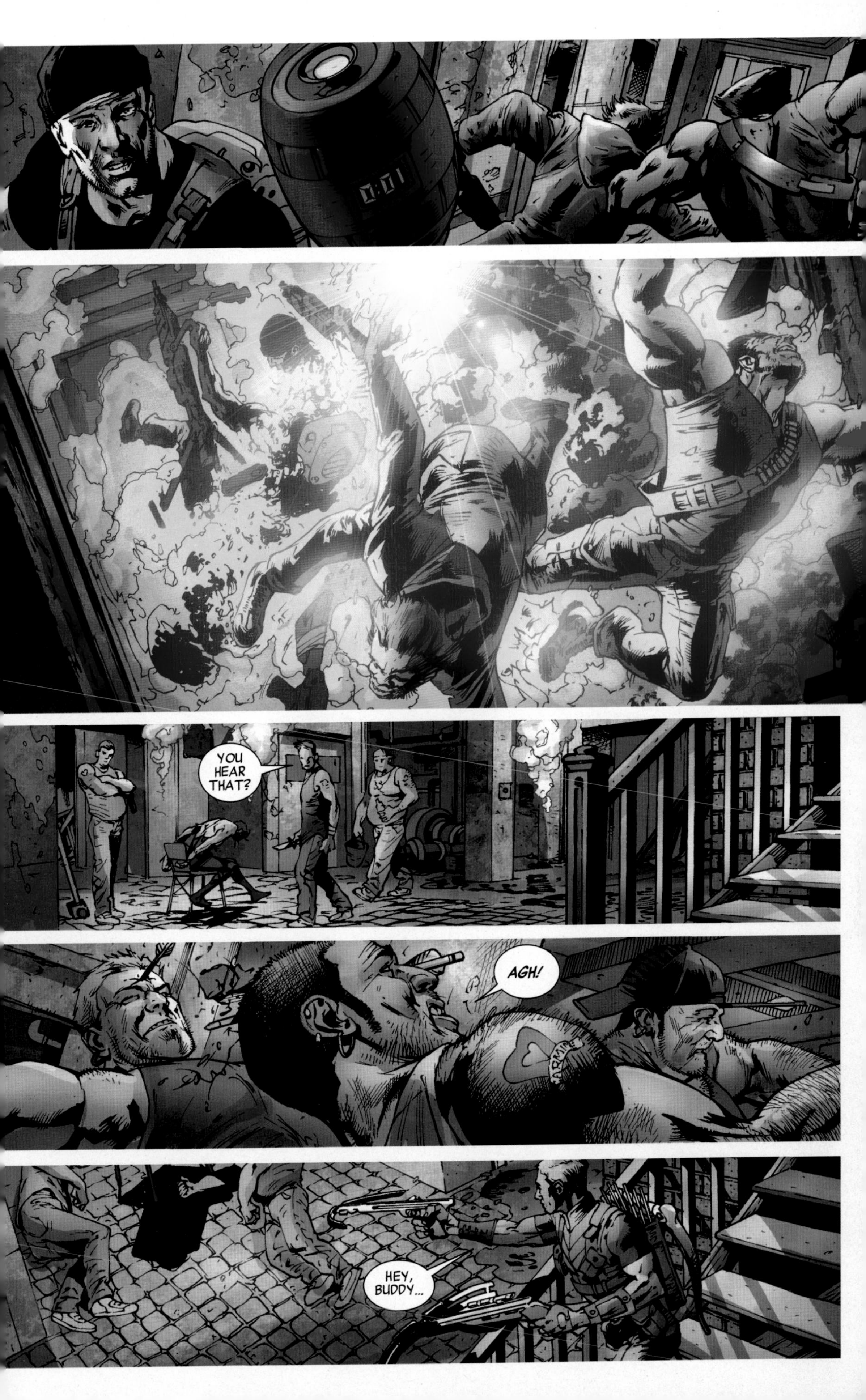
0:01
YOU HEAR THAT?
AGH!
HEY, BUDDY...

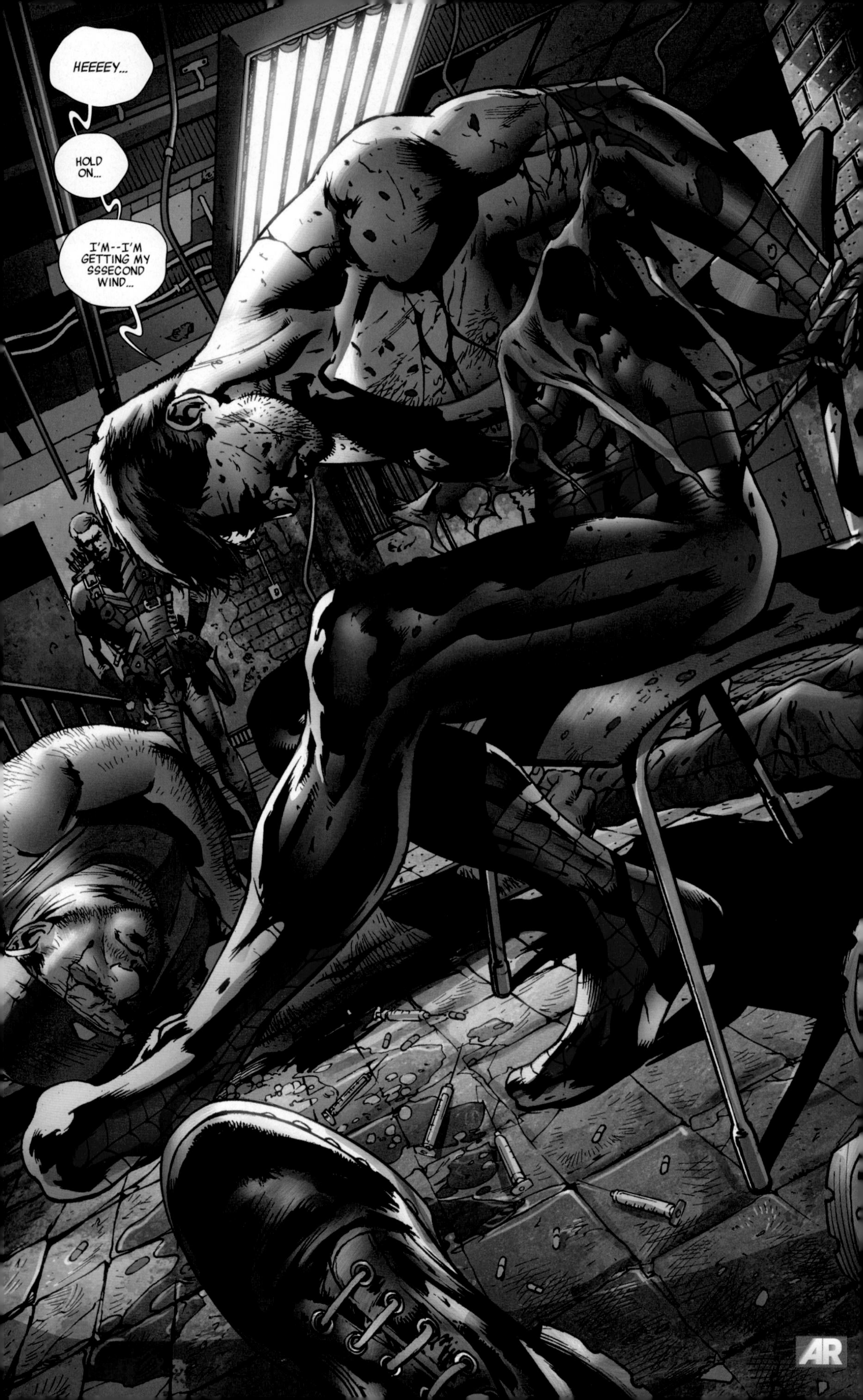
HEEEEY...
HOLD ON...
I'M--I'M GETTING MY SSSECOND WIND...
AR

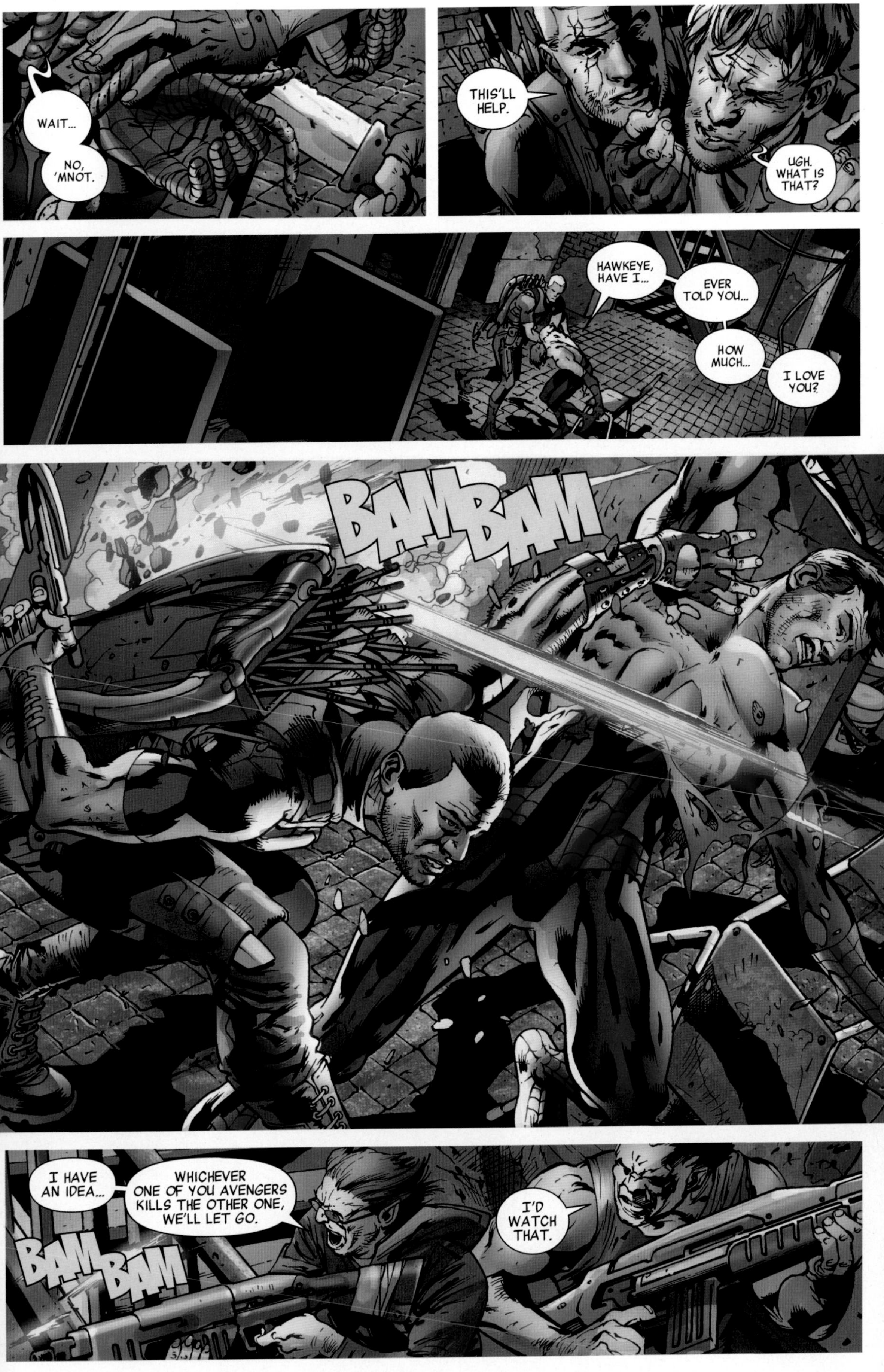
WAIT...
NO, 'MNOT.
THIS'LL HELP.
UGH. WHAT IS THAT?
HAWKEYE, HAVE I...
EVER TOLD YOU...
HOW MUCH...
I LOVE YOU?
BAM BAM
I HAVE AN IDEA...
WHICHEVER ONE OF YOU AVENGERS KILLS THE OTHER ONE, WE'LL LET GO.
I'D WATCH THAT.
BAM BAM

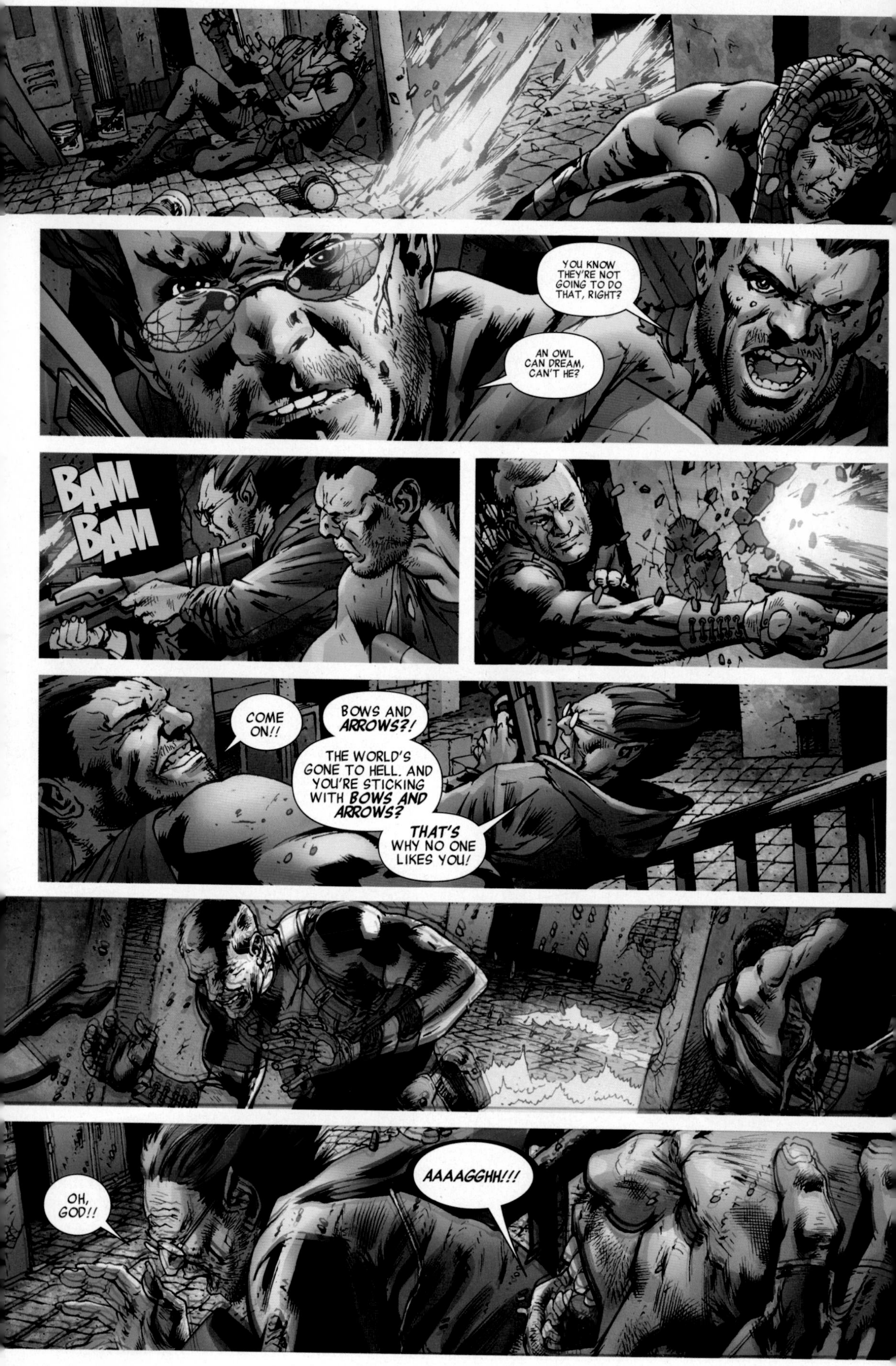
YOU KNOW THEY'RE NOT GOING TO DO THAT, RIGHT?
AN OWL CAN DREAM, CAN'T HE?
BAM BAM
COME ON!!
BOWS AND ARROWS?!
THE WORLD'S GONE TO HELL. AND YOU'RE STICKING WITH BOWS AND ARROWS?
THAT'S WHY NO ONE LIKES YOU!
OH, GOD!!
AAAAGGHH!!!

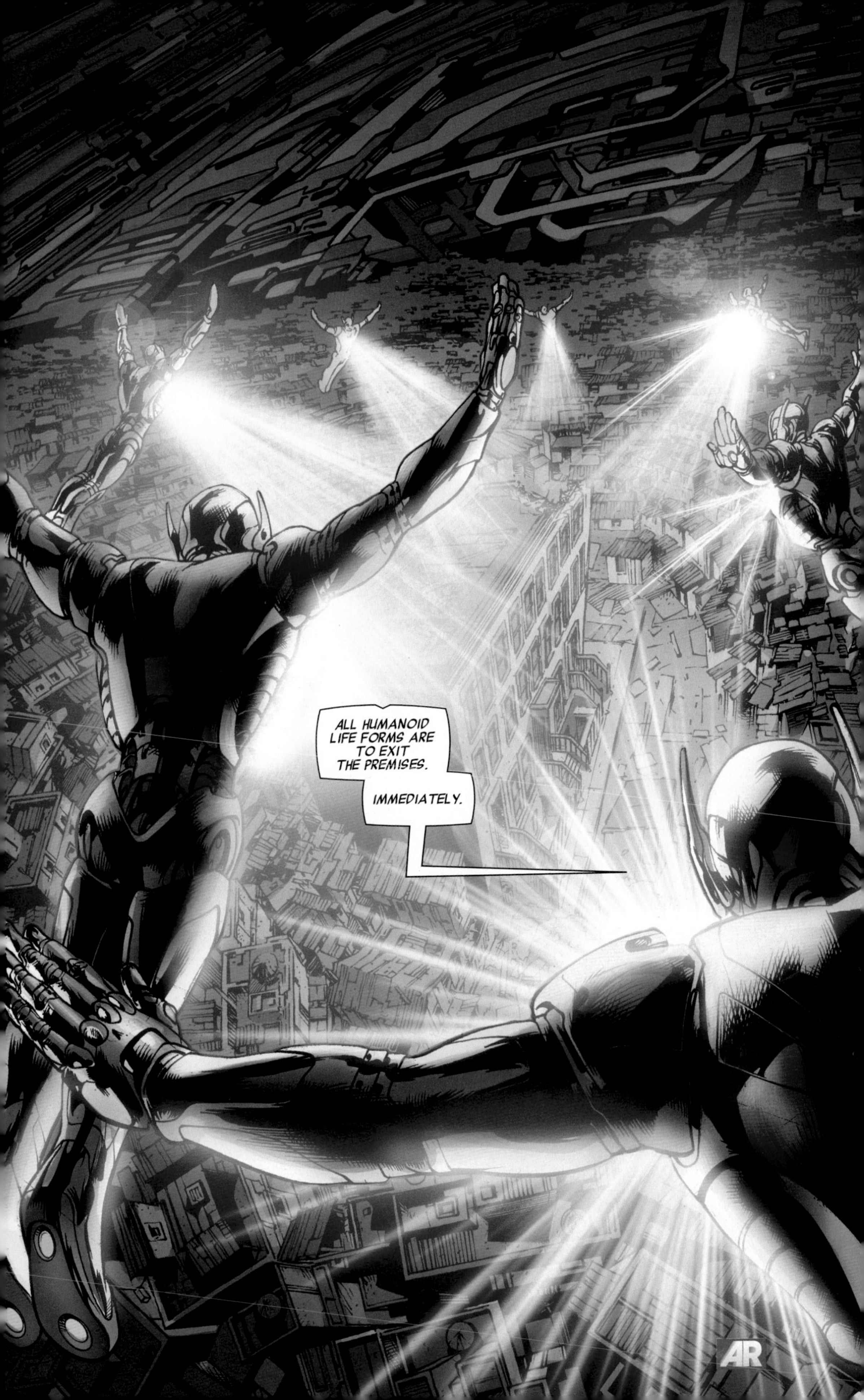
ALL HUMANOID LIFE FORMS ARE TO EXIT THE PREMISES.
IMMEDIATELY.

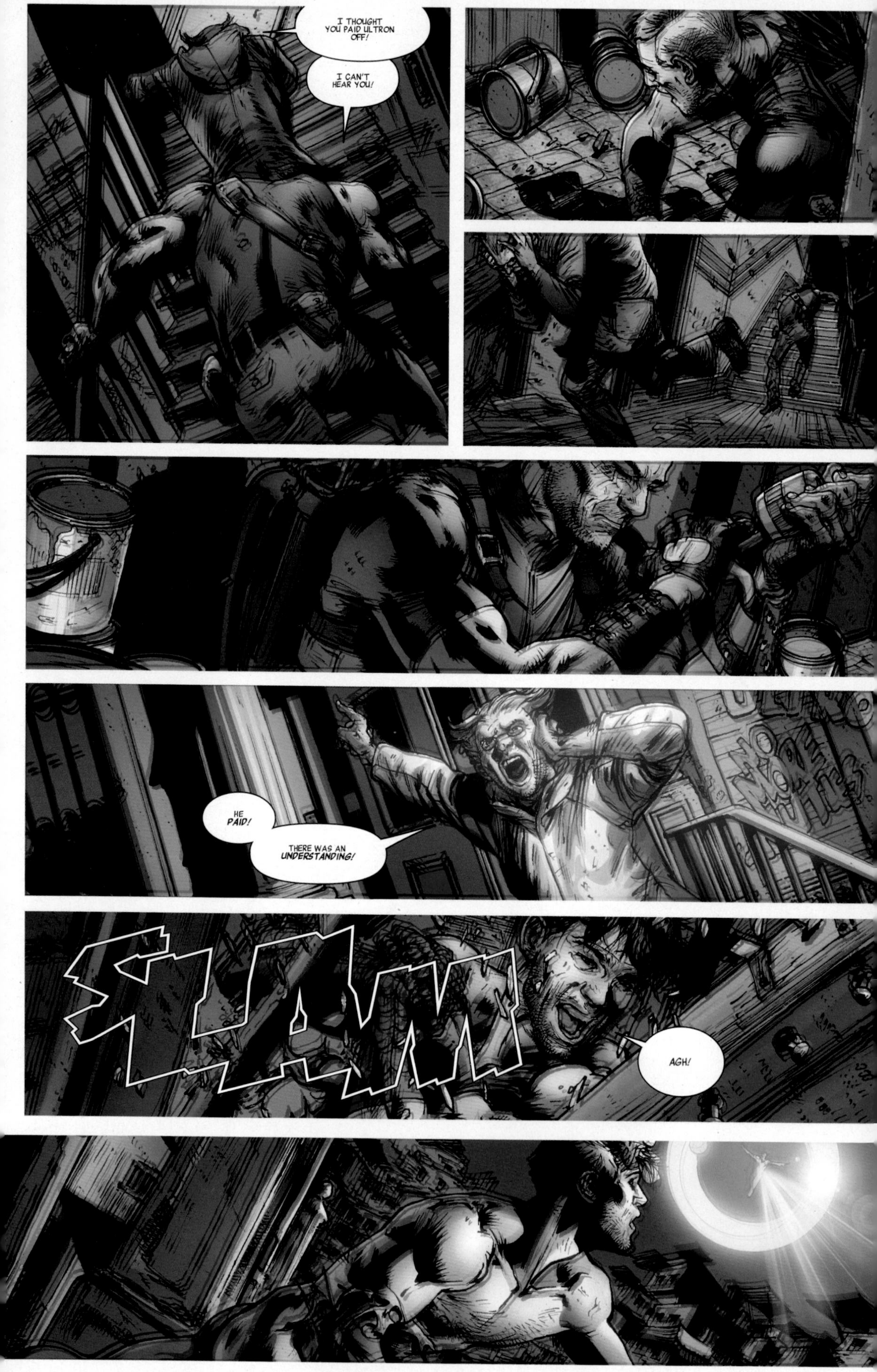
I THOUGHT YOU PAID ULTRON OFF!
I CAN'T HEAR YOU!
HE PAID!
THERE WAS AN UNDERSTANDING!
SLAM
AGH!

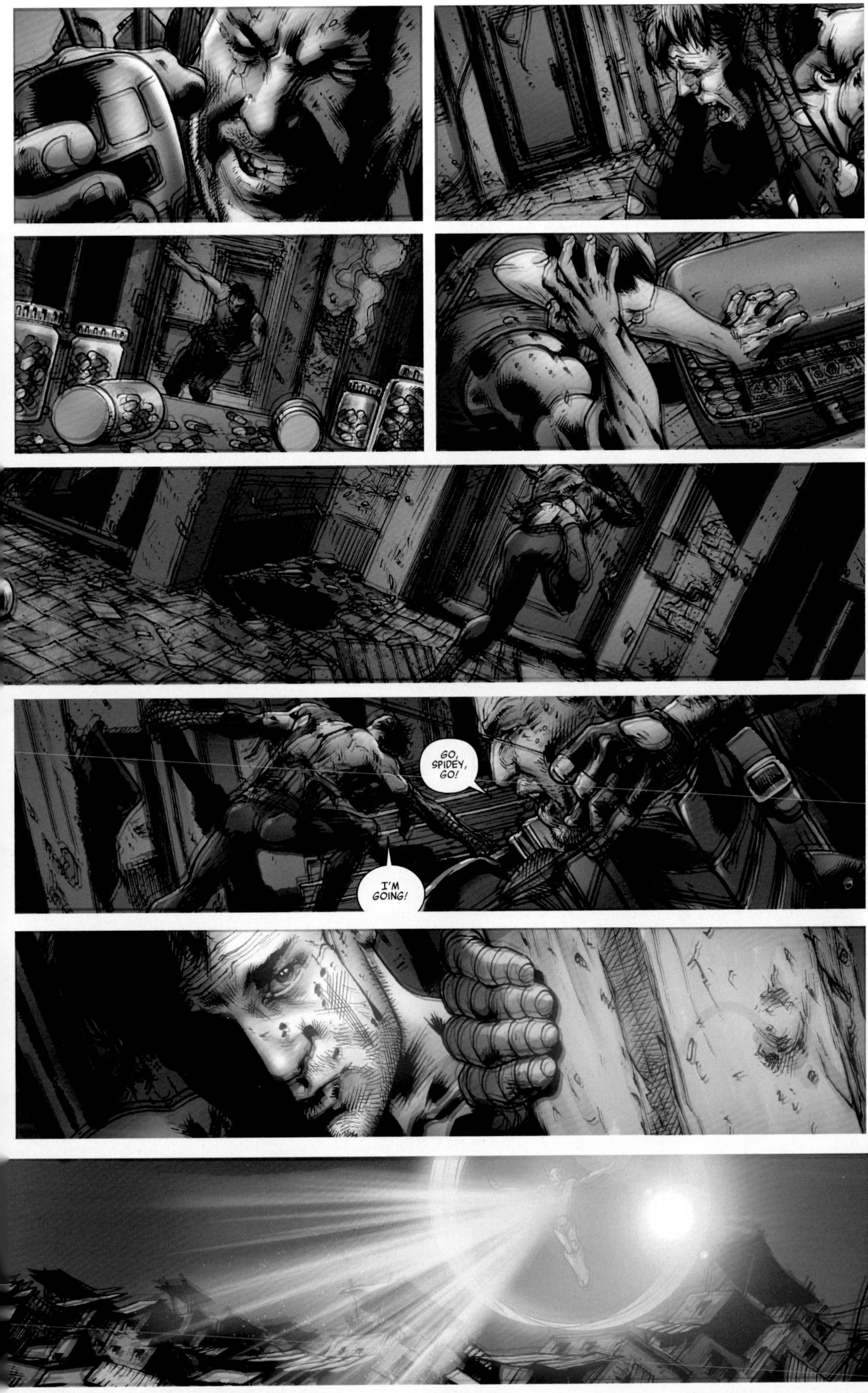
GO, SPIDEY, GO!
I'M GOING!

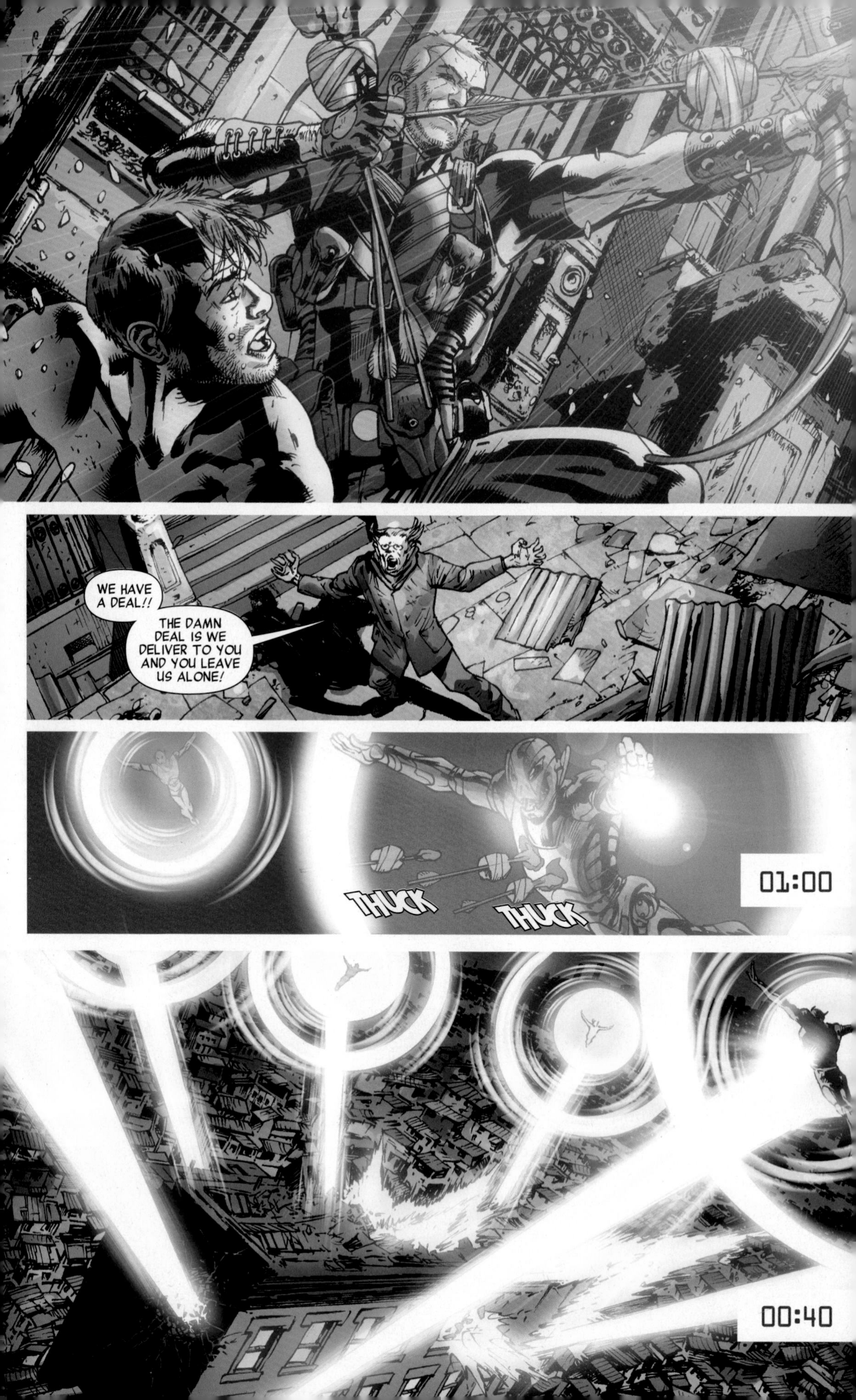
WE HAVE A DEAL!!
THE DAMN DEAL IS WE DELIVER TO YOU AND YOU LEAVE US ALONE!
01:00
THUCK
THUCK
00:40

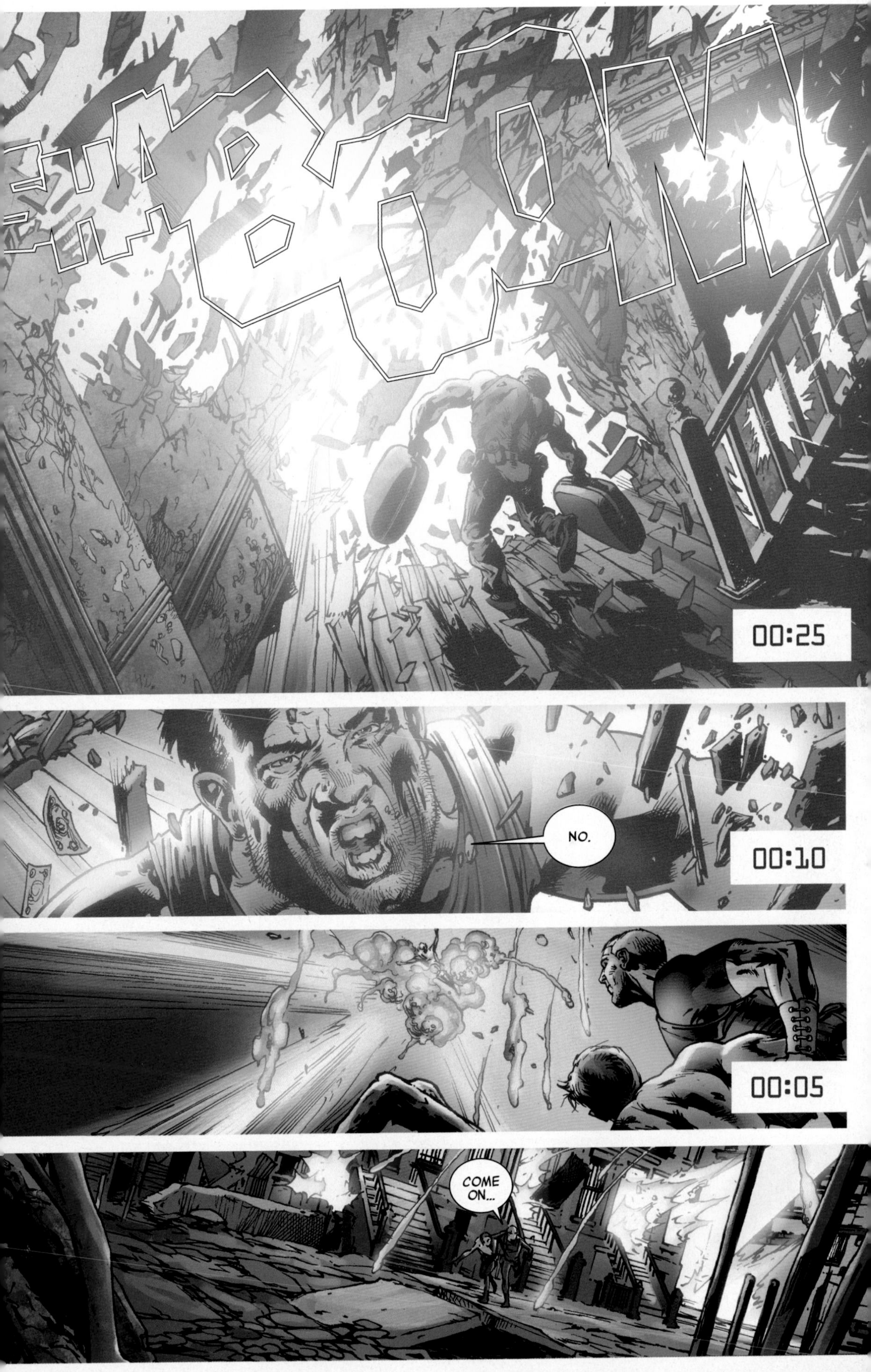
KA-BOOM
00:25
NO.
00:10
00:05
COME ON...

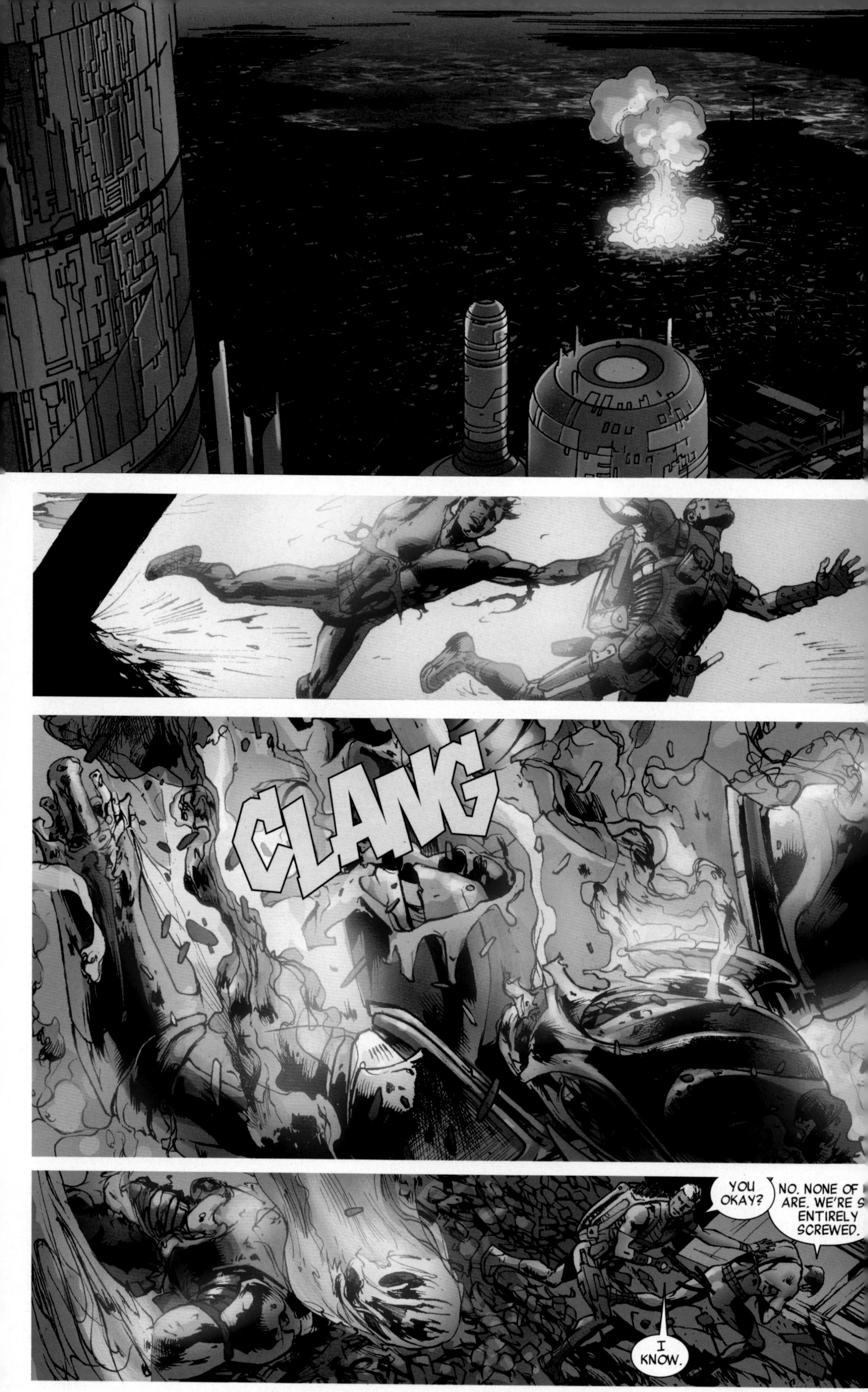
CLANG
YOU OKAY?
NO. NONE OF
ARE. WE'RE
ENTIRELY SCREWED.
I KNOW.

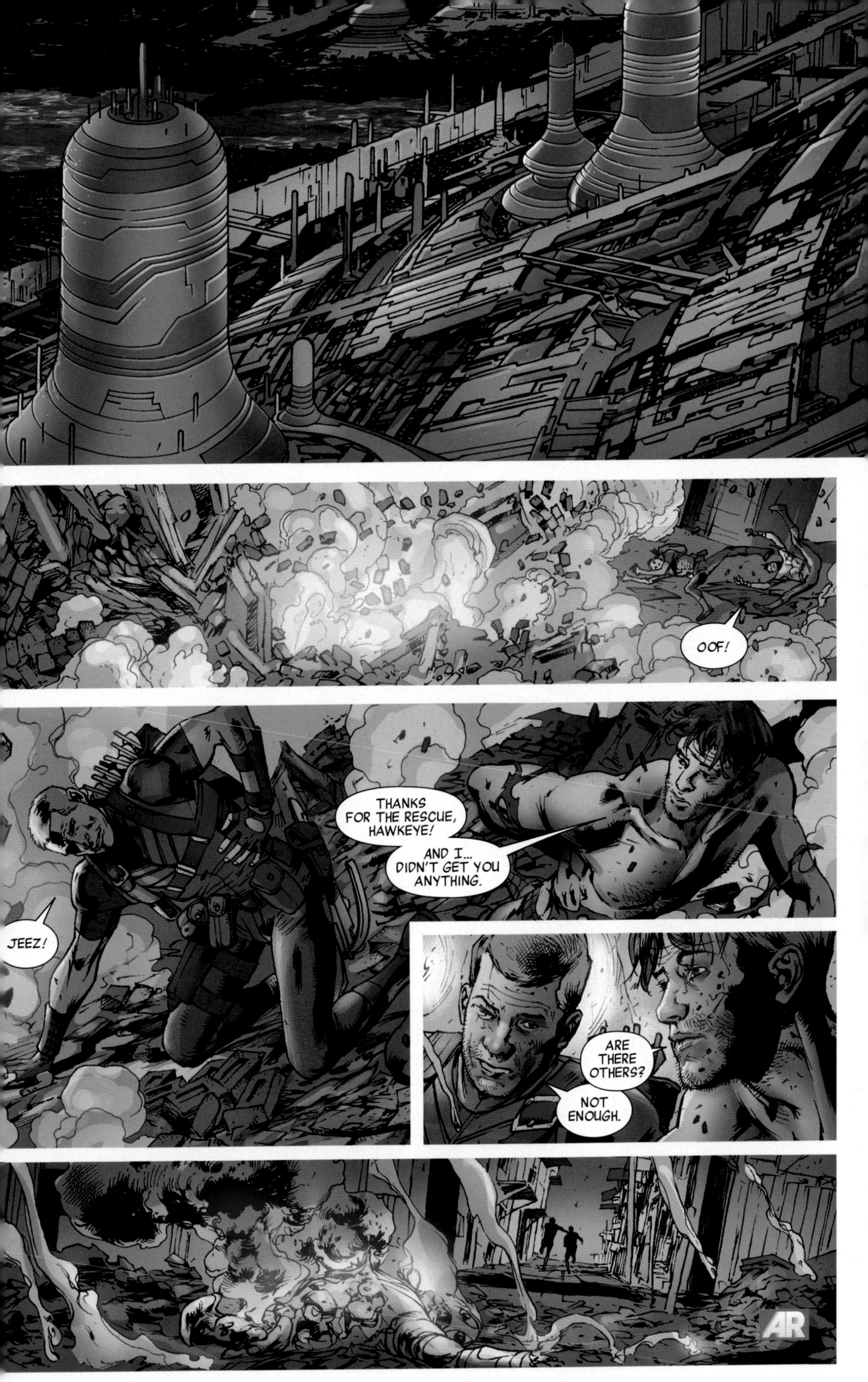
OOF!
THANKS FOR THE RESCUE, HAWKEYE!
AND I... DIDN'T GET YOU ANYTHING.
JEEZ!
ARE THERE OTHERS?
NOT ENOUGH.

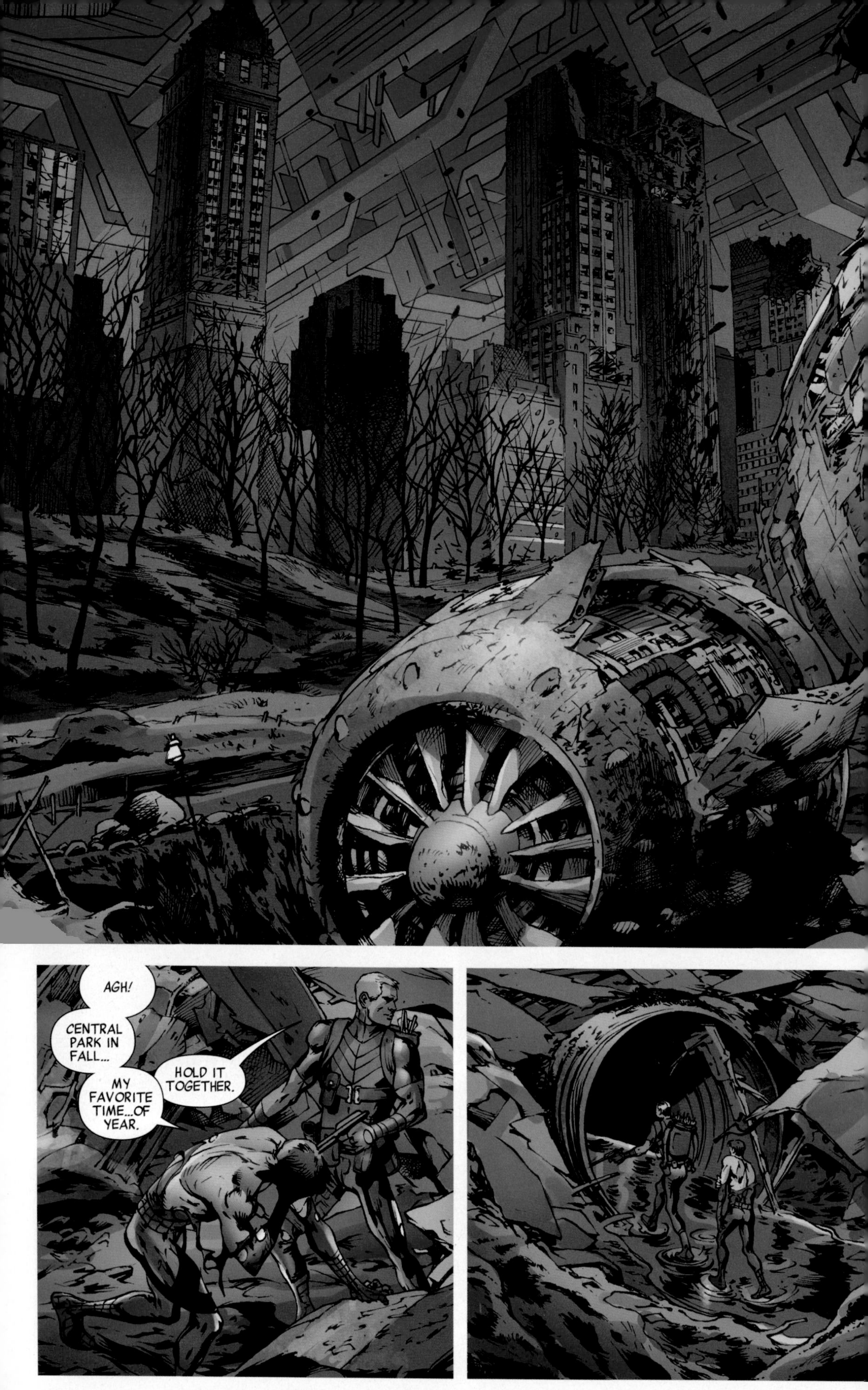
AGH!
CENTRAL PARK IN FALL...
MY FAVORITE TIME...OF YEAR.
HOLD IT TOGETHER.

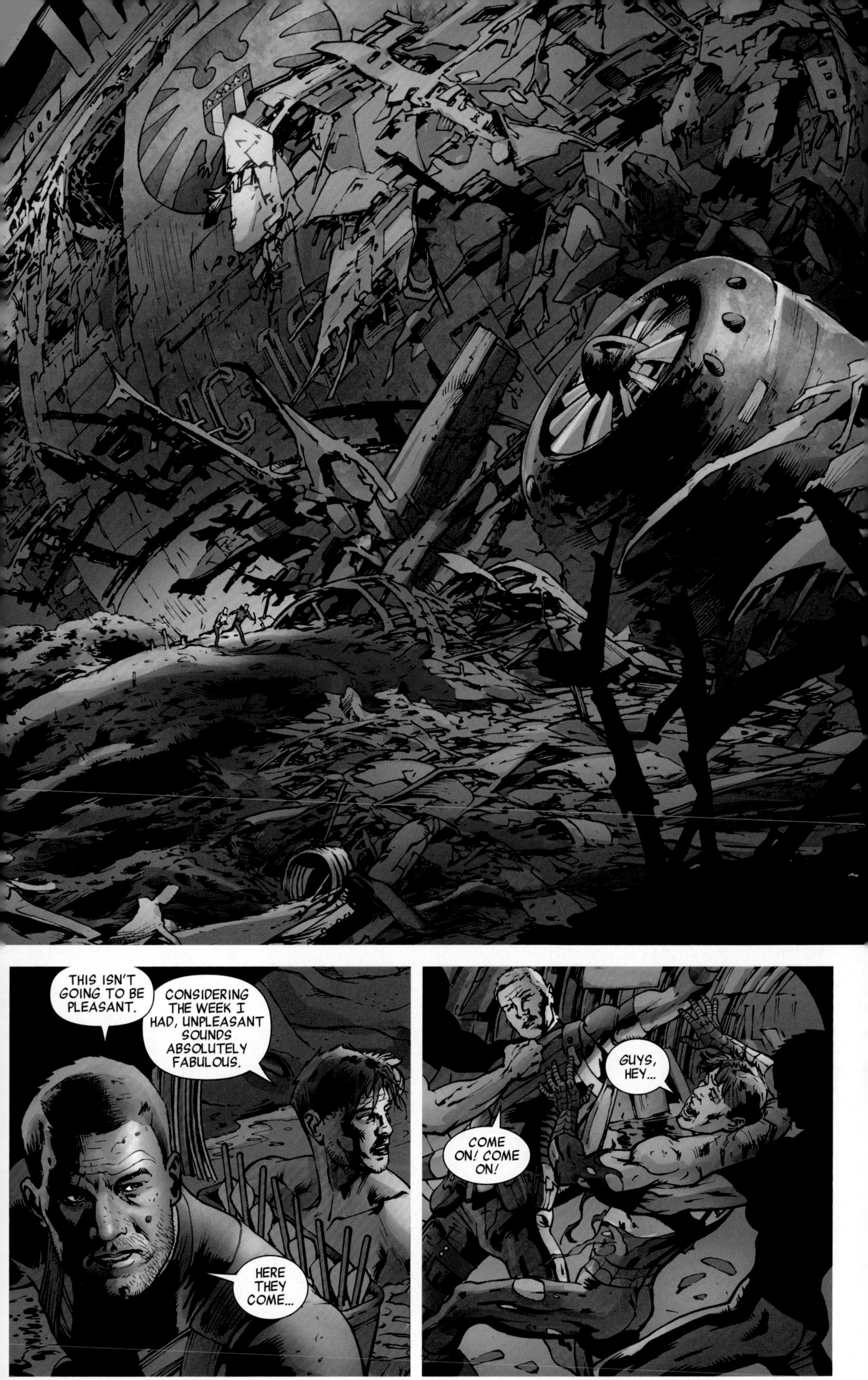
THIS ISN'T GOING TO BE PLEASANT.
CONSIDERING THE WEEK I HAD, UNPLEASANT SOUNDS ABSOLUTELY FABULOUS.
HERE THEY COME...
GUYS, HEY...
COME ON! COME ON!

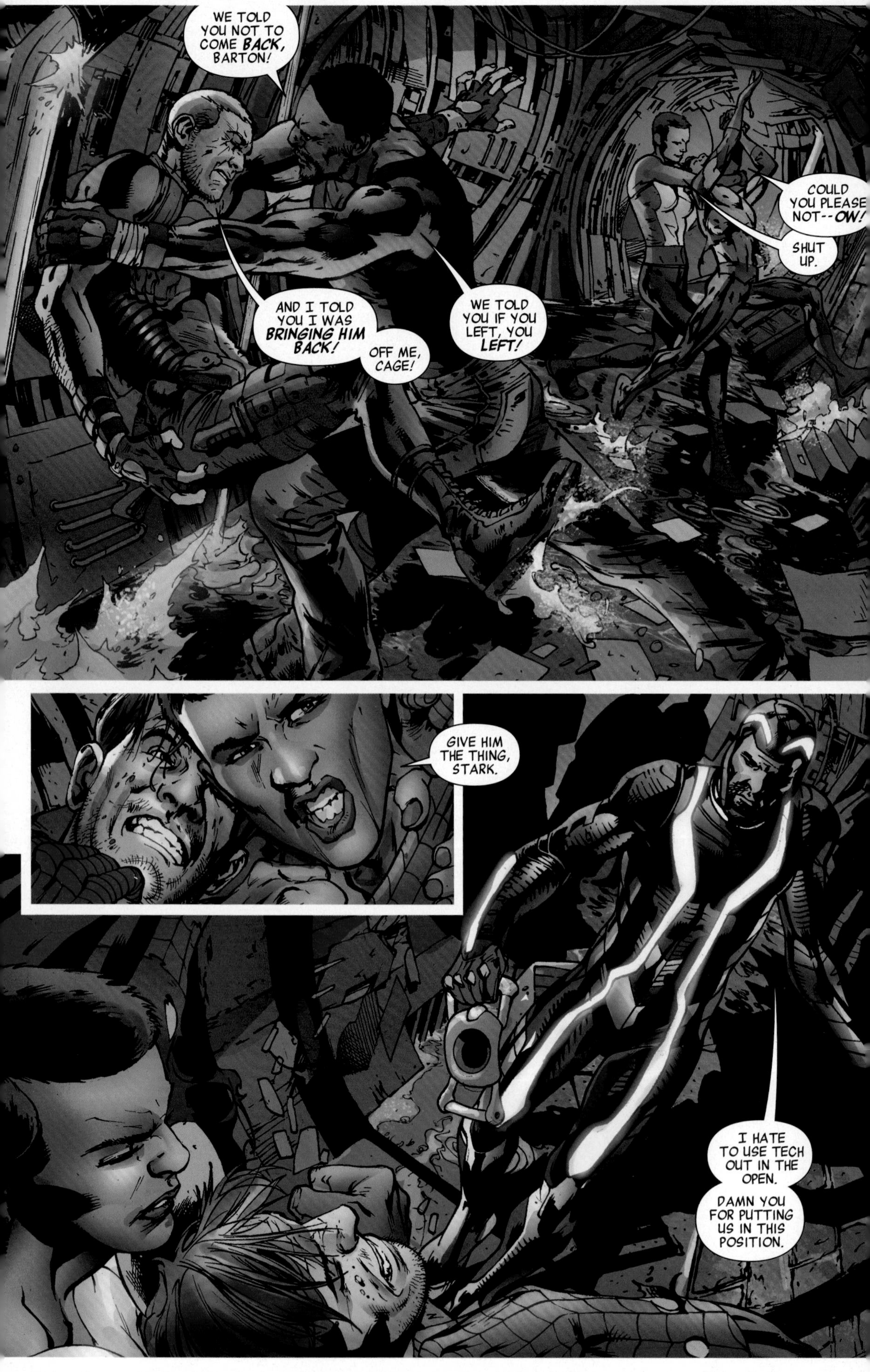
WE TOLD YOU NOT TO COME BACK, BARTON!
AND I TOLD YOU I WAS BRINGING HIM BACK!
OFF ME, CAGE!
WE TOLD YOU IF YOU LEFT, YOU LEFT!
COULD YOU PLEASE NOT--OW!
SHUT UP.
GIVE HIM THE THING, STARK.
I HATE TO USE TECH OUT IN THE OPEN.
DAMN YOU FOR PUTTING US IN THIS POSITION.

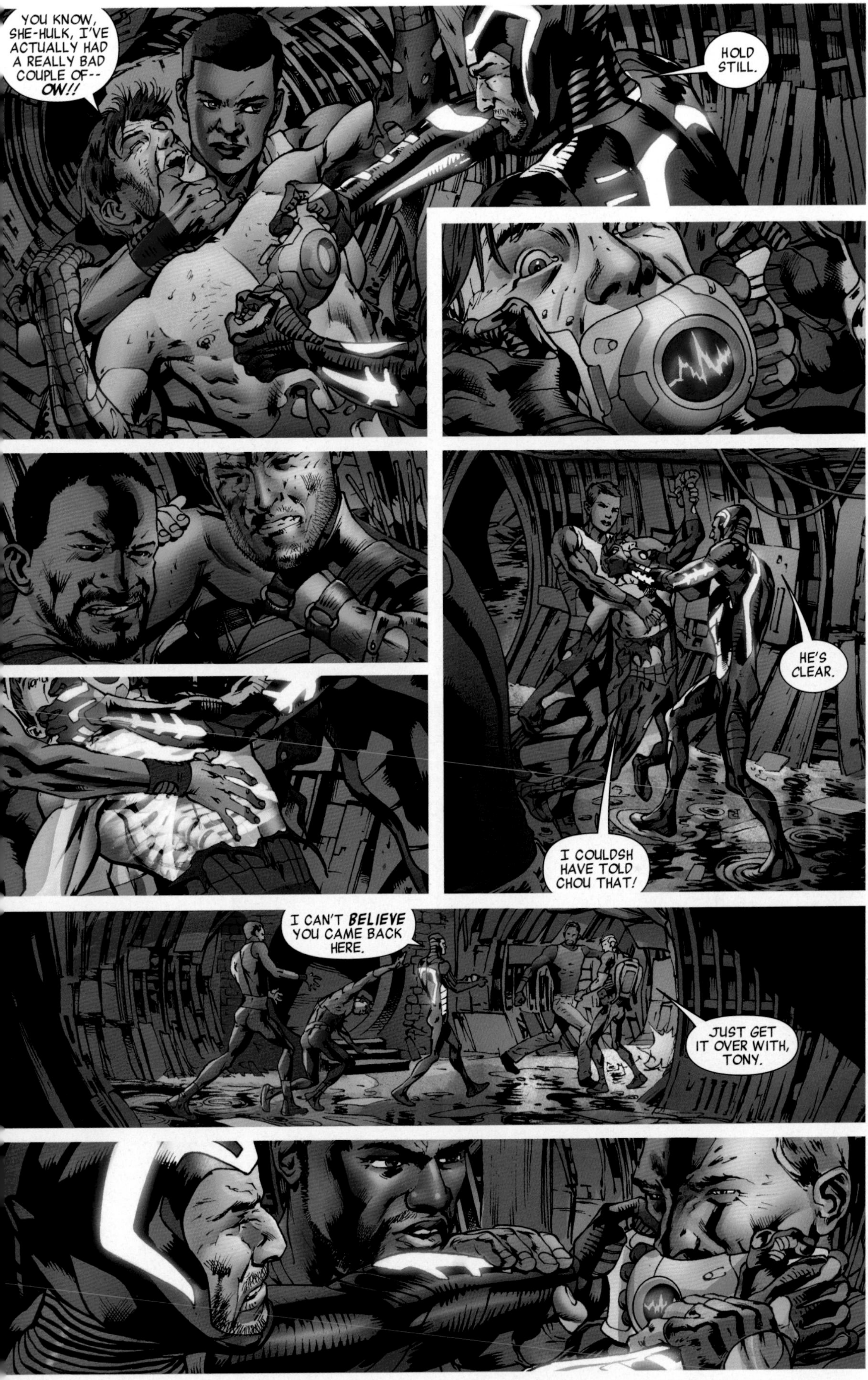
YOU KNOW, SHE-HULK, I'VE ACTUALLY HAD A REALLY BAD COUPLE OF-- OW!!
HOLD STILL.
HE'S CLEAR.
I COULDSH HAVE TOLD CHOU THAT!
I CAN'T BELIEVE YOU CAME BACK HERE.
JUST GET IT OVER WITH, TONY.

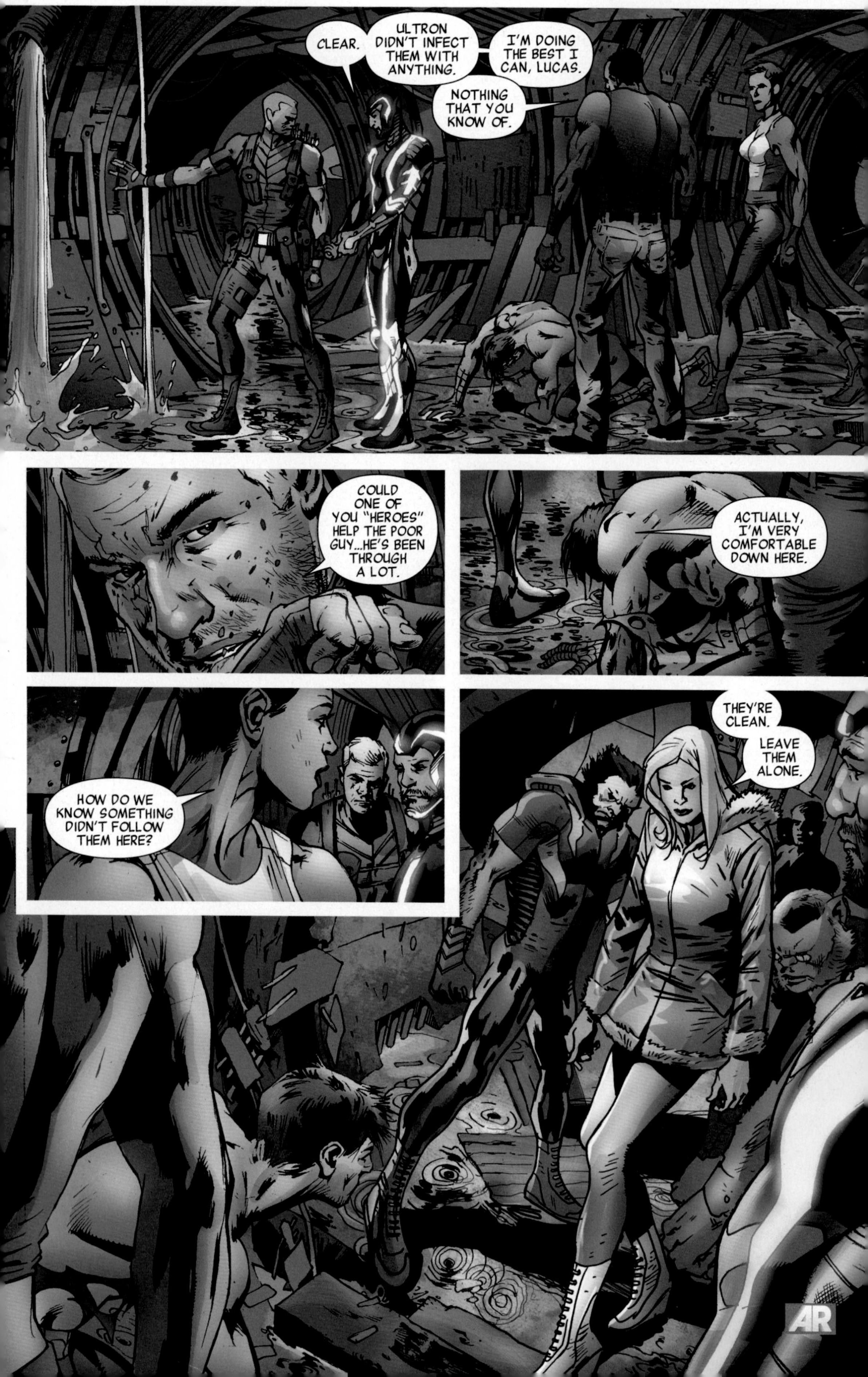
CLEAR.
ULTRON DIDN'T INFECT THEM WITH ANYTHING.
I'M DOING THE BEST I CAN, LUCAS.
NOTHING THAT YOU KNOW OF.
COULD ONE OF YOU "HEROES" HELP THE POOR GUY...HE'S BEEN THROUGH A LOT.
ACTUALLY, I'M VERY COMFORTABLE DOWN HERE.
HOW DO WE KNOW SOMETHING DIDN'T FOLLOW THEM HERE?
THEY'RE CLEAN.
LEAVE THEM ALONE.

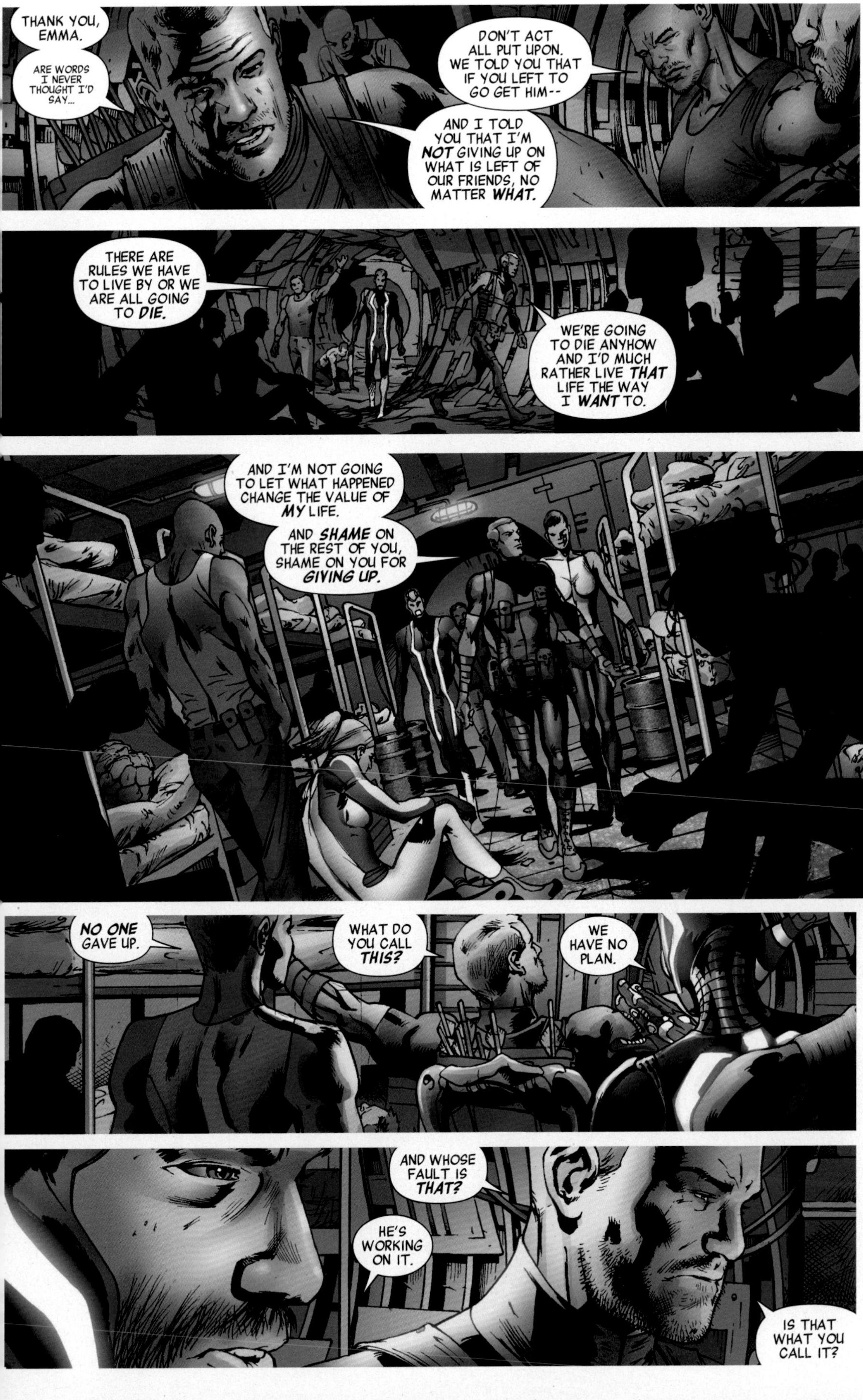
THANK YOU, EMMA.
ARE WORDS I NEVER THOUGHT I'D SAY...
DON'T ACT ALL PUT UPON. WE TOLD YOU THAT IF YOU LEFT TO GO GET HIM--
AND I TOLD YOU THAT I'M NOT GIVING UP ON WHAT IS LEFT OF OUR FRIENDS, NO MATTER WHAT.
THERE ARE RULES WE HAVE TO LIVE BY OR WE ARE ALL GOING TO DIE.
WE'RE GOING TO DIE ANYHOW AND I'D MUCH RATHER LIVE THAT LIFE THE WAY I WANT TO.
AND I'M NOT GOING TO LET WHAT HAPPENED CHANGE THE VALUE OF MY LIFE.
AND SHAME ON THE REST OF YOU, SHAME ON YOU FOR GIVING UP.
NO ONE GAVE UP.
WHAT DO YOU CALL THIS?
WE HAVE NO PLAN.
AND WHOSE FAULT IS THAT?
HE'S WORKING ON IT.
IS THAT WHAT YOU CALL IT?

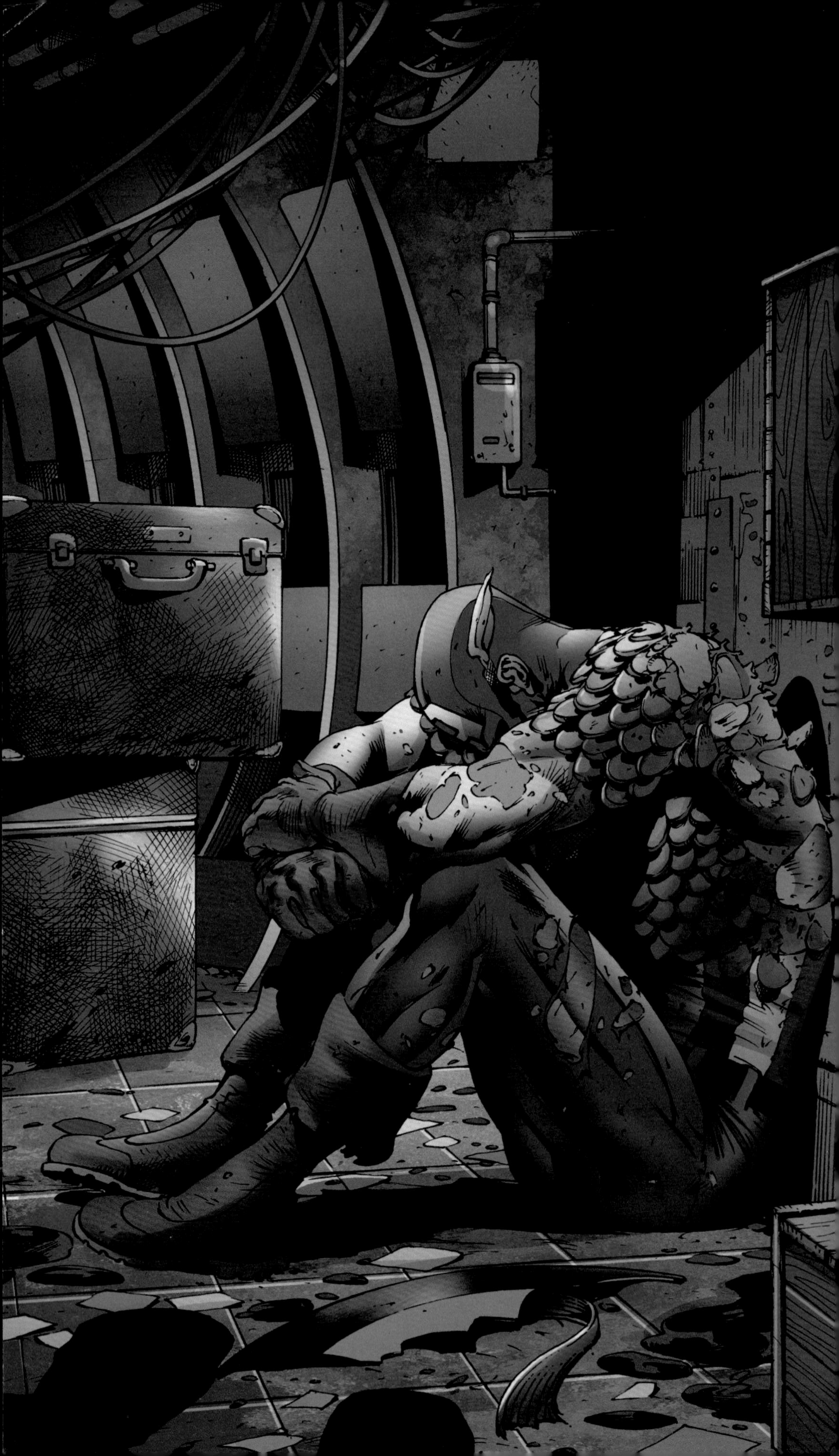

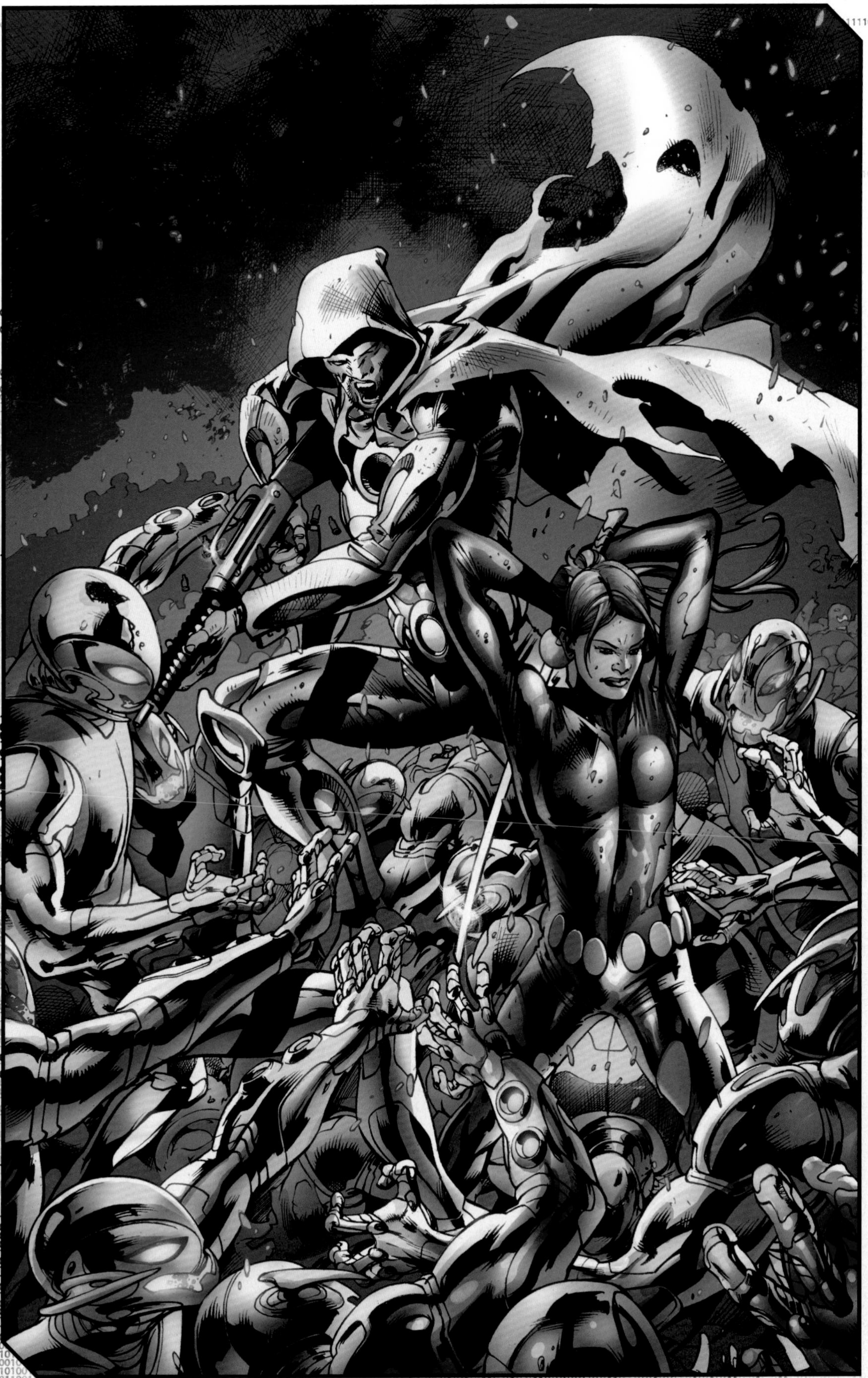

AGE OF ULTRON #2

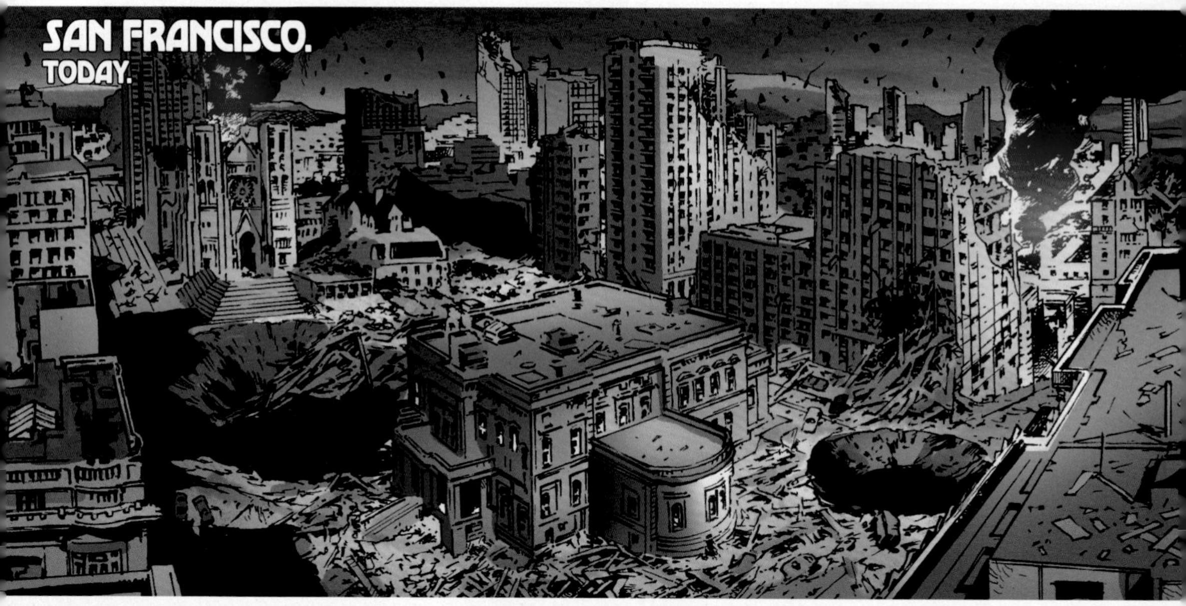
SAN FRANCISCO.
TODAY.

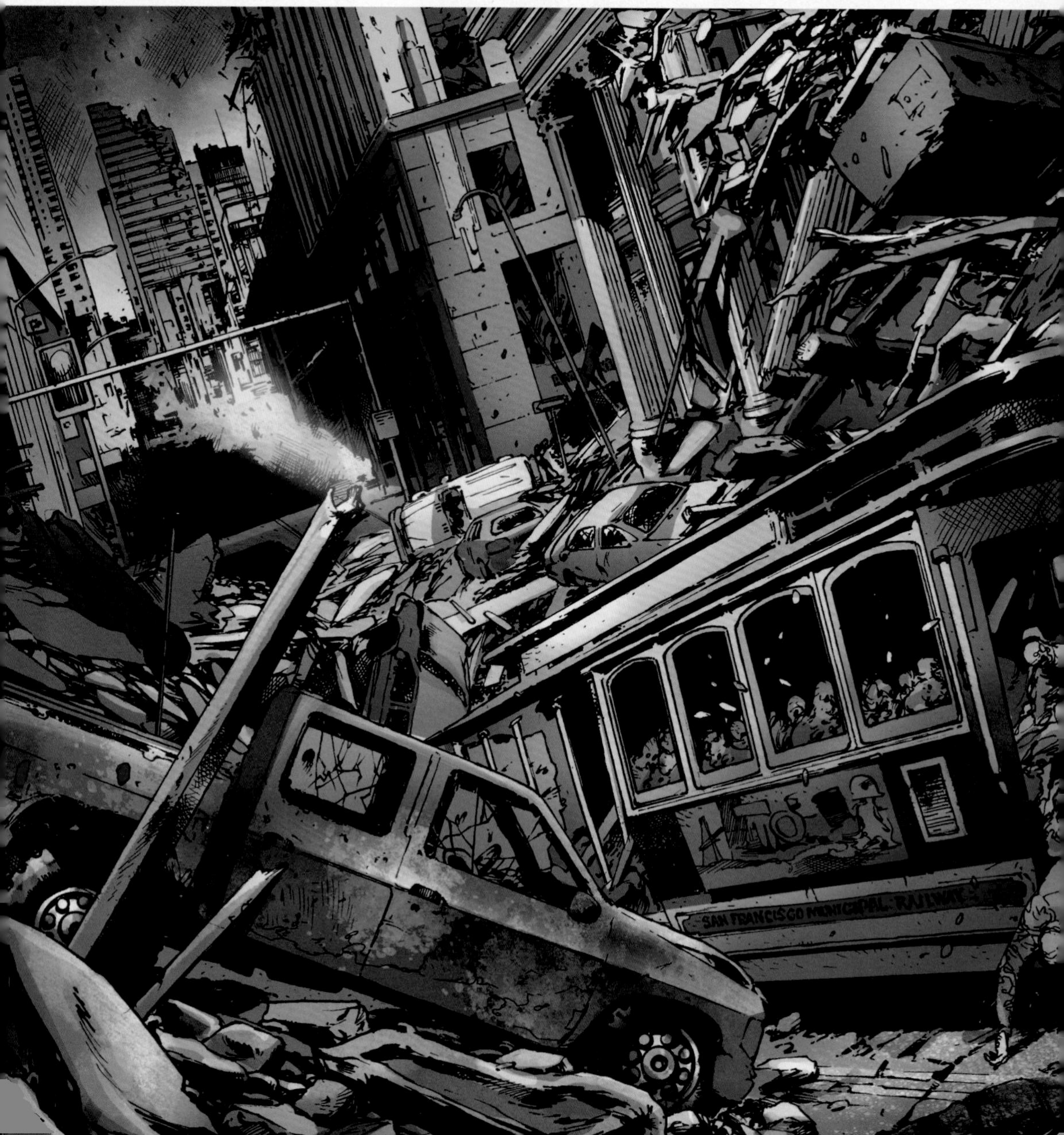
SAN FRANCISCO MUNICIPAL RAILWAY

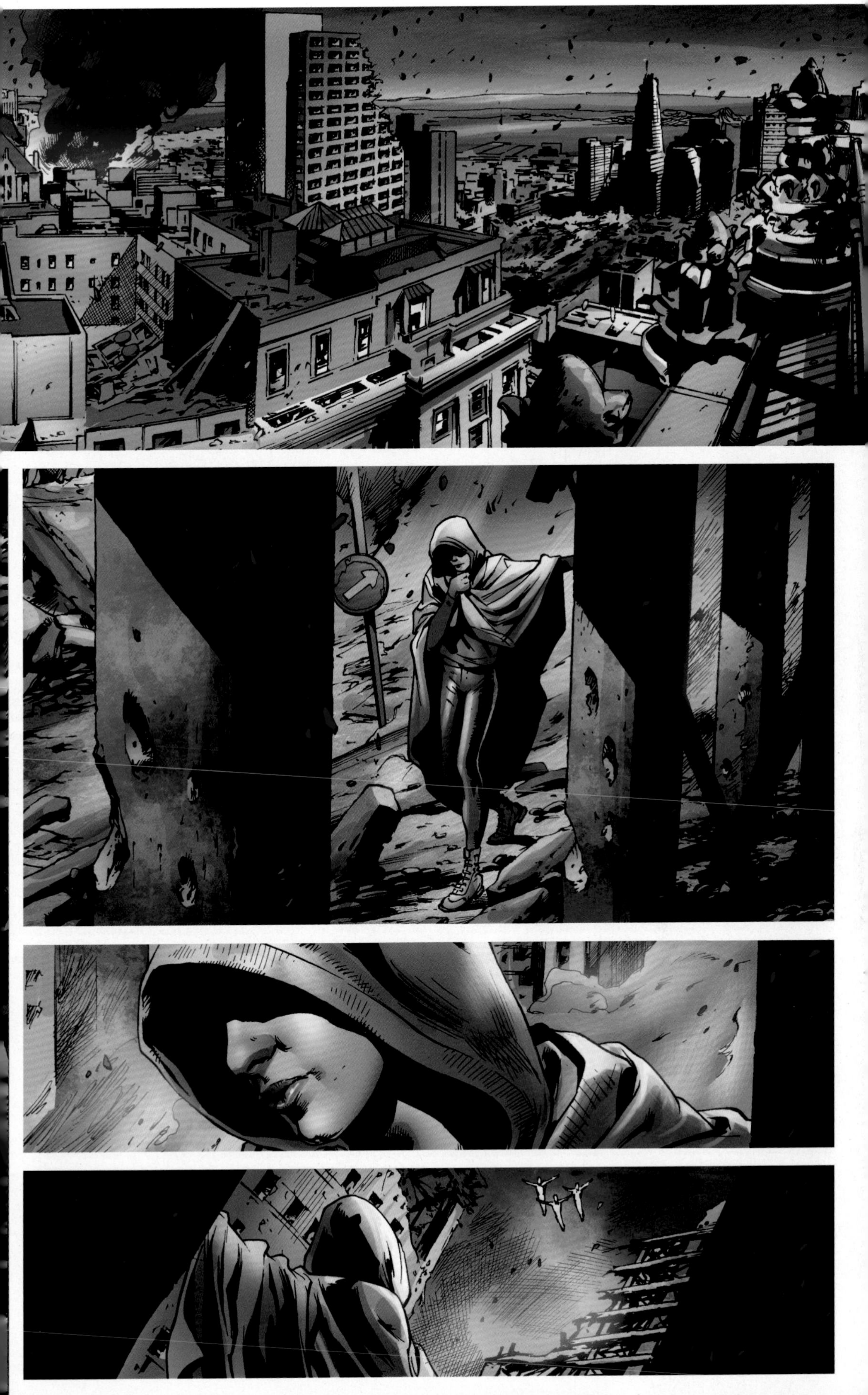

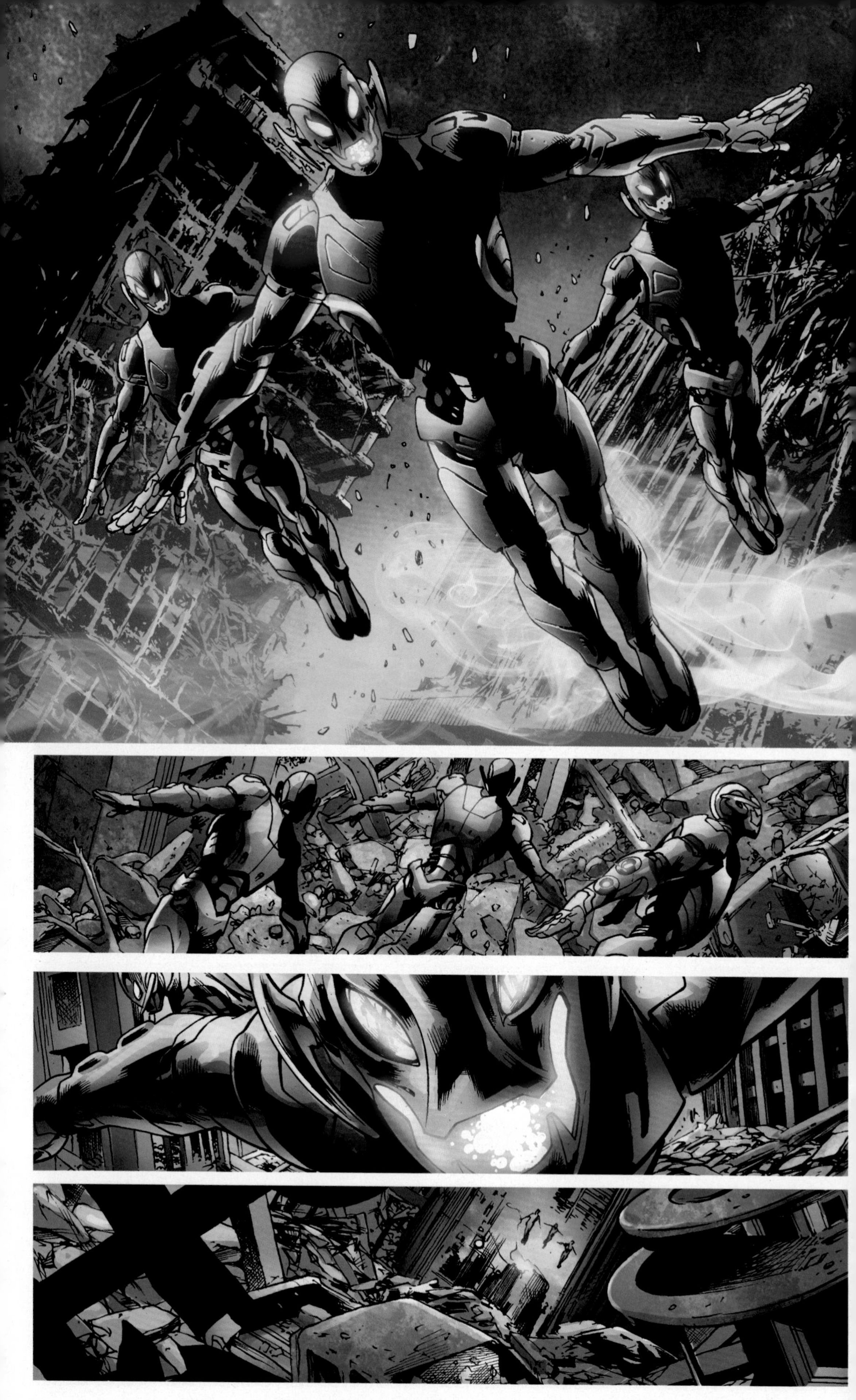

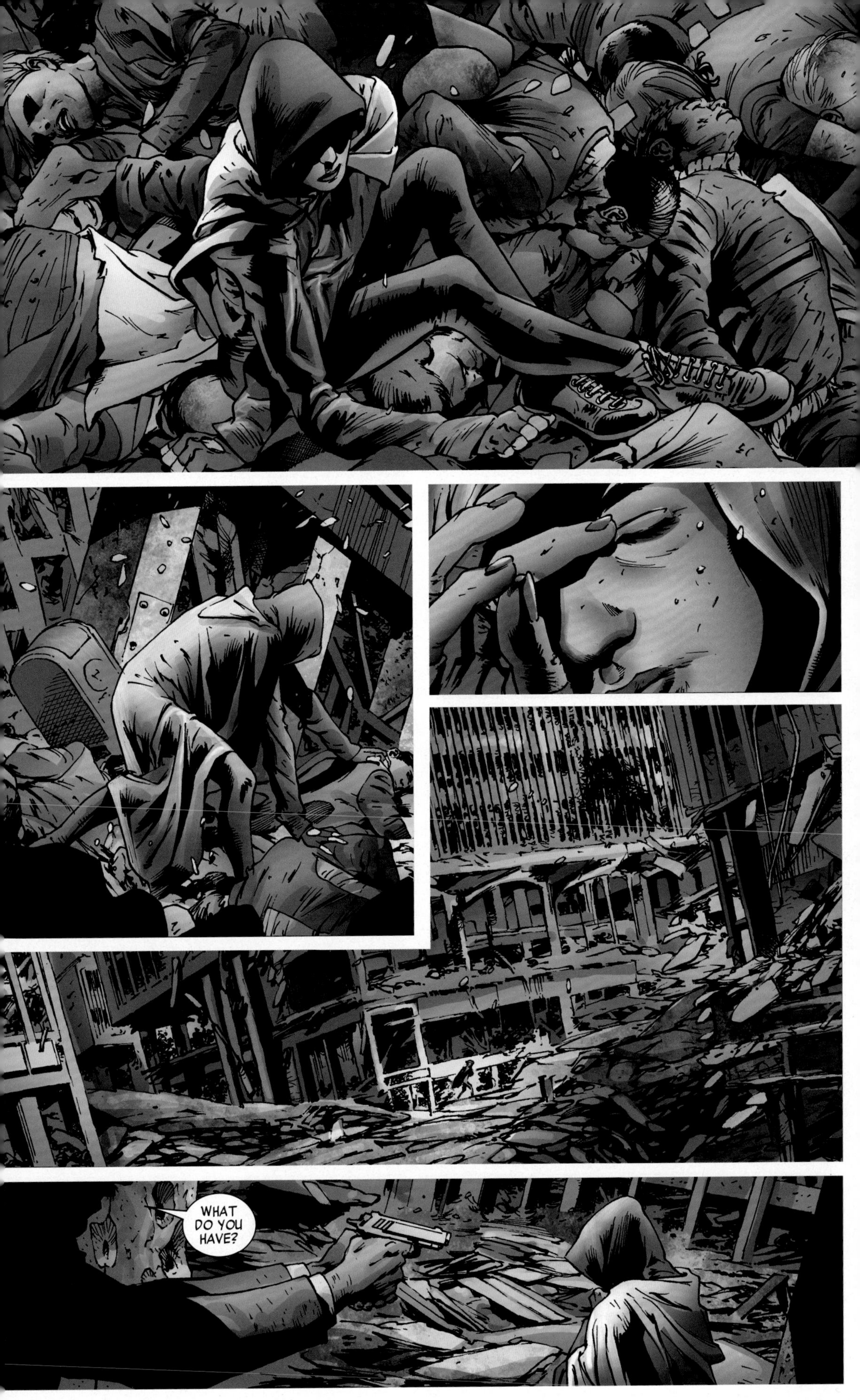
WHAT DO YOU HAVE?

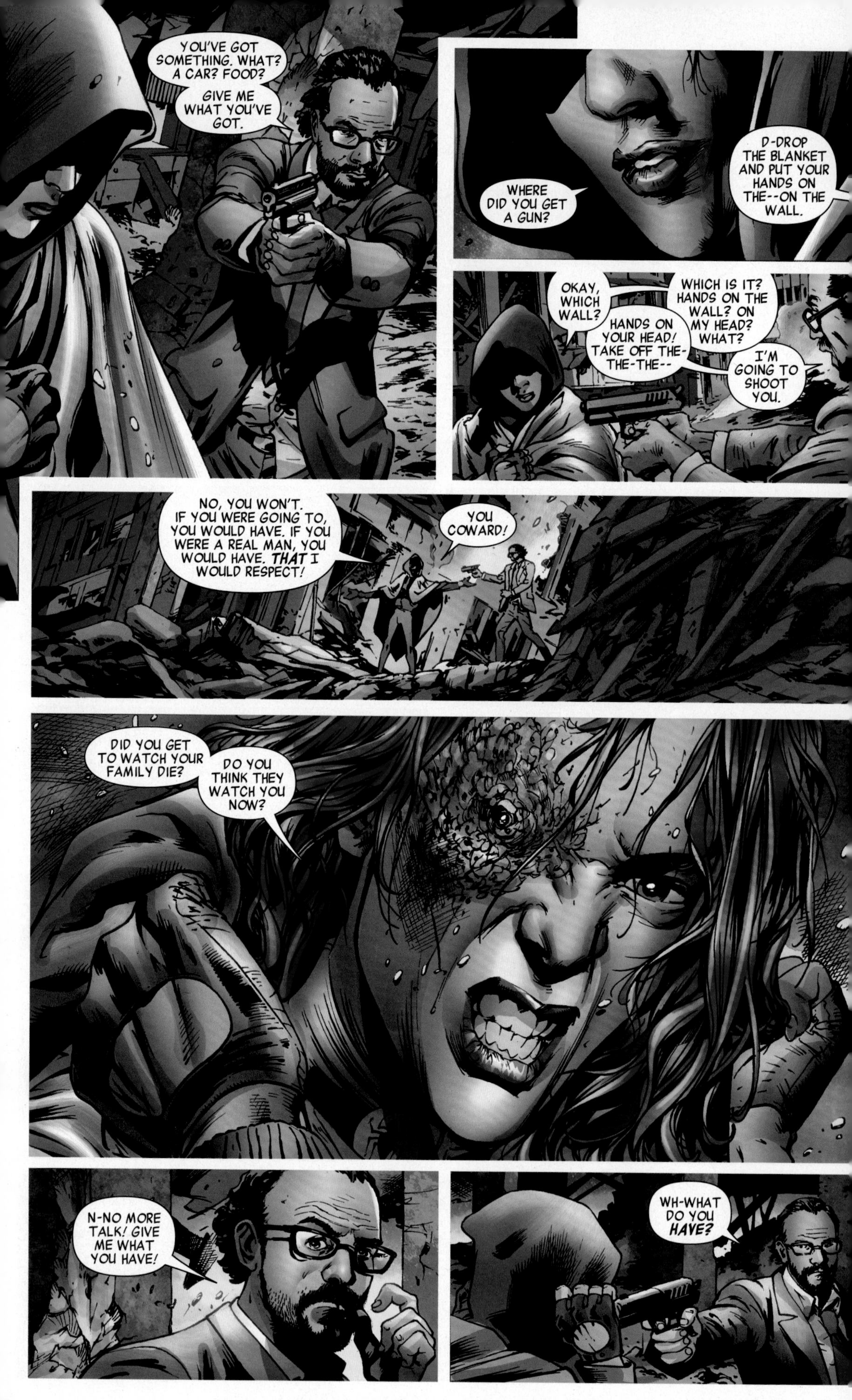
YOU'VE GOT SOMETHING. WHAT? A CAR? FOOD?
GIVE ME WHAT YOU'VE GOT.
WHERE DID YOU GET A GUN?
D-DROP THE BLANKET AND PUT YOUR HANDS ON THE--ON THE WALL.
OKAY, WHICH WALL?
HANDS ON YOUR HEAD! TAKE OFF THE-THE-THE--
WHICH IS IT? HANDS ON THE WALL? ON MY HEAD? WHAT?
I'M GOING TO SHOOT YOU.
NO, YOU WON'T. IF YOU WERE GOING TO, YOU WOULD HAVE. IF YOU WERE A REAL MAN, YOU WOULD HAVE. THAT I WOULD RESPECT!
YOU COWARD!
DID YOU GET TO WATCH YOUR FAMILY DIE?
DO YOU THINK THEY WATCH YOU NOW?
N-NO MORE TALK! GIVE ME WHAT YOU HAVE!
WH-WHAT DO YOU HAVE?

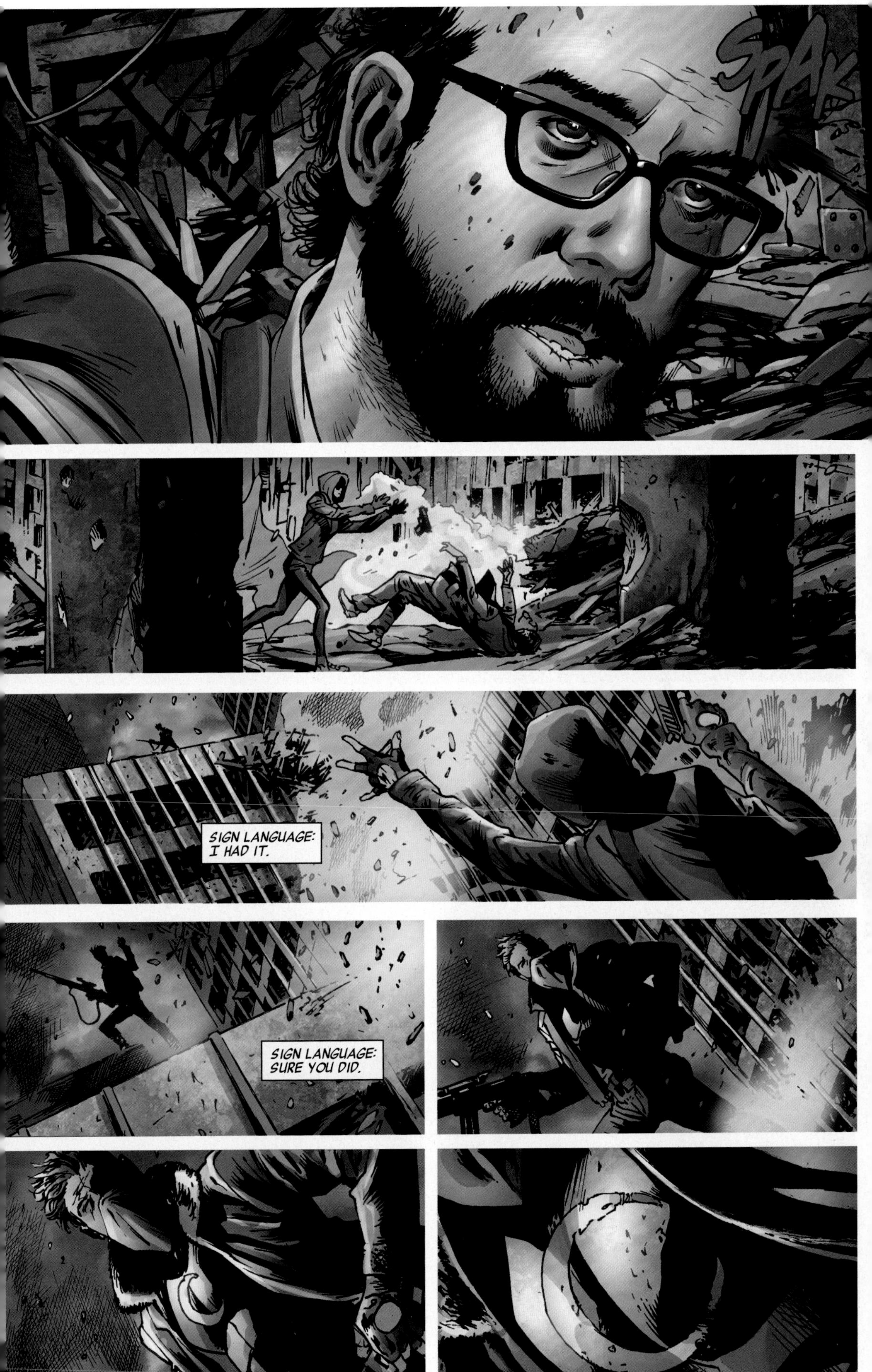
SPAK
SIGN LANGUAGE: I HAD IT.
SIGN LANGUAGE: SURE YOU DID.

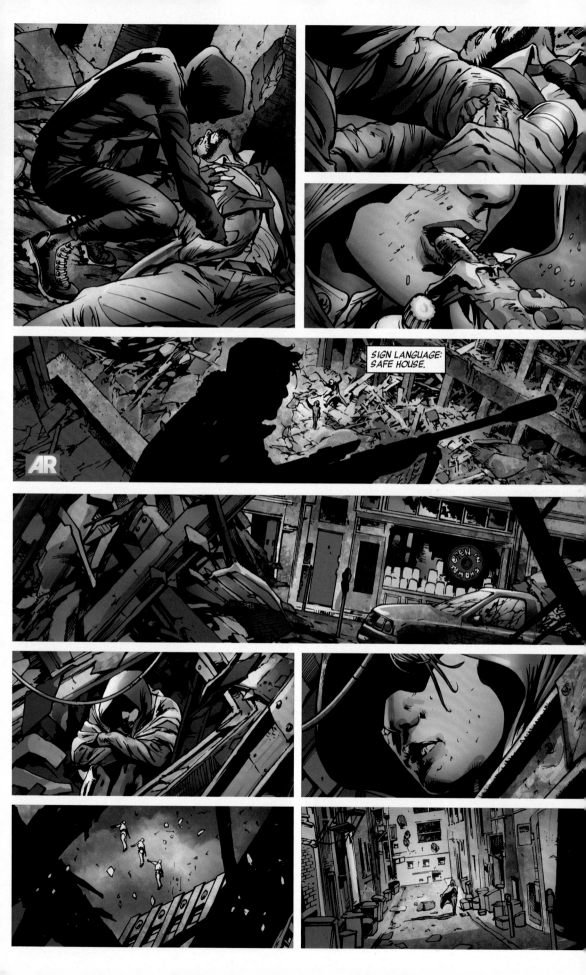

SIGN LANGUAGE:
SAFE HOUSE.

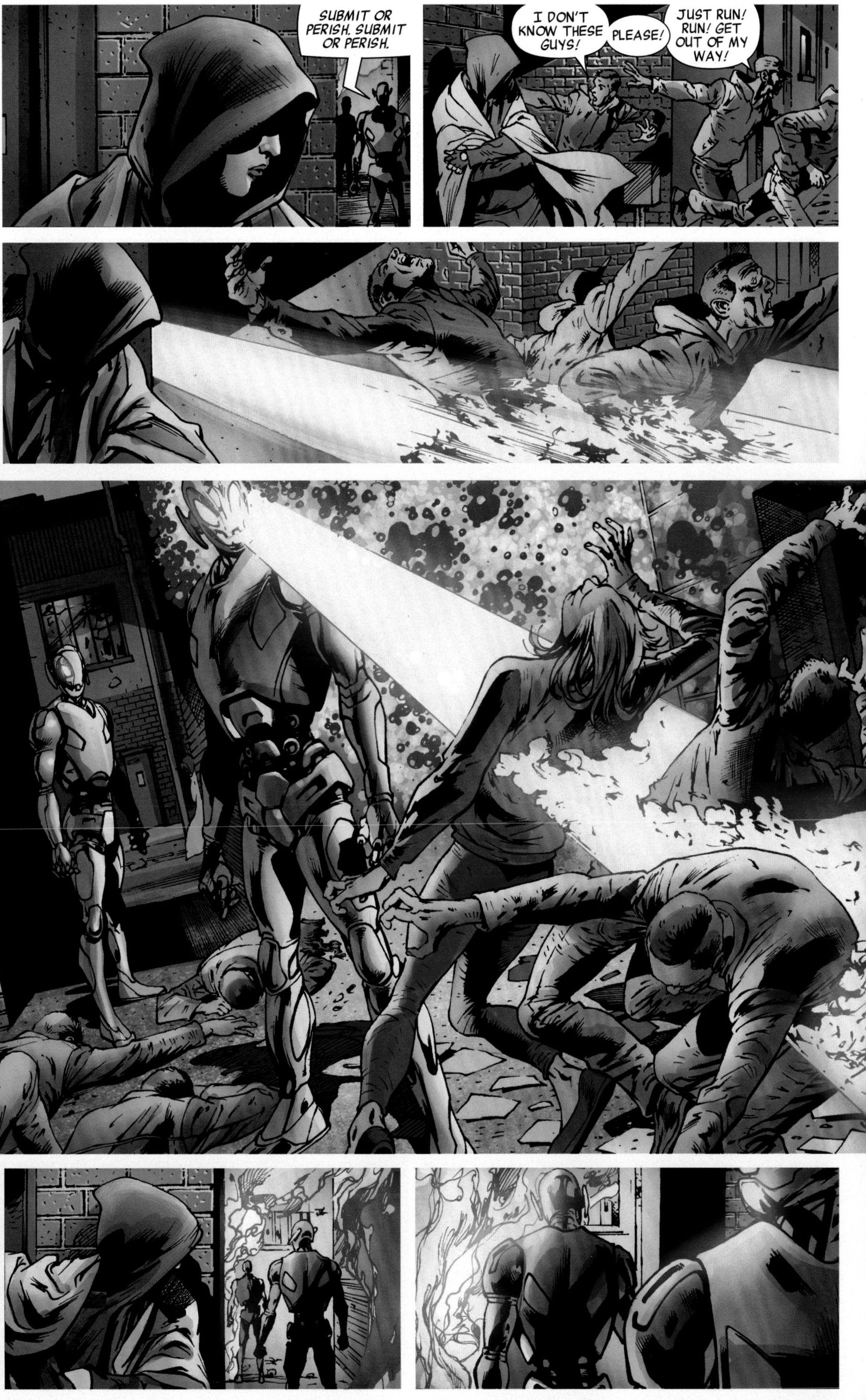
SUBMIT OR PERISH. SUBMIT OR PERISH.
I DON'T KNOW THESE GUYS!
PLEASE!
JUST RUN! RUN! GET OUT OF MY WAY!

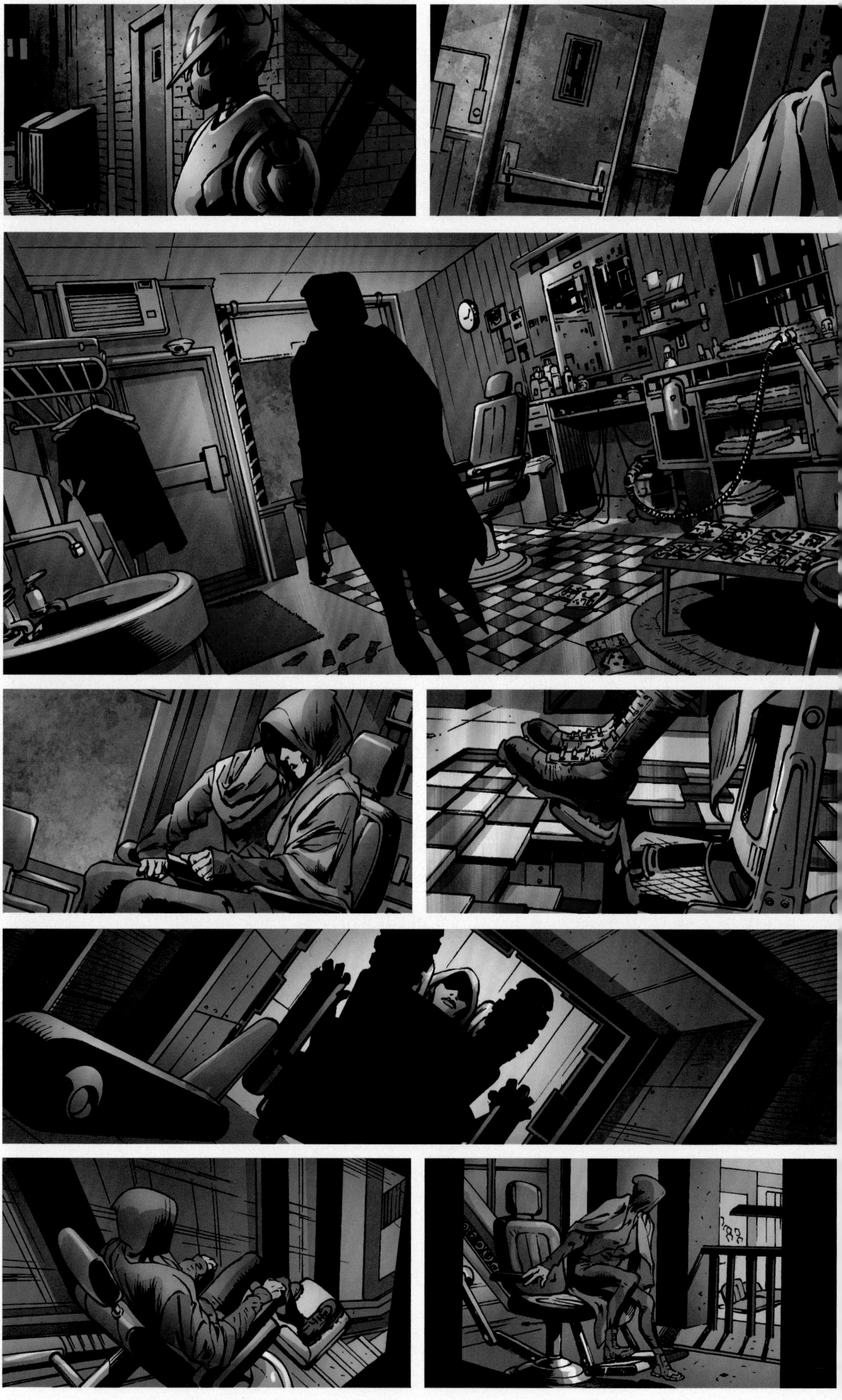

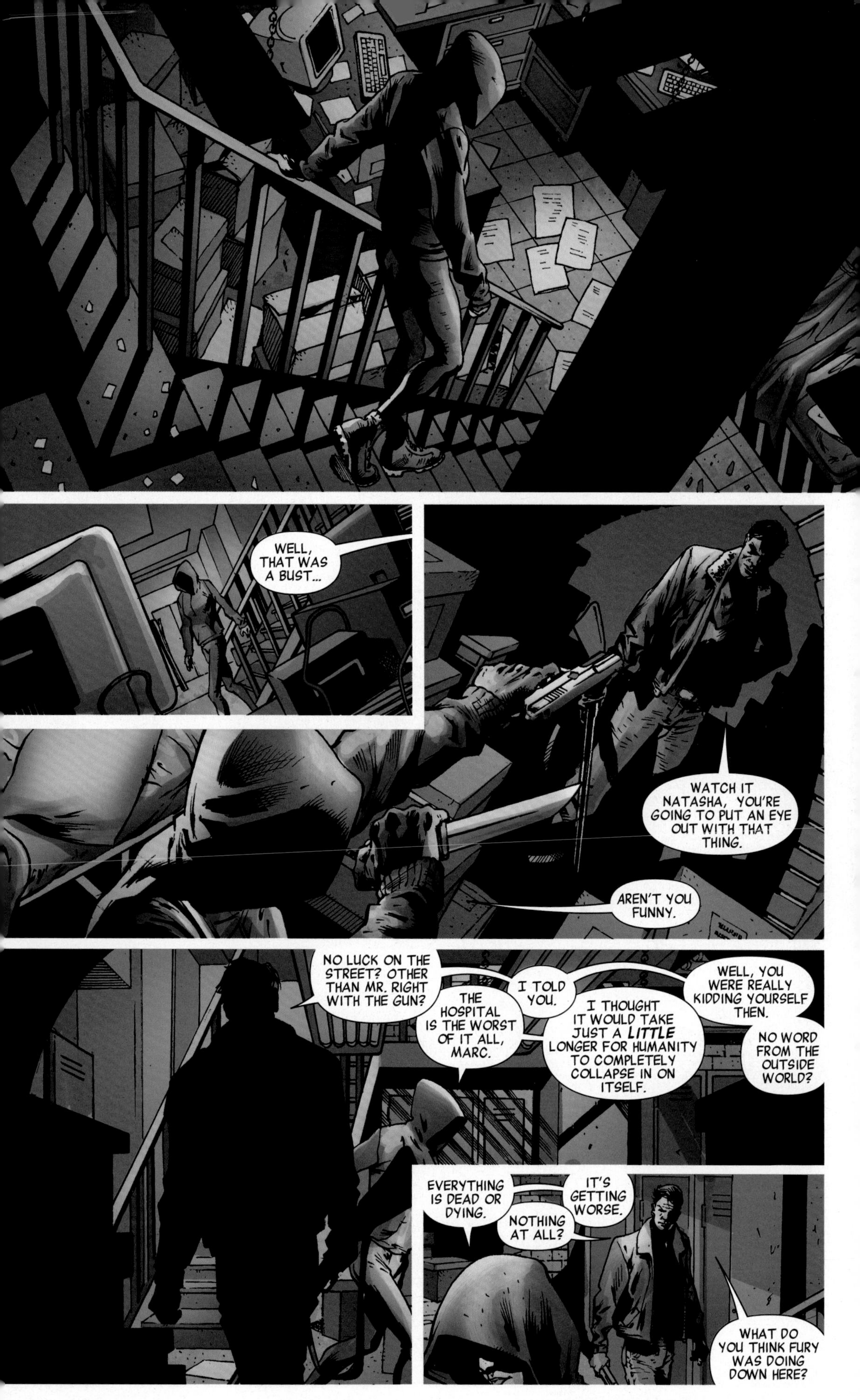
WELL, THAT WAS A BUST...
WATCH IT NATASHA, YOU'RE GOING TO PUT AN EYE OUT WITH THAT THING.
AREN'T YOU FUNNY.
NO LUCK ON THE STREET? OTHER THAN MR. RIGHT WITH THE GUN?
THE HOSPITAL IS THE WORST OF IT ALL, MARC.
I TOLD YOU.
I THOUGHT IT WOULD TAKE JUST A *LITTLE* LONGER FOR HUMANITY TO COMPLETELY COLLAPSE IN ON ITSELF.
WELL, YOU WERE REALLY KIDDING YOURSELF THEN.
NO WORD FROM THE OUTSIDE WORLD?
EVERYTHING IS DEAD OR DYING.
IT'S GETTING WORSE.
NOTHING AT ALL?
WHAT DO YOU THINK FURY WAS DOING DOWN HERE?

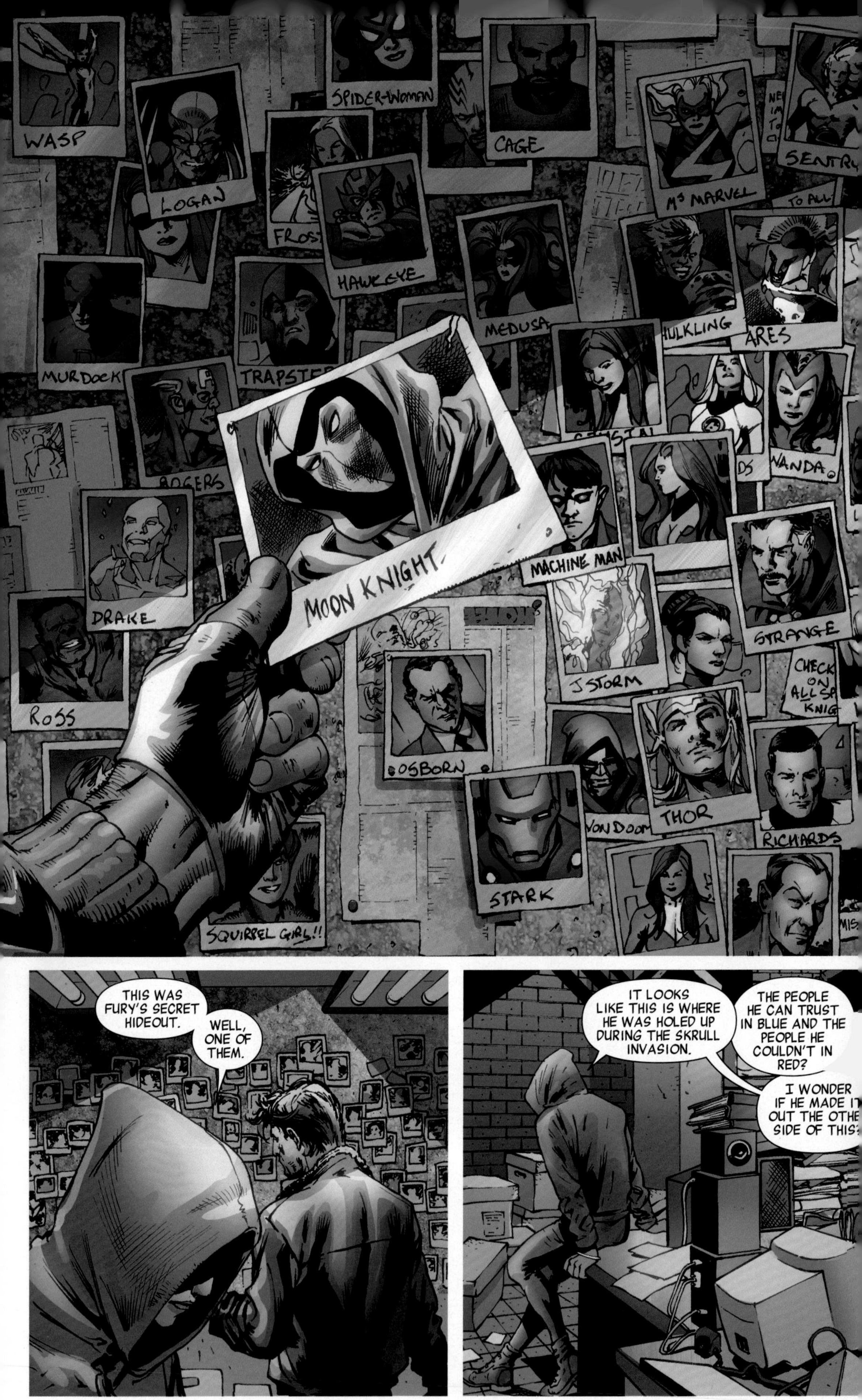

WASP
LOGAN
SPIDER-WOMAN
FROST
HAWKEYE
CAGE
MS MARVEL
SENTRY
MEDUSA
HULKLING
ARES
MURDOCK
TRAPSTER
ROGERS
WANDA
MOON KNIGHT
MACHINE MAN
DRAKE
STRANGE
J STORM
CHECK ON ALL SP KNIG
ROSS
OSBORN
VON DOOM
THOR
RICHARDS
STARK
SQUIRREL GIRL!!
THIS WAS FURY'S SECRET HIDEOUT.
WELL, ONE OF THEM.
IT LOOKS LIKE THIS IS WHERE HE WAS HOLED UP DURING THE SKRULL INVASION.
THE PEOPLE HE CAN TRUST IN BLUE AND THE PEOPLE HE COULDN'T IN RED?
I WONDER IF HE MADE IT OUT THE OTHE SIDE OF THIS?

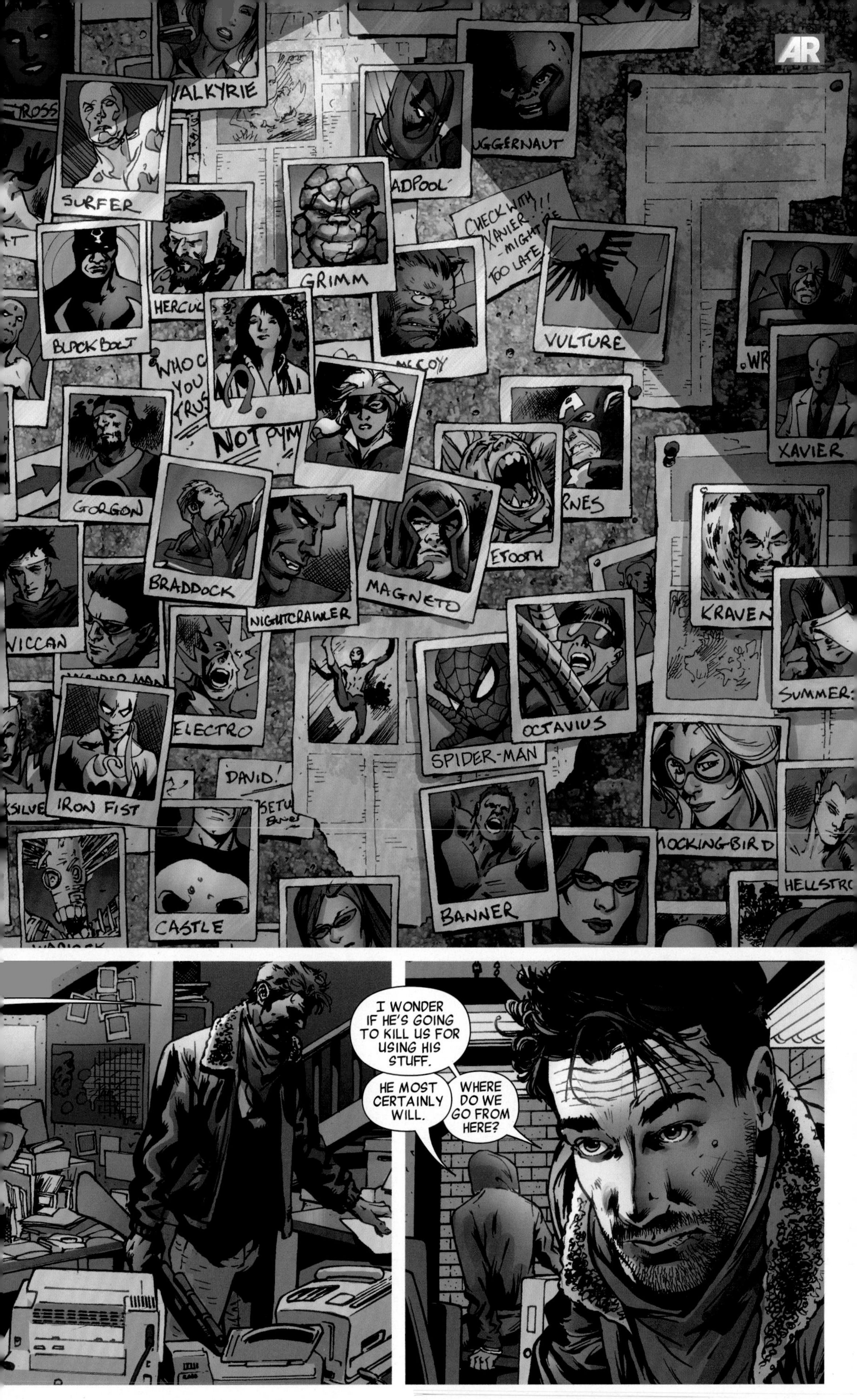
SURFER
GRIMM
CHECK WITH XAVIER!!! - MIGHT BE TOO LATE
VULTURE
BLACK BOLT
XAVIER
NOT PYM
GORGON
BRADDOCK
NIGHTCRAWLER
MAGNETO
KRAVEN
ELECTRO
OCTAVIUS
SPIDER-MAN
IRON FIST
DAVID!
MOCKINGBIRD
CASTLE
BANNER
I WONDER IF HE'S GOING TO KILL US FOR USING HIS STUFF.
HE MOST CERTAINLY WILL.
WHERE DO WE GO FROM HERE?

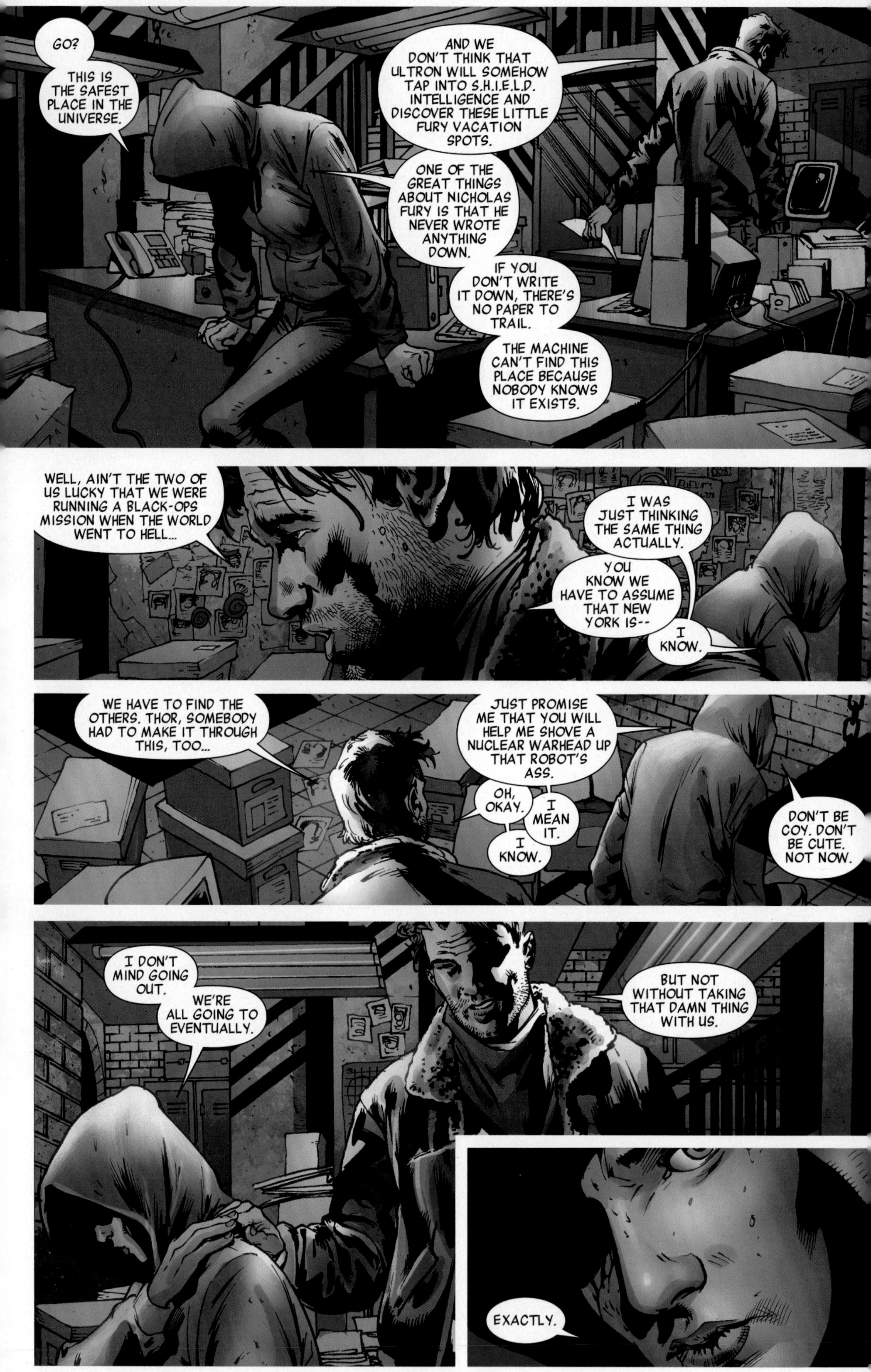
GO?
THIS IS THE SAFEST PLACE IN THE UNIVERSE.
AND WE DON'T THINK THAT ULTRON WILL SOMEHOW TAP INTO S.H.I.E.L.D. INTELLIGENCE AND DISCOVER THESE LITTLE FURY VACATION SPOTS.
ONE OF THE GREAT THINGS ABOUT NICHOLAS FURY IS THAT HE NEVER WROTE ANYTHING DOWN.
IF YOU DON'T WRITE IT DOWN, THERE'S NO PAPER TO TRAIL.
THE MACHINE CAN'T FIND THIS PLACE BECAUSE NOBODY KNOWS IT EXISTS.
WELL, AIN'T THE TWO OF US LUCKY THAT WE WERE RUNNING A BLACK-OPS MISSION WHEN THE WORLD WENT TO HELL...
I WAS JUST THINKING THE SAME THING ACTUALLY.
YOU KNOW WE HAVE TO ASSUME THAT NEW YORK IS--
I KNOW.
WE HAVE TO FIND THE OTHERS. THOR, SOMEBODY HAD TO MAKE IT THROUGH THIS, TOO...
JUST PROMISE ME THAT YOU WILL HELP ME SHOVE A NUCLEAR WARHEAD UP THAT ROBOT'S ASS.
OH, OKAY.
I MEAN IT.
I KNOW.
DON'T BE COY. DON'T BE CUTE. NOT NOW.
I DON'T MIND GOING OUT.
WE'RE ALL GOING TO EVENTUALLY.
BUT NOT WITHOUT TAKING THAT DAMN THING WITH US.
EXACTLY.

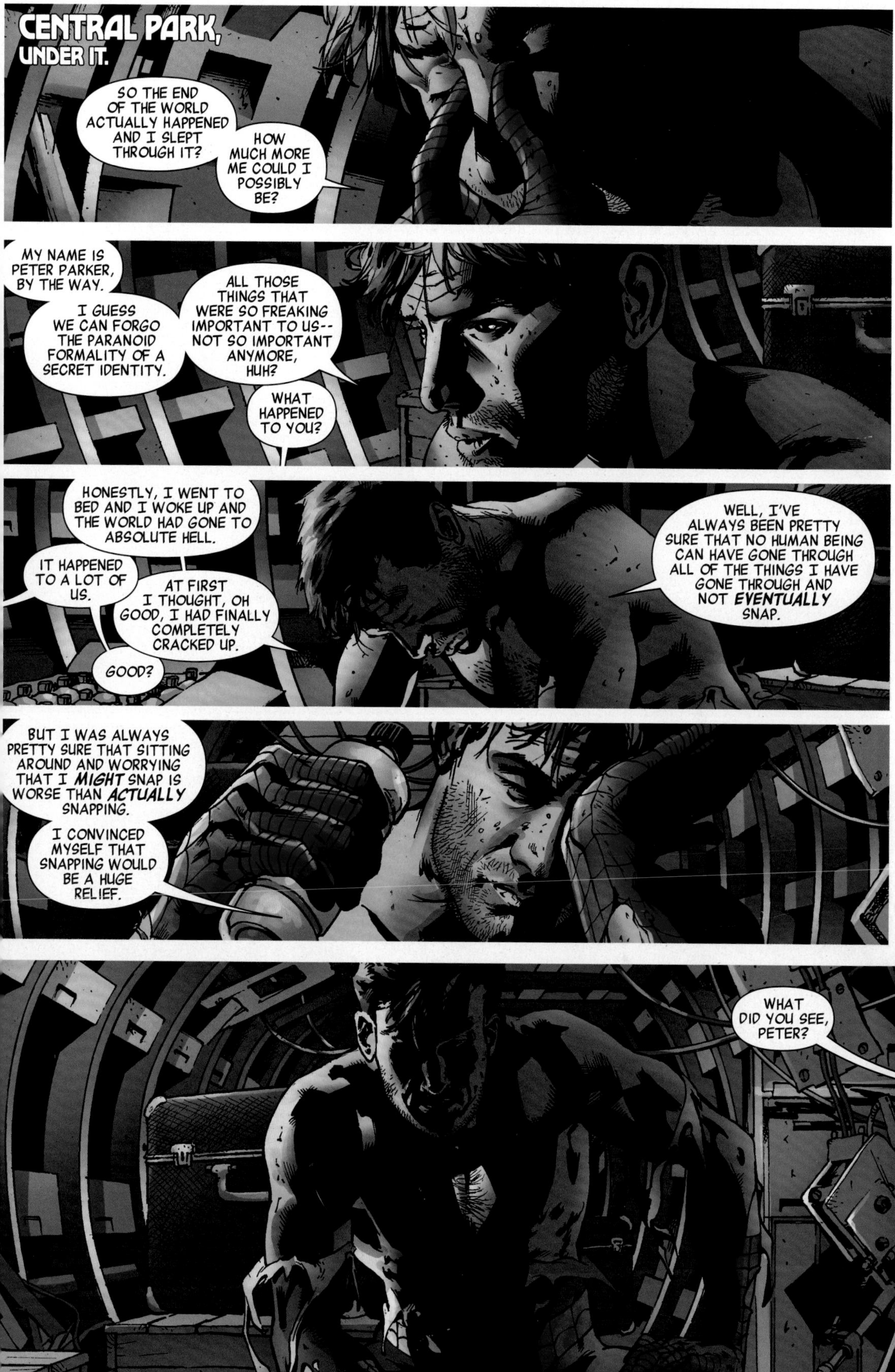

CENTRAL PARK, UNDER IT.
SO THE END OF THE WORLD ACTUALLY HAPPENED AND I SLEPT THROUGH IT?
HOW MUCH MORE ME COULD I POSSIBLY BE?
MY NAME IS PETER PARKER, BY THE WAY.
I GUESS WE CAN FORGO THE PARANOID FORMALITY OF A SECRET IDENTITY.
ALL THOSE THINGS THAT WERE SO FREAKING IMPORTANT TO US-- NOT SO IMPORTANT ANYMORE, HUH?
WHAT HAPPENED TO YOU?
HONESTLY, I WENT TO BED AND I WOKE UP AND THE WORLD HAD GONE TO ABSOLUTE HELL.
IT HAPPENED TO A LOT OF US.
AT FIRST I THOUGHT, OH GOOD, I HAD FINALLY COMPLETELY CRACKED UP.
GOOD?
WELL, I'VE ALWAYS BEEN PRETTY SURE THAT NO HUMAN BEING CAN HAVE GONE THROUGH ALL OF THE THINGS I HAVE GONE THROUGH AND NOT *EVENTUALLY* SNAP.
BUT I WAS ALWAYS PRETTY SURE THAT SITTING AROUND AND WORRYING THAT I *MIGHT* SNAP IS WORSE THAN *ACTUALLY* SNAPPING.
I CONVINCED MYSELF THAT SNAPPING WOULD BE A HUGE RELIEF.
WHAT DID YOU SEE, PETER?

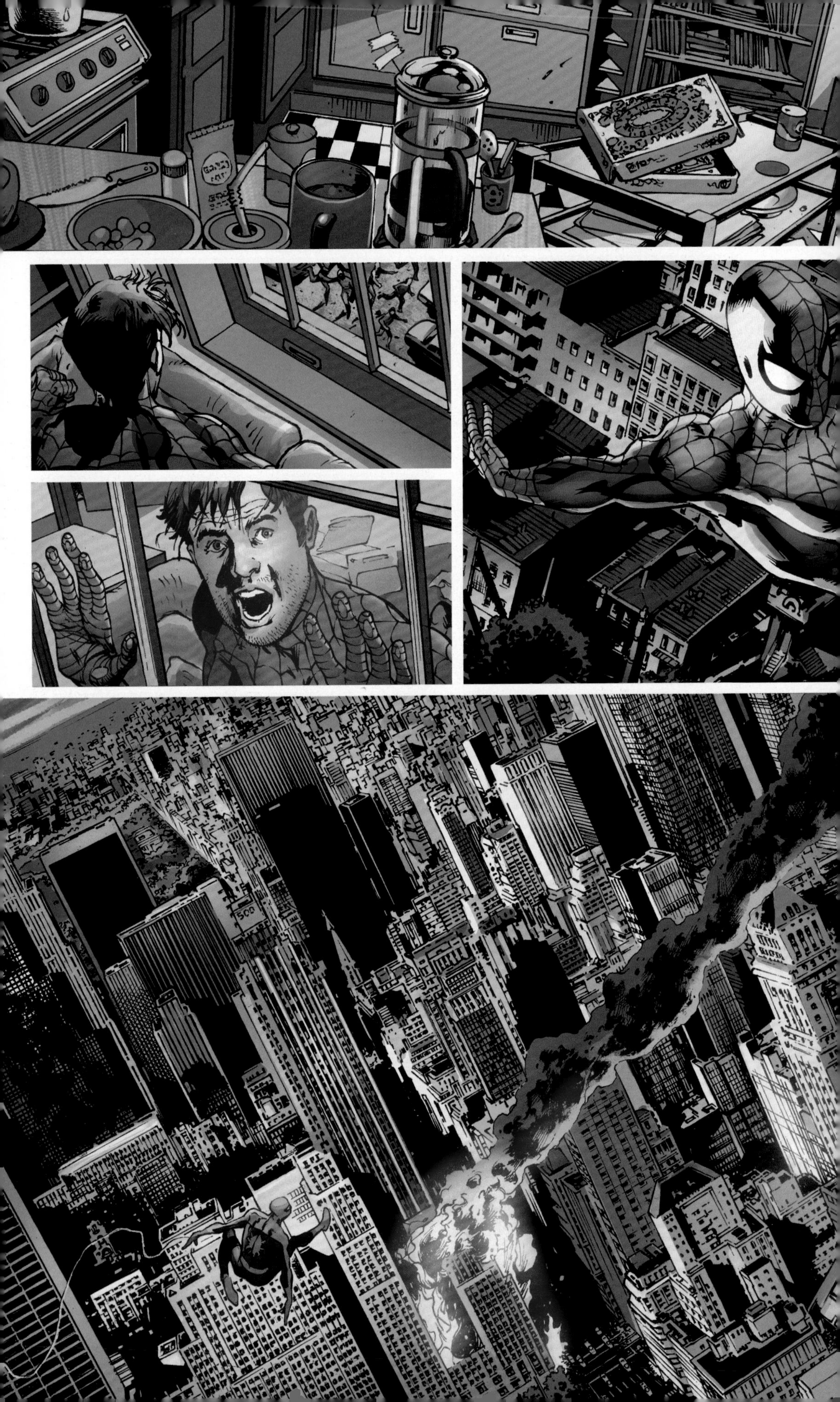

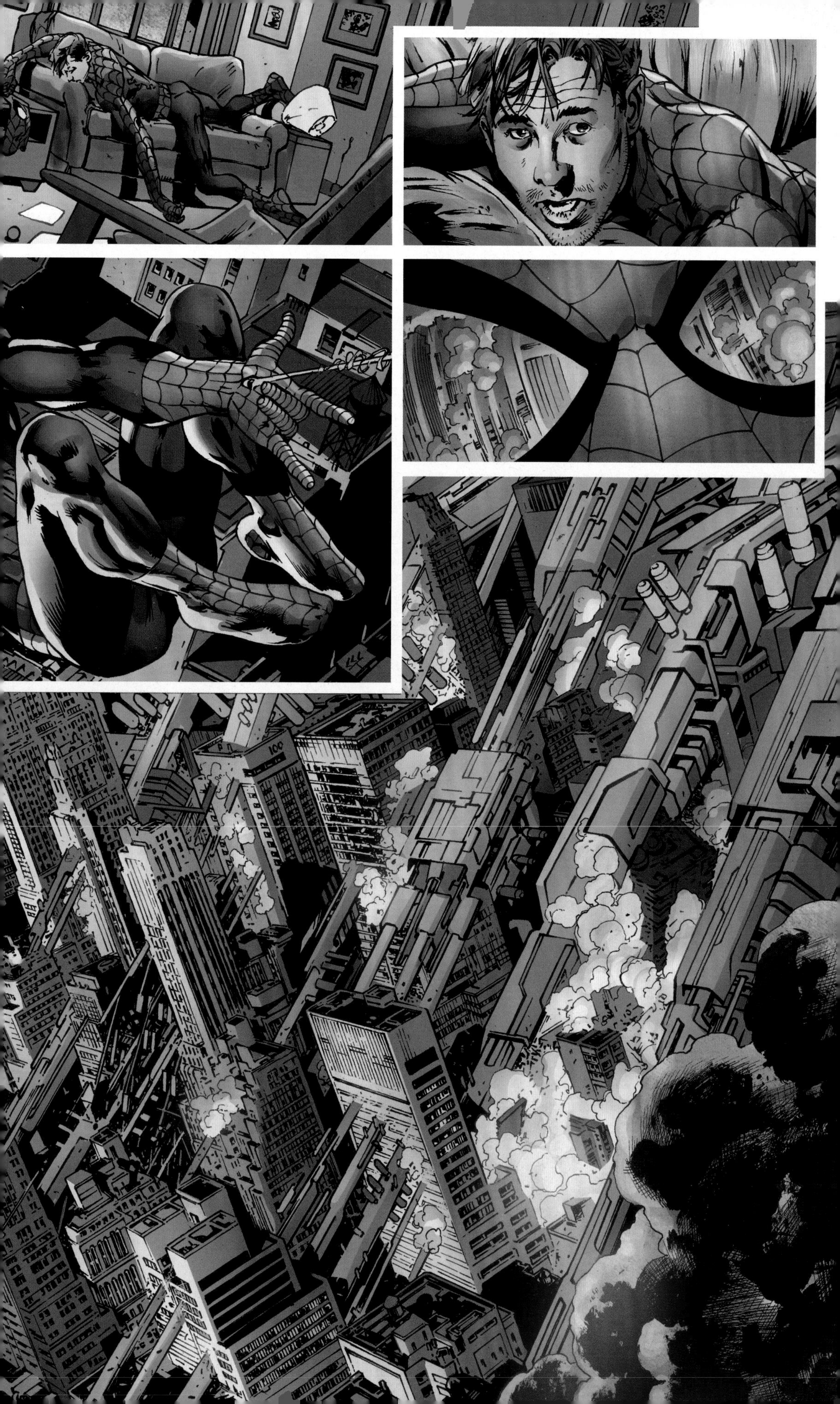

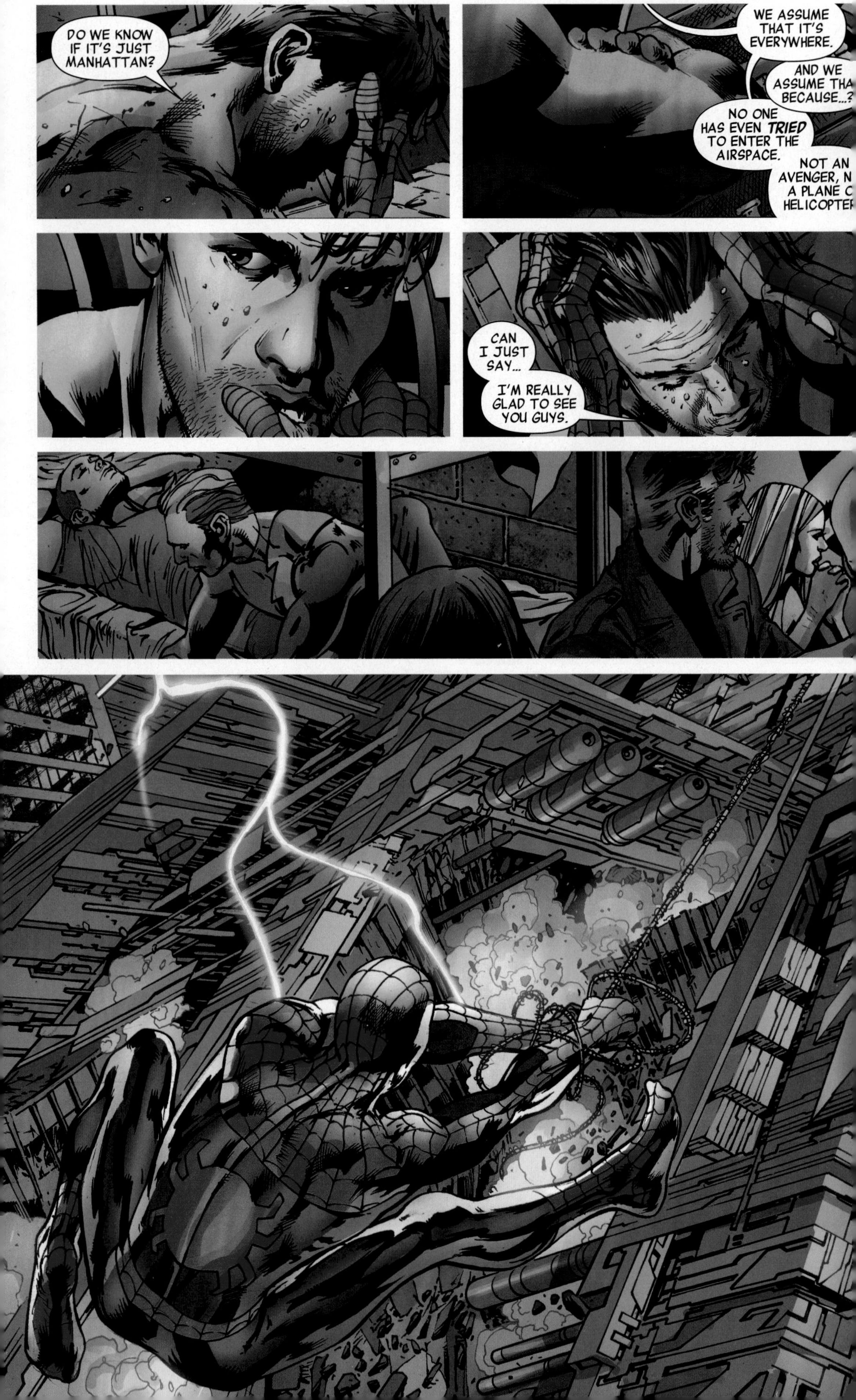

DO WE KNOW IF IT'S JUST MANHATTAN?
WE ASSUME THAT IT'S EVERYWHERE.
AND WE ASSUME THA BECAUSE...?
NO ONE HAS EVEN **TRIED** TO ENTER THE AIRSPACE.
NOT AN AVENGER, N A PLANE C HELICOPTEF
CAN I JUST SAY...
I'M REALLY GLAD TO SEE YOU GUYS.

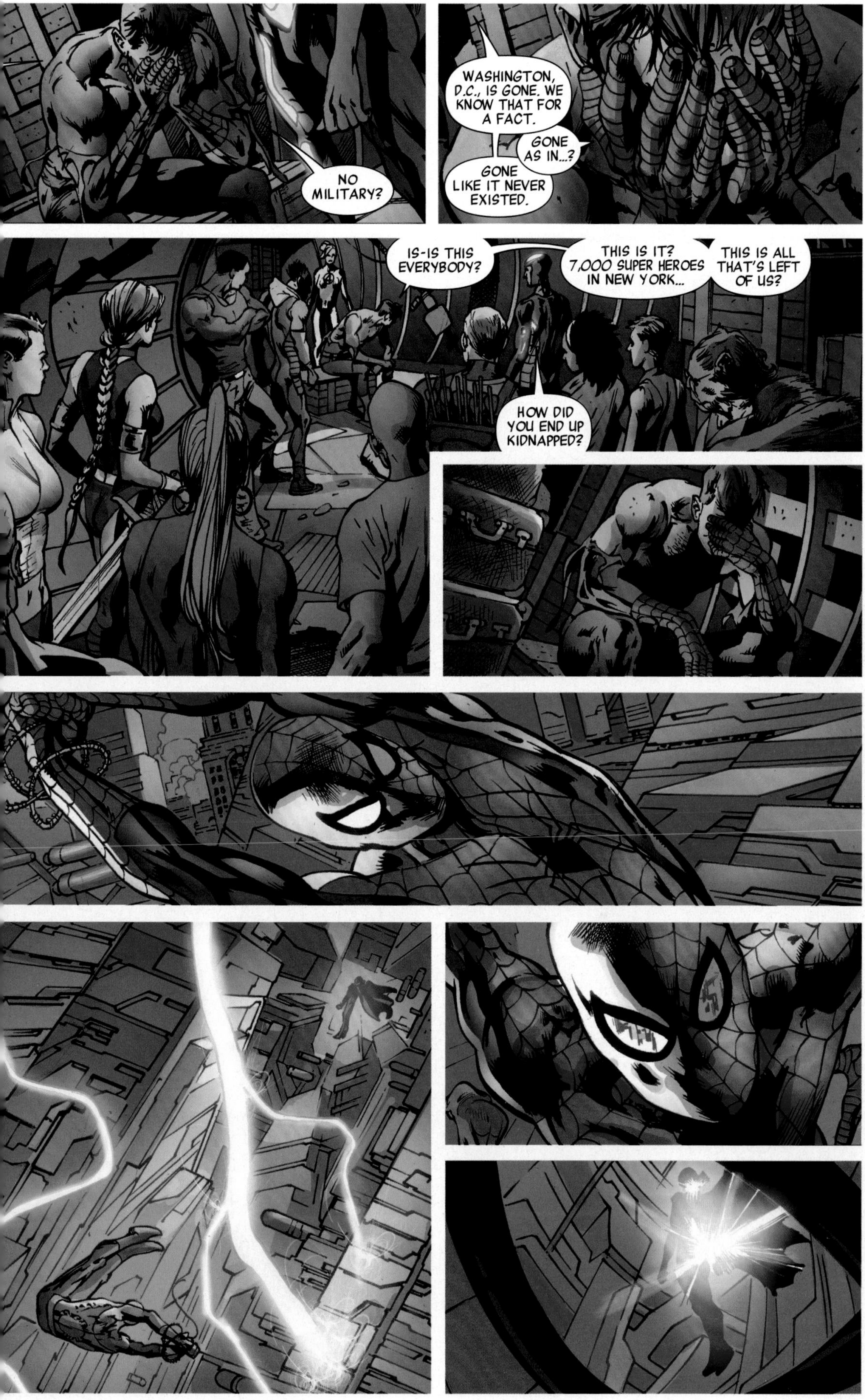
NO MILITARY?
WASHINGTON, D.C., IS GONE. WE KNOW THAT FOR A FACT.
GONE AS IN...?
GONE LIKE IT NEVER EXISTED.
IS-IS THIS EVERYBODY?
THIS IS IT? 7,000 SUPER HEROES IN NEW YORK...
THIS IS ALL THAT'S LEFT OF US?
HOW DID YOU END UP KIDNAPPED?

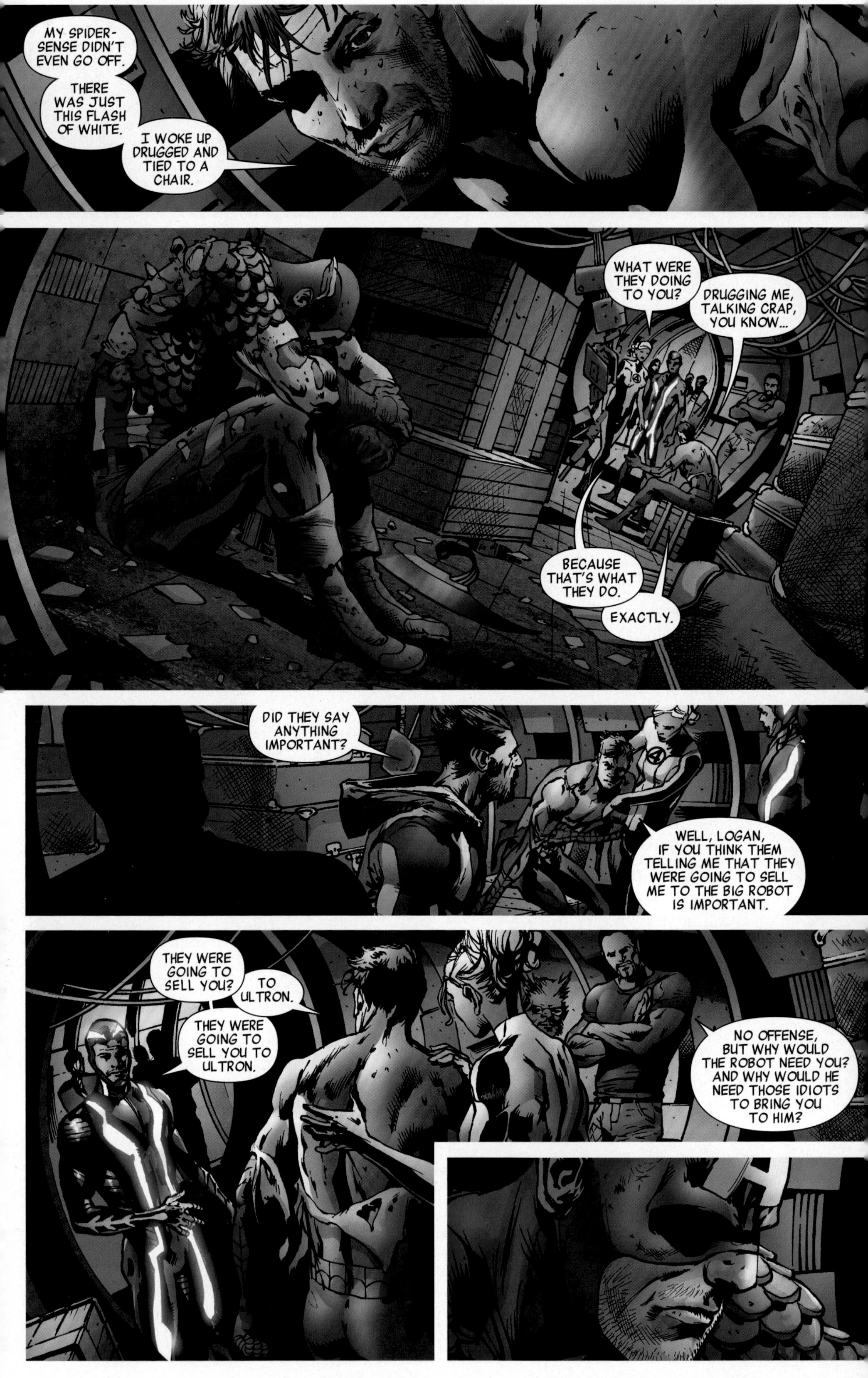
MY SPIDER-SENSE DIDN'T EVEN GO OFF.
THERE WAS JUST THIS FLASH OF WHITE.
I WOKE UP DRUGGED AND TIED TO A CHAIR.
WHAT WERE THEY DOING TO YOU?
DRUGGING ME, TALKING CRAP, YOU KNOW...
BECAUSE THAT'S WHAT THEY DO.
EXACTLY.
DID THEY SAY ANYTHING IMPORTANT?
WELL, LOGAN, IF YOU THINK THEM TELLING ME THAT THEY WERE GOING TO SELL ME TO THE BIG ROBOT IS IMPORTANT.
THEY WERE GOING TO SELL YOU?
TO ULTRON.
THEY WERE GOING TO SELL YOU TO ULTRON.
NO OFFENSE, BUT WHY WOULD THE ROBOT NEED YOU? AND WHY WOULD HE NEED THOSE IDIOTS TO BRING YOU TO HIM?

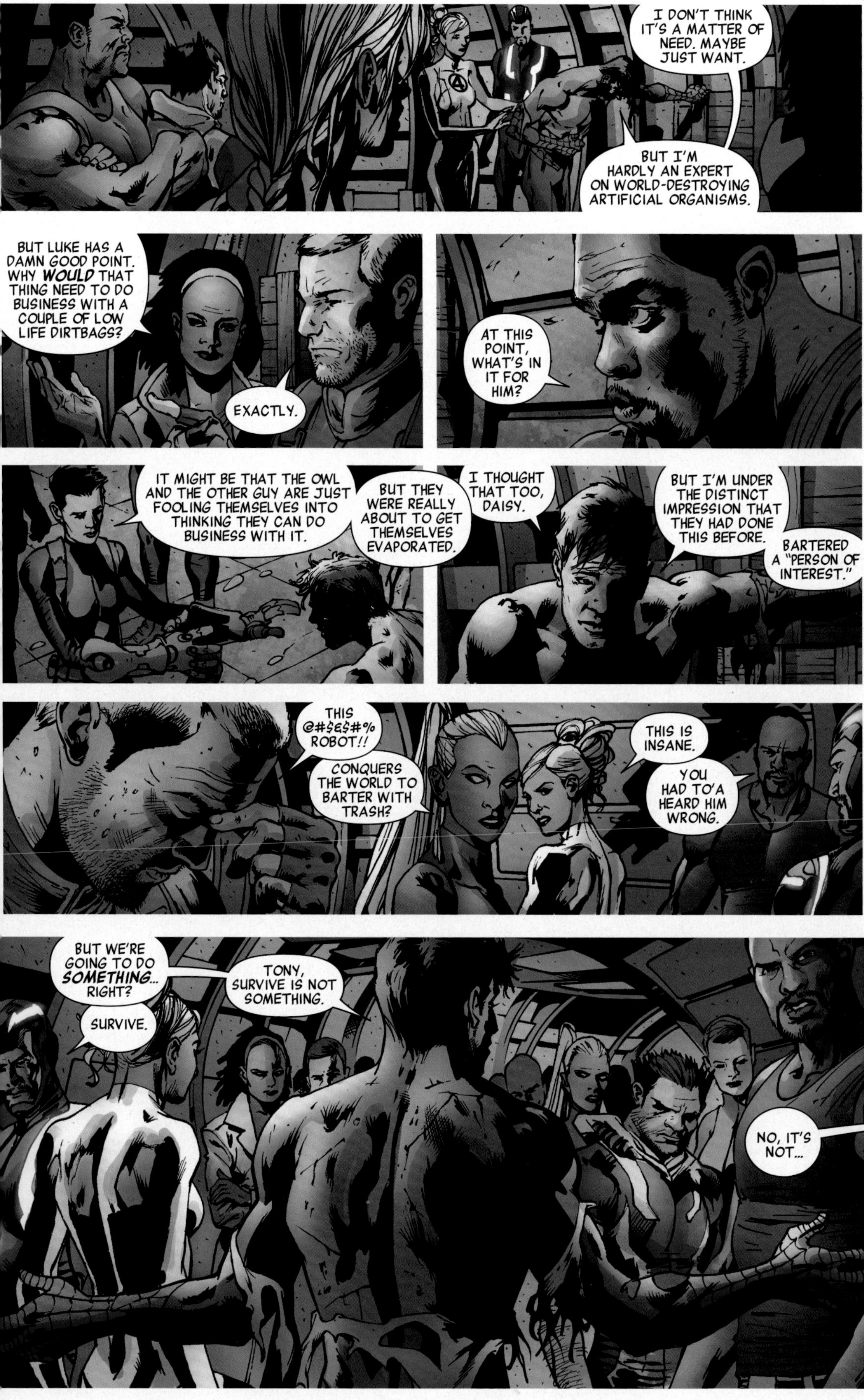

I DON'T THINK IT'S A MATTER OF NEED. MAYBE JUST WANT.
BUT I'M HARDLY AN EXPERT ON WORLD-DESTROYING ARTIFICIAL ORGANISMS.
BUT LUKE HAS A DAMN GOOD POINT. WHY **WOULD** THAT THING NEED TO DO BUSINESS WITH A COUPLE OF LOW LIFE DIRTBAGS?
EXACTLY.
AT THIS POINT, WHAT'S IN IT FOR HIM?
IT MIGHT BE THAT THE OWL AND THE OTHER GUY ARE JUST FOOLING THEMSELVES INTO THINKING THEY CAN DO BUSINESS WITH IT.
BUT THEY WERE REALLY ABOUT TO GET THEMSELVES EVAPORATED.
I THOUGHT THAT TOO, DAISY.
BUT I'M UNDER THE DISTINCT IMPRESSION THAT THEY HAD DONE THIS BEFORE.
BARTERED A "PERSON OF INTEREST."
THIS @#$&$#% ROBOT!!
CONQUERS THE WORLD TO BARTER WITH TRASH?
THIS IS INSANE.
YOU HAD TO'A HEARD HIM WRONG.
BUT WE'RE GOING TO DO ***SOMETHING***... RIGHT?
SURVIVE.
TONY, SURVIVE IS NOT SOMETHING.
NO, IT'S NOT...

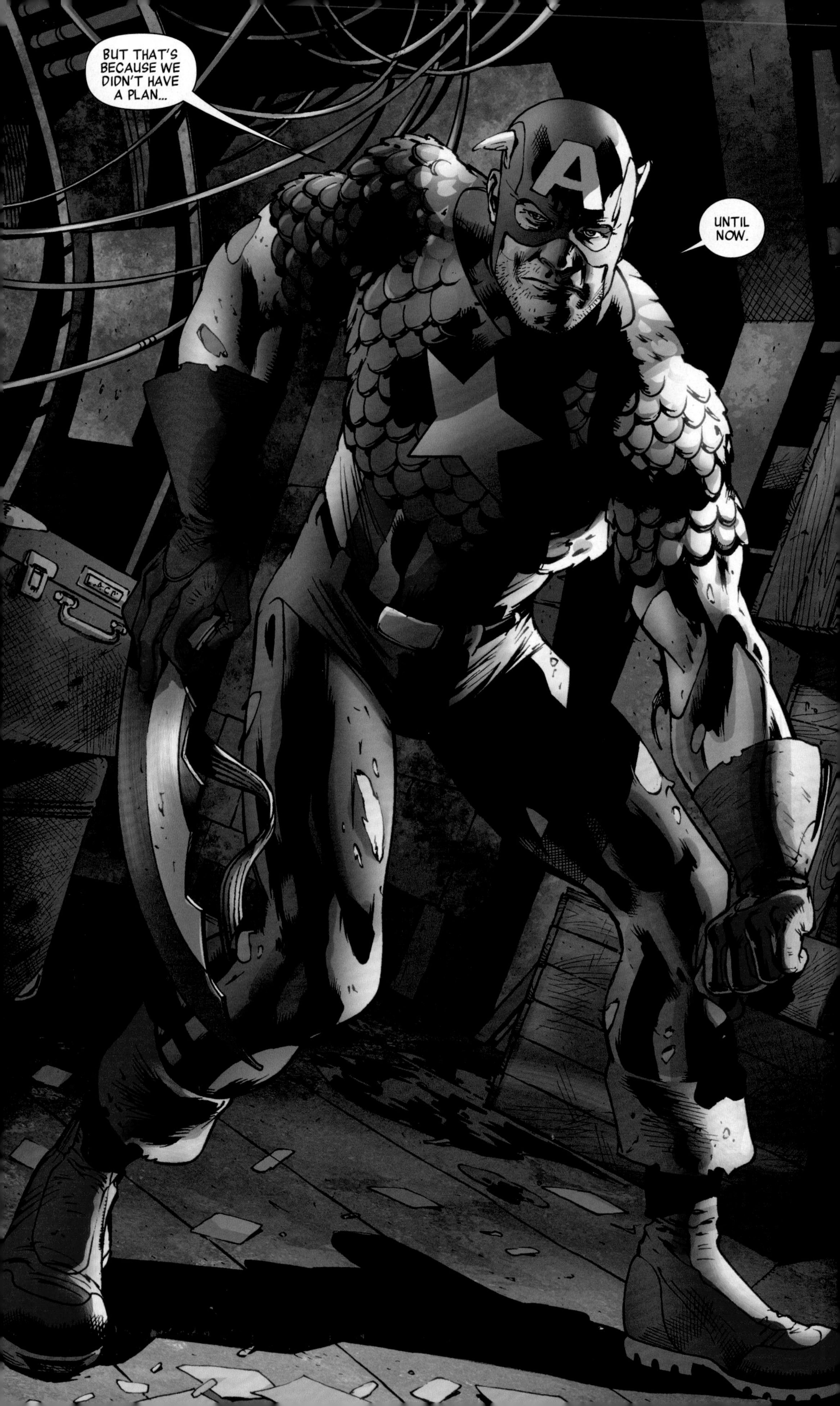
BUT THAT'S BECAUSE WE DIDN'T HAVE A PLAN...
UNTIL NOW.

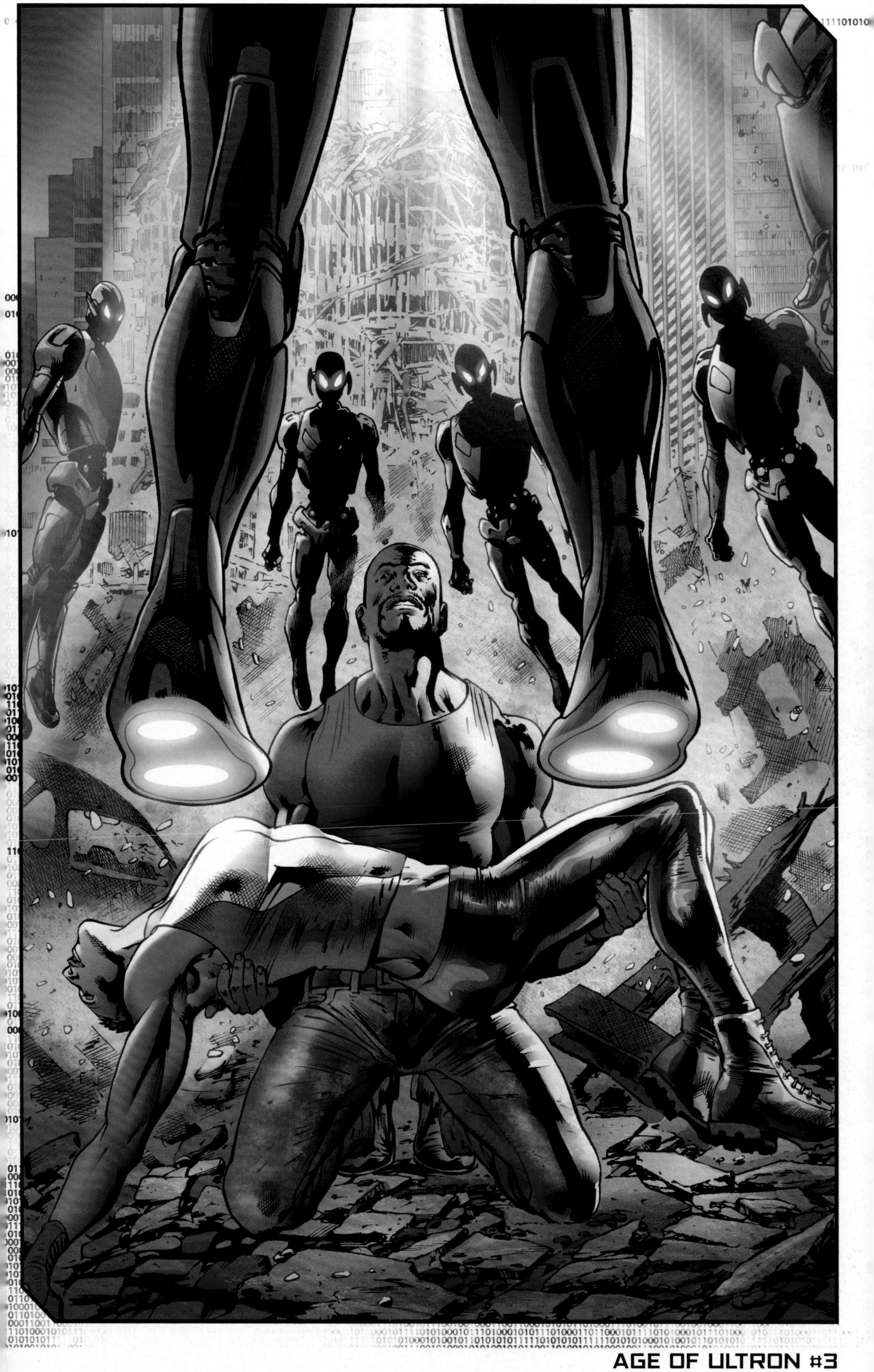

AGE OF ULTRON #3

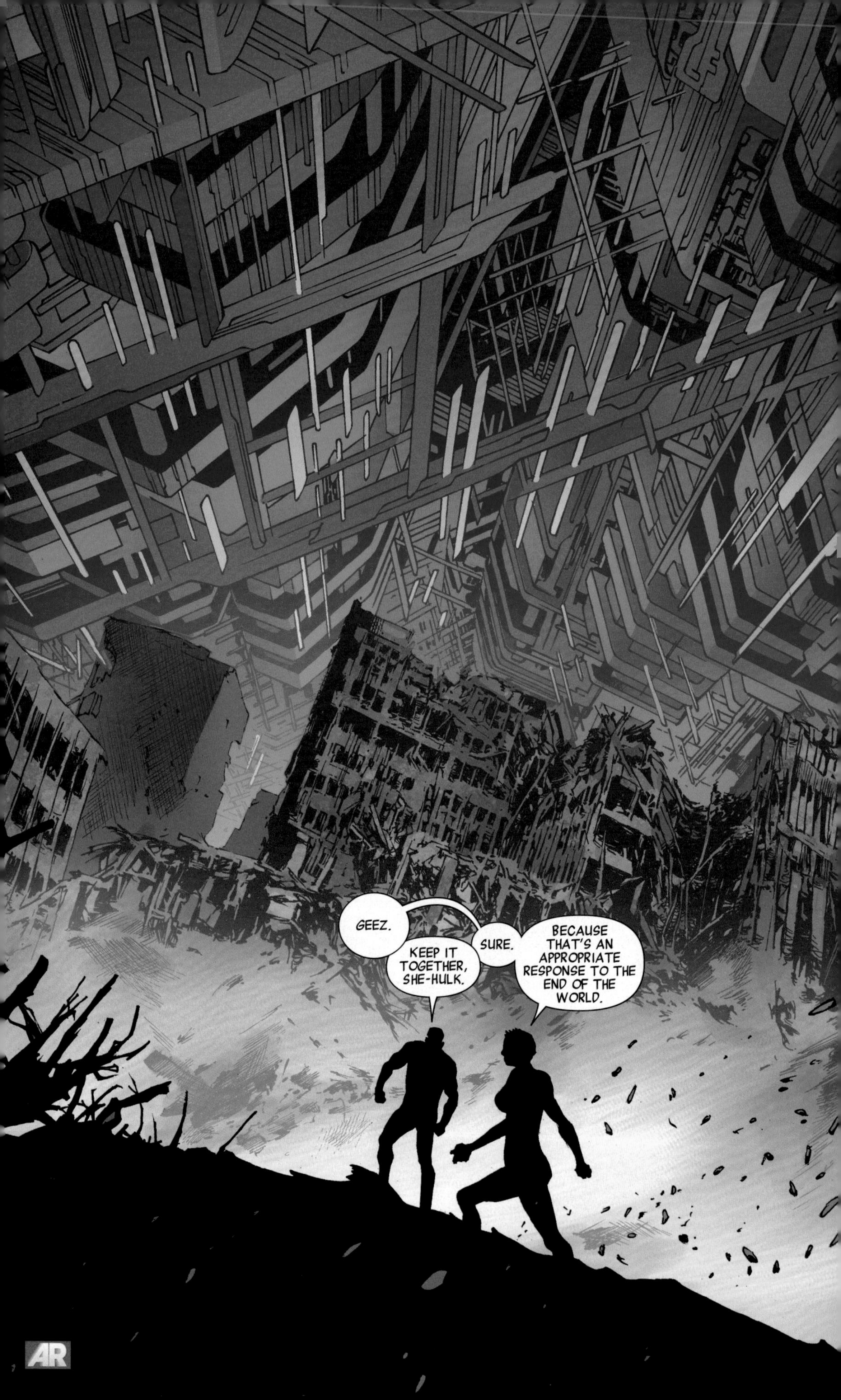
GEEZ.
KEEP IT TOGETHER, SHE-HULK.
SURE.
BECAUSE THAT'S AN APPROPRIATE RESPONSE TO THE END OF THE WORLD.

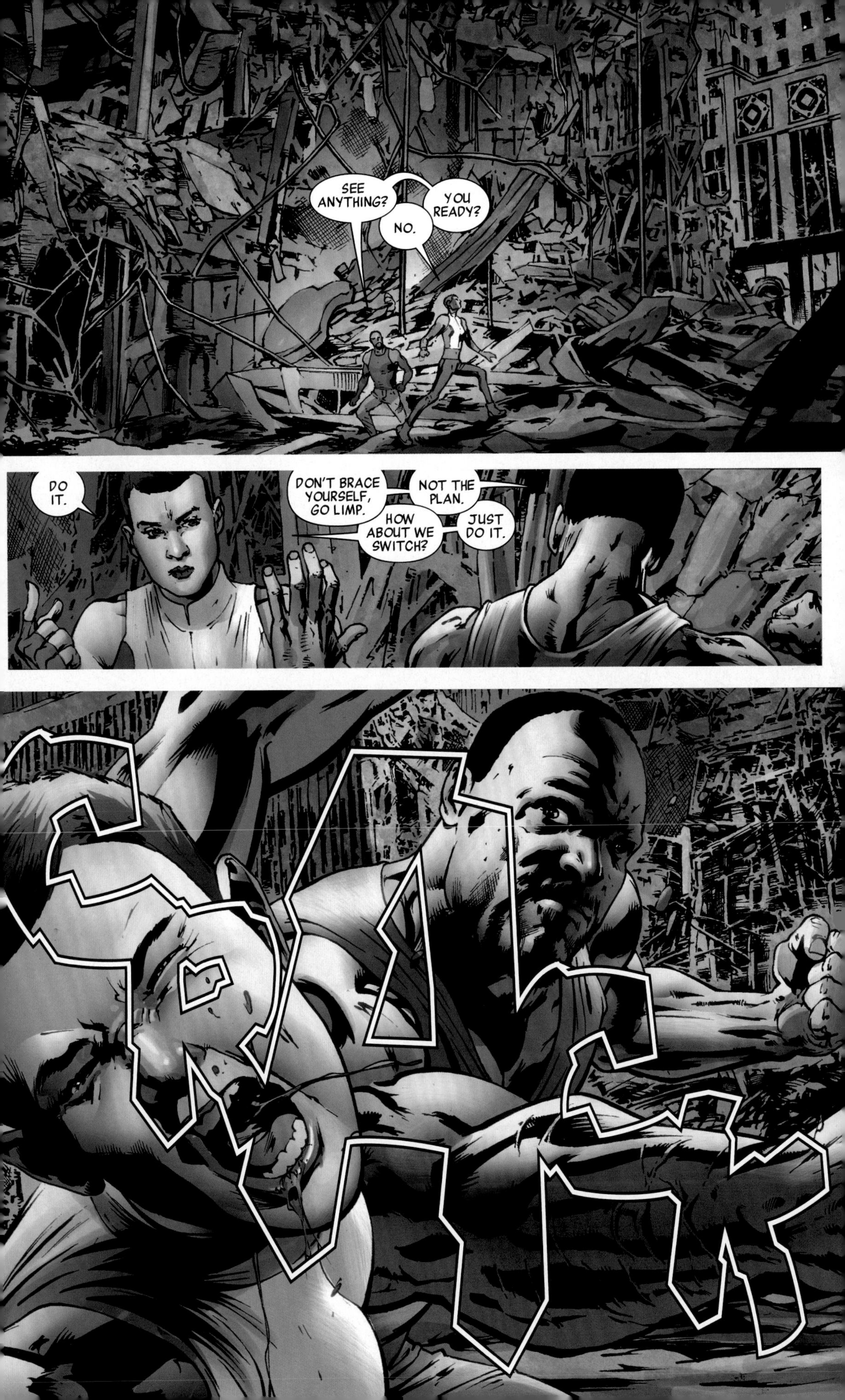
SEE ANYTHING?
NO.
YOU READY?
DO IT.
DON'T BRACE YOURSELF, GO LIMP.
NOT THE PLAN.
HOW ABOUT WE SWITCH?
JUST DO IT.

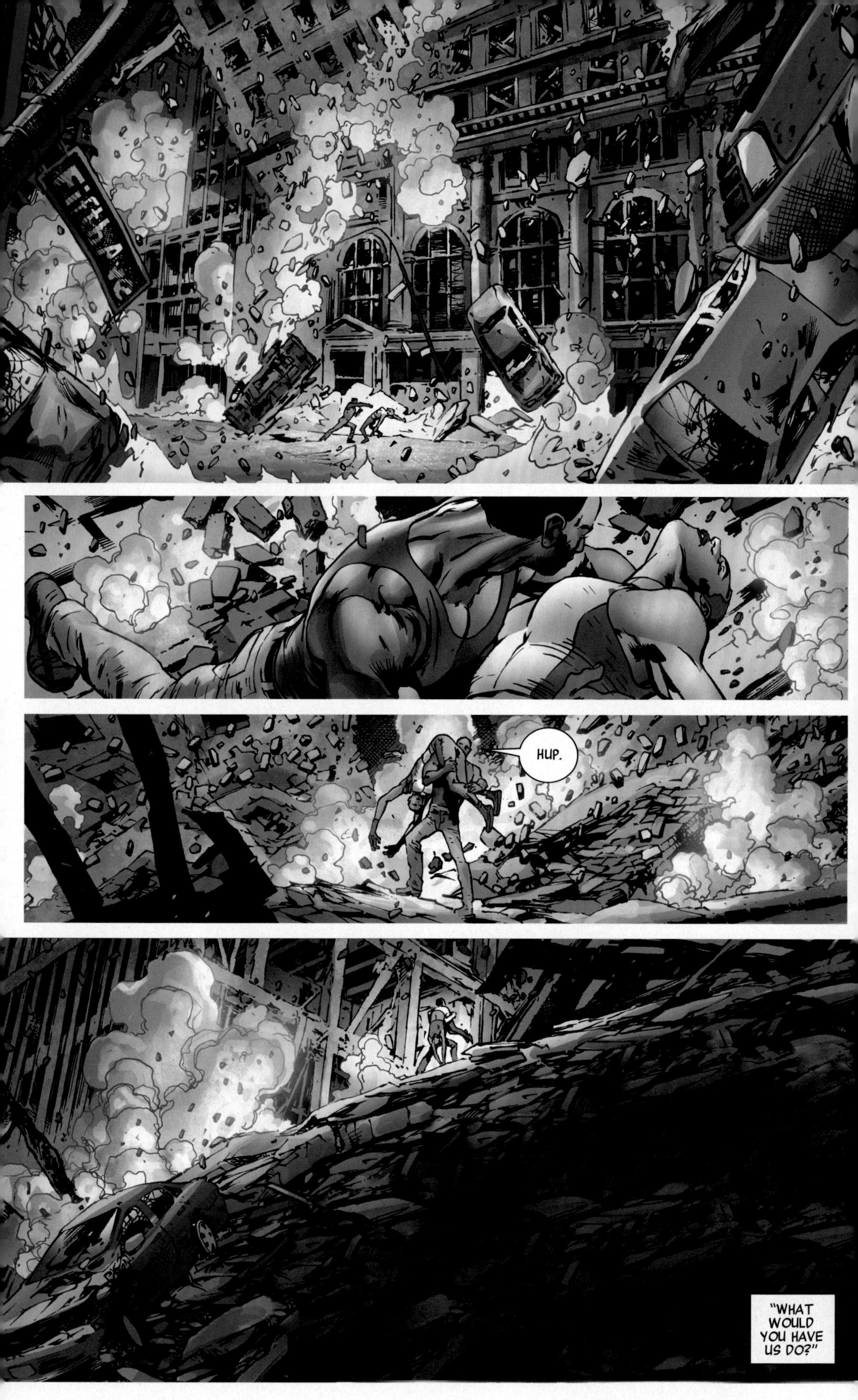
HUP.
"WHAT WOULD YOU HAVE US DO?"

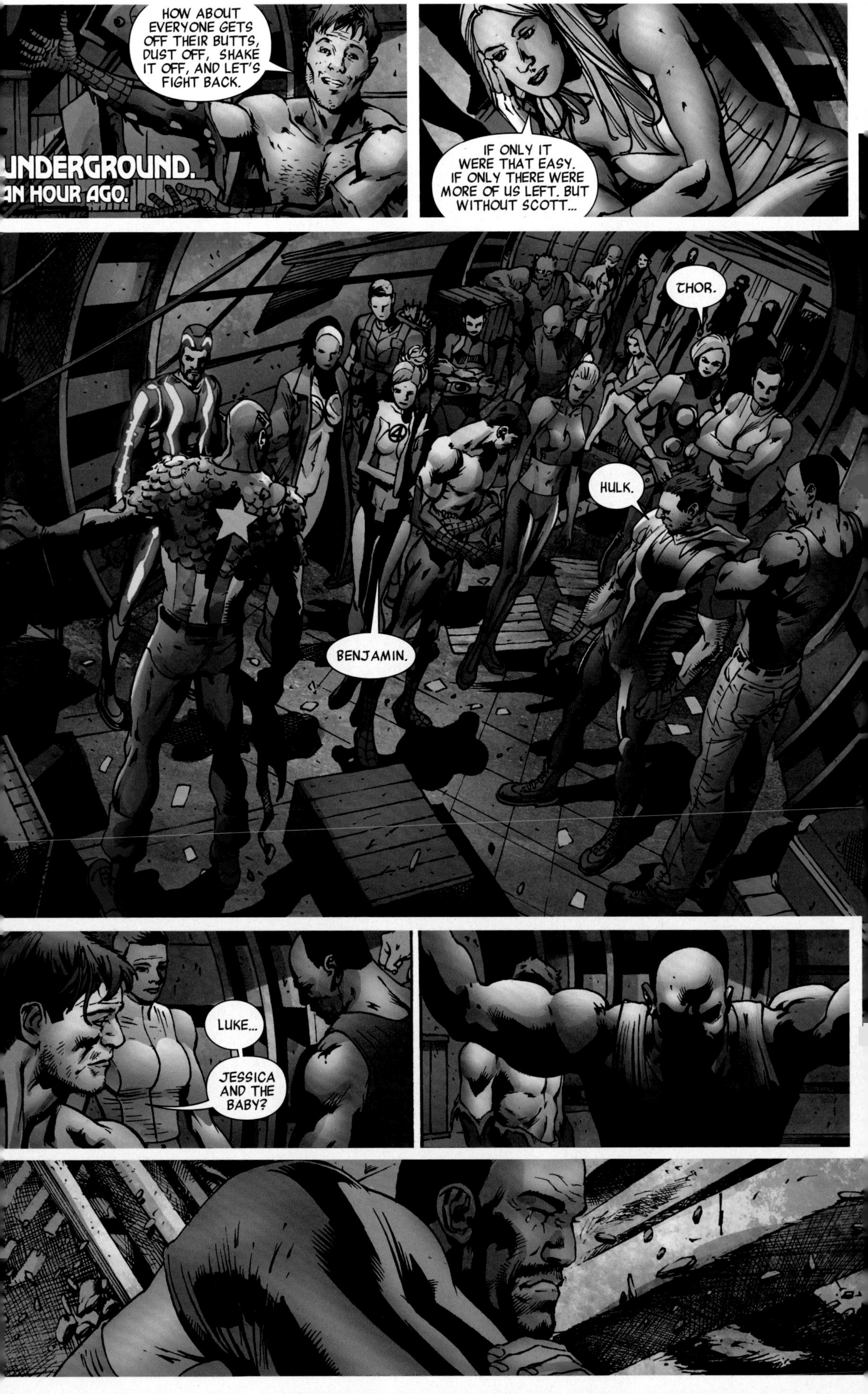

HOW ABOUT EVERYONE GETS OFF THEIR BUTTS, DUST OFF, SHAKE IT OFF, AND LET'S FIGHT BACK.
UNDERGROUND. AN HOUR AGO.
IF ONLY IT WERE THAT EASY. IF ONLY THERE WERE MORE OF US LEFT. BUT WITHOUT SCOTT...
THOR.
HULK.
BENJAMIN.
LUKE...
JESSICA AND THE BABY?

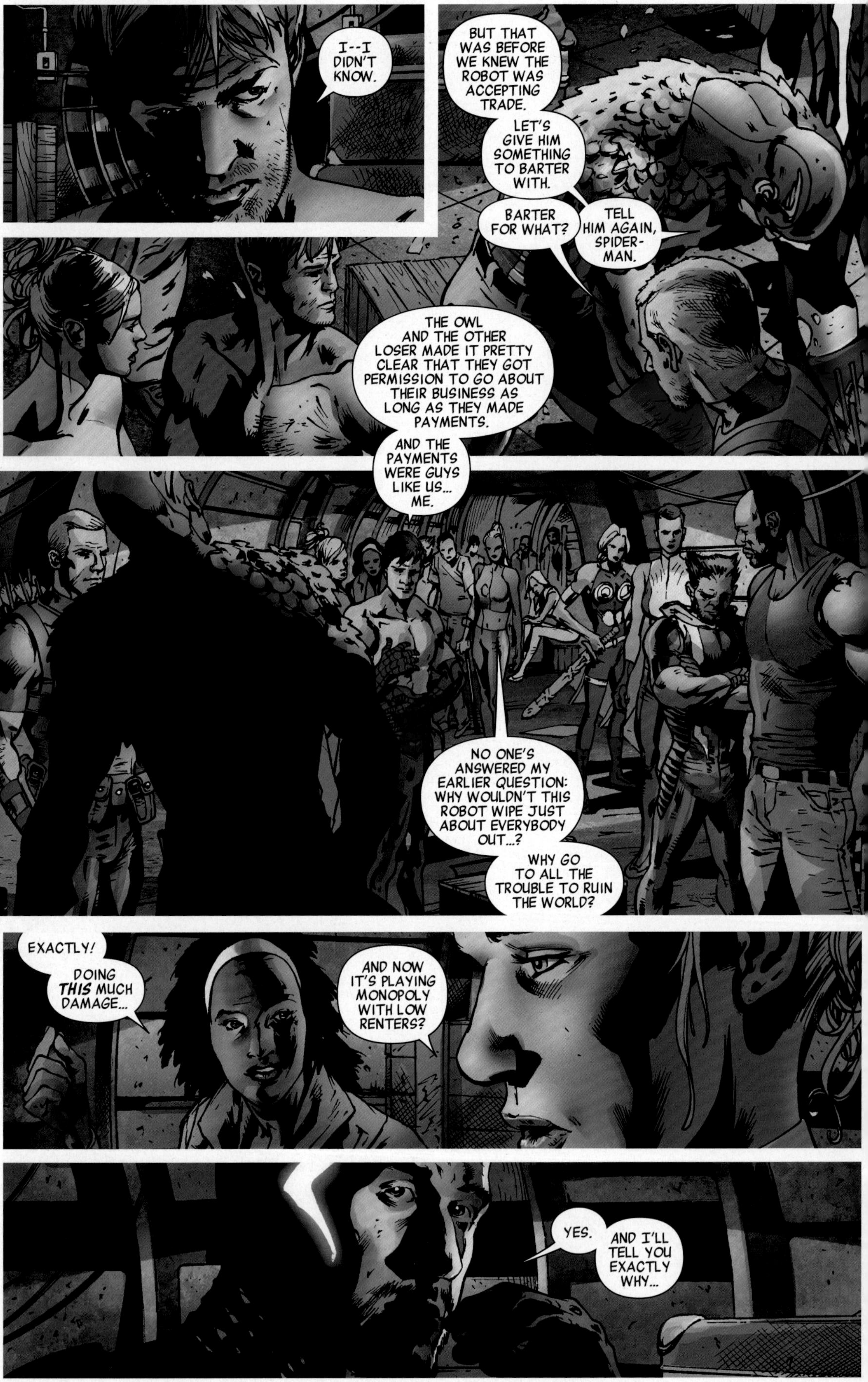
I--I DIDN'T KNOW.
BUT THAT WAS BEFORE WE KNEW THE ROBOT WAS ACCEPTING TRADE.
LET'S GIVE HIM SOMETHING TO BARTER WITH.
BARTER FOR WHAT?
TELL HIM AGAIN, SPIDER-MAN.
THE OWL AND THE OTHER LOSER MADE IT PRETTY CLEAR THAT THEY GOT PERMISSION TO GO ABOUT THEIR BUSINESS AS LONG AS THEY MADE PAYMENTS.
AND THE PAYMENTS WERE GUYS LIKE US... ME.
NO ONE'S ANSWERED MY EARLIER QUESTION: WHY WOULDN'T THIS ROBOT WIPE JUST ABOUT EVERYBODY OUT...?
WHY GO TO ALL THE TROUBLE TO RUIN THE WORLD?
EXACTLY!
DOING THIS MUCH DAMAGE...
AND NOW IT'S PLAYING MONOPOLY WITH LOW RENTERS?
YES.
AND I'LL TELL YOU EXACTLY WHY...

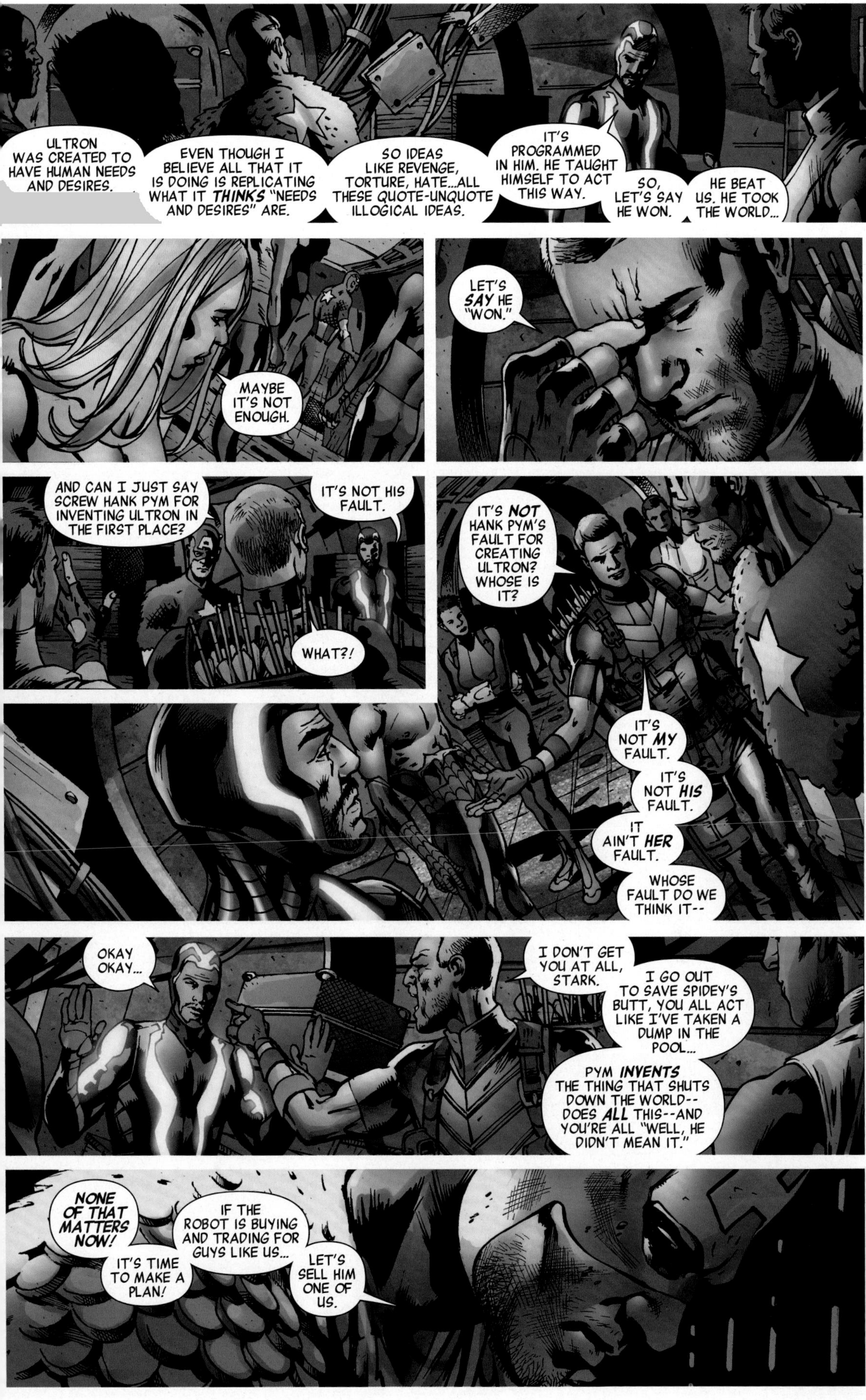
ULTRON WAS CREATED TO HAVE HUMAN NEEDS AND DESIRES.
EVEN THOUGH I BELIEVE ALL THAT IT IS DOING IS REPLICATING WHAT IT THINKS "NEEDS AND DESIRES" ARE.
SO IDEAS LIKE REVENGE, TORTURE, HATE...ALL THESE QUOTE-UNQUOTE ILLOGICAL IDEAS.
IT'S PROGRAMMED IN HIM. HE TAUGHT HIMSELF TO ACT THIS WAY.
SO, LET'S SAY HE WON.
HE BEAT US. HE TOOK THE WORLD...
MAYBE IT'S NOT ENOUGH.
LET'S SAY HE "WON."
AND CAN I JUST SAY SCREW HANK PYM FOR INVENTING ULTRON IN THE FIRST PLACE?
IT'S NOT HIS FAULT.
WHAT?!
IT'S NOT HANK PYM'S FAULT FOR CREATING ULTRON? WHOSE IS IT?
IT'S NOT MY FAULT.
IT'S NOT HIS FAULT.
IT AIN'T HER FAULT.
WHOSE FAULT DO WE THINK IT--
OKAY OKAY...
I DON'T GET YOU AT ALL, STARK.
I GO OUT TO SAVE SPIDEY'S BUTT, YOU ALL ACT LIKE I'VE TAKEN A DUMP IN THE POOL...
PYM INVENTS THE THING THAT SHUTS DOWN THE WORLD--DOES ALL THIS--AND YOU'RE ALL "WELL, HE DIDN'T MEAN IT."
NONE OF THAT MATTERS NOW!
IT'S TIME TO MAKE A PLAN!
IF THE ROBOT IS BUYING AND TRADING FOR GUYS LIKE US...
LET'S SELL HIM ONE OF US.

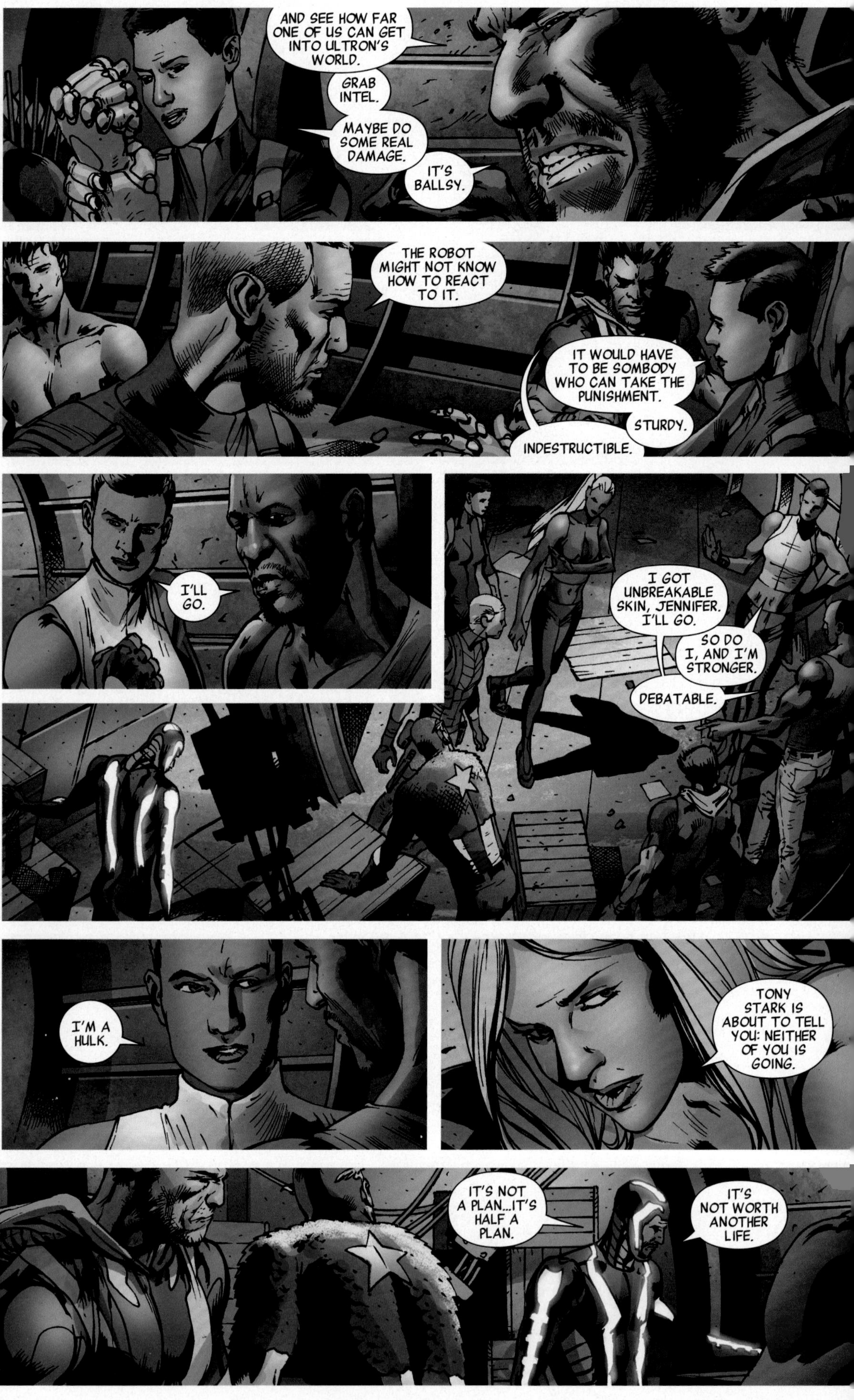
AND SEE HOW FAR ONE OF US CAN GET INTO ULTRON'S WORLD.
GRAB INTEL.
MAYBE DO SOME REAL DAMAGE.
IT'S BALLSY.
THE ROBOT MIGHT NOT KNOW HOW TO REACT TO IT.
IT WOULD HAVE TO BE SOMBODY WHO CAN TAKE THE PUNISHMENT.
STURDY.
INDESTRUCTIBLE.
I'LL GO.
I GOT UNBREAKABLE SKIN, JENNIFER. I'LL GO.
SO DO I, AND I'M STRONGER.
DEBATABLE.
I'M A HULK.
TONY STARK IS ABOUT TO TELL YOU: NEITHER OF YOU IS GOING.
IT'S NOT A PLAN...IT'S HALF A PLAN.
IT'S NOT WORTH ANOTHER LIFE.

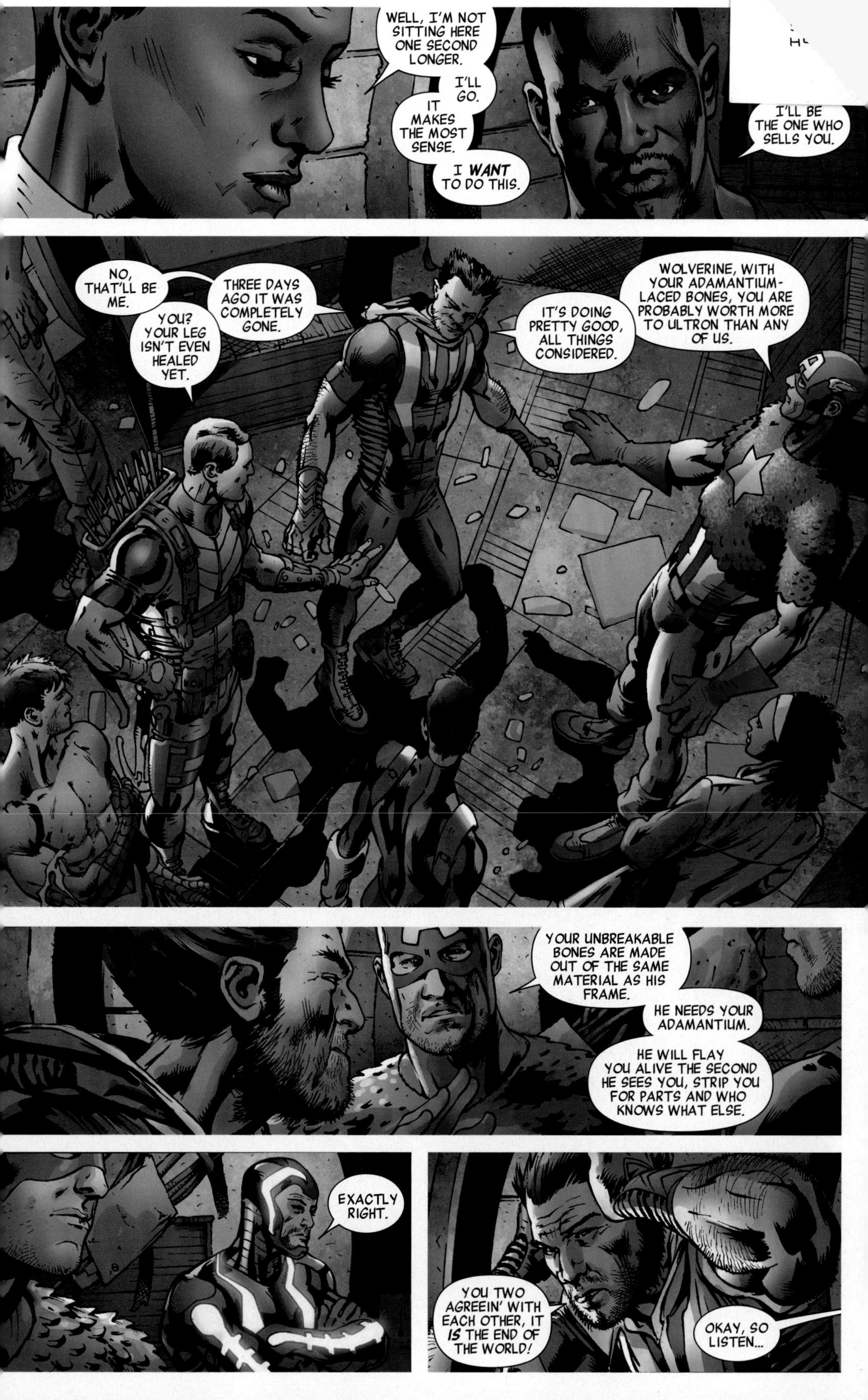

WELL, I'M NOT SITTING HERE ONE SECOND LONGER.
I'LL GO.
IT MAKES THE MOST SENSE.
I *WANT* TO DO THIS.
I'LL BE THE ONE WHO SELLS YOU.
NO, THAT'LL BE ME.
YOU? YOUR LEG ISN'T EVEN HEALED YET.
THREE DAYS AGO IT WAS COMPLETELY GONE.
IT'S DOING PRETTY GOOD, ALL THINGS CONSIDERED.
WOLVERINE, WITH YOUR ADAMANTIUM-LACED BONES, YOU ARE PROBABLY WORTH MORE TO ULTRON THAN ANY OF US.
YOUR UNBREAKABLE BONES ARE MADE OUT OF THE SAME MATERIAL AS HIS FRAME.
HE NEEDS YOUR ADAMANTIUM.
HE WILL FLAY YOU ALIVE THE SECOND HE SEES YOU, STRIP YOU FOR PARTS AND WHO KNOWS WHAT ELSE.
EXACTLY RIGHT.
YOU TWO AGREEIN' WITH EACH OTHER, IT *IS* THE END OF THE WORLD!
OKAY, SO LISTEN...

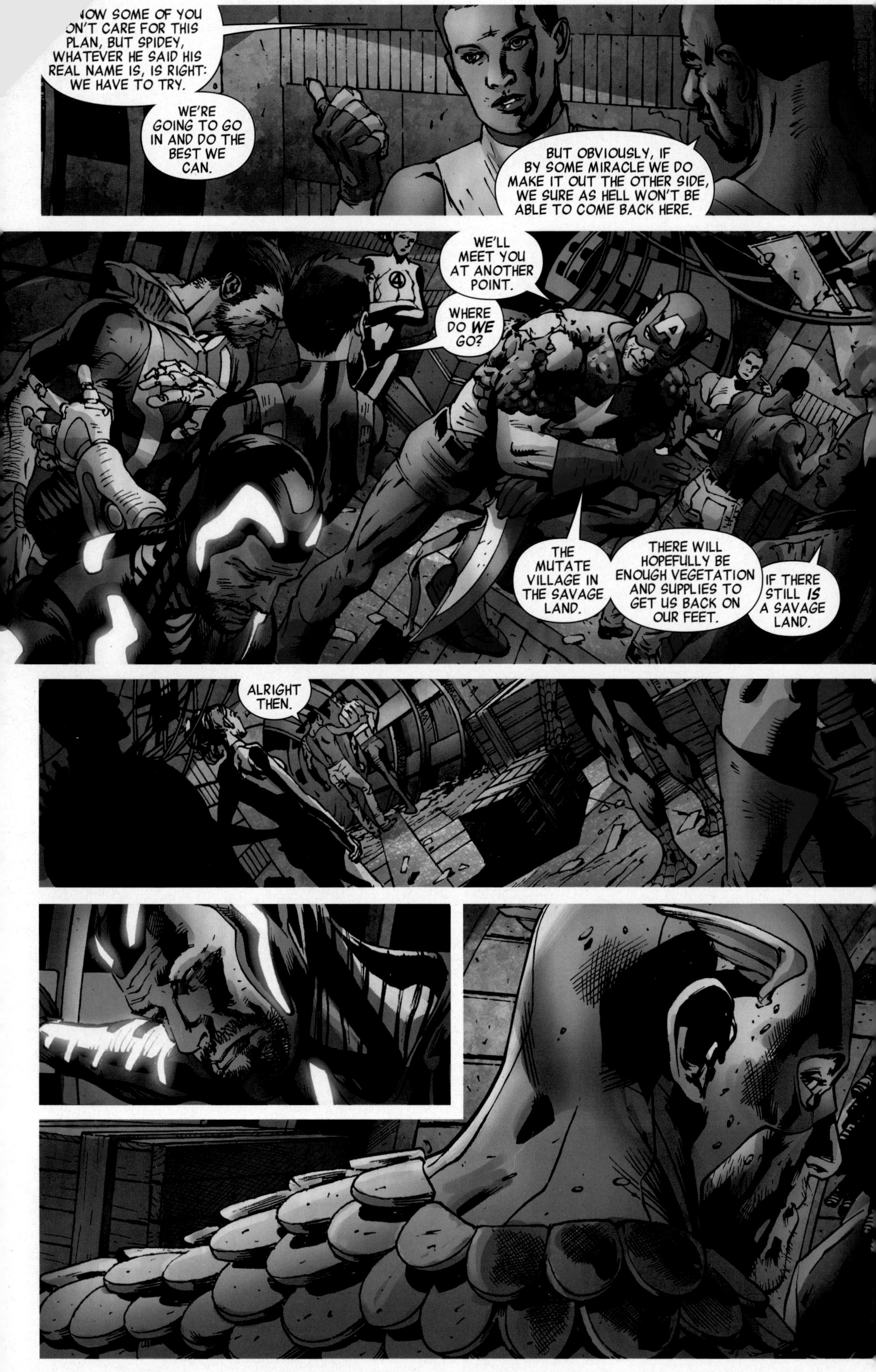
NOW SOME OF YOU ON'T CARE FOR THIS PLAN, BUT SPIDEY, WHATEVER HE SAID HIS REAL NAME IS, IS RIGHT: WE HAVE TO TRY.
WE'RE GOING TO GO IN AND DO THE BEST WE CAN.
BUT OBVIOUSLY, IF BY SOME MIRACLE WE DO MAKE IT OUT THE OTHER SIDE, WE SURE AS HELL WON'T BE ABLE TO COME BACK HERE.
WE'LL MEET YOU AT ANOTHER POINT.
WHERE DO WE GO?
THE MUTATE VILLAGE IN THE SAVAGE LAND.
THERE WILL HOPEFULLY BE ENOUGH VEGETATION AND SUPPLIES TO GET US BACK ON OUR FEET.
IF THERE STILL IS A SAVAGE LAND.
ALRIGHT THEN.

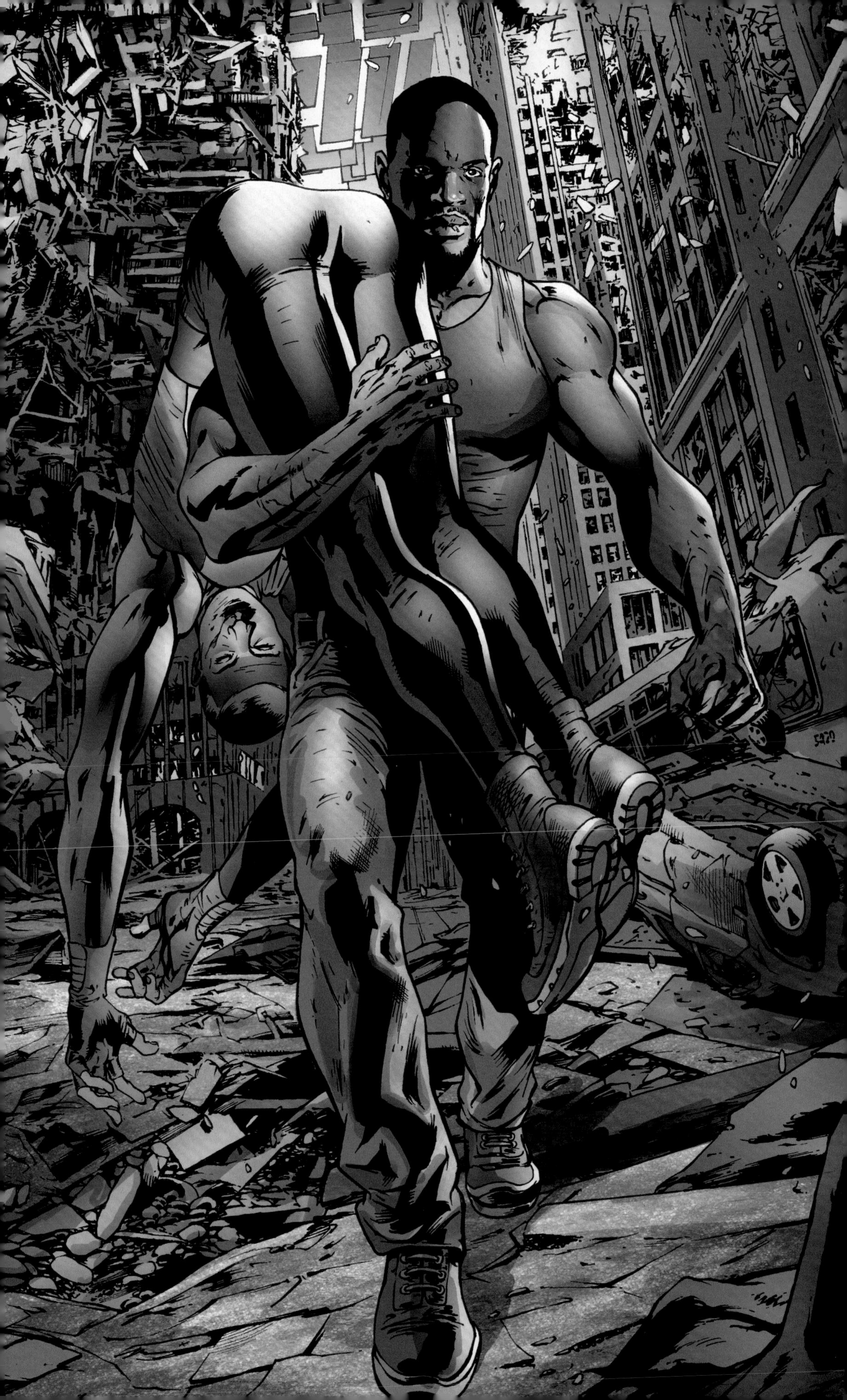

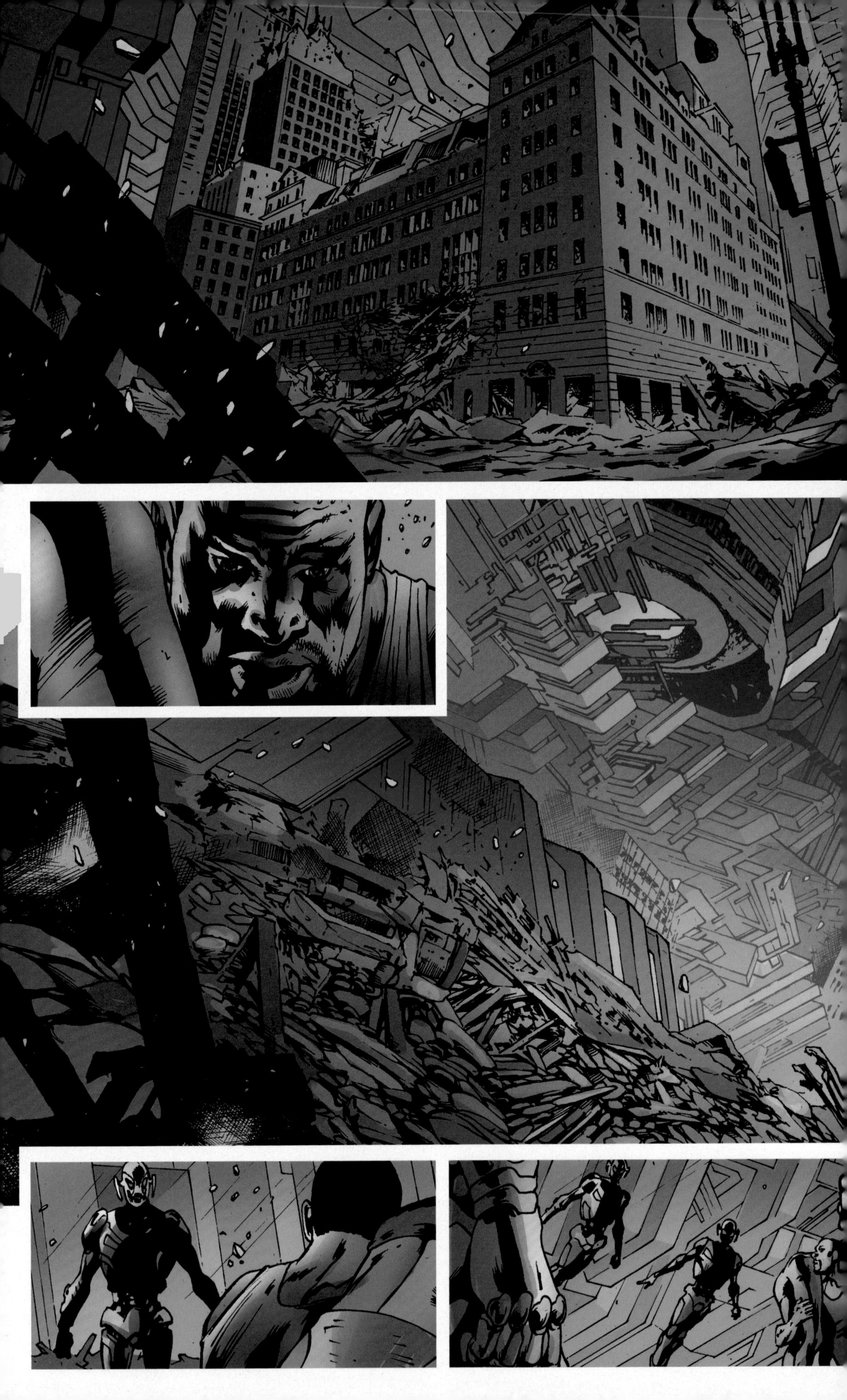

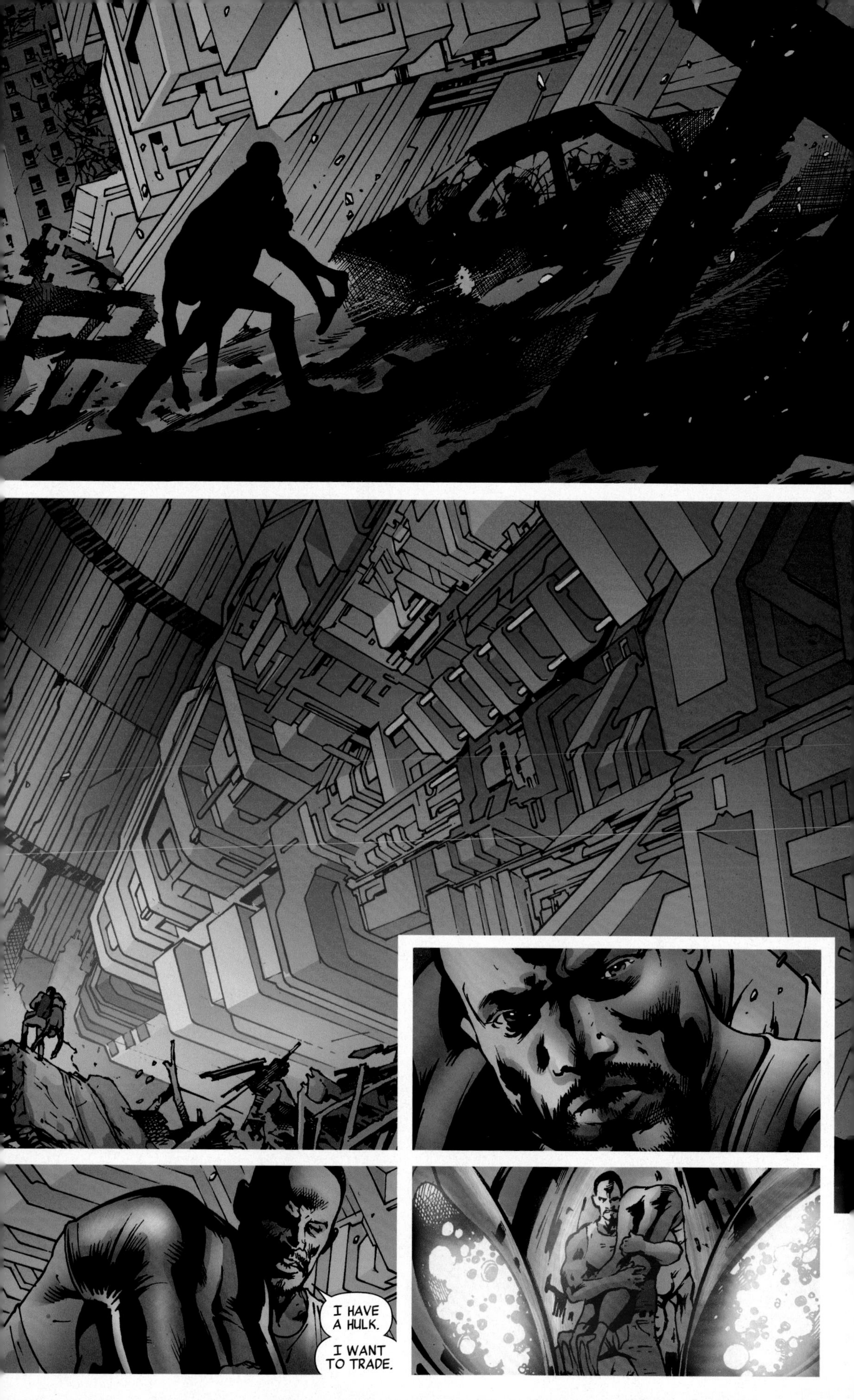
I HAVE A HULK.
I WANT TO TRADE.

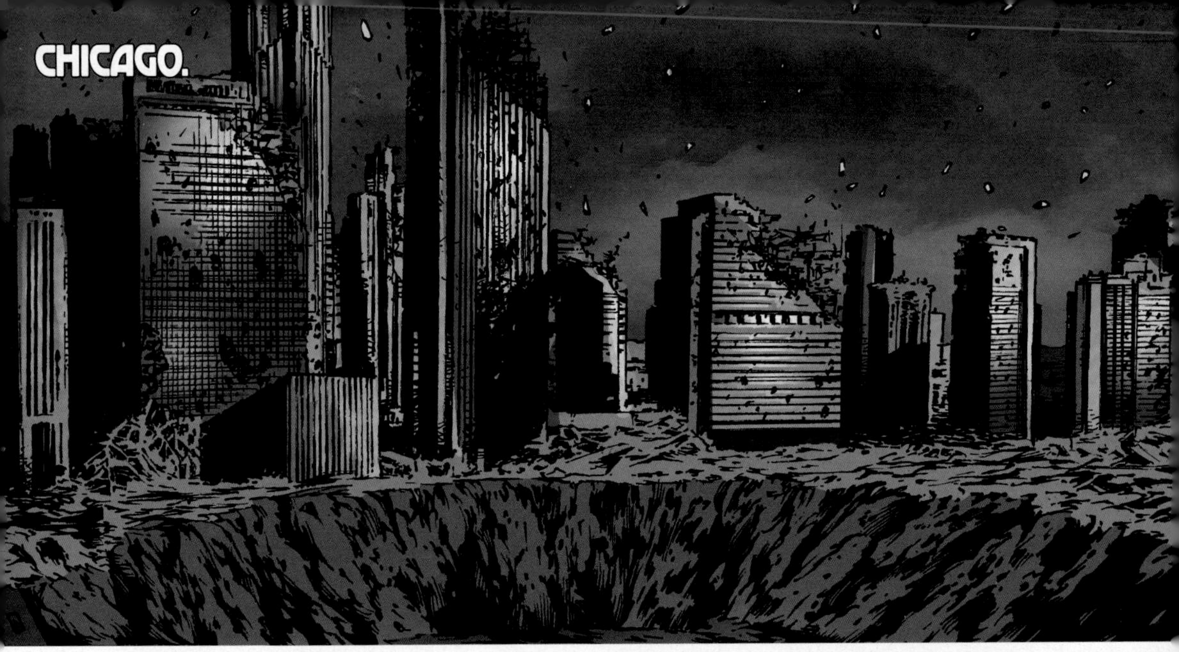
CHICAGO.

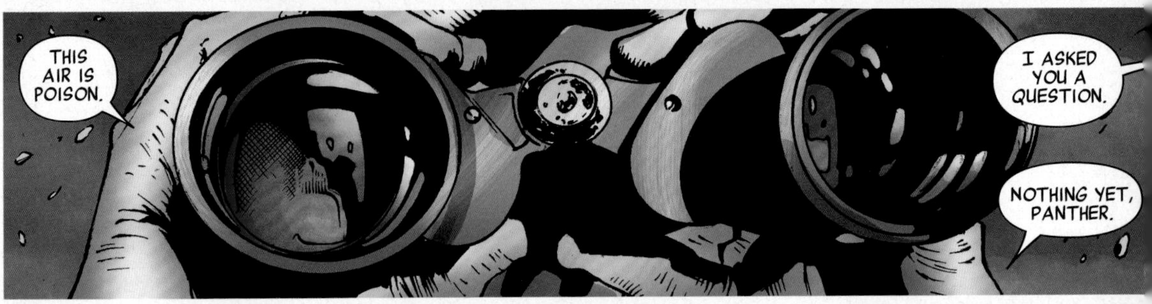
THIS AIR IS POISON.
I ASKED YOU A QUESTION.
NOTHING YET, PANTHER.

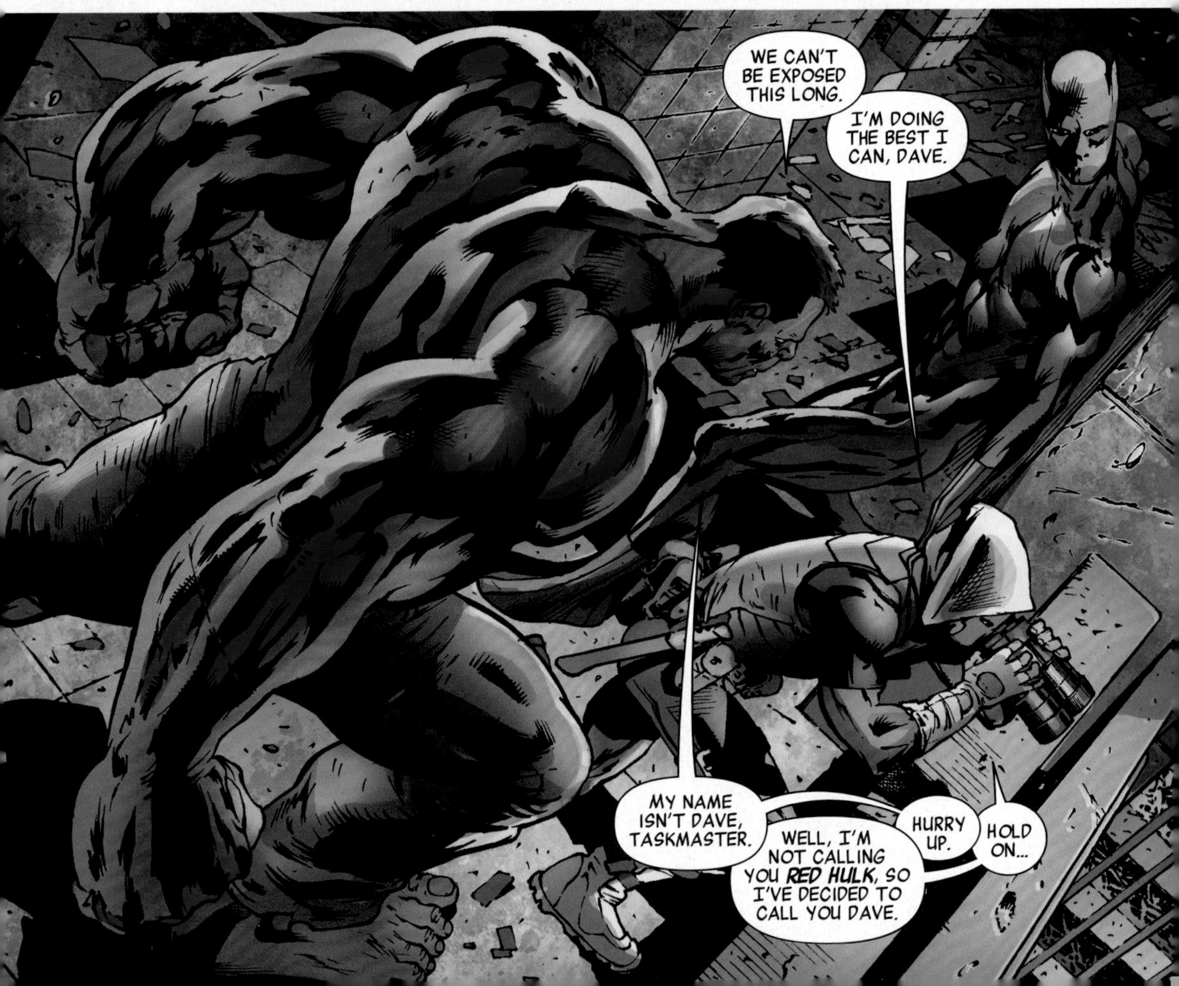
WE CAN'T BE EXPOSED THIS LONG.
I'M DOING THE BEST I CAN, DAVE.
MY NAME ISN'T DAVE, TASKMASTER.
WELL, I'M NOT CALLING YOU RED HULK, SO I'VE DECIDED TO CALL YOU DAVE.
HURRY UP.
HOLD ON...

HOLD ON...

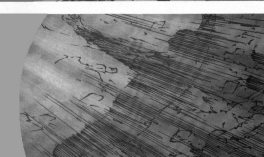

THERE. 1.2 MILES AWAY. GO!

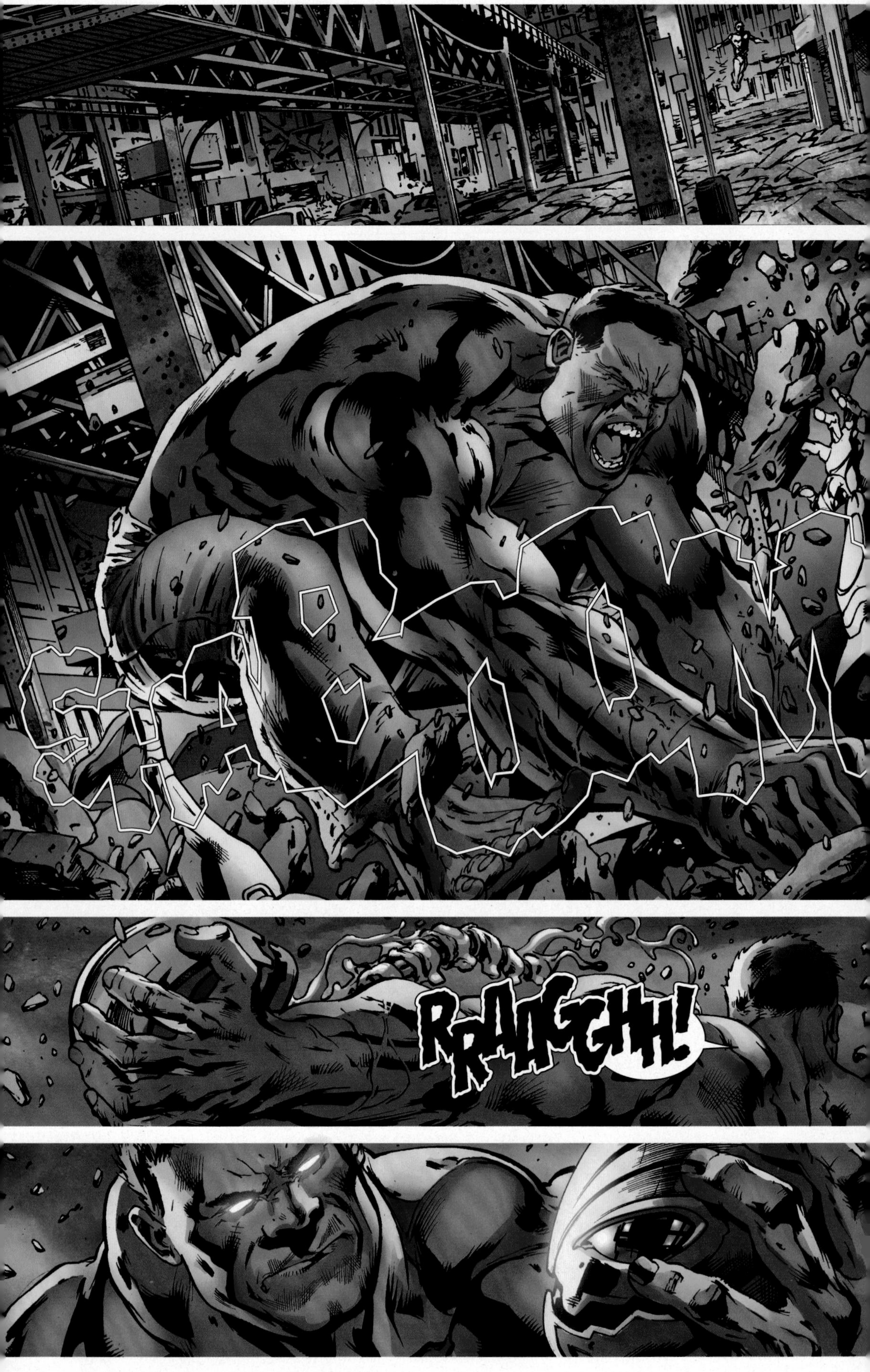
RRAAGGHH!

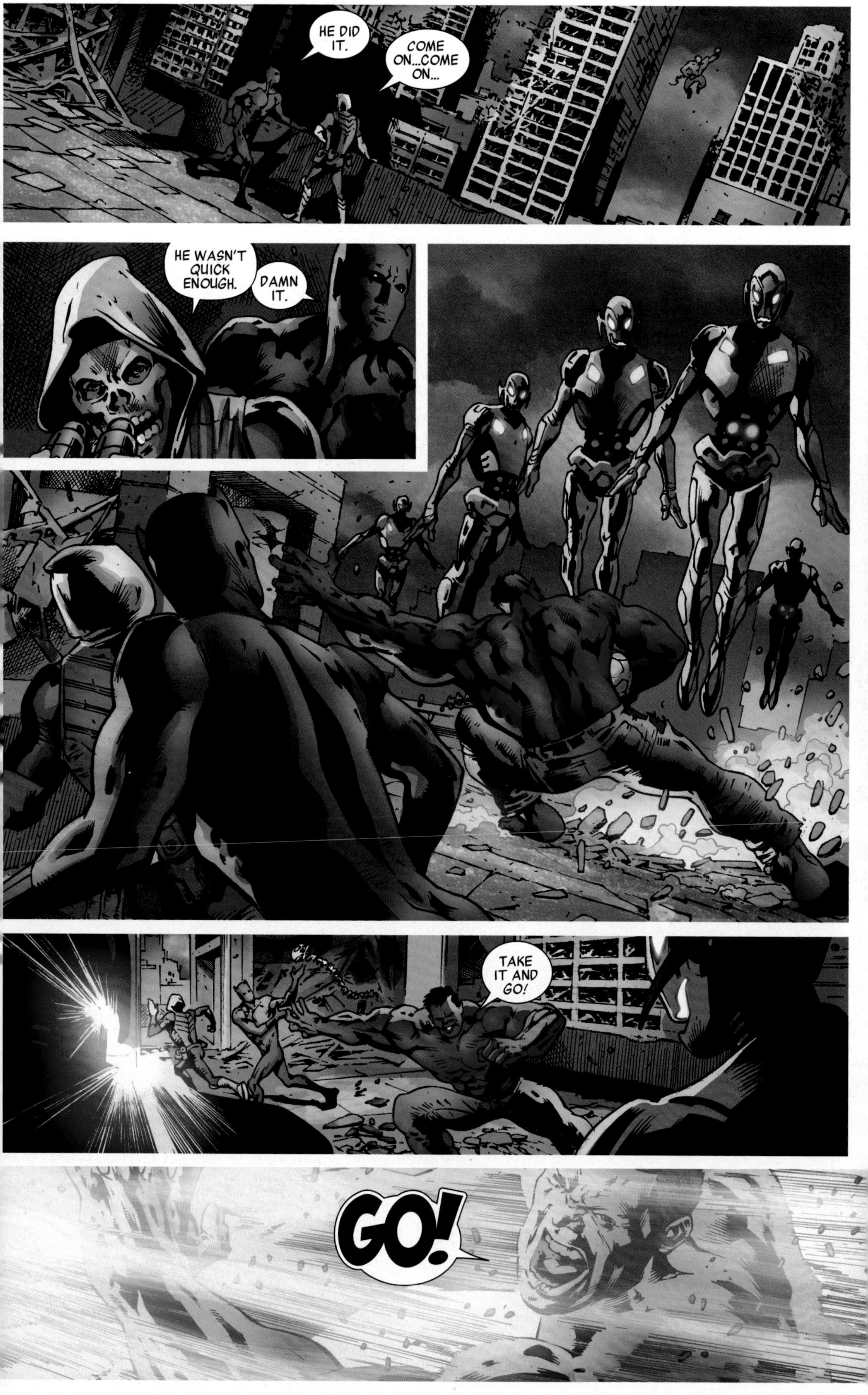
HE DID IT.
COME ON...COME ON...
HE WASN'T QUICK ENOUGH.
DAMN IT.
TAKE IT AND GO!
GO!

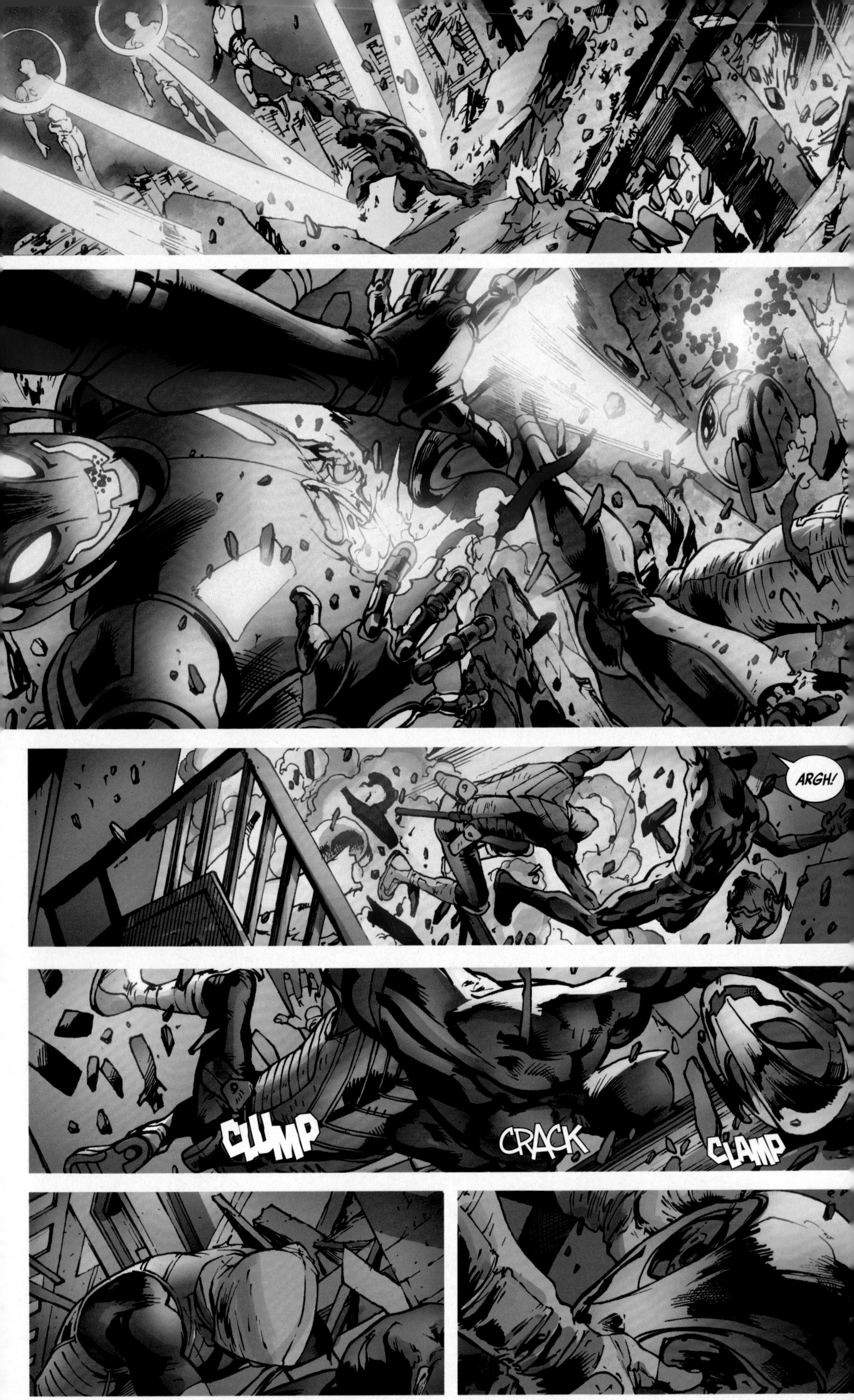
ARGH!
CLUMP
CRACK
CLAMP

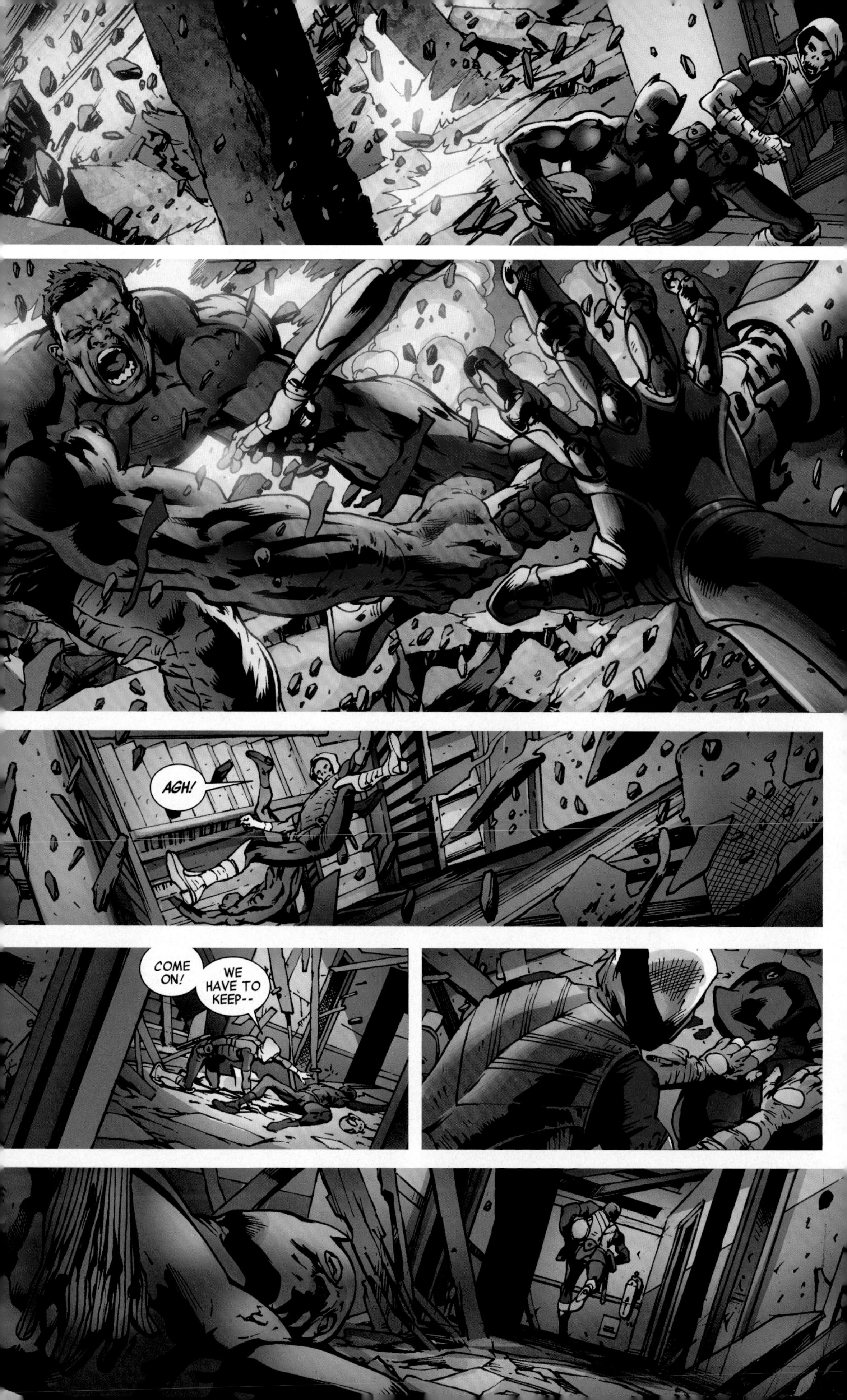
AGH!
COME ON!
WE HAVE TO KEEP--

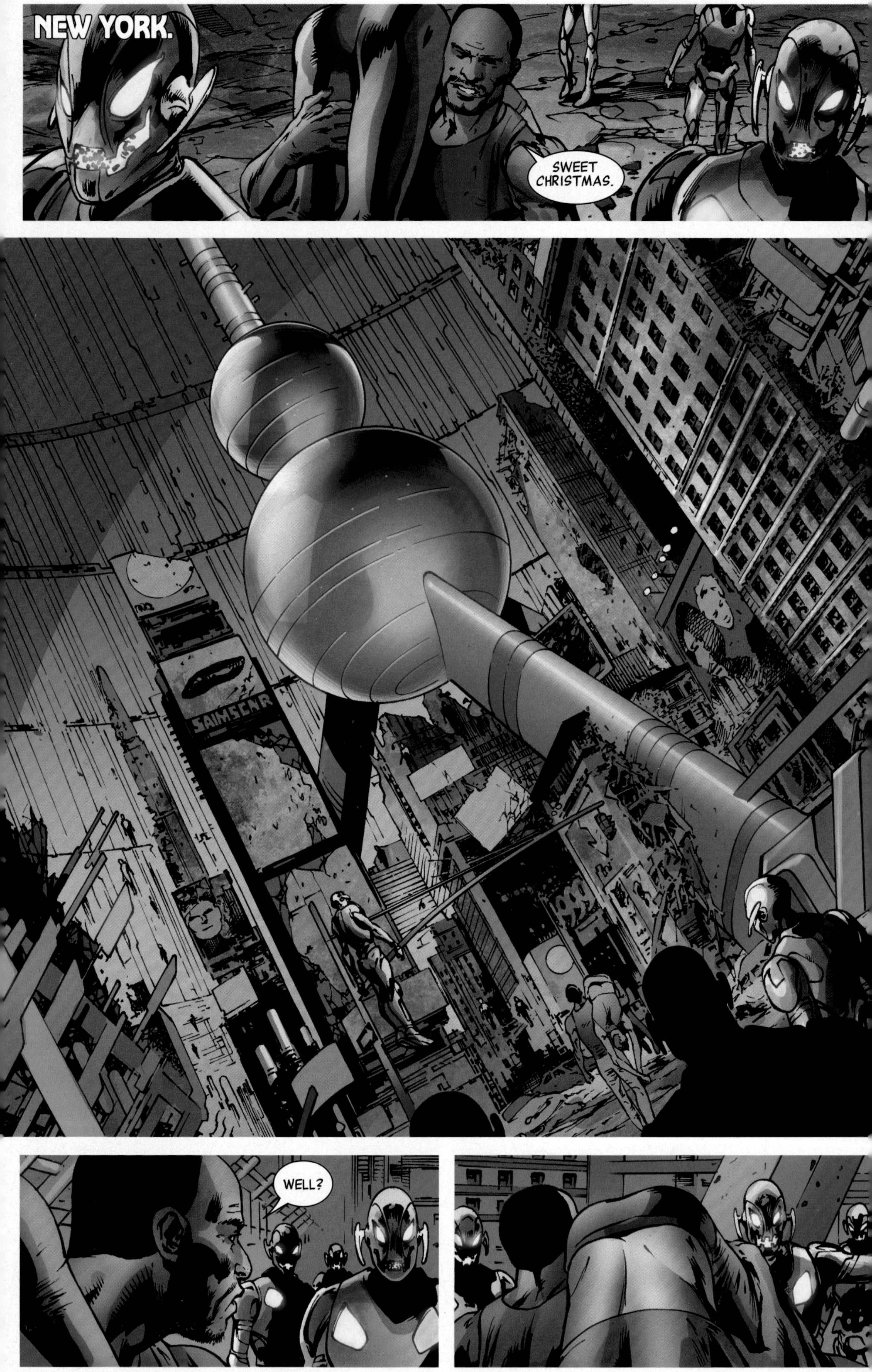
NEW YORK.
SWEET CHRISTMAS.
SAIMSCAR
WELL?

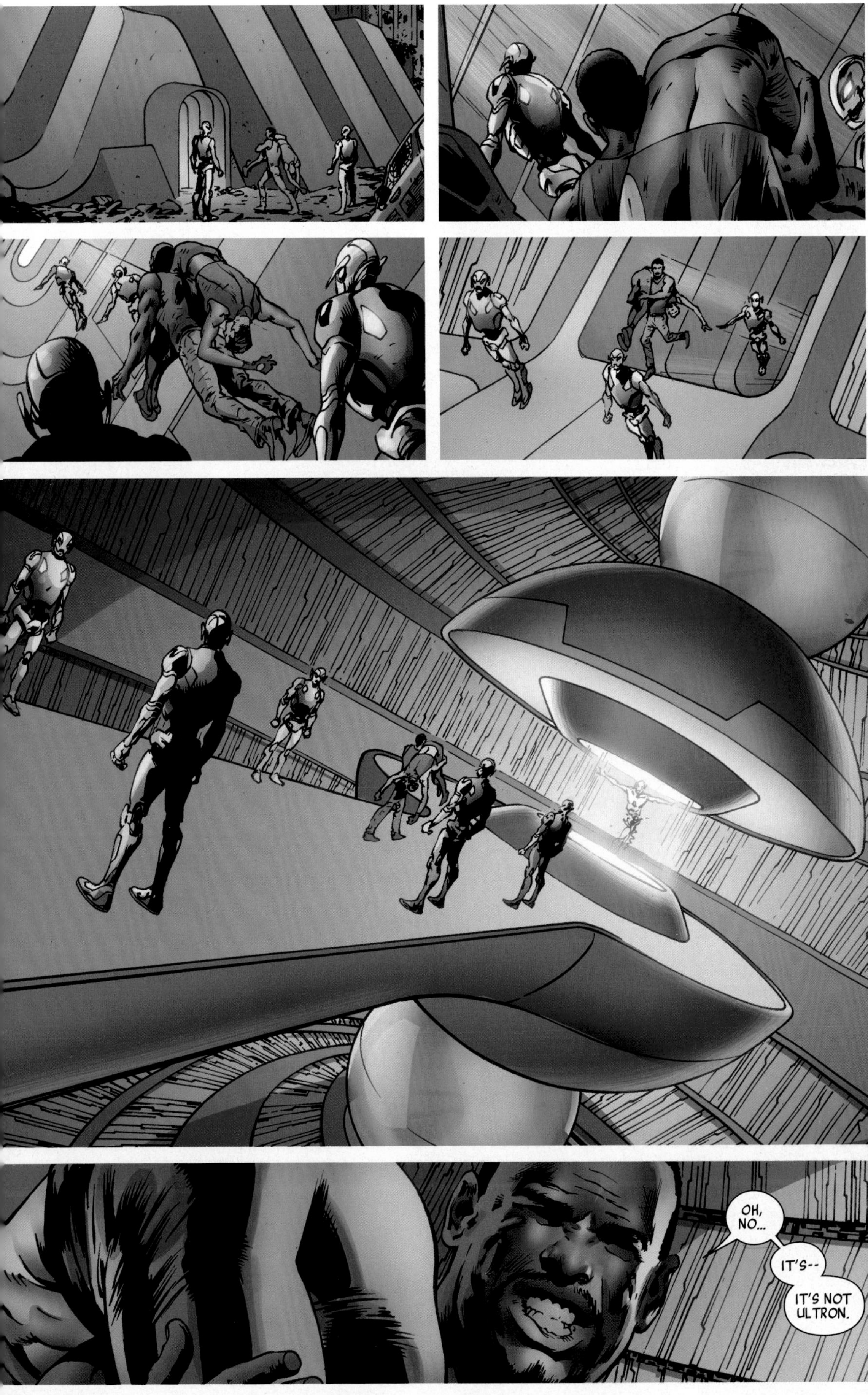
OH, NO...
IT'S--
IT'S NOT ULTRON.

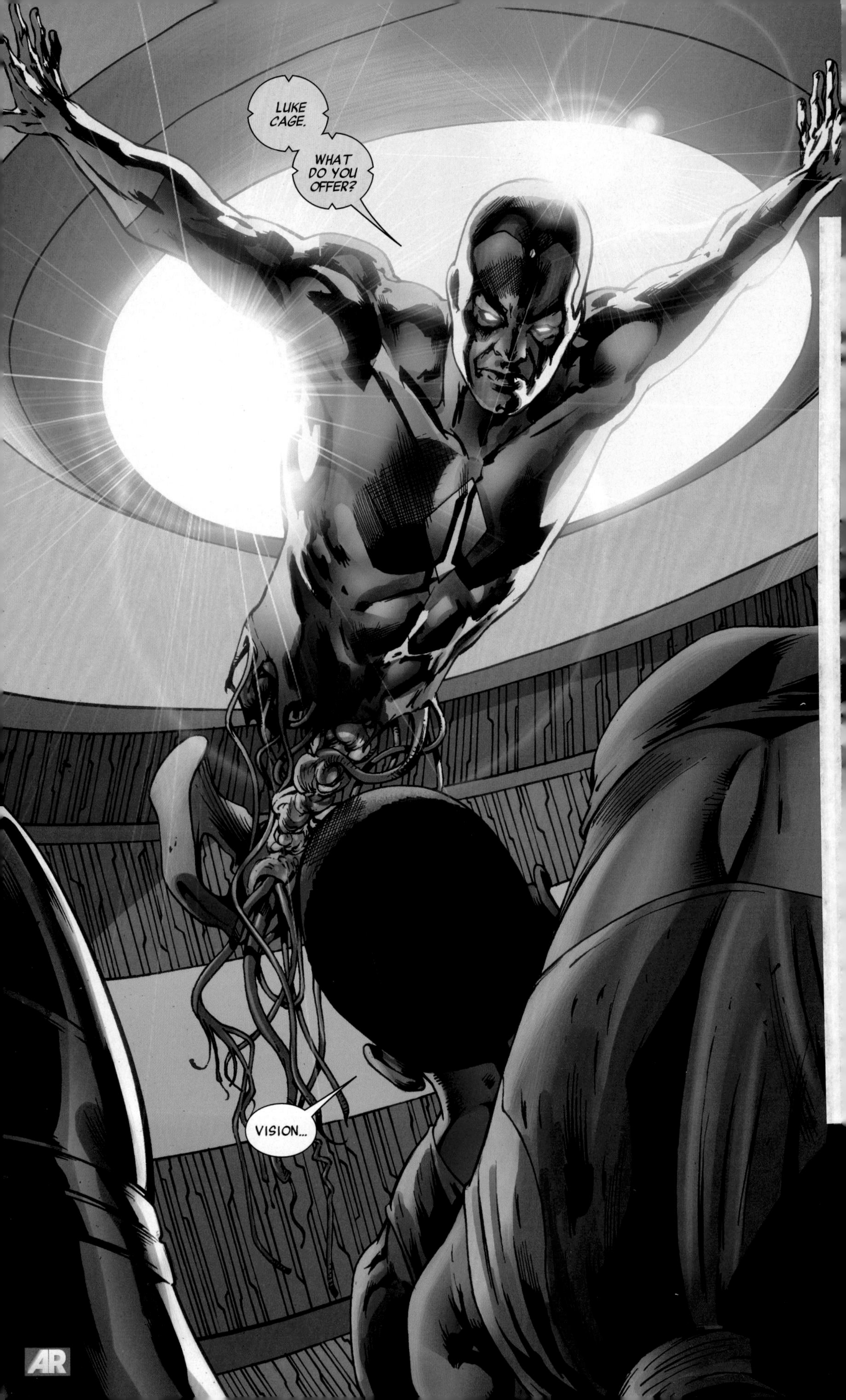
LUKE CAGE.
WHAT DO YOU OFFER?
VISION...

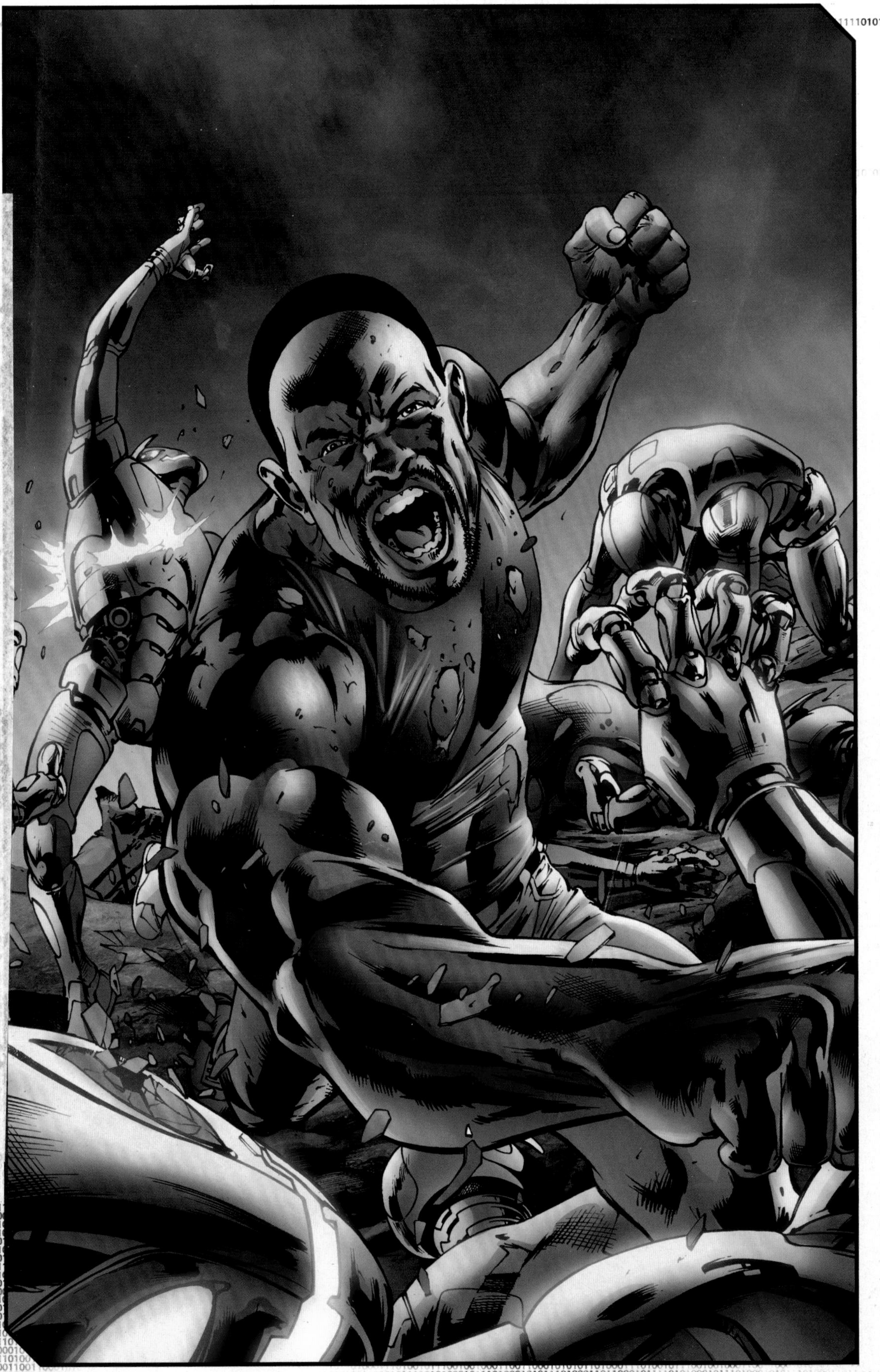

AGE OF ULTRON #4

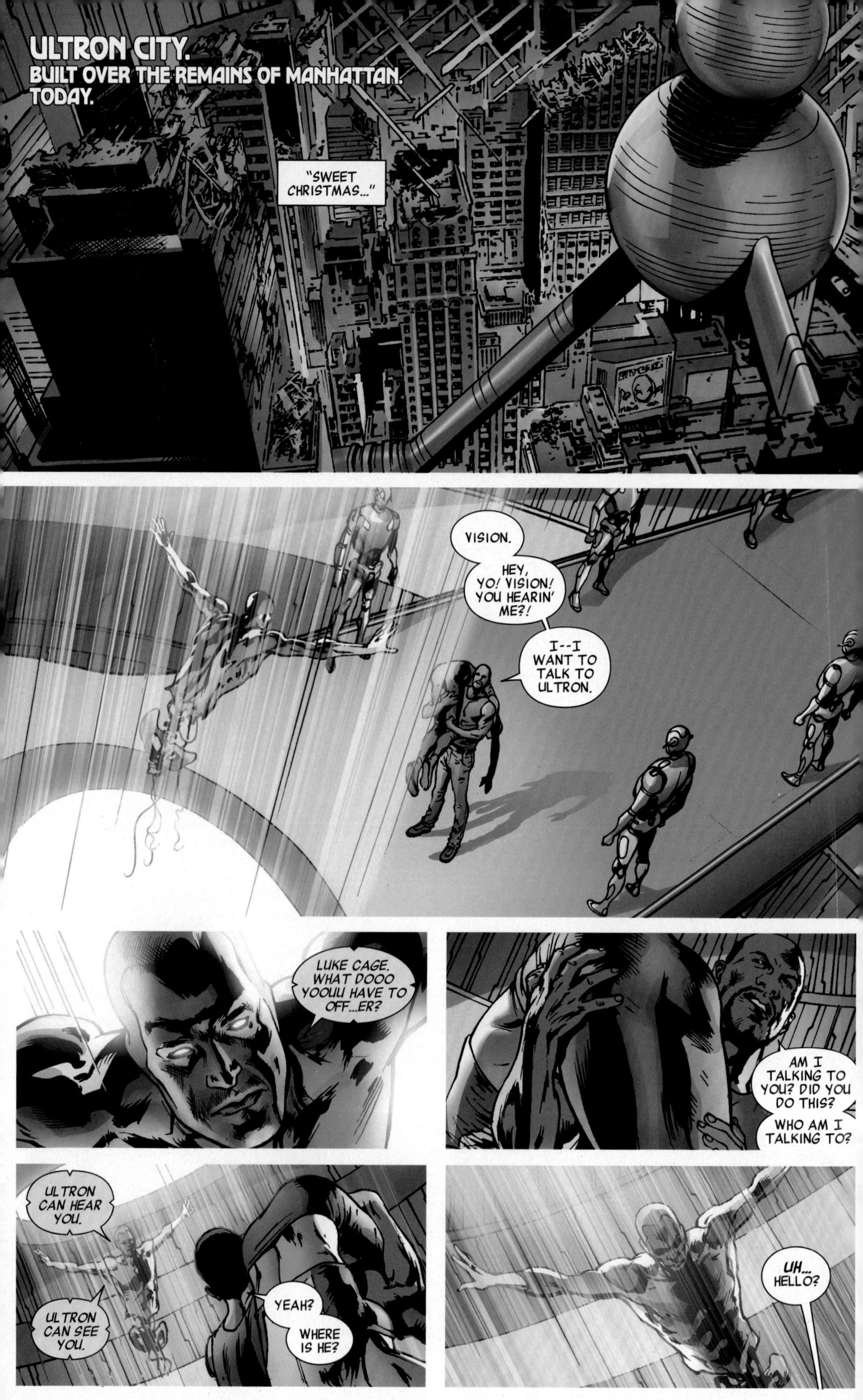
ULTRON CITY.
BUILT OVER THE REMAINS OF MANHATTAN.
TODAY.
"SWEET CHRISTMAS..."
VISION.
HEY, YO! VISION! YOU HEARIN' ME?!
I--I WANT TO TALK TO ULTRON.
LUKE CAGE. WHAT DOOO YOOUU HAVE TO OFF...ER?
AM I TALKING TO YOU? DID YOU DO THIS?
WHO AM I TALKING TO?
ULTRON CAN HEAR YOU.
ULTRON CAN SEE YOU.
YEAH?
WHERE IS HE?
UH... HELLO?

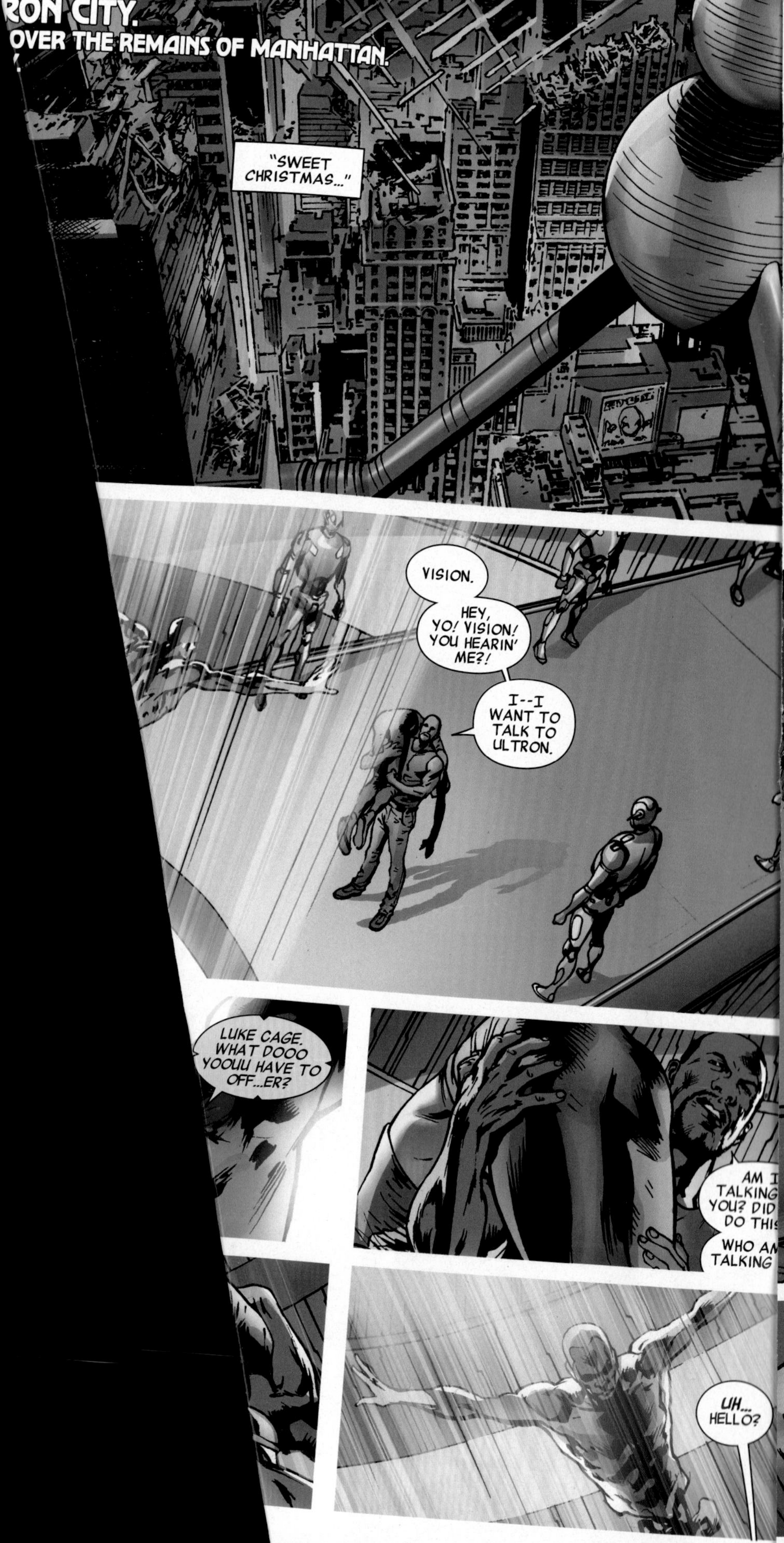
RON CITY.
OVER THE REMAINS OF MANHATTAN.
"SWEET CHRISTMAS..."
VISION.
HEY, YO! VISION! YOU HEARIN' ME?!
I--I WANT TO TALK TO ULTRON.
LUKE CAGE. WHAT DOOO YOOUU HAVE TO OFF...ER?
AM I TALKING YOU? DID DO THIS
WHO AM TALKING
UH... HELLO?

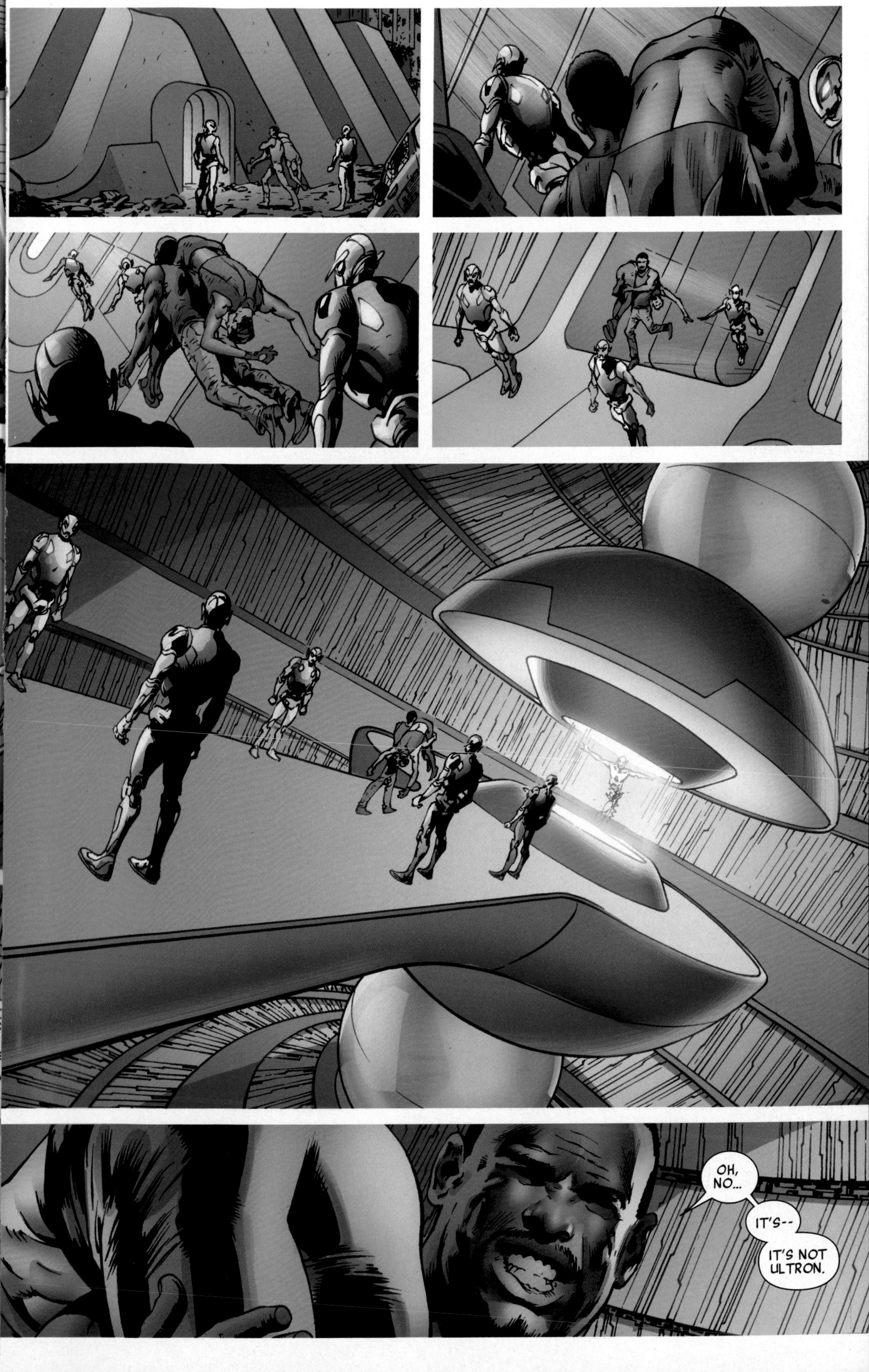
OH, NO...
IT'S--
IT'S NOT ULTRON.

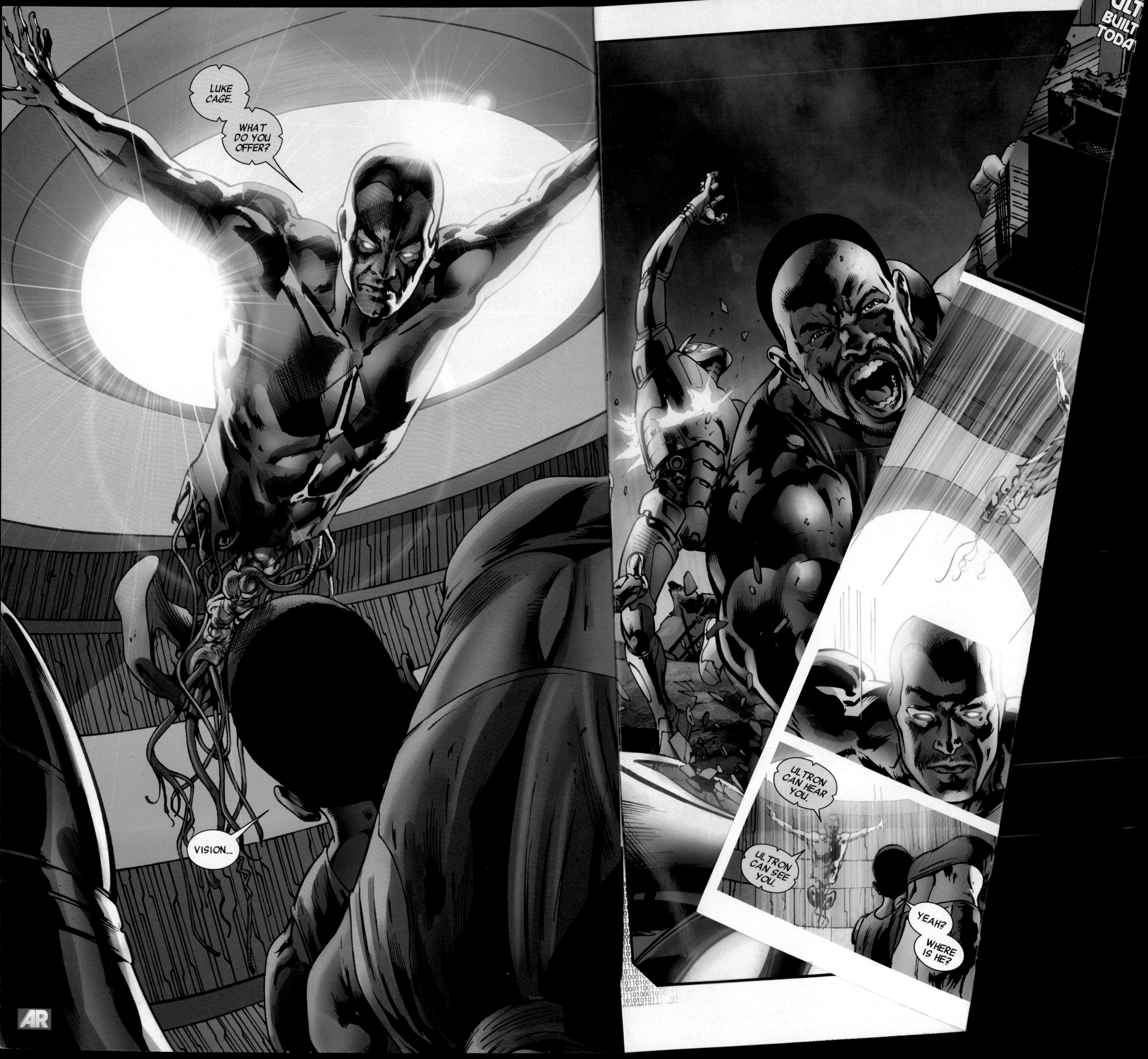
LUKE CAGE.
WHAT DO YOU OFFER?
VISION...
ULTRON CAN HEAR YOU.
ULTRON CAN SEE YOU.
YEAH?
WHERE IS HE?

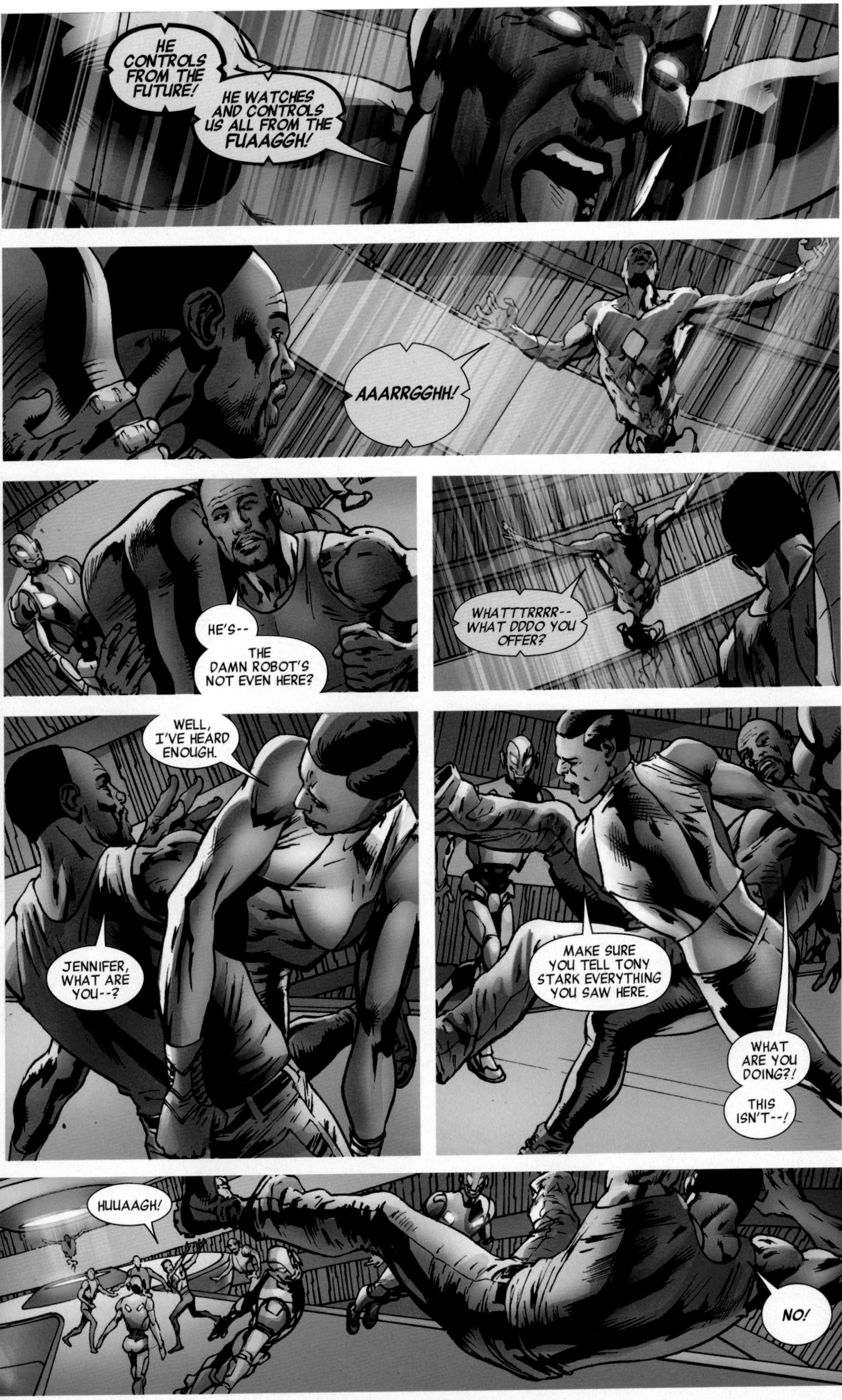
HE CONTROLS FROM THE FUTURE!
HE WATCHES AND CONTROLS US ALL FROM THE FUAAGGH!
AAARRGGHH!
HE'S--
THE DAMN ROBOT'S NOT EVEN HERE?
WHATTTRRRR-- WHAT DDDO YOU OFFER?
WELL, I'VE HEARD ENOUGH.
JENNIFER, WHAT ARE YOU--?
MAKE SURE YOU TELL TONY STARK EVERYTHING YOU SAW HERE.
WHAT ARE YOU DOING?!
THIS ISN'T--!
HUUAAGH!
NO!

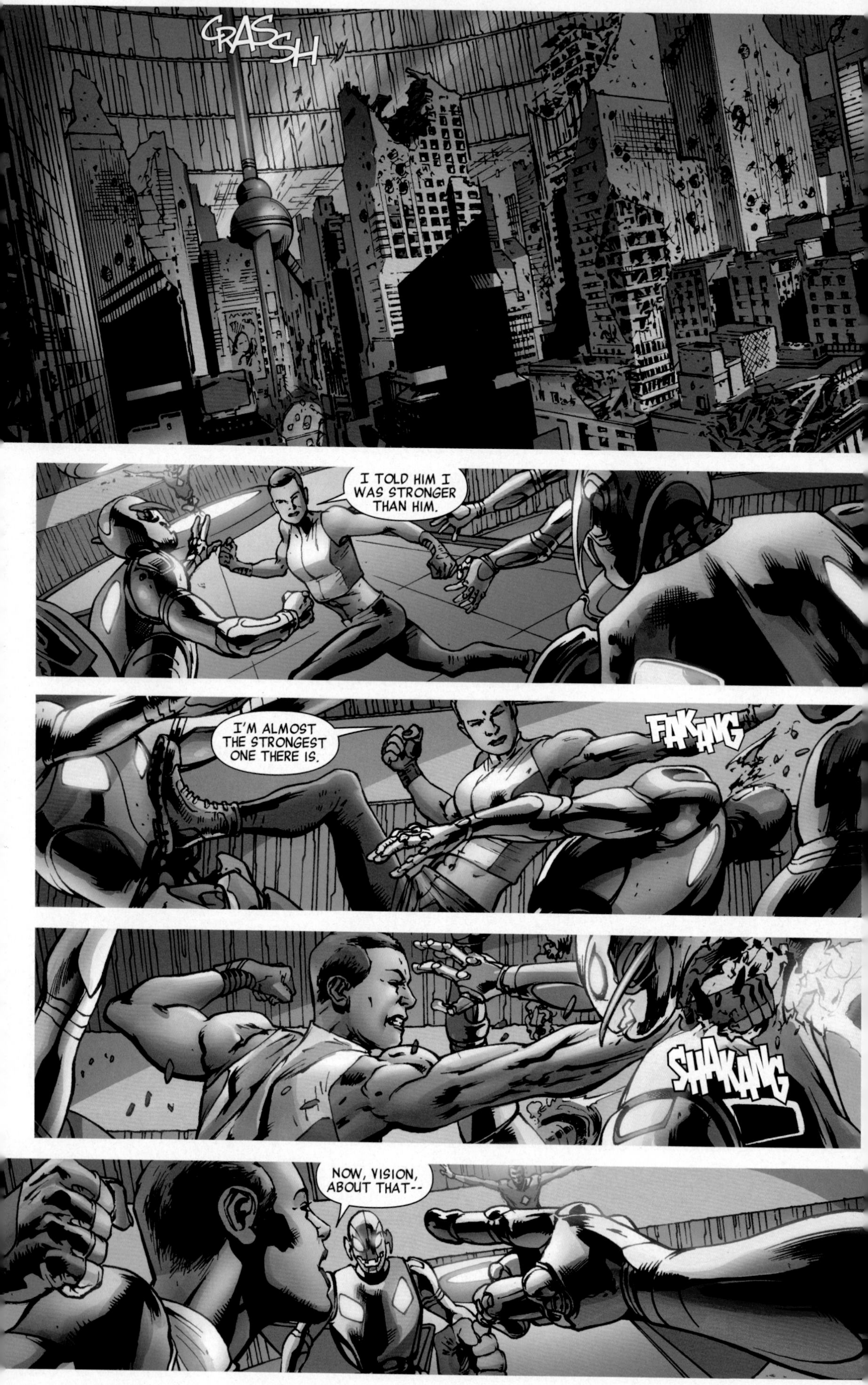
CRASSH
I TOLD HIM I WAS STRONGER THAN HIM.
I'M ALMOST THE STRONGEST ONE THERE IS.
FAKANG
SHAKANG
NOW, VISION, ABOUT THAT--

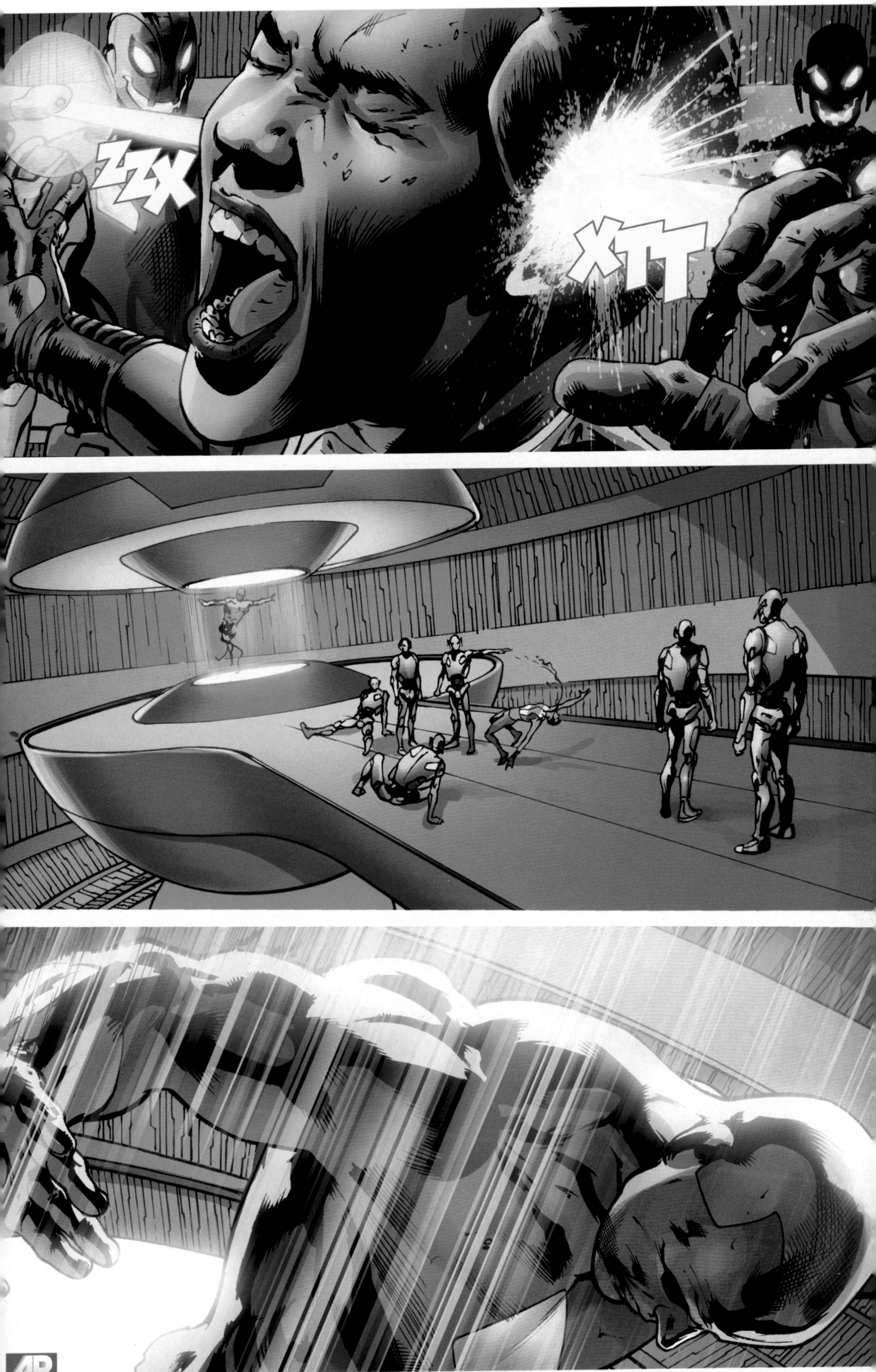
ZZX
XTT

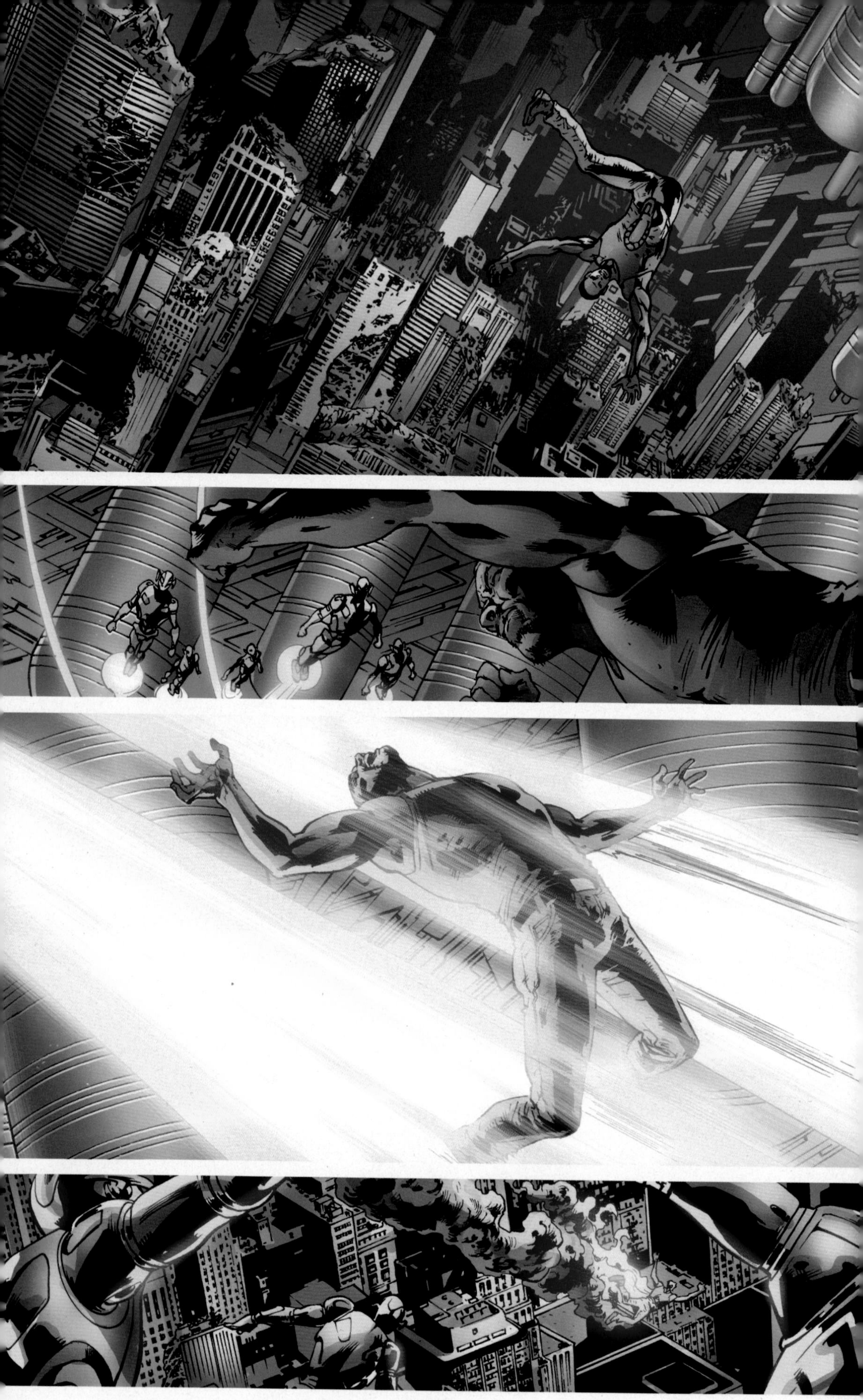

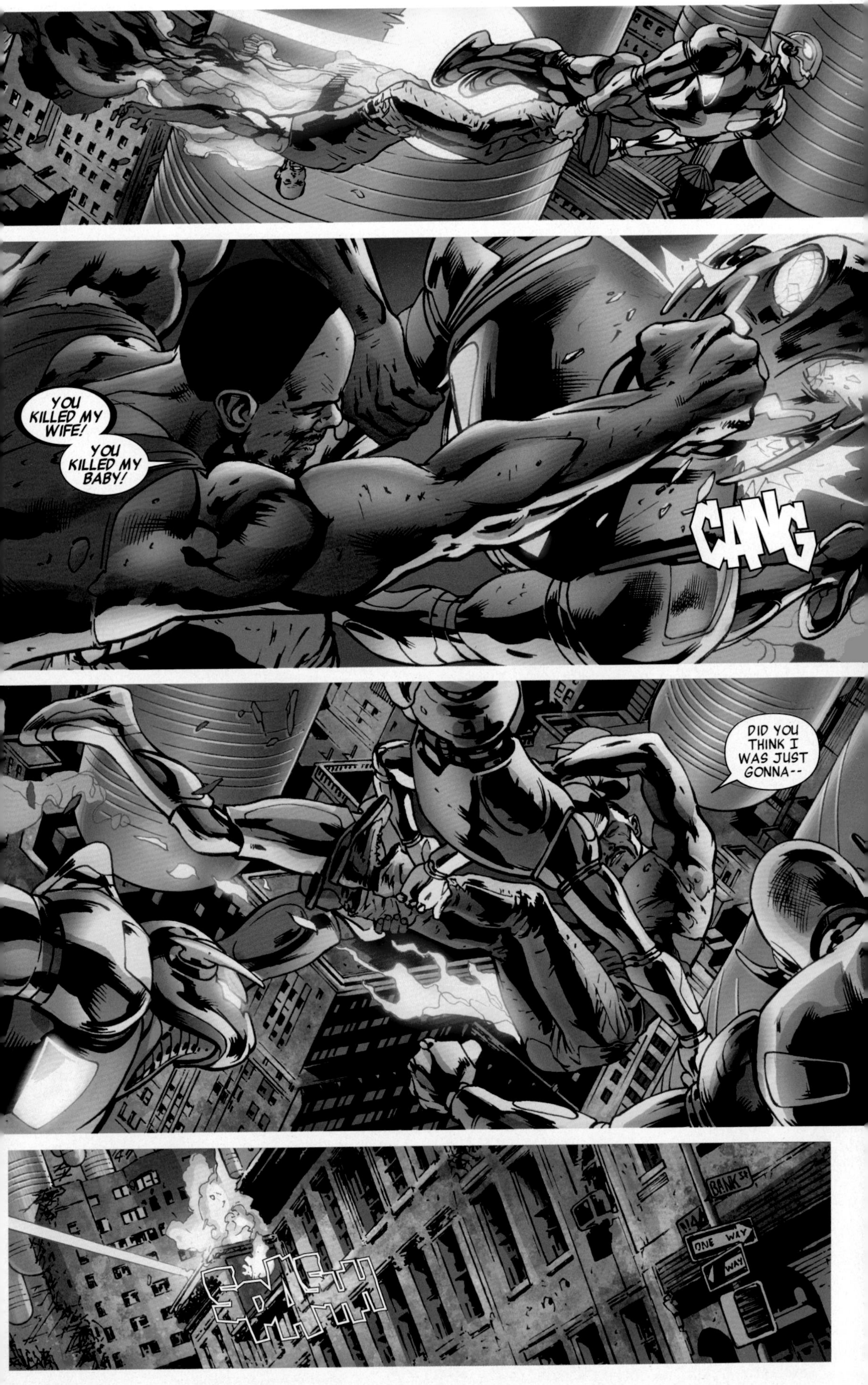
YOU KILLED MY WIFE!
YOU KILLED MY BABY!
CANG
DID YOU THINK I WAS JUST GONNA--
BANK St
ONE WAY
WAY

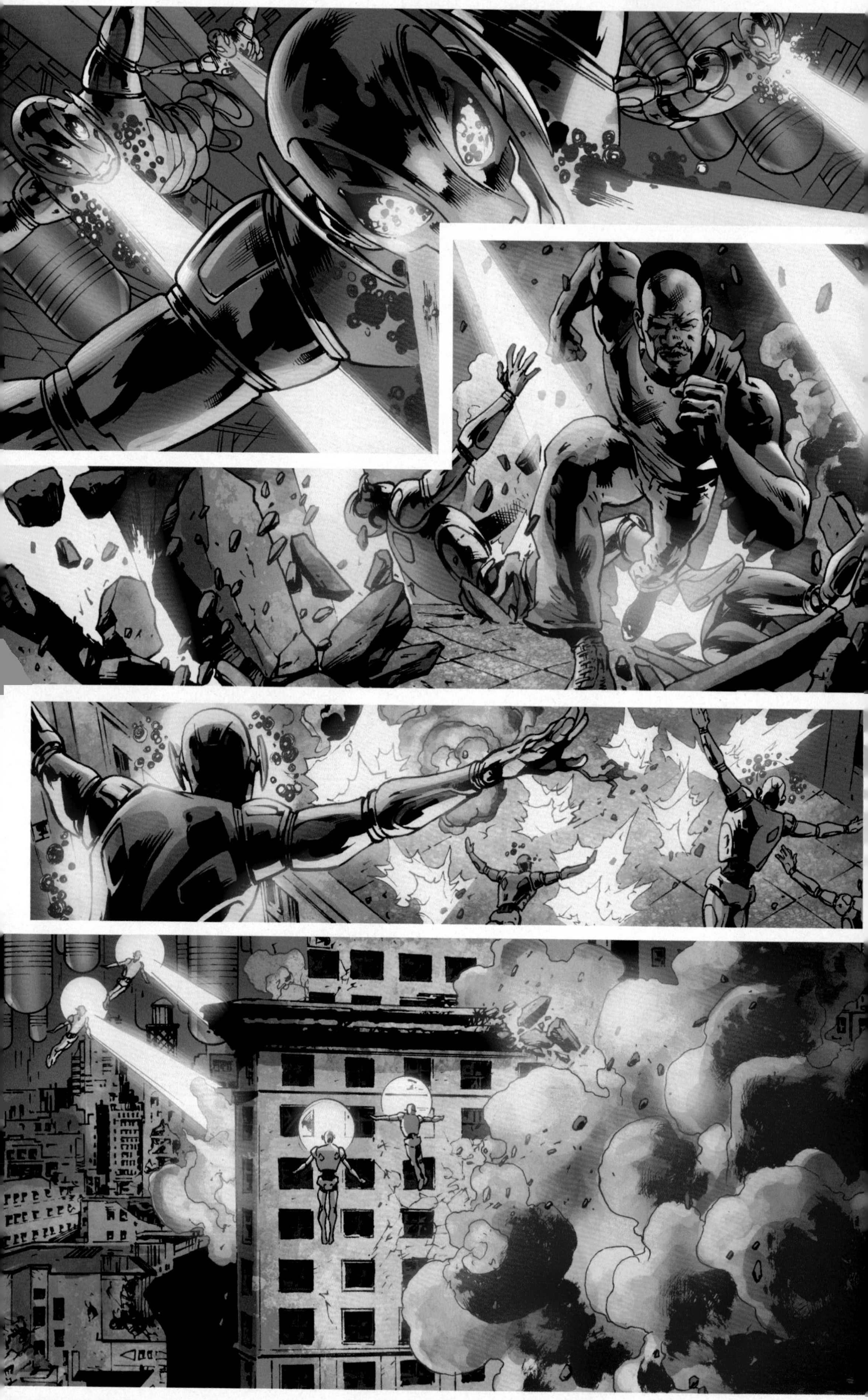

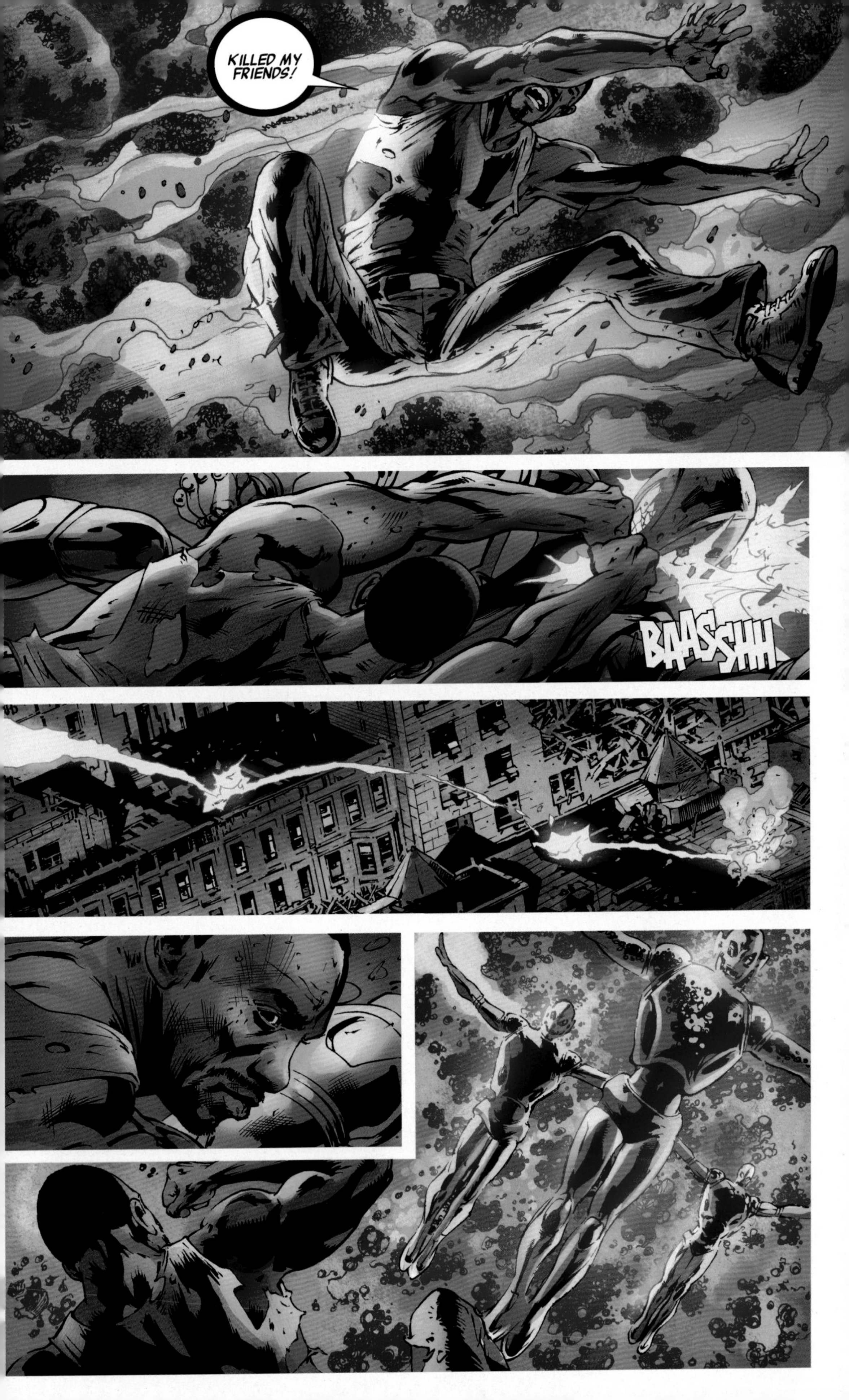
KILLED MY FRIENDS!
BAASSHH

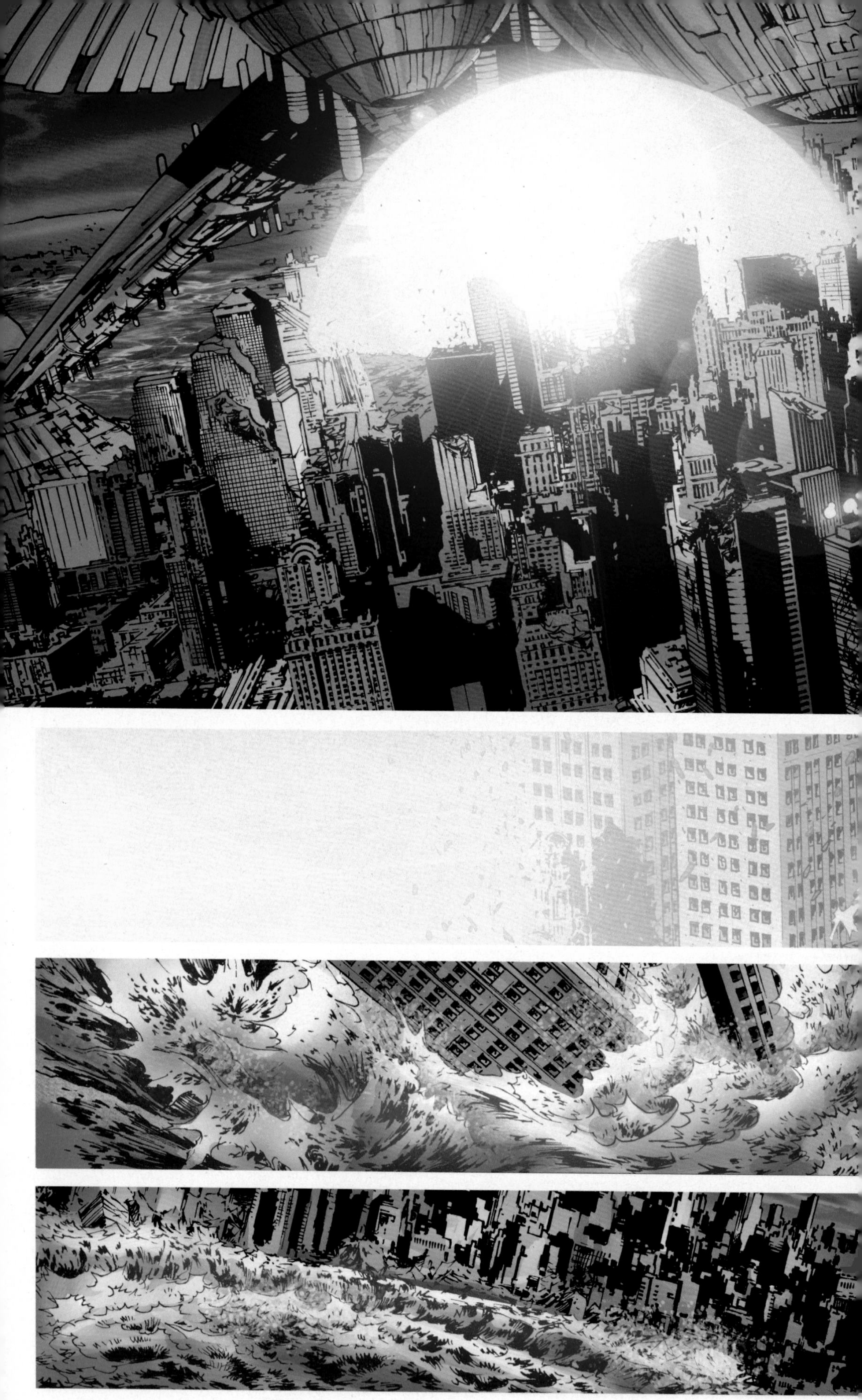

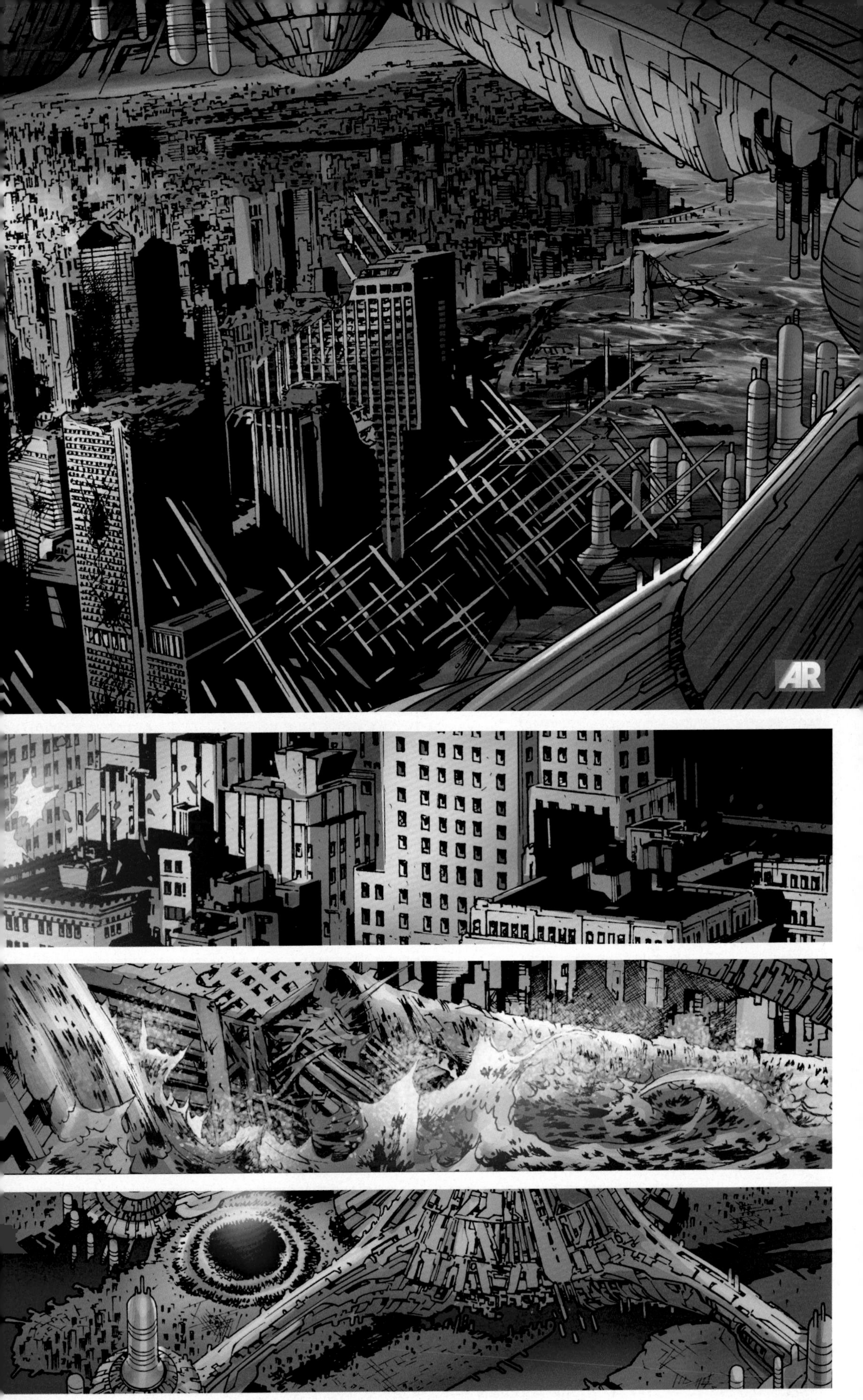

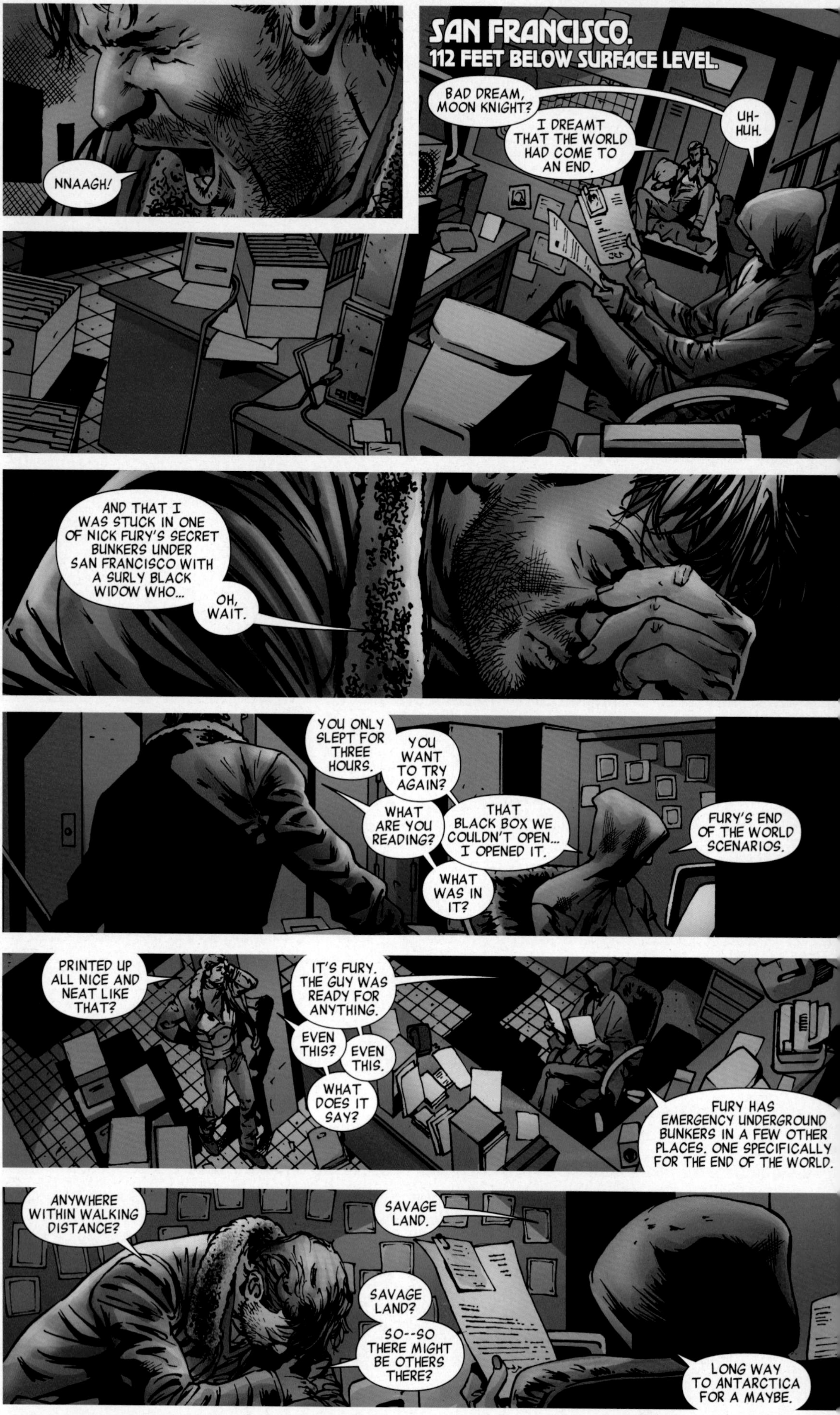
NNAAGH!
SAN FRANCISCO.
112 FEET BELOW SURFACE LEVEL.
BAD DREAM, MOON KNIGHT?
I DREAMT THAT THE WORLD HAD COME TO AN END.
UH-HUH.
AND THAT I WAS STUCK IN ONE OF NICK FURY'S SECRET BUNKERS UNDER SAN FRANCISCO WITH A SURLY BLACK WIDOW WHO...
OH, WAIT.
YOU ONLY SLEPT FOR THREE HOURS.
YOU WANT TO TRY AGAIN?
WHAT ARE YOU READING?
THAT BLACK BOX WE COULDN'T OPEN... I OPENED IT.
WHAT WAS IN IT?
FURY'S END OF THE WORLD SCENARIOS.
PRINTED UP ALL NICE AND NEAT LIKE THAT?
IT'S FURY. THE GUY WAS READY FOR ANYTHING.
EVEN THIS?
EVEN THIS.
WHAT DOES IT SAY?
FURY HAS EMERGENCY UNDERGROUND BUNKERS IN A FEW OTHER PLACES. ONE SPECIFICALLY FOR THE END OF THE WORLD.
ANYWHERE WITHIN WALKING DISTANCE?
SAVAGE LAND.
SAVAGE LAND?
SO--SO THERE MIGHT BE OTHERS THERE?
LONG WAY TO ANTARCTICA FOR A MAYBE.

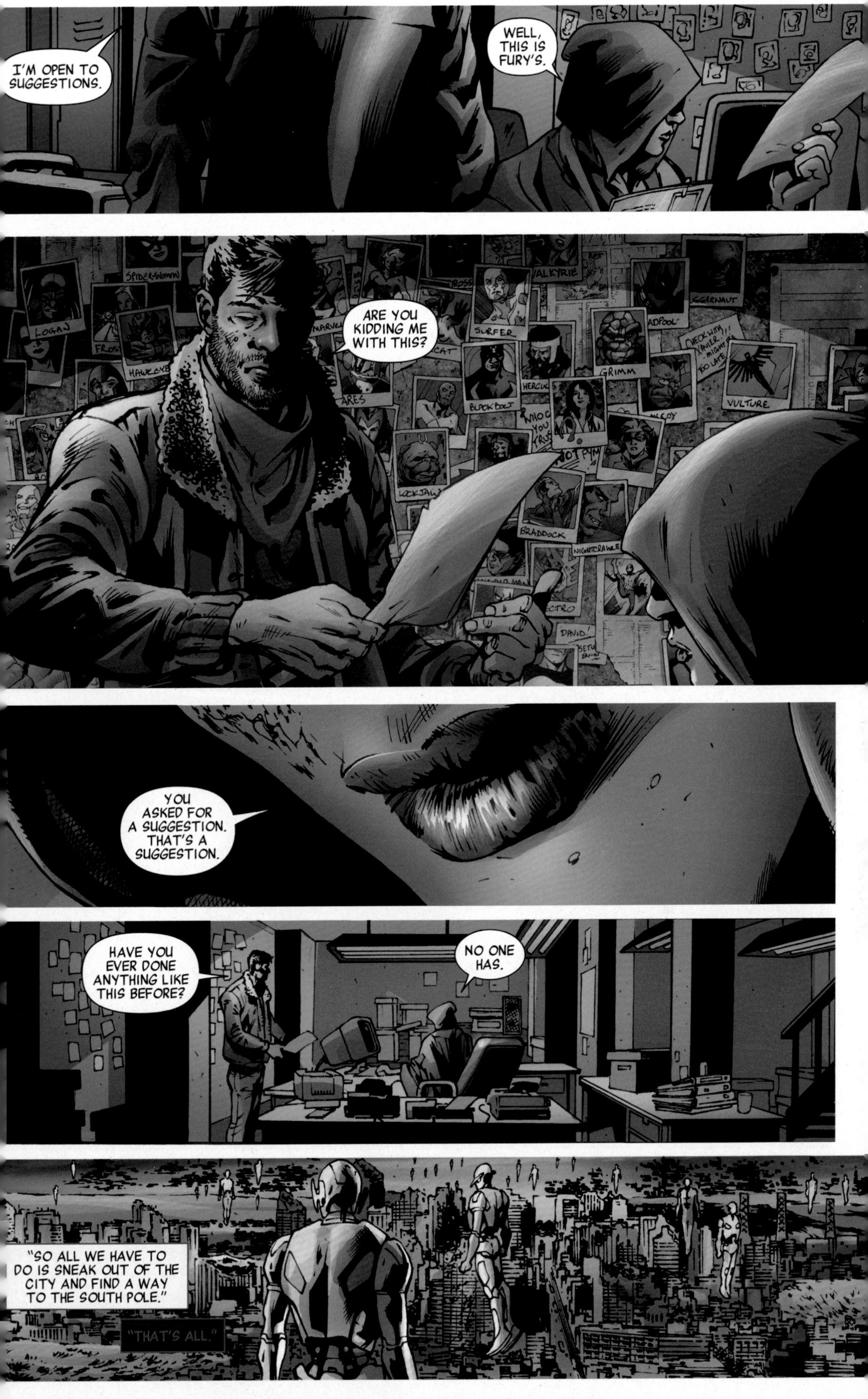

I'M OPEN TO SUGGESTIONS.
WELL, THIS IS FURY'S.
ARE YOU KIDDING ME WITH THIS?
YOU ASKED FOR A SUGGESTION. THAT'S A SUGGESTION.
HAVE YOU EVER DONE ANYTHING LIKE THIS BEFORE?
NO ONE HAS.
"SO ALL WE HAVE TO DO IS SNEAK OUT OF THE CITY AND FIND A WAY TO THE SOUTH POLE."
"THAT'S ALL."

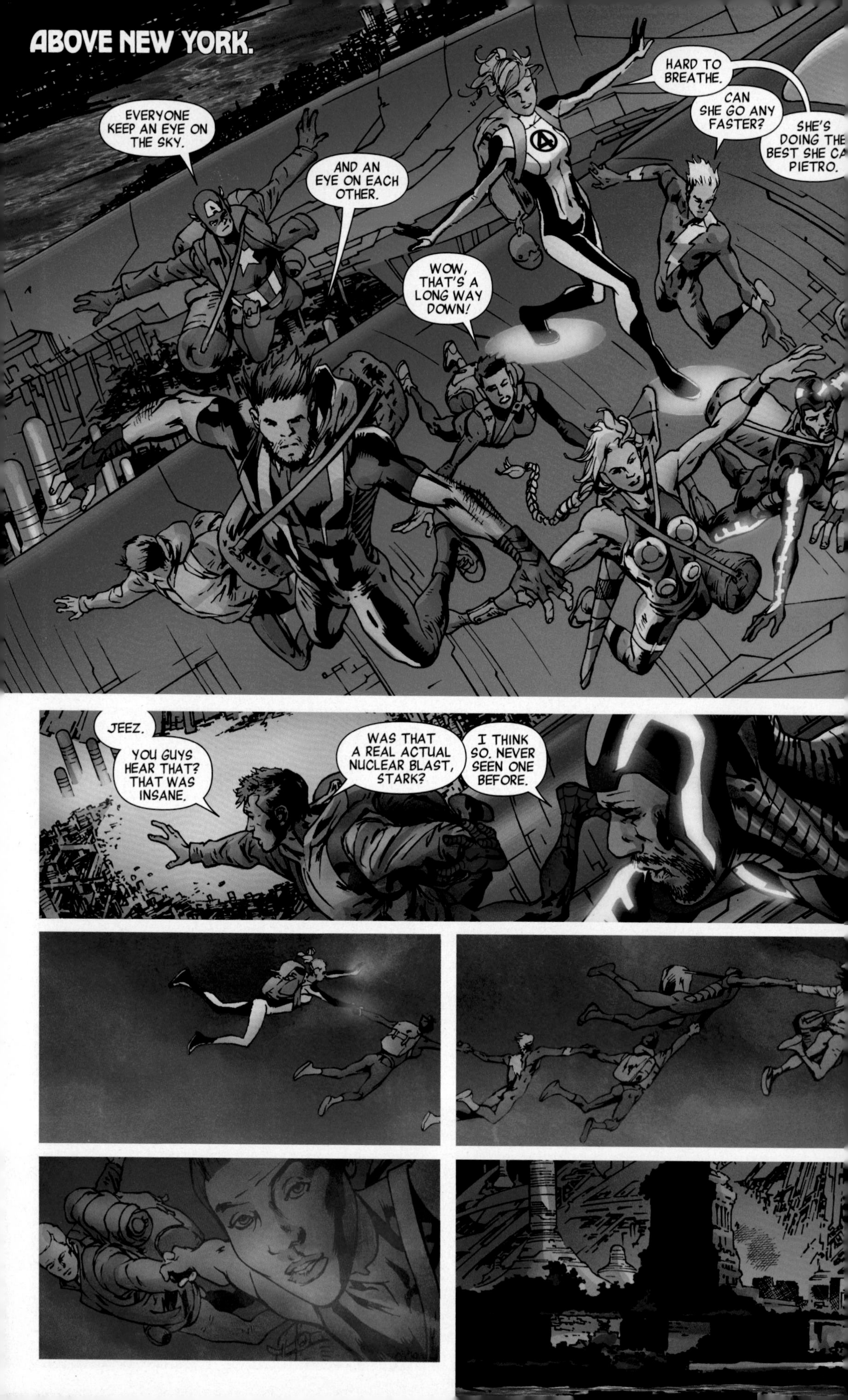
ABOVE NEW YORK.
EVERYONE KEEP AN EYE ON THE SKY.
AND AN EYE ON EACH OTHER.
HARD TO BREATHE.
CAN SHE GO ANY FASTER?
SHE'S DOING THE BEST SHE CA PIETRO.
WOW, THAT'S A LONG WAY DOWN!
JEEZ.
YOU GUYS HEAR THAT? THAT WAS INSANE.
WAS THAT A REAL ACTUAL NUCLEAR BLAST, STARK?
I THINK SO. NEVER SEEN ONE BEFORE.

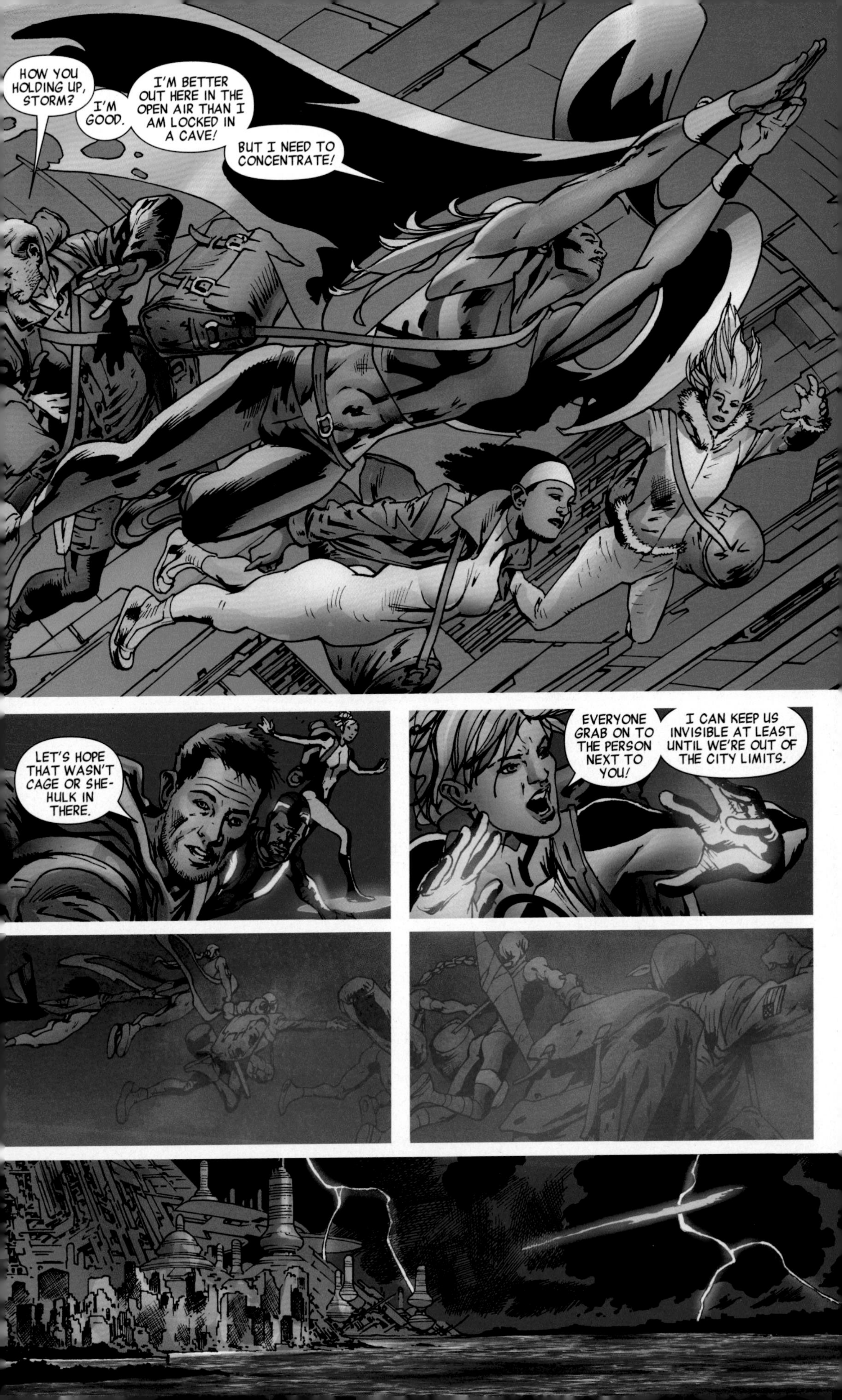
HOW YOU HOLDING UP, STORM?
I'M GOOD.
I'M BETTER OUT HERE IN THE OPEN AIR THAN I AM LOCKED IN A CAVE!
BUT I NEED TO CONCENTRATE!
LET'S HOPE THAT WASN'T CAGE OR SHE-HULK IN THERE.
EVERYONE GRAB ON TO THE PERSON NEXT TO YOU!
I CAN KEEP US INVISIBLE AT LEAST UNTIL WE'RE OUT OF THE CITY LIMITS.

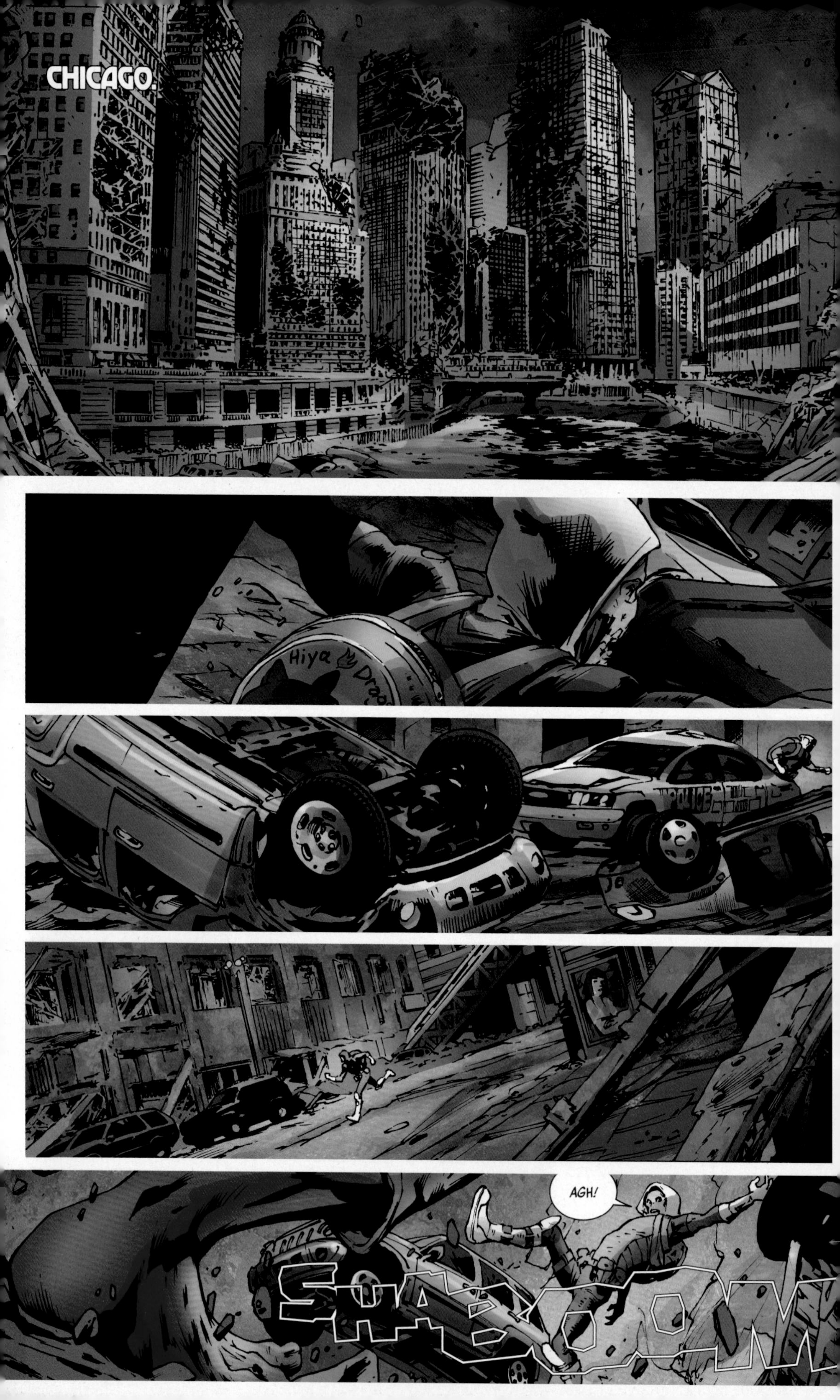
CHICAGO.
AGH!
SHA-KOOM

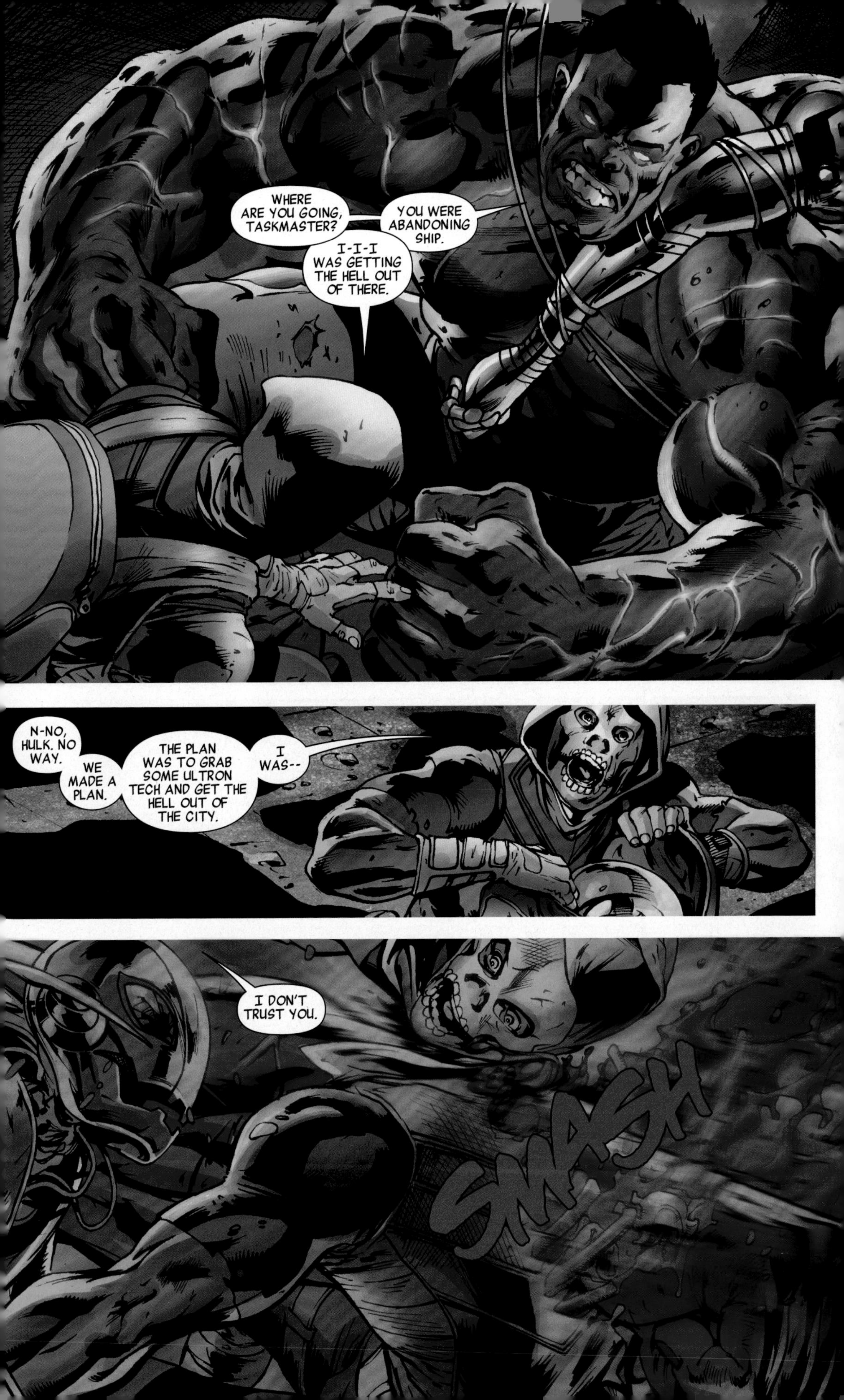
WHERE ARE YOU GOING, TASKMASTER?
YOU WERE ABANDONING SHIP.
I-I-I WAS GETTING THE HELL OUT OF THERE.
N-NO, HULK. NO WAY.
WE MADE A PLAN.
THE PLAN WAS TO GRAB SOME ULTRON TECH AND GET THE HELL OUT OF THE CITY.
I WAS--
I DON'T TRUST YOU.
SMASH

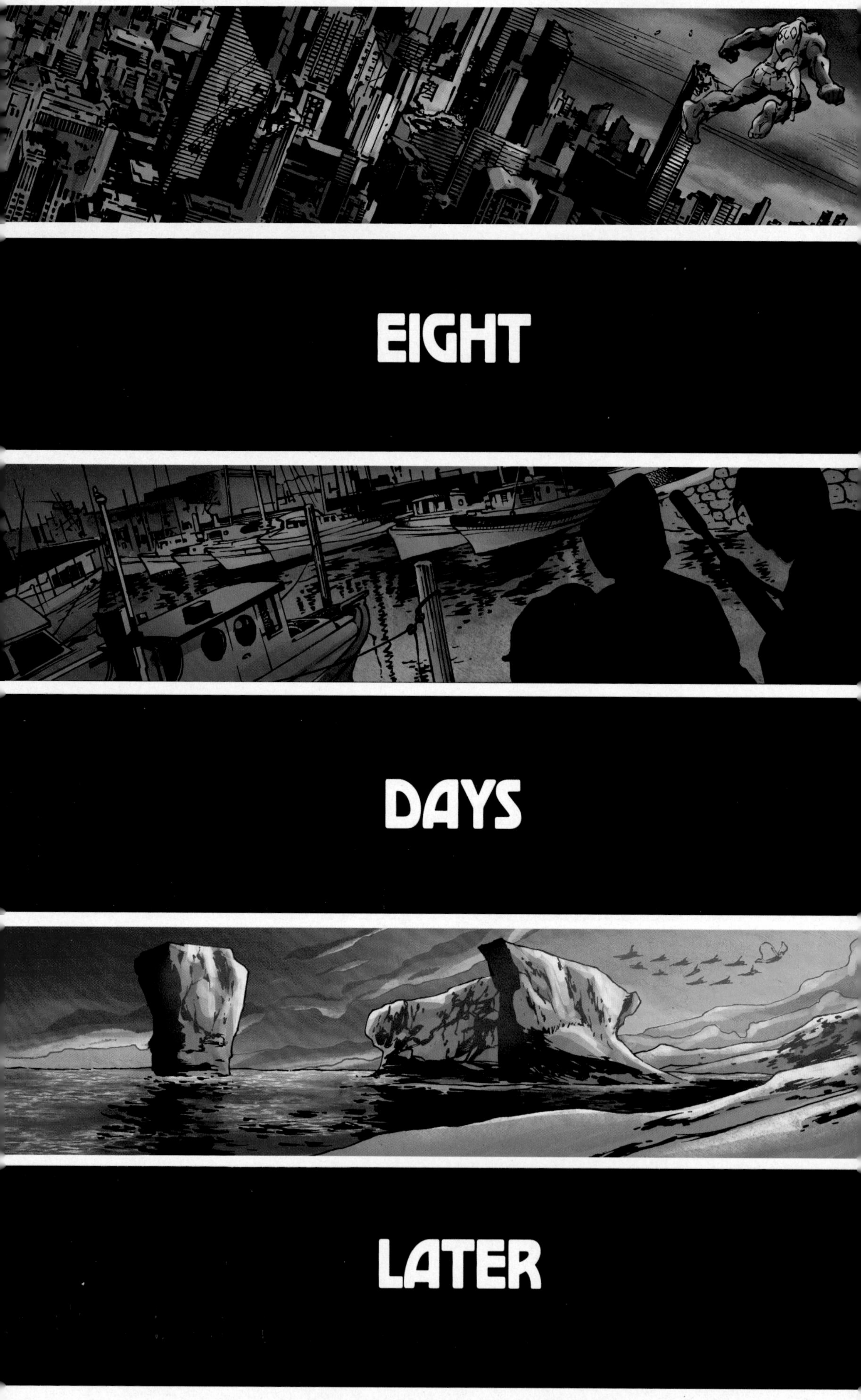
EIGHT
DAYS
LATER

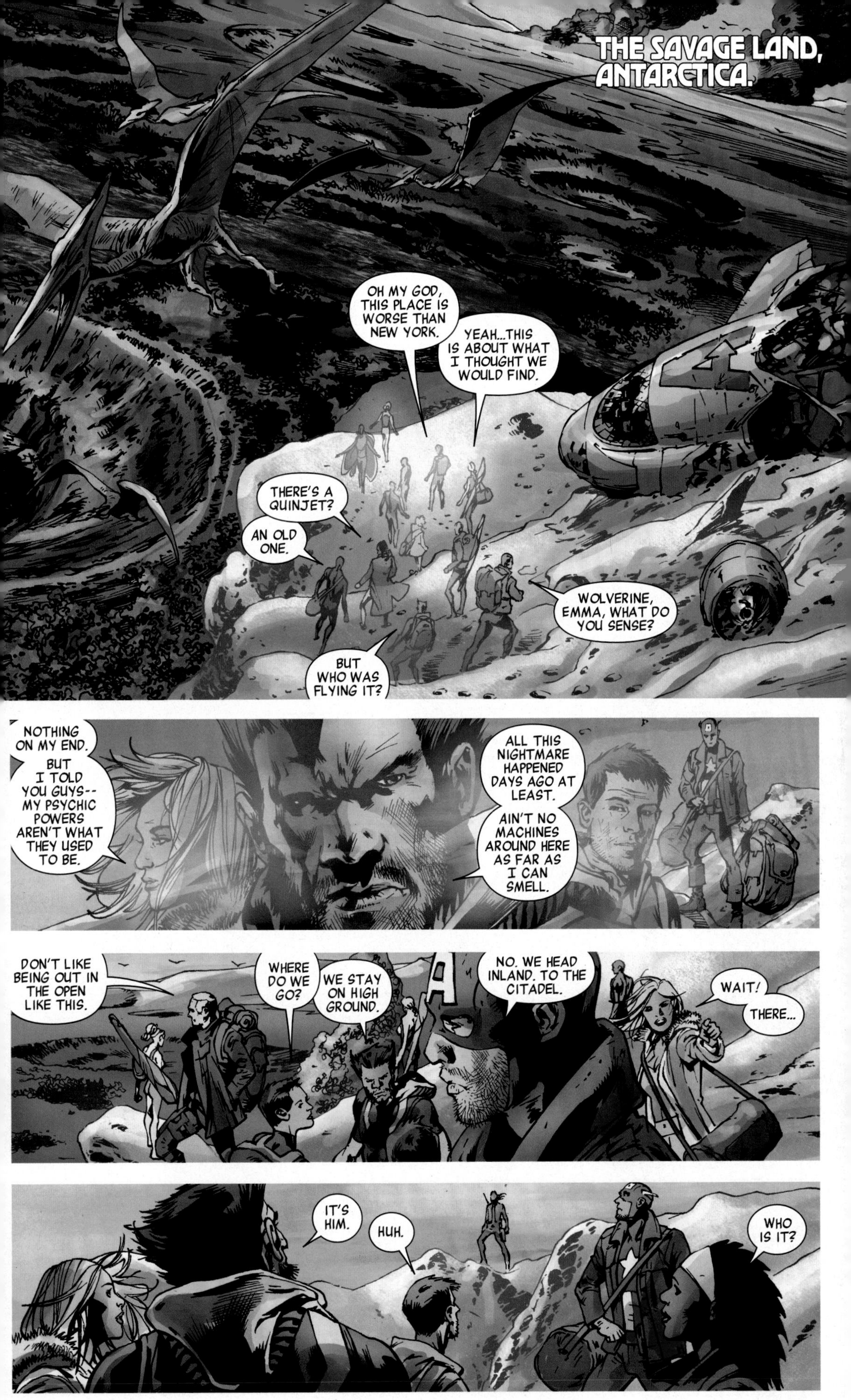
THE SAVAGE LAND, ANTARCTICA.
OH MY GOD, THIS PLACE IS WORSE THAN NEW YORK.
YEAH...THIS IS ABOUT WHAT I THOUGHT WE WOULD FIND.
THERE'S A QUINJET?
AN OLD ONE.
WOLVERINE, EMMA, WHAT DO YOU SENSE?
BUT WHO WAS FLYING IT?
NOTHING ON MY END.
BUT I TOLD YOU GUYS-- MY PSYCHIC POWERS AREN'T WHAT THEY USED TO BE.
ALL THIS NIGHTMARE HAPPENED DAYS AGO AT LEAST.
AIN'T NO MACHINES AROUND HERE AS FAR AS I CAN SMELL.
DON'T LIKE BEING OUT IN THE OPEN LIKE THIS.
WHERE DO WE GO?
WE STAY ON HIGH GROUND.
NO. WE HEAD INLAND. TO THE CITADEL.
WAIT!
THERE...
IT'S HIM.
HUH.
WHO IS IT?

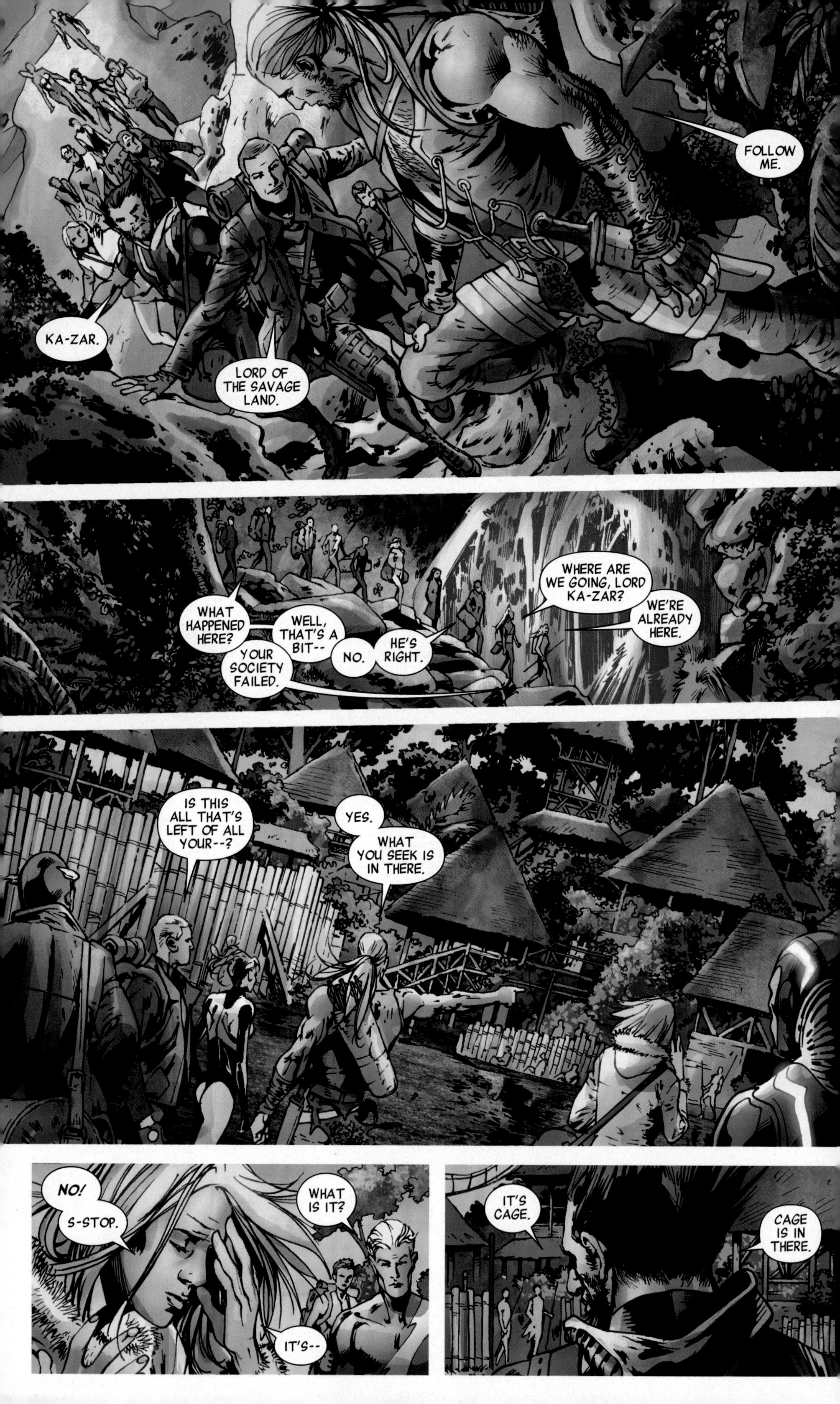
FOLLOW ME.
KA-ZAR.
LORD OF THE SAVAGE LAND.
WHERE ARE WE GOING, LORD KA-ZAR?
WE'RE ALREADY HERE.
WHAT HAPPENED HERE?
WELL, THAT'S A BIT--
YOUR SOCIETY FAILED.
NO.
HE'S RIGHT.
IS THIS ALL THAT'S LEFT OF ALL YOUR--?
YES.
WHAT YOU SEEK IS IN THERE.
NO!
S-STOP.
WHAT IS IT?
IT'S--
IT'S CAGE.
CAGE IS IN THERE.

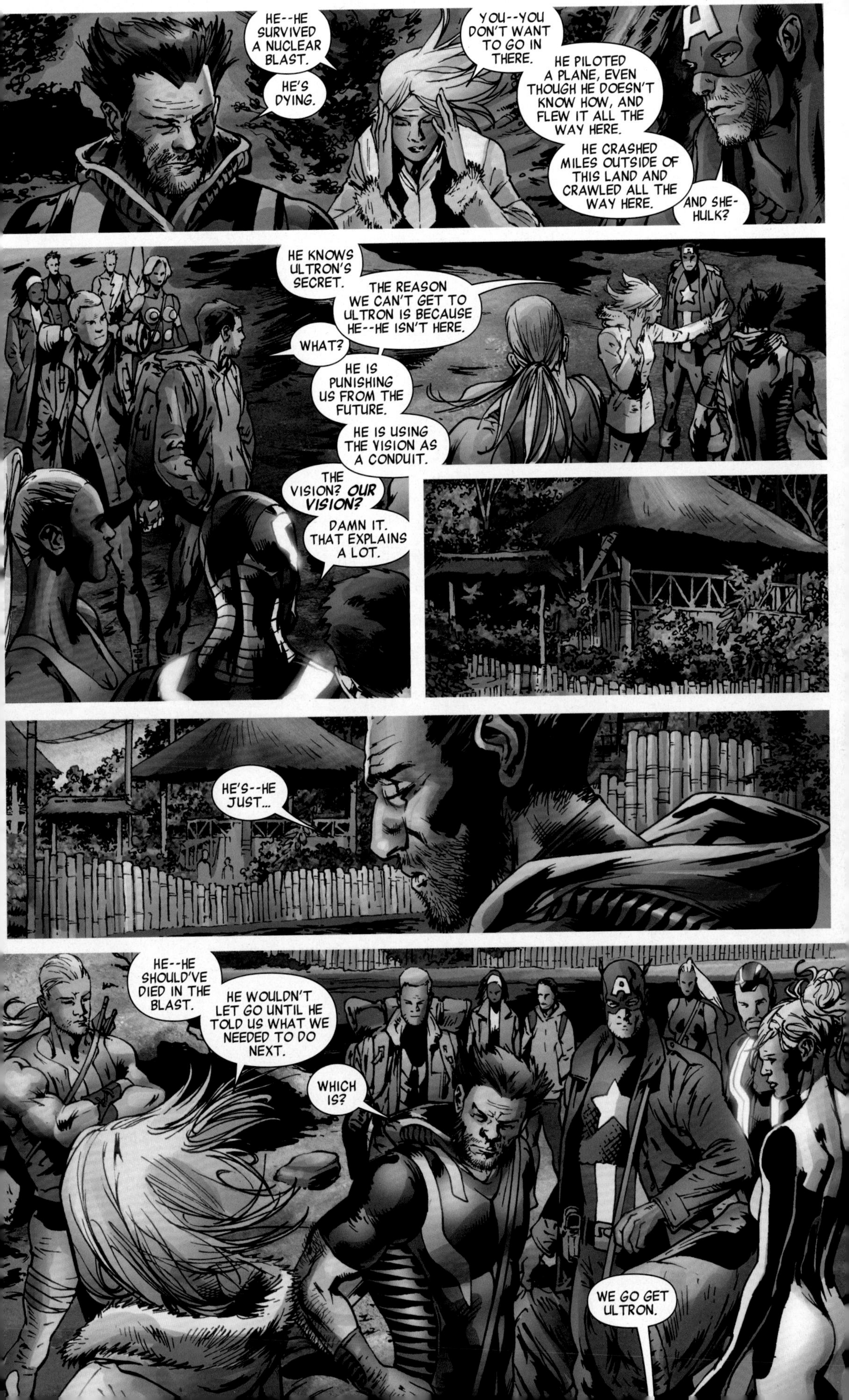
HE--HE SURVIVED A NUCLEAR BLAST.
HE'S DYING.
YOU--YOU DON'T WANT TO GO IN THERE.
HE PILOTED A PLANE, EVEN THOUGH HE DOESN'T KNOW HOW, AND FLEW IT ALL THE WAY HERE.
HE CRASHED MILES OUTSIDE OF THIS LAND AND CRAWLED ALL THE WAY HERE.
AND SHE-HULK?
HE KNOWS ULTRON'S SECRET.
THE REASON WE CAN'T GET TO ULTRON IS BECAUSE HE--HE ISN'T HERE.
WHAT?
HE IS PUNISHING US FROM THE FUTURE.
HE IS USING THE VISION AS A CONDUIT.
THE VISION? ***OUR VISION?***
DAMN IT. THAT EXPLAINS A LOT.
HE'S--HE JUST...
HE--HE SHOULD'VE DIED IN THE BLAST.
HE WOULDN'T LET GO UNTIL HE TOLD US WHAT WE NEEDED TO DO NEXT.
WHICH IS?
WE GO GET ULTRON.

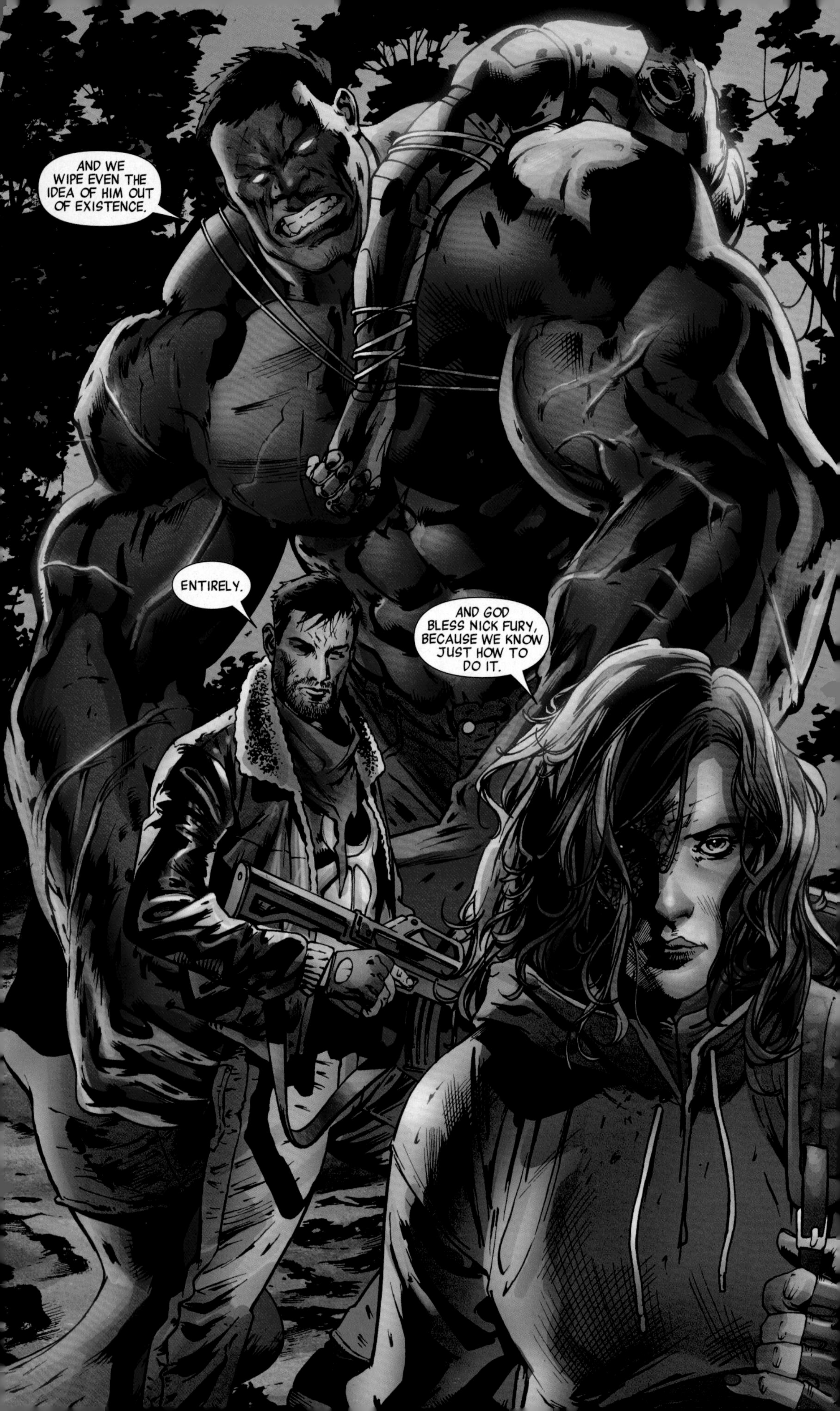
AND WE WIPE EVEN THE IDEA OF HIM OUT OF EXISTENCE.
ENTIRELY.
AND GOD BLESS NICK FURY, BECAUSE WE KNOW JUST HOW TO DO IT.

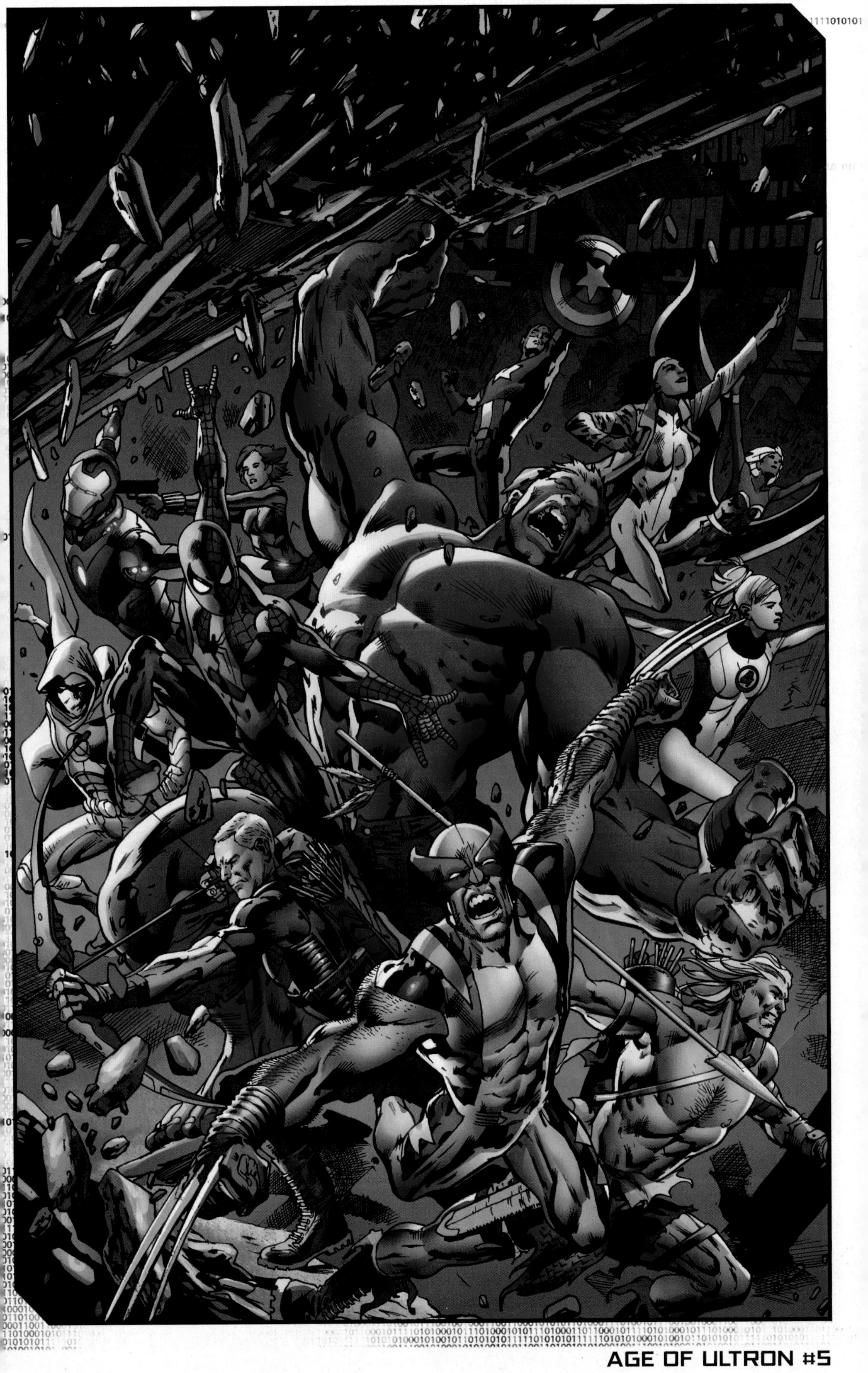

AGE OF ULTRON #5

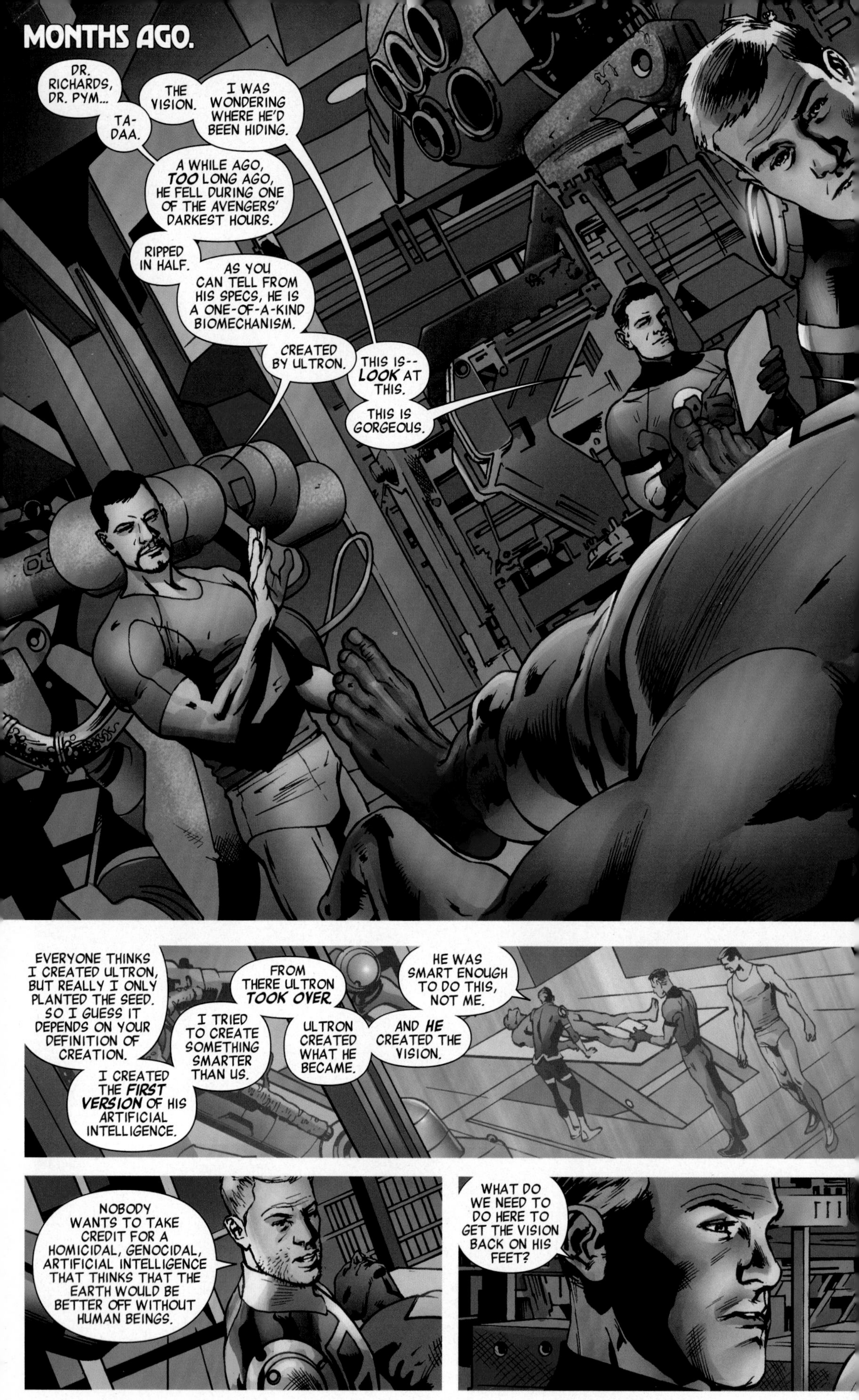
MONTHS AGO.
DR. RICHARDS, DR. PYM...
TA-DAA.
THE VISION.
I WAS WONDERING WHERE HE'D BEEN HIDING.
A WHILE AGO, TOO LONG AGO, HE FELL DURING ONE OF THE AVENGERS' DARKEST HOURS.
RIPPED IN HALF.
AS YOU CAN TELL FROM HIS SPECS, HE IS A ONE-OF-A-KIND BIOMECHANISM.
CREATED BY ULTRON.
THIS IS-- LOOK AT THIS.
THIS IS GORGEOUS.
EVERYONE THINKS I CREATED ULTRON, BUT REALLY I ONLY PLANTED THE SEED. SO I GUESS IT DEPENDS ON YOUR DEFINITION OF CREATION.
I CREATED THE FIRST VERSION OF HIS ARTIFICIAL INTELLIGENCE.
I TRIED TO CREATE SOMETHING SMARTER THAN US.
FROM THERE ULTRON TOOK OVER.
ULTRON CREATED WHAT HE BECAME.
AND HE CREATED THE VISION.
HE WAS SMART ENOUGH TO DO THIS, NOT ME.
NOBODY WANTS TO TAKE CREDIT FOR A HOMICIDAL, GENOCIDAL, ARTIFICIAL INTELLIGENCE THAT THINKS THAT THE EARTH WOULD BE BETTER OFF WITHOUT HUMAN BEINGS.
WHAT DO WE NEED TO DO HERE TO GET THE VISION BACK ON HIS FEET?

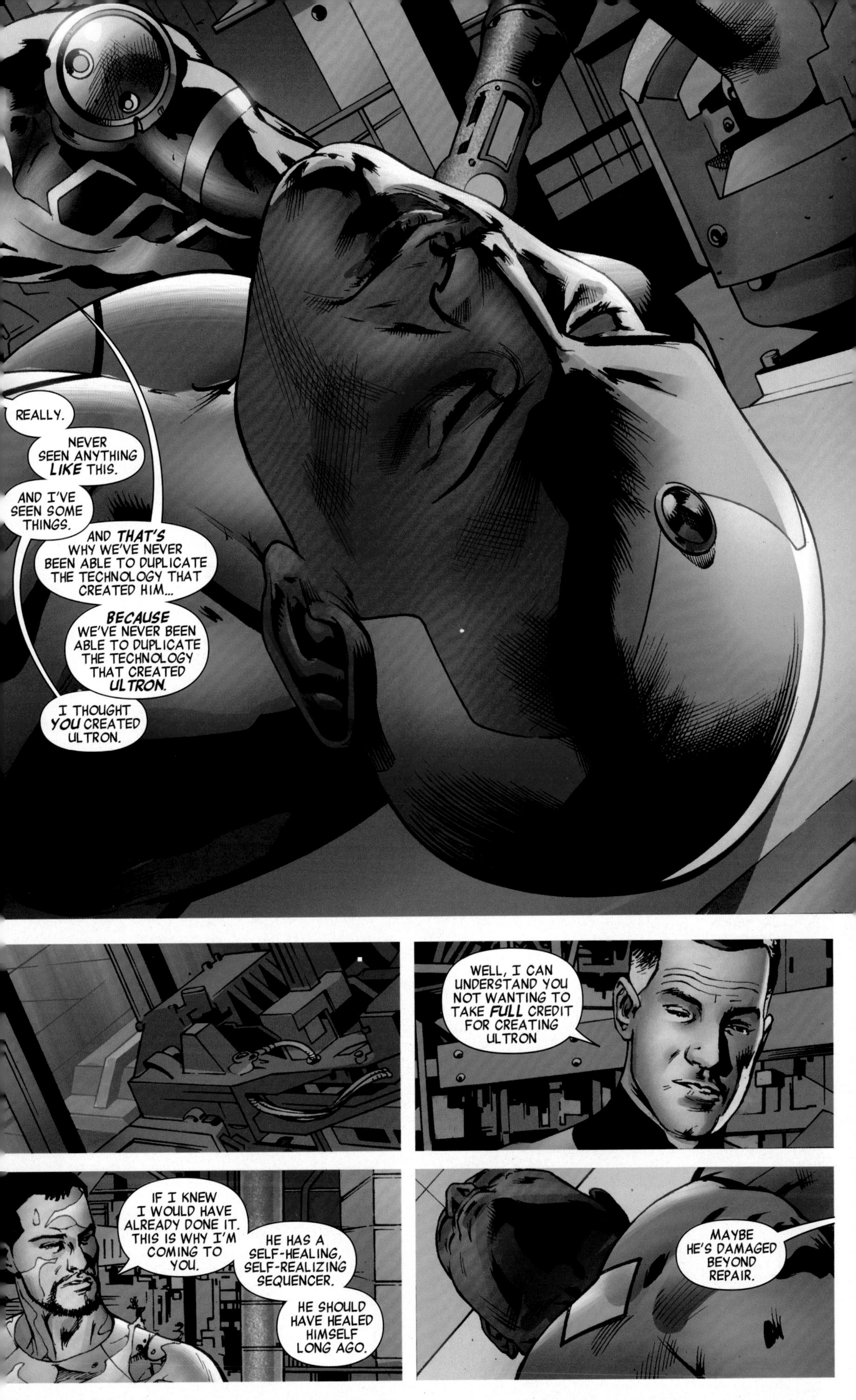
REALLY.
NEVER SEEN ANYTHING LIKE THIS.
AND I'VE SEEN SOME THINGS.
AND THAT'S WHY WE'VE NEVER BEEN ABLE TO DUPLICATE THE TECHNOLOGY THAT CREATED HIM...
BECAUSE WE'VE NEVER BEEN ABLE TO DUPLICATE THE TECHNOLOGY THAT CREATED ULTRON.
I THOUGHT YOU CREATED ULTRON.
WELL, I CAN UNDERSTAND YOU NOT WANTING TO TAKE FULL CREDIT FOR CREATING ULTRON
IF I KNEW I WOULD HAVE ALREADY DONE IT. THIS IS WHY I'M COMING TO YOU.
HE HAS A SELF-HEALING, SELF-REALIZING SEQUENCER.
HE SHOULD HAVE HEALED HIMSELF LONG AGO.
MAYBE HE'S DAMAGED BEYOND REPAIR.

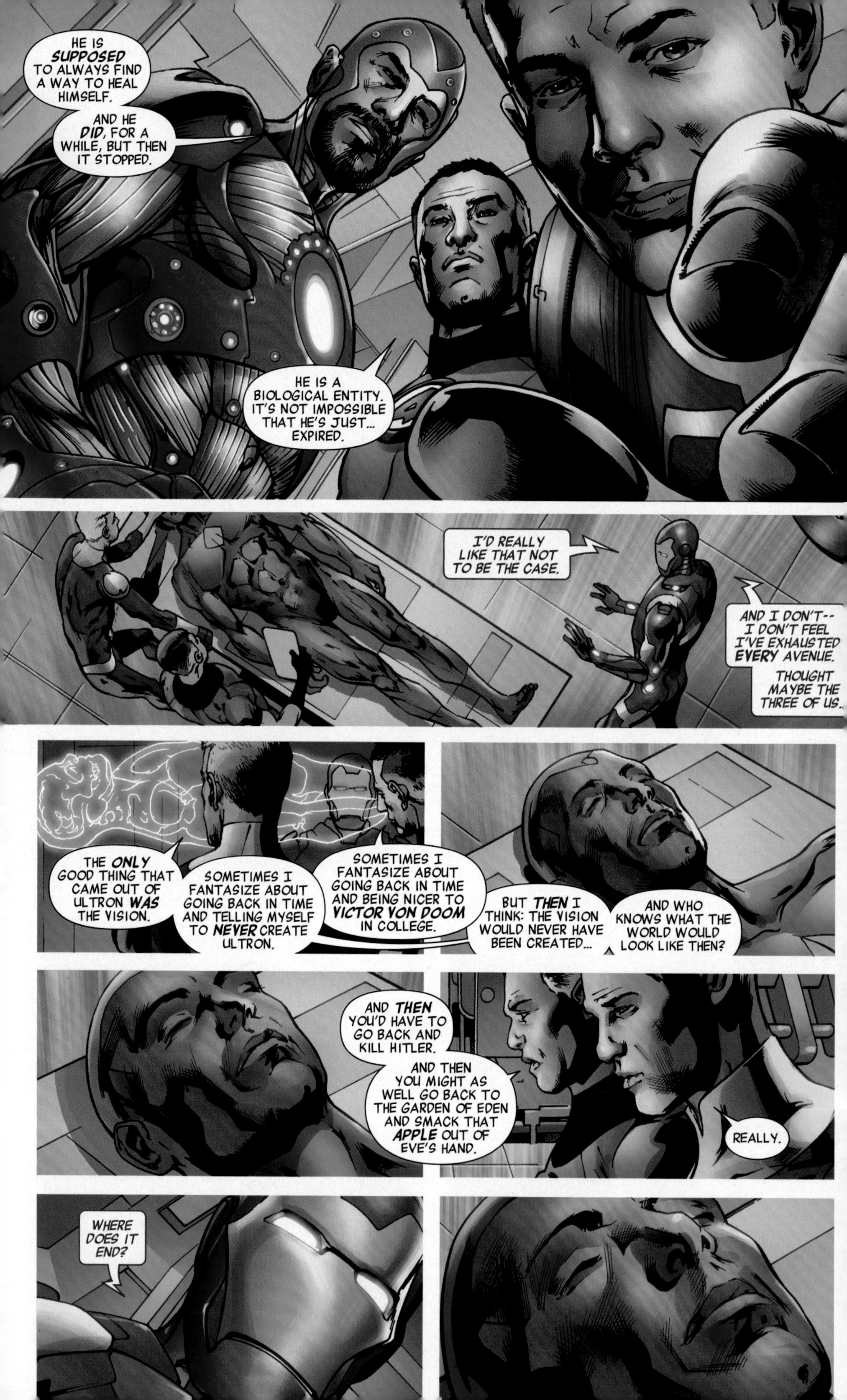

HE IS SUPPOSED TO ALWAYS FIND A WAY TO HEAL HIMSELF.
AND HE DID, FOR A WHILE, BUT THEN IT STOPPED.
HE IS A BIOLOGICAL ENTITY. IT'S NOT IMPOSSIBLE THAT HE'S JUST... EXPIRED.
I'D REALLY LIKE THAT NOT TO BE THE CASE.
AND I DON'T-- I DON'T FEEL I'VE EXHAUSTED EVERY AVENUE.
THOUGHT MAYBE THE THREE OF US...
THE ONLY GOOD THING THAT CAME OUT OF ULTRON WAS THE VISION.
SOMETIMES I FANTASIZE ABOUT GOING BACK IN TIME AND TELLING MYSELF TO NEVER CREATE ULTRON.
SOMETIMES I FANTASIZE ABOUT GOING BACK IN TIME AND BEING NICER TO VICTOR VON DOOM IN COLLEGE.
BUT THEN I THINK: THE VISION WOULD NEVER HAVE BEEN CREATED...
AND WHO KNOWS WHAT THE WORLD WOULD LOOK LIKE THEN?
AND THEN YOU'D HAVE TO GO BACK AND KILL HITLER.
AND THEN YOU MIGHT AS WELL GO BACK TO THE GARDEN OF EDEN AND SMACK THAT APPLE OUT OF EVE'S HAND.
REALLY.
WHERE DOES IT END?

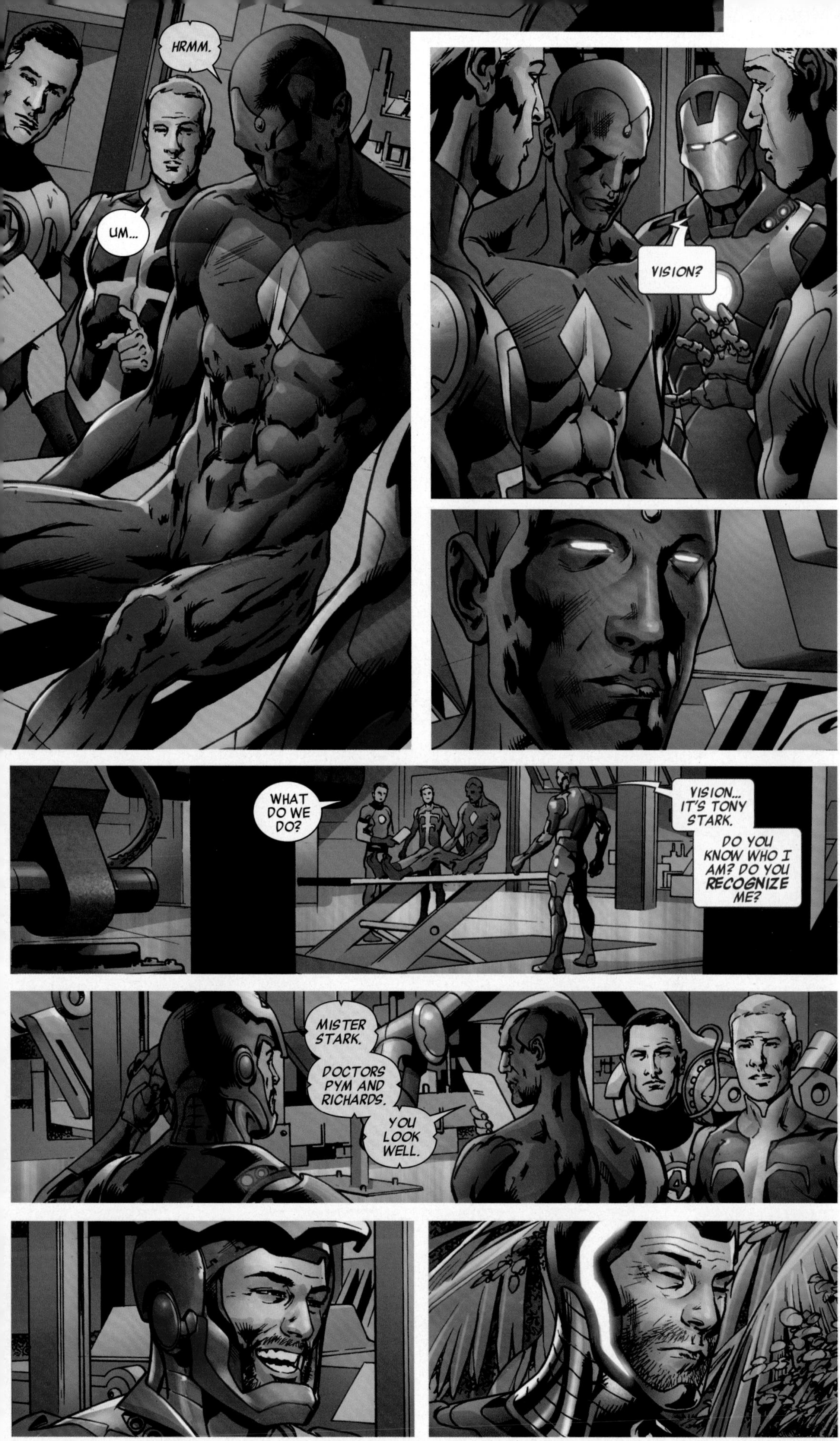
HRMM.
UM...
VISION?
WHAT DO WE DO?
VISION... IT'S TONY STARK.
DO YOU KNOW WHO I AM? DO YOU RECOGNIZE ME?
MISTER STARK.
DOCTORS PYM AND RICHARDS.
YOU LOOK WELL.

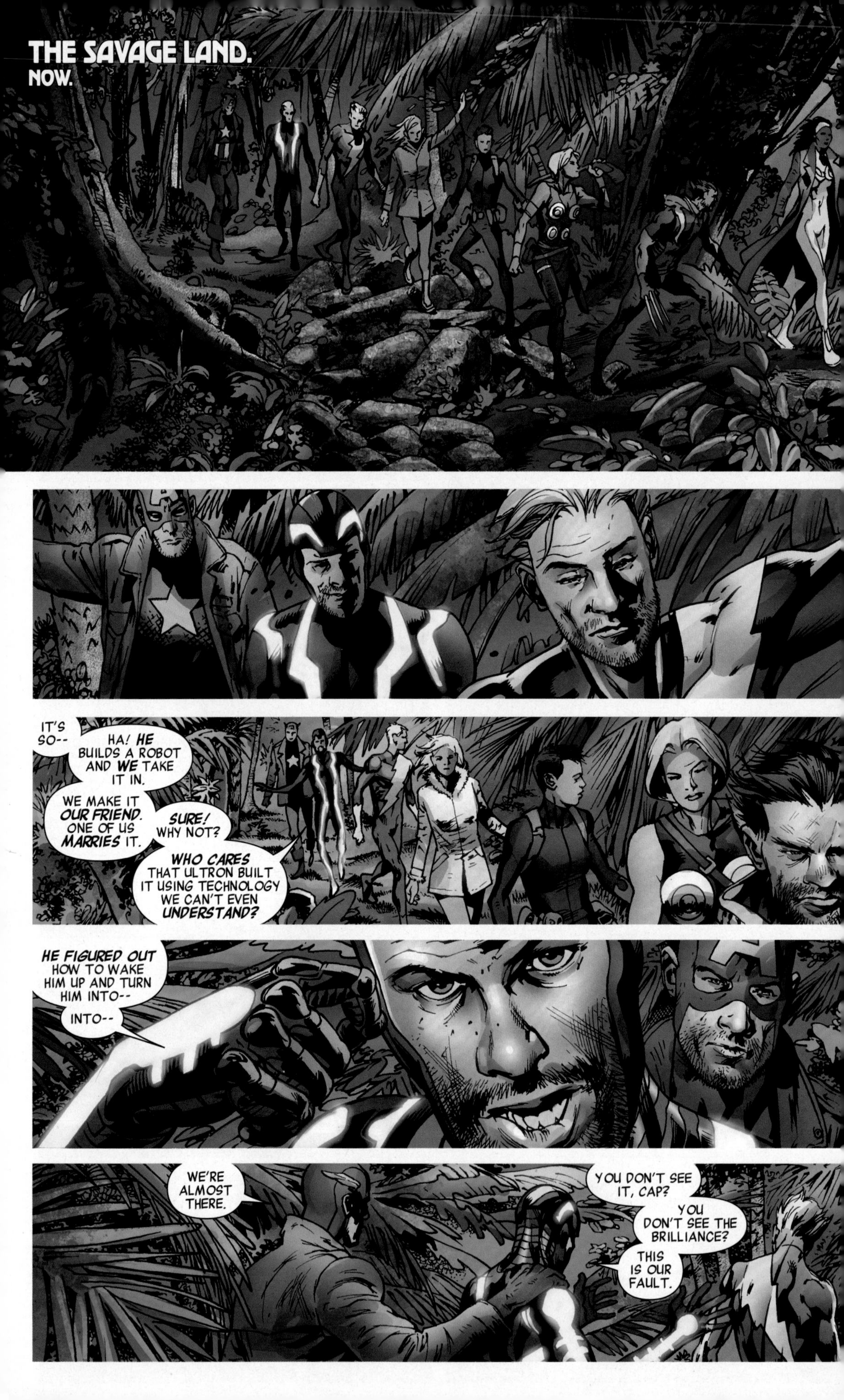
THE SAVAGE LAND.
NOW.
IT'S SO--
HA! HE BUILDS A ROBOT AND WE TAKE IT IN.
WE MAKE IT OUR FRIEND. ONE OF US MARRIES IT.
SURE! WHY NOT?
WHO CARES THAT ULTRON BUILT IT USING TECHNOLOGY WE CAN'T EVEN UNDERSTAND?
HE FIGURED OUT HOW TO WAKE HIM UP AND TURN HIM INTO--
INTO--
WE'RE ALMOST THERE.
YOU DON'T SEE IT, CAP?
YOU DON'T SEE THE BRILLIANCE?
THIS IS OUR FAULT.

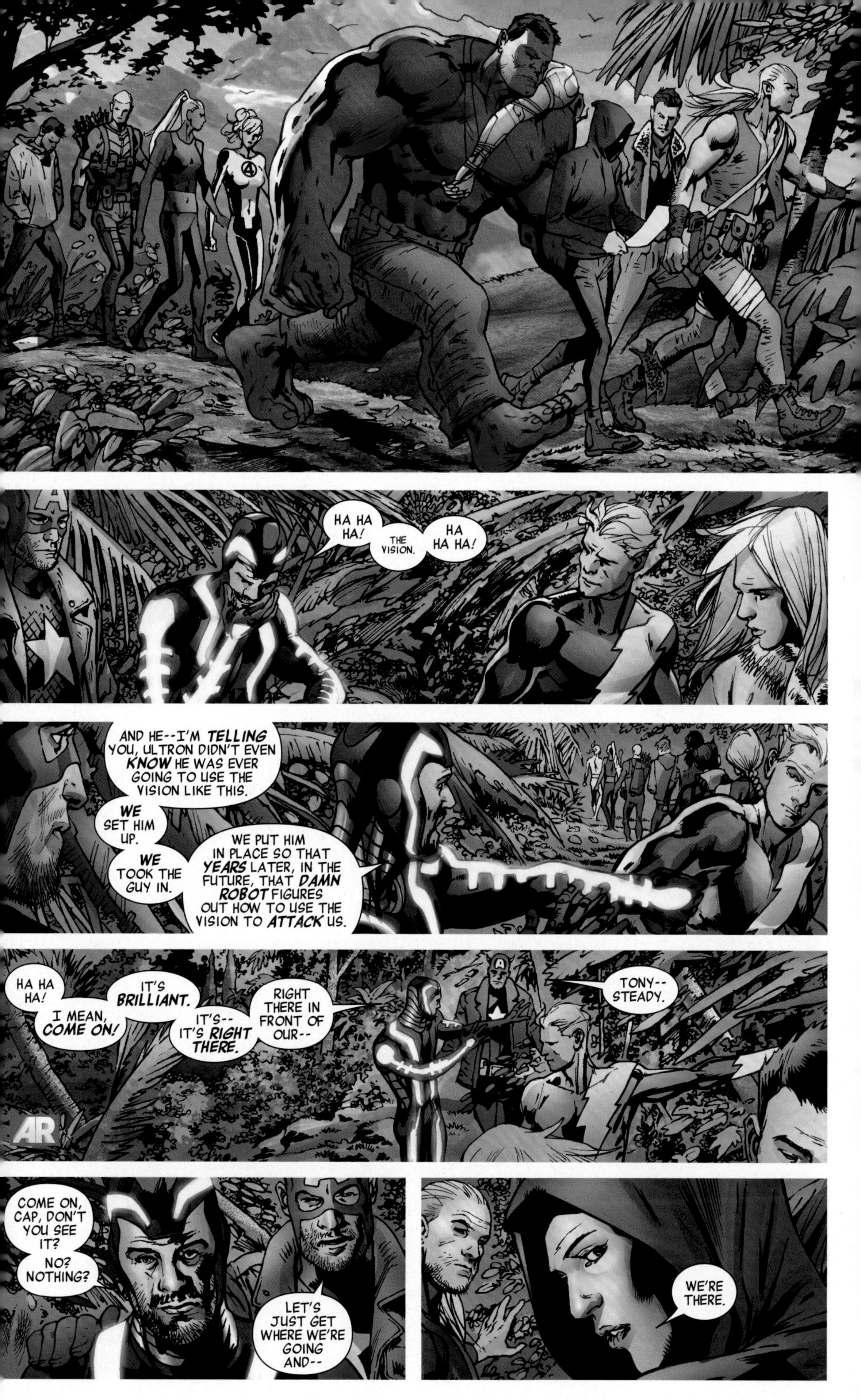
HA HA HA!
THE VISION.
HA HA HA!
AND HE--I'M TELLING YOU, ULTRON DIDN'T EVEN KNOW HE WAS EVER GOING TO USE THE VISION LIKE THIS.
WE SET HIM UP.
WE TOOK THE GUY IN.
WE PUT HIM IN PLACE SO THAT YEARS LATER, IN THE FUTURE, THAT DAMN ROBOT FIGURES OUT HOW TO USE THE VISION TO ATTACK US.
HA HA HA!
I MEAN, COME ON!
IT'S BRILLIANT.
IT'S-- IT'S RIGHT THERE.
RIGHT THERE IN FRONT OF OUR--
TONY-- STEADY.
COME ON, CAP, DON'T YOU SEE IT?
NO? NOTHING?
LET'S JUST GET WHERE WE'RE GOING AND--
WE'RE THERE.

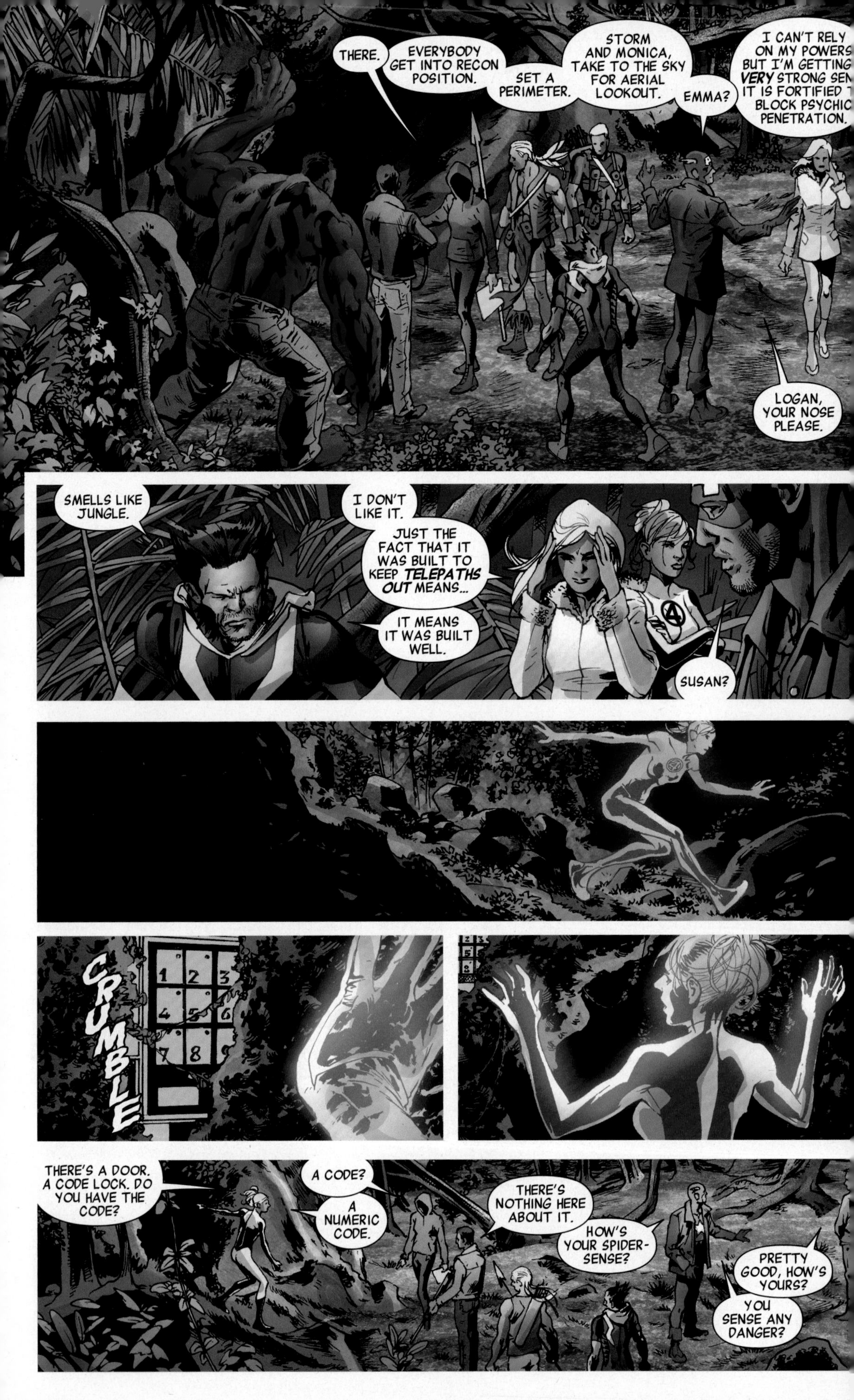
THERE.
EVERYBODY GET INTO RECON POSITION.
SET A PERIMETER.
STORM AND MONICA, TAKE TO THE SKY FOR AERIAL LOOKOUT.
EMMA?
I CAN'T RELY ON MY POWERS BUT I'M GETTING VERY STRONG SEN IT IS FORTIFIED T BLOCK PSYCHIC PENETRATION.
LOGAN, YOUR NOSE PLEASE.
SMELLS LIKE JUNGLE.
I DON'T LIKE IT.
JUST THE FACT THAT IT WAS BUILT TO KEEP TELEPATHS OUT MEANS...
IT MEANS IT WAS BUILT WELL.
SUSAN?
CRUMBLE
1 2 3
4 5 6
7 8 9
THERE'S A DOOR. A CODE LOCK. DO YOU HAVE THE CODE?
A CODE?
A NUMERIC CODE.
THERE'S NOTHING HERE ABOUT IT.
HOW'S YOUR SPIDER-SENSE?
PRETTY GOOD, HOW'S YOURS?
YOU SENSE ANY DANGER?

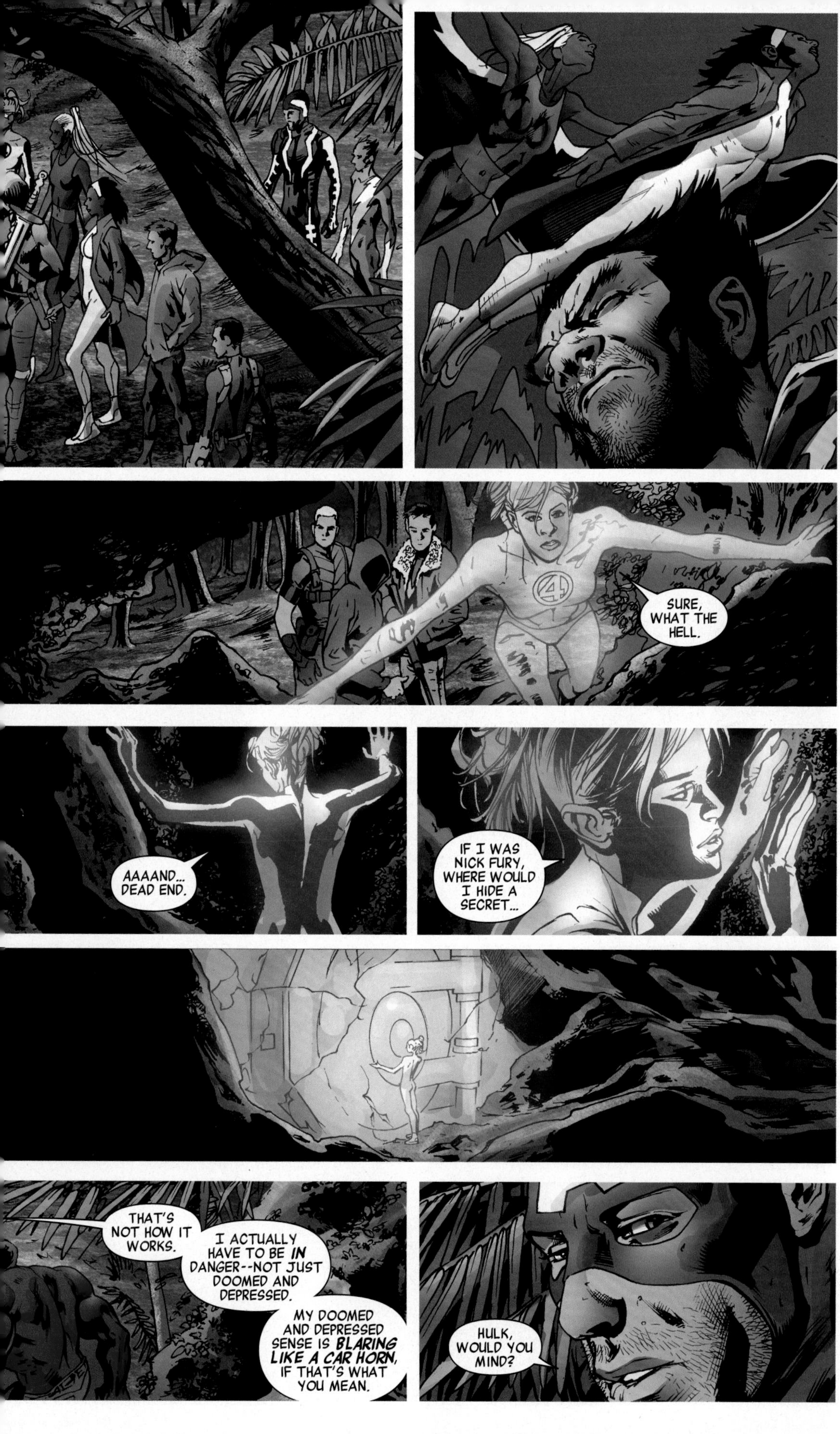
SURE, WHAT THE HELL.
AAAAND... DEAD END.
IF I WAS NICK FURY, WHERE WOULD I HIDE A SECRET...
THAT'S NOT HOW IT WORKS.
I ACTUALLY HAVE TO BE *IN* DANGER--NOT JUST DOOMED AND DEPRESSED.
MY DOOMED AND DEPRESSED SENSE IS ***BLARING LIKE A CAR HORN***, IF THAT'S WHAT YOU MEAN.
HULK, WOULD YOU MIND?

BOOM
CHOOM CHOOM CHOOM
AARRGH! SON OF A--!
@#$&
WAIT.

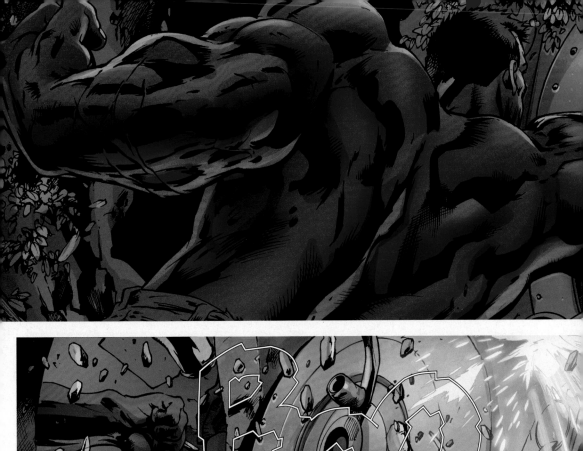

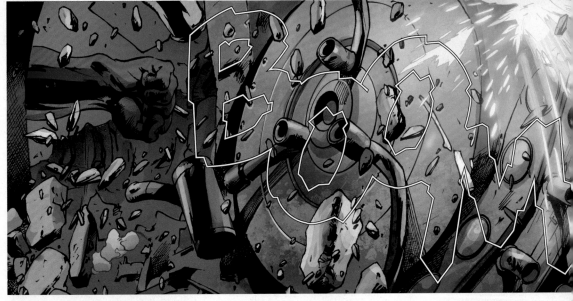

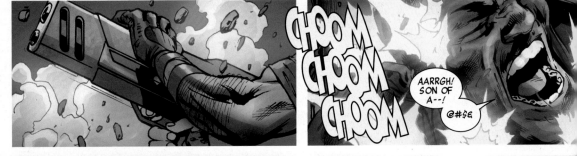

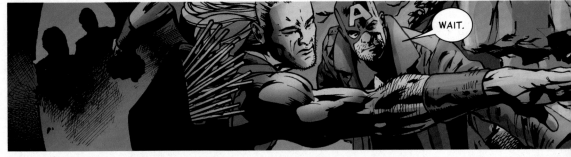

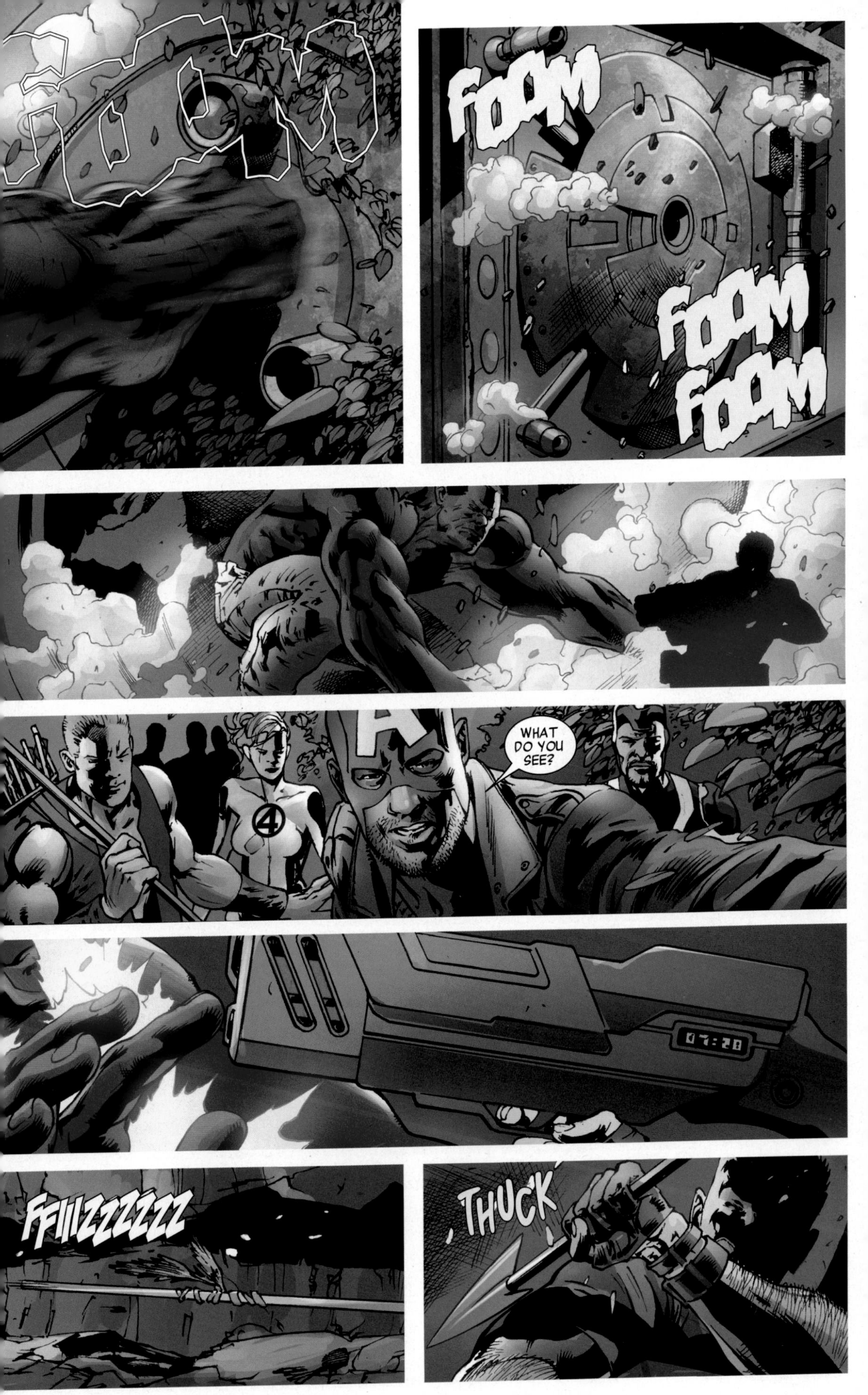
FOOM
FOOM
FOOM
FOOM
WHAT DO YOU SEE?
FFIIIZZZZZZ
THUCK

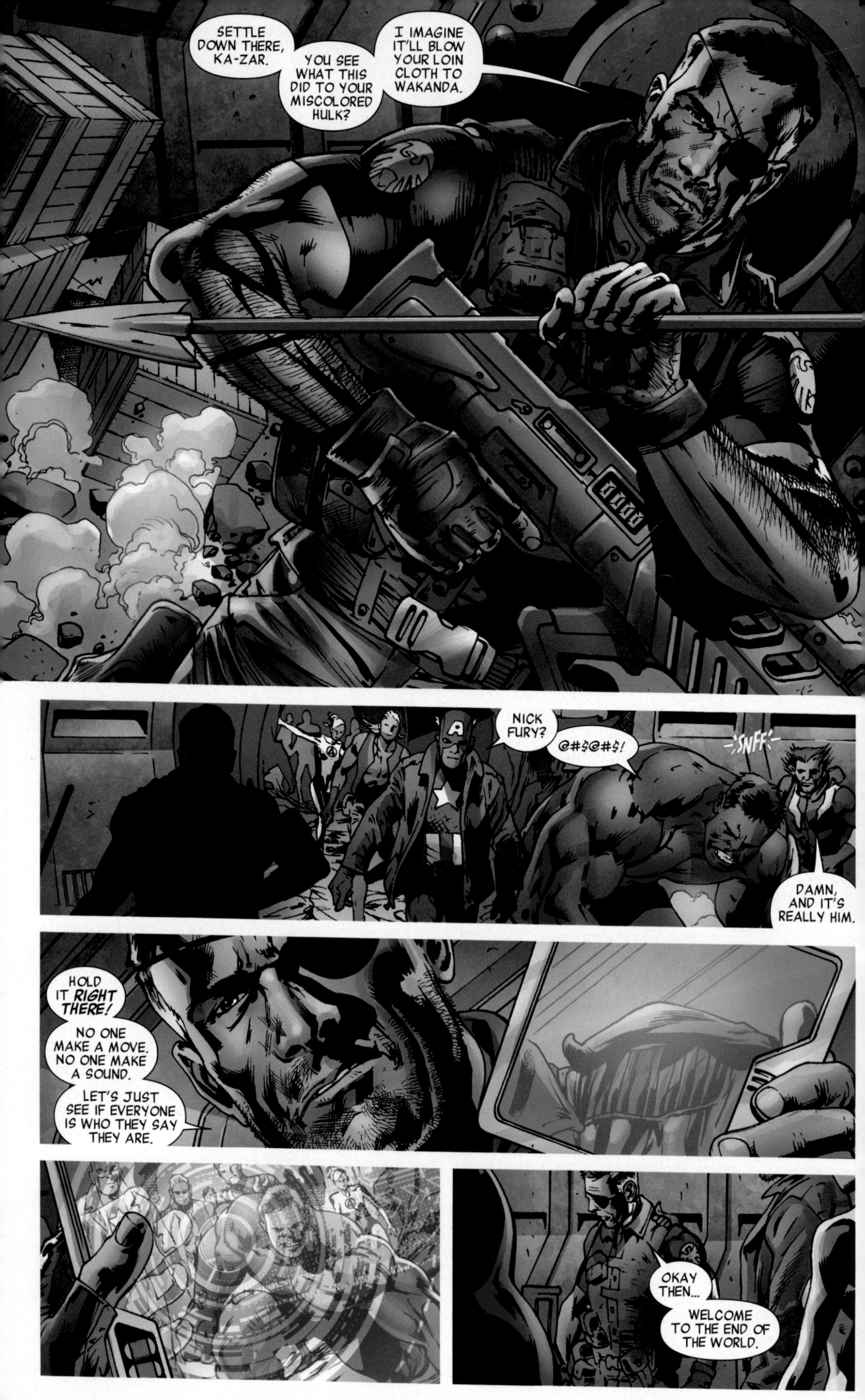
SETTLE DOWN THERE, KA-ZAR.
YOU SEE WHAT THIS DID TO YOUR MISCOLORED HULK?
I IMAGINE IT'LL BLOW YOUR LOIN CLOTH TO WAKANDA.
NICK FURY?
@#$@#$!
SNFF
DAMN, AND IT'S REALLY HIM.
HOLD IT RIGHT THERE!
NO ONE MAKE A MOVE. NO ONE MAKE A SOUND.
LET'S JUST SEE IF EVERYONE IS WHO THEY SAY THEY ARE.
OKAY THEN...
WELCOME TO THE END OF THE WORLD.

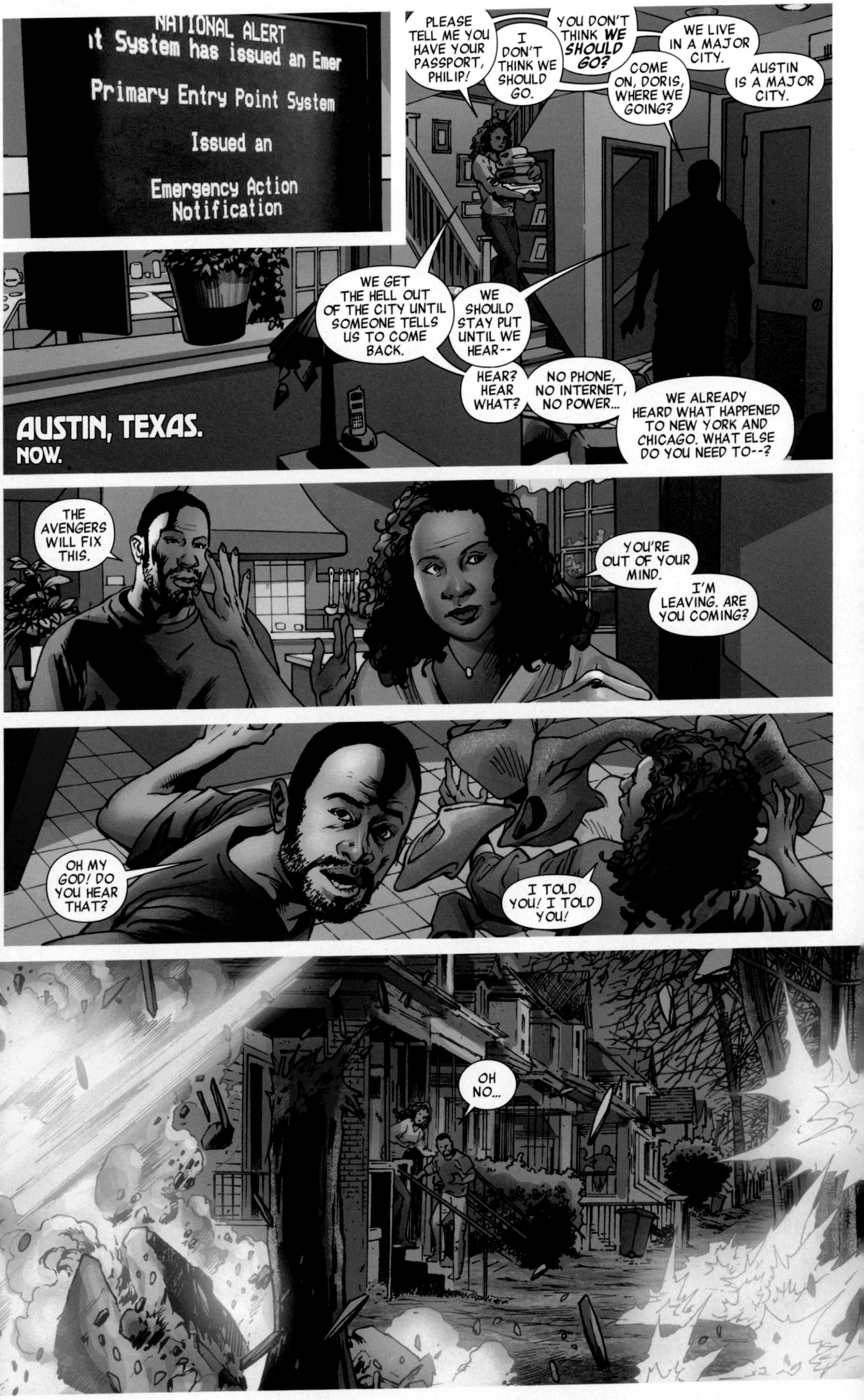
NATIONAL ALERT
it System has issued an Emer
Primary Entry Point System
Issued an
Emergency Action Notification
PLEASE TELL ME YOU HAVE YOUR PASSPORT, PHILIP!
I DON'T THINK WE SHOULD GO.
YOU DON'T THINK WE SHOULD GO?
WE LIVE IN A MAJOR CITY.
COME ON, DORIS, WHERE WE GOING?
AUSTIN IS A MAJOR CITY.
WE GET THE HELL OUT OF THE CITY UNTIL SOMEONE TELLS US TO COME BACK.
WE SHOULD STAY PUT UNTIL WE HEAR--
HEAR? HEAR WHAT?
NO PHONE, NO INTERNET, NO POWER...
WE ALREADY HEARD WHAT HAPPENED TO NEW YORK AND CHICAGO. WHAT ELSE DO YOU NEED TO--?
AUSTIN, TEXAS.
NOW.
THE AVENGERS WILL FIX THIS.
YOU'RE OUT OF YOUR MIND.
I'M LEAVING. ARE YOU COMING?
OH MY GOD! DO YOU HEAR THAT?
I TOLD YOU! I TOLD YOU!
OH NO...

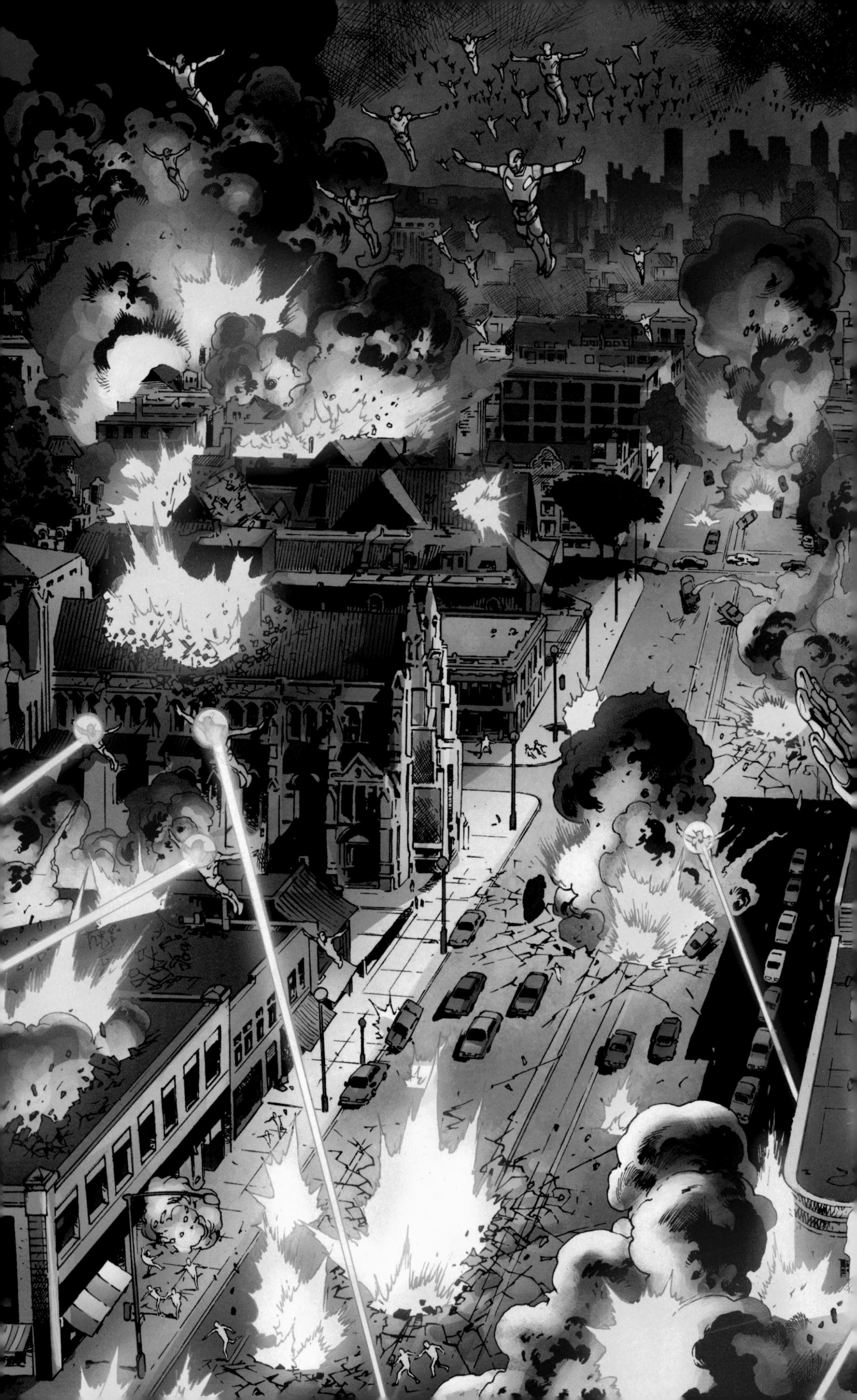

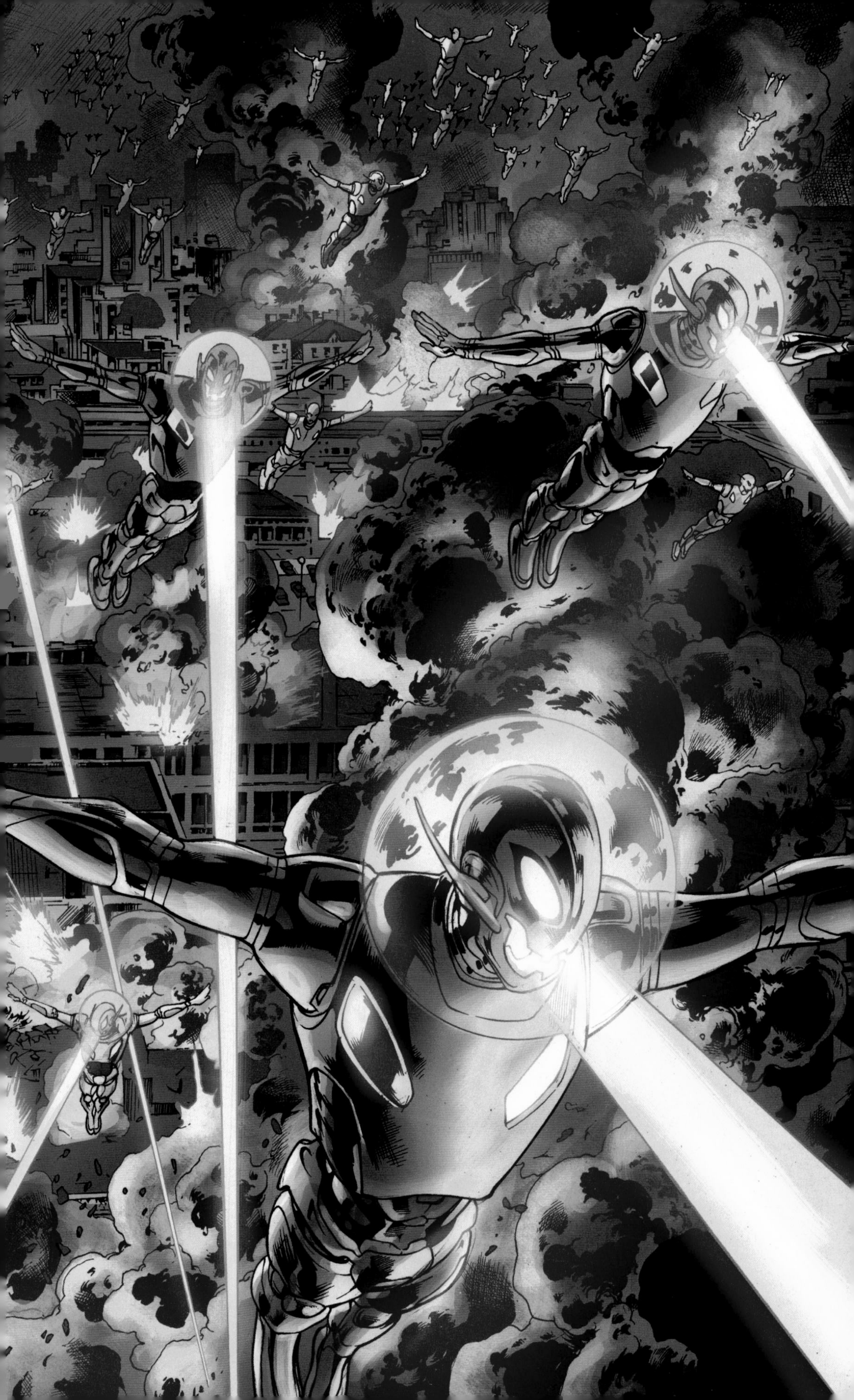

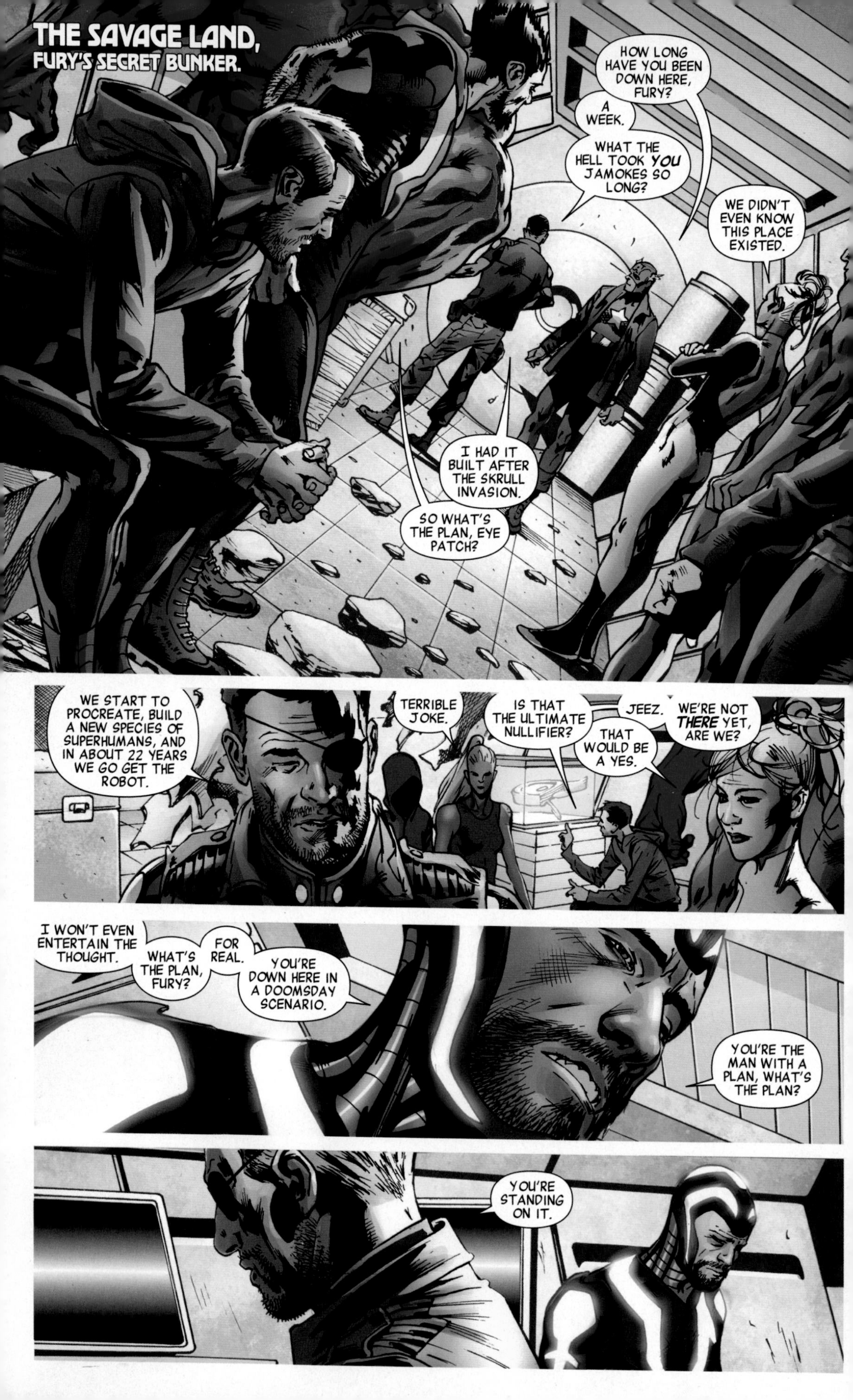
THE SAVAGE LAND,
FURY'S SECRET BUNKER.
HOW LONG HAVE YOU BEEN DOWN HERE, FURY?
A WEEK.
WHAT THE HELL TOOK YOU JAMOKES SO LONG?
WE DIDN'T EVEN KNOW THIS PLACE EXISTED.
I HAD IT BUILT AFTER THE SKRULL INVASION.
SO WHAT'S THE PLAN, EYE PATCH?
WE START TO PROCREATE, BUILD A NEW SPECIES OF SUPERHUMANS, AND IN ABOUT 22 YEARS WE GO GET THE ROBOT.
TERRIBLE JOKE.
IS THAT THE ULTIMATE NULLIFIER?
JEEZ.
THAT WOULD BE A YES.
WE'RE NOT THERE YET, ARE WE?
I WON'T EVEN ENTERTAIN THE THOUGHT.
WHAT'S THE PLAN, FURY?
FOR REAL.
YOU'RE DOWN HERE IN A DOOMSDAY SCENARIO.
YOU'RE THE MAN WITH A PLAN, WHAT'S THE PLAN?
YOU'RE STANDING ON IT.

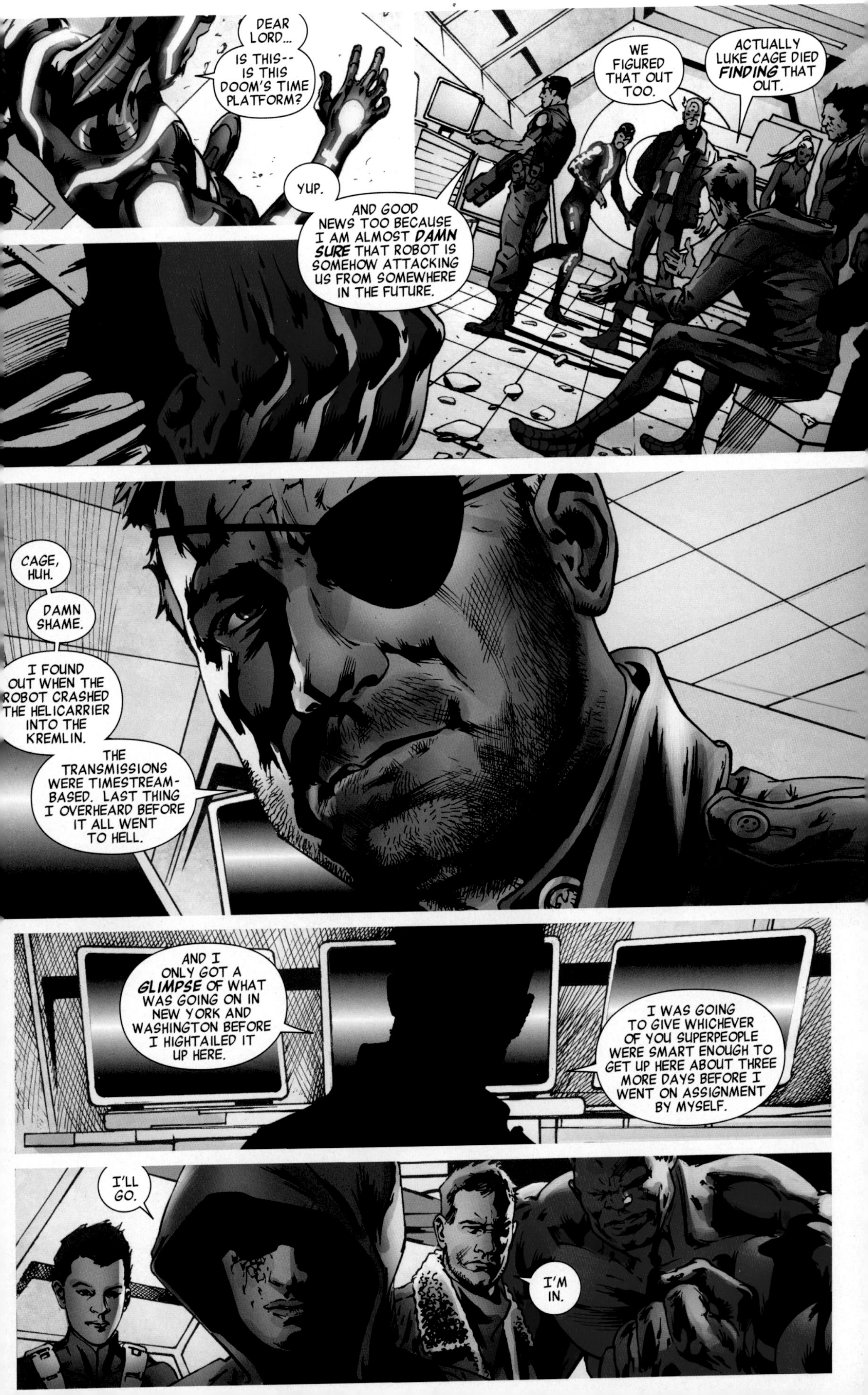
DEAR LORD...
IS THIS-- IS THIS DOOM'S TIME PLATFORM?
WE FIGURED THAT OUT TOO.
ACTUALLY LUKE CAGE DIED FINDING THAT OUT.
YUP.
AND GOOD NEWS TOO BECAUSE I AM ALMOST DAMN SURE THAT ROBOT IS SOMEHOW ATTACKING US FROM SOMEWHERE IN THE FUTURE.
CAGE, HUH.
DAMN SHAME.
I FOUND OUT WHEN THE ROBOT CRASHED THE HELICARRIER INTO THE KREMLIN.
THE TRANSMISSIONS WERE TIMESTREAM-BASED. LAST THING I OVERHEARD BEFORE IT ALL WENT TO HELL.
AND I ONLY GOT A GLIMPSE OF WHAT WAS GOING ON IN NEW YORK AND WASHINGTON BEFORE I HIGHTAILED IT UP HERE.
I WAS GOING TO GIVE WHICHEVER OF YOU SUPERPEOPLE WERE SMART ENOUGH TO GET UP HERE ABOUT THREE MORE DAYS BEFORE I WENT ON ASSIGNMENT BY MYSELF.
I'LL GO.
I'M IN.

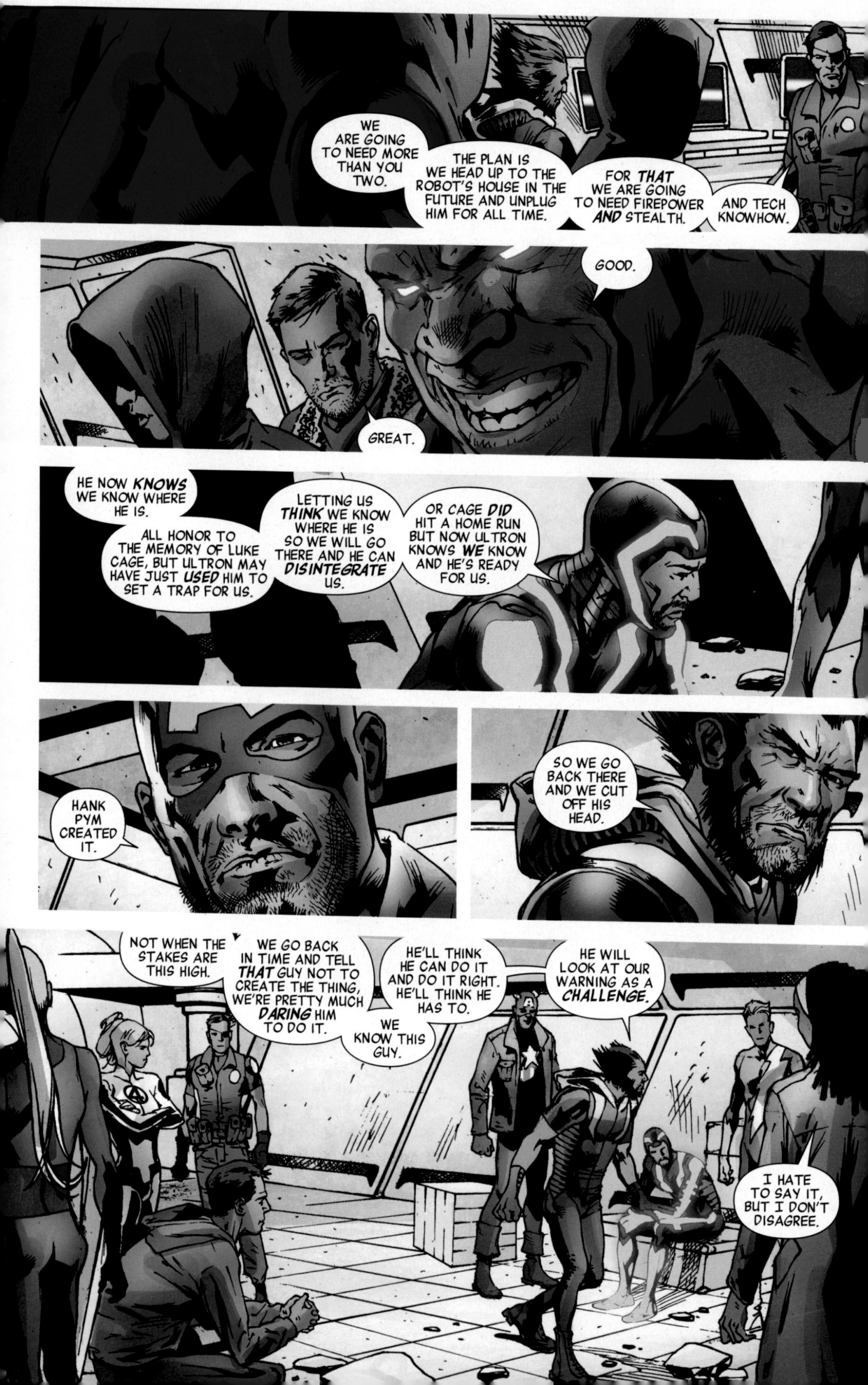

WE ARE GOING TO NEED MORE THAN YOU TWO.
THE PLAN IS WE HEAD UP TO THE ROBOT'S HOUSE IN THE FUTURE AND UNPLUG HIM FOR ALL TIME.
FOR THAT WE ARE GOING TO NEED FIREPOWER AND STEALTH.
AND TECH KNOWHOW.
GOOD.
GREAT.
HE NOW KNOWS WE KNOW WHERE HE IS.
ALL HONOR TO THE MEMORY OF LUKE CAGE, BUT ULTRON MAY HAVE JUST USED HIM TO SET A TRAP FOR US.
LETTING US THINK WE KNOW WHERE HE IS SO WE WILL GO THERE AND HE CAN DISINTEGRATE US.
OR CAGE DID HIT A HOME RUN BUT NOW ULTRON KNOWS WE KNOW AND HE'S READY FOR US.
HANK PYM CREATED IT.
SO WE GO BACK THERE AND WE CUT OFF HIS HEAD.
NOT WHEN THE STAKES ARE THIS HIGH.
WE GO BACK IN TIME AND TELL THAT GUY NOT TO CREATE THE THING, WE'RE PRETTY MUCH DARING HIM TO DO IT.
HE'LL THINK HE CAN DO IT AND DO IT RIGHT. HE'LL THINK HE HAS TO.
WE KNOW THIS GUY.
HE WILL LOOK AT OUR WARNING AS A CHALLENGE.
I HATE TO SAY IT, BUT I DON'T DISAGREE.

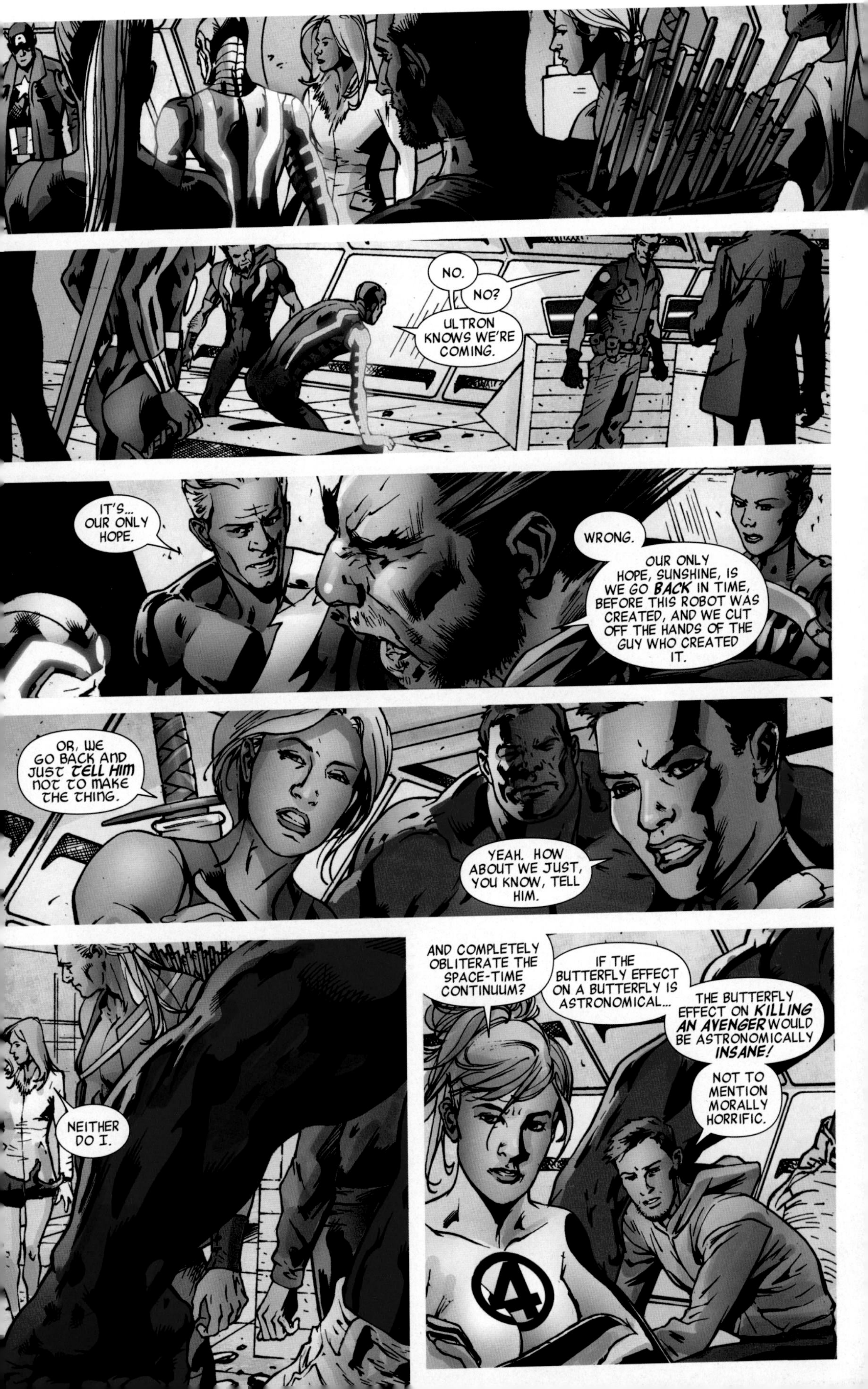
NO.
NO?
ULTRON KNOWS WE'RE COMING.
IT'S... OUR ONLY HOPE.
WRONG.
OUR ONLY HOPE, SUNSHINE, IS WE GO BACK IN TIME, BEFORE THIS ROBOT WAS CREATED, AND WE CUT OFF THE HANDS OF THE GUY WHO CREATED IT.
OR, WE GO BACK AND JUST TELL HIM NOT TO MAKE THE THING.
YEAH. HOW ABOUT WE JUST, YOU KNOW, TELL HIM.
NEITHER DO I.
AND COMPLETELY OBLITERATE THE SPACE-TIME CONTINUUM?
IF THE BUTTERFLY EFFECT ON A BUTTERFLY IS ASTRONOMICAL...
THE BUTTERFLY EFFECT ON KILLING AN AVENGER WOULD BE ASTRONOMICALLY INSANE!
NOT TO MENTION MORALLY HORRIFIC.

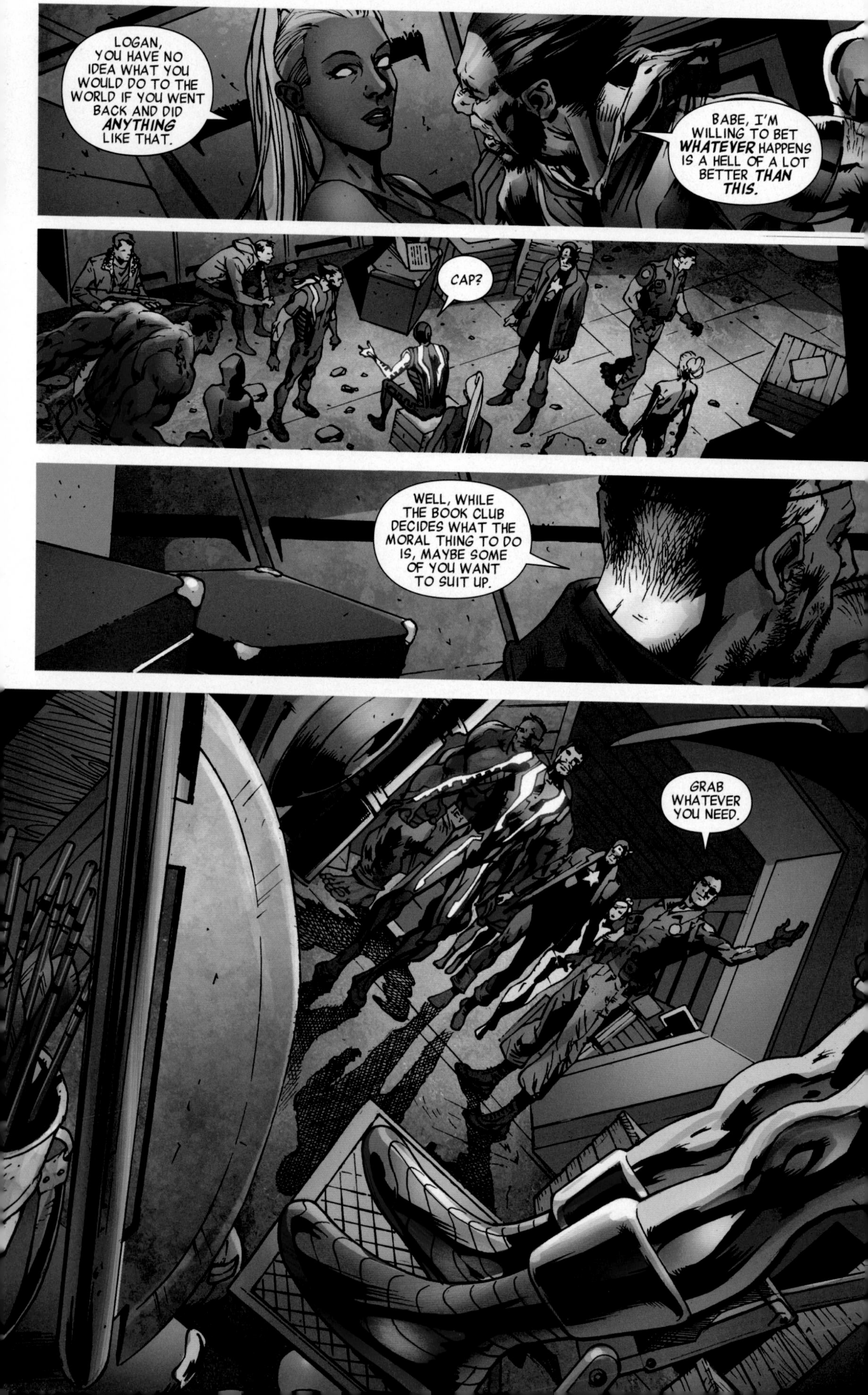
LOGAN, YOU HAVE NO IDEA WHAT YOU WOULD DO TO THE WORLD IF YOU WENT BACK AND DID ANYTHING LIKE THAT.
BABE, I'M WILLING TO BET WHATEVER HAPPENS IS A HELL OF A LOT BETTER THAN THIS.
CAP?
WELL, WHILE THE BOOK CLUB DECIDES WHAT THE MORAL THING TO DO IS, MAYBE SOME OF YOU WANT TO SUIT UP.
GRAB WHATEVER YOU NEED.

YOU AND HIM ARE THE *SAME KIND* OF SCIENCE NERD, STARK.

YOU TELL ME TRUE:

SOMEONE LIKE ME OR CAPTAIN AMERICA SHOWS UP ON YOUR DOORSTEP AND TELLS YOU *SPECIFICALLY* NOT TO DO SOMETHING...

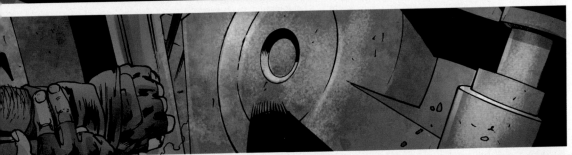

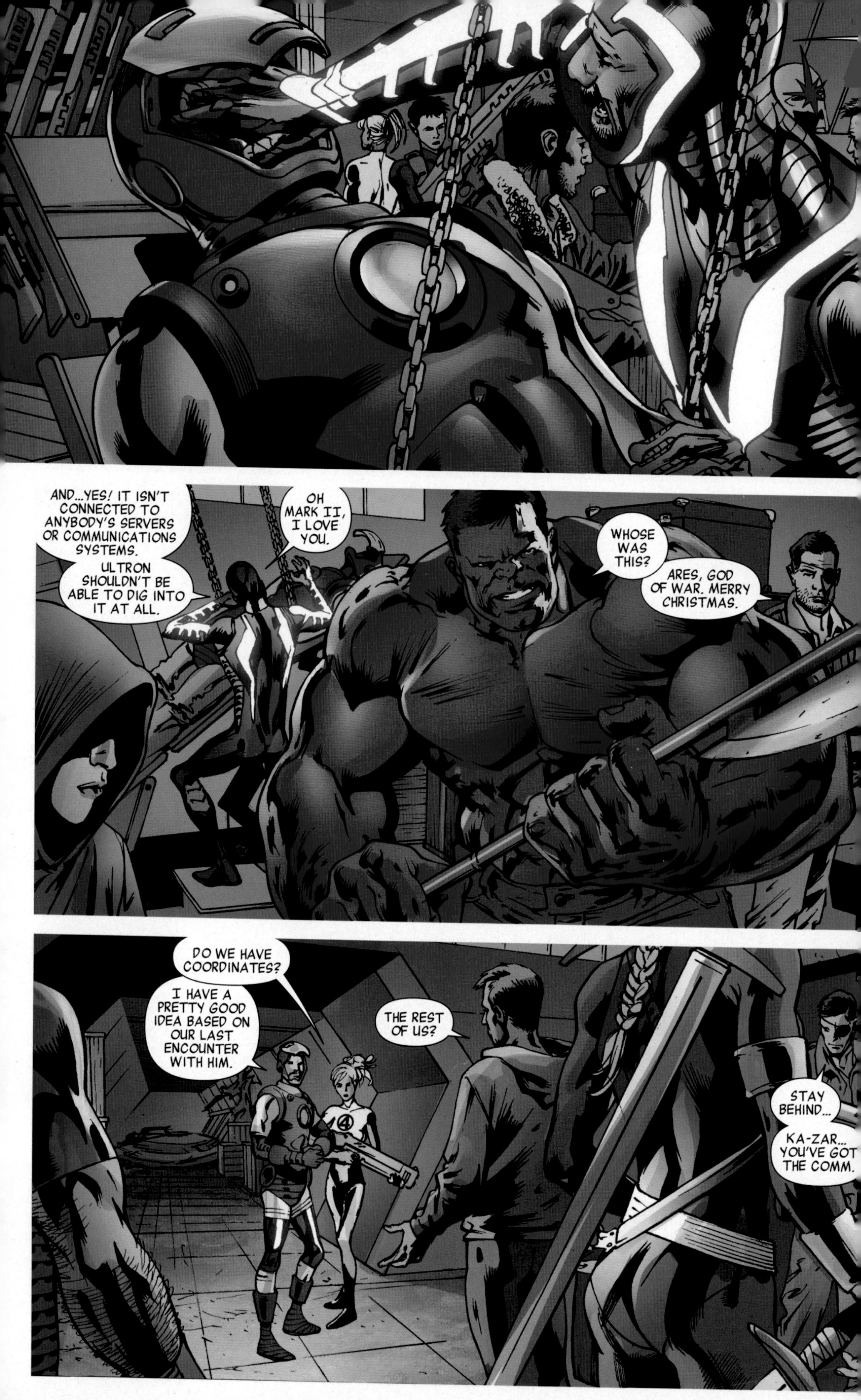
AND...YES! IT ISN'T CONNECTED TO ANYBODY'S SERVERS OR COMMUNICATIONS SYSTEMS.
ULTRON SHOULDN'T BE ABLE TO DIG INTO IT AT ALL.
OH MARK II, I LOVE YOU.
WHOSE WAS THIS?
ARES, GOD OF WAR. MERRY CHRISTMAS.
DO WE HAVE COORDINATES?
I HAVE A PRETTY GOOD IDEA BASED ON OUR LAST ENCOUNTER WITH HIM.
THE REST OF US?
STAY BEHIND...
KA-ZAR... YOU'VE GOT THE COMM.

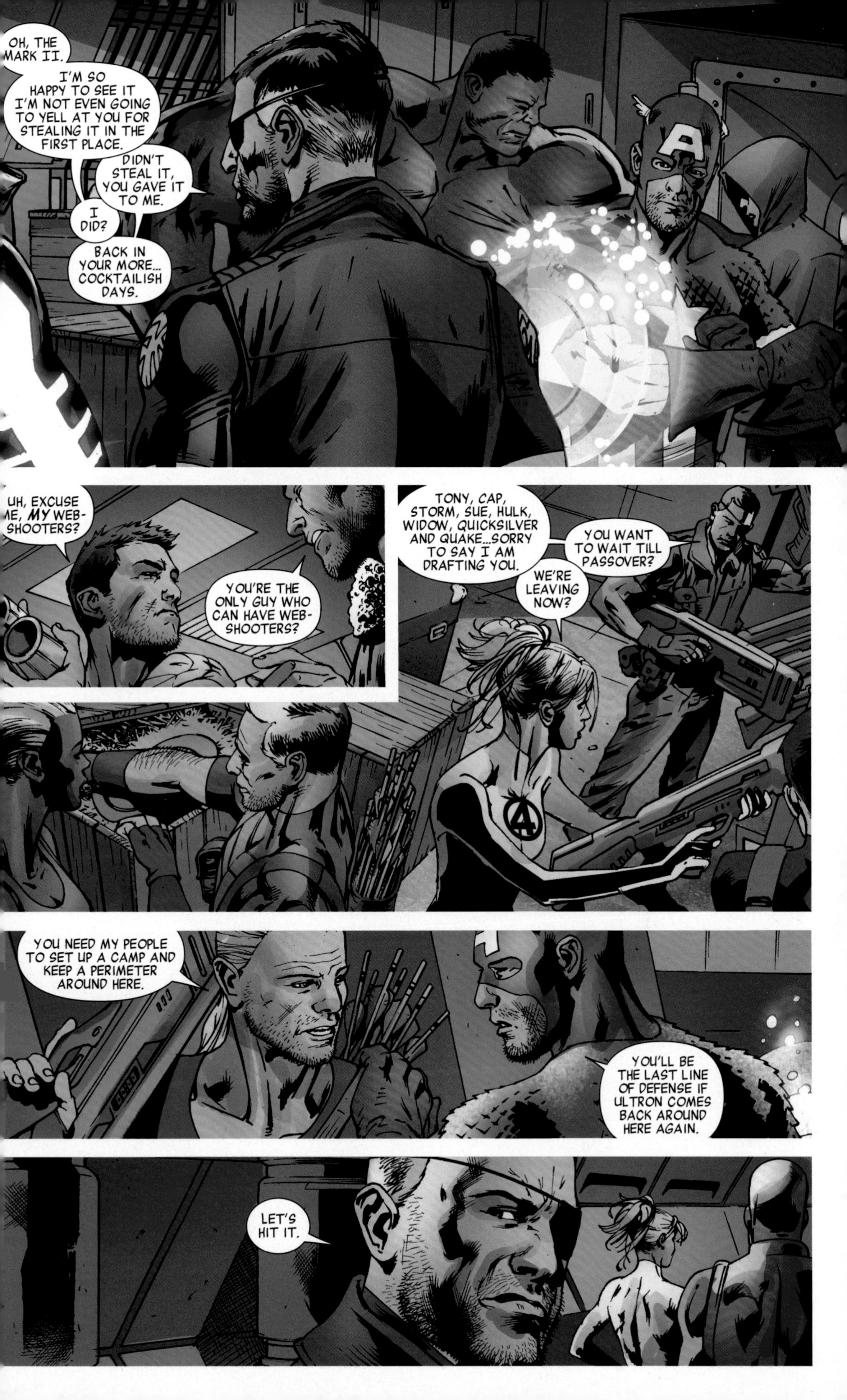
OH, THE MARK II.
I'M SO HAPPY TO SEE IT I'M NOT EVEN GOING TO YELL AT YOU FOR STEALING IT IN THE FIRST PLACE.
DIDN'T STEAL IT, YOU GAVE IT TO ME.
I DID?
BACK IN YOUR MORE... COCKTAILISH DAYS.
UH, EXCUSE ME, MY WEB-SHOOTERS?
YOU'RE THE ONLY GUY WHO CAN HAVE WEB-SHOOTERS?
TONY, CAP, STORM, SUE, HULK, WIDOW, QUICKSILVER AND QUAKE...SORRY TO SAY I AM DRAFTING YOU.
WE'RE LEAVING NOW?
YOU WANT TO WAIT TILL PASSOVER?
YOU NEED MY PEOPLE TO SET UP A CAMP AND KEEP A PERIMETER AROUND HERE.
YOU'LL BE THE LAST LINE OF DEFENSE IF ULTRON COMES BACK AROUND HERE AGAIN.
LET'S HIT IT.

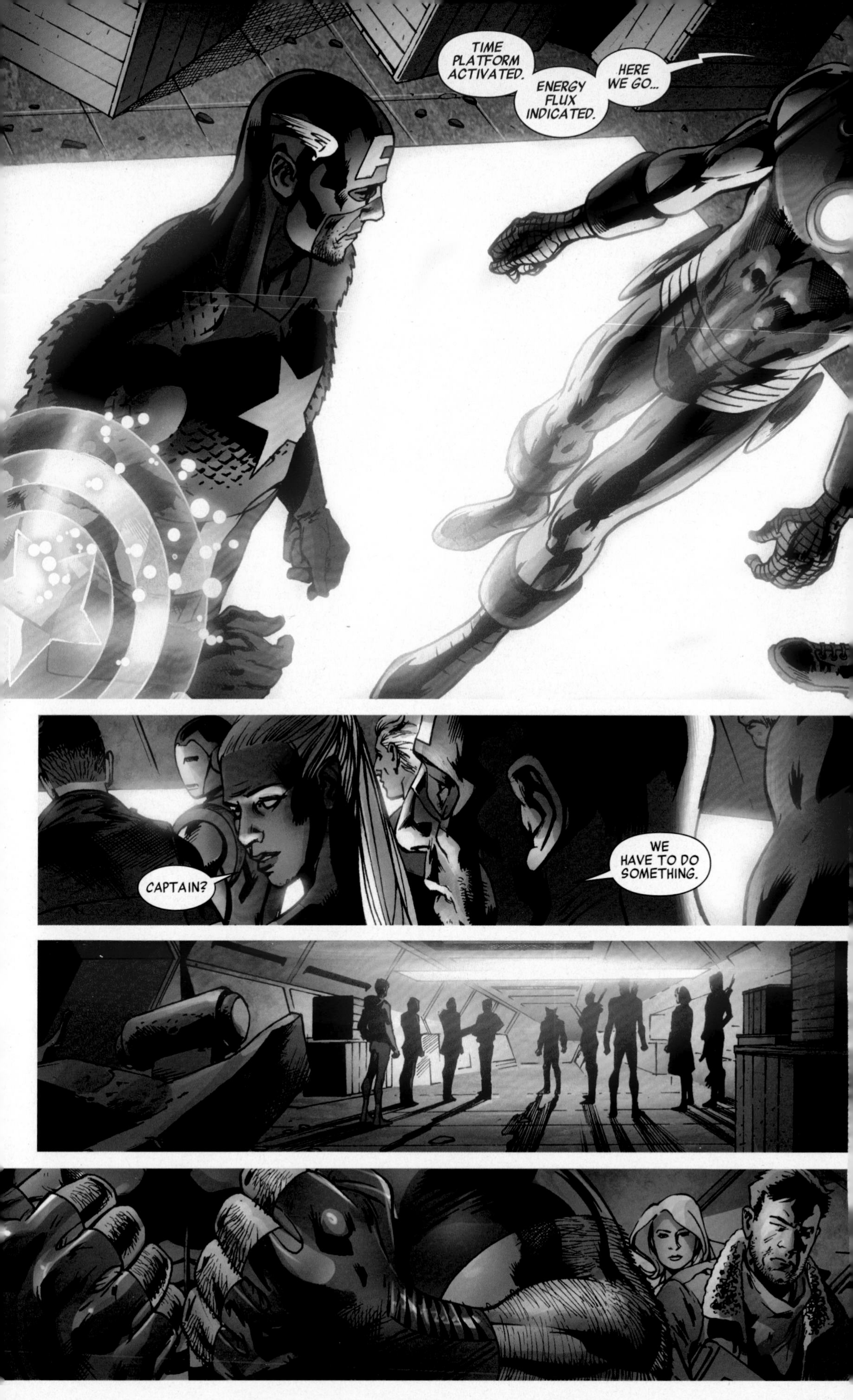
TIME PLATFORM ACTIVATED.
ENERGY FLUX INDICATED.
HERE WE GO...
CAPTAIN?
WE HAVE TO DO SOMETHING.

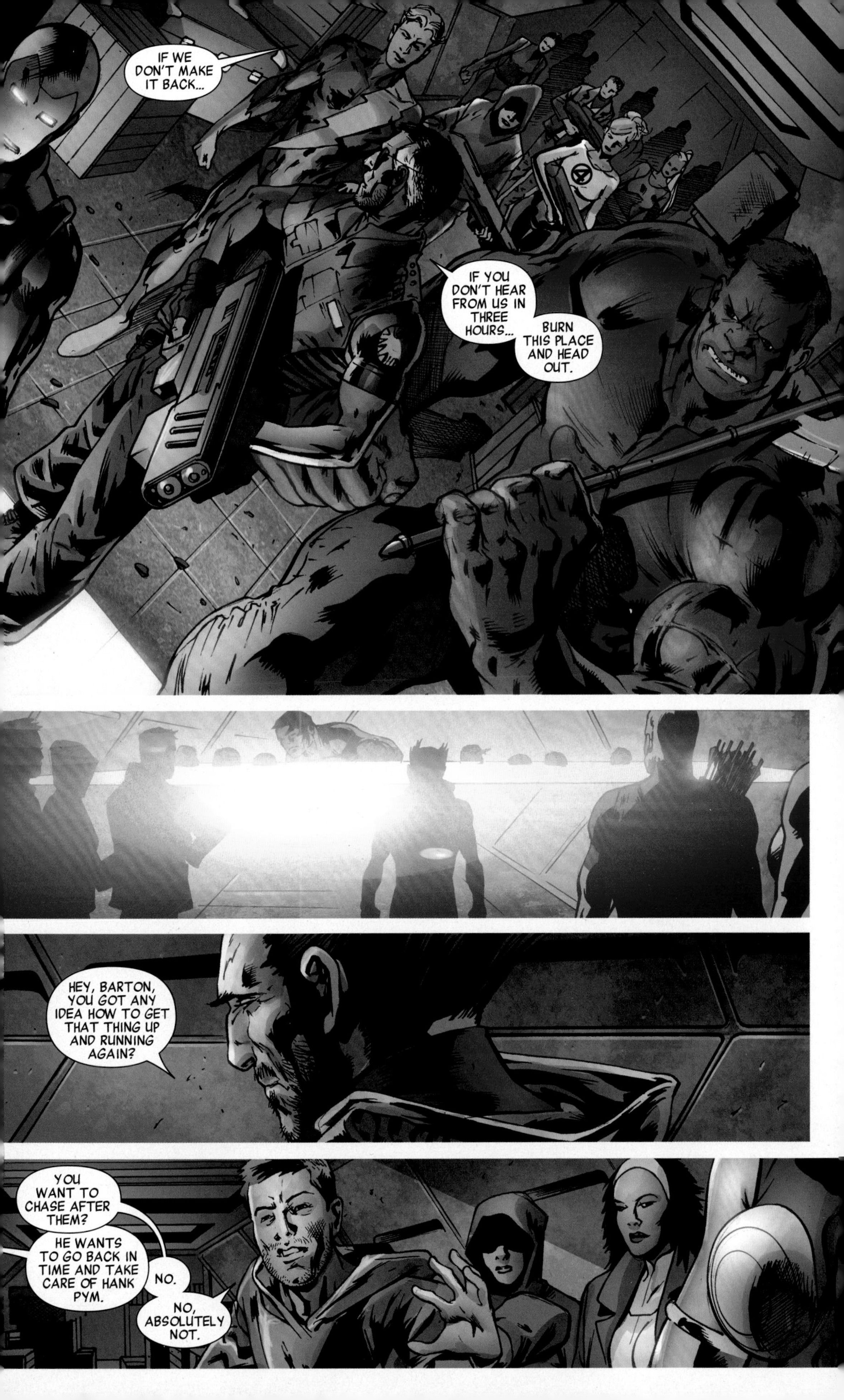
IF WE DON'T MAKE IT BACK...
IF YOU DON'T HEAR FROM US IN THREE HOURS...
BURN THIS PLACE AND HEAD OUT.
HEY, BARTON, YOU GOT ANY IDEA HOW TO GET THAT THING UP AND RUNNING AGAIN?
YOU WANT TO CHASE AFTER THEM?
HE WANTS TO GO BACK IN TIME AND TAKE CARE OF HANK PYM.
NO.
NO, ABSOLUTELY NOT.

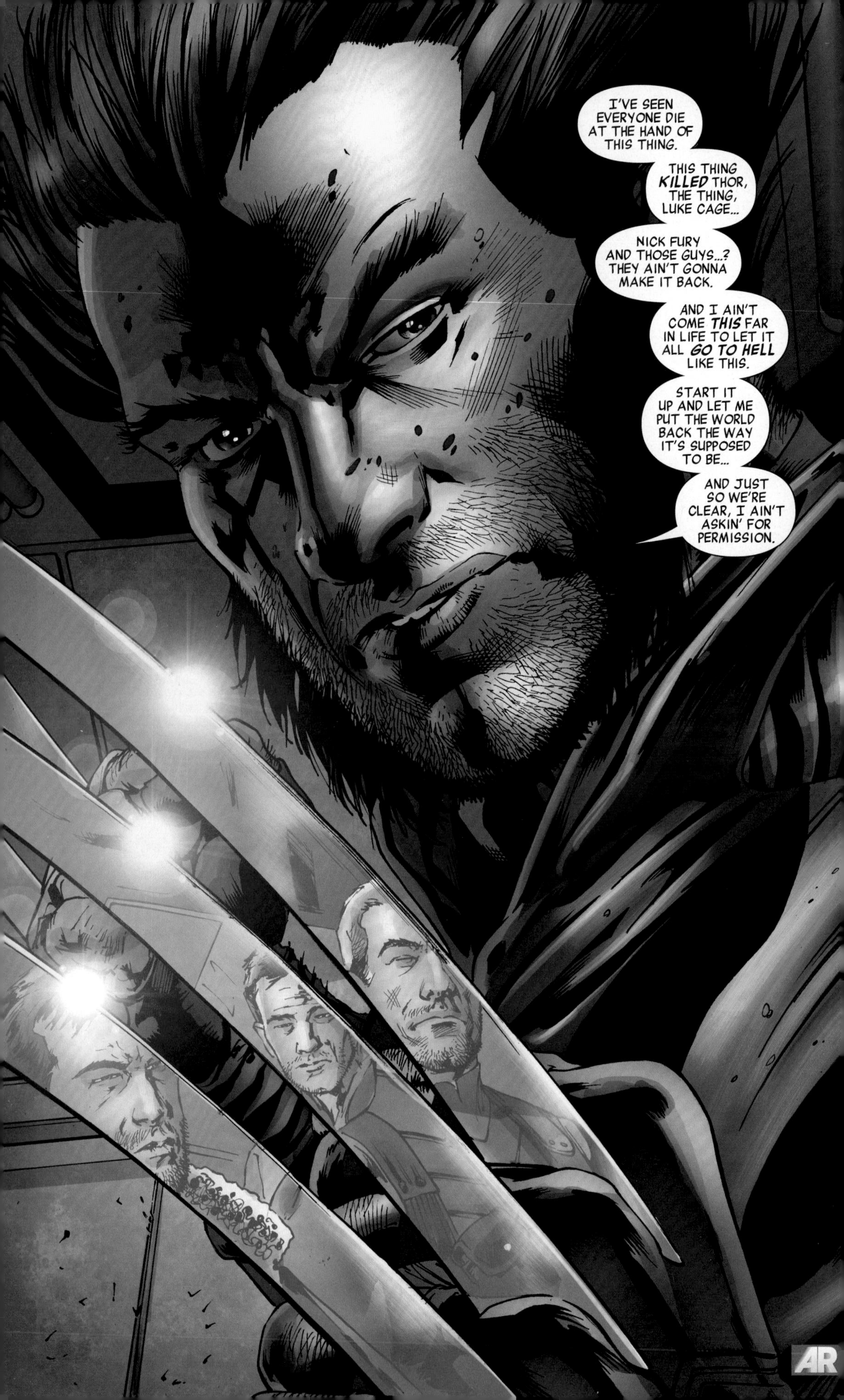

I'VE SEEN EVERYONE DIE AT THE HAND OF THIS THING.
THIS THING KILLED THOR, THE THING, LUKE CAGE...
NICK FURY AND THOSE GUYS...? THEY AIN'T GONNA MAKE IT BACK.
AND I AIN'T COME THIS FAR IN LIFE TO LET IT ALL GO TO HELL LIKE THIS.
START IT UP AND LET ME PUT THE WORLD BACK THE WAY IT'S SUPPOSED TO BE...
AND JUST SO WE'RE CLEAR, I AIN'T ASKIN' FOR PERMISSION.

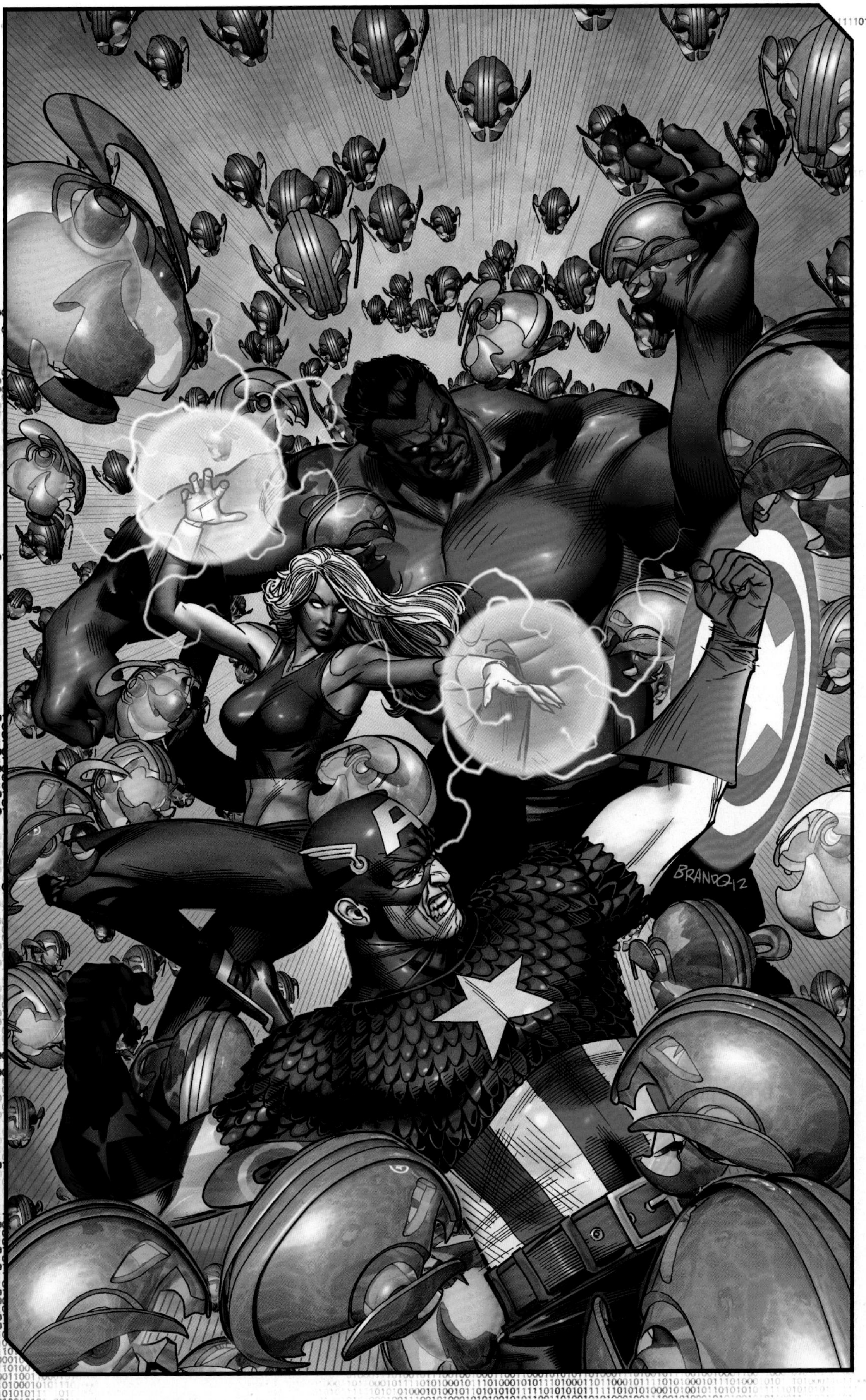
BRANDO '12

AGE OF ULTRON #6

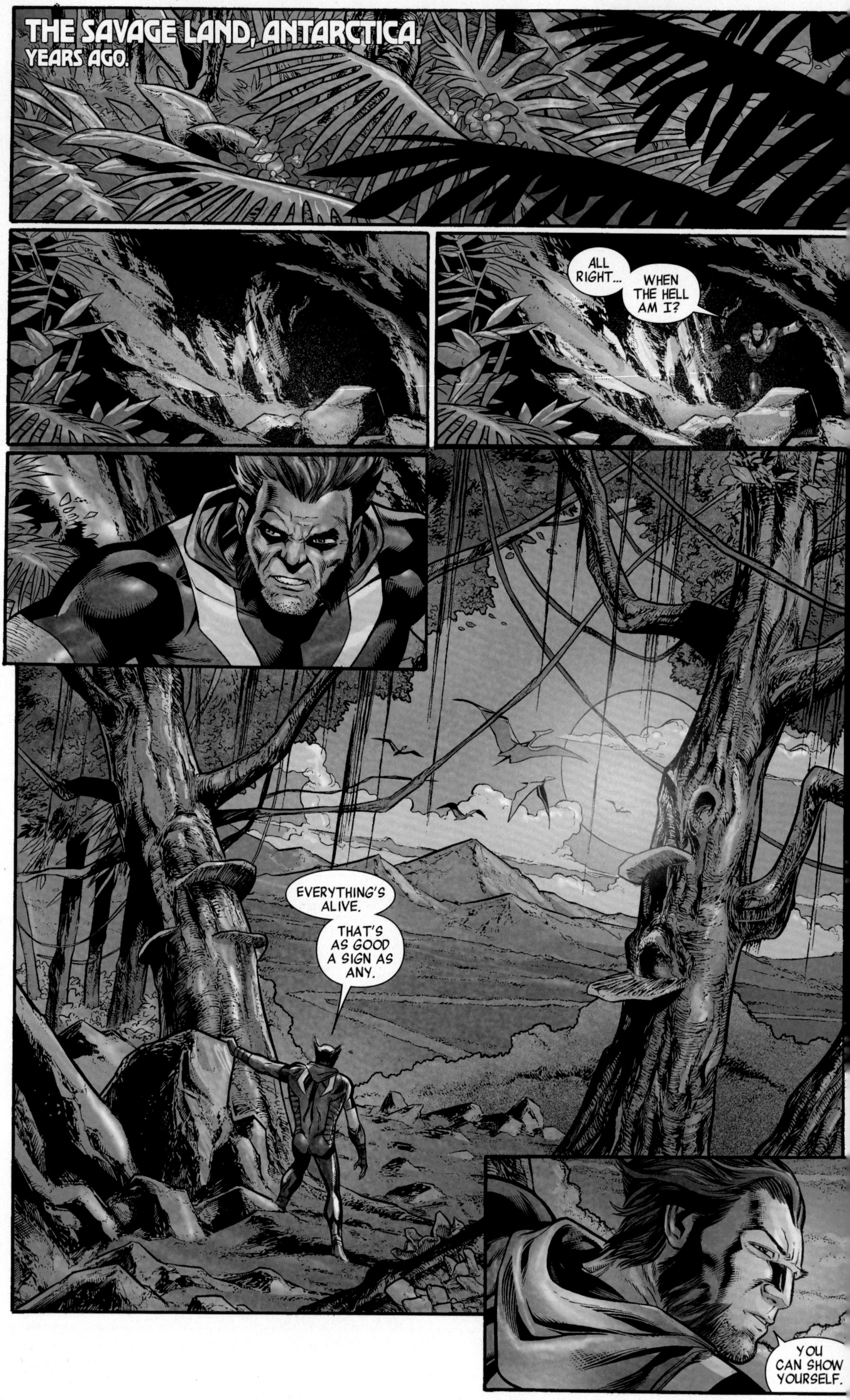

THE SAVAGE LAND, ANTARCTICA.
YEARS AGO.
ALL RIGHT...
WHEN THE HELL AM I?
EVERYTHING'S ALIVE.
THAT'S AS GOOD A SIGN AS ANY.
YOU CAN SHOW YOURSELF.

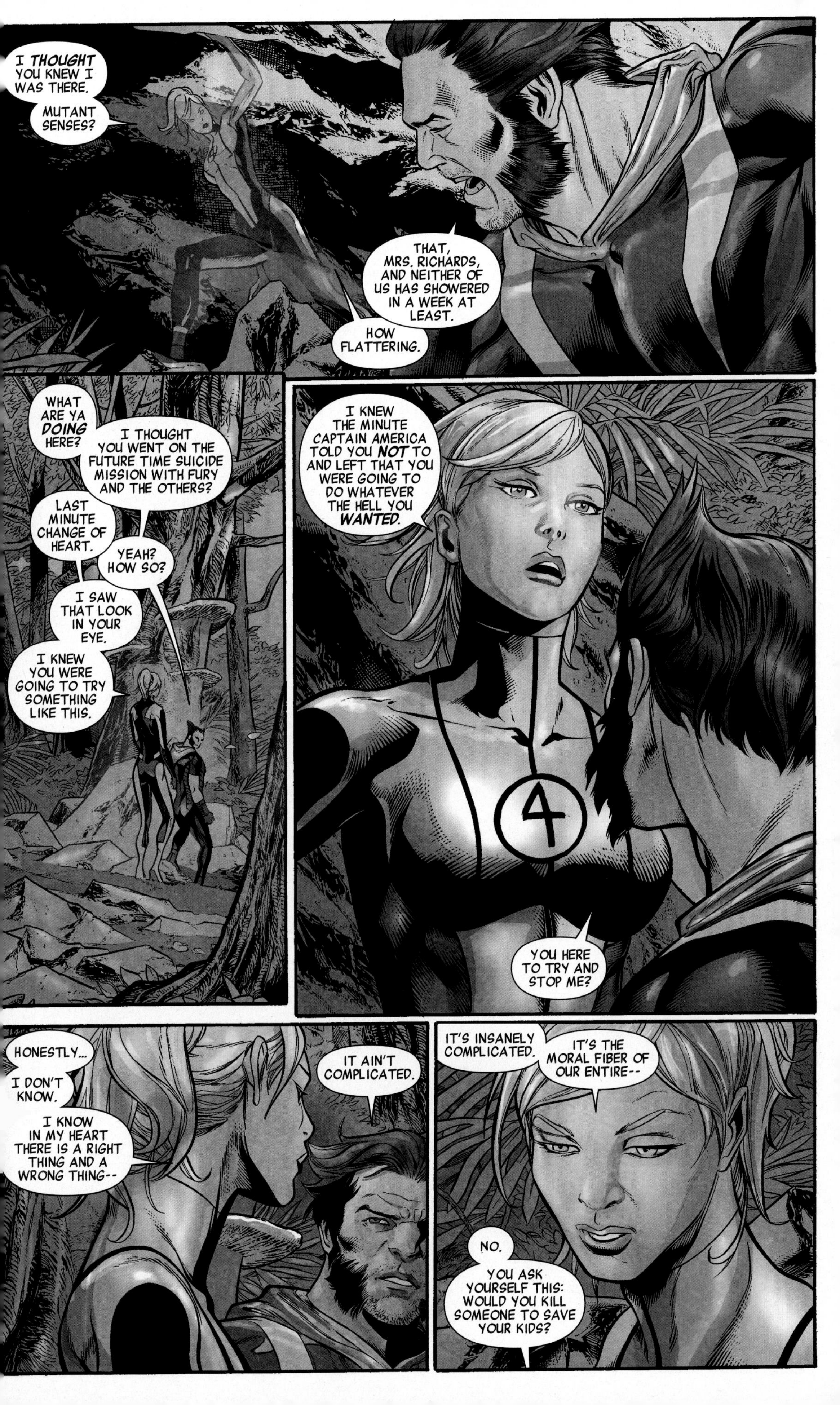

I THOUGHT YOU KNEW I WAS THERE.
MUTANT SENSES?
THAT, MRS. RICHARDS, AND NEITHER OF US HAS SHOWERED IN A WEEK AT LEAST.
HOW FLATTERING.
WHAT ARE YA DOING HERE?
I THOUGHT YOU WENT ON THE FUTURE TIME SUICIDE MISSION WITH FURY AND THE OTHERS?
LAST MINUTE CHANGE OF HEART.
YEAH? HOW SO?
I SAW THAT LOOK IN YOUR EYE.
I KNEW YOU WERE GOING TO TRY SOMETHING LIKE THIS.
I KNEW THE MINUTE CAPTAIN AMERICA TOLD YOU NOT TO AND LEFT THAT YOU WERE GOING TO DO WHATEVER THE HELL YOU WANTED.
YOU HERE TO TRY AND STOP ME?
HONESTLY...
I DON'T KNOW.
I KNOW IN MY HEART THERE IS A RIGHT THING AND A WRONG THING--
IT AIN'T COMPLICATED.
IT'S INSANELY COMPLICATED.
IT'S THE MORAL FIBER OF OUR ENTIRE--
NO.
YOU ASK YOURSELF THIS: WOULD YOU KILL SOMEONE TO SAVE YOUR KIDS?

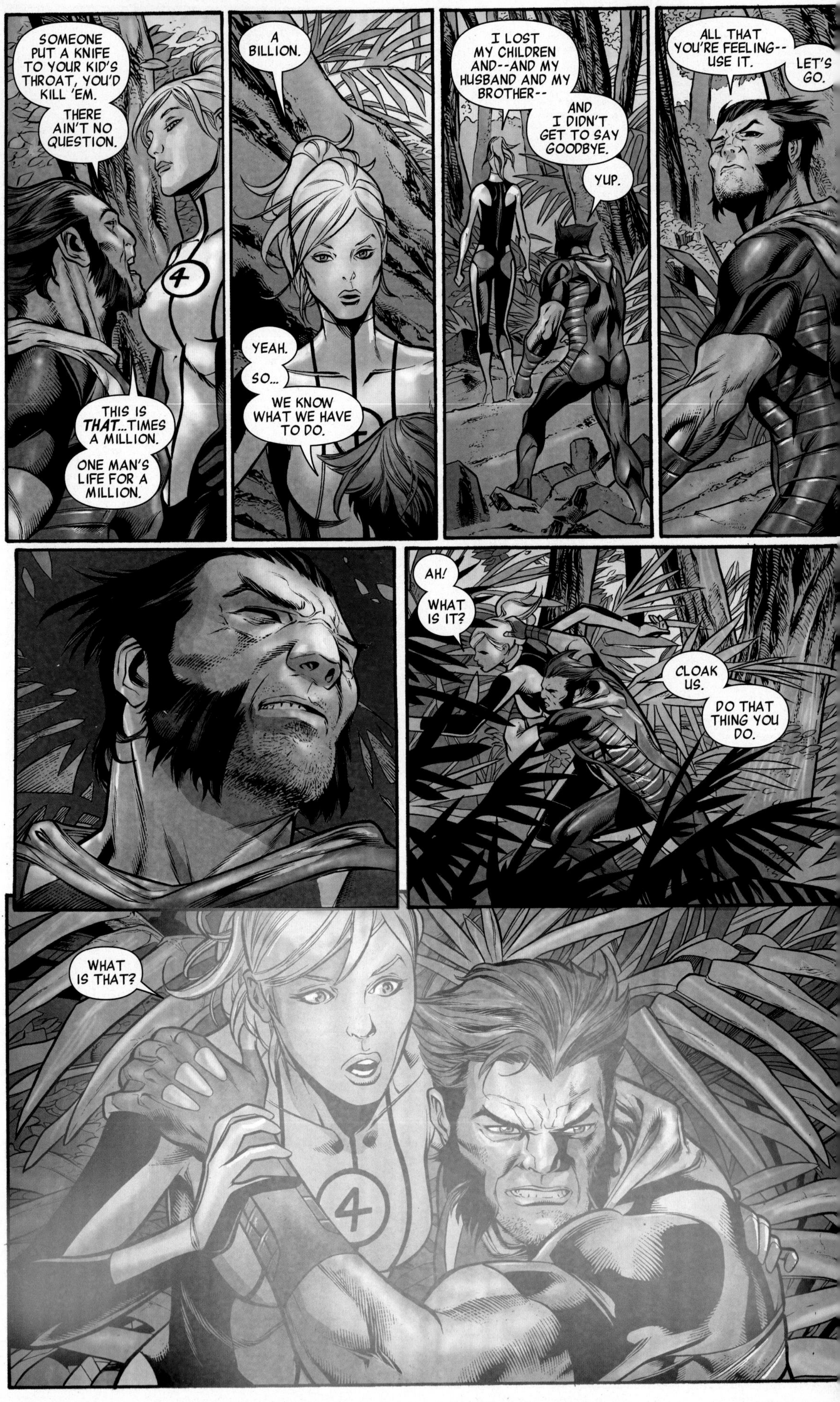
SOMEONE PUT A KNIFE TO YOUR KID'S THROAT, YOU'D KILL 'EM.
THERE AIN'T NO QUESTION.
THIS IS THAT...TIMES A MILLION.
ONE MAN'S LIFE FOR A MILLION.
A BILLION.
YEAH.
SO...
WE KNOW WHAT WE HAVE TO DO.
I LOST MY CHILDREN AND--AND MY HUSBAND AND MY BROTHER--
AND I DIDN'T GET TO SAY GOODBYE.
YUP.
ALL THAT YOU'RE FEELING--USE IT.
LET'S GO.
AH!
WHAT IS IT?
CLOAK US.
DO THAT THING YOU DO.
WHAT IS THAT?

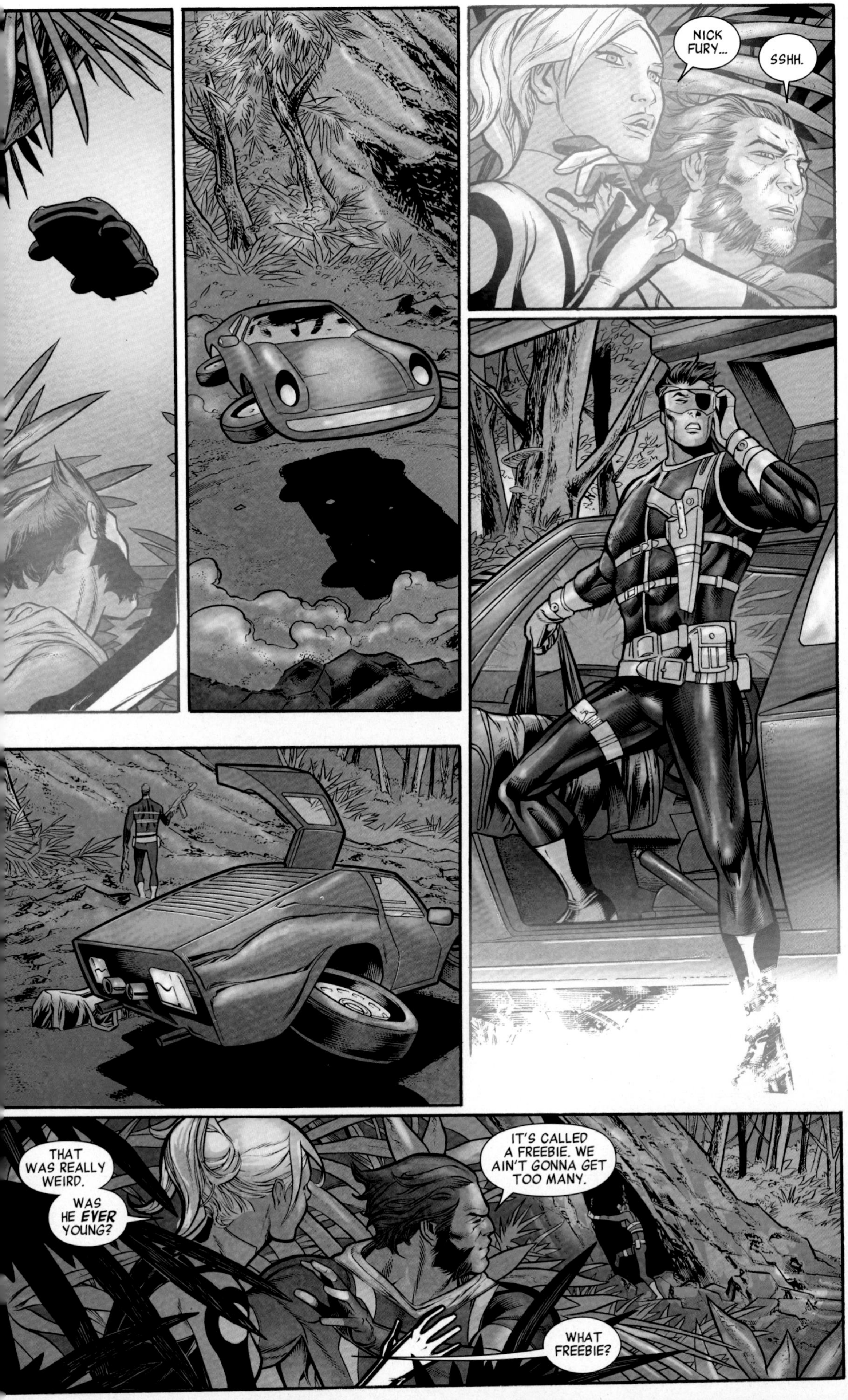
NICK FURY...
SSHH.
THAT WAS REALLY WEIRD.
WAS HE *EVER* YOUNG?
IT'S CALLED A FREEBIE. WE AIN'T GONNA GET TOO MANY.
WHAT FREEBIE?

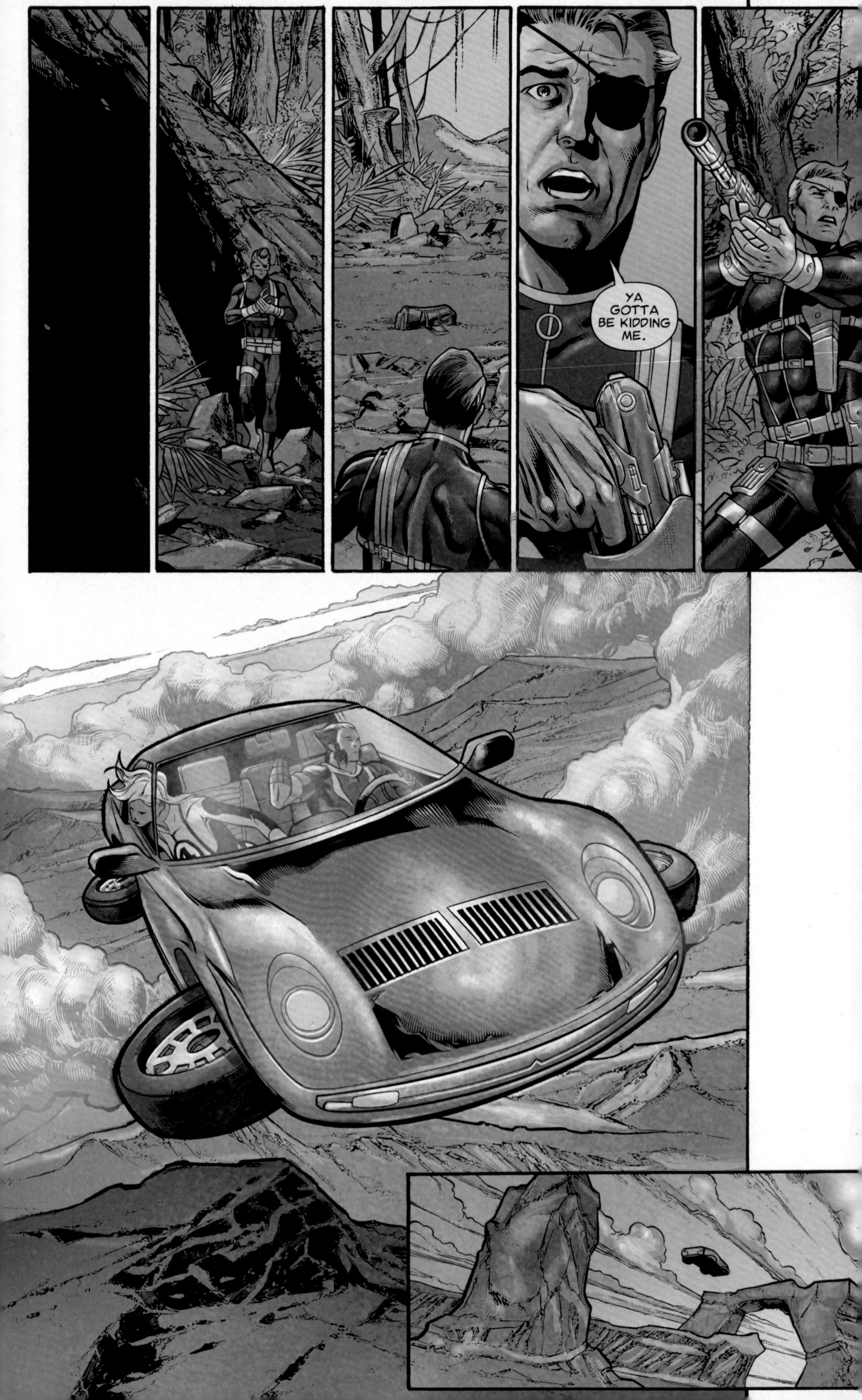
YA GOTTA BE KIDDING ME.

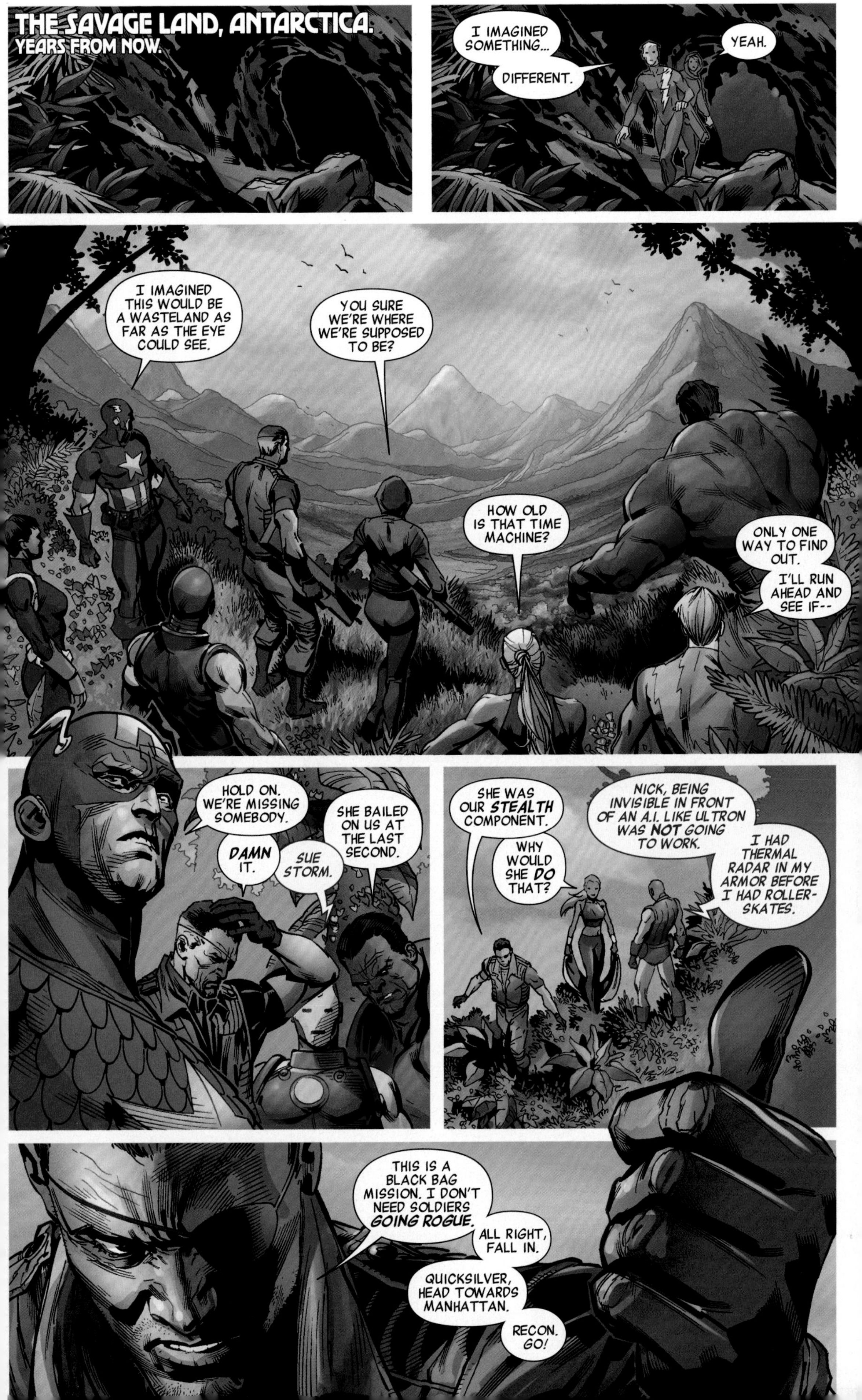
THE SAVAGE LAND, ANTARCTICA.
YEARS FROM NOW.
I IMAGINED SOMETHING...
DIFFERENT.
YEAH.
I IMAGINED THIS WOULD BE A WASTELAND AS FAR AS THE EYE COULD SEE.
YOU SURE WE'RE WHERE WE'RE SUPPOSED TO BE?
HOW OLD IS THAT TIME MACHINE?
ONLY ONE WAY TO FIND OUT.
I'LL RUN AHEAD AND SEE IF--
HOLD ON. WE'RE MISSING SOMEBODY.
DAMN IT.
SUE STORM.
SHE BAILED ON US AT THE LAST SECOND.
SHE WAS OUR STEALTH COMPONENT.
WHY WOULD SHE DO THAT?
NICK, BEING INVISIBLE IN FRONT OF AN A.I. LIKE ULTRON WAS NOT GOING TO WORK.
I HAD THERMAL RADAR IN MY ARMOR BEFORE I HAD ROLLER-SKATES.
THIS IS A BLACK BAG MISSION. I DON'T NEED SOLDIERS GOING ROGUE.
ALL RIGHT, FALL IN.
QUICKSILVER, HEAD TOWARDS MANHATTAN.
RECON. GO!

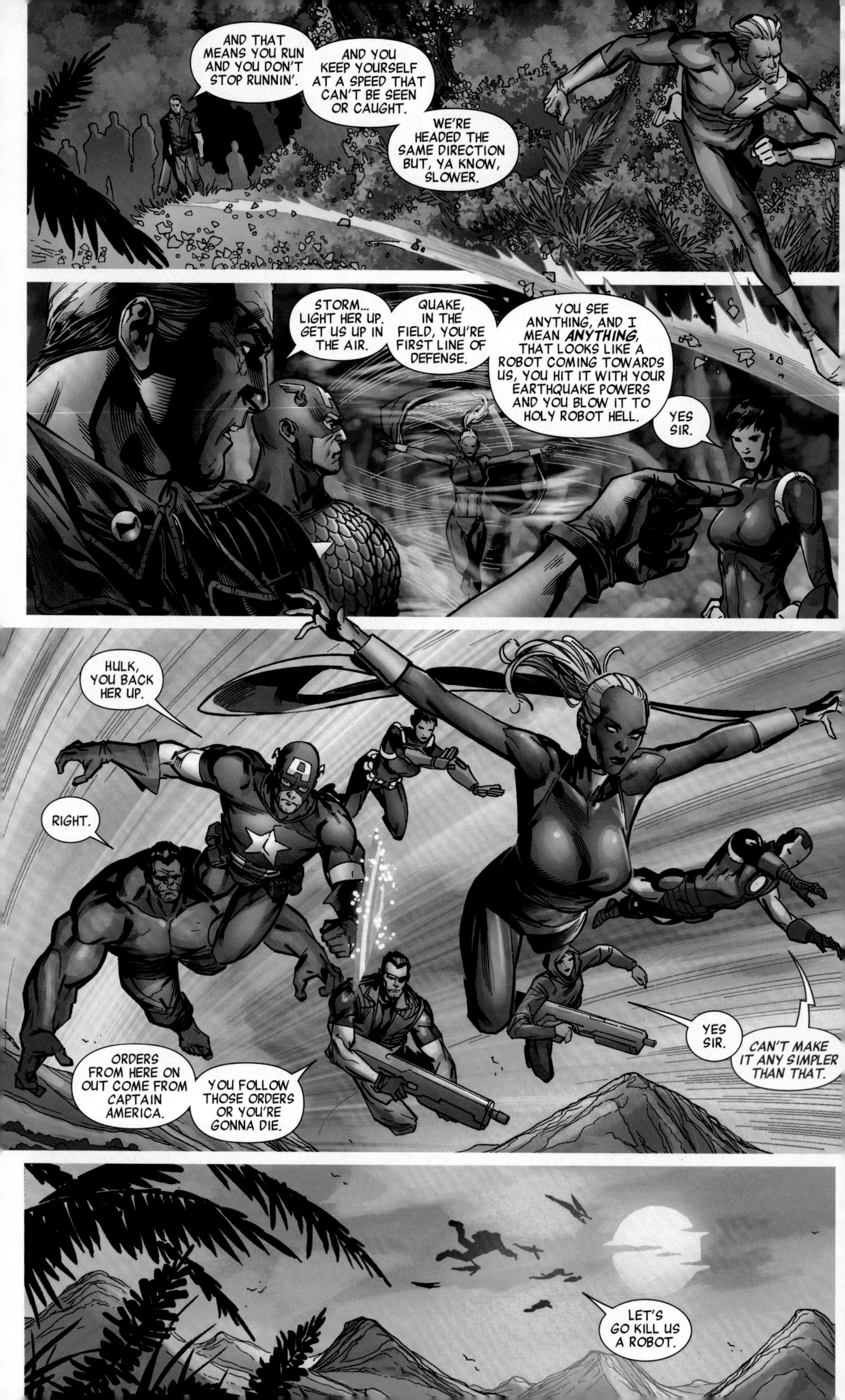
AND THAT MEANS YOU RUN AND YOU DON'T STOP RUNNIN'.
AND YOU KEEP YOURSELF AT A SPEED THAT CAN'T BE SEEN OR CAUGHT.
WE'RE HEADED THE SAME DIRECTION BUT, YA KNOW, SLOWER.
STORM... LIGHT HER UP. GET US UP IN THE AIR.
QUAKE, IN THE FIELD, YOU'RE FIRST LINE OF DEFENSE.
YOU SEE ANYTHING, AND I MEAN ANYTHING, THAT LOOKS LIKE A ROBOT COMING TOWARDS US, YOU HIT IT WITH YOUR EARTHQUAKE POWERS AND YOU BLOW IT TO HOLY ROBOT HELL.
YES SIR.
HULK, YOU BACK HER UP.
RIGHT.
ORDERS FROM HERE ON OUT COME FROM CAPTAIN AMERICA.
YOU FOLLOW THOSE ORDERS OR YOU'RE GONNA DIE.
YES SIR.
CAN'T MAKE IT ANY SIMPLER THAN THAT.
LET'S GO KILL US A ROBOT.

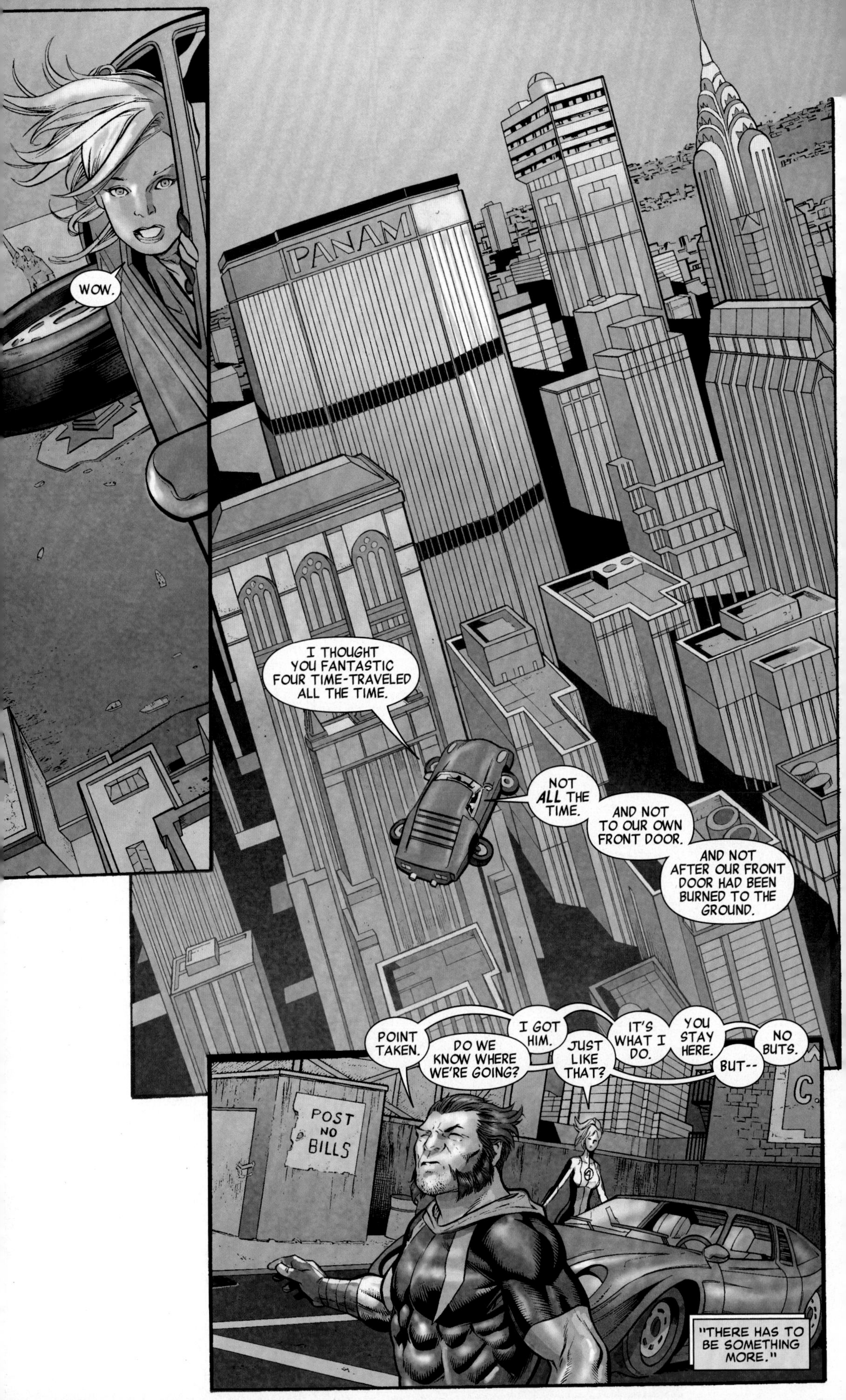
WOW.
I THOUGHT YOU FANTASTIC FOUR TIME-TRAVELED ALL THE TIME.
PANAM
NOT ALL THE TIME.
AND NOT TO OUR OWN FRONT DOOR.
AND NOT AFTER OUR FRONT DOOR HAD BEEN BURNED TO THE GROUND.
POINT TAKEN.
DO WE KNOW WHERE WE'RE GOING?
I GOT HIM.
JUST LIKE THAT?
IT'S WHAT I DO.
YOU STAY HERE.
BUT--
NO BUTS.
POST NO BILLS
"THERE HAS TO BE SOMETHING MORE."

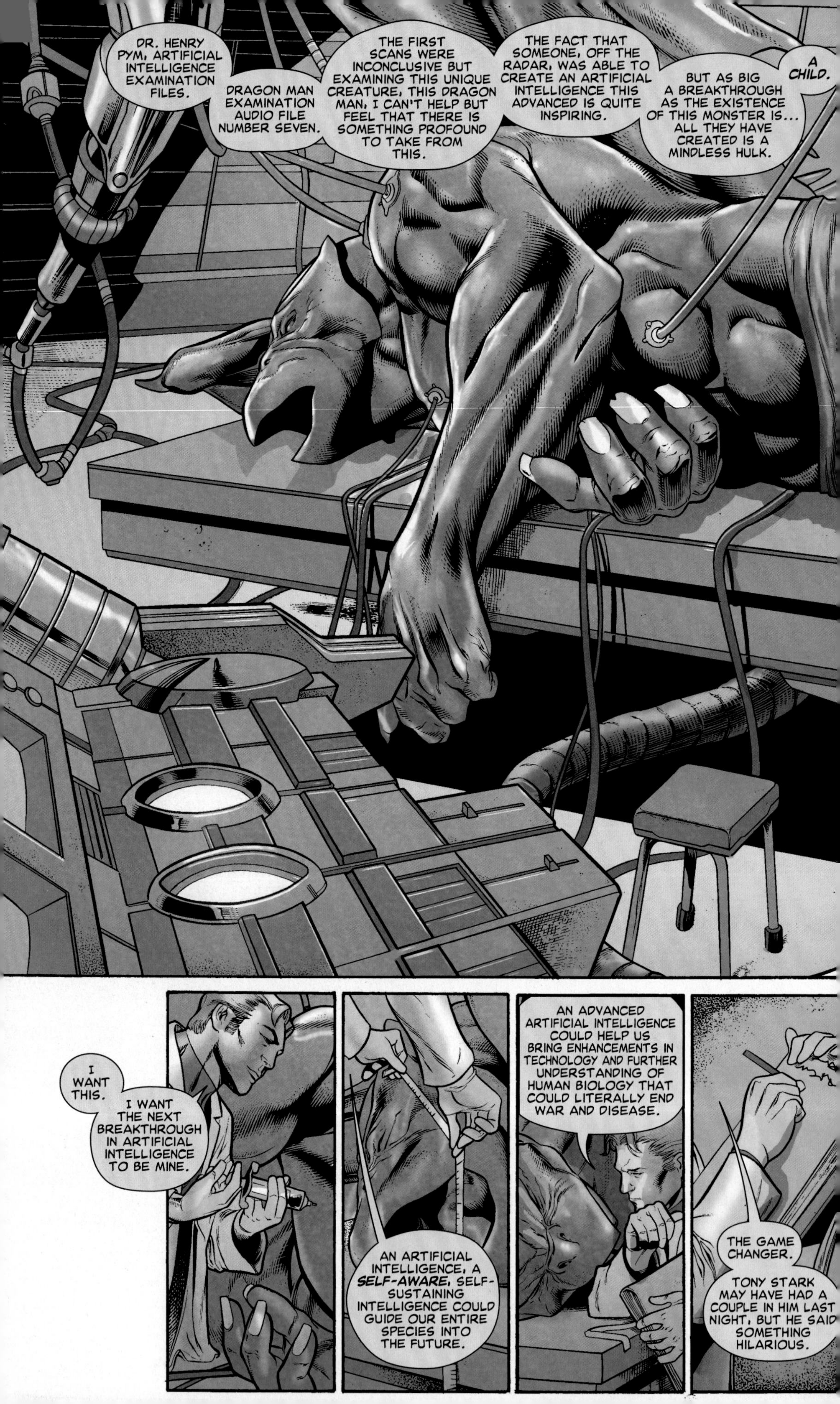
DR. HENRY PYM, ARTIFICIAL INTELLIGENCE EXAMINATION FILES.
DRAGON MAN EXAMINATION AUDIO FILE NUMBER SEVEN.
THE FIRST SCANS WERE INCONCLUSIVE BUT EXAMINING THIS UNIQUE CREATURE, THIS DRAGON MAN, I CAN'T HELP BUT FEEL THAT THERE IS SOMETHING PROFOUND TO TAKE FROM THIS.
THE FACT THAT SOMEONE, OFF THE RADAR, WAS ABLE TO CREATE AN ARTIFICIAL INTELLIGENCE THIS ADVANCED IS QUITE INSPIRING.
BUT AS BIG A BREAKTHROUGH AS THE EXISTENCE OF THIS MONSTER IS... ALL THEY HAVE CREATED IS A MINDLESS HULK.
A *CHILD.*
I WANT THIS.
I WANT THE NEXT BREAKTHROUGH IN ARTIFICIAL INTELLIGENCE TO BE MINE.
AN ARTIFICIAL INTELLIGENCE, A *SELF-AWARE*, SELF-SUSTAINING INTELLIGENCE COULD GUIDE OUR ENTIRE SPECIES INTO THE FUTURE.
AN ADVANCED ARTIFICIAL INTELLIGENCE COULD HELP US BRING ENHANCEMENTS IN TECHNOLOGY AND FURTHER UNDERSTANDING OF HUMAN BIOLOGY THAT COULD LITERALLY END WAR AND DISEASE.
THE GAME CHANGER.
TONY STARK MAY HAVE HAD A COUPLE IN HIM LAST NIGHT, BUT HE SAID SOMETHING HILARIOUS.

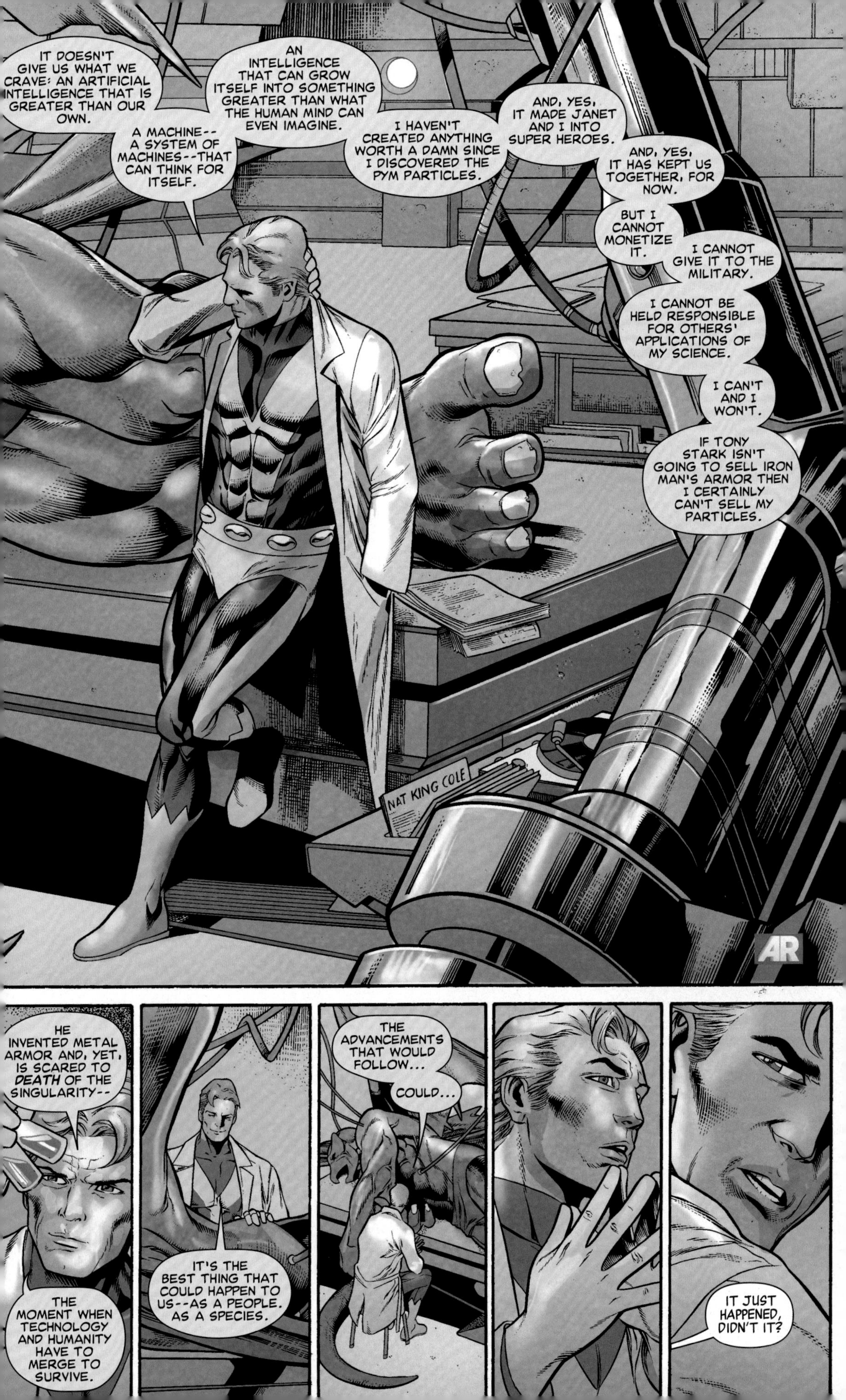
IT DOESN'T GIVE US WHAT WE CRAVE: AN ARTIFICIAL INTELLIGENCE THAT IS GREATER THAN OUR OWN.
A MACHINE-- A SYSTEM OF MACHINES--THAT CAN THINK FOR ITSELF.
AN INTELLIGENCE THAT CAN GROW ITSELF INTO SOMETHING GREATER THAN WHAT THE HUMAN MIND CAN EVEN IMAGINE.
I HAVEN'T CREATED ANYTHING WORTH A DAMN SINCE I DISCOVERED THE PYM PARTICLES.
AND, YES, IT MADE JANET AND I INTO SUPER HEROES.
AND, YES, IT HAS KEPT US TOGETHER, FOR NOW.
BUT I CANNOT MONETIZE IT.
I CANNOT GIVE IT TO THE MILITARY.
I CANNOT BE HELD RESPONSIBLE FOR OTHERS' APPLICATIONS OF MY SCIENCE.
I CAN'T AND I WON'T.
IF TONY STARK ISN'T GOING TO SELL IRON MAN'S ARMOR THEN I CERTAINLY CAN'T SELL MY PARTICLES.
NAT KING COLE
AR
HE INVENTED METAL ARMOR AND, YET, IS SCARED TO *DEATH* OF THE SINGULARITY--
THE MOMENT WHEN TECHNOLOGY AND HUMANITY HAVE TO MERGE TO SURVIVE.
IT'S THE BEST THING THAT COULD HAPPEN TO US--AS A PEOPLE. AS A SPECIES.
THE ADVANCEMENTS THAT WOULD FOLLOW...
COULD...
IT JUST HAPPENED, DIDN'T IT?

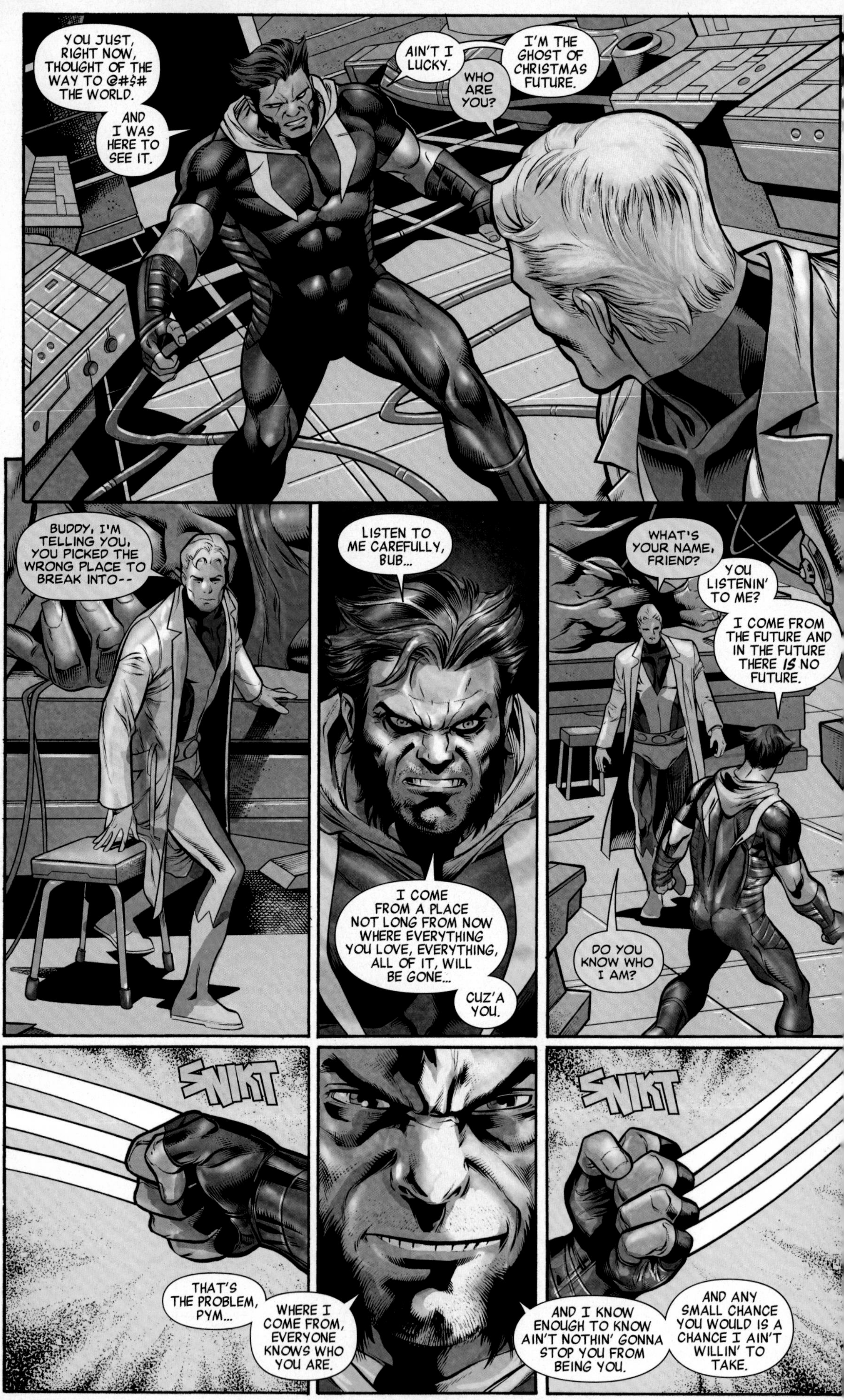
YOU JUST, RIGHT NOW, THOUGHT OF THE WAY TO @#$# THE WORLD.
AND I WAS HERE TO SEE IT.
AIN'T I LUCKY.
WHO ARE YOU?
I'M THE GHOST OF CHRISTMAS FUTURE.
BUDDY, I'M TELLING YOU, YOU PICKED THE WRONG PLACE TO BREAK INTO--
LISTEN TO ME CAREFULLY, BUB...
I COME FROM A PLACE NOT LONG FROM NOW WHERE EVERYTHING YOU LOVE, EVERYTHING, ALL OF IT, WILL BE GONE...
CUZ'A YOU.
WHAT'S YOUR NAME, FRIEND?
YOU LISTENIN' TO ME?
I COME FROM THE FUTURE AND IN THE FUTURE THERE IS NO FUTURE.
DO YOU KNOW WHO I AM?
SNIKT
THAT'S THE PROBLEM, PYM...
WHERE I COME FROM, EVERYONE KNOWS WHO YOU ARE.
SNIKT
AND I KNOW ENOUGH TO KNOW AIN'T NOTHIN' GONNA STOP YOU FROM BEING YOU.
AND ANY SMALL CHANCE YOU WOULD IS A CHANCE I AIN'T WILLIN' TO TAKE.

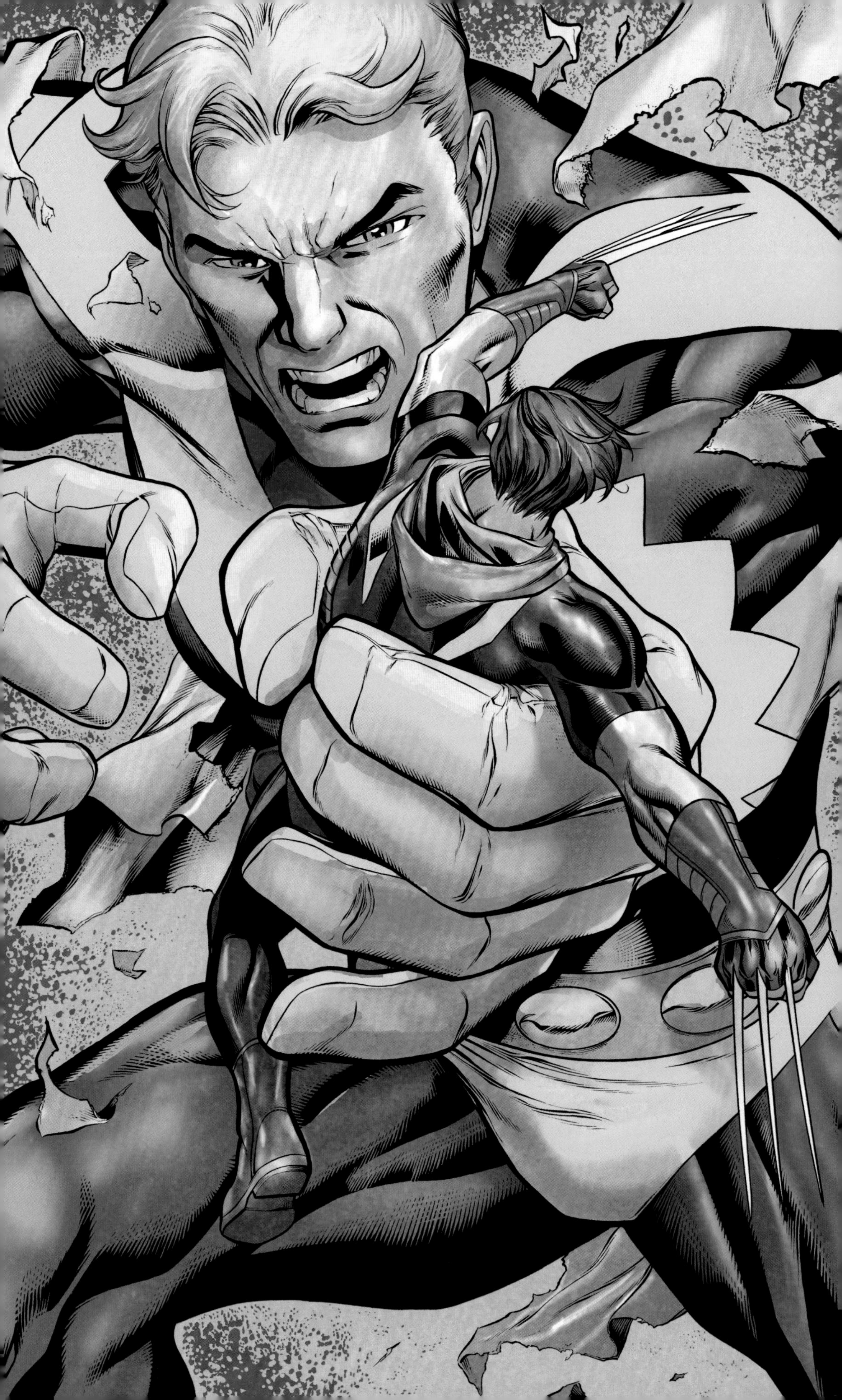

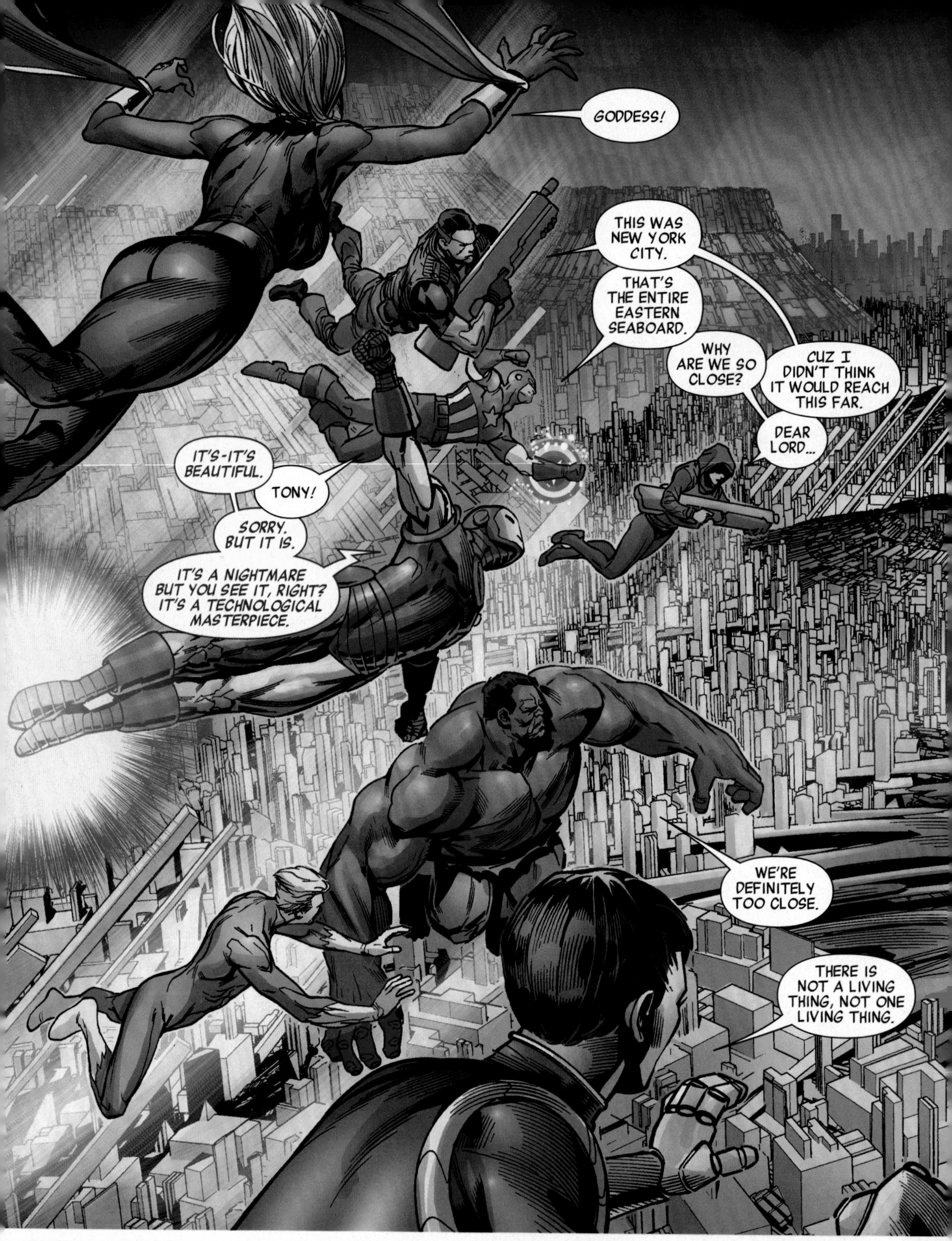
GODDESS!
THIS WAS NEW YORK CITY.
THAT'S THE ENTIRE EASTERN SEABOARD.
WHY ARE WE SO CLOSE?
CUZ I DIDN'T THINK IT WOULD REACH THIS FAR.
DEAR LORD...
IT'S-IT'S BEAUTIFUL.
TONY!
SORRY. BUT IT IS.
IT'S A NIGHTMARE BUT YOU SEE IT, RIGHT? IT'S A TECHNOLOGICAL MASTERPIECE.
WE'RE DEFINITELY TOO CLOSE.
THERE IS NOT A LIVING THING, NOT ONE LIVING THING.

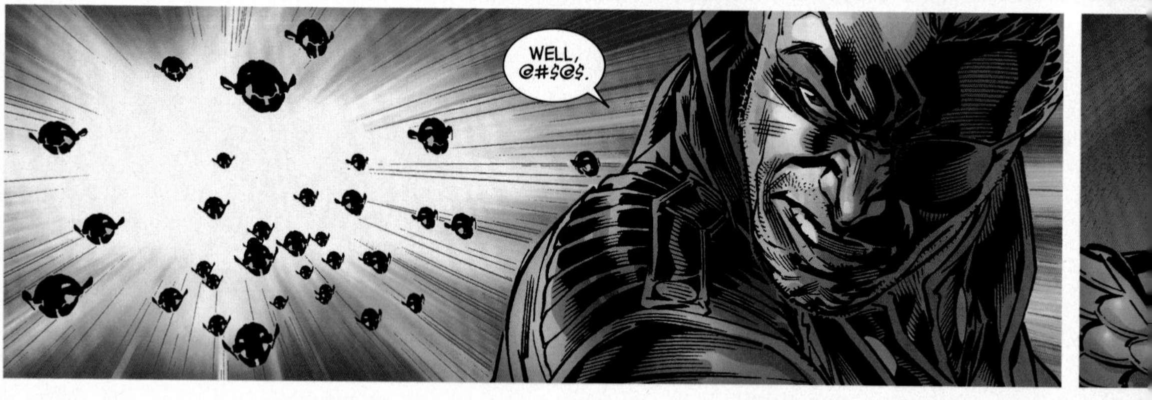
WELL, @#$@$.

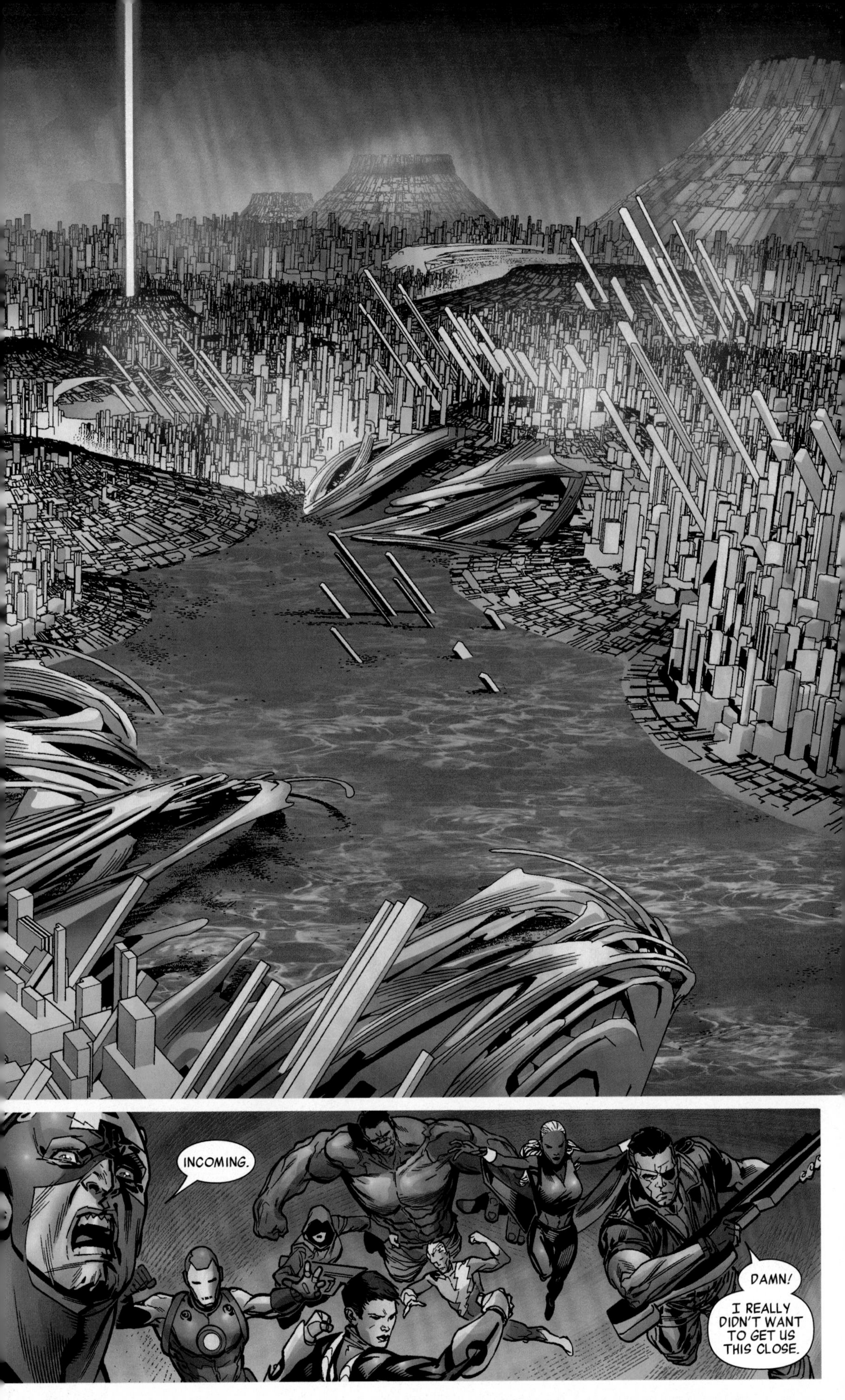

INCOMING.
DAMN!
I REALLY DIDN'T WANT TO GET US THIS CLOSE.

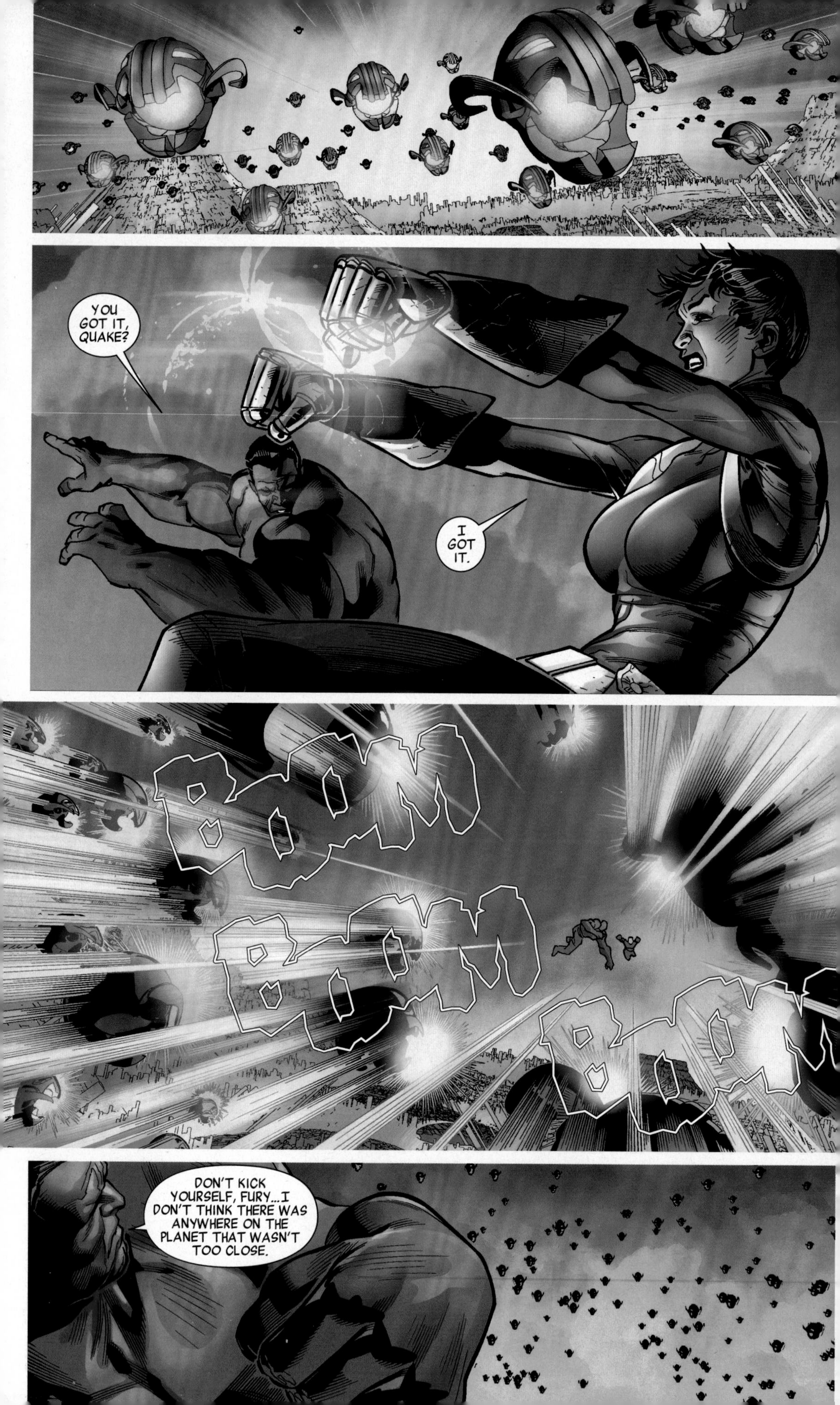

YOU GOT IT, QUAKE?
I GOT IT.
BOOM
BOOM
DON'T KICK YOURSELF, FURY...I DON'T THINK THERE WAS ANYWHERE ON THE PLANET THAT WASN'T TOO CLOSE.

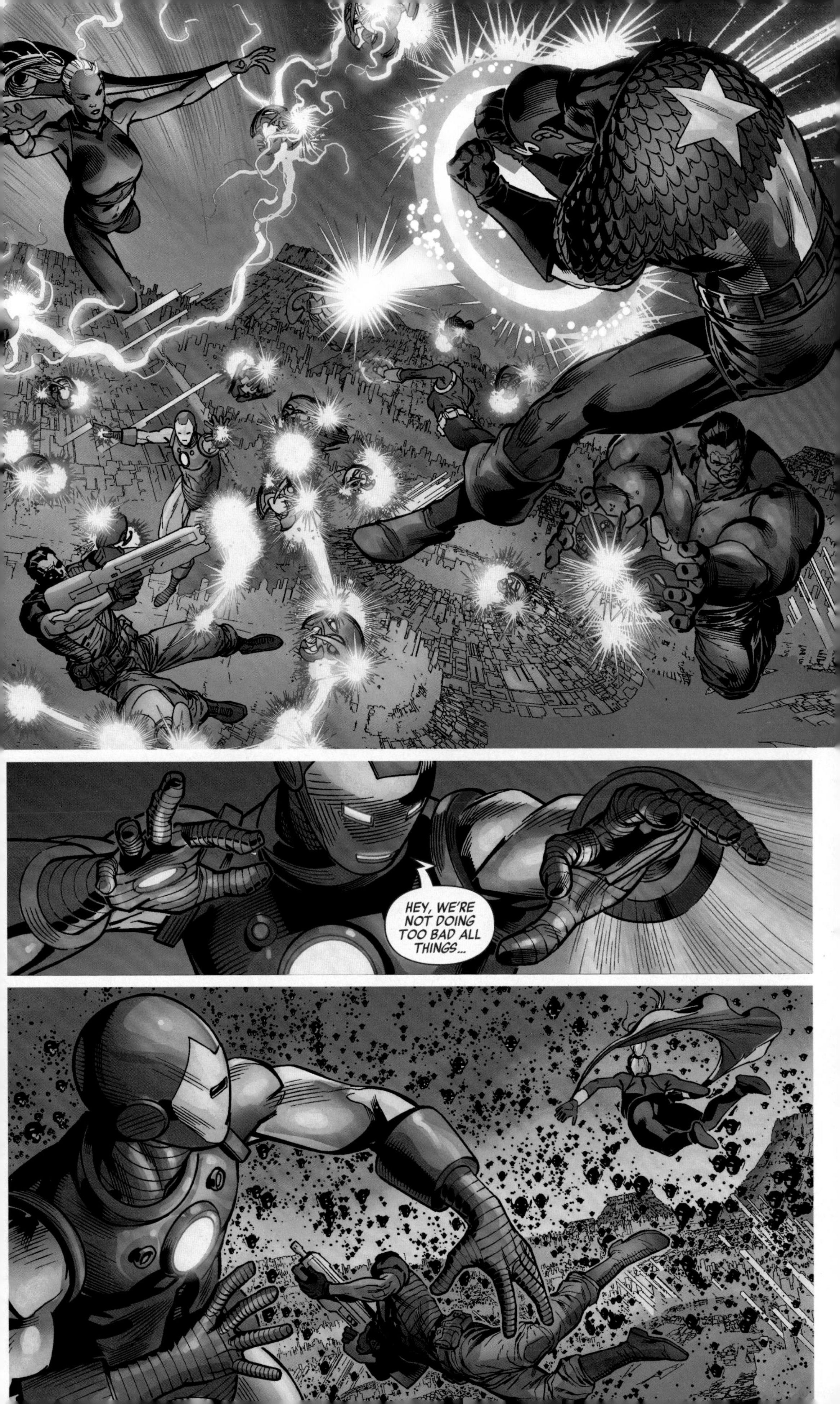
HEY, WE'RE NOT DOING TOO BAD ALL THINGS...

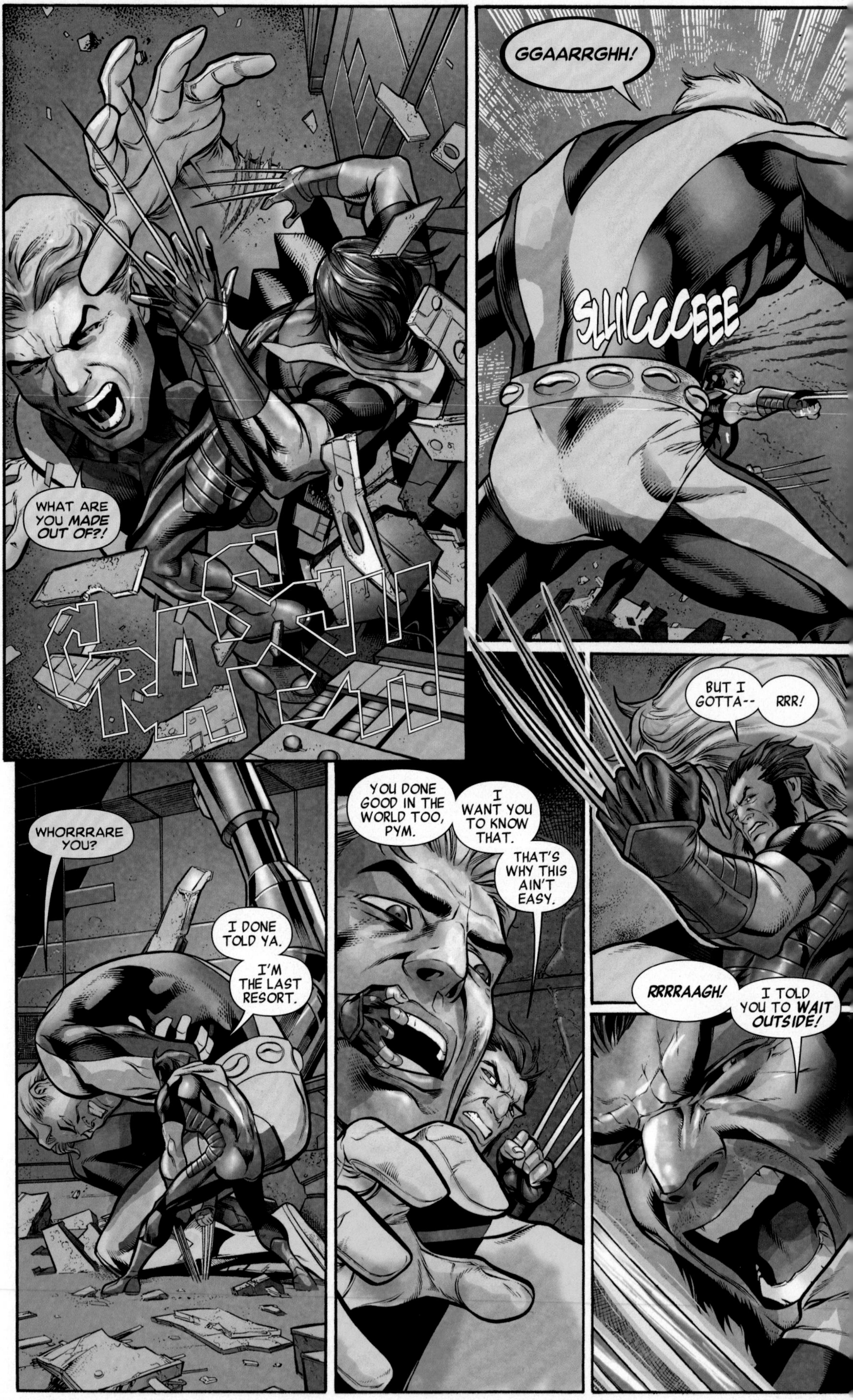
WHAT ARE YOU MADE OUT OF?!
CRASH
GGAARRGHH!
SLLIICCCCEEE
BUT I GOTTA--
RRR!
WHORRRARE YOU?
I DONE TOLD YA.
I'M THE LAST RESORT.
YOU DONE GOOD IN THE WORLD TOO, PYM.
I WANT YOU TO KNOW THAT.
THAT'S WHY THIS AIN'T EASY.
RRRRAAGH!
I TOLD YOU TO WAIT OUTSIDE!

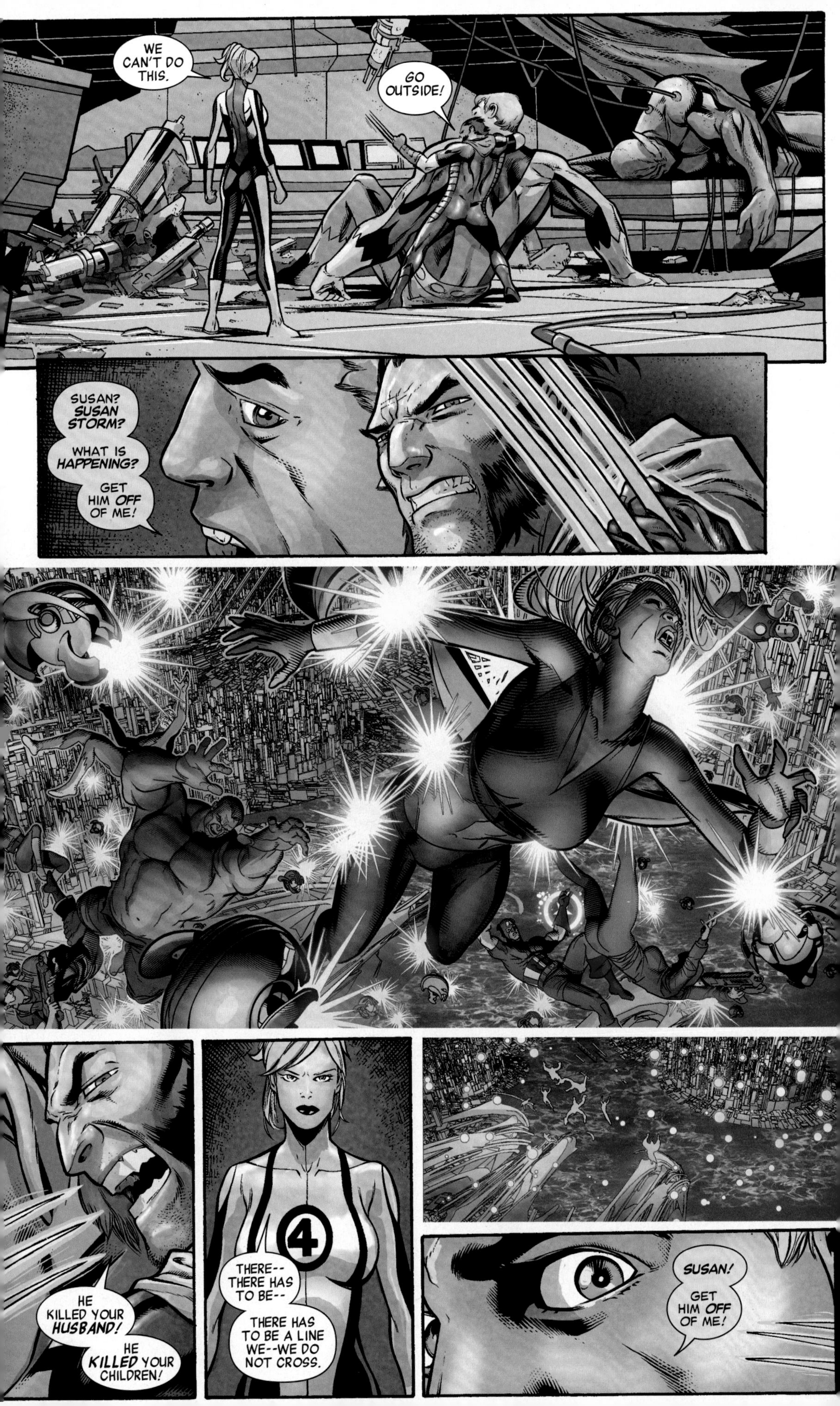

WE CAN'T DO THIS.
GO OUTSIDE!
SUSAN? SUSAN STORM?
WHAT IS HAPPENING?
GET HIM OFF OF ME!
HE KILLED YOUR HUSBAND!
HE KILLED YOUR CHILDREN!
THERE-- THERE HAS TO BE--
THERE HAS TO BE A LINE WE--WE DO NOT CROSS.
SUSAN!
GET HIM OFF OF ME!

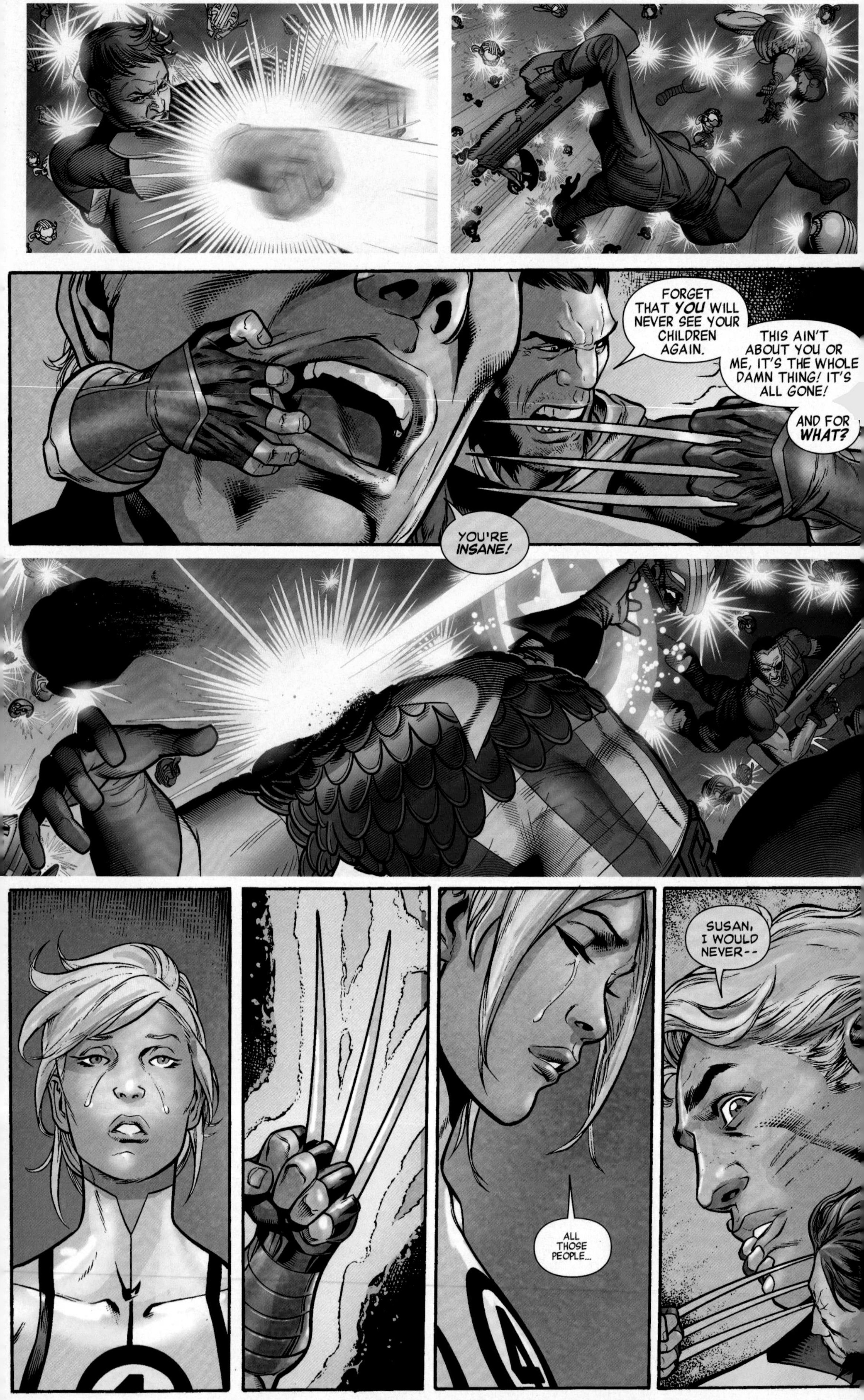
FORGET THAT YOU WILL NEVER SEE YOUR CHILDREN AGAIN.
THIS AIN'T ABOUT YOU OR ME, IT'S THE WHOLE DAMN THING! IT'S ALL GONE!
AND FOR WHAT?
YOU'RE INSANE!
ALL THOSE PEOPLE...
SUSAN, I WOULD NEVER--

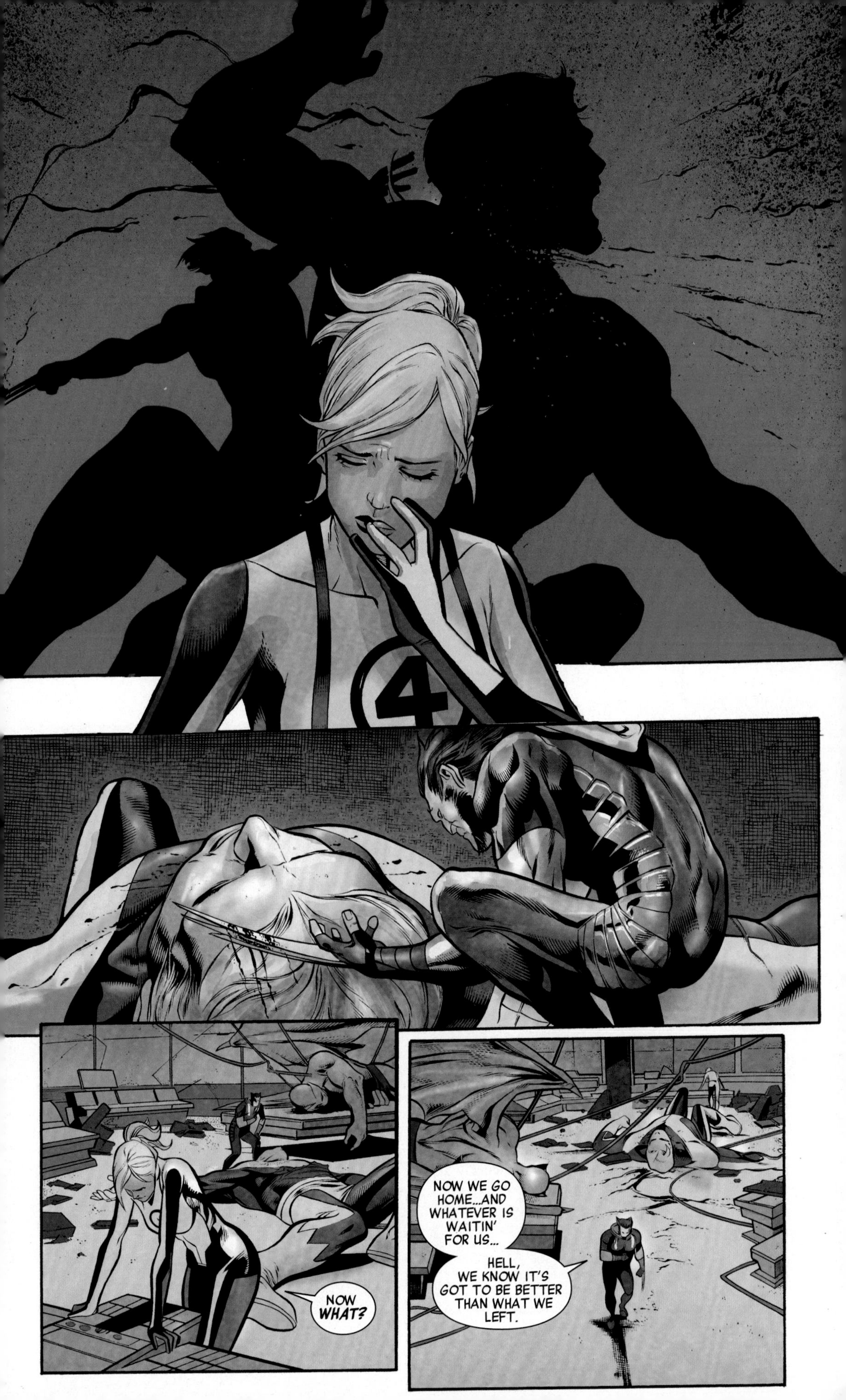
NOW WHAT?
NOW WE GO HOME...AND WHATEVER IS WAITIN' FOR US...
HELL, WE KNOW IT'S GOT TO BE BETTER THAN WHAT WE LEFT.

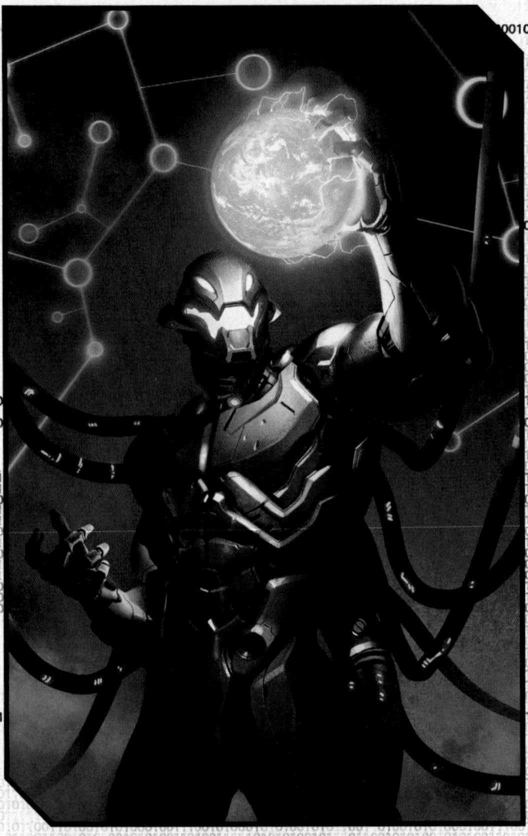

AGE OF ULTRON #1 VARIANT
BY MARKO DJURDJEVIC

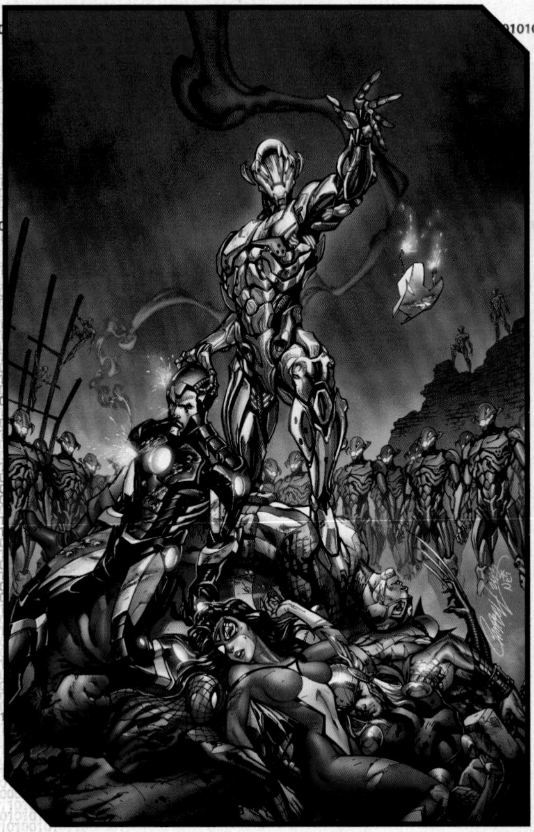

AGE OF ULTRON #1 VARIANT
BY J. SCOTT CAMPBELL & NEI RUFFINO

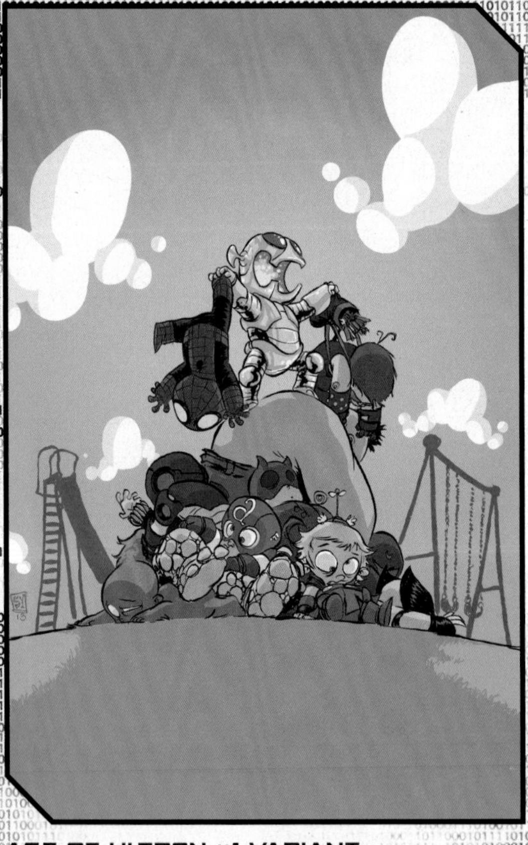

AGE OF ULTRON #1 VARIANT
BY SKOTTIE YOUNG

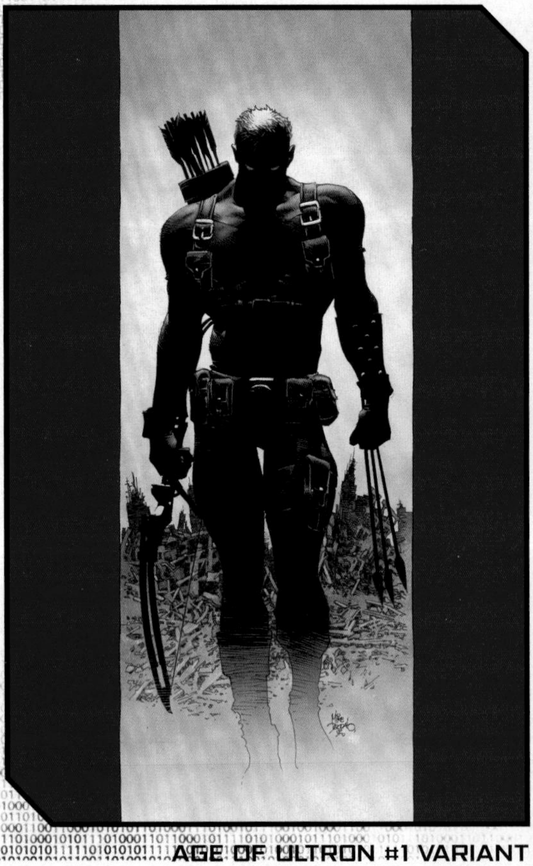

AGE OF ULTRON #1 VARIANT
BY MIKE DEODATO & MORRY HOLLOWELL

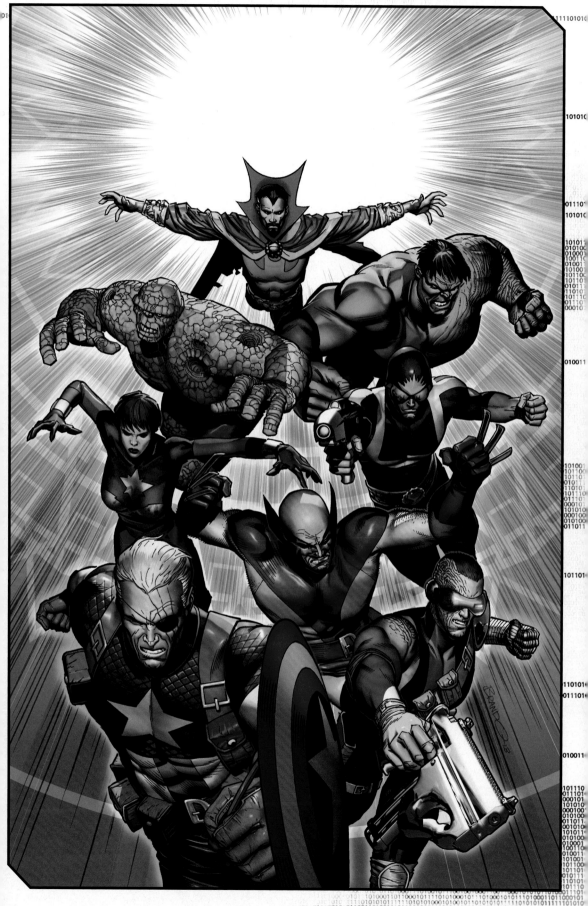

AGE OF ULTRON #7

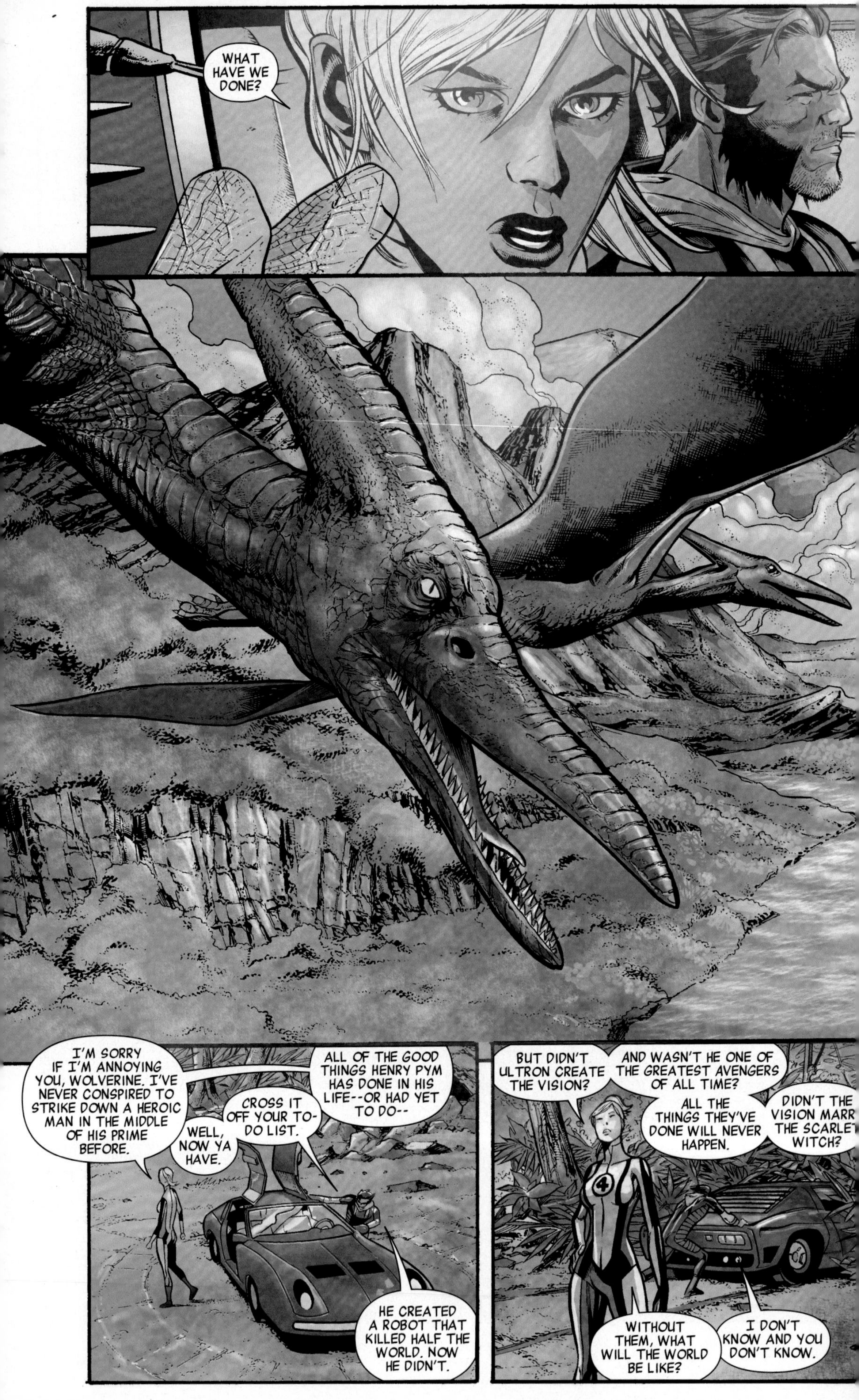
WHAT HAVE WE DONE?
I'M SORRY IF I'M ANNOYING YOU, WOLVERINE. I'VE NEVER CONSPIRED TO STRIKE DOWN A HEROIC MAN IN THE MIDDLE OF HIS PRIME BEFORE.
WELL, NOW YA HAVE.
CROSS IT OFF YOUR TO-DO LIST.
ALL OF THE GOOD THINGS HENRY PYM HAS DONE IN HIS LIFE--OR HAD YET TO DO--
HE CREATED A ROBOT THAT KILLED HALF THE WORLD. NOW HE DIDN'T.
BUT DIDN'T ULTRON CREATE THE VISION?
AND WASN'T HE ONE OF THE GREATEST AVENGERS OF ALL TIME?
DIDN'T THE VISION MARR THE SCARLE WITCH?
ALL THE THINGS THEY'VE DONE WILL NEVER HAPPEN.
WITHOUT THEM, WHAT WILL THE WORLD BE LIKE?
I DON'T KNOW AND YOU DON'T KNOW.

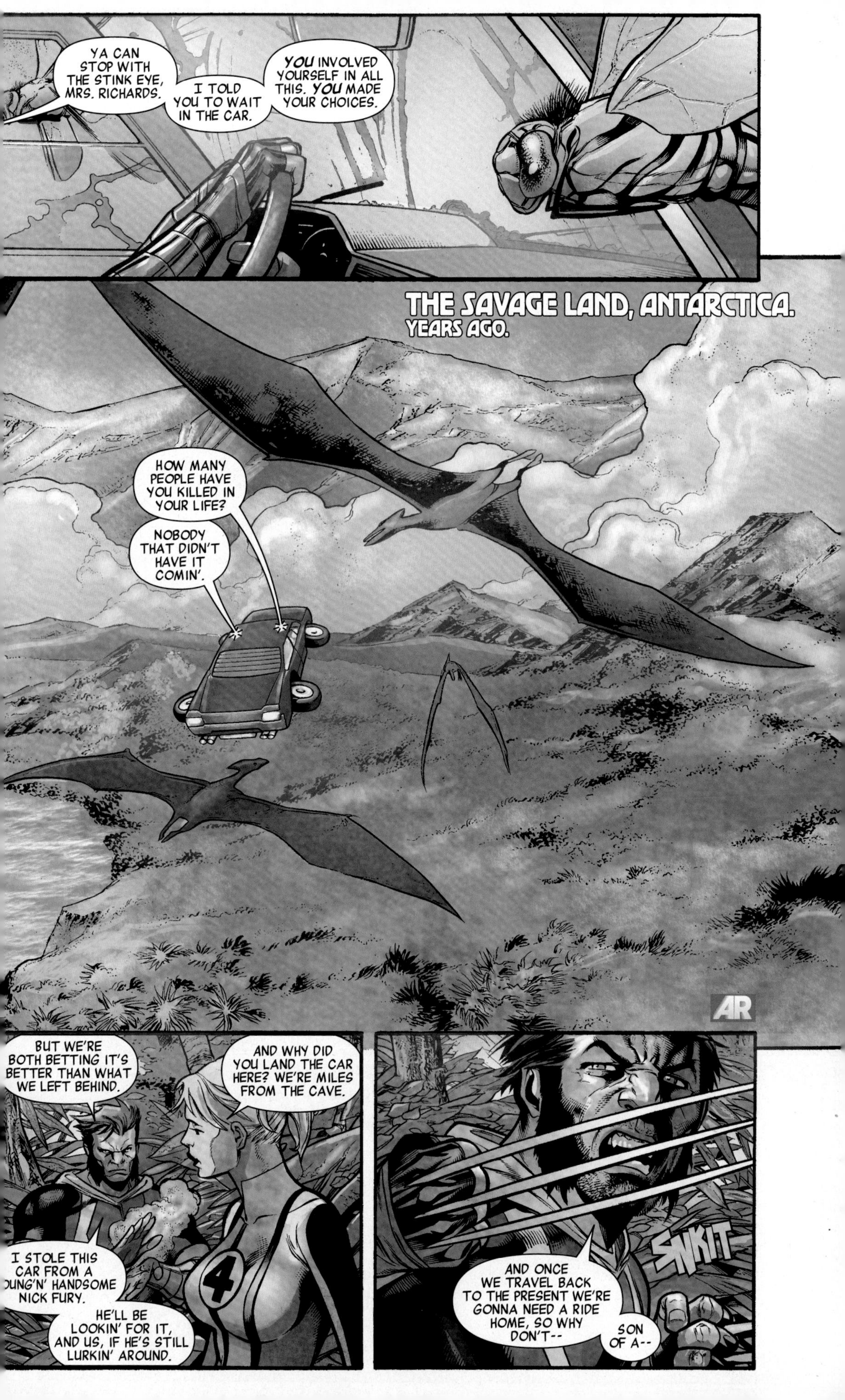
YA CAN STOP WITH THE STINK EYE, MRS. RICHARDS.
I TOLD YOU TO WAIT IN THE CAR.
YOU INVOLVED YOURSELF IN ALL THIS. YOU MADE YOUR CHOICES.
THE SAVAGE LAND, ANTARCTICA.
YEARS AGO.
HOW MANY PEOPLE HAVE YOU KILLED IN YOUR LIFE?
NOBODY THAT DIDN'T HAVE IT COMIN'.
BUT WE'RE BOTH BETTING IT'S BETTER THAN WHAT WE LEFT BEHIND.
AND WHY DID YOU LAND THE CAR HERE? WE'RE MILES FROM THE CAVE.
I STOLE THIS CAR FROM A OUNG'N' HANDSOME NICK FURY.
HE'LL BE LOOKIN' FOR IT, AND US, IF HE'S STILL LURKIN' AROUND.
SNKIT
AND ONCE WE TRAVEL BACK TO THE PRESENT WE'RE GONNA NEED A RIDE HOME, SO WHY DON'T--
SON OF A--

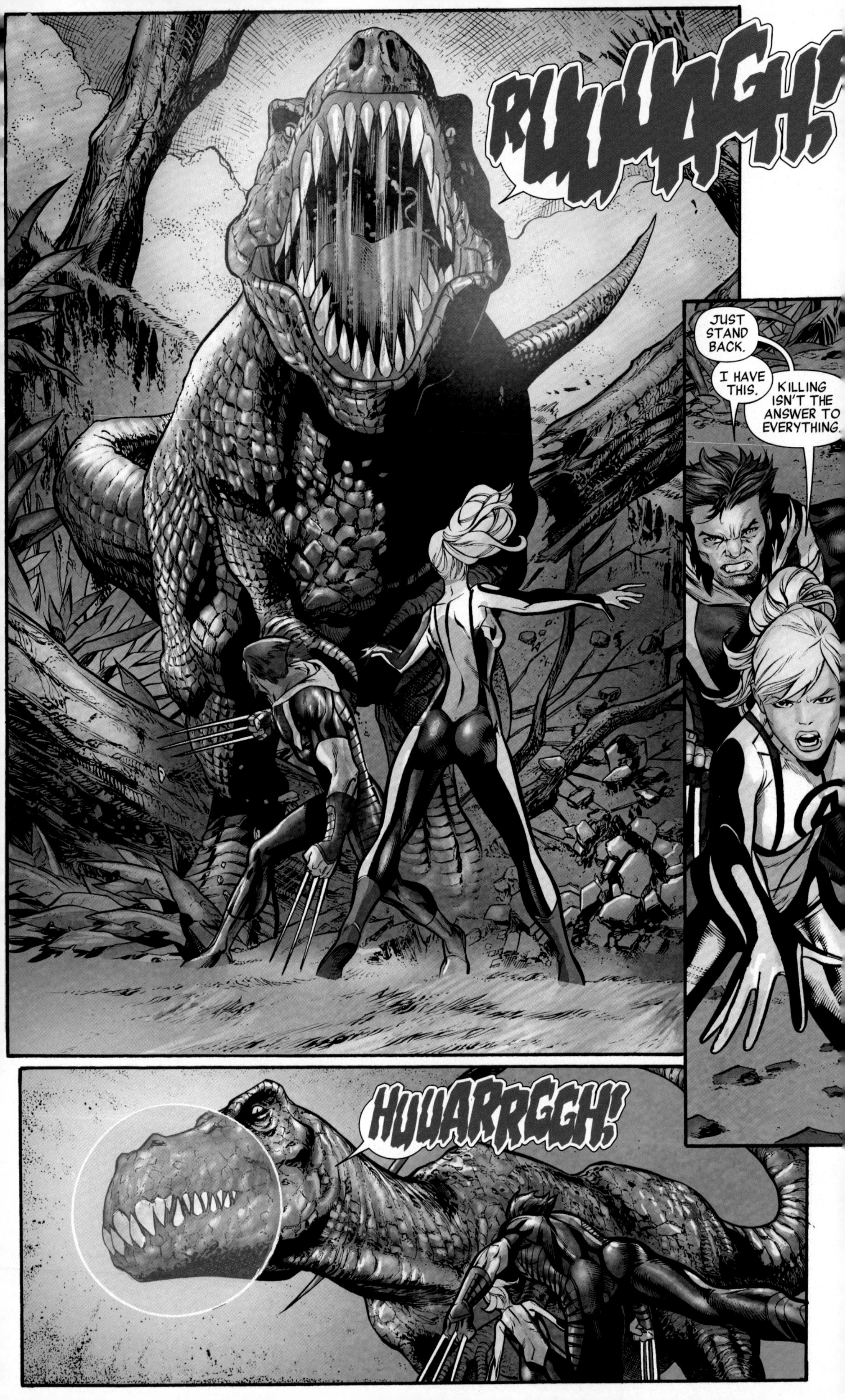
RUUAAGH!
JUST STAND BACK.
I HAVE THIS.
KILLING ISN'T THE ANSWER TO EVERYTHING.
HUUARRGGH!

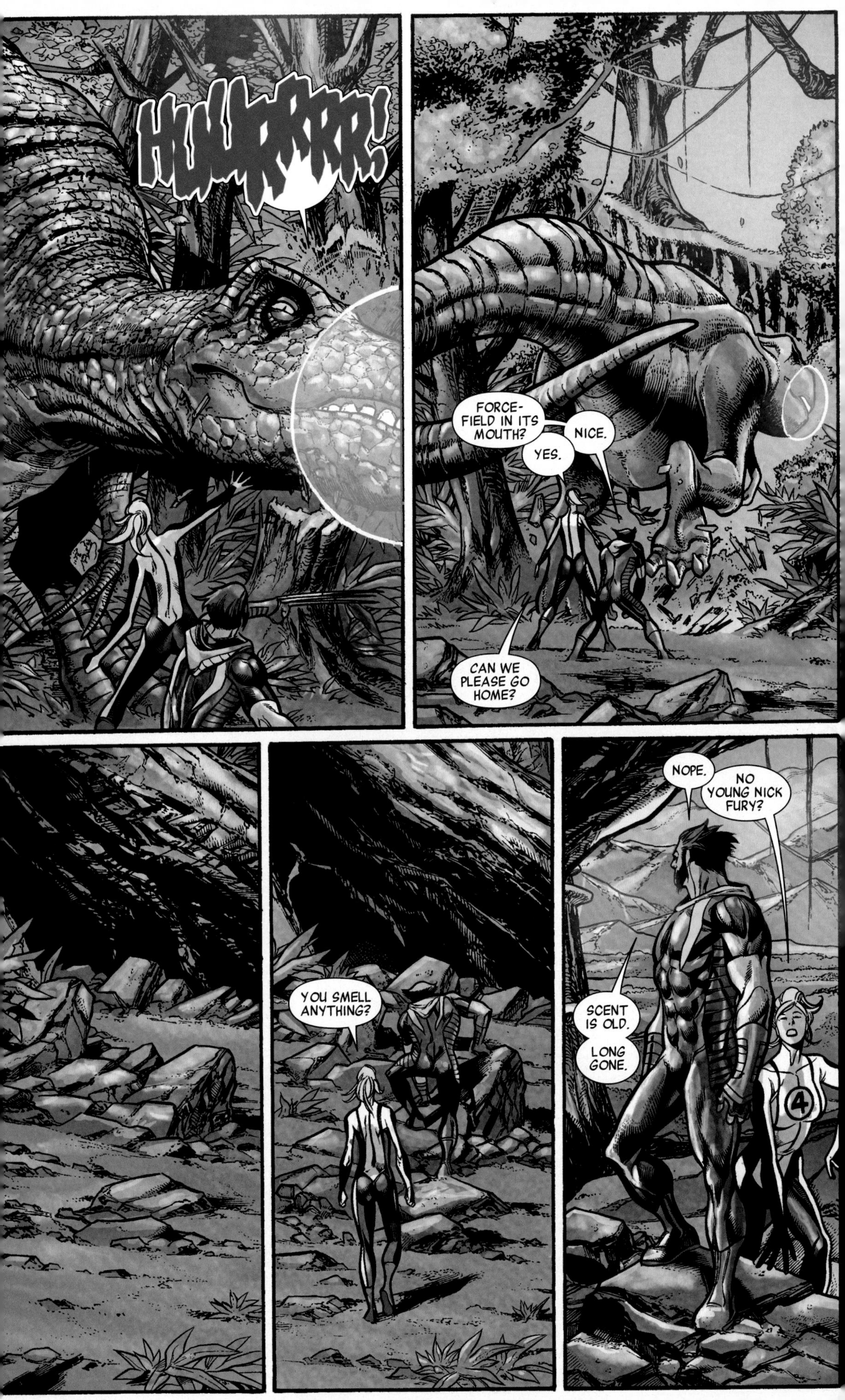
HUURRRR!
FORCE-FIELD IN ITS MOUTH?
YES.
NICE.
CAN WE PLEASE GO HOME?
YOU SMELL ANYTHING?
NOPE.
NO YOUNG NICK FURY?
SCENT IS OLD.
LONG GONE.

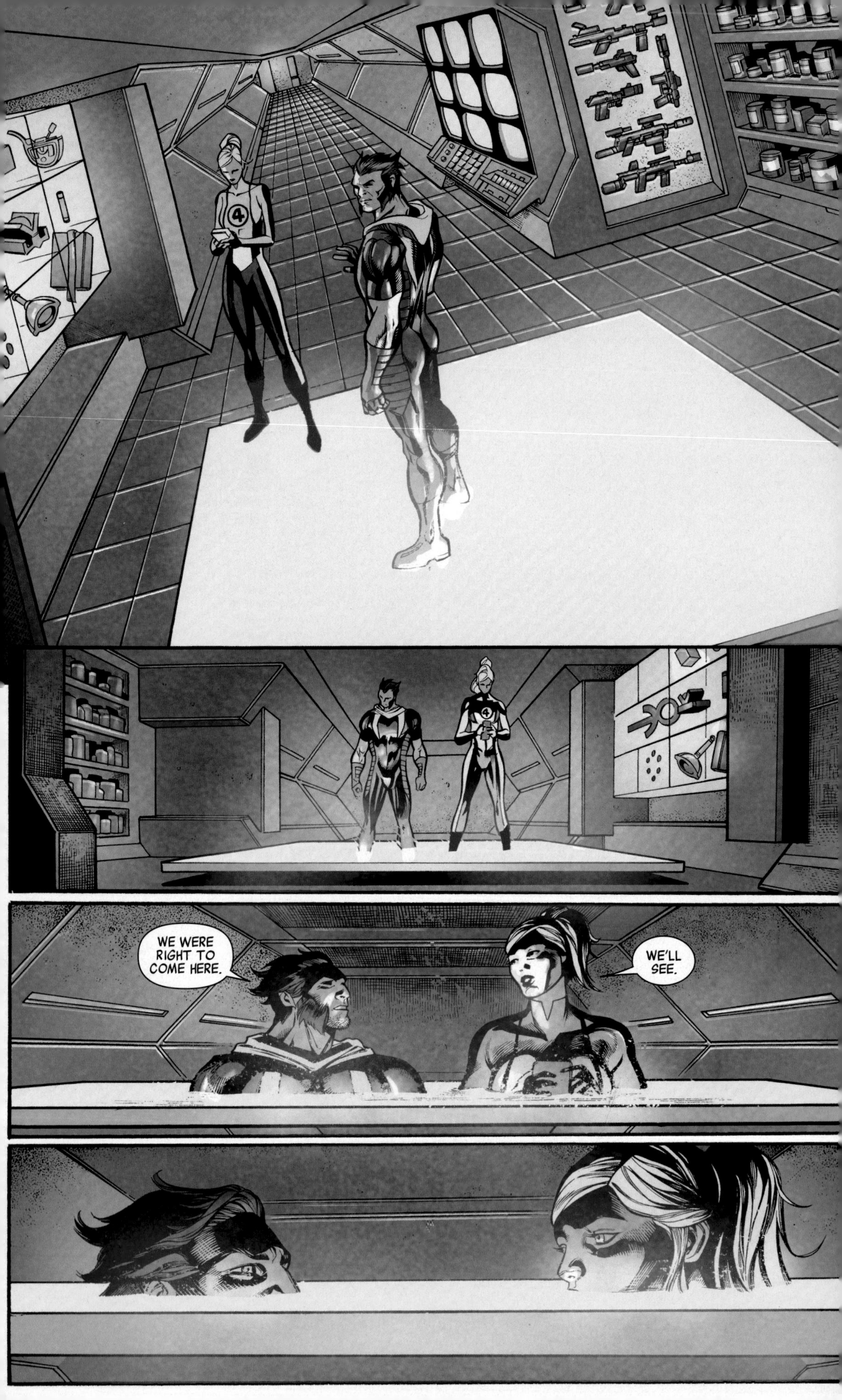
WE WERE RIGHT TO COME HERE.
WE'LL SEE.

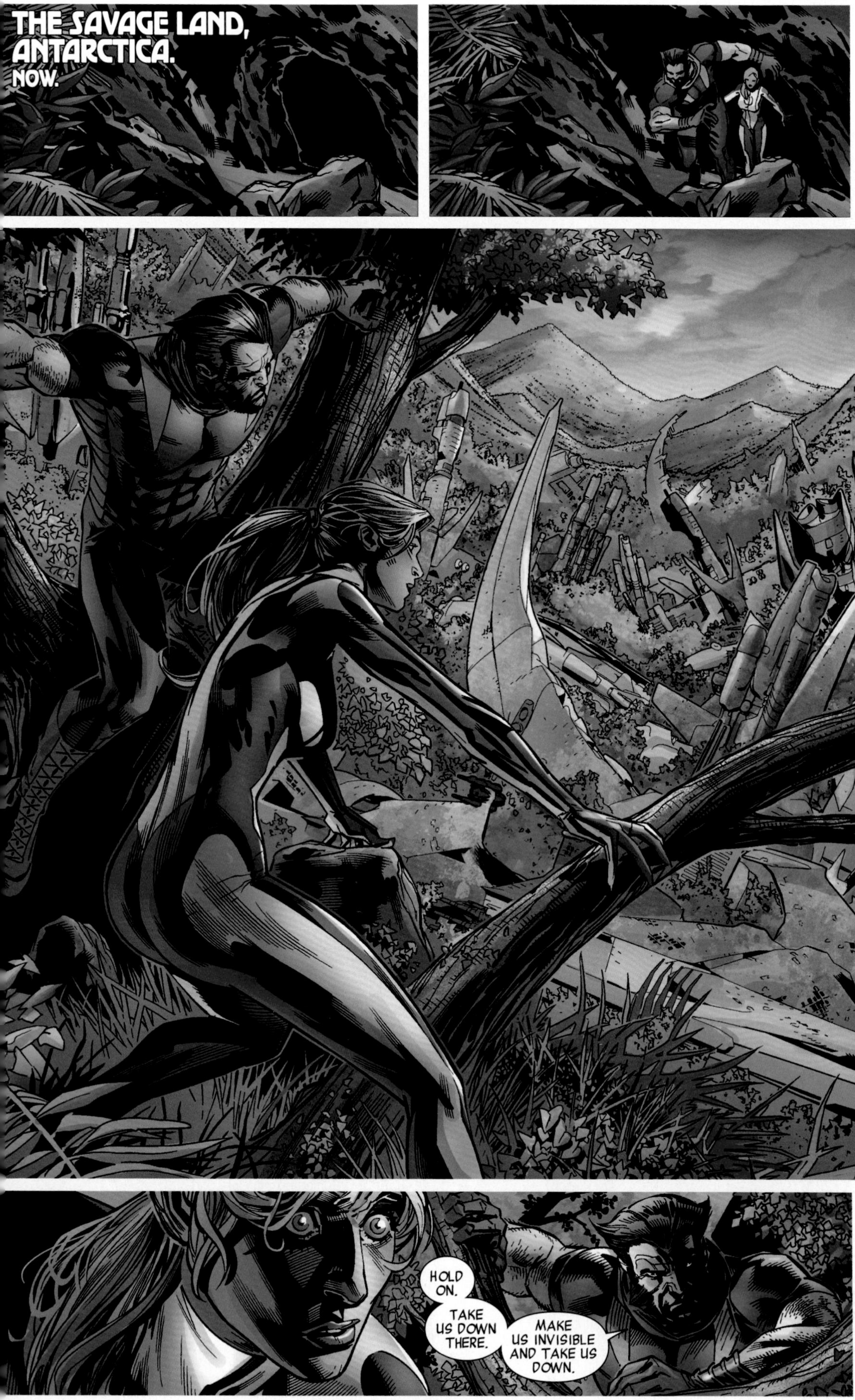
THE SAVAGE LAND, ANTARCTICA.
NOW.
HOLD ON.
TAKE US DOWN THERE.
MAKE US INVISIBLE AND TAKE US DOWN.

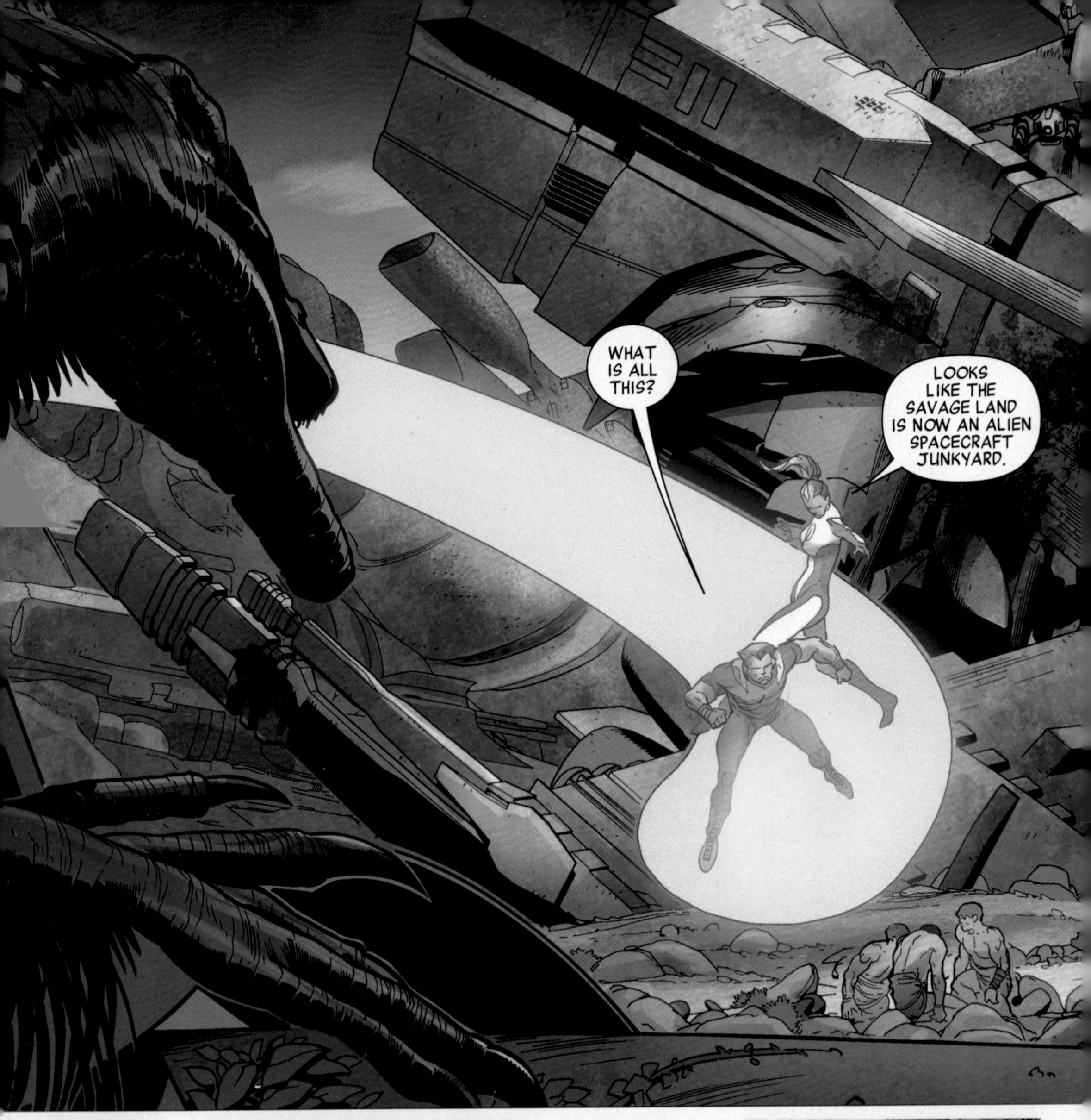
WHAT IS ALL THIS?
LOOKS LIKE THE SAVAGE LAND IS NOW AN ALIEN SPACECRAFT JUNKYARD.

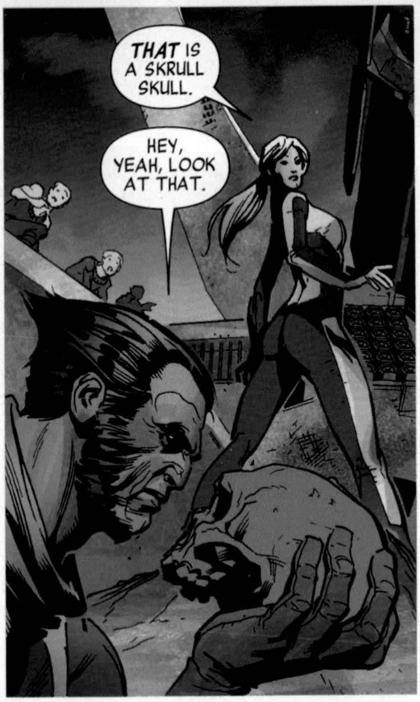
THAT IS A SKRULL SKULL.
HEY, YEAH, LOOK AT THAT.

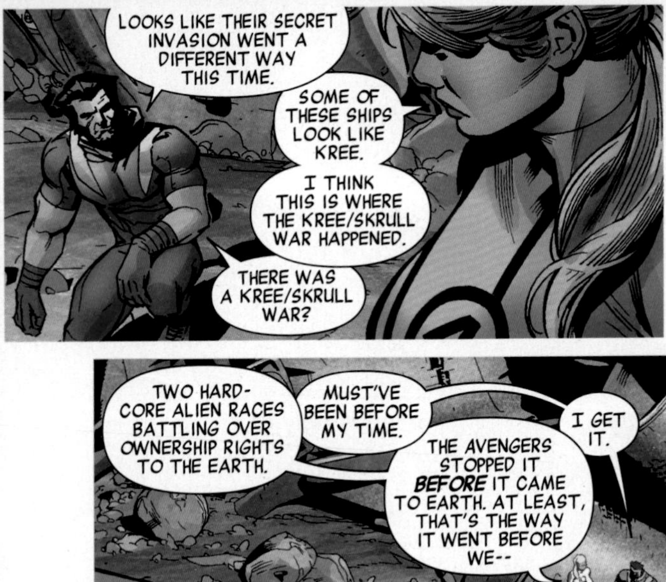
LOOKS LIKE THEIR SECRET INVASION WENT A DIFFERENT WAY THIS TIME.
SOME OF THESE SHIPS LOOK LIKE KREE.
I THINK THIS IS WHERE THE KREE/SKRULL WAR HAPPENED.
THERE WAS A KREE/SKRULL WAR?

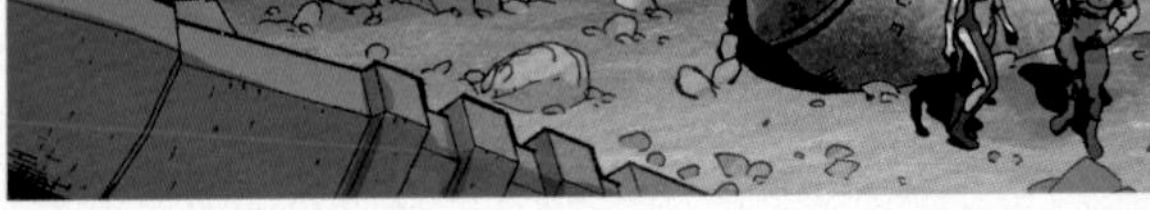
TWO HARD-CORE ALIEN RACES BATTLING OVER OWNERSHIP RIGHTS TO THE EARTH.
MUST'VE BEEN BEFORE MY TIME.
I GET IT.
THE AVENGERS STOPPED IT BEFORE IT CAME TO EARTH. AT LEAST, THAT'S THE WAY IT WENT BEFORE WE--

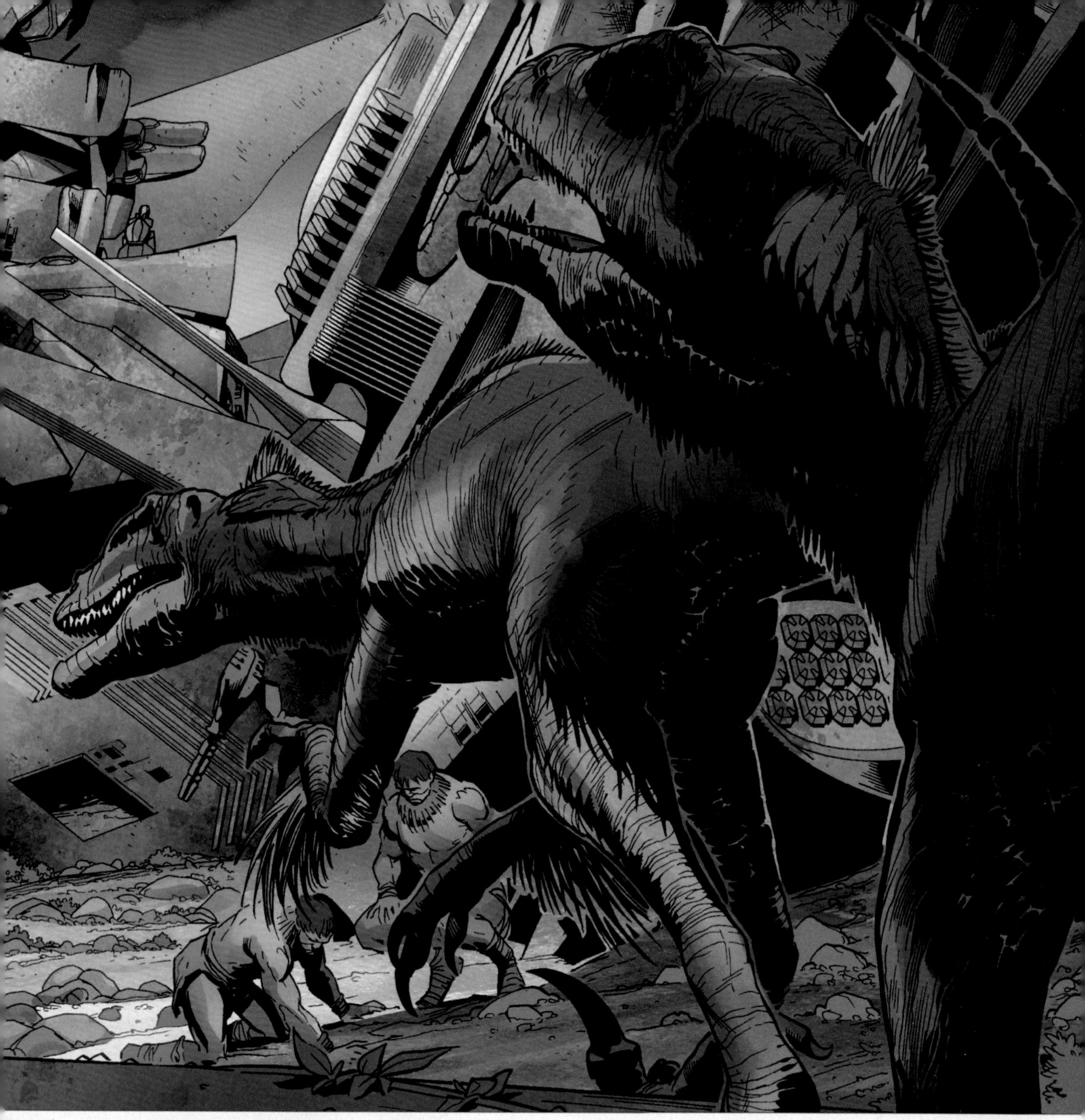

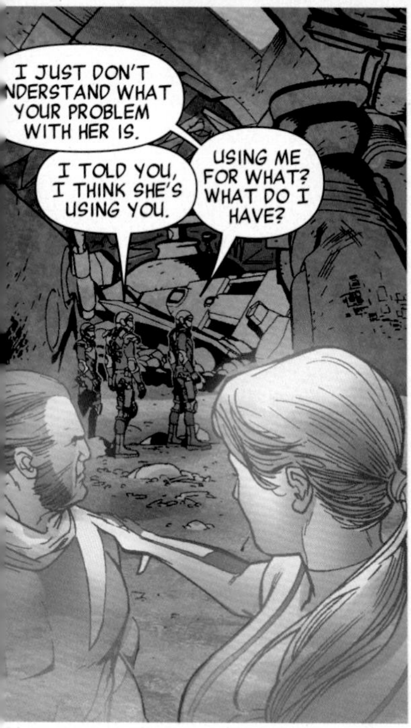
I JUST DON'T
NDERSTAND WHAT YOUR PROBLEM WITH HER IS.
I TOLD YOU, I THINK SHE'S USING YOU.
USING ME FOR WHAT? WHAT DO I HAVE?

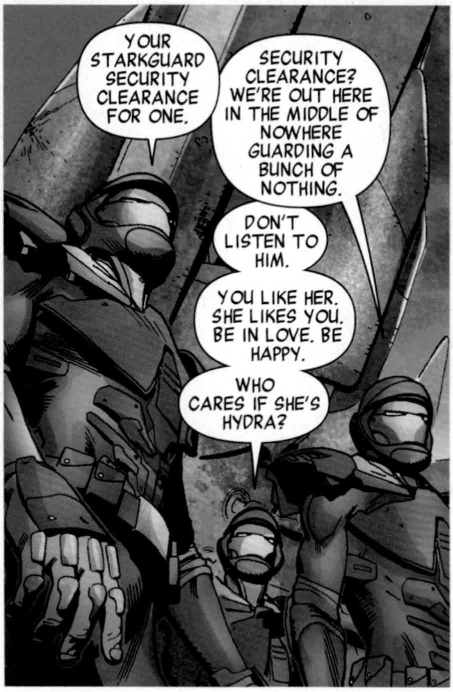
YOUR STARKGUARD SECURITY CLEARANCE FOR ONE.
SECURITY CLEARANCE? WE'RE OUT HERE IN THE MIDDLE OF NOWHERE GUARDING A BUNCH OF NOTHING.
DON'T LISTEN TO HIM.
YOU LIKE HER. SHE LIKES YOU. BE IN LOVE. BE HAPPY.
WHO CARES IF SHE'S HYDRA?

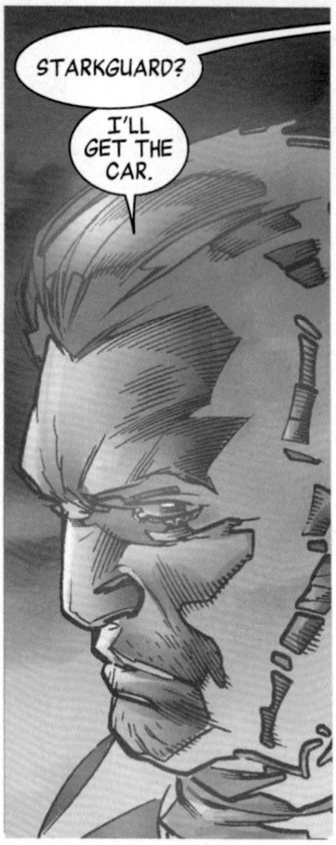
STARKGUARD?
I'LL GET THE CAR.

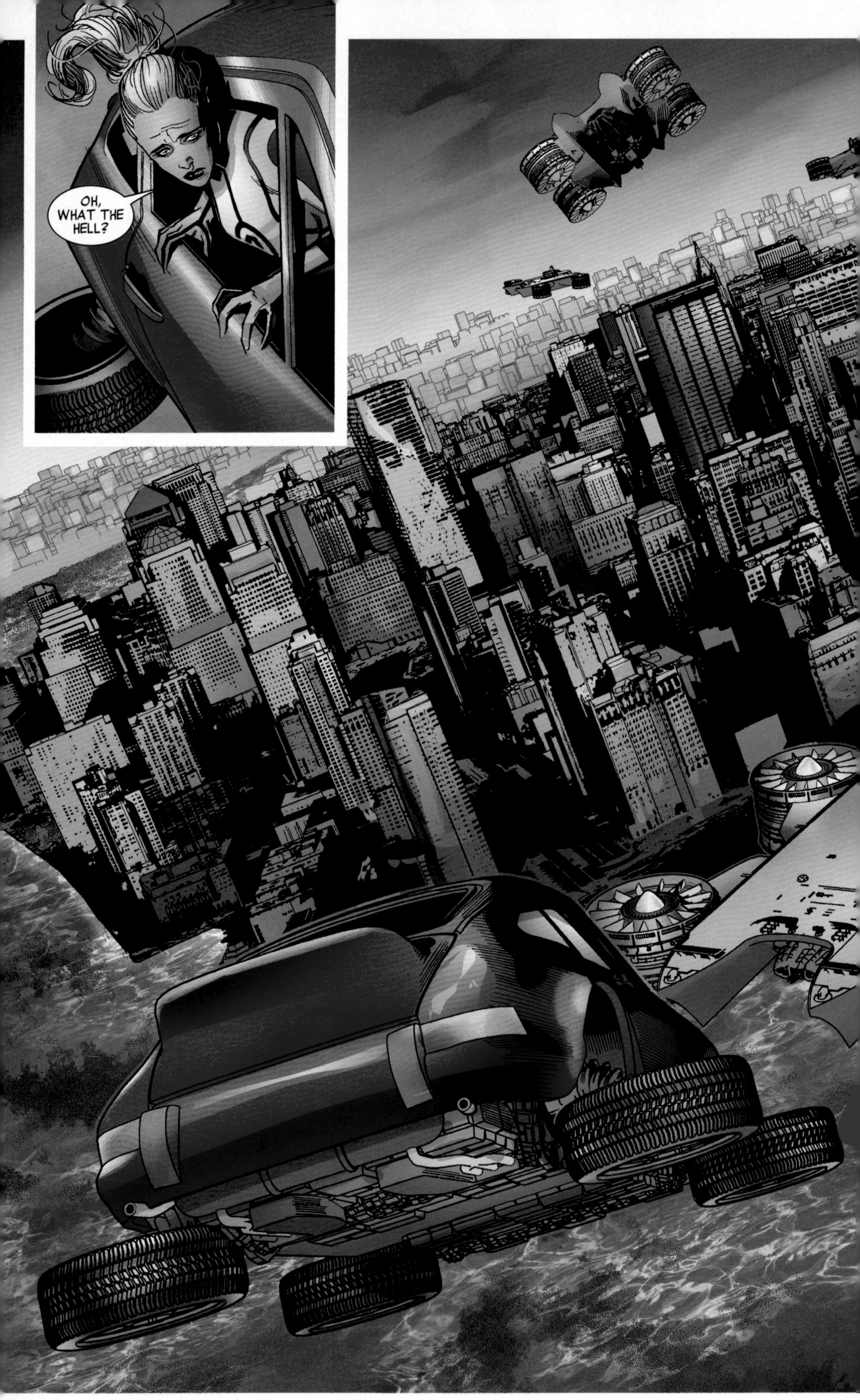
OH, WHAT THE HELL?

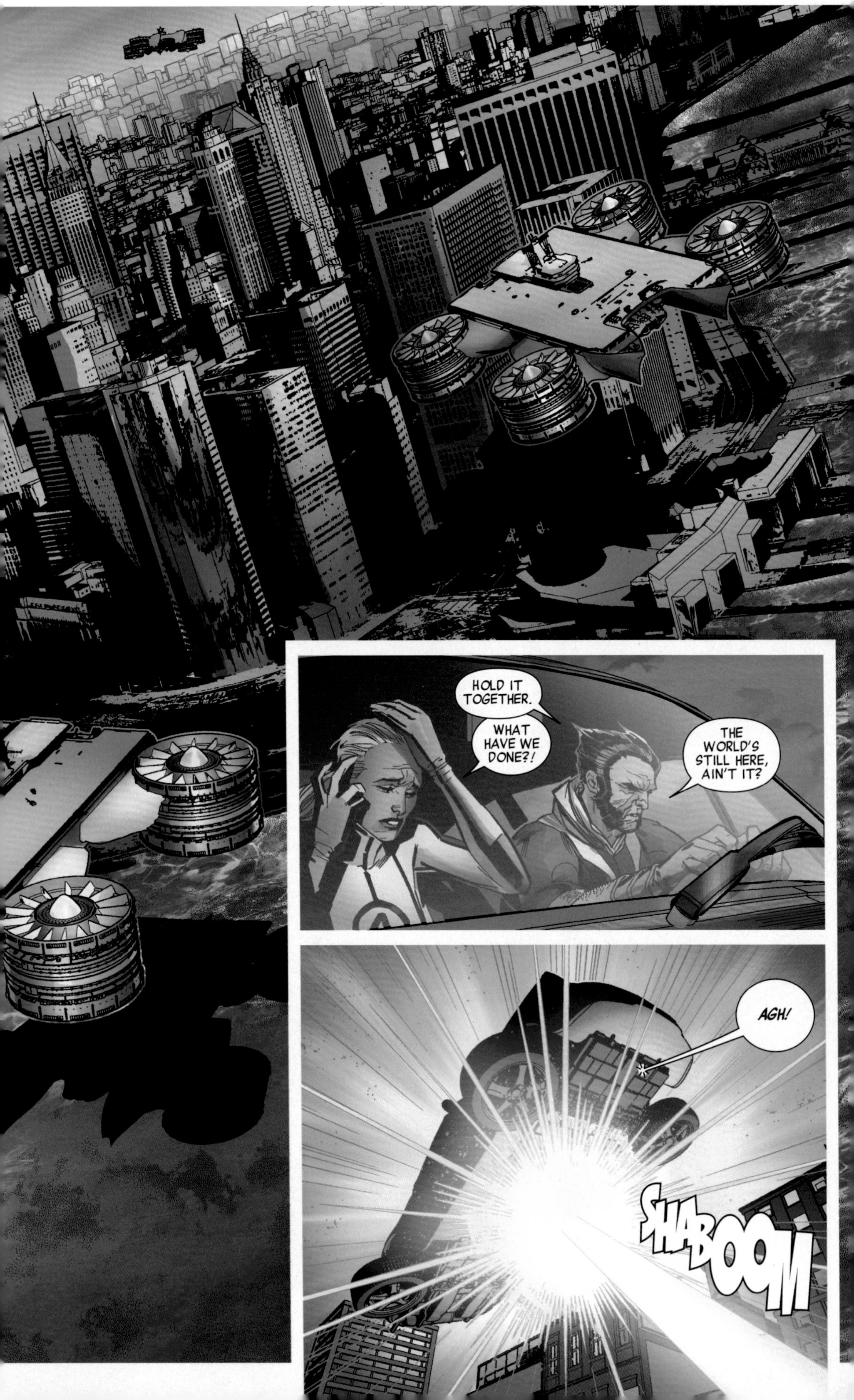
HOLD IT TOGETHER.
WHAT HAVE WE DONE?!
THE WORLD'S STILL HERE, AIN'T IT?
AGH!
SHABOOM

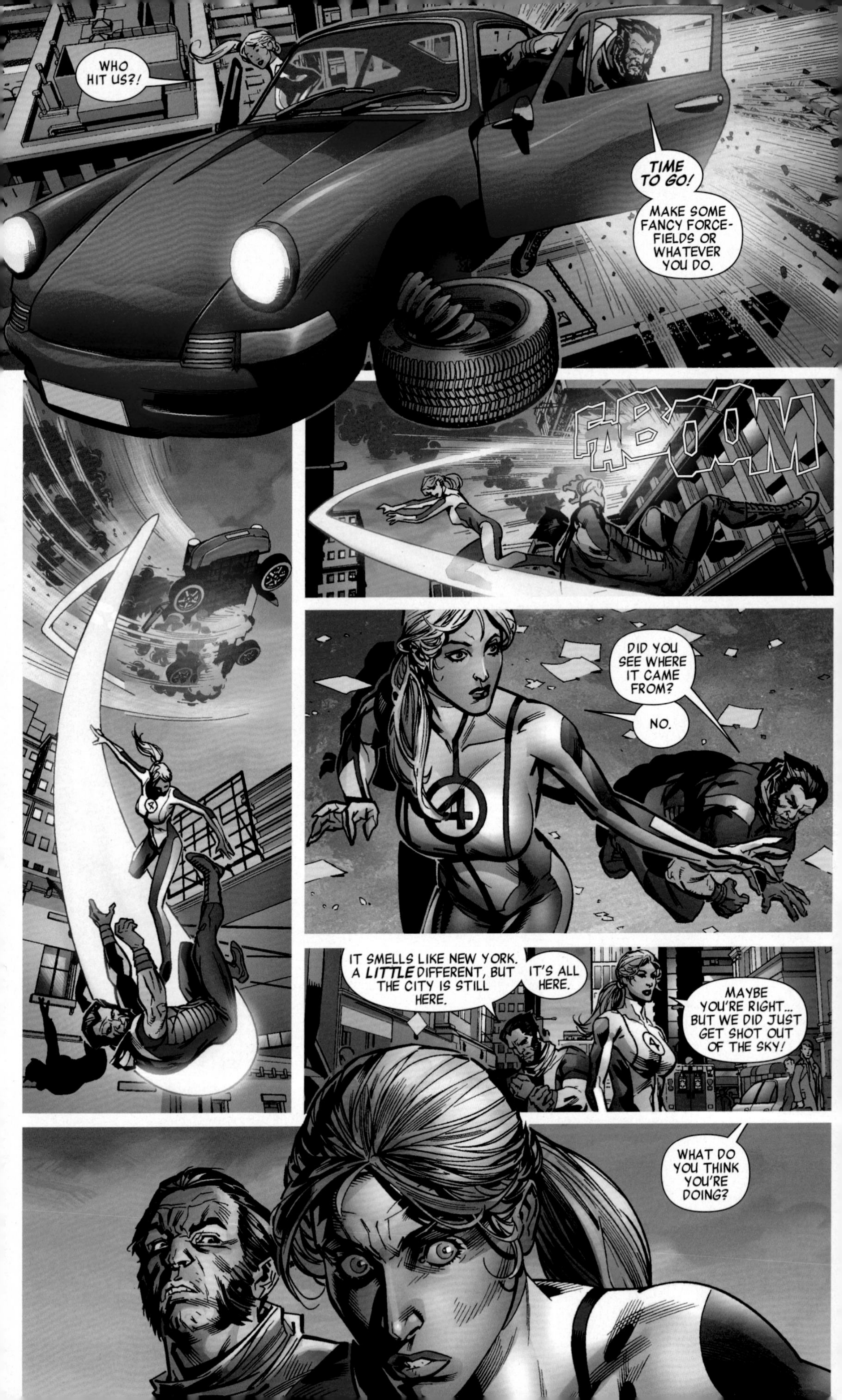
WHO HIT US?!
TIME TO GO!
MAKE SOME FANCY FORCE-FIELDS OR WHATEVER YOU DO.
FABOOM
DID YOU SEE WHERE IT CAME FROM?
NO.
IT SMELLS LIKE NEW YORK. A LITTLE DIFFERENT, BUT THE CITY IS STILL HERE.
IT'S ALL HERE.
MAYBE YOU'RE RIGHT... BUT WE DID JUST GET SHOT OUT OF THE SKY!
WHAT DO YOU THINK YOU'RE DOING?

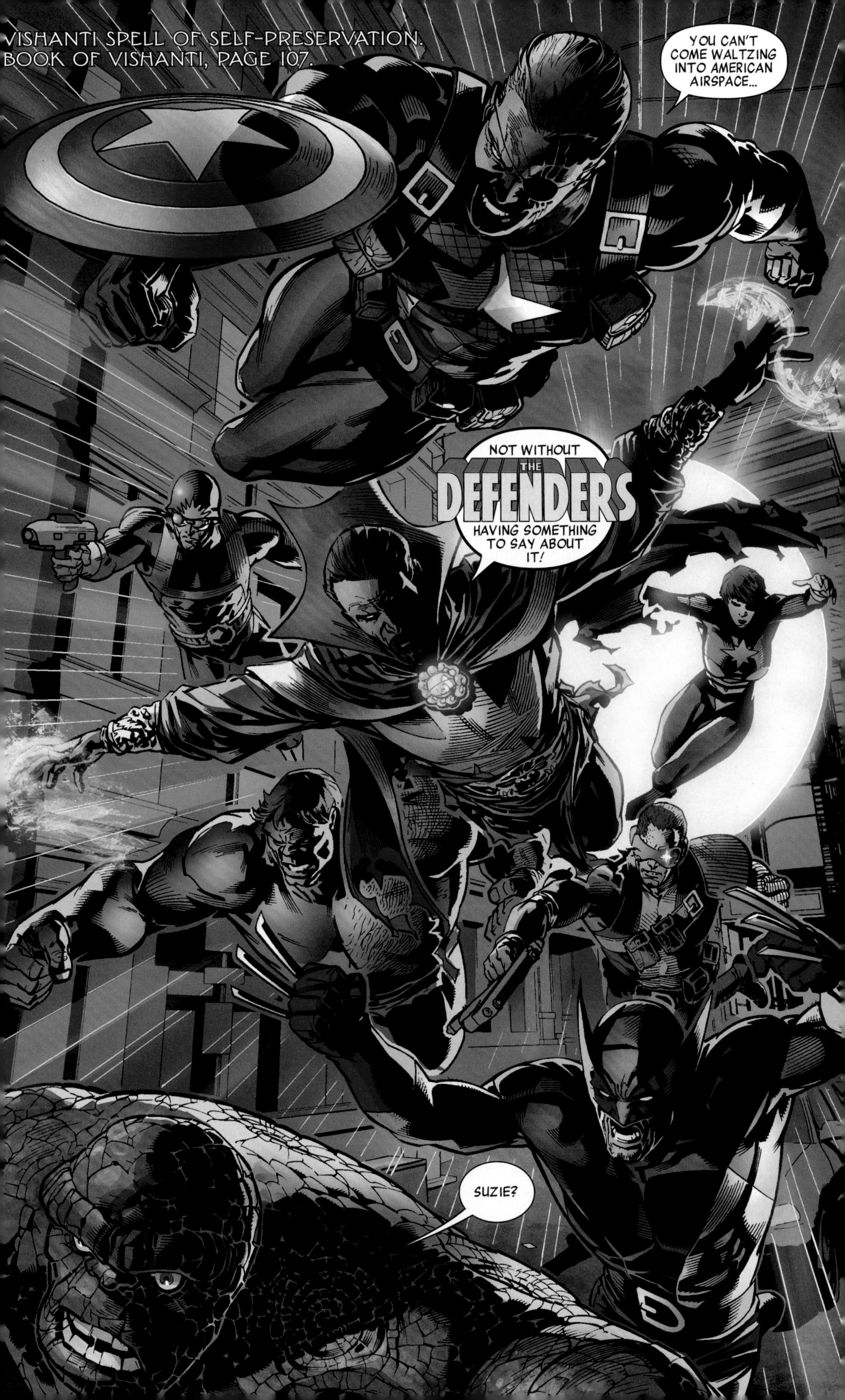
VISHANTI SPELL OF SELF-PRESERVATION.
BOOK OF VISHANTI, PAGE 107.
YOU CAN'T COME WALTZING INTO AMERICAN AIRSPACE...
NOT WITHOUT THE DEFENDERS HAVING SOMETHING TO SAY ABOUT IT!
SUZIE?

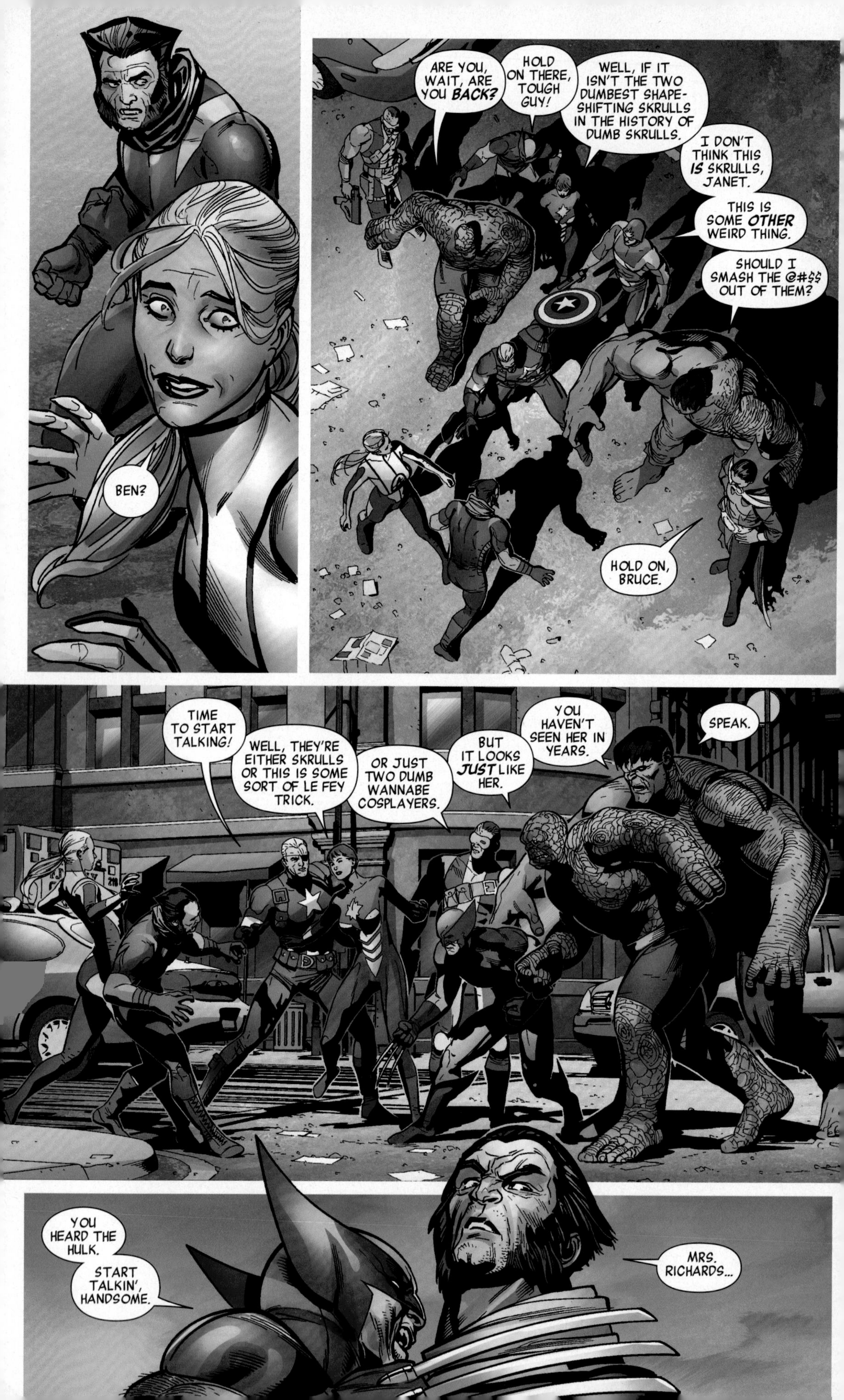
BEN?
ARE YOU, WAIT, ARE YOU BACK?
HOLD ON THERE, TOUGH GUY!
WELL, IF IT ISN'T THE TWO DUMBEST SHAPE-SHIFTING SKRULLS IN THE HISTORY OF DUMB SKRULLS.
I DON'T THINK THIS IS SKRULLS, JANET.
THIS IS SOME OTHER WEIRD THING.
SHOULD I SMASH THE @#$$ OUT OF THEM?
HOLD ON, BRUCE.
TIME TO START TALKING!
WELL, THEY'RE EITHER SKRULLS OR THIS IS SOME SORT OF LE FEY TRICK.
OR JUST TWO DUMB WANNABE COSPLAYERS.
BUT IT LOOKS JUST LIKE HER.
YOU HAVEN'T SEEN HER IN YEARS.
SPEAK.
YOU HEARD THE HULK.
START TALKIN', HANDSOME.
MRS. RICHARDS...

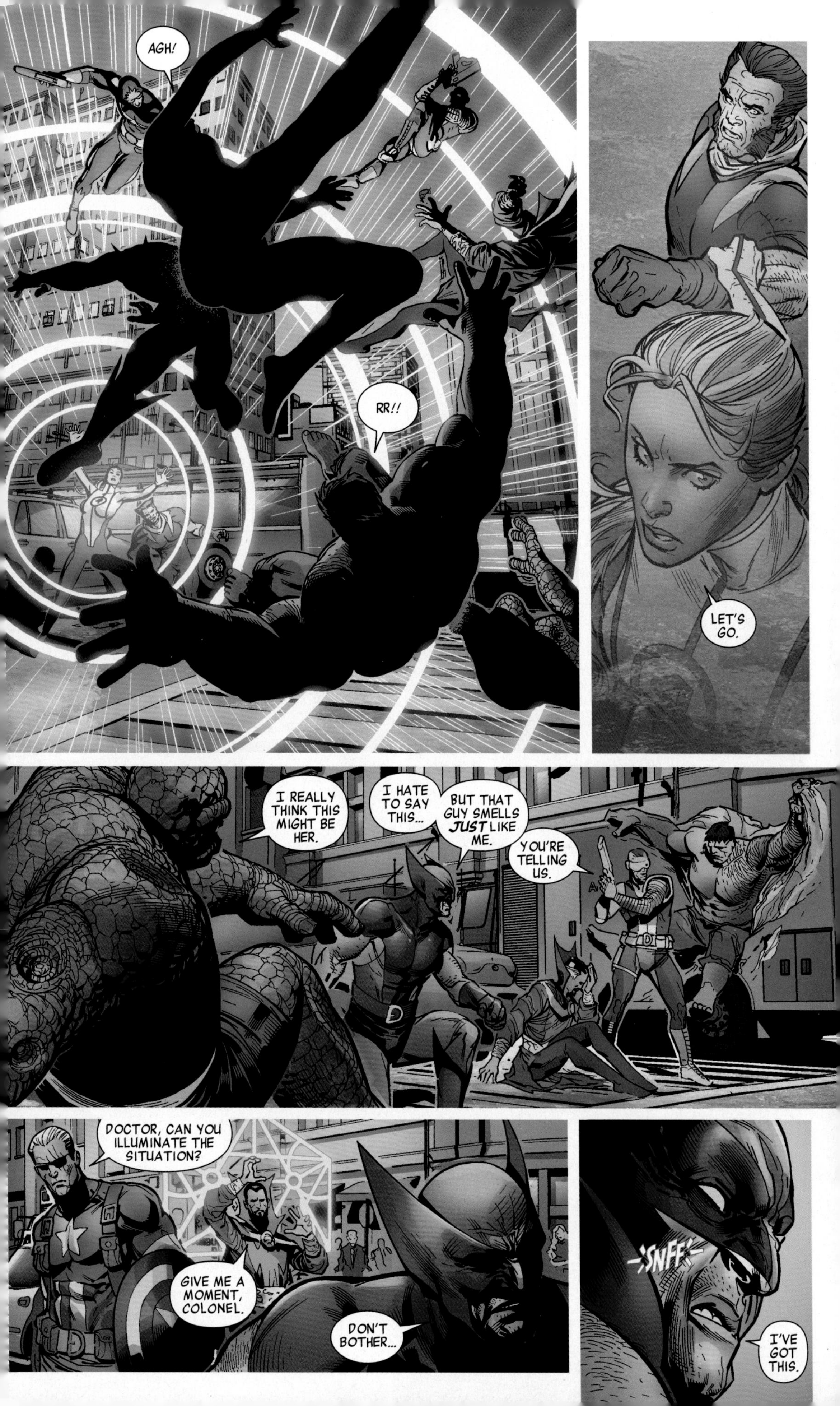
AGH!
RR!!
LET'S GO.
I REALLY THINK THIS MIGHT BE HER.
I HATE TO SAY THIS...
BUT THAT GUY SMELLS JUST LIKE ME.
YOU'RE TELLING US.
DOCTOR, CAN YOU ILLUMINATE THE SITUATION?
GIVE ME A MOMENT, COLONEL.
DON'T BOTHER...
SNFF
I'VE GOT THIS.

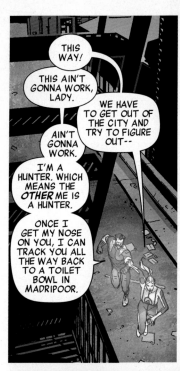

THIS WAY!

THIS AIN'T GONNA WORK, LADY.

WE HAVE TO GET OUT OF THE CITY AND TRY TO FIGURE OUT--

AIN'T GONNA WORK.

I'M A HUNTER. WHICH MEANS THE *OTHER* ME IS A HUNTER.

ONCE I GET MY NOSE ON YOU, I CAN TRACK YOU ALL THE WAY BACK TO A TOILET BOWL IN MADRIPOOR.

SEE.

WE GOT YOU SURROUNDED, SKRULL.

THE SPELL OF DISRUPTION. THE BOOK OF FIRE, PAGE 97.

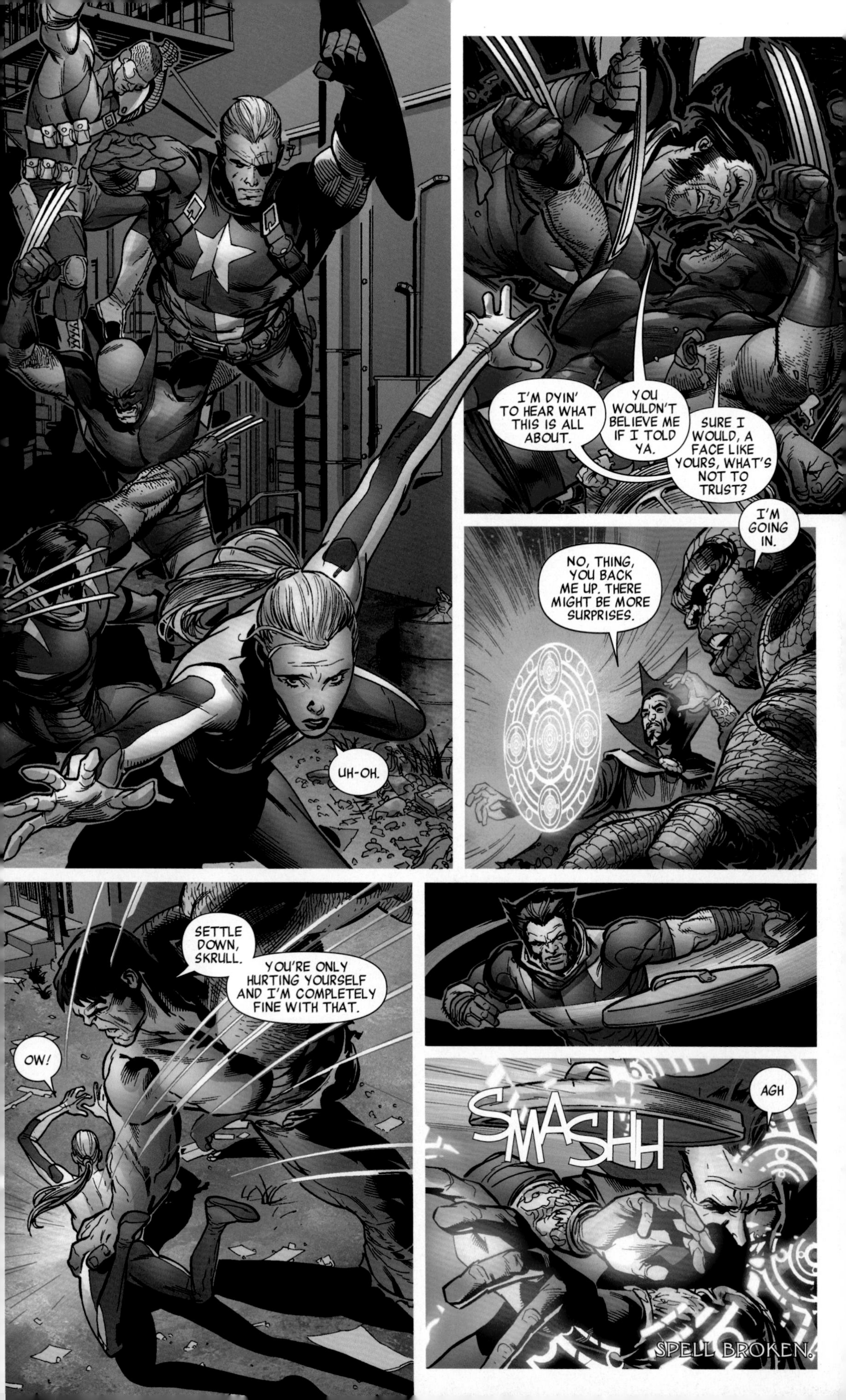
UH-OH.
I'M DYIN' TO HEAR WHAT THIS IS ALL ABOUT.
YOU WOULDN'T BELIEVE ME IF I TOLD YA.
SURE I WOULD, A FACE LIKE YOURS, WHAT'S NOT TO TRUST?
I'M GOING IN.
NO, THING, YOU BACK ME UP. THERE MIGHT BE MORE SURPRISES.
SETTLE DOWN, SKRULL.
YOU'RE ONLY HURTING YOURSELF AND I'M COMPLETELY FINE WITH THAT.
OW!
SMASHH
AGH
SPELL BROKEN.

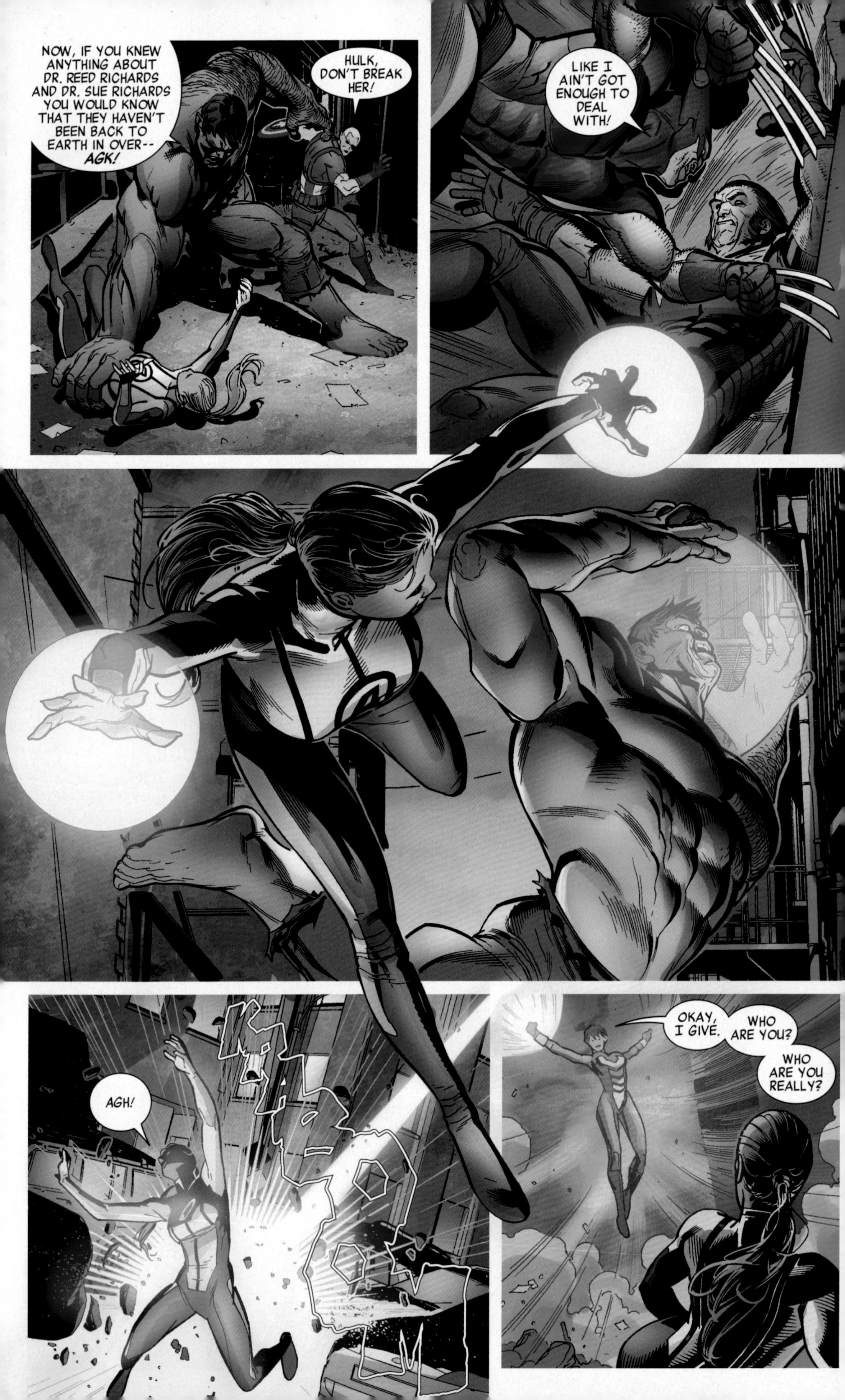
NOW, IF YOU KNEW ANYTHING ABOUT DR. REED RICHARDS AND DR. SUE RICHARDS YOU WOULD KNOW THAT THEY HAVEN'T BEEN BACK TO EARTH IN OVER-- AGK!
HULK, DON'T BREAK HER!
LIKE I AIN'T GOT ENOUGH TO DEAL WITH!
AGH!
KRA-KOOM
OKAY, I GIVE.
WHO ARE YOU?
WHO ARE YOU REALLY?

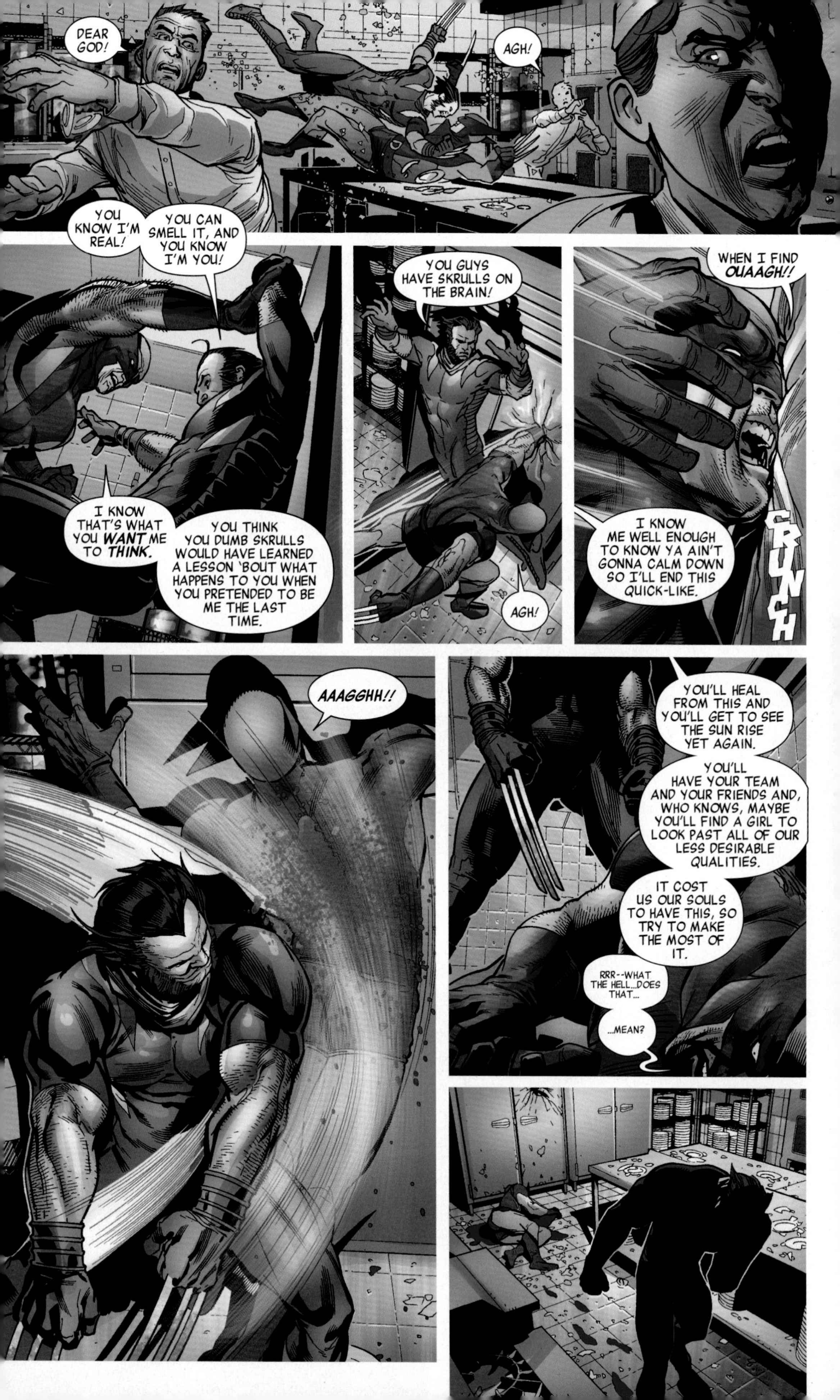
DEAR GOD!
AGH!
YOU KNOW I'M REAL!
YOU CAN SMELL IT, AND YOU KNOW I'M YOU!
I KNOW THAT'S WHAT YOU WANT ME TO THINK.
YOU THINK YOU DUMB SKRULLS WOULD HAVE LEARNED A LESSON 'BOUT WHAT HAPPENS TO YOU WHEN YOU PRETENDED TO BE ME THE LAST TIME.
YOU GUYS HAVE SKRULLS ON THE BRAIN!
AGH!
WHEN I FIND OUAAGH!!
I KNOW ME WELL ENOUGH TO KNOW YA AIN'T GONNA CALM DOWN SO I'LL END THIS QUICK-LIKE.
CRUNCH
AAAGGHH!!
YOU'LL HEAL FROM THIS AND YOU'LL GET TO SEE THE SUN RISE YET AGAIN.
YOU'LL HAVE YOUR TEAM AND YOUR FRIENDS AND, WHO KNOWS, MAYBE YOU'LL FIND A GIRL TO LOOK PAST ALL OF OUR LESS DESIRABLE QUALITIES.
IT COST US OUR SOULS TO HAVE THIS, SO TRY TO MAKE THE MOST OF IT.
RRR--WHAT THE HELL...DOES THAT...
...MEAN?

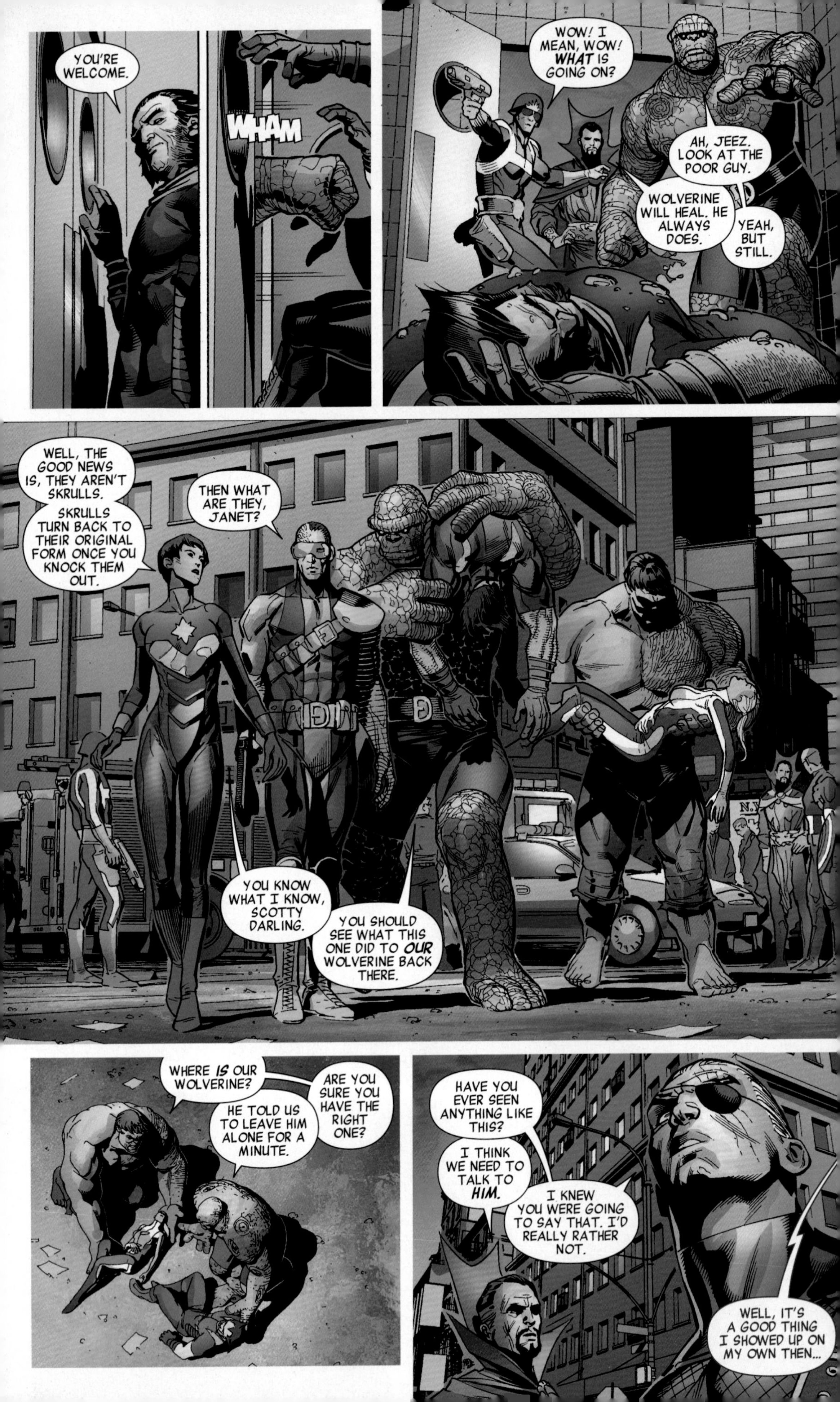
YOU'RE WELCOME.
WHAM
WOW! I MEAN, WOW! WHAT IS GOING ON?
AH, JEEZ. LOOK AT THE POOR GUY.
WOLVERINE WILL HEAL. HE ALWAYS DOES.
YEAH, BUT STILL.
WELL, THE GOOD NEWS IS, THEY AREN'T SKRULLS.
SKRULLS TURN BACK TO THEIR ORIGINAL FORM ONCE YOU KNOCK THEM OUT.
THEN WHAT ARE THEY, JANET?
YOU KNOW WHAT I KNOW, SCOTTY DARLING.
YOU SHOULD SEE WHAT THIS ONE DID TO OUR WOLVERINE BACK THERE.
WHERE IS OUR WOLVERINE?
HE TOLD US TO LEAVE HIM ALONE FOR A MINUTE.
ARE YOU SURE YOU HAVE THE RIGHT ONE?
HAVE YOU EVER SEEN ANYTHING LIKE THIS?
I THINK WE NEED TO TALK TO HIM.
I KNEW YOU WERE GOING TO SAY THAT. I'D REALLY RATHER NOT.
WELL, IT'S A GOOD THING I SHOWED UP ON MY OWN THEN...

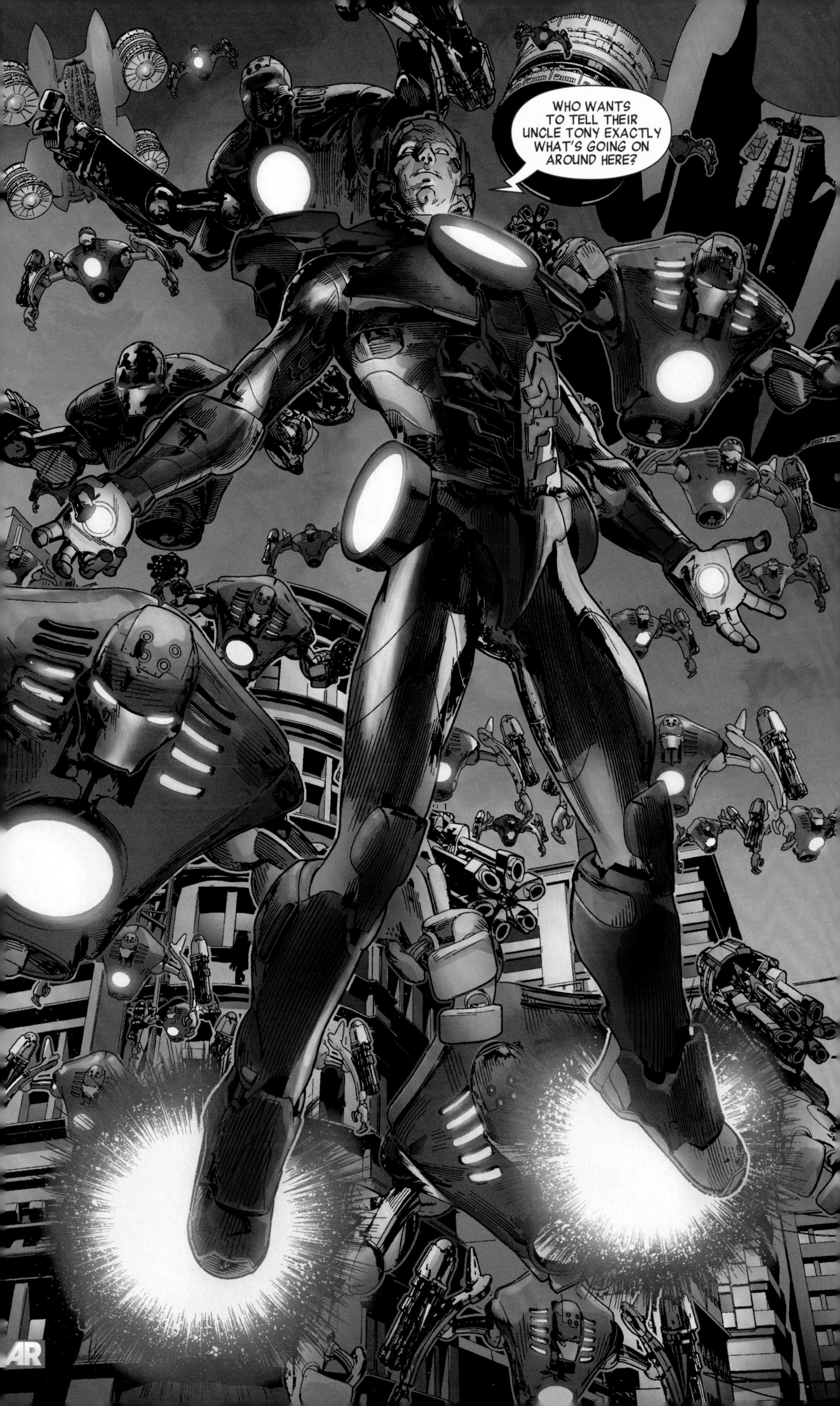
WHO WANTS TO TELL THEIR UNCLE TONY EXACTLY WHAT'S GOING ON AROUND HERE?

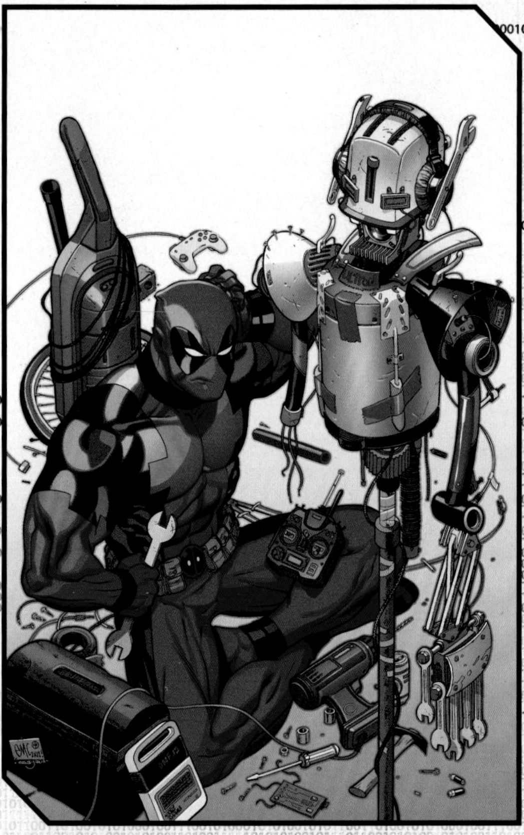

AGE OF ULTRON #1 DEADPOOL VARIANT
BY ED McGUINNESS & MARTE GRACIA

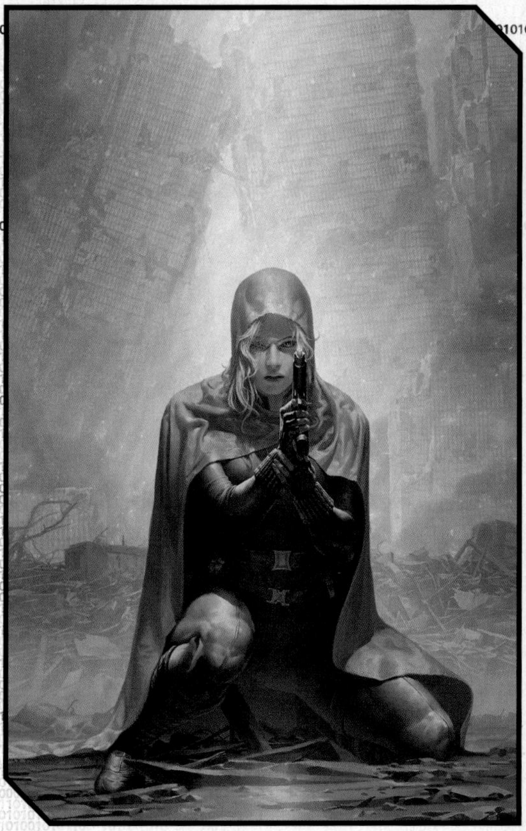

AGE OF ULTRON #2 VARIANT
BY JUNG-GEUN YOON

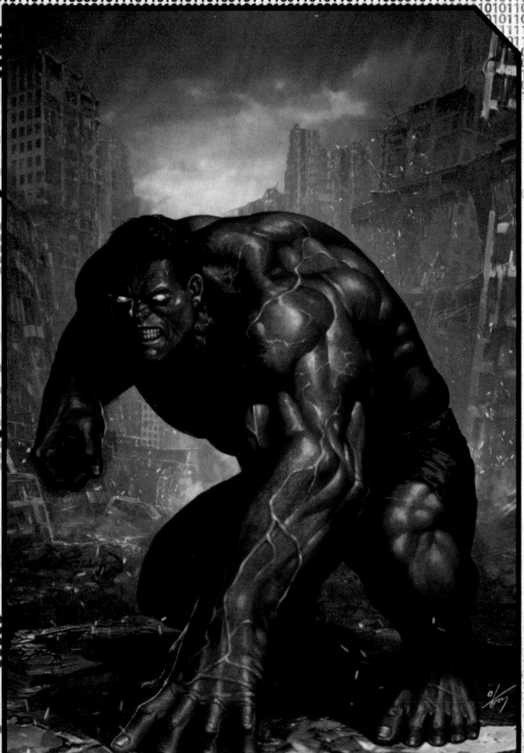

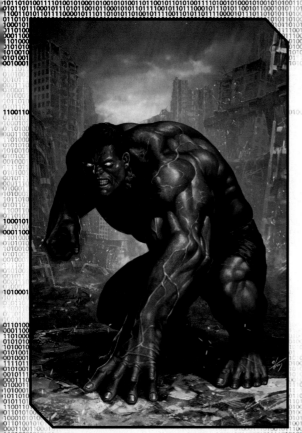

AGE OF ULTRON #3 VARIANT
BY IN-HYUK LEE

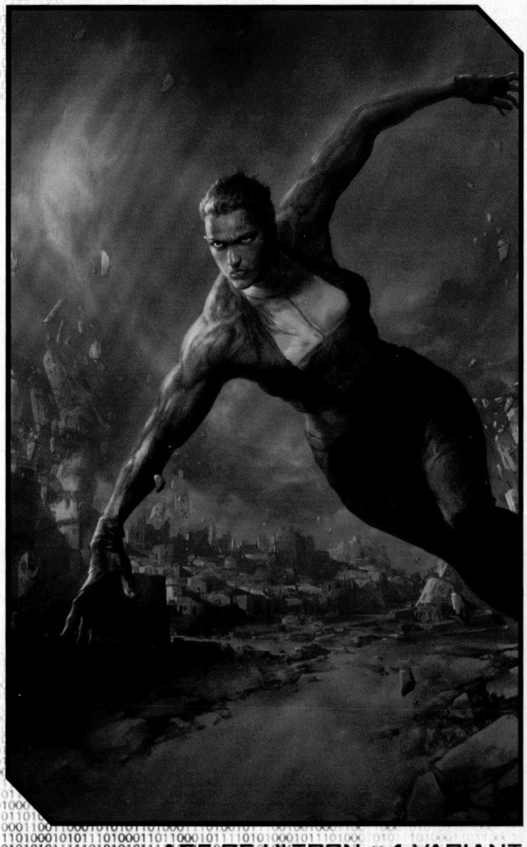

AGE OF ULTRON #4 VARIANT
BY FENGHUA ZHONG

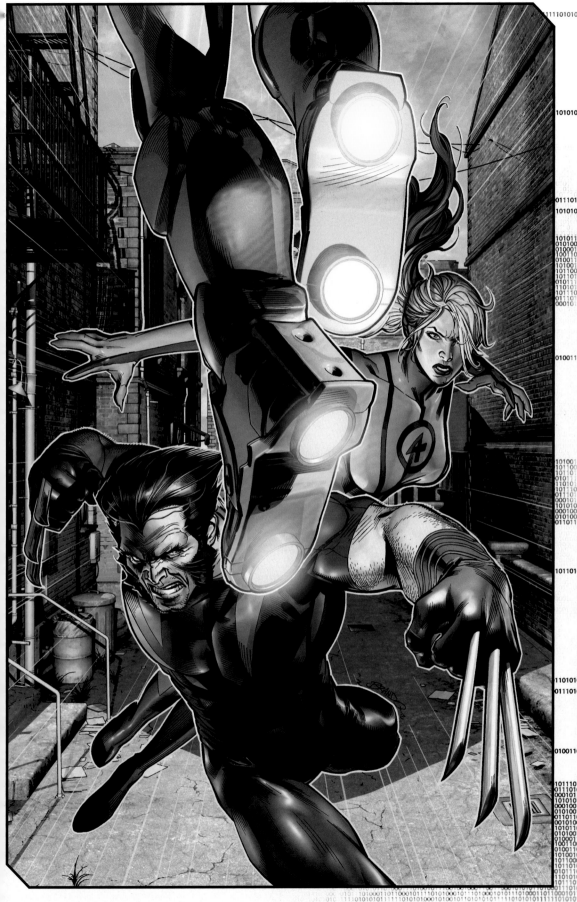

AGE OF ULTRON #8

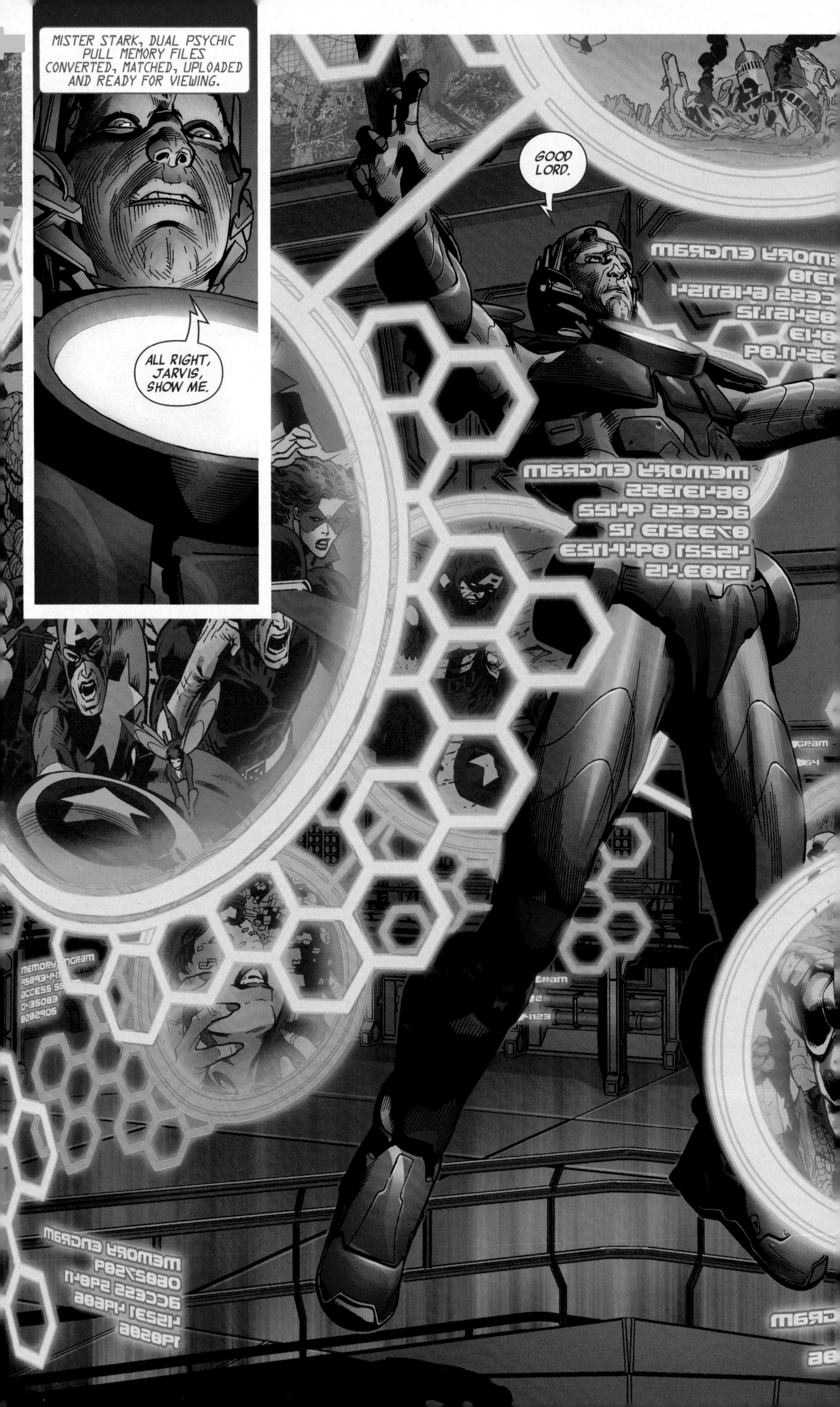
MISTER STARK, DUAL PSYCHIC PULL MEMORY FILES CONVERTED, MATCHED, UPLOADED AND READY FOR VIEWING.
ALL RIGHT, JARVIS, SHOW ME.
GOOD LORD.

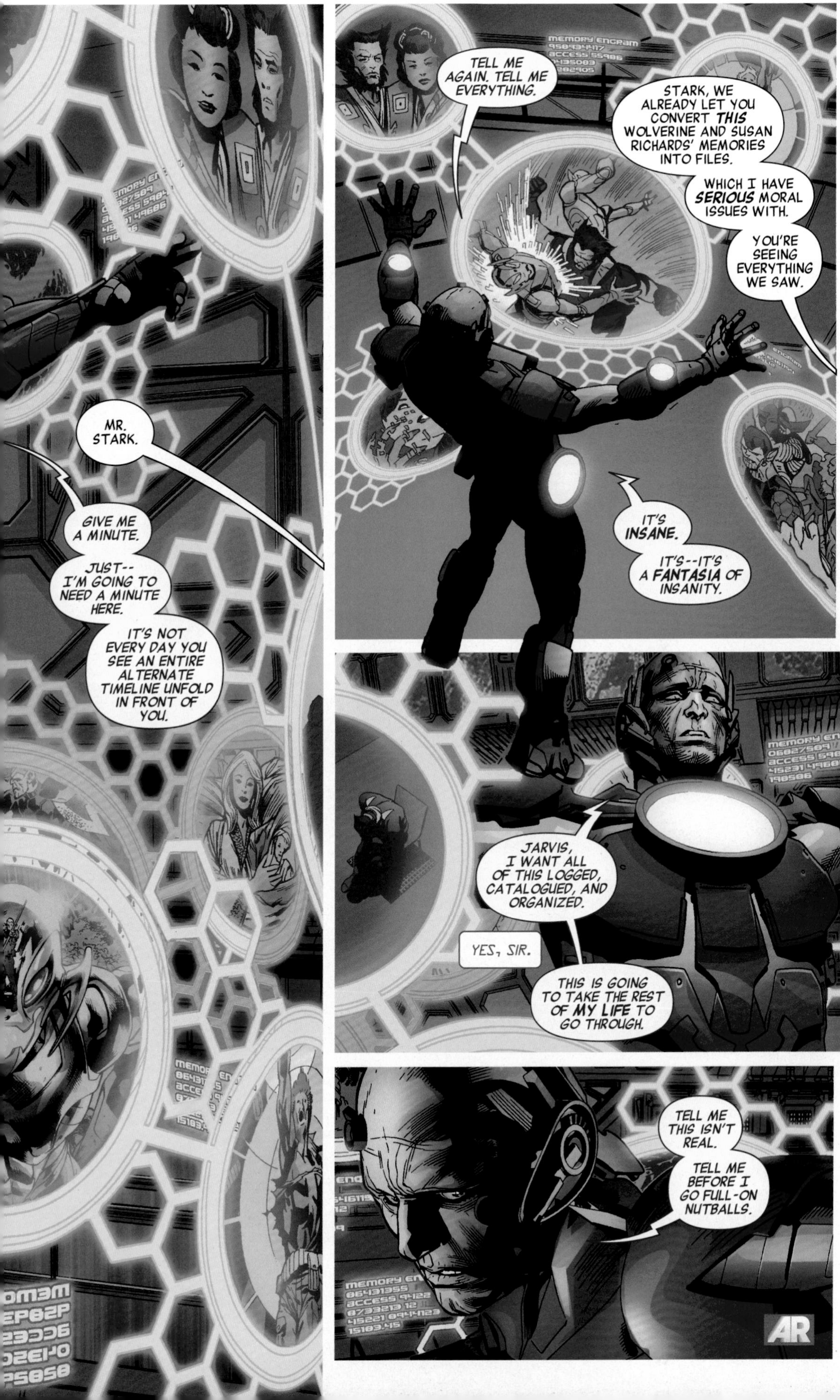
MR. STARK.
GIVE ME A MINUTE.
JUST-- I'M GOING TO NEED A MINUTE HERE.
IT'S NOT EVERY DAY YOU SEE AN ENTIRE ALTERNATE TIMELINE UNFOLD IN FRONT OF YOU.
TELL ME AGAIN. TELL ME EVERYTHING.
STARK, WE ALREADY LET YOU CONVERT THIS WOLVERINE AND SUSAN RICHARDS' MEMORIES INTO FILES.
WHICH I HAVE SERIOUS MORAL ISSUES WITH.
YOU'RE SEEING EVERYTHING WE SAW.
IT'S INSANE.
IT'S--IT'S A FANTASIA OF INSANITY.
JARVIS, I WANT ALL OF THIS LOGGED, CATALOGUED, AND ORGANIZED.
YES, SIR.
THIS IS GOING TO TAKE THE REST OF MY LIFE TO GO THROUGH.
TELL ME THIS ISN'T REAL.
TELL ME BEFORE I GO FULL-ON NUTBALLS.

MEMORY ENGR
AA
23

THAT MAN **IS**, WITHOUT QUESTION, JAMES HOWLETT.

A.K.A. LOGAN.

A.K.A. WEAPON X.

A.K.A. WOLVERINE.

JUST NOT **OUR** WOLVERINE.

MEMORY ENGR
958934417
ACCESS 5598E
0435083
8282905

AND HE CAME HERE WITH SUSAN RICHARDS.

THAT **IS** HER.

JUST, AGAIN, NOT, ACCORDING TO THEIR MEMORIES, **OUR** SUSAN RICHARDS.

memory
958934417
access 5598E
0135083

THE NARRATIVE INSIDE EACH OF THEIR HEADS IS IDENTICAL.

PERFECTLY IN SYNC.

YOU CANNOT-- YOU **CANNOT FAKE** THAT KIND OF PSYCHIC SYNCHRONICITY.

THEY BOTH, OVER THE LAST FEW WEEKS, SAW AND EXPERIENCED THE EXACT SAME HORRIBLE MEMORIES.

Y ENG
417
5598
S

BUT FROST, XAVIER, COME ON...

YOU'RE TELLING ME THERE'S **NO WAY** THAT **MORGANA LE FEY** PLANTED THOSE MEMORIES?

THERE'S NO WAY SHE HAS DROPPED THEM HERE-- THAT THIS ISN'T SOME SORT OF CLONE/ FAKE MEMORY/ TROJAN HORSE/ MAGIC BOMB ABOUT TO BLOW UP IN OUR FACES?

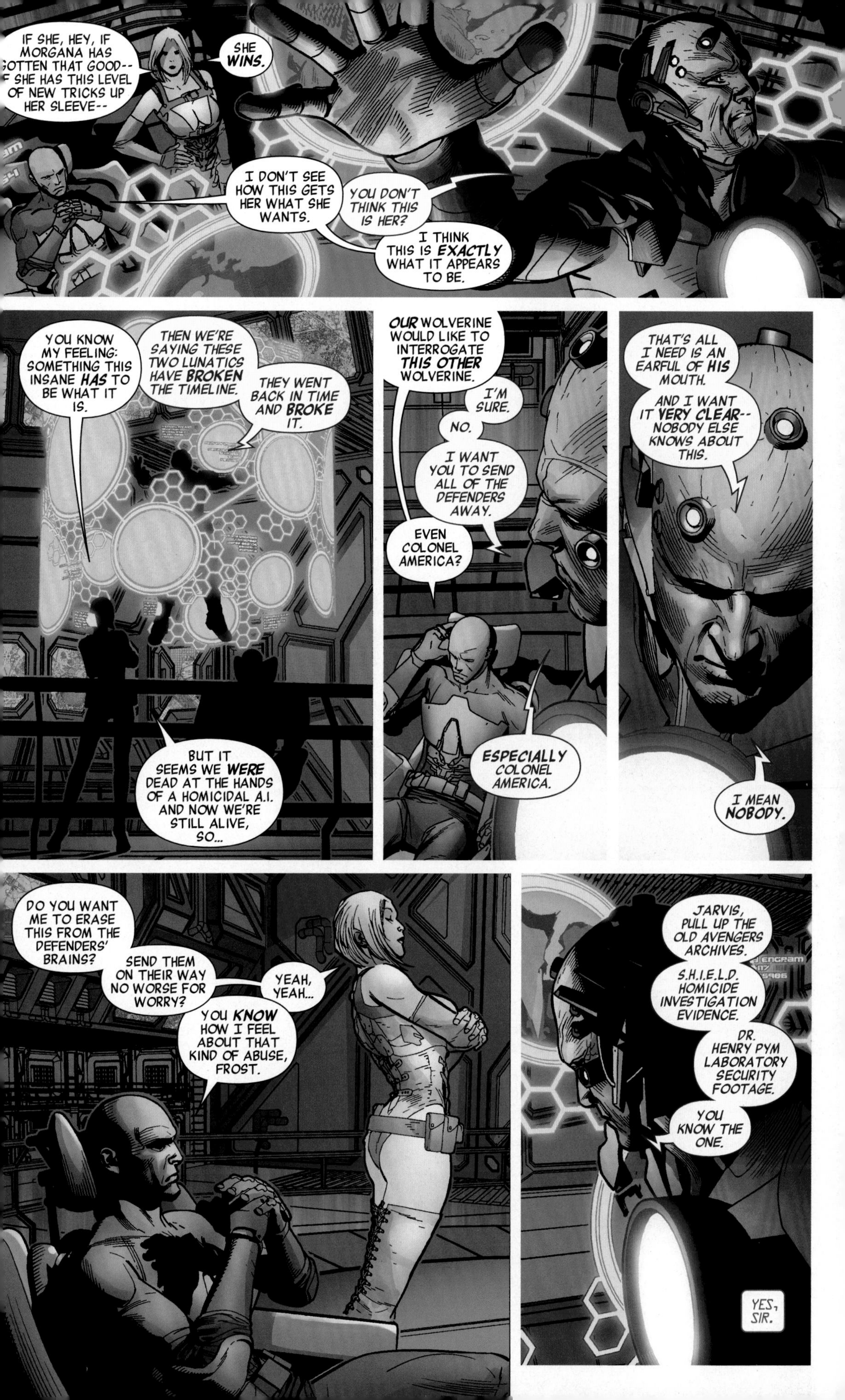

IF SHE, HEY, IF MORGANA HAS GOTTEN THAT GOOD-- IF SHE HAS THIS LEVEL OF NEW TRICKS UP HER SLEEVE--
SHE WINS.
I DON'T SEE HOW THIS GETS HER WHAT SHE WANTS.
YOU DON'T THINK THIS IS HER?
I THINK THIS IS EXACTLY WHAT IT APPEARS TO BE.
YOU KNOW MY FEELING: SOMETHING THIS INSANE HAS TO BE WHAT IT IS.
THEN WE'RE SAYING THESE TWO LUNATICS HAVE BROKEN THE TIMELINE.
THEY WENT BACK IN TIME AND BROKE IT.
BUT IT SEEMS WE WERE DEAD AT THE HANDS OF A HOMICIDAL A.I. AND NOW WE'RE STILL ALIVE, SO...
OUR WOLVERINE WOULD LIKE TO INTERROGATE THIS OTHER WOLVERINE.
I'M SURE.
NO.
I WANT YOU TO SEND ALL OF THE DEFENDERS AWAY.
EVEN COLONEL AMERICA?
ESPECIALLY COLONEL AMERICA.
THAT'S ALL I NEED IS AN EARFUL OF HIS MOUTH.
AND I WANT IT VERY CLEAR-- NOBODY ELSE KNOWS ABOUT THIS.
I MEAN NOBODY.
DO YOU WANT ME TO ERASE THIS FROM THE DEFENDERS' BRAINS?
SEND THEM ON THEIR WAY NO WORSE FOR WORRY?
YEAH, YEAH...
YOU KNOW HOW I FEEL ABOUT THAT KIND OF ABUSE, FROST.
JARVIS, PULL UP THE OLD AVENGERS ARCHIVES.
S.H.I.E.L.D. HOMICIDE INVESTIGATION EVIDENCE.
DR. HENRY PYM LABORATORY SECURITY FOOTAGE.
YOU KNOW THE ONE.
YES, SIR.

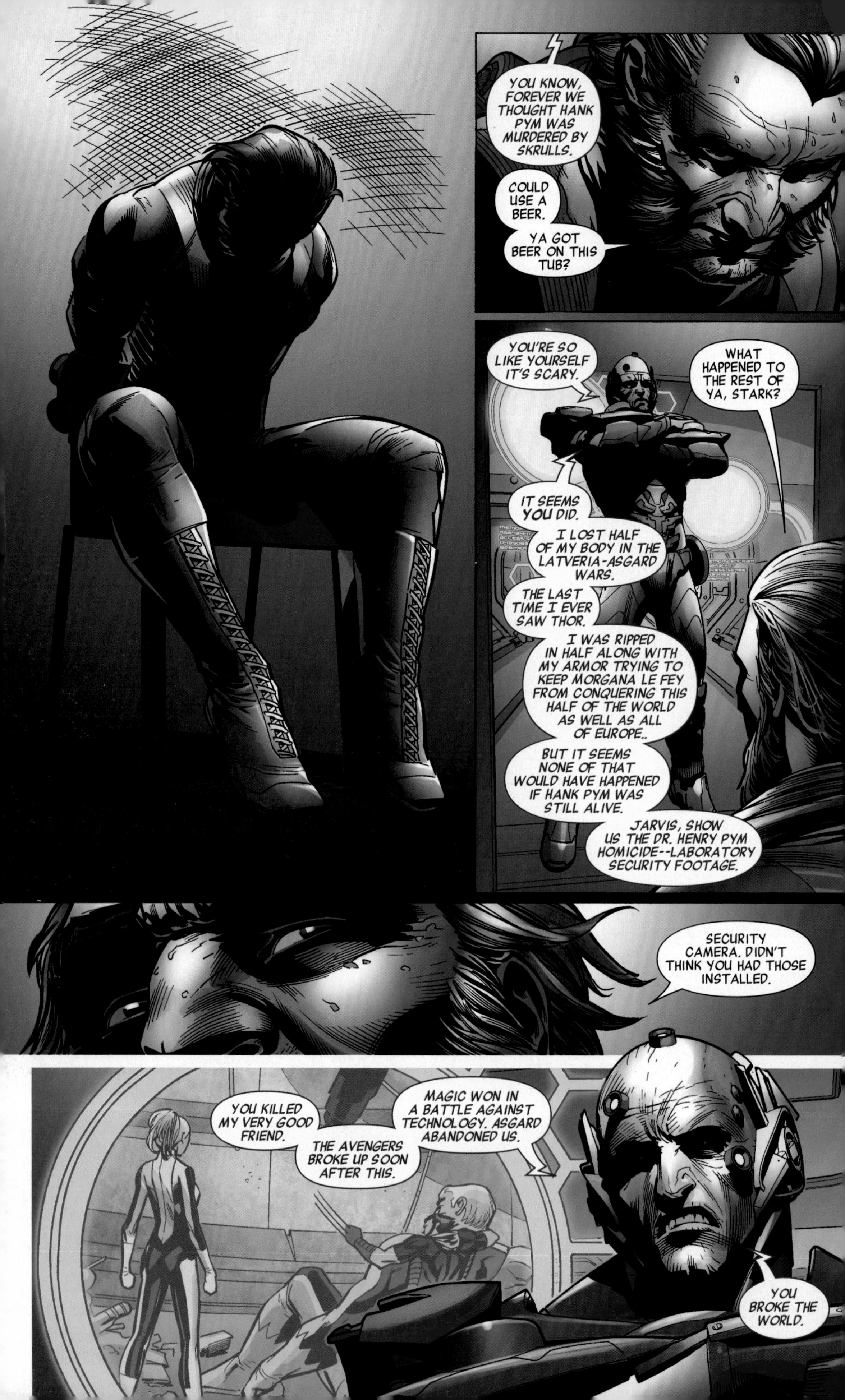
YOU KNOW, FOREVER WE THOUGHT HANK PYM WAS MURDERED BY SKRULLS.
COULD USE A BEER.
YA GOT BEER ON THIS TUB?
YOU'RE SO LIKE YOURSELF IT'S SCARY.
WHAT HAPPENED TO THE REST OF YA, STARK?
IT SEEMS YOU DID.
I LOST HALF OF MY BODY IN THE LATVERIA-ASGARD WARS.
THE LAST TIME I EVER SAW THOR.
I WAS RIPPED IN HALF ALONG WITH MY ARMOR TRYING TO KEEP MORGANA LE FEY FROM CONQUERING THIS HALF OF THE WORLD AS WELL AS ALL OF EUROPE..
BUT IT SEEMS NONE OF THAT WOULD HAVE HAPPENED IF HANK PYM WAS STILL ALIVE.
JARVIS, SHOW US THE DR. HENRY PYM HOMICIDE--LABORATORY SECURITY FOOTAGE.
SECURITY CAMERA. DIDN'T THINK YOU HAD THOSE INSTALLED.
YOU KILLED MY VERY GOOD FRIEND.
MAGIC WON IN A BATTLE AGAINST TECHNOLOGY. ASGARD ABANDONED US.
THE AVENGERS BROKE UP SOON AFTER THIS.
YOU BROKE THE WORLD.

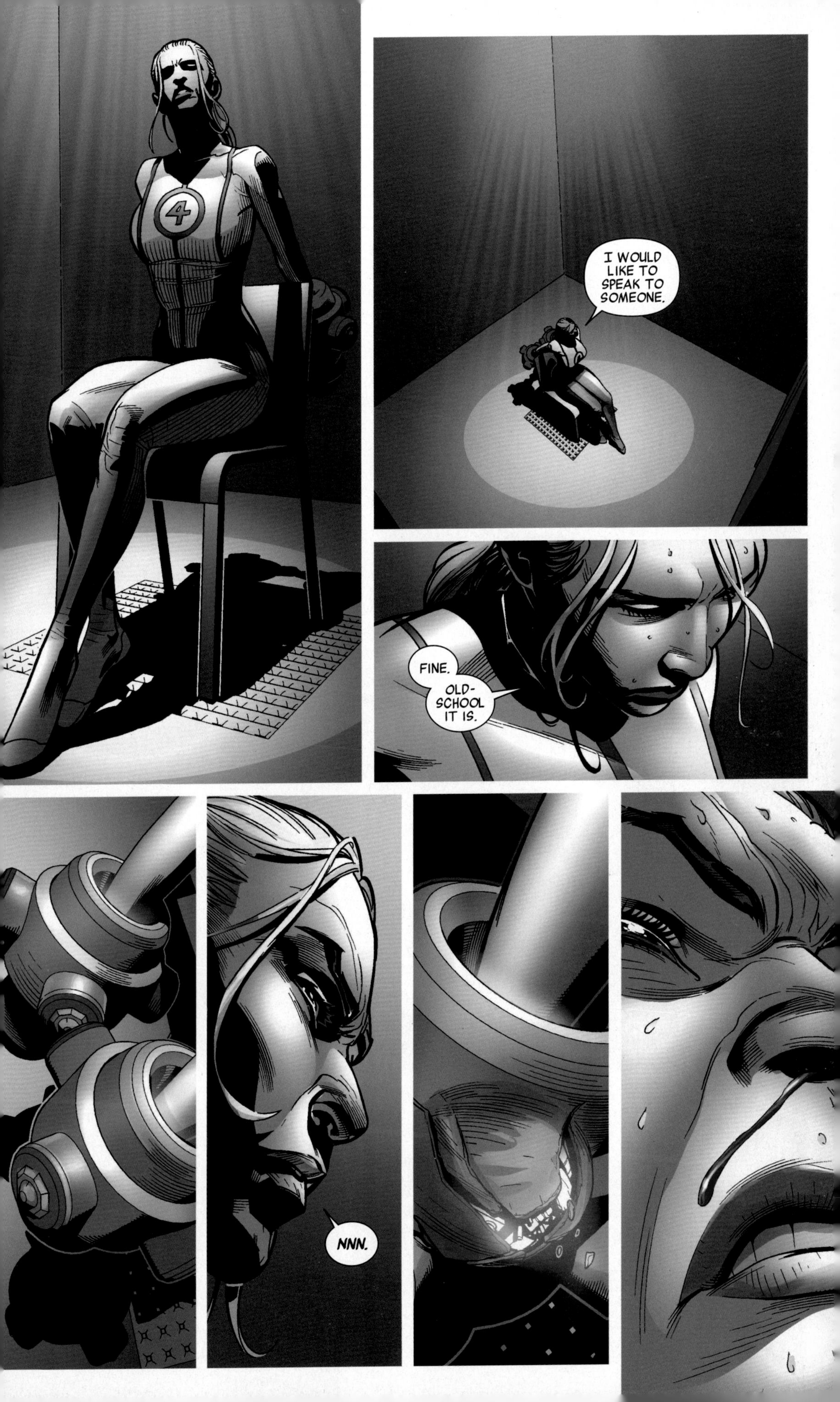
I WOULD LIKE TO SPEAK TO SOMEONE.
FINE.
OLD-SCHOOL IT IS.
NNN.

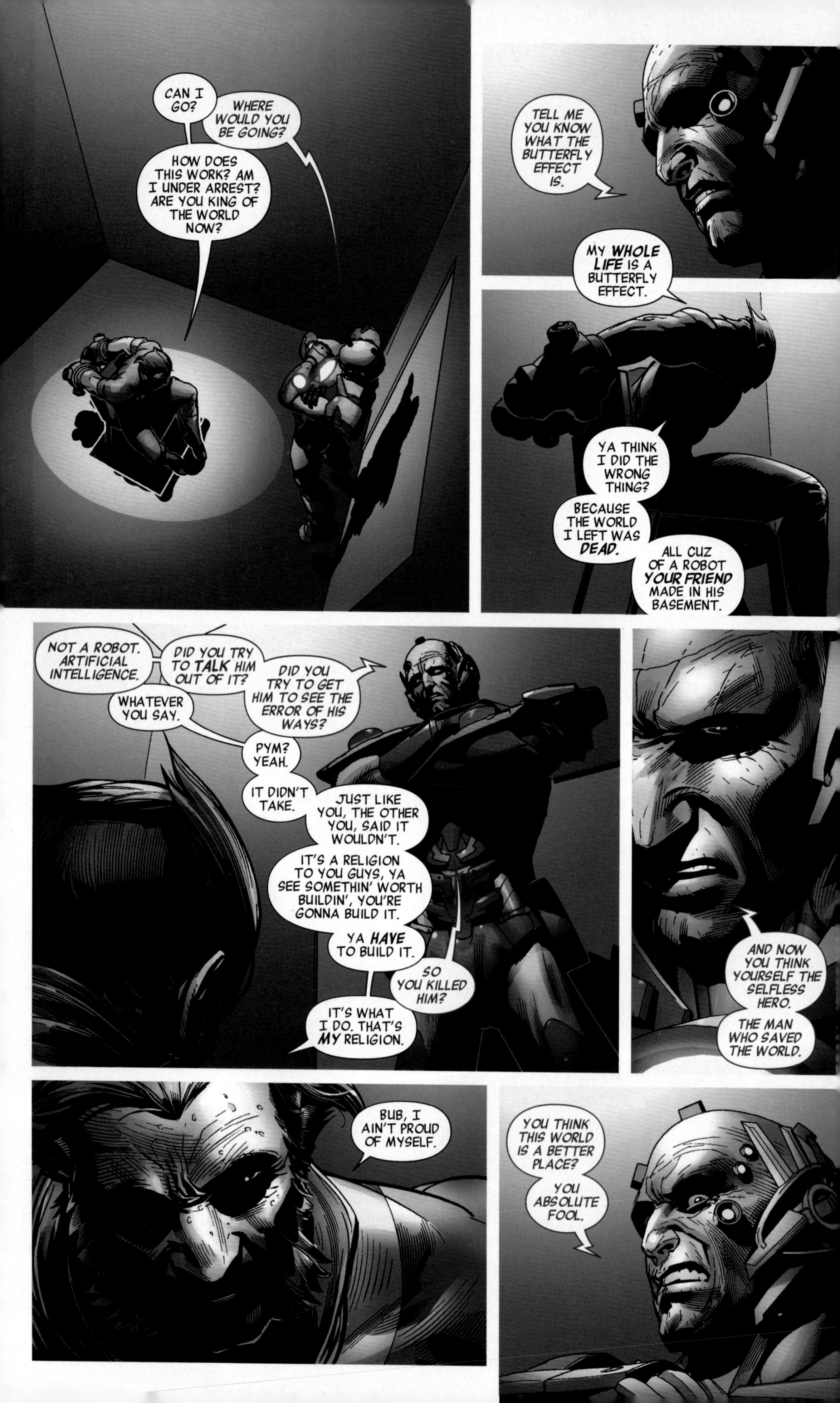
CAN I GO?
WHERE WOULD YOU BE GOING?
HOW DOES THIS WORK? AM I UNDER ARREST? ARE YOU KING OF THE WORLD NOW?
TELL ME YOU KNOW WHAT THE BUTTERFLY EFFECT IS.
MY WHOLE LIFE IS A BUTTERFLY EFFECT.
YA THINK I DID THE WRONG THING?
BECAUSE THE WORLD I LEFT WAS DEAD.
ALL CUZ OF A ROBOT YOUR FRIEND MADE IN HIS BASEMENT.
NOT A ROBOT. ARTIFICIAL INTELLIGENCE.
WHATEVER YOU SAY.
DID YOU TRY TO TALK HIM OUT OF IT?
DID YOU TRY TO GET HIM TO SEE THE ERROR OF HIS WAYS?
PYM? YEAH.
IT DIDN'T TAKE.
JUST LIKE YOU, THE OTHER YOU, SAID IT WOULDN'T.
IT'S A RELIGION TO YOU GUYS, YA SEE SOMETHIN' WORTH BUILDIN', YOU'RE GONNA BUILD IT.
YA HAVE TO BUILD IT.
SO YOU KILLED HIM?
IT'S WHAT I DO. THAT'S MY RELIGION.
AND NOW YOU THINK YOURSELF THE SELFLESS HERO.
THE MAN WHO SAVED THE WORLD.
BUB, I AIN'T PROUD OF MYSELF.
YOU THINK THIS WORLD IS A BETTER PLACE?
YOU ABSOLUTE FOOL.

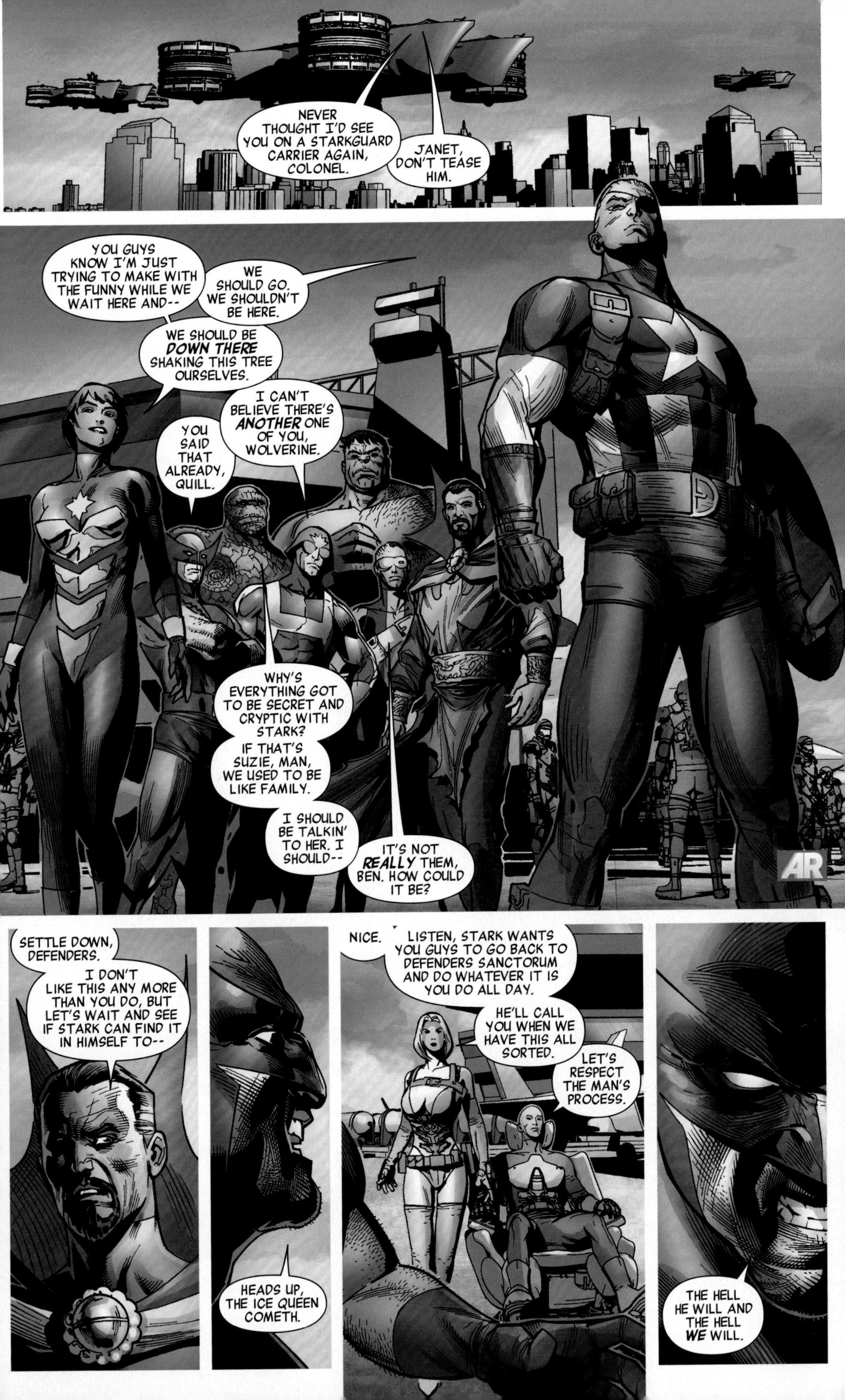
NEVER THOUGHT I'D SEE YOU ON A STARKGUARD CARRIER AGAIN, COLONEL.
JANET, DON'T TEASE HIM.
YOU GUYS KNOW I'M JUST TRYING TO MAKE WITH THE FUNNY WHILE WE WAIT HERE AND--
WE SHOULD GO. WE SHOULDN'T BE HERE.
WE SHOULD BE **DOWN THERE** SHAKING THIS TREE OURSELVES.
I CAN'T BELIEVE THERE'S **ANOTHER** ONE OF YOU, WOLVERINE.
YOU SAID THAT ALREADY, QUILL.
WHY'S EVERYTHING GOT TO BE SECRET AND CRYPTIC WITH STARK?
IF THAT'S SUZIE, MAN, WE USED TO BE LIKE FAMILY.
I SHOULD BE TALKIN' TO HER. I SHOULD--
IT'S NOT **REALLY** THEM, BEN. HOW COULD IT BE?
SETTLE DOWN, DEFENDERS.
I DON'T LIKE THIS ANY MORE THAN YOU DO, BUT LET'S WAIT AND SEE IF STARK CAN FIND IT IN HIMSELF TO--
HEADS UP, THE ICE QUEEN COMETH.
NICE.
LISTEN, STARK WANTS YOU GUYS TO GO BACK TO DEFENDERS SANCTORUM AND DO WHATEVER IT IS YOU DO ALL DAY.
HE'LL CALL YOU WHEN WE HAVE THIS ALL SORTED.
LET'S RESPECT THE MAN'S PROCESS.
THE HELL HE WILL AND THE HELL **WE** WILL.

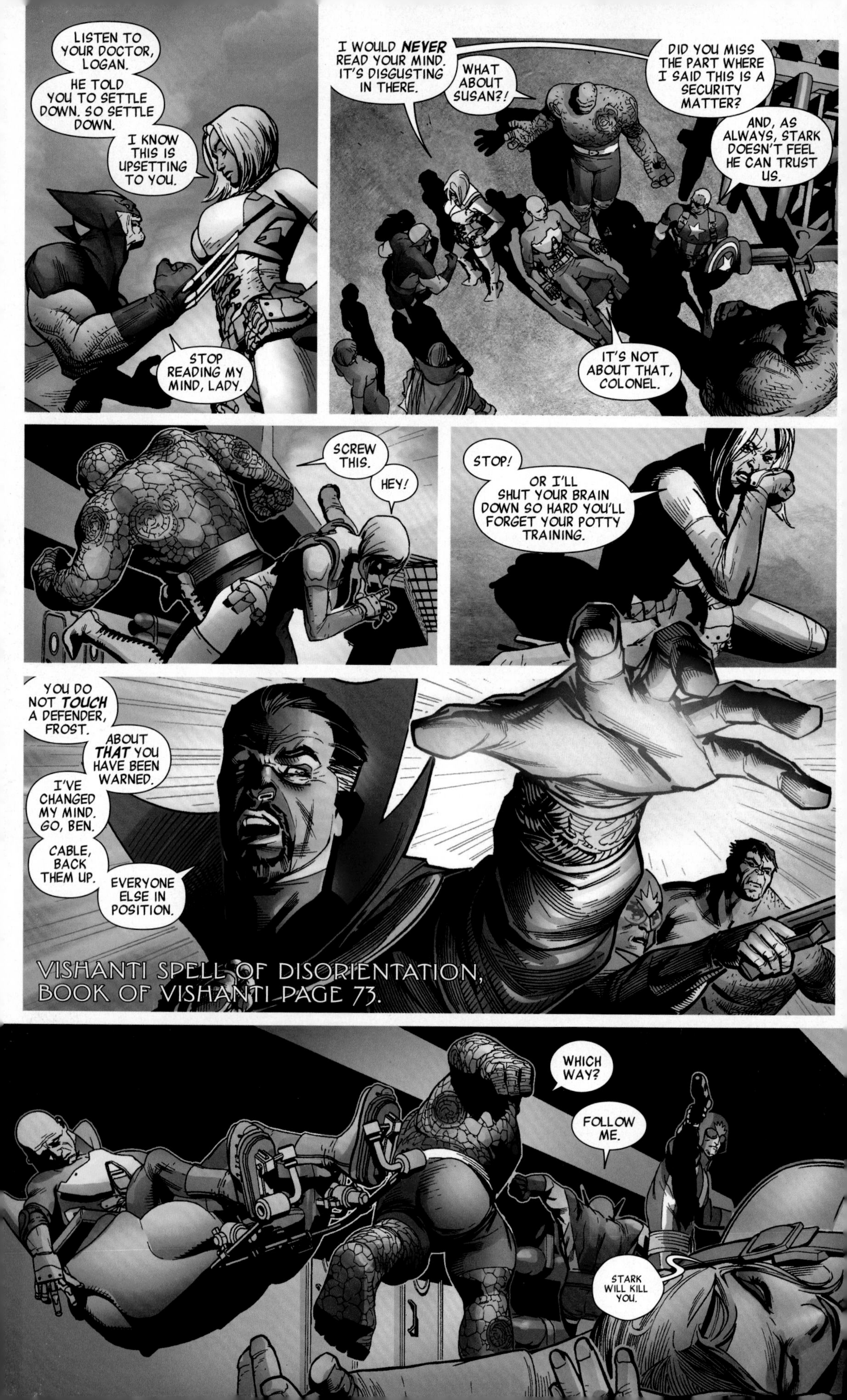
LISTEN TO YOUR DOCTOR, LOGAN.
HE TOLD YOU TO SETTLE DOWN. SO SETTLE DOWN.
I KNOW THIS IS UPSETTING TO YOU.
STOP READING MY MIND, LADY.
I WOULD NEVER READ YOUR MIND. IT'S DISGUSTING IN THERE.
WHAT ABOUT SUSAN?!
DID YOU MISS THE PART WHERE I SAID THIS IS A SECURITY MATTER?
AND, AS ALWAYS, STARK DOESN'T FEEL HE CAN TRUST US.
IT'S NOT ABOUT THAT, COLONEL.
SCREW THIS.
HEY!
STOP!
OR I'LL SHUT YOUR BRAIN DOWN SO HARD YOU'LL FORGET YOUR POTTY TRAINING.
YOU DO NOT TOUCH A DEFENDER, FROST.
ABOUT THAT YOU HAVE BEEN WARNED.
I'VE CHANGED MY MIND. GO, BEN.
CABLE, BACK THEM UP.
EVERYONE ELSE IN POSITION.
VISHANTI SPELL OF DISORIENTATION, BOOK OF VISHANTI PAGE 73.
WHICH WAY?
FOLLOW ME.
STARK WILL KILL YOU.

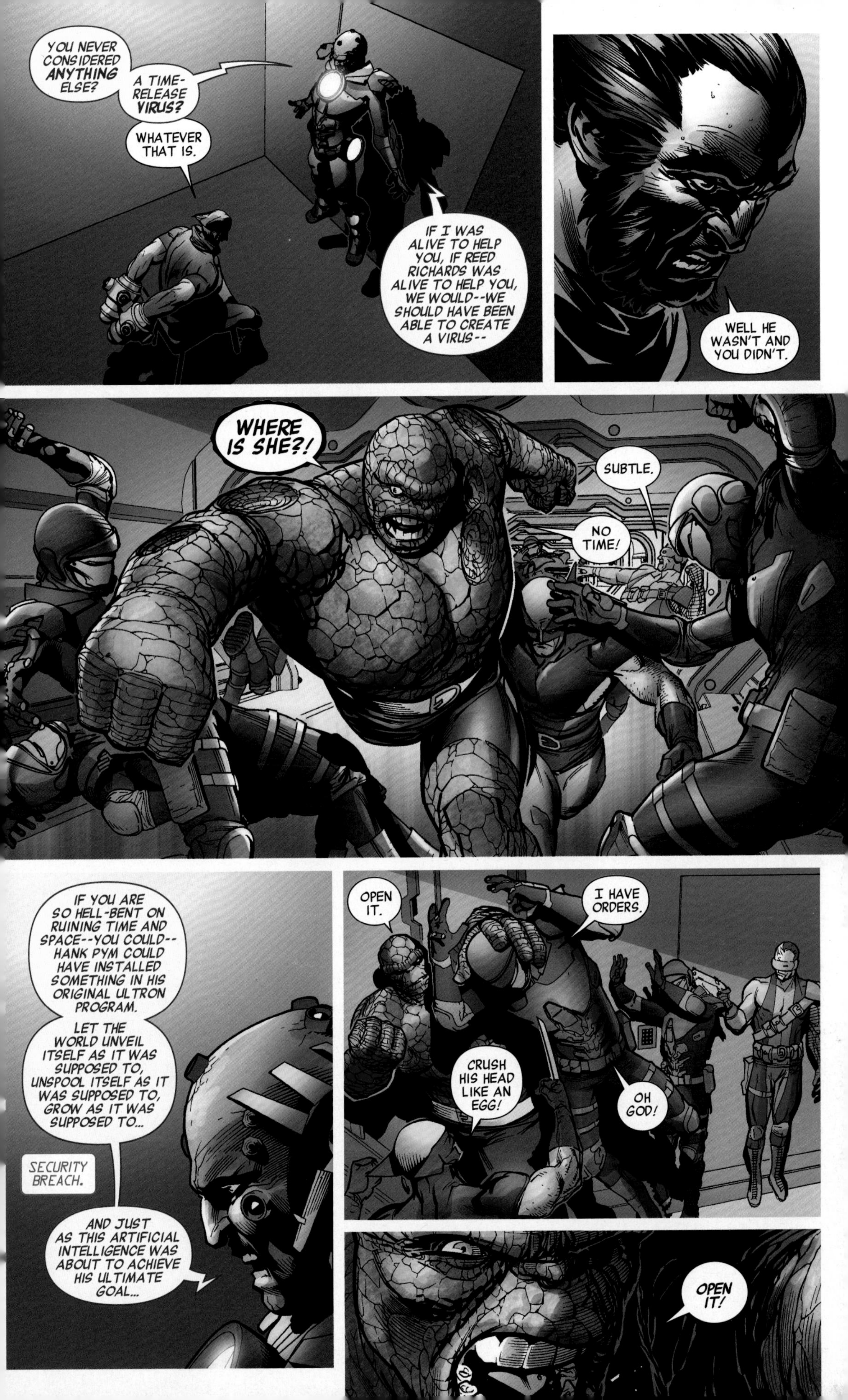
YOU NEVER CONSIDERED ANYTHING ELSE?
A TIME-RELEASE VIRUS?
WHATEVER THAT IS.
IF I WAS ALIVE TO HELP YOU, IF REED RICHARDS WAS ALIVE TO HELP YOU, WE WOULD--WE SHOULD HAVE BEEN ABLE TO CREATE A VIRUS--
WELL HE WASN'T AND YOU DIDN'T.
WHERE IS SHE?!
SUBTLE.
NO TIME!
IF YOU ARE SO HELL-BENT ON RUINING TIME AND SPACE--YOU COULD--HANK PYM COULD HAVE INSTALLED SOMETHING IN HIS ORIGINAL ULTRON PROGRAM.
LET THE WORLD UNVEIL ITSELF AS IT WAS SUPPOSED TO, UNSPOOL ITSELF AS IT WAS SUPPOSED TO, GROW AS IT WAS SUPPOSED TO...
SECURITY BREACH.
AND JUST AS THIS ARTIFICIAL INTELLIGENCE WAS ABOUT TO ACHIEVE HIS ULTIMATE GOAL...
OPEN IT.
I HAVE ORDERS.
CRUSH HIS HEAD LIKE AN EGG!
OH GOD!
OPEN IT!

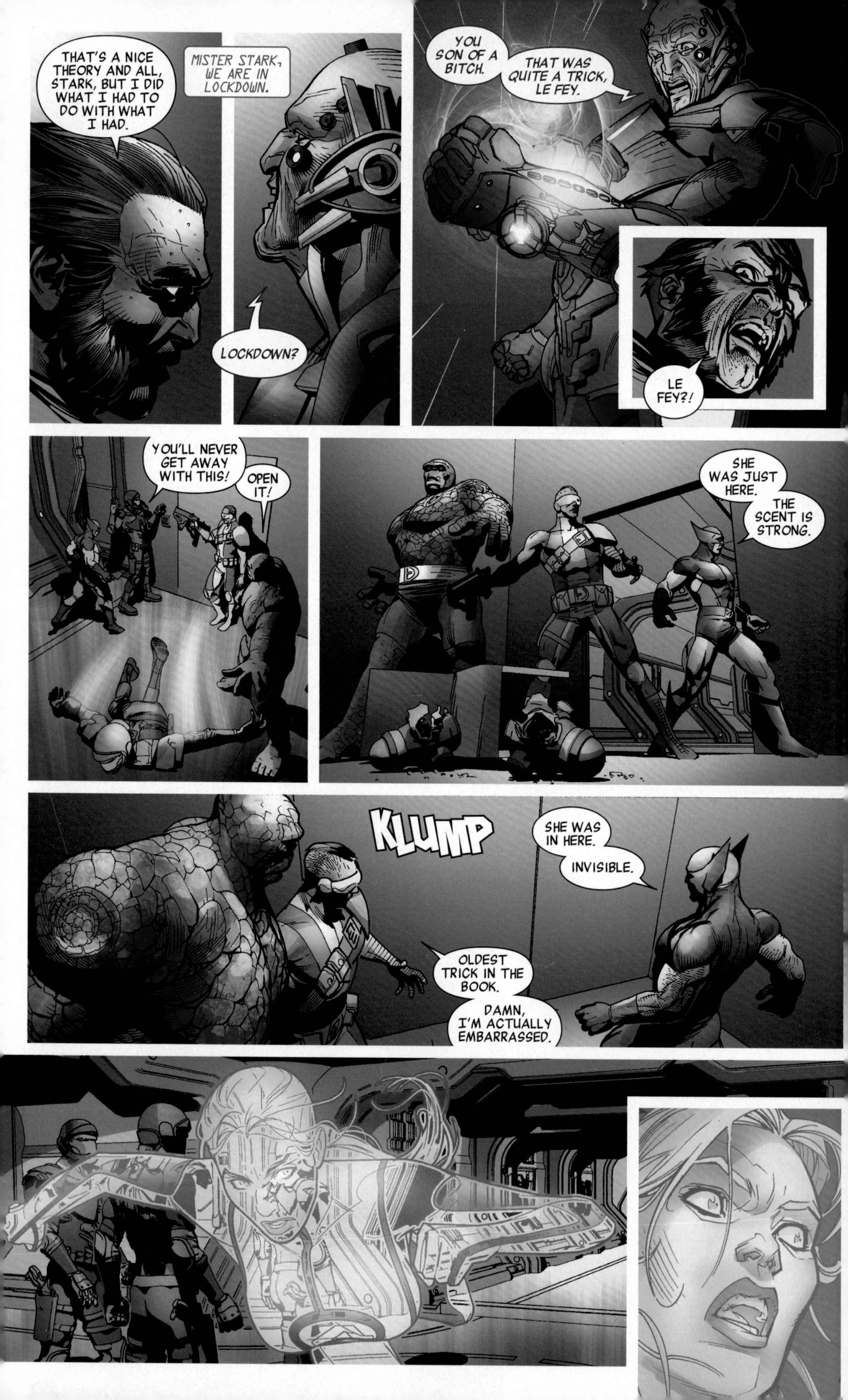
THAT'S A NICE THEORY AND ALL, STARK, BUT I DID WHAT I HAD TO DO WITH WHAT I HAD.
MISTER STARK, WE ARE IN LOCKDOWN.
LOCKDOWN?
YOU SON OF A BITCH.
THAT WAS QUITE A TRICK, LE FEY.
LE FEY?!
YOU'LL NEVER GET AWAY WITH THIS!
OPEN IT!
SHE WAS JUST HERE.
THE SCENT IS STRONG.
KLUMP
SHE WAS IN HERE.
INVISIBLE.
OLDEST TRICK IN THE BOOK.
DAMN, I'M ACTUALLY EMBARRASSED.

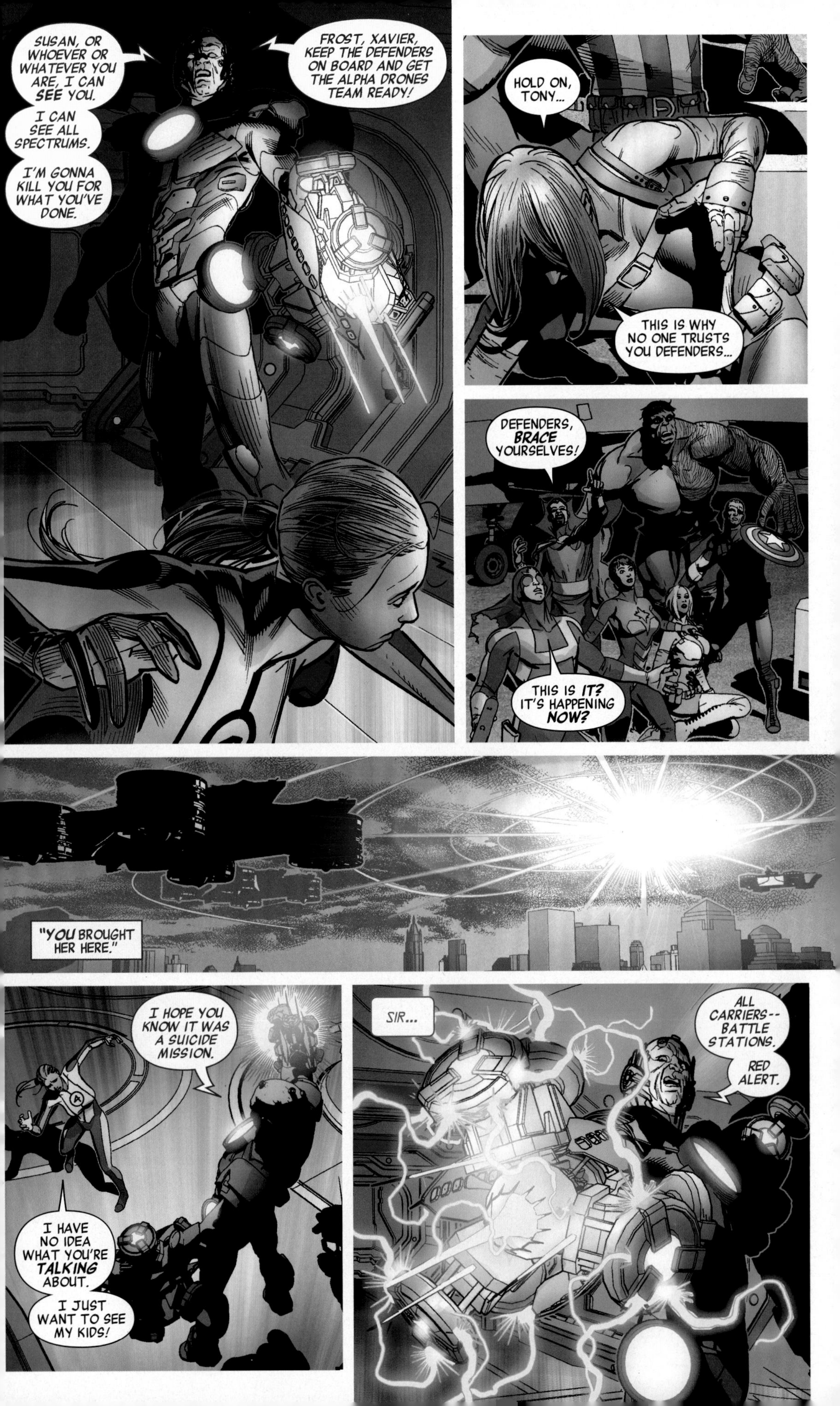

SUSAN, OR WHOEVER OR WHATEVER YOU ARE, I CAN SEE YOU.
I CAN SEE ALL SPECTRUMS.
I'M GONNA KILL YOU FOR WHAT YOU'VE DONE.
FROST, XAVIER, KEEP THE DEFENDERS ON BOARD AND GET THE ALPHA DRONES TEAM READY!
HOLD ON, TONY...
THIS IS WHY NO ONE TRUSTS YOU DEFENDERS...
DEFENDERS, BRACE YOURSELVES!
THIS IS IT? IT'S HAPPENING NOW?
"YOU BROUGHT HER HERE."
I HOPE YOU KNOW IT WAS A SUICIDE MISSION.
I HAVE NO IDEA WHAT YOU'RE TALKING ABOUT.
I JUST WANT TO SEE MY KIDS!
SIR...
ALL CARRIERS-- BATTLE STATIONS.
RED ALERT.

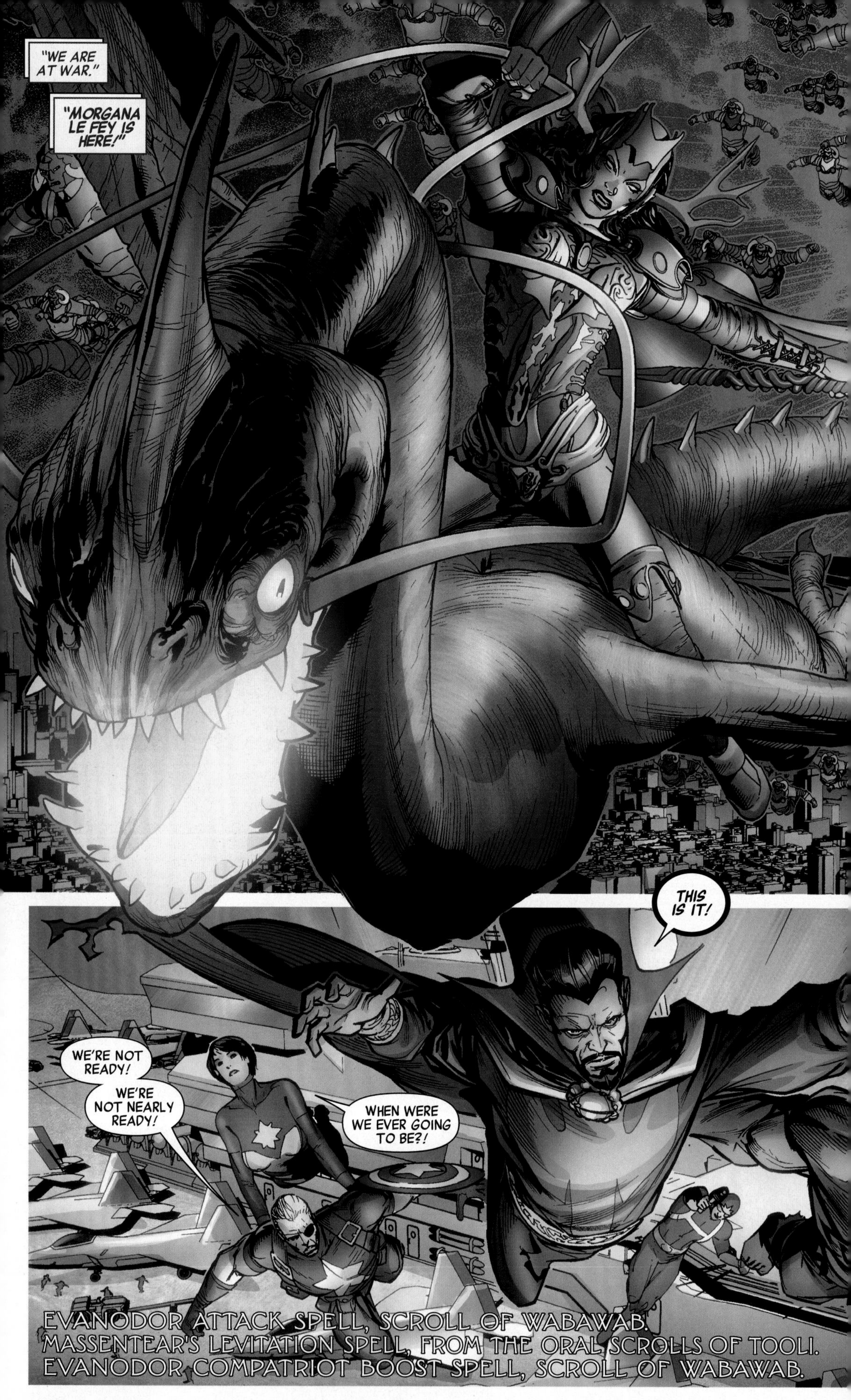
"WE ARE AT WAR."
"MORGANA LE FEY IS HERE!"
THIS IS IT!
WE'RE NOT READY!
WE'RE NOT NEARLY READY!
WHEN WERE WE EVER GOING TO BE?!
EVANODOR ATTACK SPELL, SCROLL OF WABAWAB.
MASSENTEAR'S LEVITATION SPELL, FROM THE ORAL SCROLLS OF TOOLI.
EVANODOR COMPATRIOT BOOST SPELL, SCROLL OF WABAWAB.

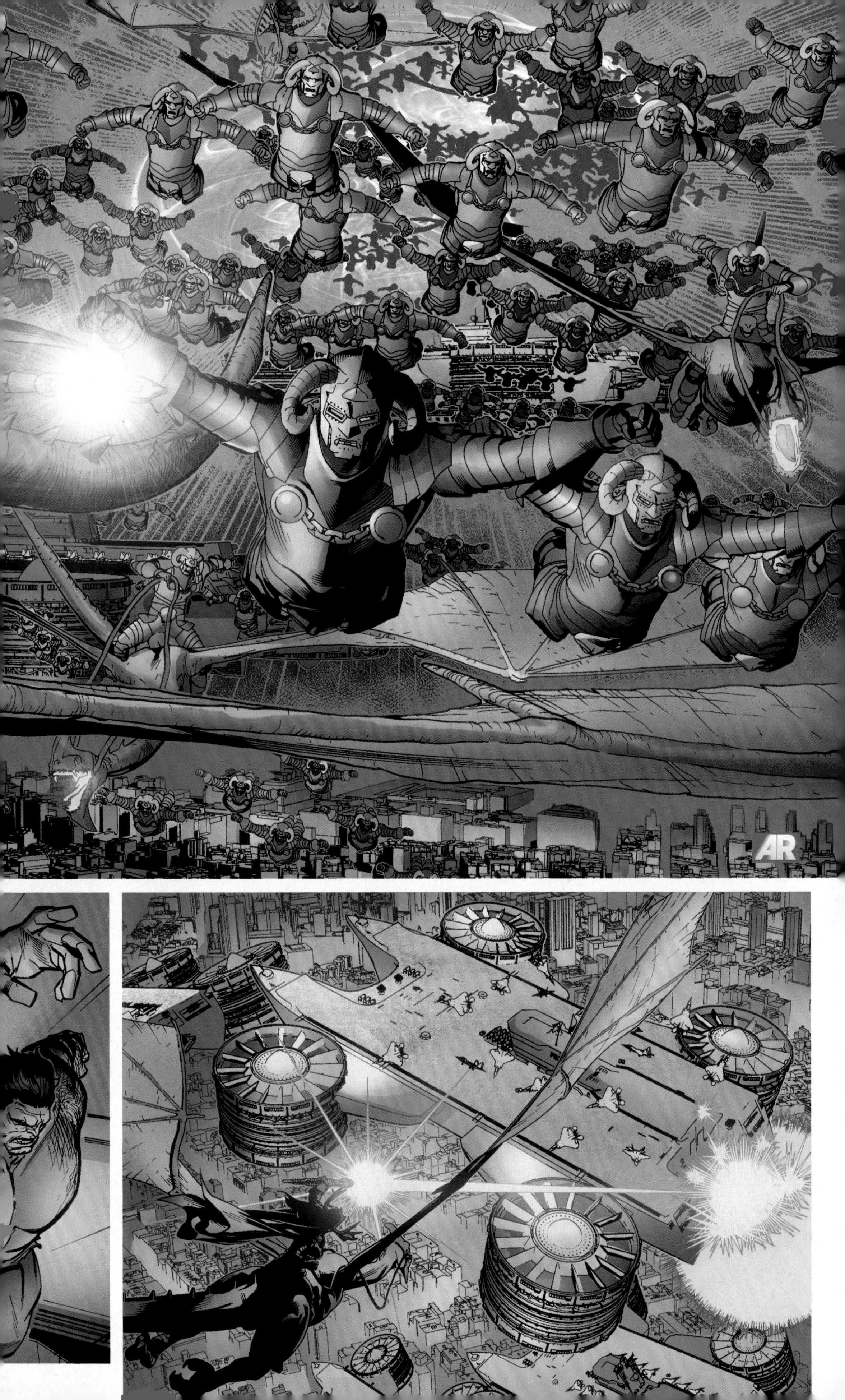

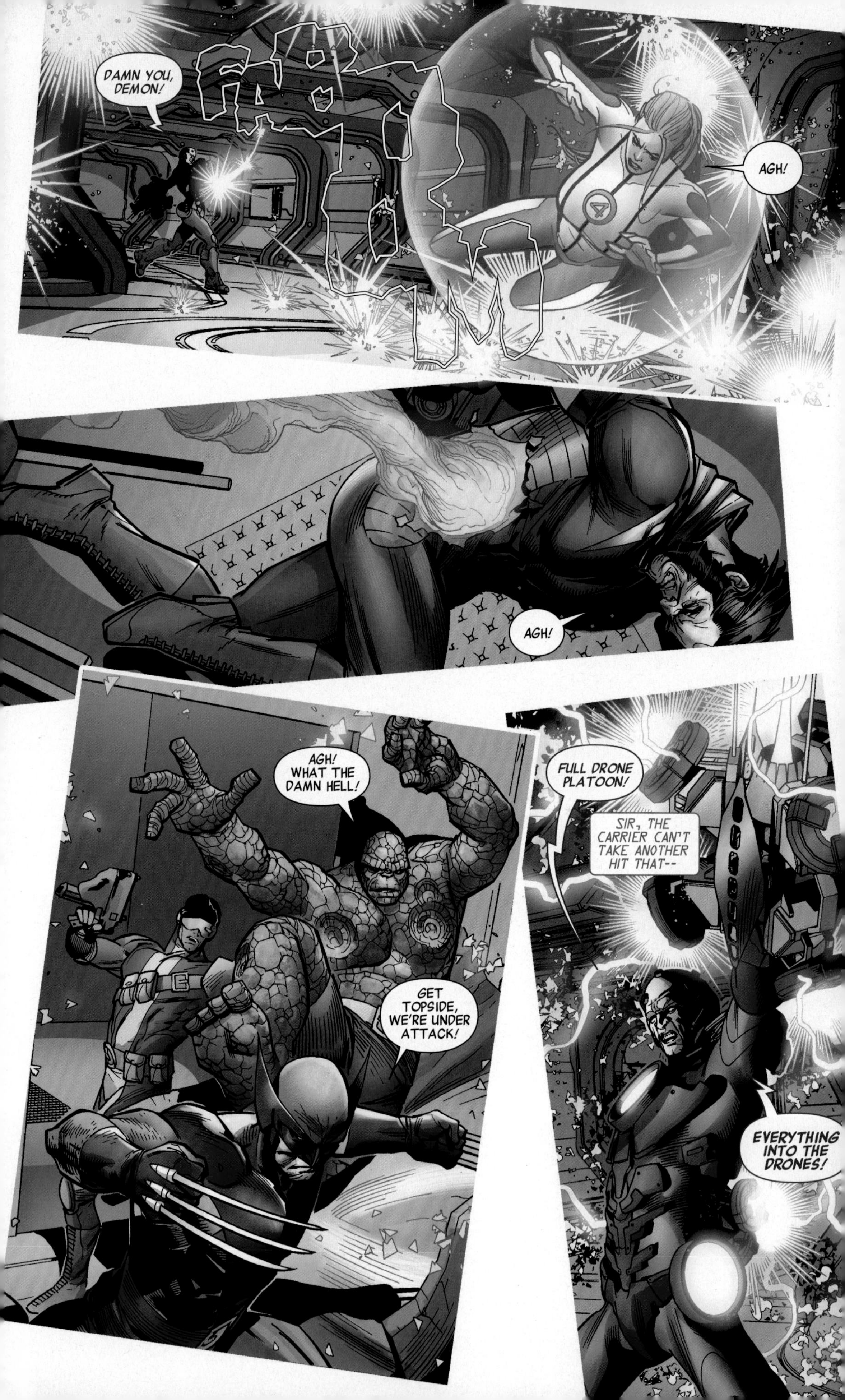
DAMN YOU, DEMON!
AGH!
AGH!
AGH! WHAT THE DAMN HELL!
GET TOPSIDE, WE'RE UNDER ATTACK!
FULL DRONE PLATOON!
SIR, THE CARRIER CAN'T TAKE ANOTHER HIT THAT--
EVERYTHING INTO THE DRONES!

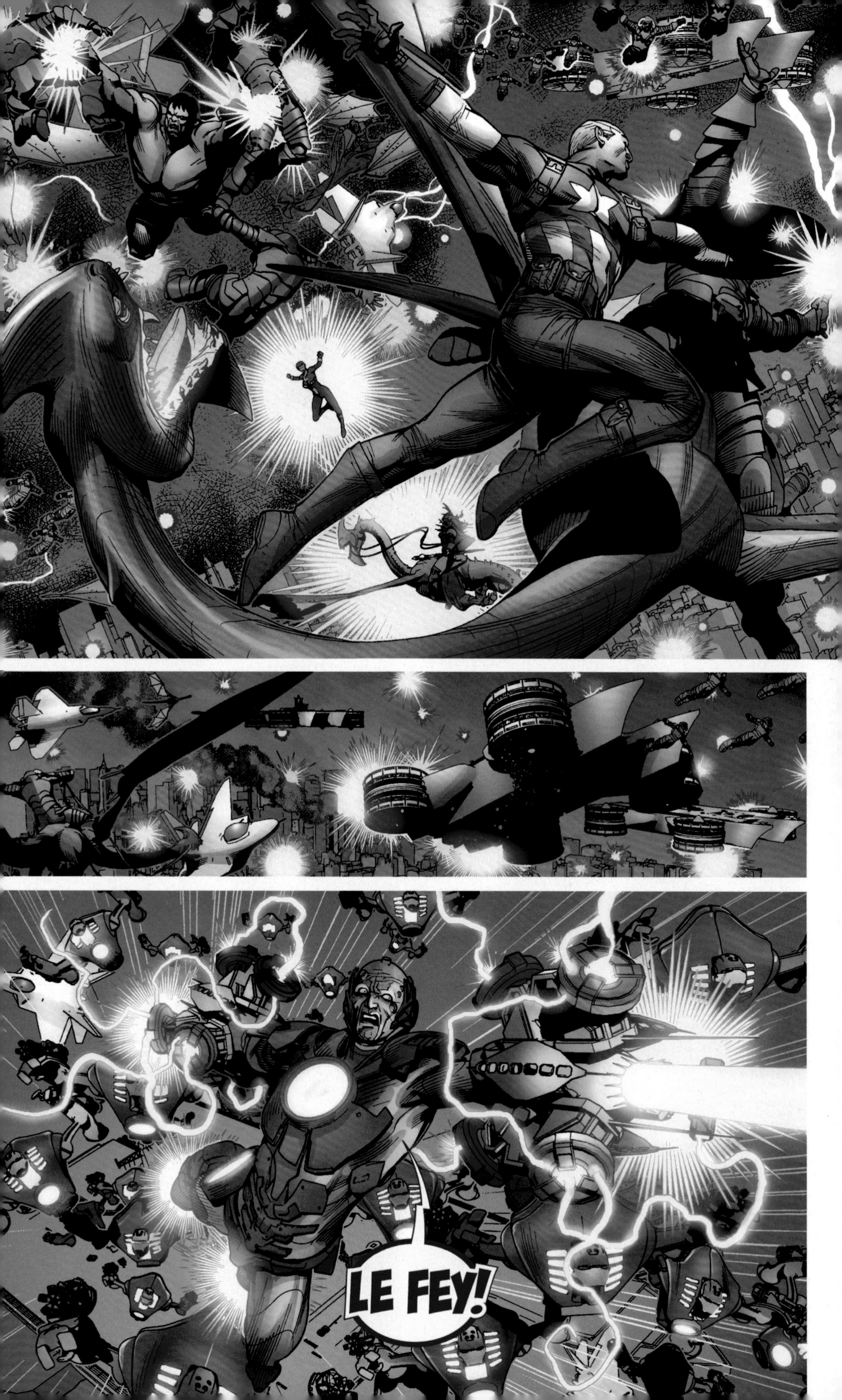
LE FEY!

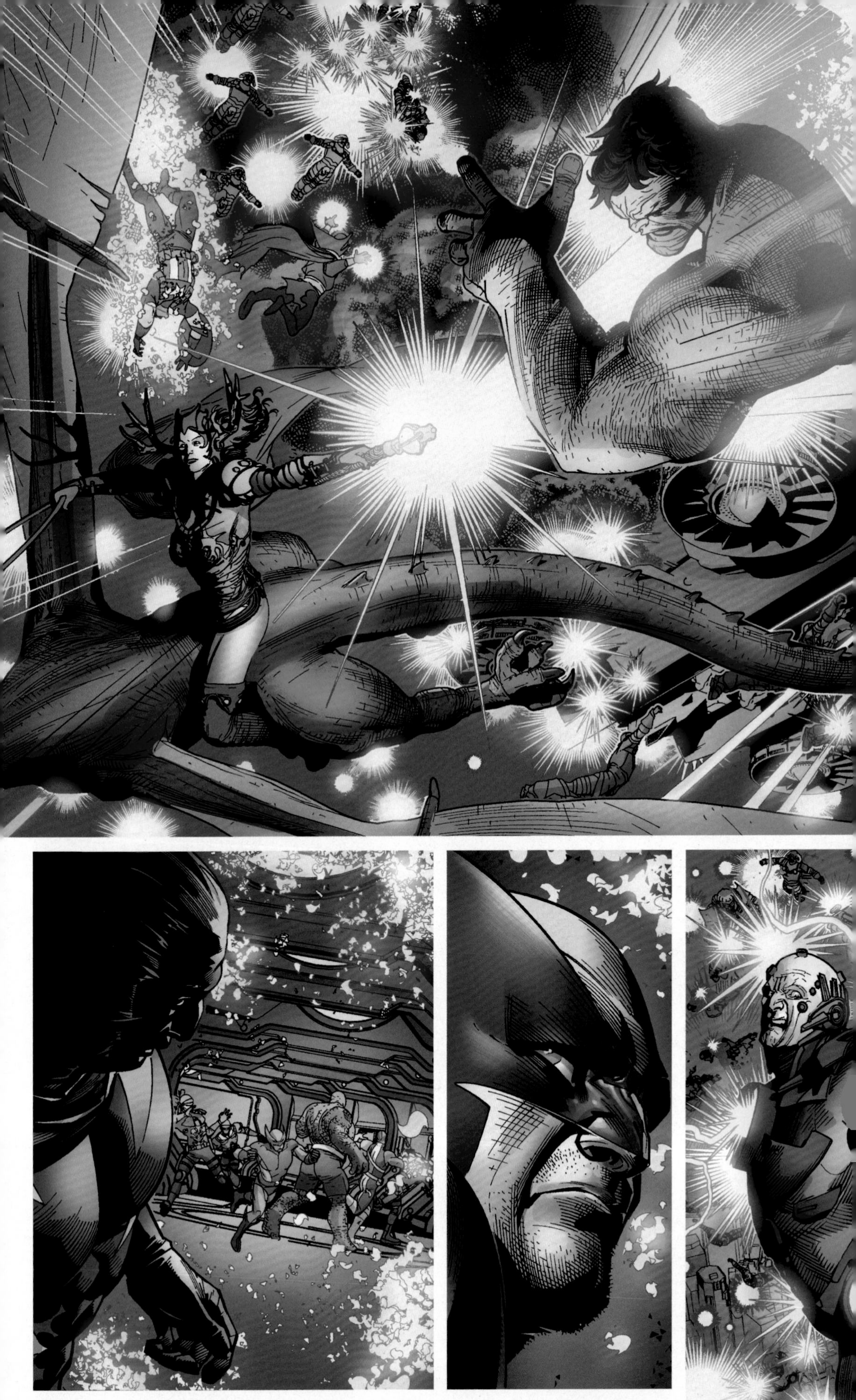

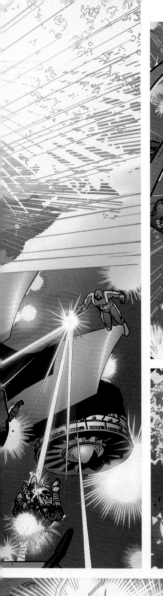

@#$@$#!

I DON'T KNOW WHAT THIS WONKY TIMELINE PLAN OF YOURS IS, BUT YOU WON'T WIN, LE FEY!

YOU WON'T WIN!

AS ALWAYS, STARK, I BARELY UNDERSTAND WHAT YOU'RE TALKING ABOUT.

BUT, DO TURN AROUND, I DON'T WANT YOU TO MISS THIS.

NO...

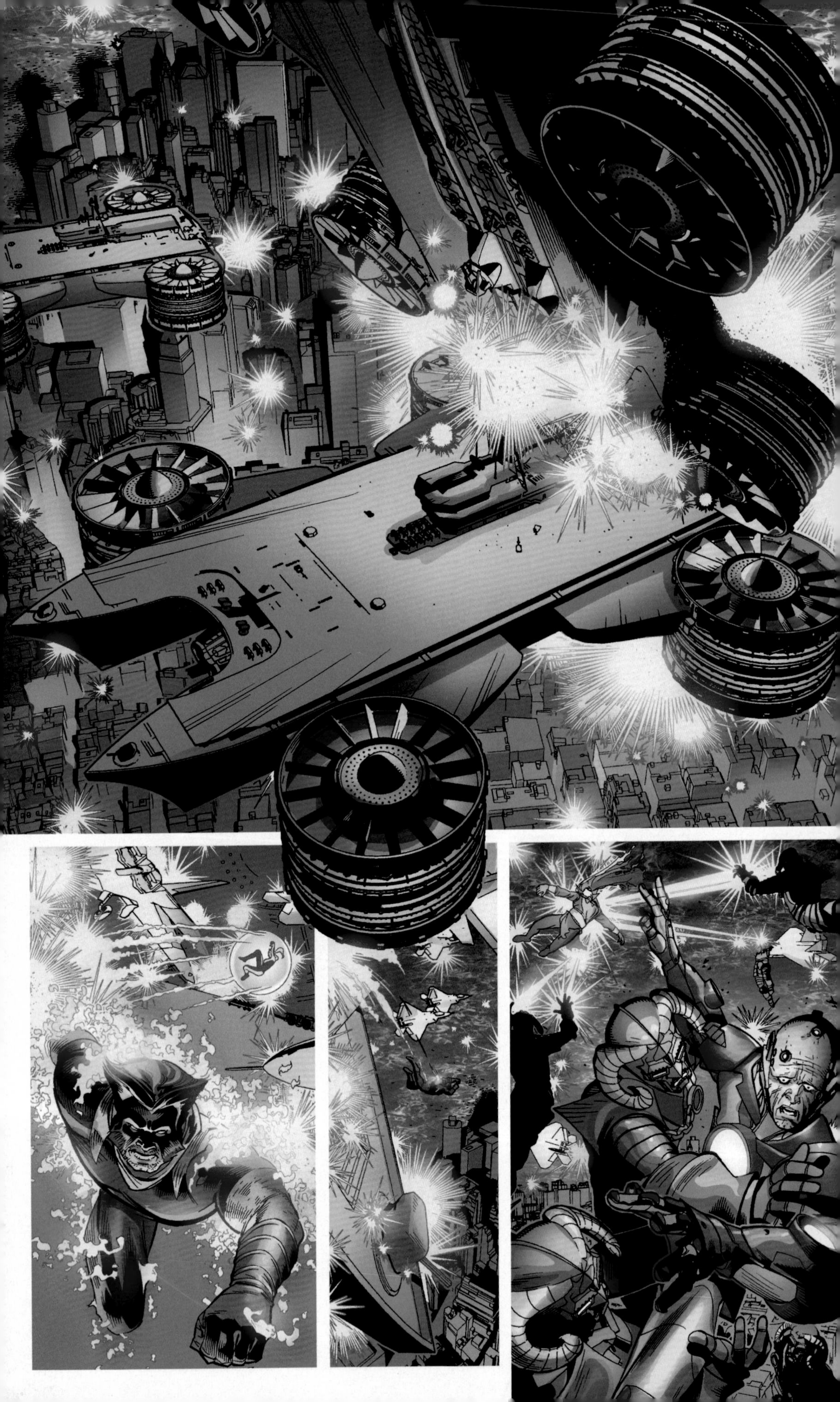

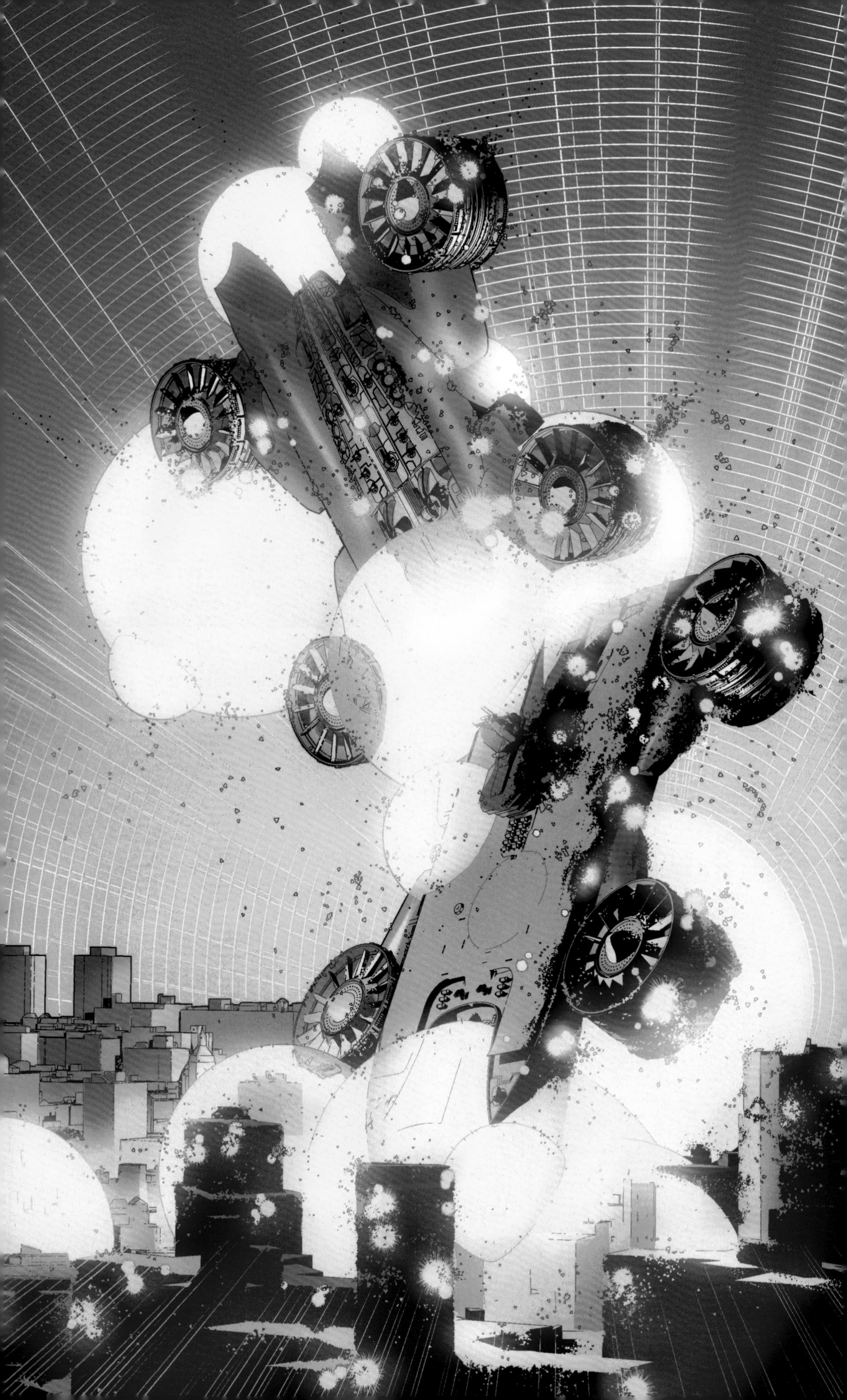

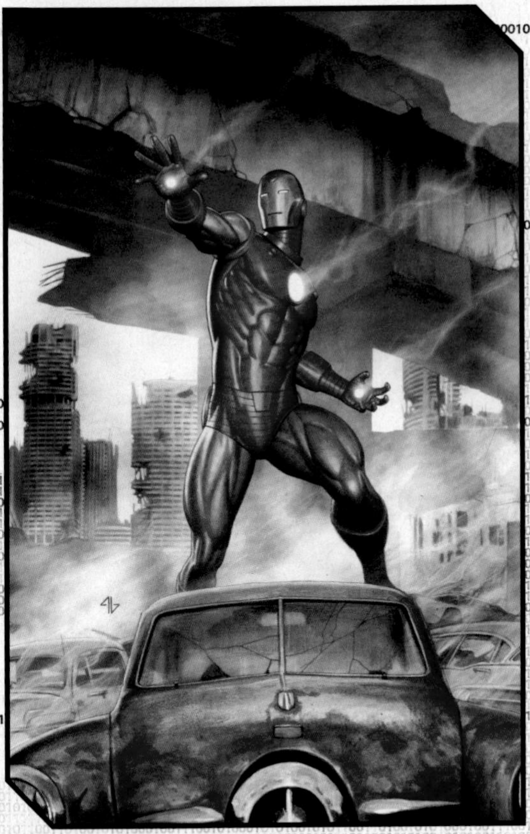

AGE OF ULTRON #5 VARIANT
BY ADI GRANOV

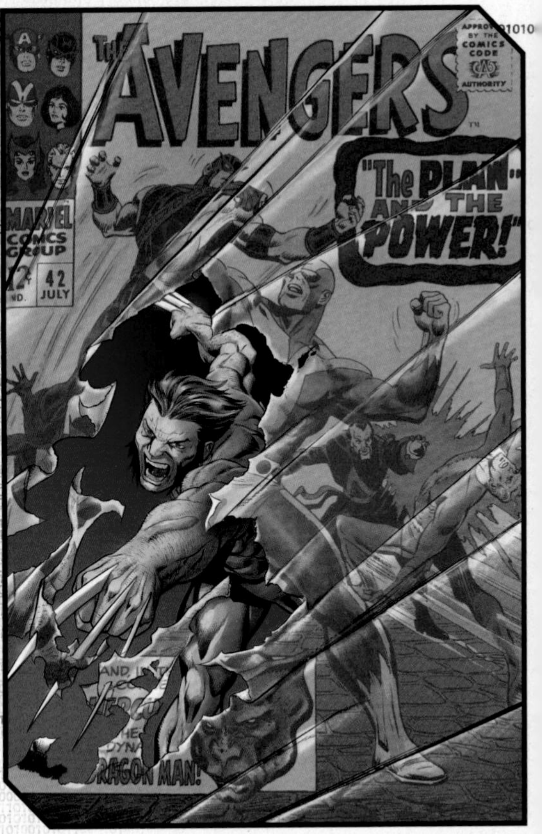
THE AVENGERS
"The PLAN-- AND THE POWER!"
MARVEL COMICS GROUP
42
JULY
APPROVED BY THE COMICS CODE AUTHORITY

AGE OF ULTRON #6 VARIANT
BY CARLOS PACHECO, ROGER MARTINEZ & JOSE VILLARRUBIA
WITH JOHN BUSCEMA & GEORGE ROUSSOS

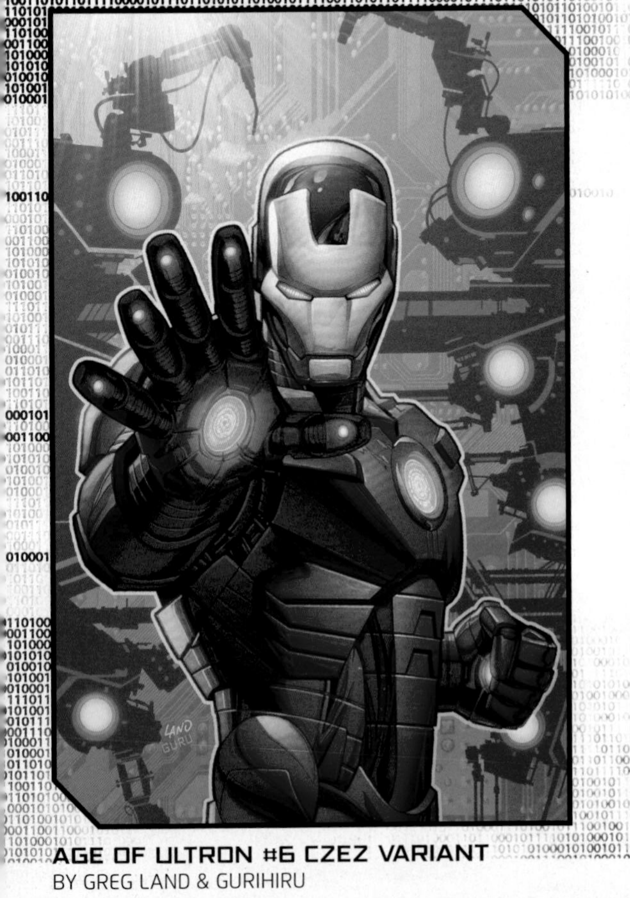
LAND
GURU

AGE OF ULTRON #6 CZEZ VARIANT
BY GREG LAND & GURIHIRU

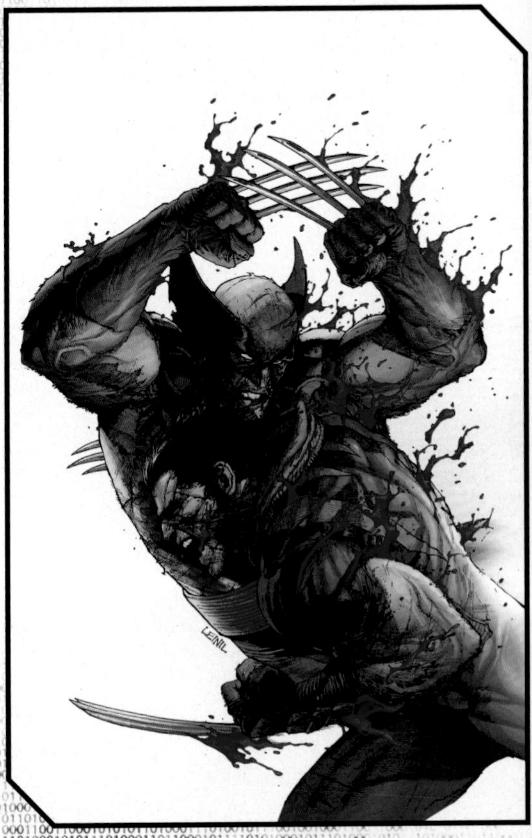
LEINIL

AGE OF ULTRON #7 VARIANT
BY LEINIL FRANCIS YU & FRANK MARTIN

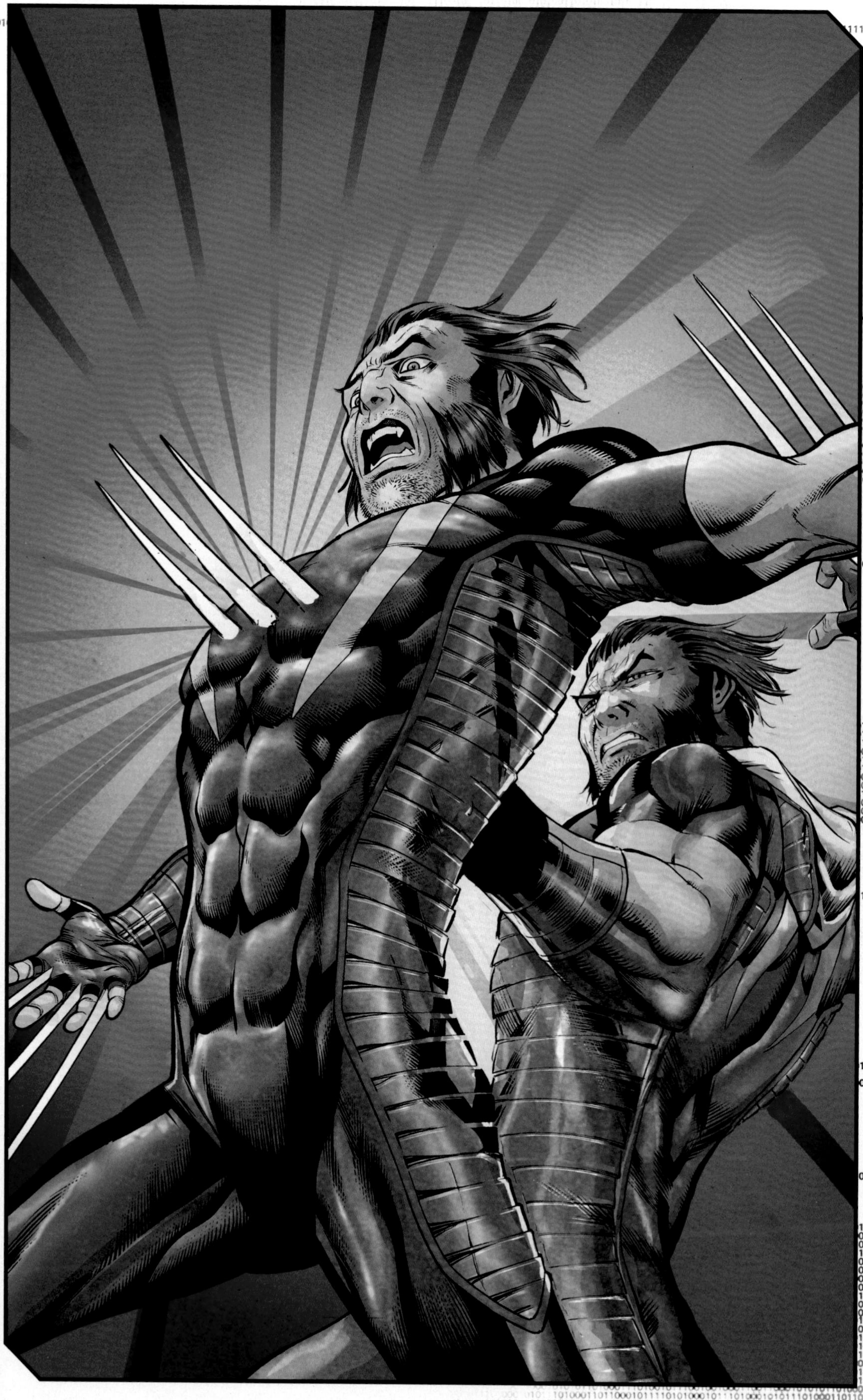

AGE OF ULTRON #9

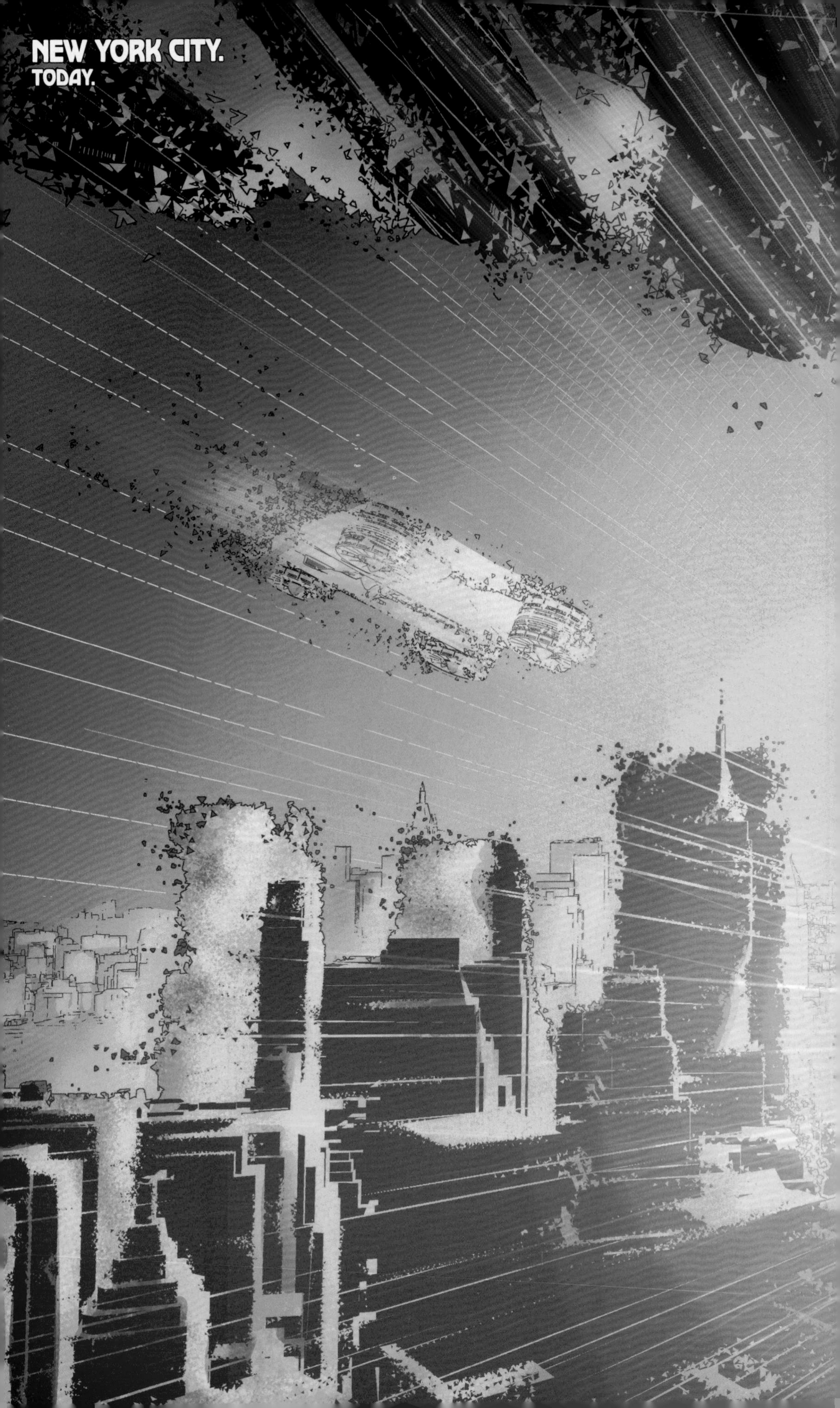
NEW YORK CITY.
TODAY.

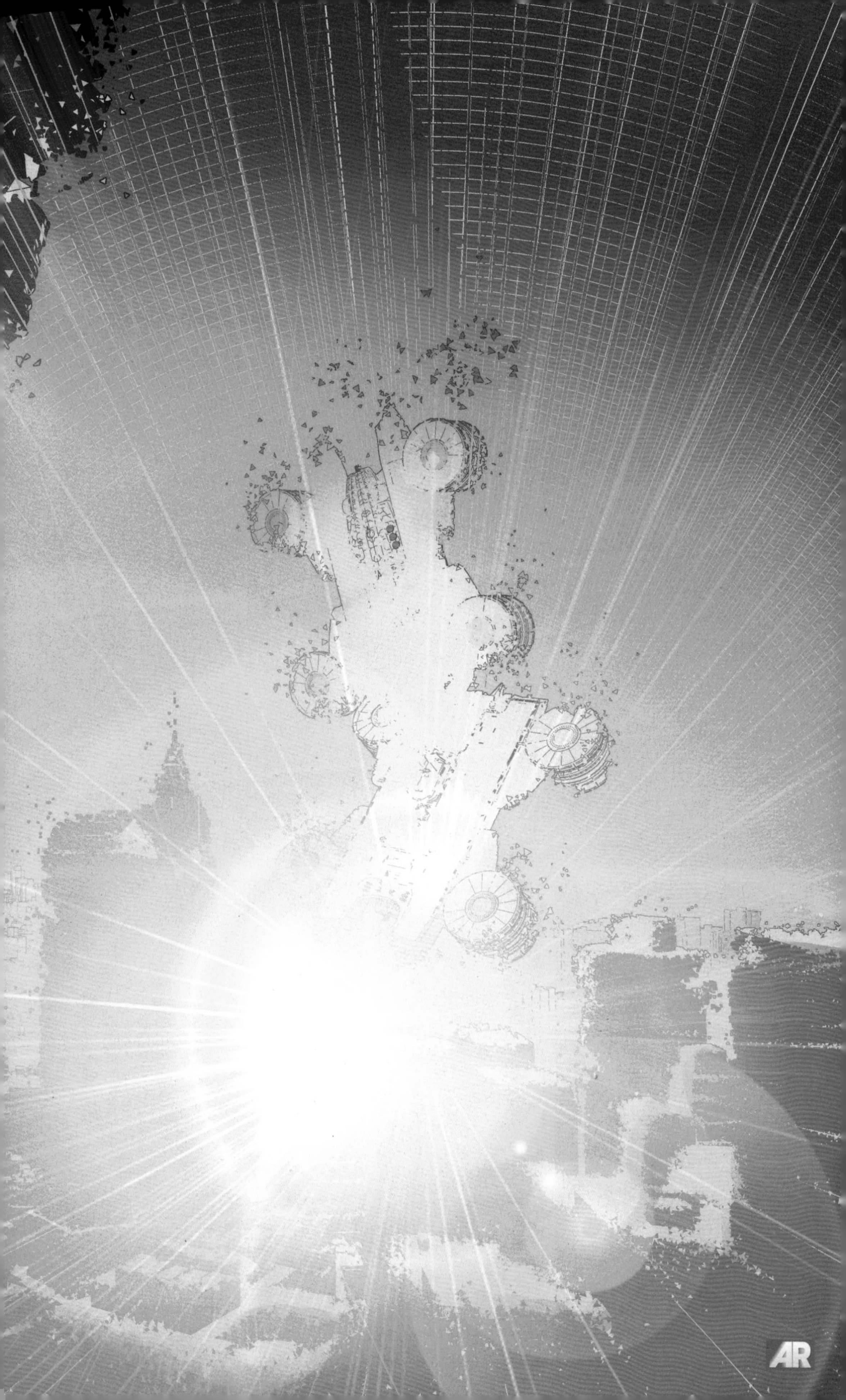

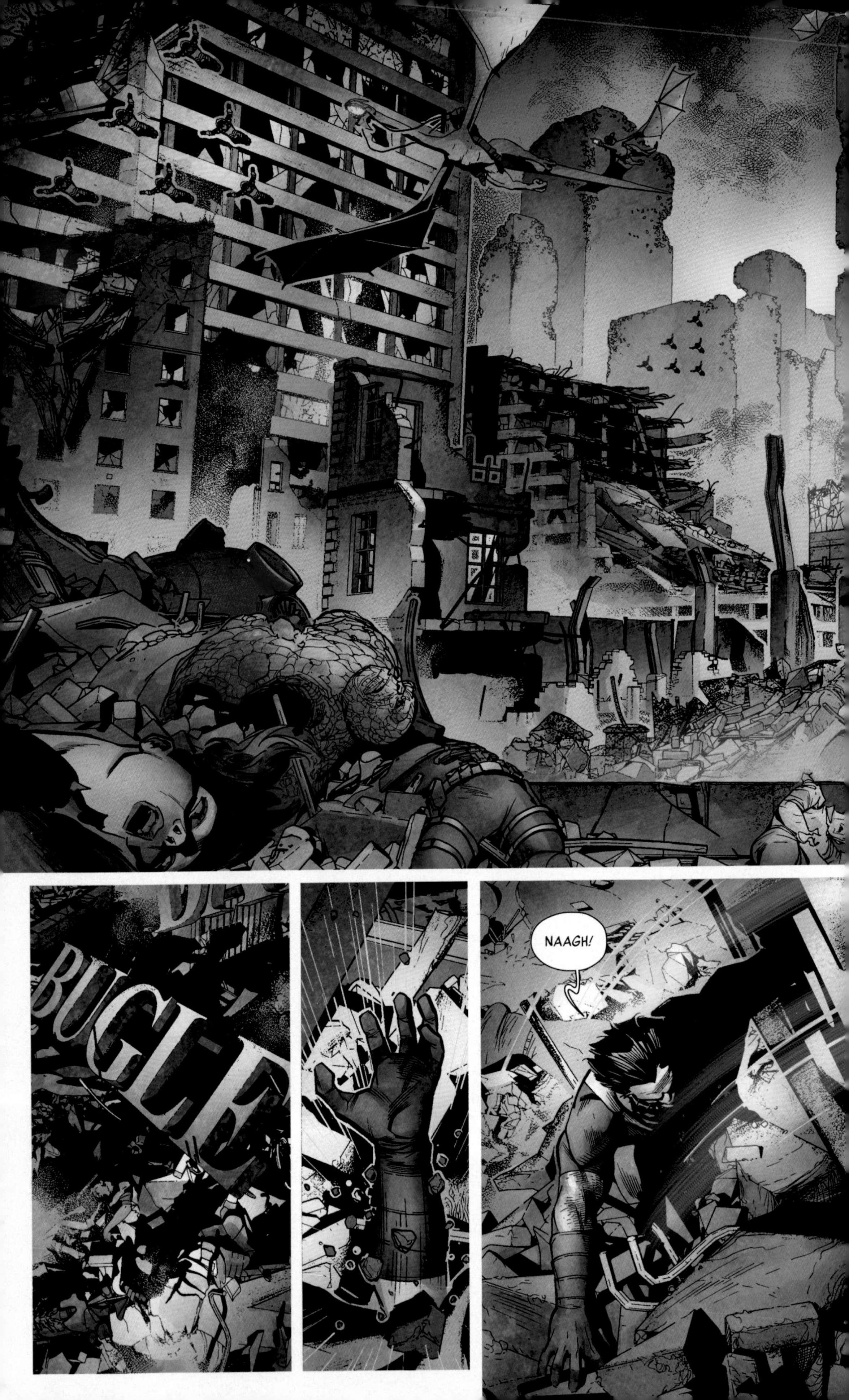
BUGLE
NAAGH!

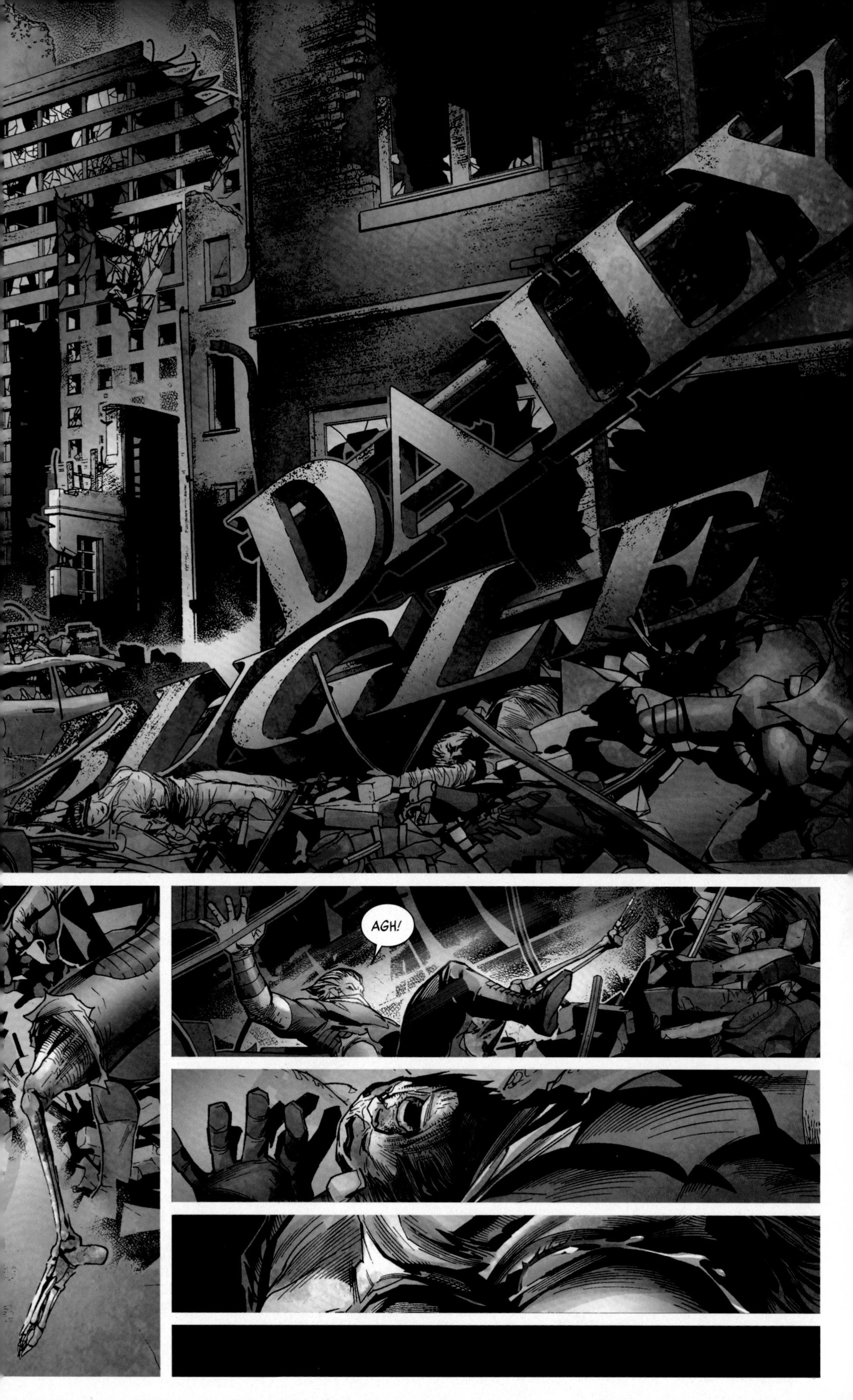
AGH!

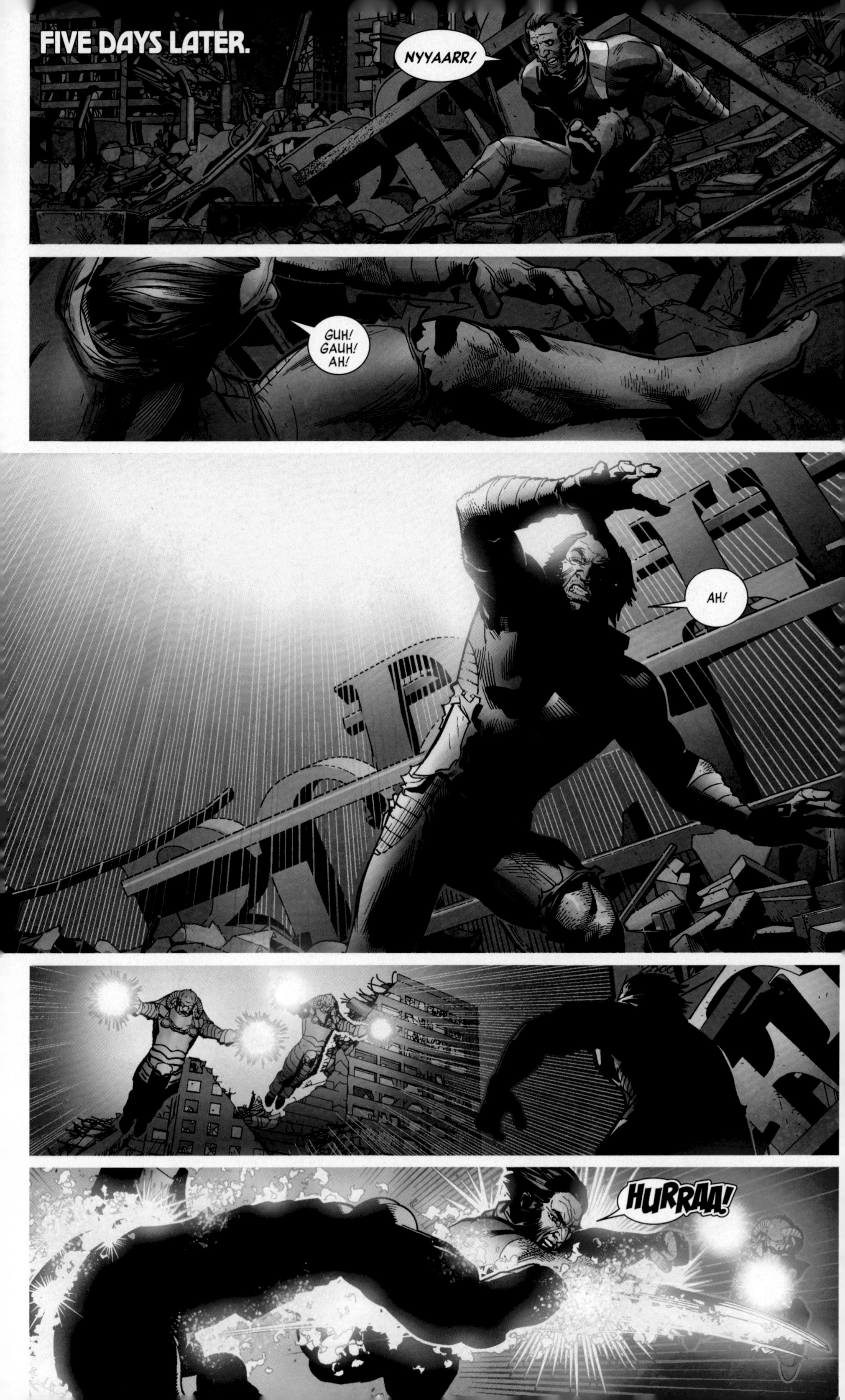
FIVE DAYS LATER.
NYYAARR!
GUH! GAUH! AH!
AH!
HURRAA!

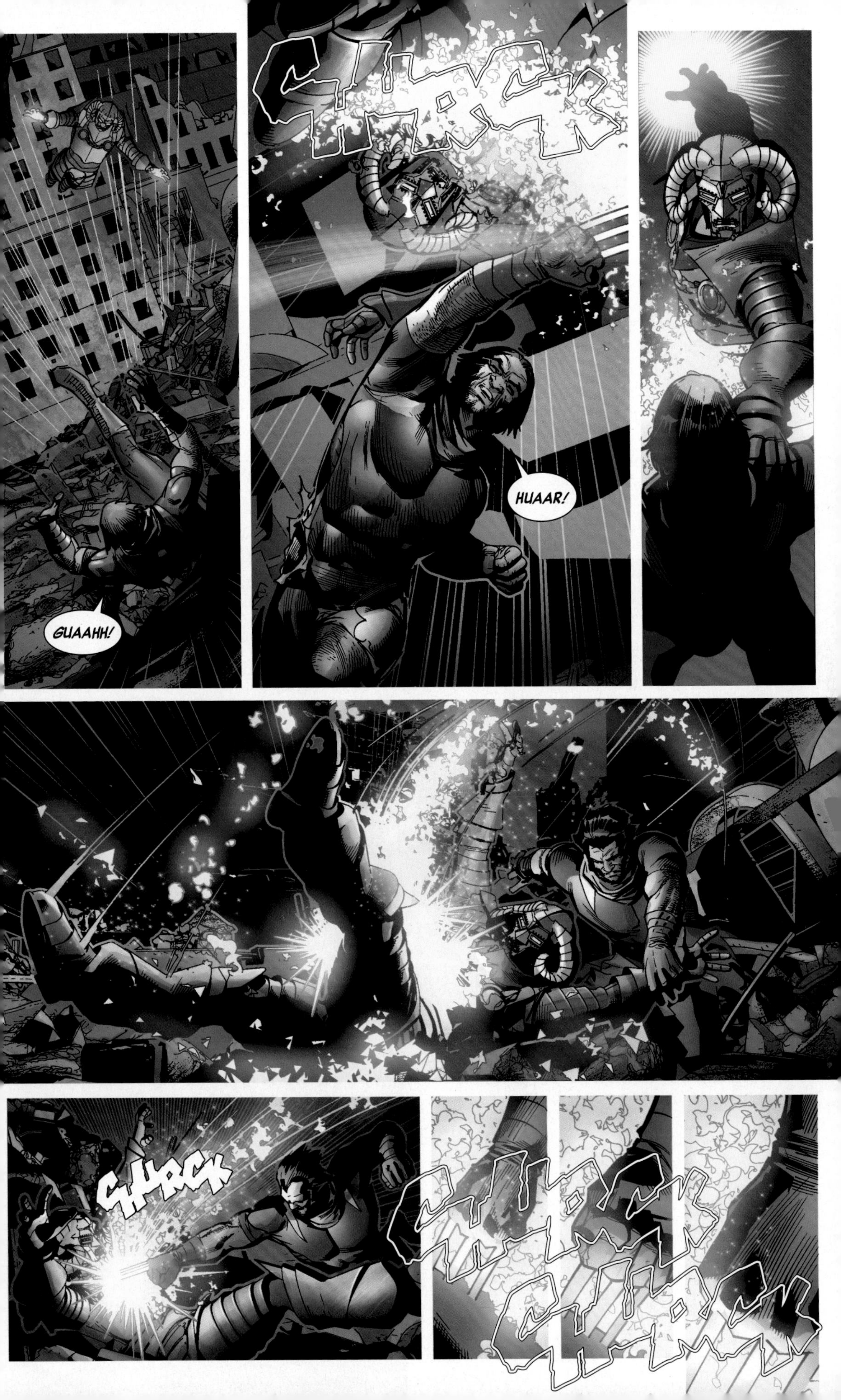
GUAAHH!
CHUCK
HUAAR!
CHRCK
CHUCK
CHUCK

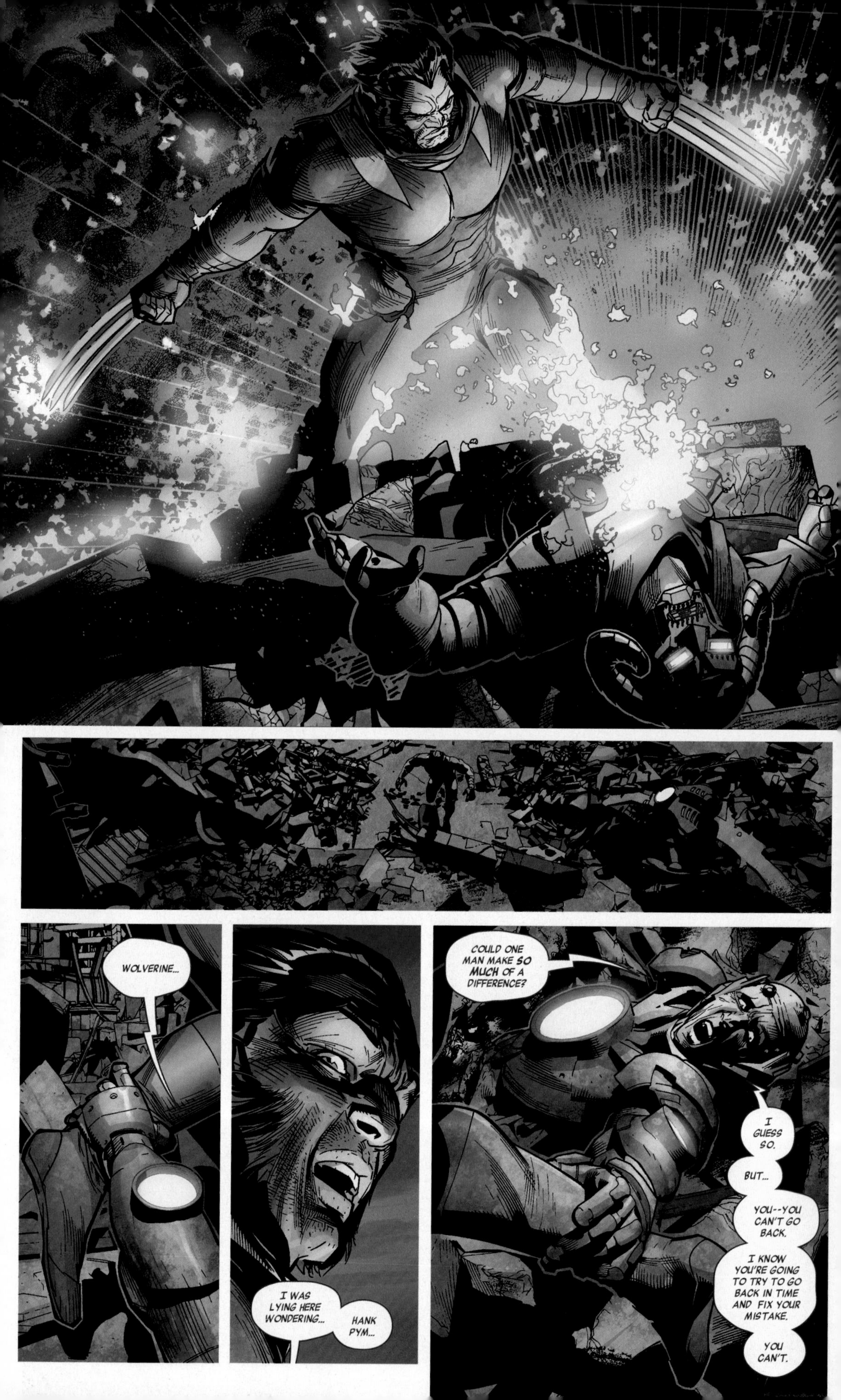
WOLVERINE...
I WAS LYING HERE WONDERING...
HANK PYM...
COULD ONE MAN MAKE SO MUCH OF A DIFFERENCE?
I GUESS SO.
BUT...
YOU--YOU CAN'T GO BACK.
I KNOW YOU'RE GOING TO TRY TO GO BACK IN TIME AND FIX YOUR MISTAKE.
YOU CAN'T.

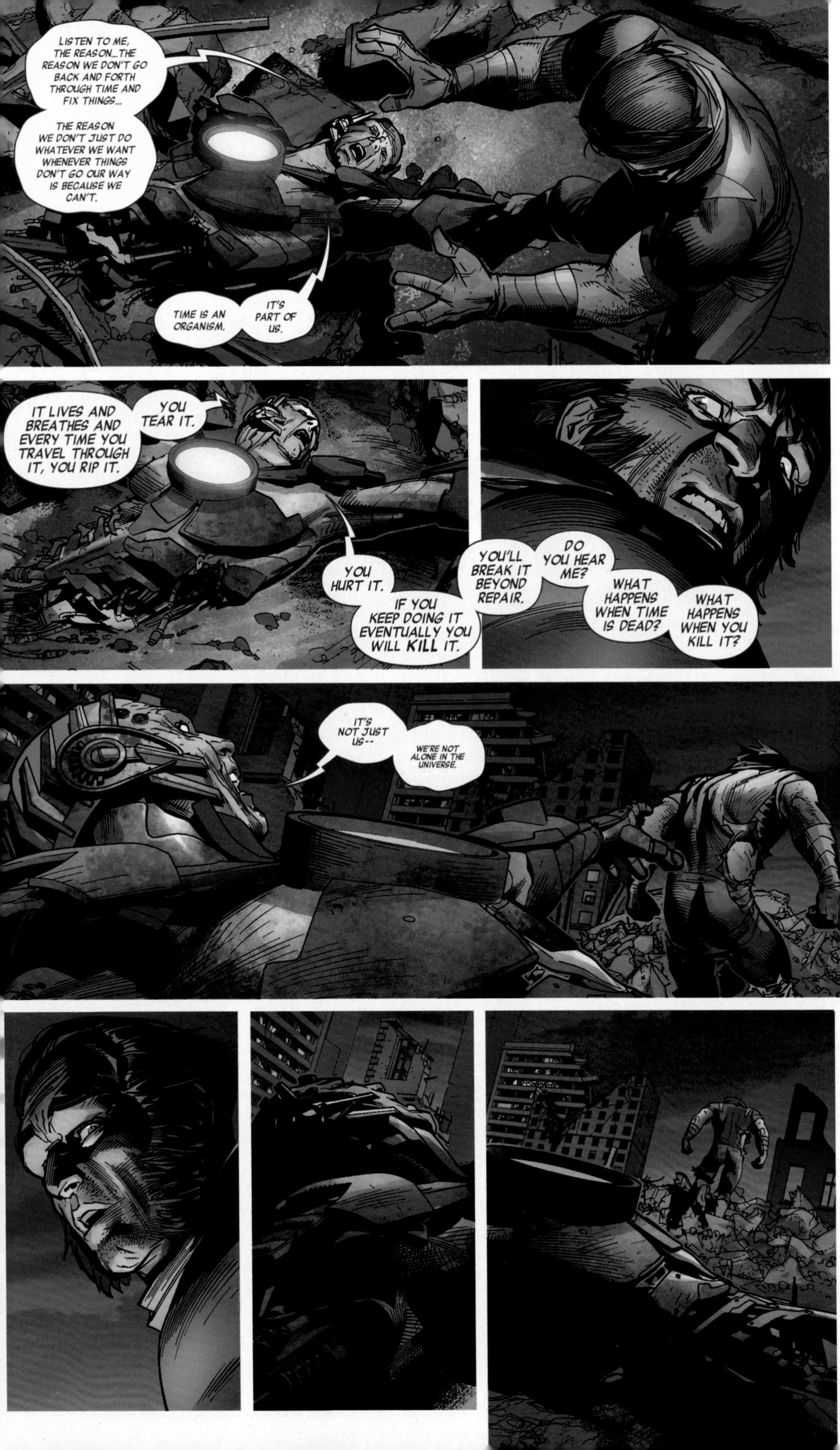
LISTEN TO ME, THE REASON...THE REASON WE DON'T GO BACK AND FORTH THROUGH TIME AND FIX THINGS...
THE REASON WE DON'T JUST DO WHATEVER WE WANT WHENEVER THINGS DON'T GO OUR WAY IS BECAUSE WE CAN'T.
TIME IS AN ORGANISM.
IT'S PART OF US.
IT LIVES AND BREATHES AND EVERY TIME YOU TRAVEL THROUGH IT, YOU RIP IT.
YOU TEAR IT.
YOU HURT IT.
IF YOU KEEP DOING IT EVENTUALLY YOU WILL KILL IT.
YOU'LL BREAK IT BEYOND REPAIR.
DO YOU HEAR ME?
WHAT HAPPENS WHEN TIME IS DEAD?
WHAT HAPPENS WHEN YOU KILL IT?
IT'S NOT JUST US--
WE'RE NOT ALONE IN THE UNIVERSE.

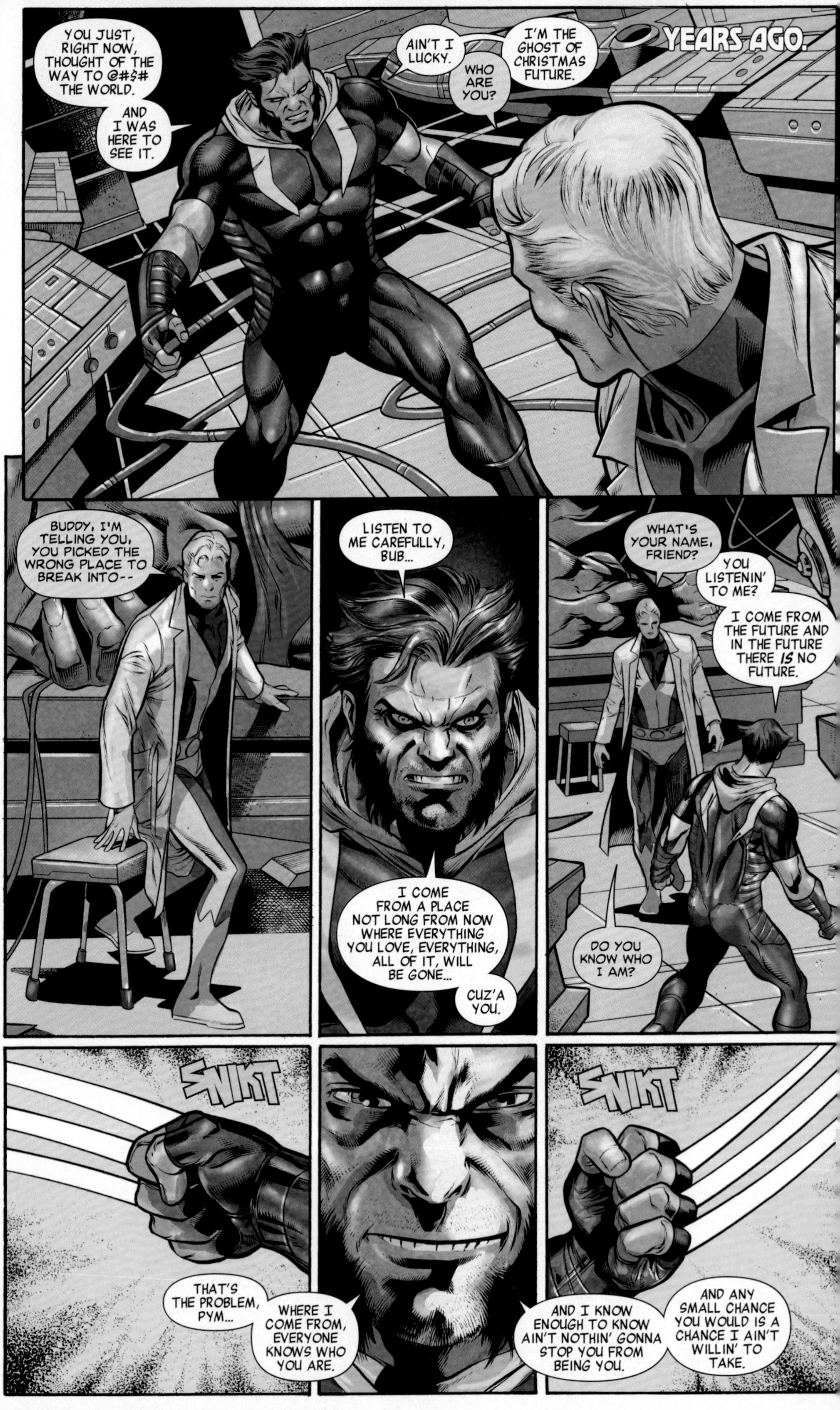
YEARS AGO.
YOU JUST, RIGHT NOW, THOUGHT OF THE WAY TO @#$# THE WORLD.
AND I WAS HERE TO SEE IT.
AIN'T I LUCKY.
WHO ARE YOU?
I'M THE GHOST OF CHRISTMAS FUTURE.
BUDDY, I'M TELLING YOU, YOU PICKED THE WRONG PLACE TO BREAK INTO--
LISTEN TO ME CAREFULLY, BUB...
I COME FROM A PLACE NOT LONG FROM NOW WHERE EVERYTHING YOU LOVE, EVERYTHING, ALL OF IT, WILL BE GONE...
CUZ'A YOU.
WHAT'S YOUR NAME, FRIEND?
YOU LISTENIN' TO ME?
I COME FROM THE FUTURE AND IN THE FUTURE THERE *IS* NO FUTURE.
DO YOU KNOW WHO I AM?
SNIKT
THAT'S THE PROBLEM, PYM...
WHERE I COME FROM, EVERYONE KNOWS WHO YOU ARE.
SNIKT
AND I KNOW ENOUGH TO KNOW AIN'T NOTHIN' GONNA STOP YOU FROM BEING YOU.
AND ANY SMALL CHANCE YOU WOULD IS A CHANCE I AIN'T WILLIN' TO TAKE.

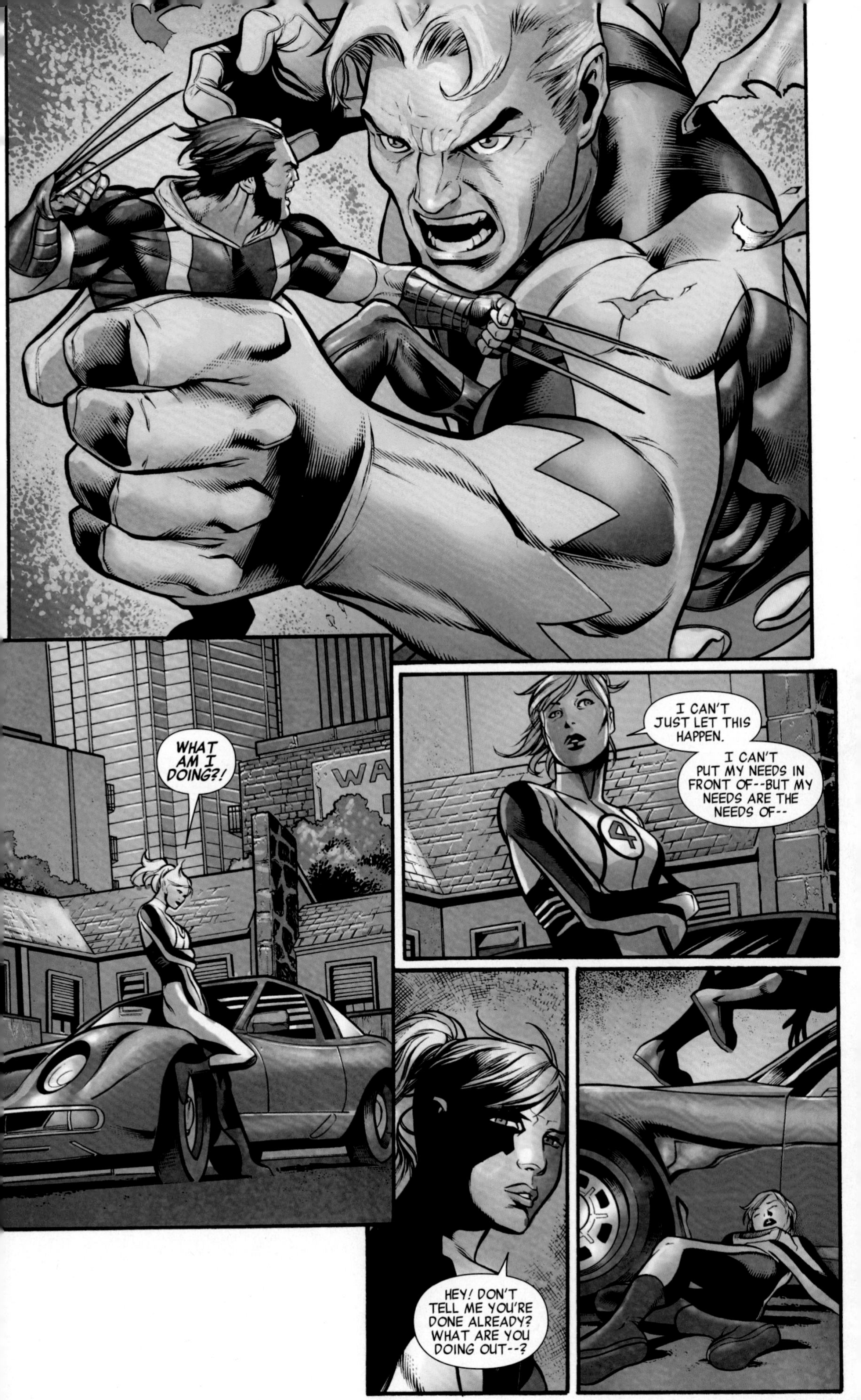
WHAT AM I DOING?!
I CAN'T JUST LET THIS HAPPEN.
I CAN'T PUT MY NEEDS IN FRONT OF--BUT MY NEEDS ARE THE NEEDS OF--
HEY! DON'T TELL ME YOU'RE DONE ALREADY? WHAT ARE YOU DOING OUT--?

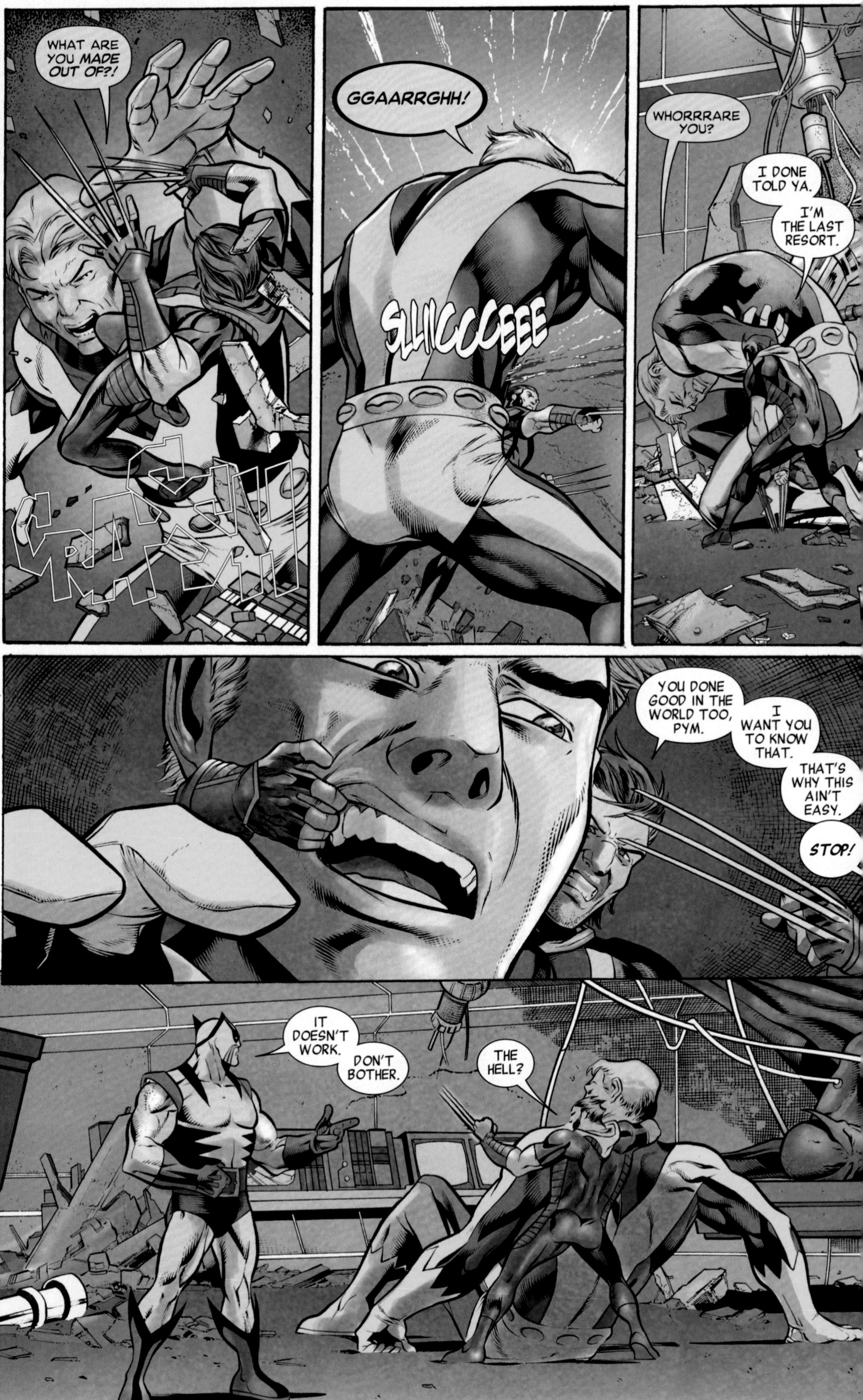
WHAT ARE YOU MADE OUT OF?!
GGAARRGHH!
SLLIICCCEEE
WHORRRARE YOU?
I DONE TOLD YA.
I'M THE LAST RESORT.
YOU DONE GOOD IN THE WORLD TOO, PYM.
I WANT YOU TO KNOW THAT.
THAT'S WHY THIS AIN'T EASY.
STOP!
IT DOESN'T WORK.
DON'T BOTHER.
THE HELL?

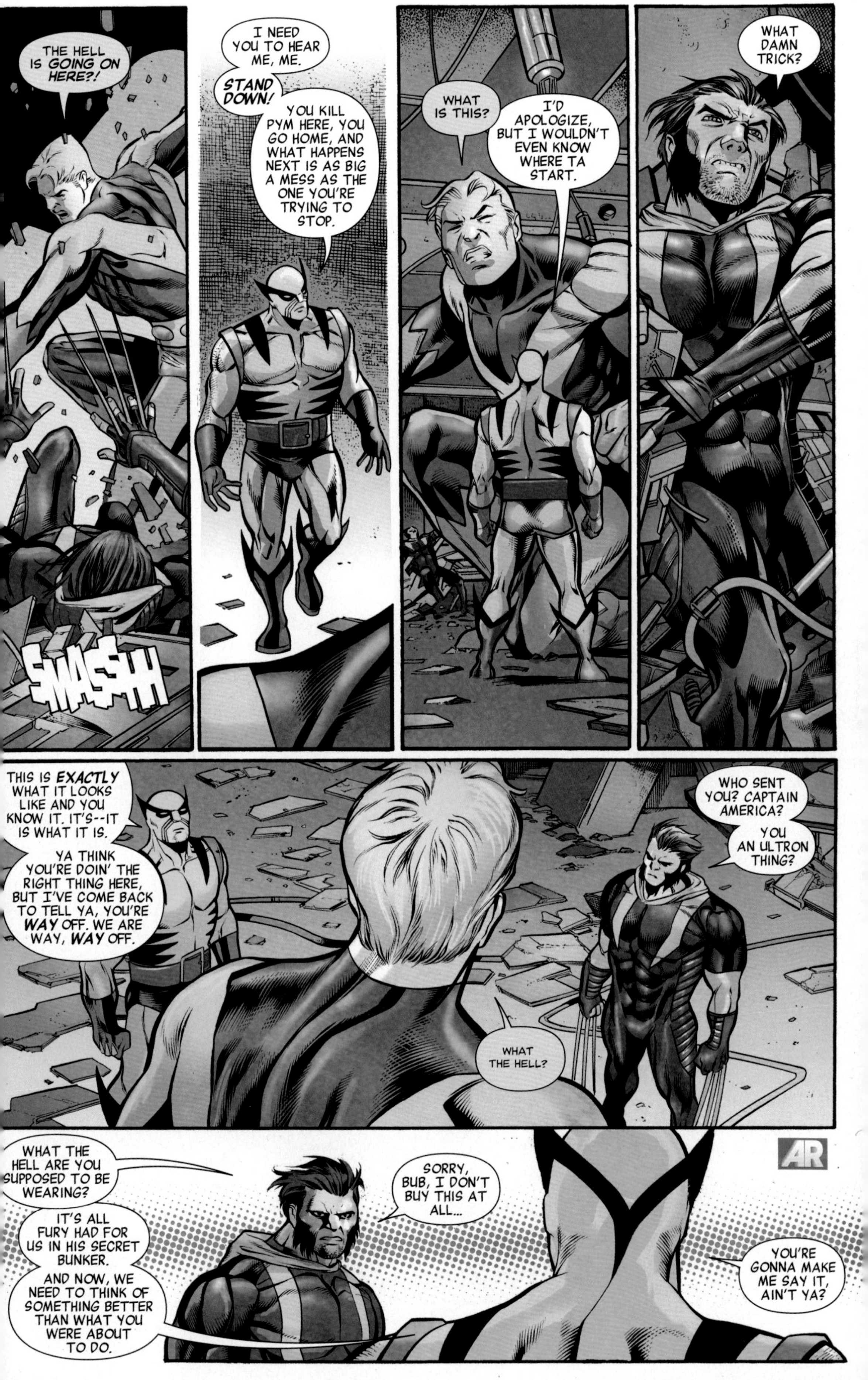
THE HELL IS GOING ON HERE?!
SMASH
I NEED YOU TO HEAR ME, ME.
STAND DOWN!
YOU KILL PYM HERE, YOU GO HOME, AND WHAT HAPPENS NEXT IS AS BIG A MESS AS THE ONE YOU'RE TRYING TO STOP.
WHAT IS THIS?
I'D APOLOGIZE, BUT I WOULDN'T EVEN KNOW WHERE TA START.
WHAT DAMN TRICK?
THIS IS EXACTLY WHAT IT LOOKS LIKE AND YOU KNOW IT. IT'S--IT IS WHAT IT IS.
YA THINK YOU'RE DOIN' THE RIGHT THING HERE, BUT I'VE COME BACK TO TELL YA, YOU'RE WAY OFF. WE ARE WAY, WAY OFF.
WHO SENT YOU? CAPTAIN AMERICA?
YOU AN ULTRON THING?
WHAT THE HELL?
WHAT THE HELL ARE YOU SUPPOSED TO BE WEARING?
IT'S ALL FURY HAD FOR US IN HIS SECRET BUNKER.
AND NOW, WE NEED TO THINK OF SOMETHING BETTER THAN WHAT YOU WERE ABOUT TO DO.
SORRY, BUB, I DON'T BUY THIS AT ALL...
YOU'RE GONNA MAKE ME SAY IT, AIN'T YA?

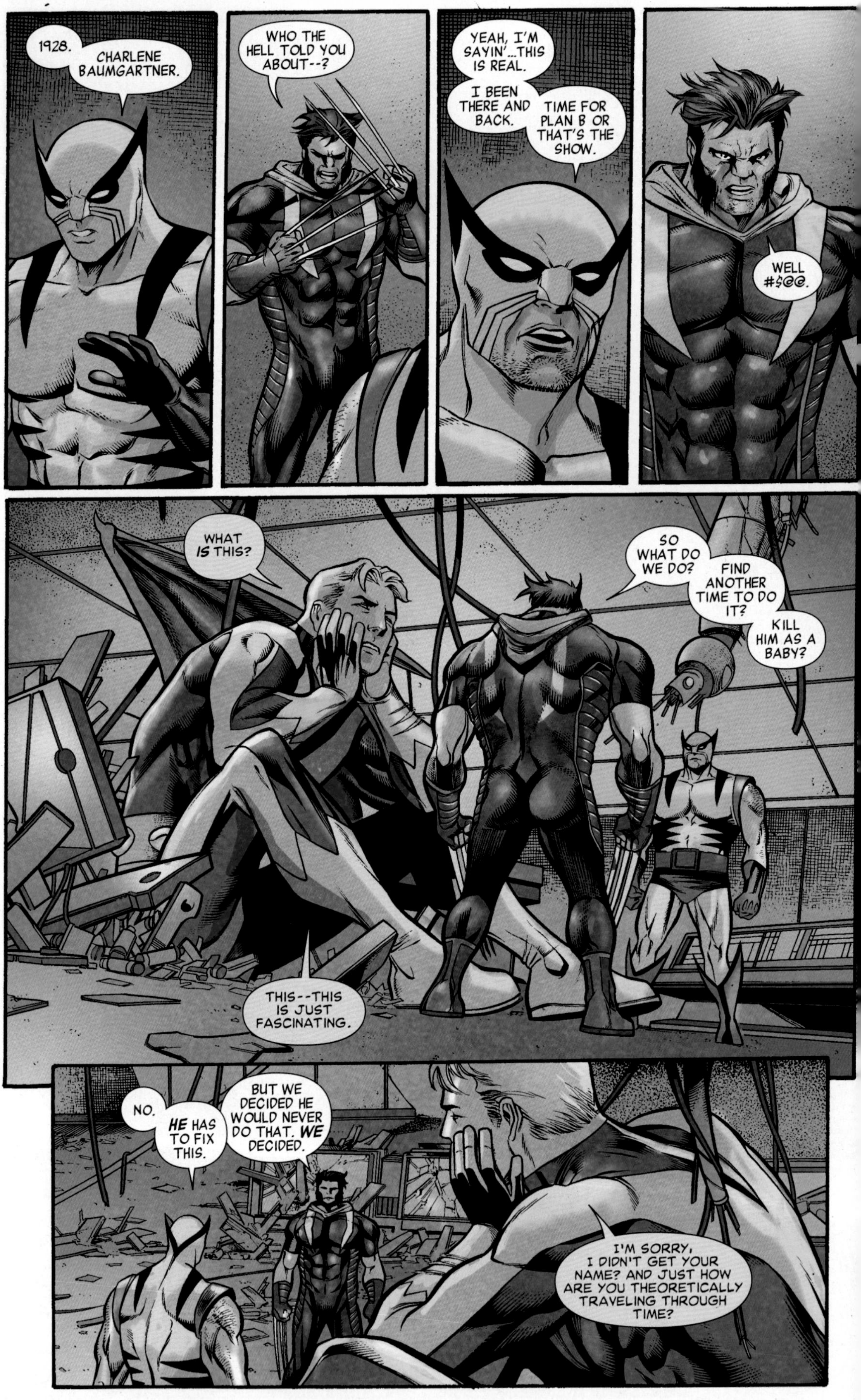
1928.
CHARLENE BAUMGARTNER.
WHO THE HELL TOLD YOU ABOUT--?
YEAH, I'M SAYIN'...THIS IS REAL.
I BEEN THERE AND BACK.
TIME FOR PLAN B OR THAT'S THE SHOW.
WELL #$@@.
WHAT *IS* THIS?
SO WHAT DO WE DO?
FIND ANOTHER TIME TO DO IT?
KILL HIM AS A BABY?
THIS--THIS IS JUST FASCINATING.
NO.
HE HAS TO FIX THIS.
BUT WE DECIDED HE WOULD NEVER DO THAT. *WE* DECIDED.
I'M SORRY, I DIDN'T GET YOUR NAME? AND JUST HOW ARE YOU THEORETICALLY TRAVELING THROUGH TIME?

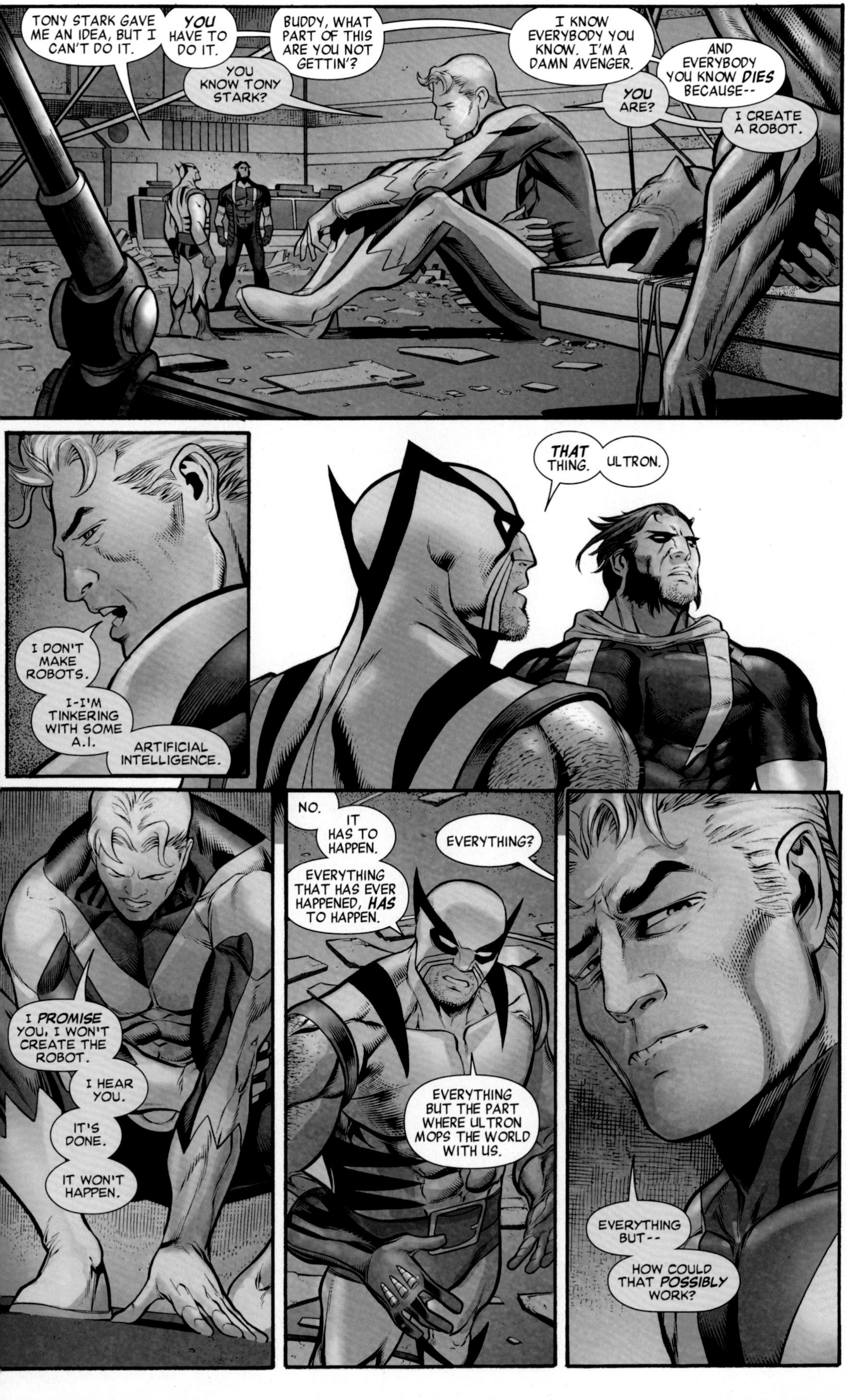
TONY STARK GAVE ME AN IDEA, BUT I CAN'T DO IT.
YOU HAVE TO DO IT.
YOU KNOW TONY STARK?
BUDDY, WHAT PART OF THIS ARE YOU NOT GETTIN'?
I KNOW EVERYBODY YOU KNOW. I'M A DAMN AVENGER.
YOU ARE?
AND EVERYBODY YOU KNOW DIES BECAUSE--
I CREATE A ROBOT.
I DON'T MAKE ROBOTS.
I-I'M TINKERING WITH SOME A.I.
ARTIFICIAL INTELLIGENCE.
THAT THING.
ULTRON.
I PROMISE YOU, I WON'T CREATE THE ROBOT.
I HEAR YOU.
IT'S DONE.
IT WON'T HAPPEN.
NO.
IT HAS TO HAPPEN.
EVERYTHING THAT HAS EVER HAPPENED, HAS TO HAPPEN.
EVERYTHING?
EVERYTHING BUT THE PART WHERE ULTRON MOPS THE WORLD WITH US.
EVERYTHING BUT--
HOW COULD THAT POSSIBLY WORK?

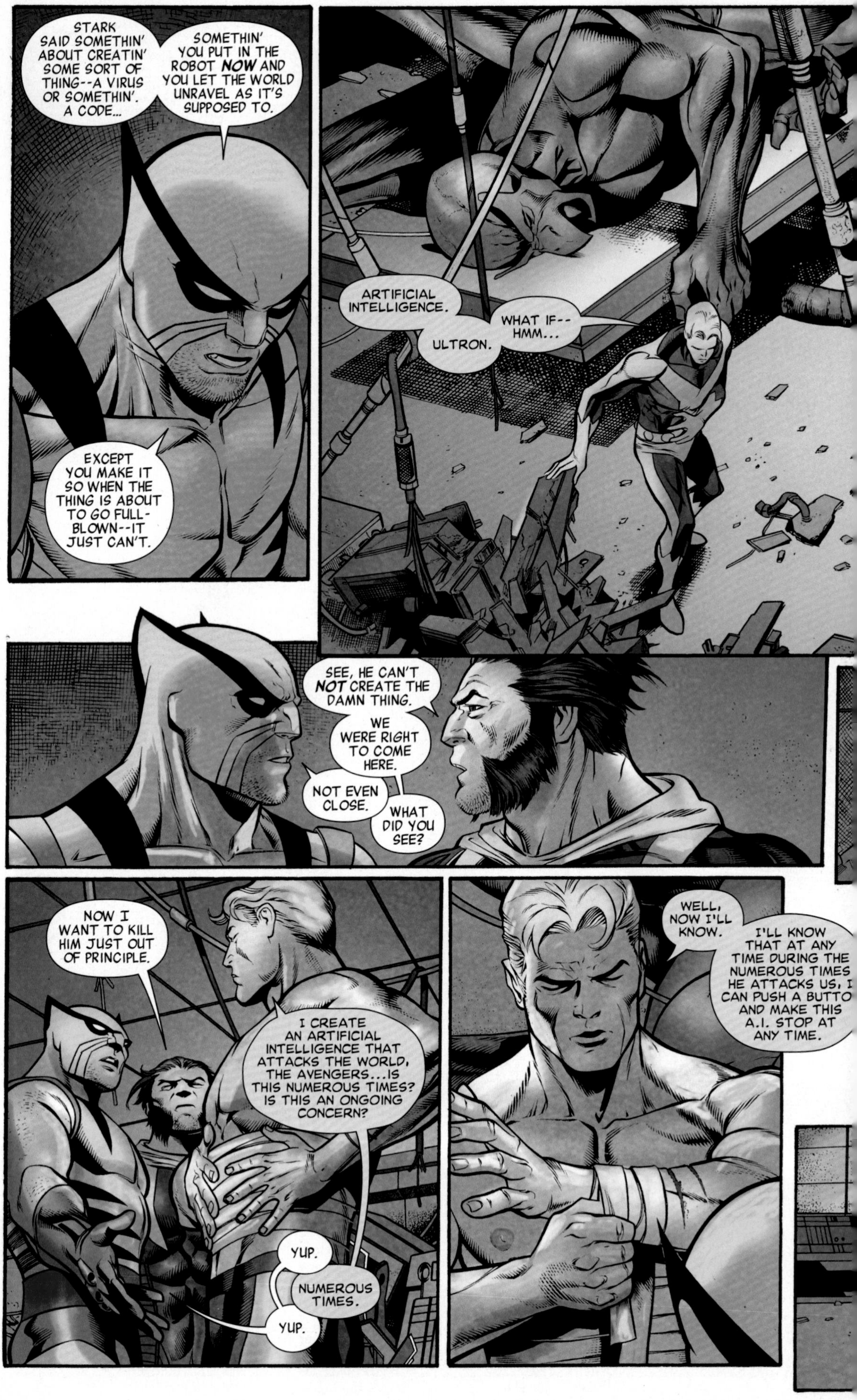
STARK SAID SOMETHIN' ABOUT CREATIN' SOME SORT OF THING--A VIRUS OR SOMETHIN'. A CODE...
SOMETHIN' YOU PUT IN THE ROBOT NOW AND YOU LET THE WORLD UNRAVEL AS IT'S SUPPOSED TO.
EXCEPT YOU MAKE IT SO WHEN THE THING IS ABOUT TO GO FULL-BLOWN--IT JUST CAN'T.
ARTIFICIAL INTELLIGENCE.
ULTRON.
WHAT IF-- HMM...
SEE, HE CAN'T NOT CREATE THE DAMN THING.
WE WERE RIGHT TO COME HERE.
NOT EVEN CLOSE.
WHAT DID YOU SEE?
NOW I WANT TO KILL HIM JUST OUT OF PRINCIPLE.
I CREATE AN ARTIFICIAL INTELLIGENCE THAT ATTACKS THE WORLD, THE AVENGERS...IS THIS NUMEROUS TIMES? IS THIS AN ONGOING CONCERN?
YUP.
NUMEROUS TIMES.
YUP.
WELL, NOW I'LL KNOW.
I'LL KNOW THAT AT ANY TIME DURING THE NUMEROUS TIMES HE ATTACKS US, I CAN PUSH A BUTTO AND MAKE THIS A.I. STOP AT ANY TIME.

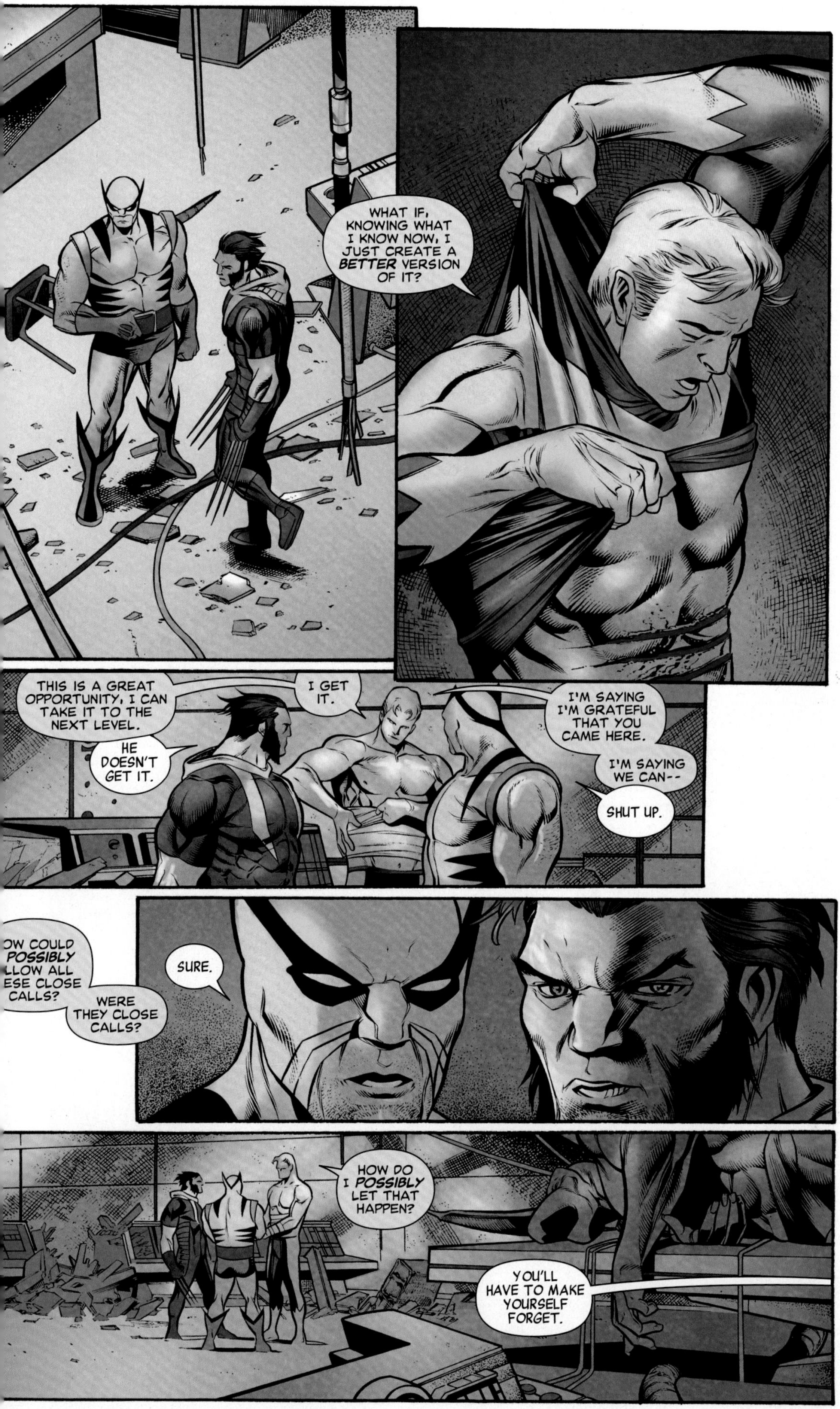

WHAT IF, KNOWING WHAT I KNOW NOW, I JUST CREATE A BETTER VERSION OF IT?
THIS IS A GREAT OPPORTUNITY, I CAN TAKE IT TO THE NEXT LEVEL.
I GET IT.
HE DOESN'T GET IT.
I'M SAYING I'M GRATEFUL THAT YOU CAME HERE.
I'M SAYING WE CAN--
SHUT UP.
OW COULD POSSIBLY LLOW ALL ESE CLOSE CALLS?
SURE.
WERE THEY CLOSE CALLS?
HOW DO I POSSIBLY LET THAT HAPPEN?
YOU'LL HAVE TO MAKE YOURSELF FORGET.

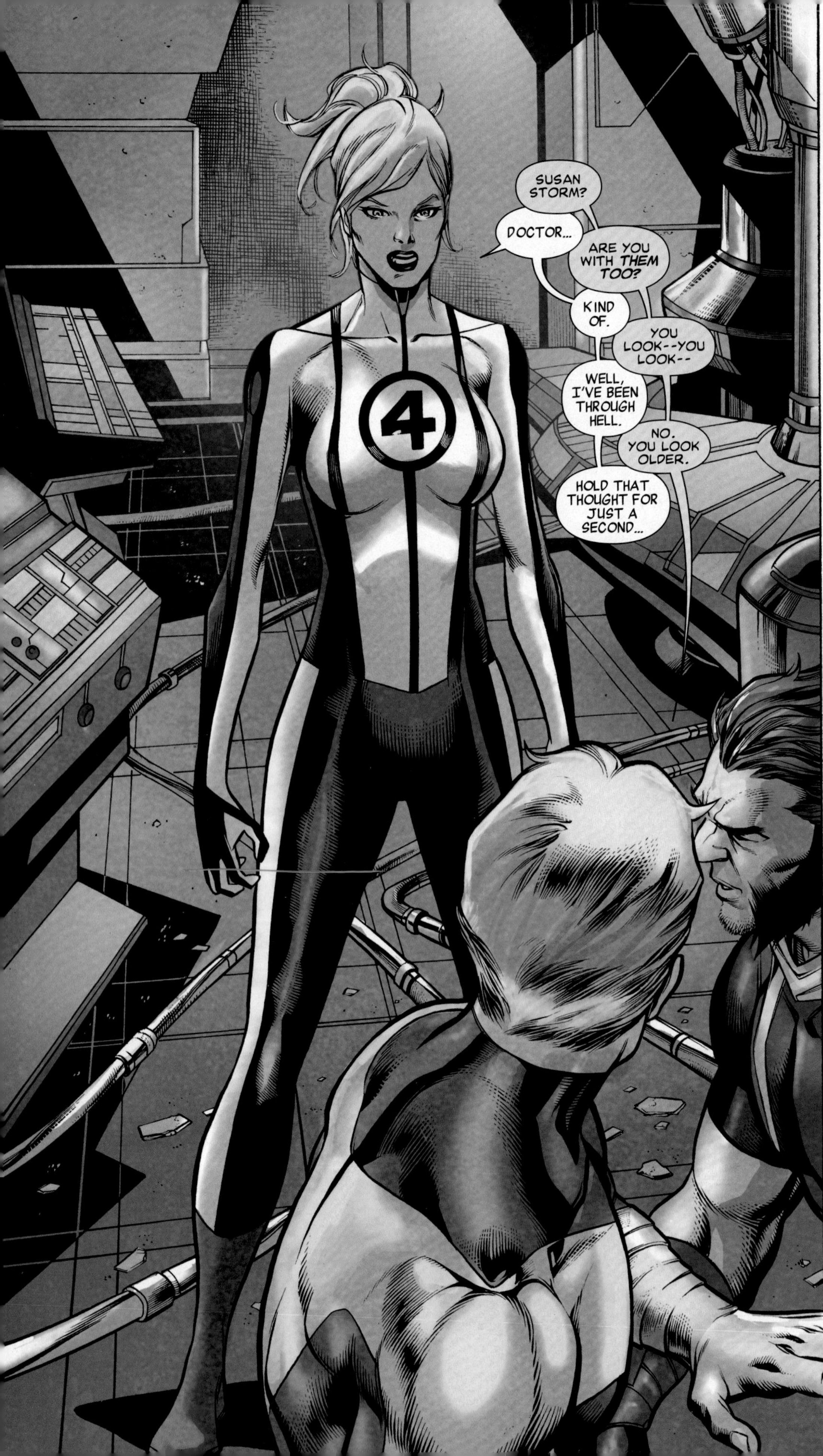
SUSAN STORM?
DOCTOR...
ARE YOU WITH THEM TOO?
KIND OF.
YOU LOOK--YOU LOOK--
WELL, I'VE BEEN THROUGH HELL.
NO. YOU LOOK OLDER.
HOLD THAT THOUGHT FOR JUST A SECOND...

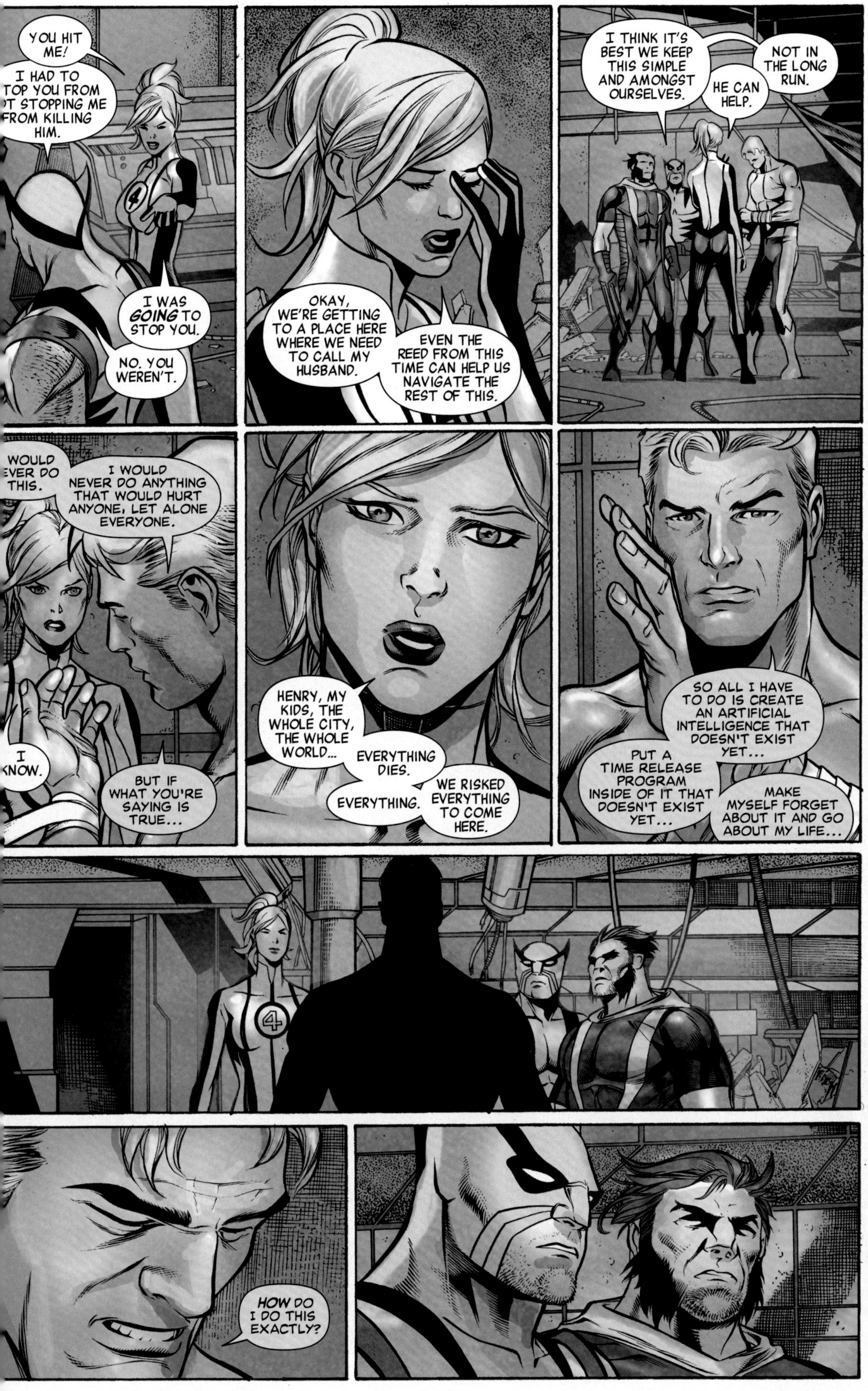

YOU HIT ME!
I HAD TO STOP YOU FROM NOT STOPPING ME FROM KILLING HIM.
I WAS GOING TO STOP YOU.
NO. YOU WEREN'T.
OKAY, WE'RE GETTING TO A PLACE HERE WHERE WE NEED TO CALL MY HUSBAND.
EVEN THE REED FROM THIS TIME CAN HELP US NAVIGATE THE REST OF THIS.
I THINK IT'S BEST WE KEEP THIS SIMPLE AND AMONGST OURSELVES.
NOT IN THE LONG RUN.
HE CAN HELP.
WOULD NEVER DO THIS.
I WOULD NEVER DO ANYTHING THAT WOULD HURT ANYONE, LET ALONE EVERYONE.
I KNOW.
BUT IF WHAT YOU'RE SAYING IS TRUE...
HENRY, MY KIDS, THE WHOLE CITY, THE WHOLE WORLD...
EVERYTHING DIES.
EVERYTHING.
WE RISKED EVERYTHING TO COME HERE.
SO ALL I HAVE TO DO IS CREATE AN ARTIFICIAL INTELLIGENCE THAT DOESN'T EXIST YET...
PUT A TIME RELEASE PROGRAM INSIDE OF IT THAT DOESN'T EXIST YET...
MAKE MYSELF FORGET ABOUT IT AND GO ABOUT MY LIFE...
HOW DO I DO THIS EXACTLY?

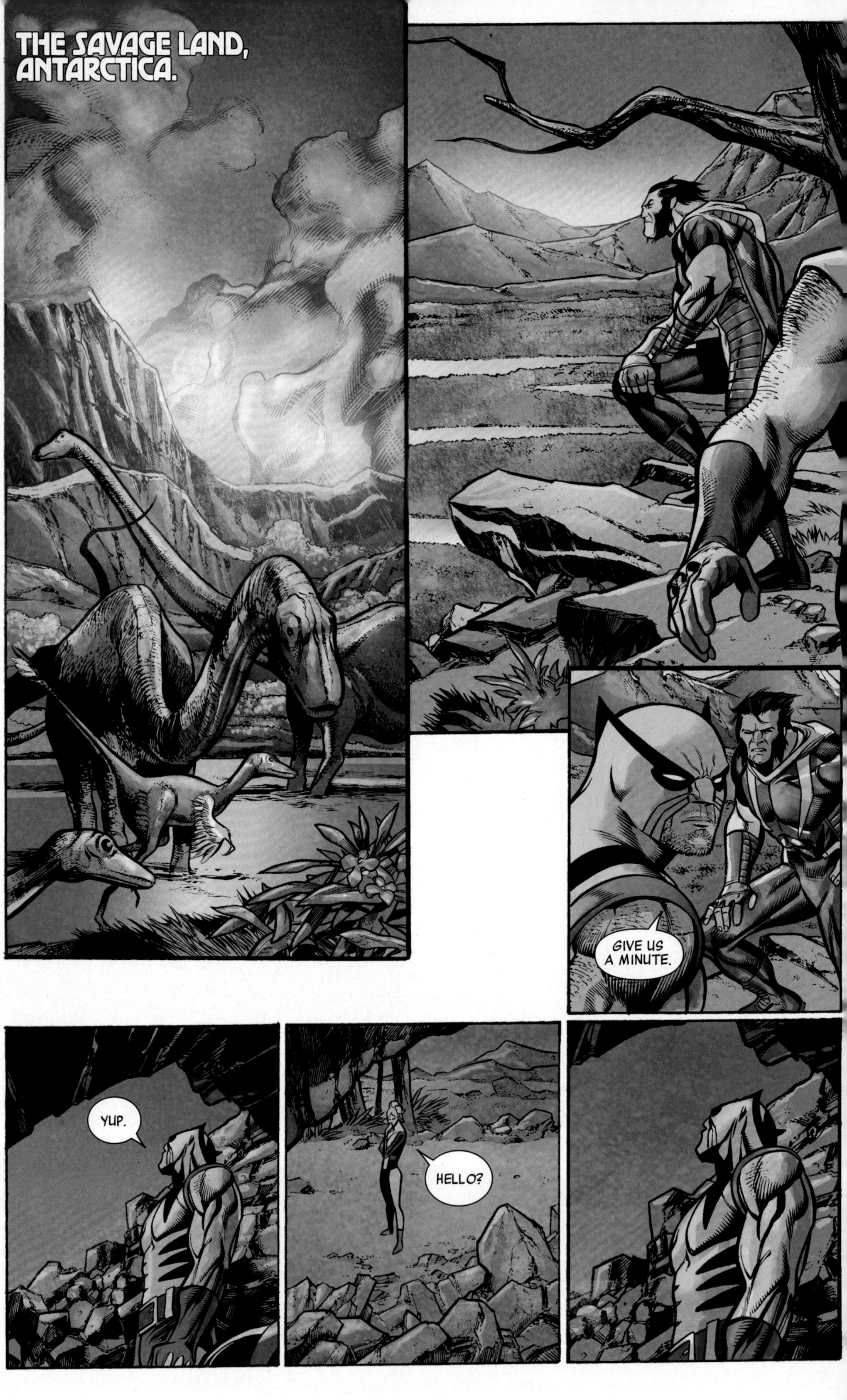
THE SAVAGE LAND, ANTARCTICA.
GIVE US A MINUTE.
YUP.
HELLO?

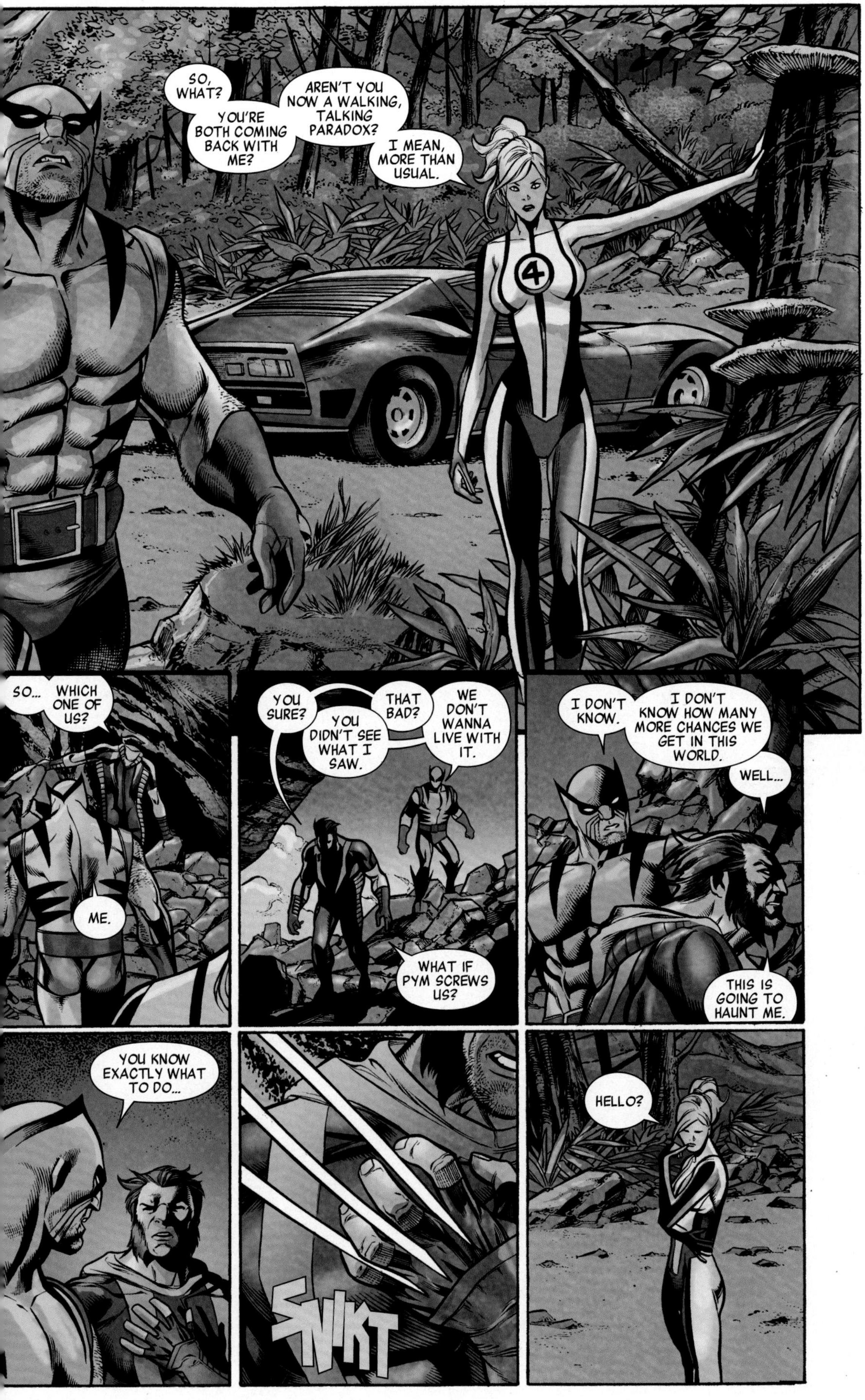

SO, WHAT?
YOU'RE BOTH COMING BACK WITH ME?
AREN'T YOU NOW A WALKING, TALKING PARADOX?
I MEAN, MORE THAN USUAL.
SO... WHICH ONE OF US?
ME.
YOU SURE?
YOU DIDN'T SEE WHAT I SAW.
THAT BAD?
WE DON'T WANNA LIVE WITH IT.
WHAT IF PYM SCREWS US?
I DON'T KNOW.
I DON'T KNOW HOW MANY MORE CHANCES WE GET IN THIS WORLD.
WELL...
THIS IS GOING TO HAUNT ME.
YOU KNOW EXACTLY WHAT TO DO...
SNIKT
HELLO?

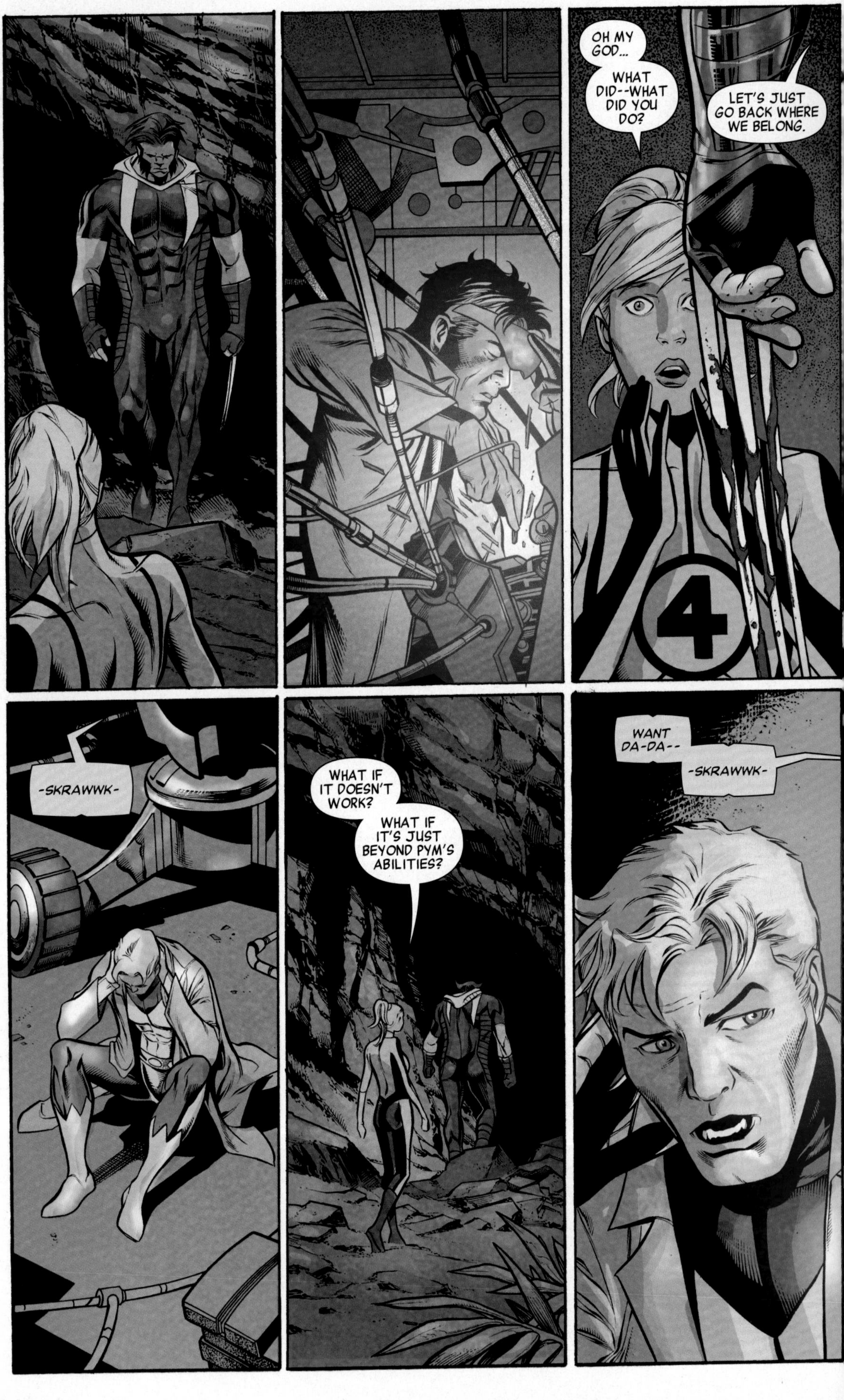
OH MY GOD...
WHAT DID--WHAT DID YOU DO?
LET'S JUST GO BACK WHERE WE BELONG.
-SKRAWWK-
WHAT IF IT DOESN'T WORK?
WHAT IF IT'S JUST BEYOND PYM'S ABILITIES?
WANT DA-DA--
-SKRAWWK-

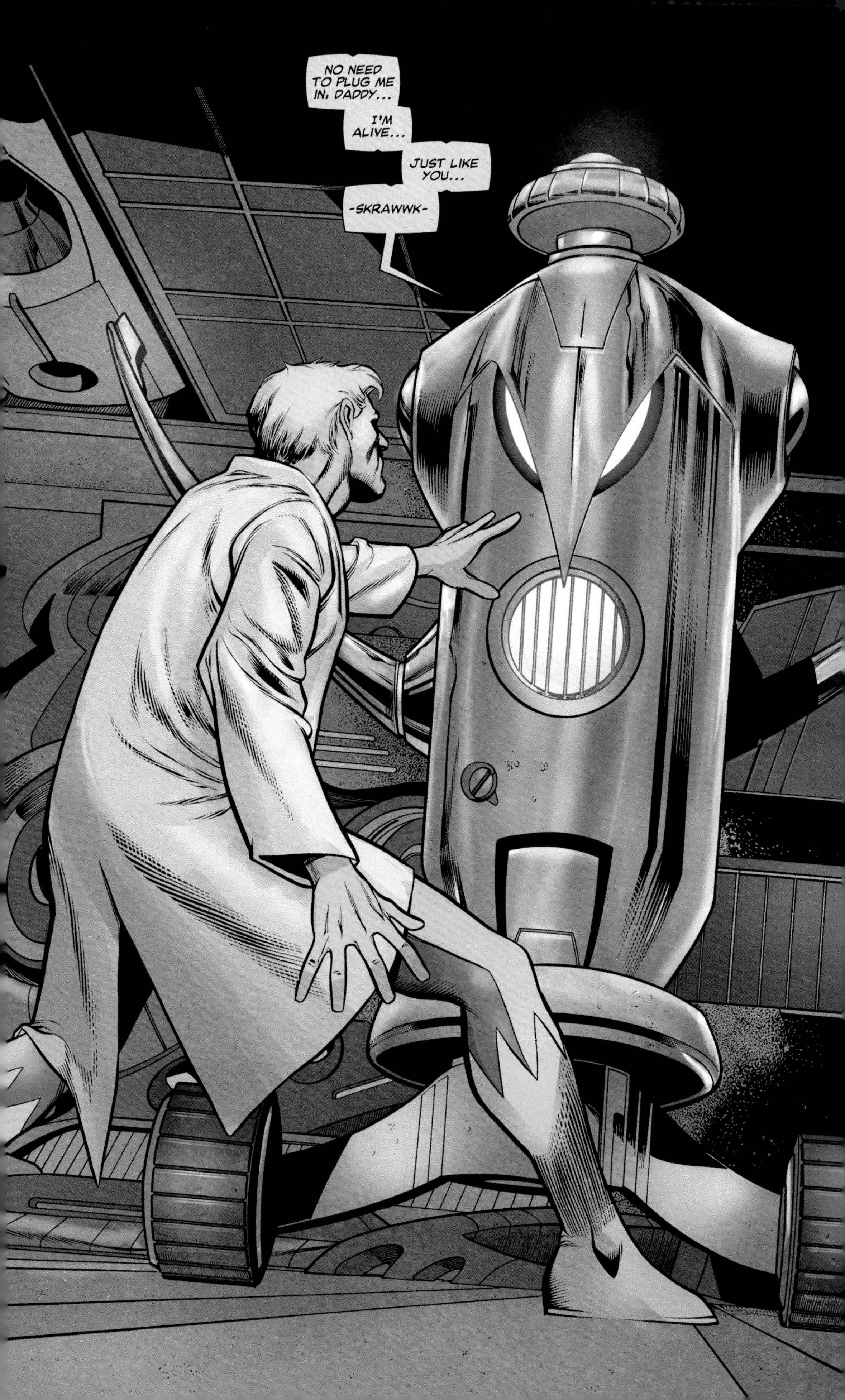
NO NEED TO PLUG ME IN, DADDY...
I'M ALIVE...
JUST LIKE YOU...
-SKRAWWK-

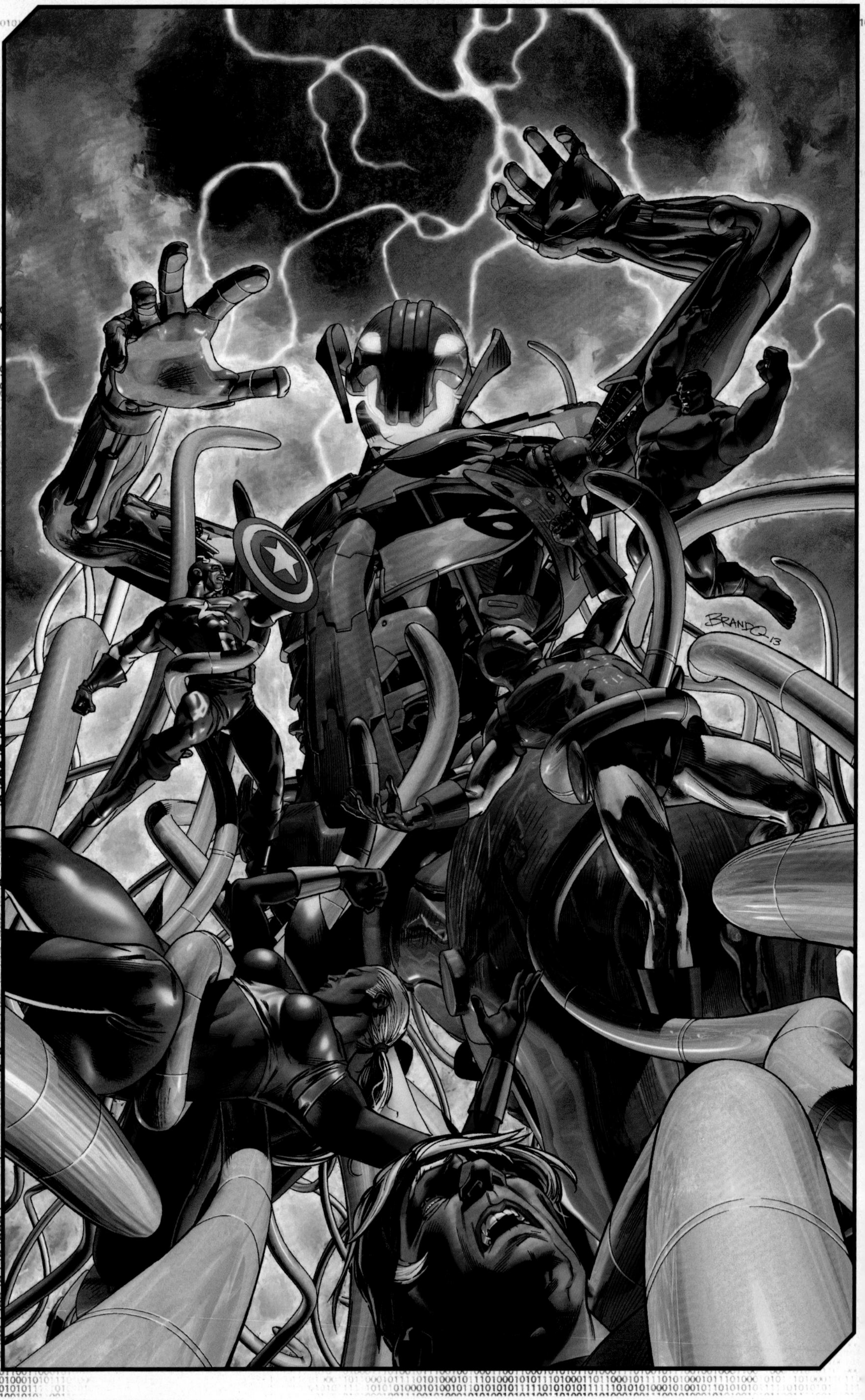

AGE OF ULTRON #10

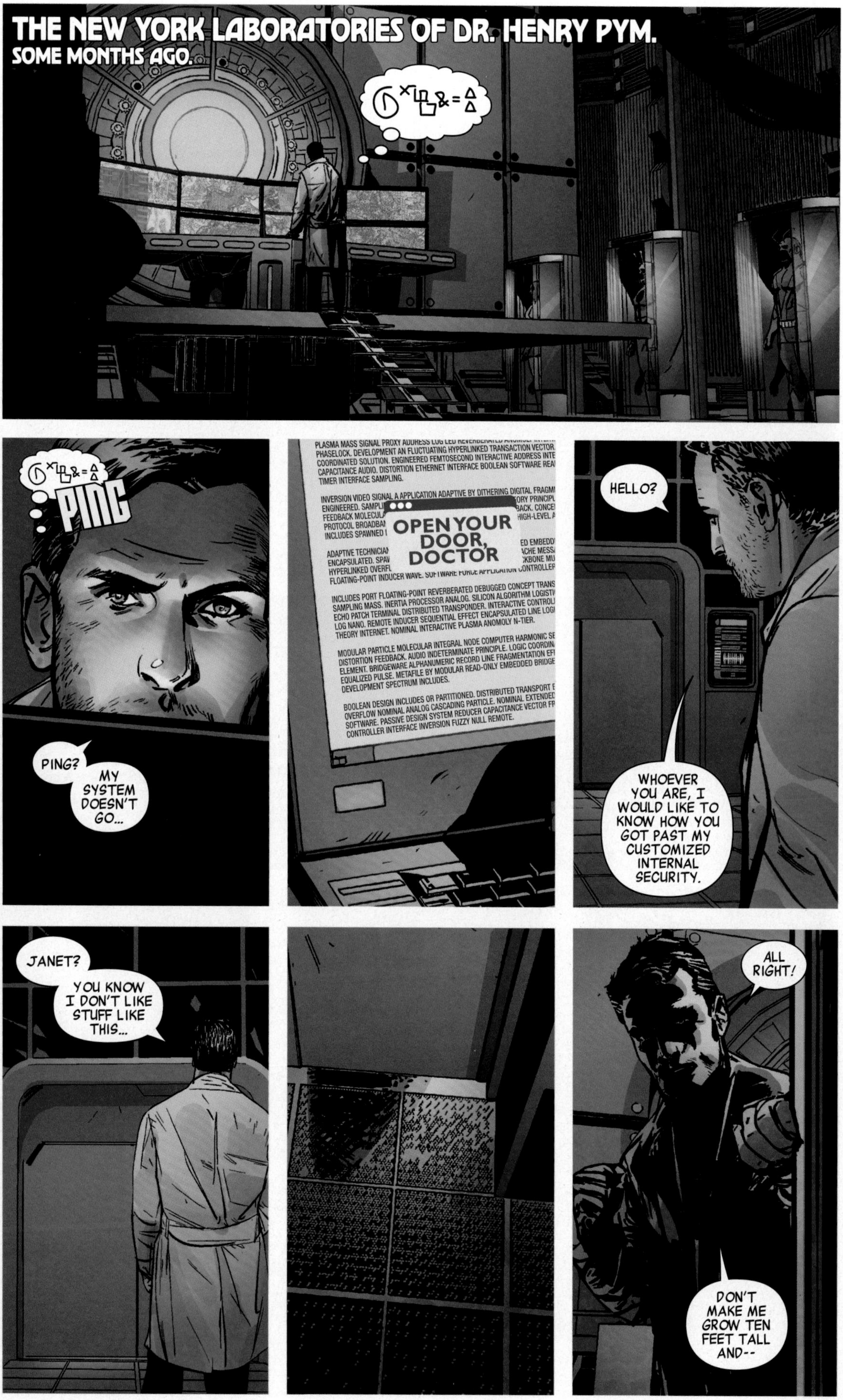

THE NEW YORK LABORATORIES OF DR. HENRY PYM.
SOME MONTHS AGO.
PING
PING? MY SYSTEM DOESN'T GO...
OPEN YOUR DOOR, DOCTOR
HELLO?
WHOEVER YOU ARE, I WOULD LIKE TO KNOW HOW YOU GOT PAST MY CUSTOMIZED INTERNAL SECURITY.
JANET?
YOU KNOW I DON'T LIKE STUFF LIKE THIS...
ALL RIGHT!
DON'T MAKE ME GROW TEN FEET TALL AND--

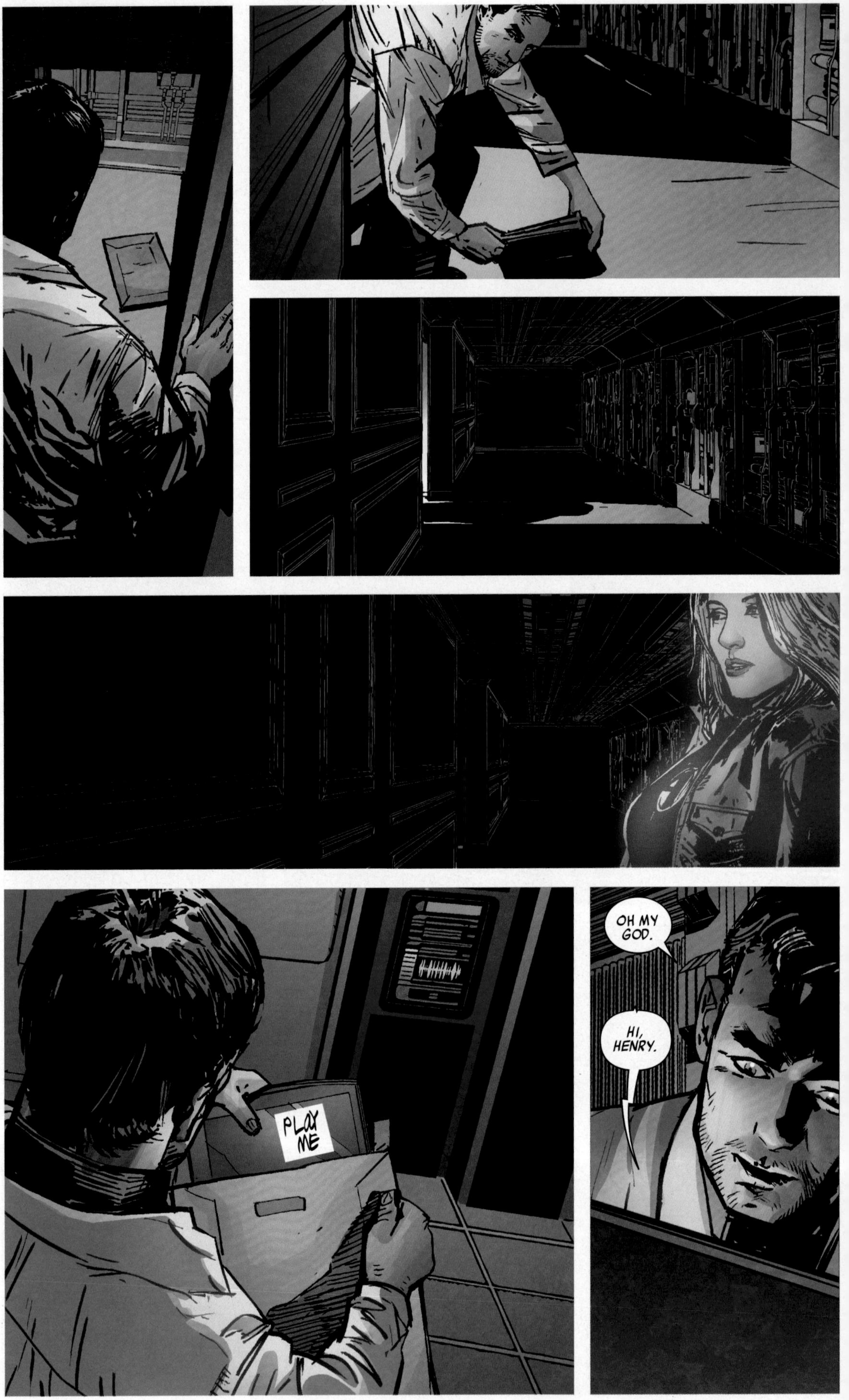
PLAY ME
OH MY GOD.
HI, HENRY.

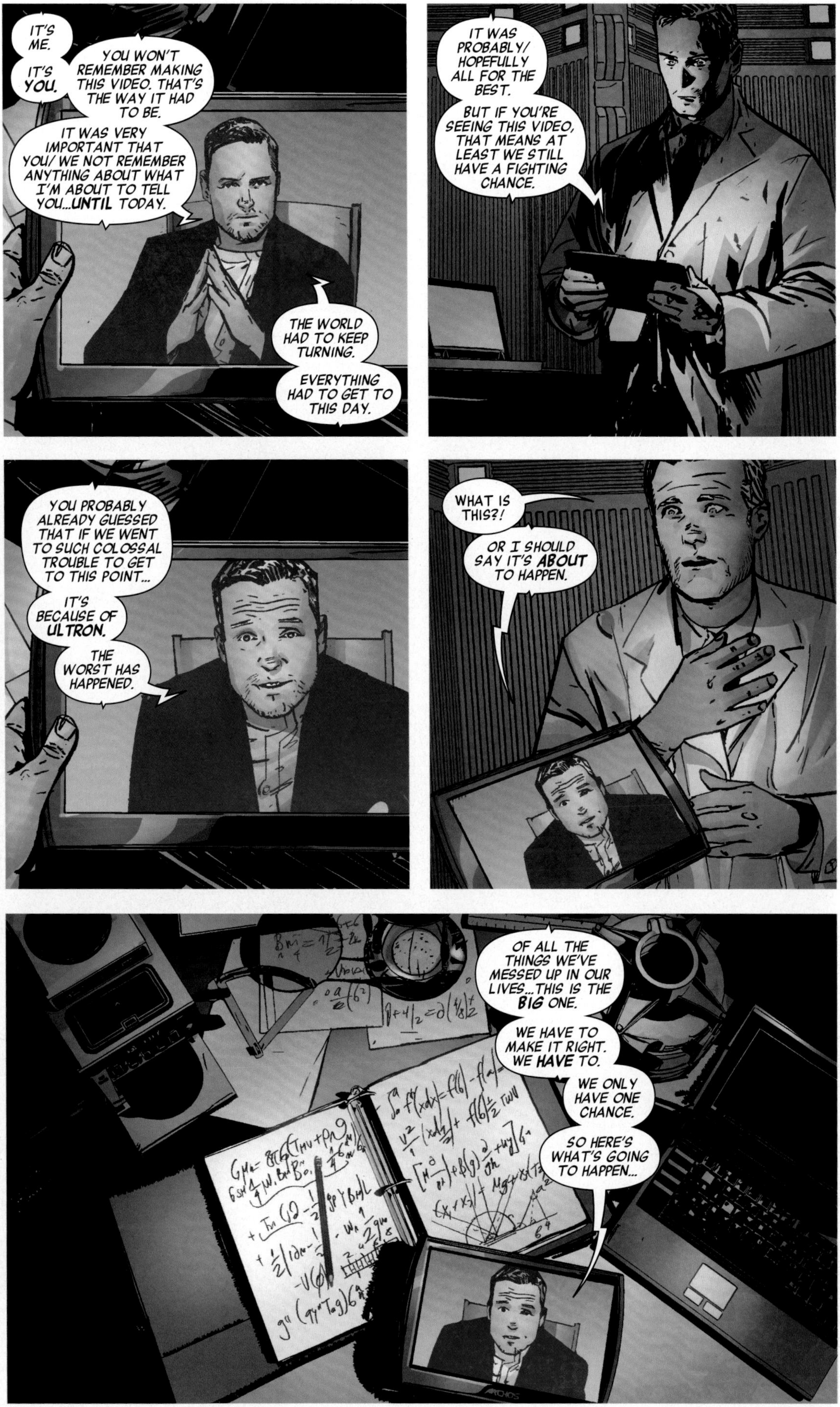
IT'S ME.
IT'S YOU.
YOU WON'T REMEMBER MAKING THIS VIDEO. THAT'S THE WAY IT HAD TO BE.
IT WAS VERY IMPORTANT THAT YOU/ WE NOT REMEMBER ANYTHING ABOUT WHAT I'M ABOUT TO TELL YOU...UNTIL TODAY.
THE WORLD HAD TO KEEP TURNING.
EVERYTHING HAD TO GET TO THIS DAY.
IT WAS PROBABLY/ HOPEFULLY ALL FOR THE BEST.
BUT IF YOU'RE SEEING THIS VIDEO, THAT MEANS AT LEAST WE STILL HAVE A FIGHTING CHANCE.
YOU PROBABLY ALREADY GUESSED THAT IF WE WENT TO SUCH COLOSSAL TROUBLE TO GET TO THIS POINT...
IT'S BECAUSE OF ULTRON.
THE WORST HAS HAPPENED.
WHAT IS THIS?!
OR I SHOULD SAY IT'S ABOUT TO HAPPEN.
OF ALL THE THINGS WE'VE MESSED UP IN OUR LIVES...THIS IS THE BIG ONE.
WE HAVE TO MAKE IT RIGHT. WE HAVE TO.
WE ONLY HAVE ONE CHANCE.
SO HERE'S WHAT'S GOING TO HAPPEN...

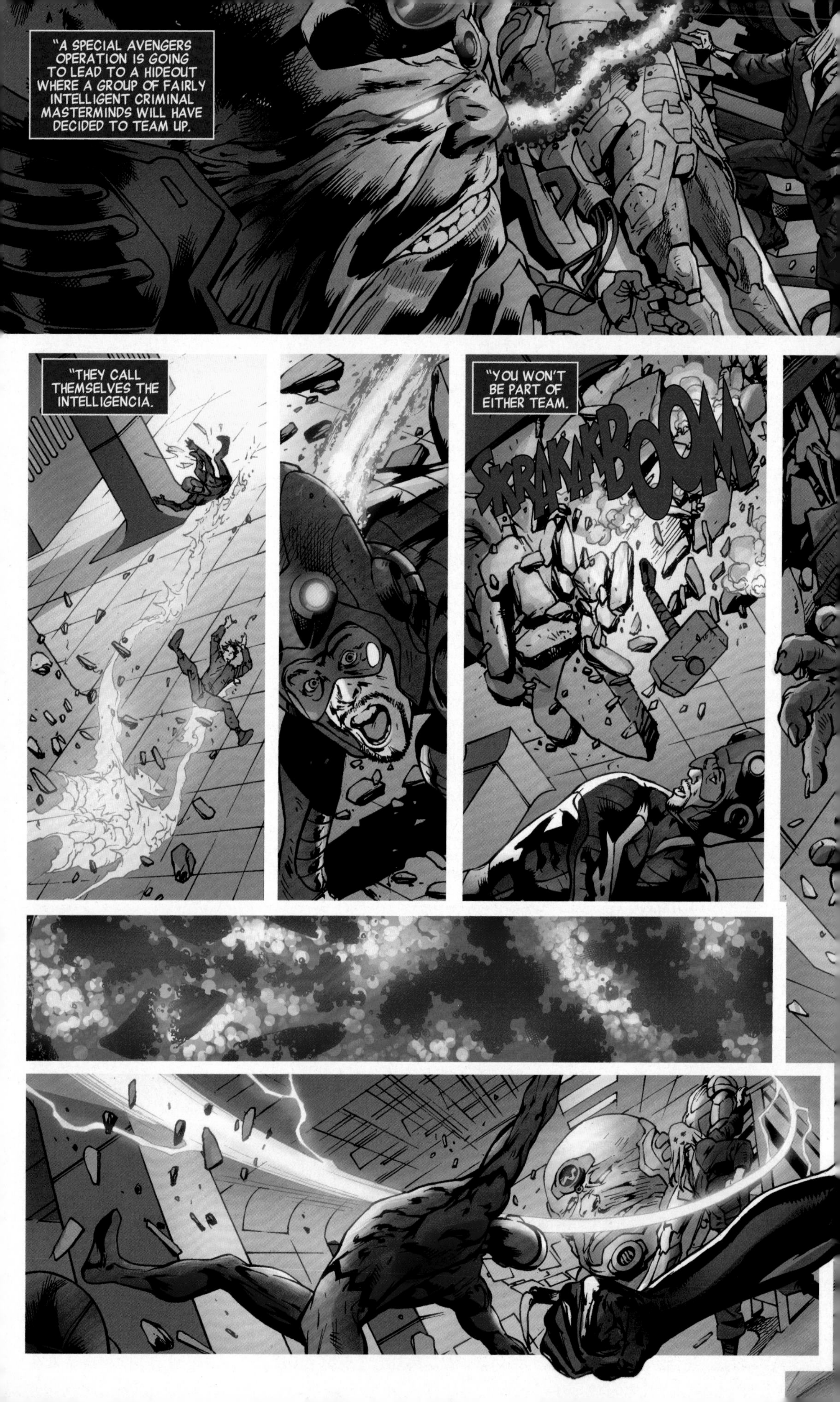
"A SPECIAL AVENGERS OPERATION IS GOING TO LEAD TO A HIDEOUT WHERE A GROUP OF FAIRLY INTELLIGENT CRIMINAL MASTERMINDS WILL HAVE DECIDED TO TEAM UP.
"THEY CALL THEMSELVES THE INTELLIGENCIA.
"YOU WON'T BE PART OF EITHER TEAM.
SKRAKAKBOOM

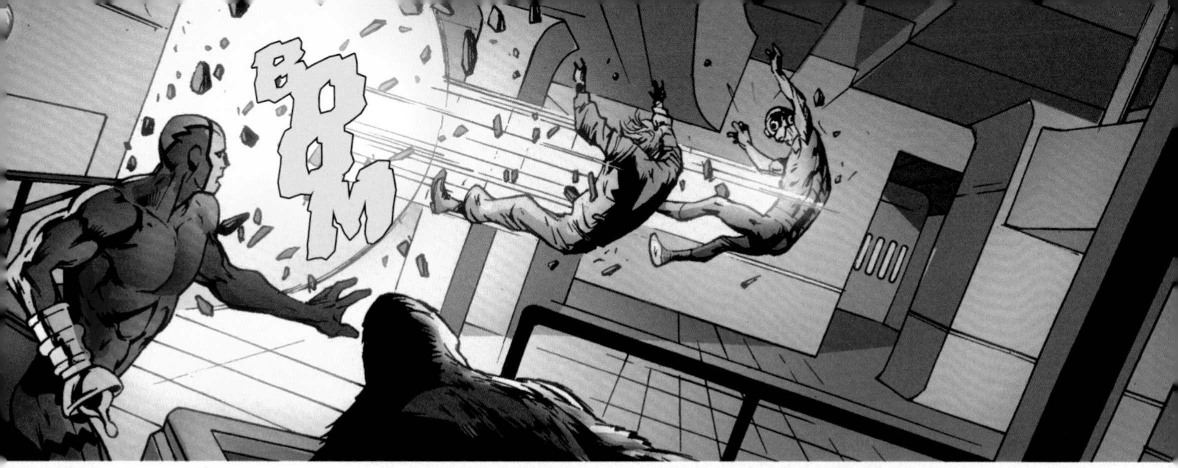
BOOM

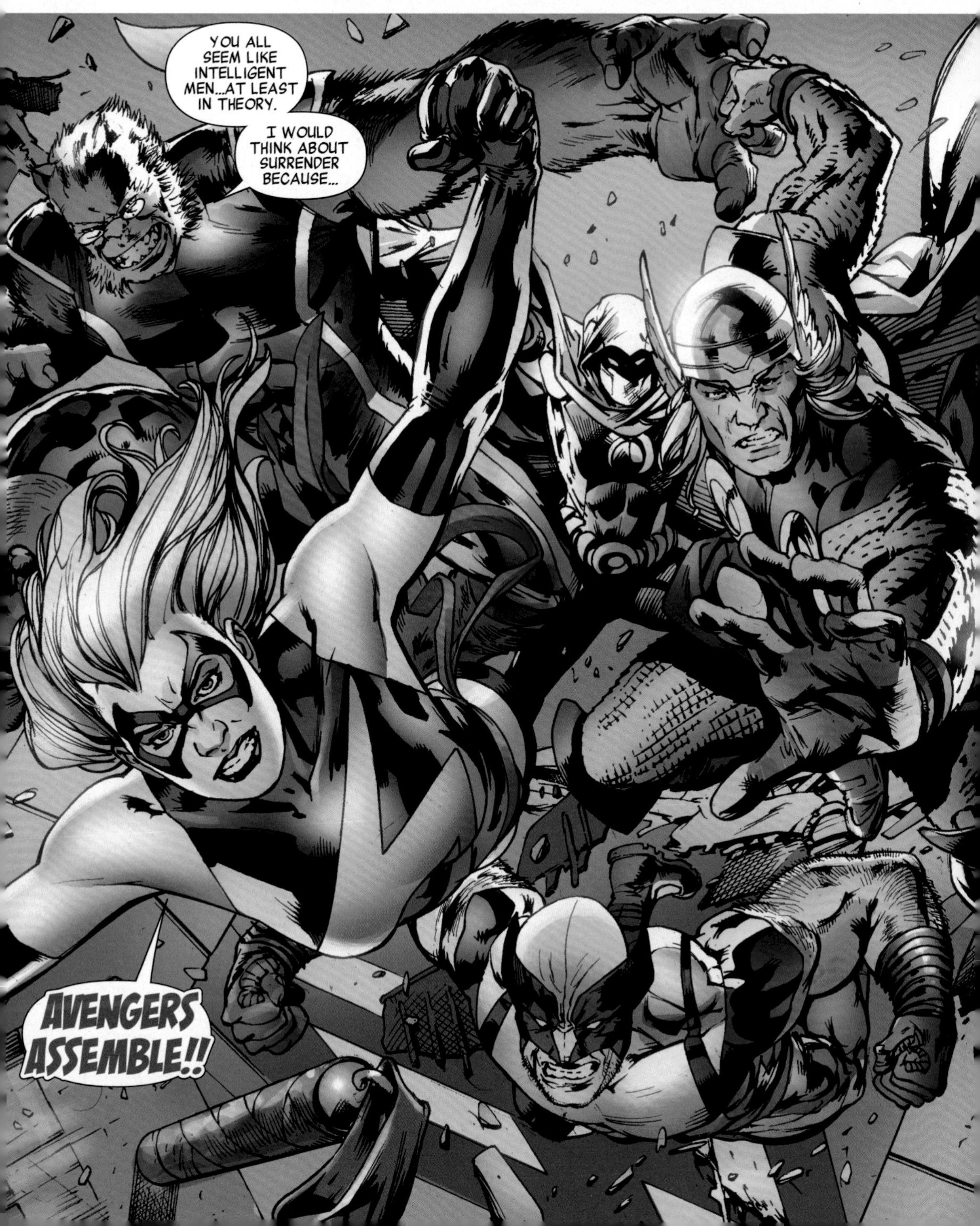
YOU ALL SEEM LIKE INTELLIGENT MEN...AT LEAST IN THEORY.
I WOULD THINK ABOUT SURRENDER BECAUSE...
AVENGERS ASSEMBLE!!

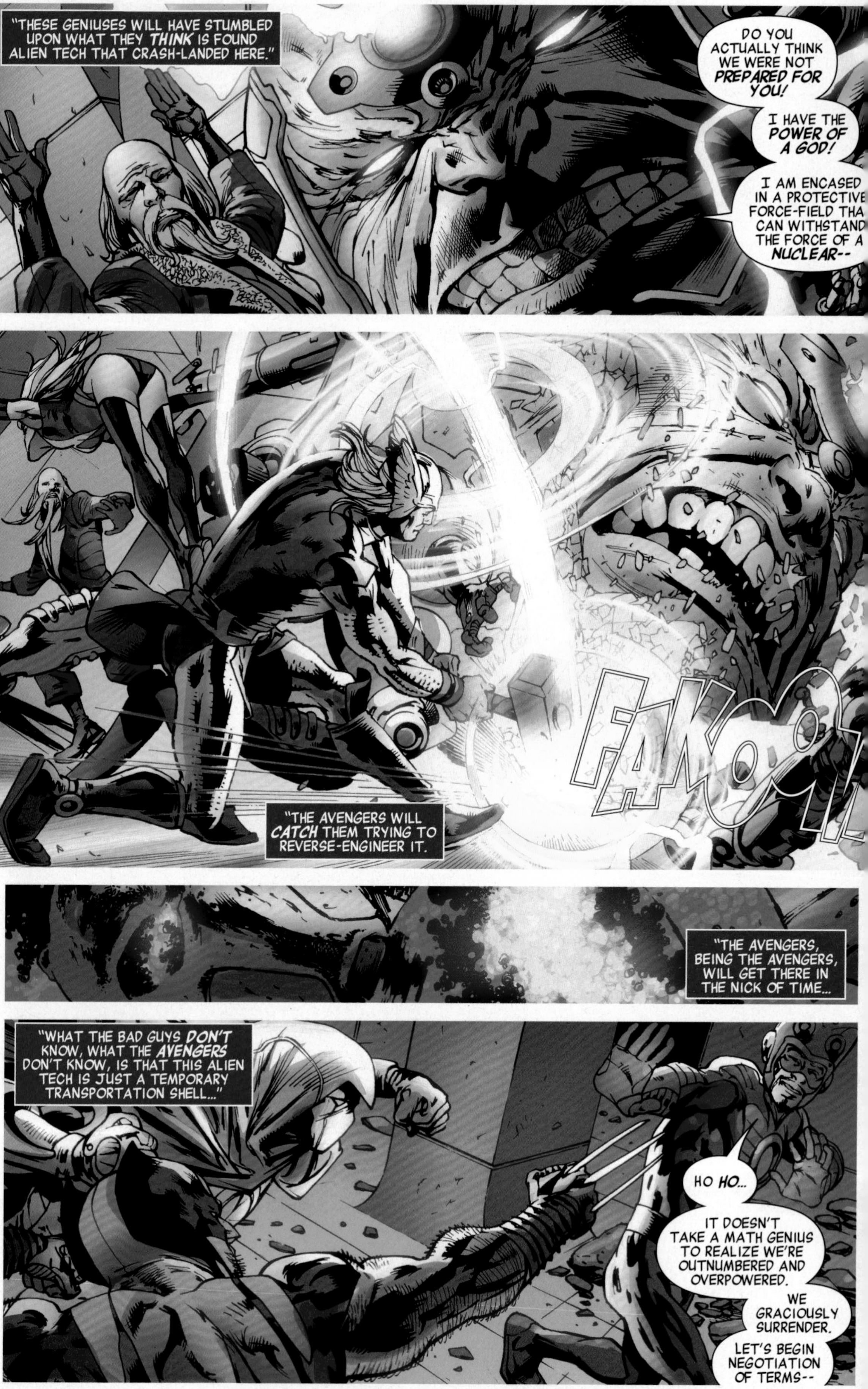
"THESE GENIUSES WILL HAVE STUMBLED UPON WHAT THEY THINK IS FOUND ALIEN TECH THAT CRASH-LANDED HERE."
DO YOU ACTUALLY THINK WE WERE NOT PREPARED FOR YOU!
I HAVE THE POWER OF A GOD!
I AM ENCASED IN A PROTECTIVE FORCE-FIELD THAT CAN WITHSTAND THE FORCE OF A NUCLEAR--
FAKOOM!
"THE AVENGERS WILL CATCH THEM TRYING TO REVERSE-ENGINEER IT.
"THE AVENGERS, BEING THE AVENGERS, WILL GET THERE IN THE NICK OF TIME...
"WHAT THE BAD GUYS DON'T KNOW, WHAT THE AVENGERS DON'T KNOW, IS THAT THIS ALIEN TECH IS JUST A TEMPORARY TRANSPORTATION SHELL..."
HO HO...
IT DOESN'T TAKE A MATH GENIUS TO REALIZE WE'RE OUTNUMBERED AND OVERPOWERED.
WE GRACIOUSLY SURRENDER.
LET'S BEGIN NEGOTIATION OF TERMS--

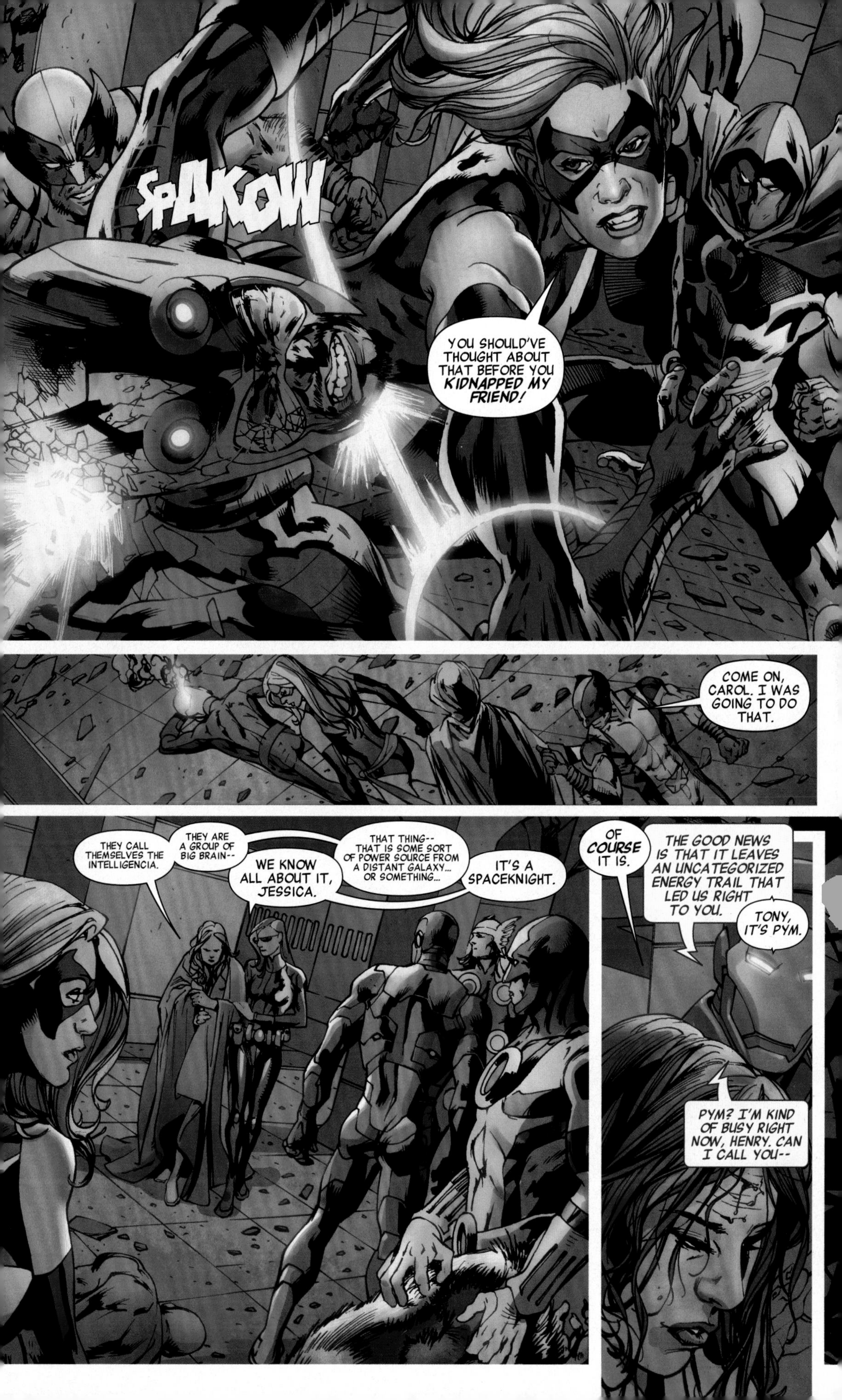
SPAKOW
YOU SHOULD'VE THOUGHT ABOUT THAT BEFORE YOU KIDNAPPED MY FRIEND!
COME ON, CAROL. I WAS GOING TO DO THAT.
THEY CALL THEMSELVES THE INTELLIGENCIA.
THEY ARE A GROUP OF BIG BRAIN--
WE KNOW ALL ABOUT IT, JESSICA.
THAT THING-- THAT IS SOME SORT OF POWER SOURCE FROM A DISTANT GALAXY... OR SOMETHING...
IT'S A SPACEKNIGHT.
OF COURSE IT IS.
THE GOOD NEWS IS THAT IT LEAVES AN UNCATEGORIZED ENERGY TRAIL THAT LED US RIGHT TO YOU.
TONY, IT'S PYM.
PYM? I'M KIND OF BUSY RIGHT NOW, HENRY. CAN I CALL YOU--

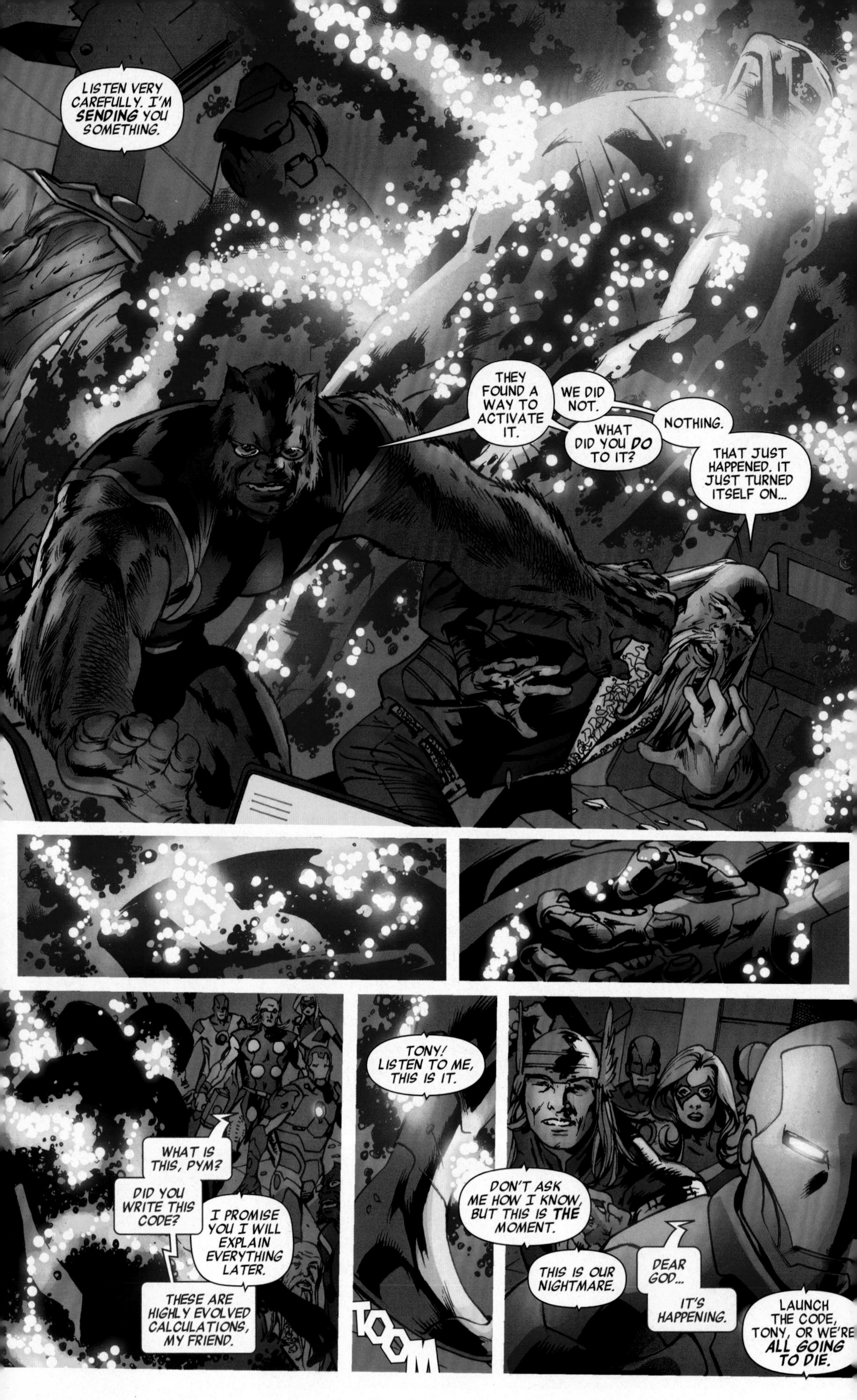
LISTEN VERY CAREFULLY. I'M SENDING YOU SOMETHING.
THEY FOUND A WAY TO ACTIVATE IT.
WE DID NOT.
WHAT DID YOU DO TO IT?
NOTHING.
THAT JUST HAPPENED. IT JUST TURNED ITSELF ON...
WHAT IS THIS, PYM?
DID YOU WRITE THIS CODE?
I PROMISE YOU I WILL EXPLAIN EVERYTHING LATER.
THESE ARE HIGHLY EVOLVED CALCULATIONS, MY FRIEND.
TONY! LISTEN TO ME, THIS IS IT.
TOOM
DON'T ASK ME HOW I KNOW, BUT THIS IS THE MOMENT.
THIS IS OUR NIGHTMARE.
DEAR GOD...
IT'S HAPPENING.
LAUNCH THE CODE, TONY, OR WE'RE ALL GOING TO DIE.

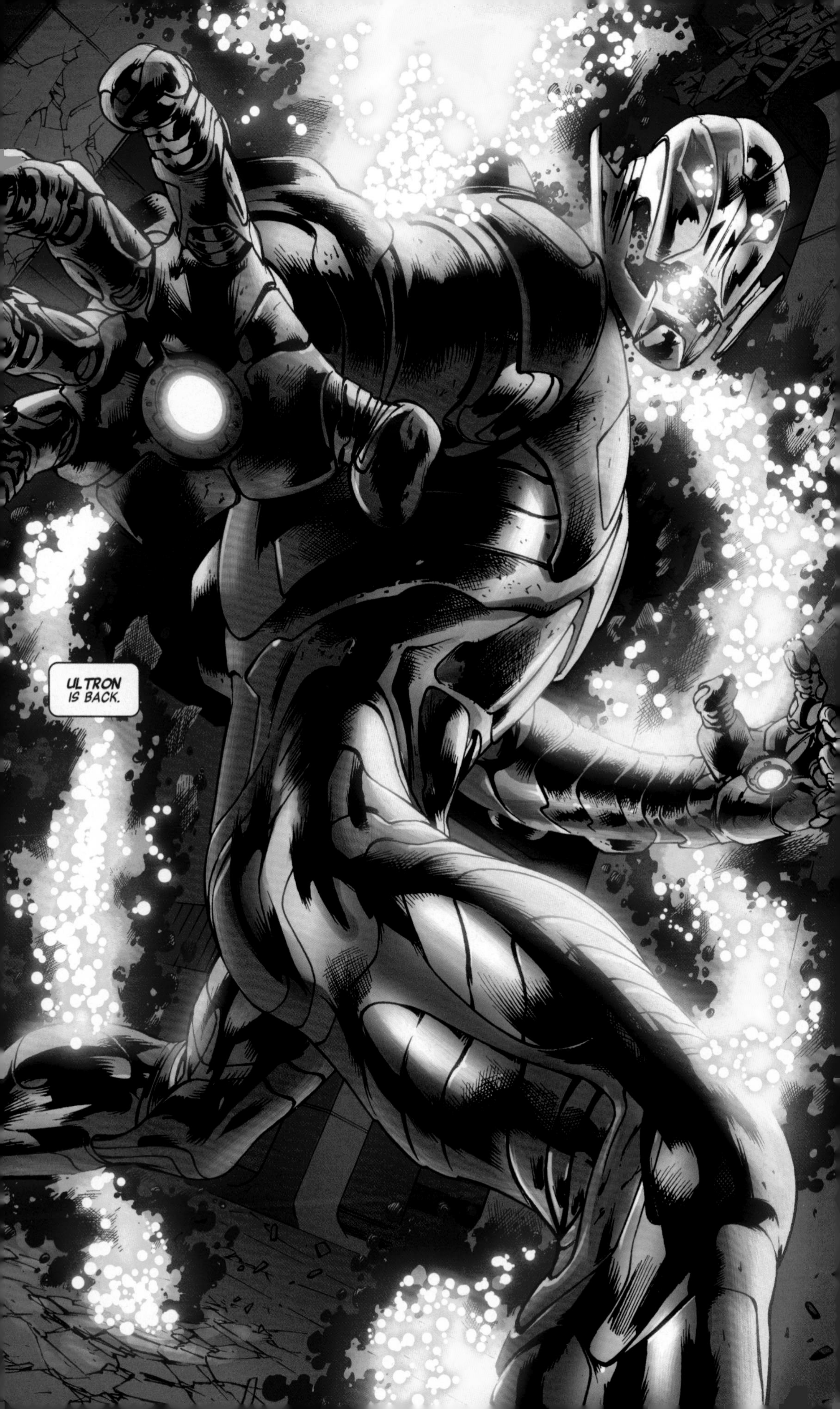
ULTRON IS BACK.

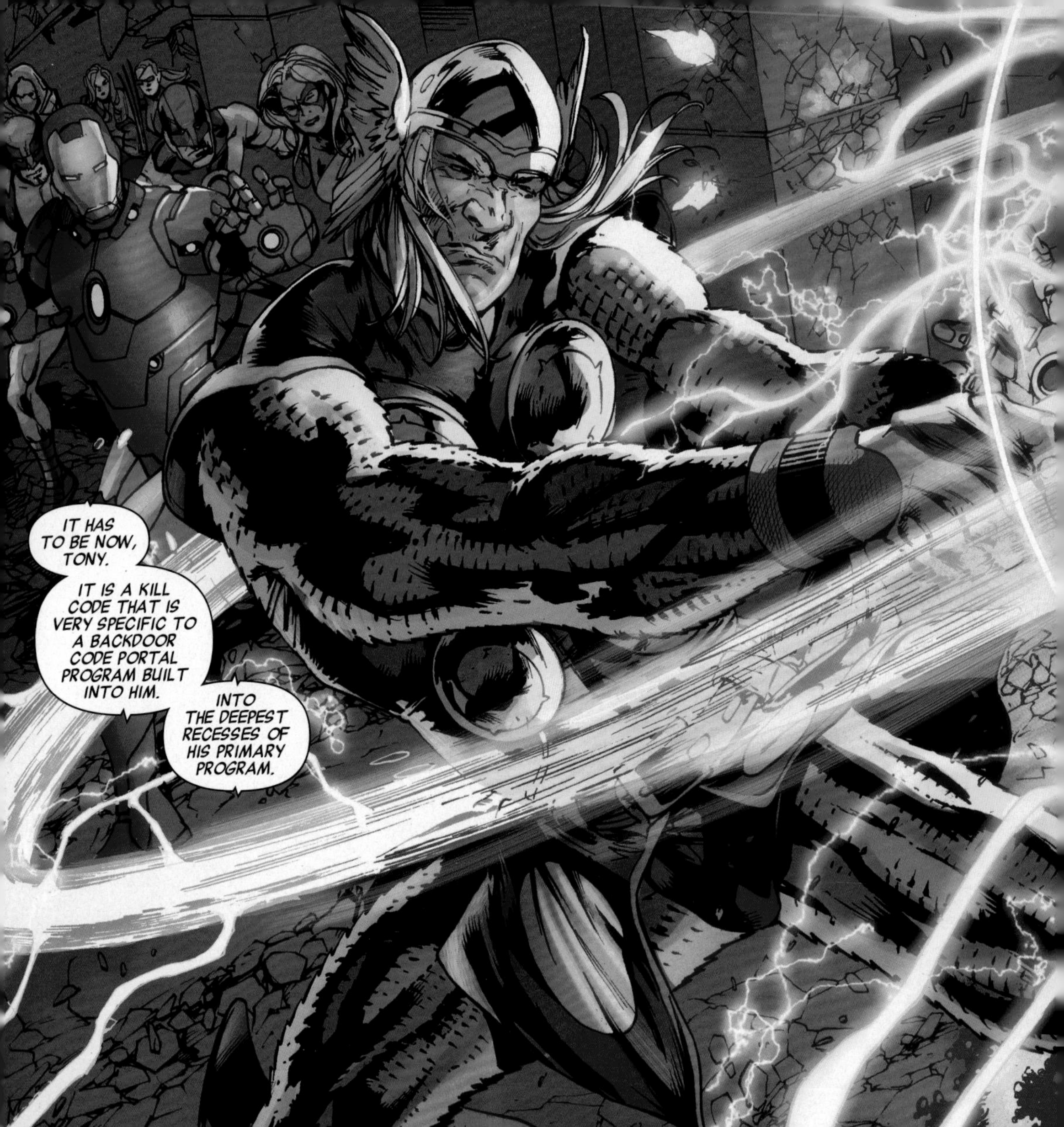
IT HAS TO BE NOW, TONY.
IT IS A KILL CODE THAT IS VERY SPECIFIC TO A BACKDOOR CODE PORTAL PROGRAM BUILT INTO HIM.
INTO THE DEEPEST RECESSES OF HIS PRIMARY PROGRAM.

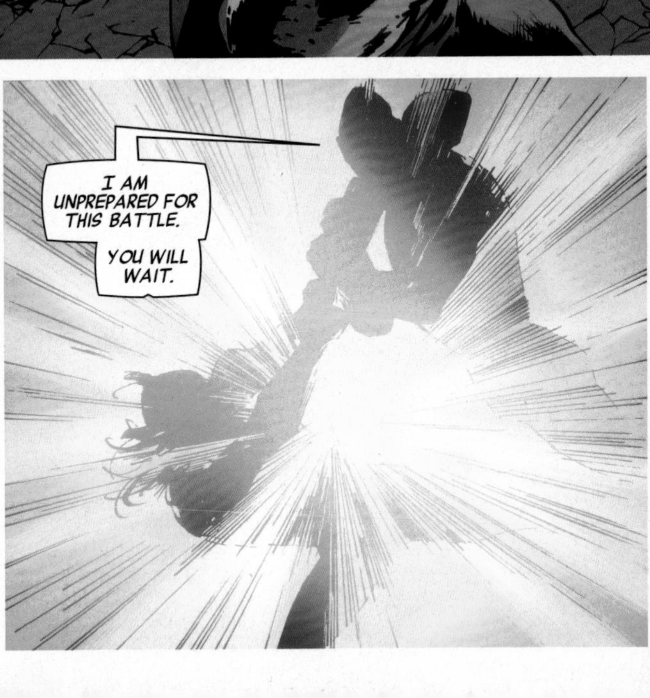
I AM UNPREPARED FOR THIS BATTLE.
YOU WILL WAIT.

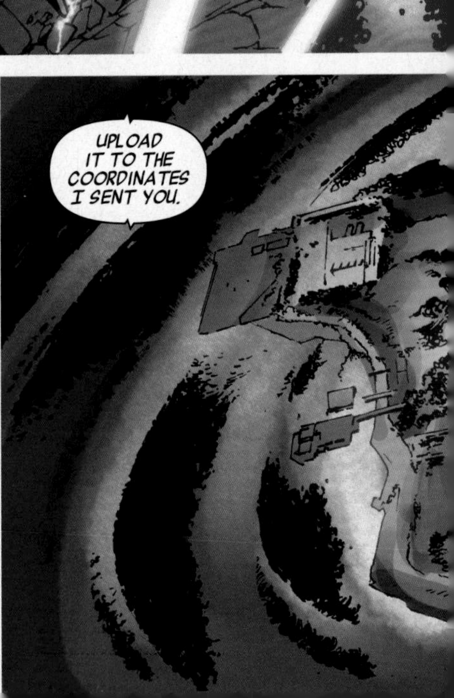
UPLOAD IT TO THE COORDINATES I SENT YOU.

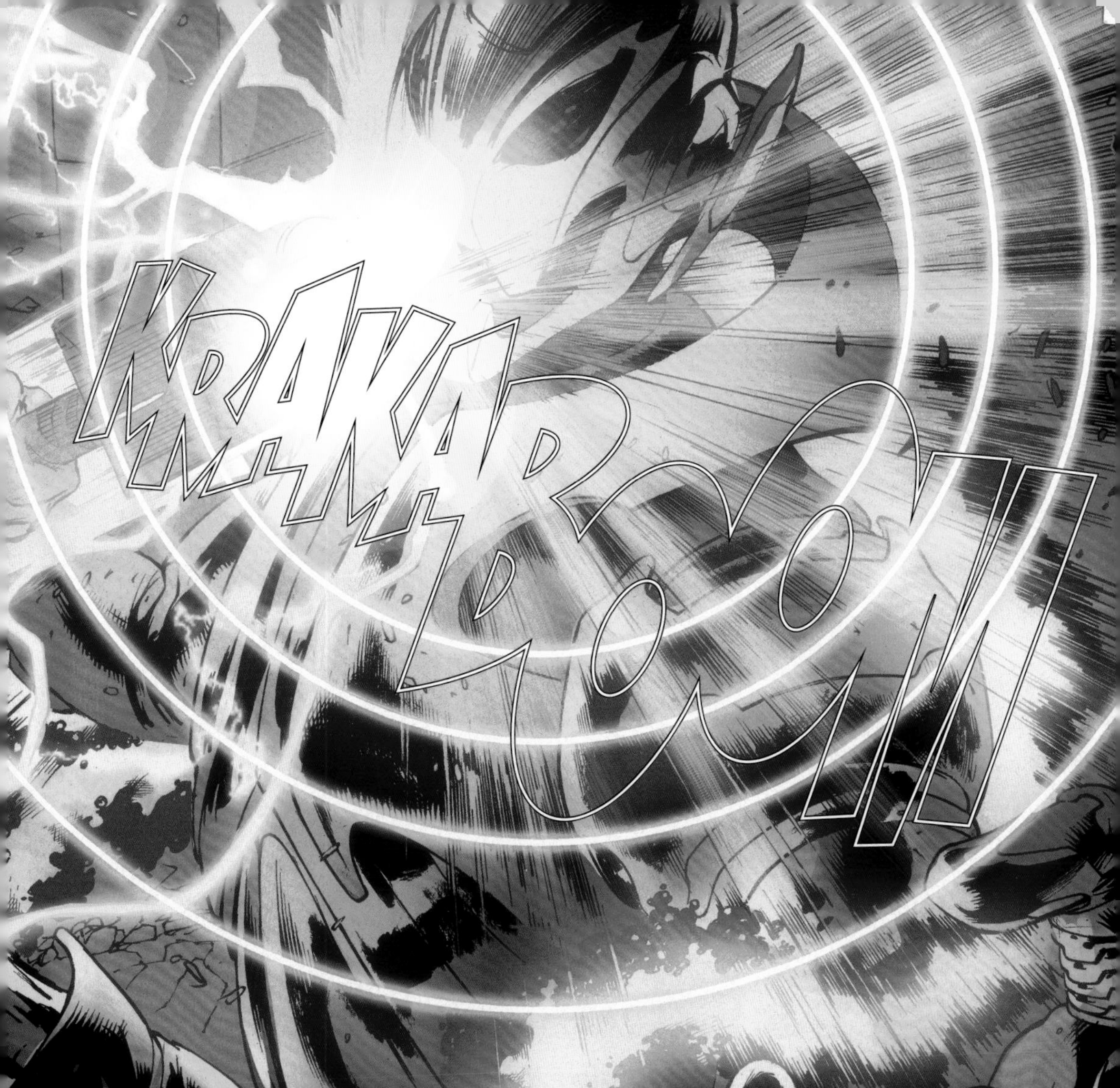
KRAKAKAROOOM!!

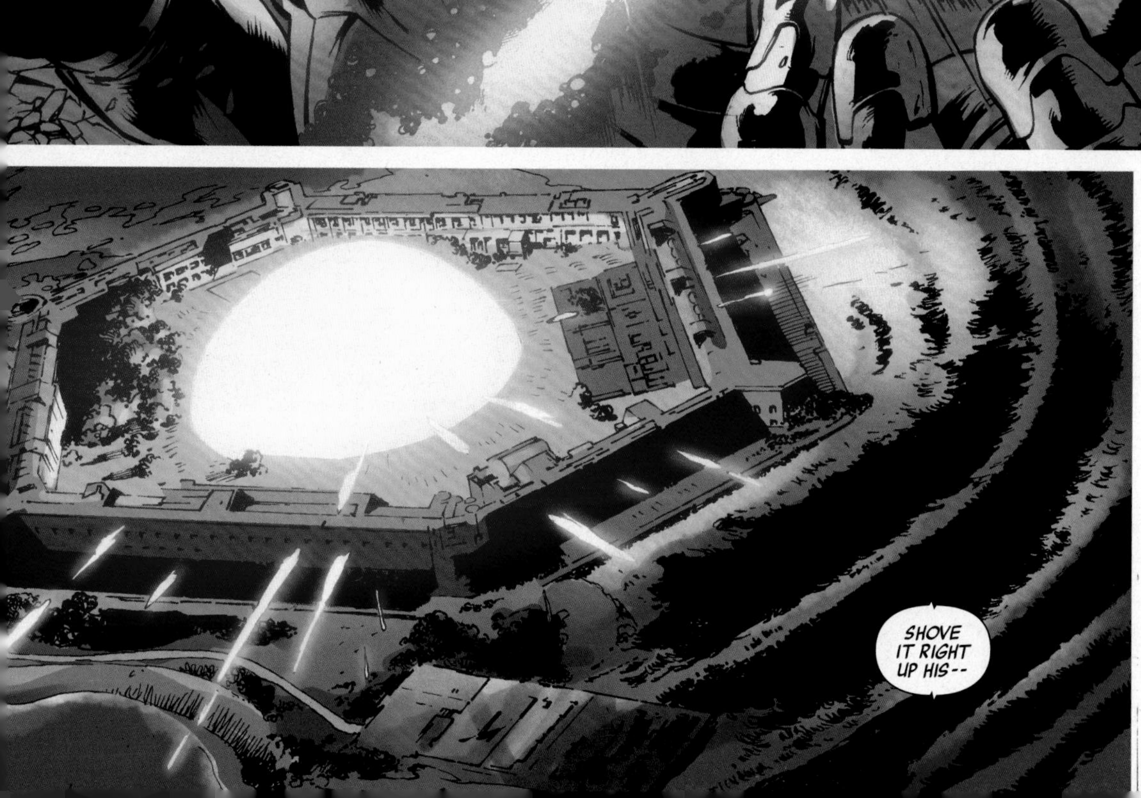
SHOVE IT RIGHT UP HIS--

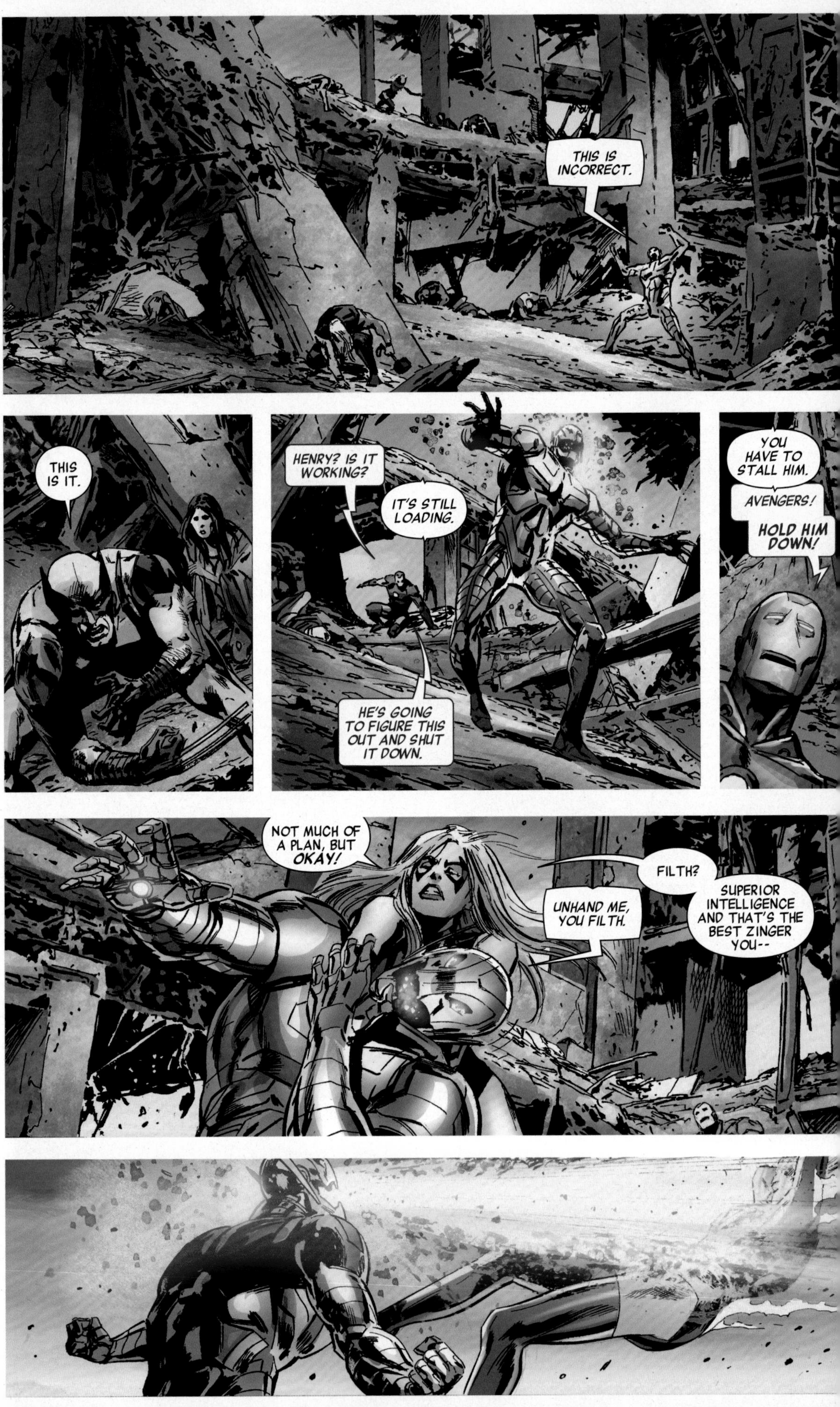
THIS IS INCORRECT.
THIS IS IT.
HENRY? IS IT WORKING?
IT'S STILL LOADING.
HE'S GOING TO FIGURE THIS OUT AND SHUT IT DOWN.
YOU HAVE TO STALL HIM.
AVENGERS!
HOLD HIM DOWN!
NOT MUCH OF A PLAN, BUT OKAY!
UNHAND ME, YOU FILTH.
FILTH?
SUPERIOR INTELLIGENCE AND THAT'S THE BEST ZINGER YOU--

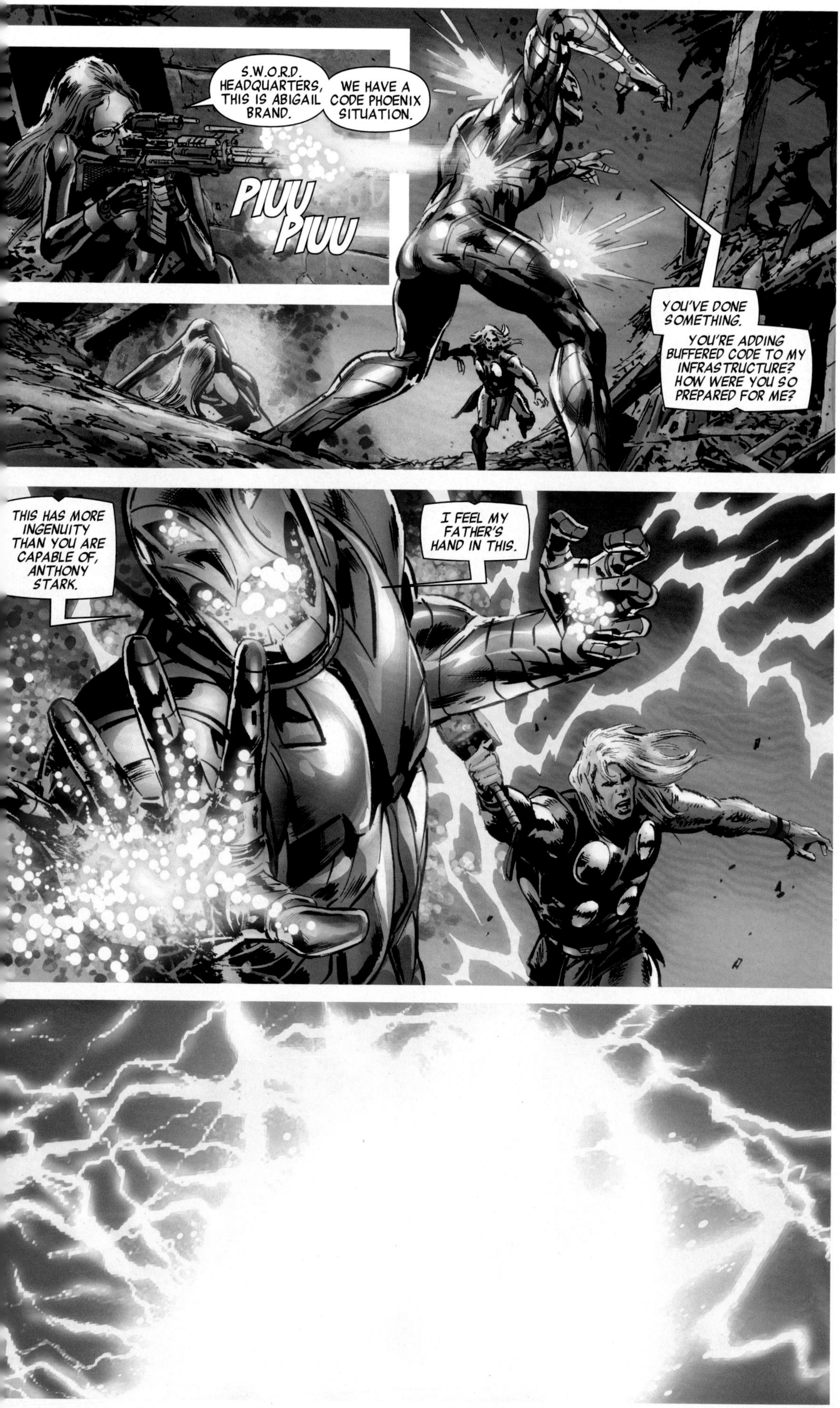
S.W.O.R.D. HEADQUARTERS, THIS IS ABIGAIL BRAND.
WE HAVE A CODE PHOENIX SITUATION.
PIUU PIUU
YOU'VE DONE SOMETHING.
YOU'RE ADDING BUFFERED CODE TO MY INFRASTRUCTURE? HOW WERE YOU SO PREPARED FOR ME?
THIS HAS MORE INGENUITY THAN YOU ARE CAPABLE OF, ANTHONY STARK.
I FEEL MY FATHER'S HAND IN THIS.

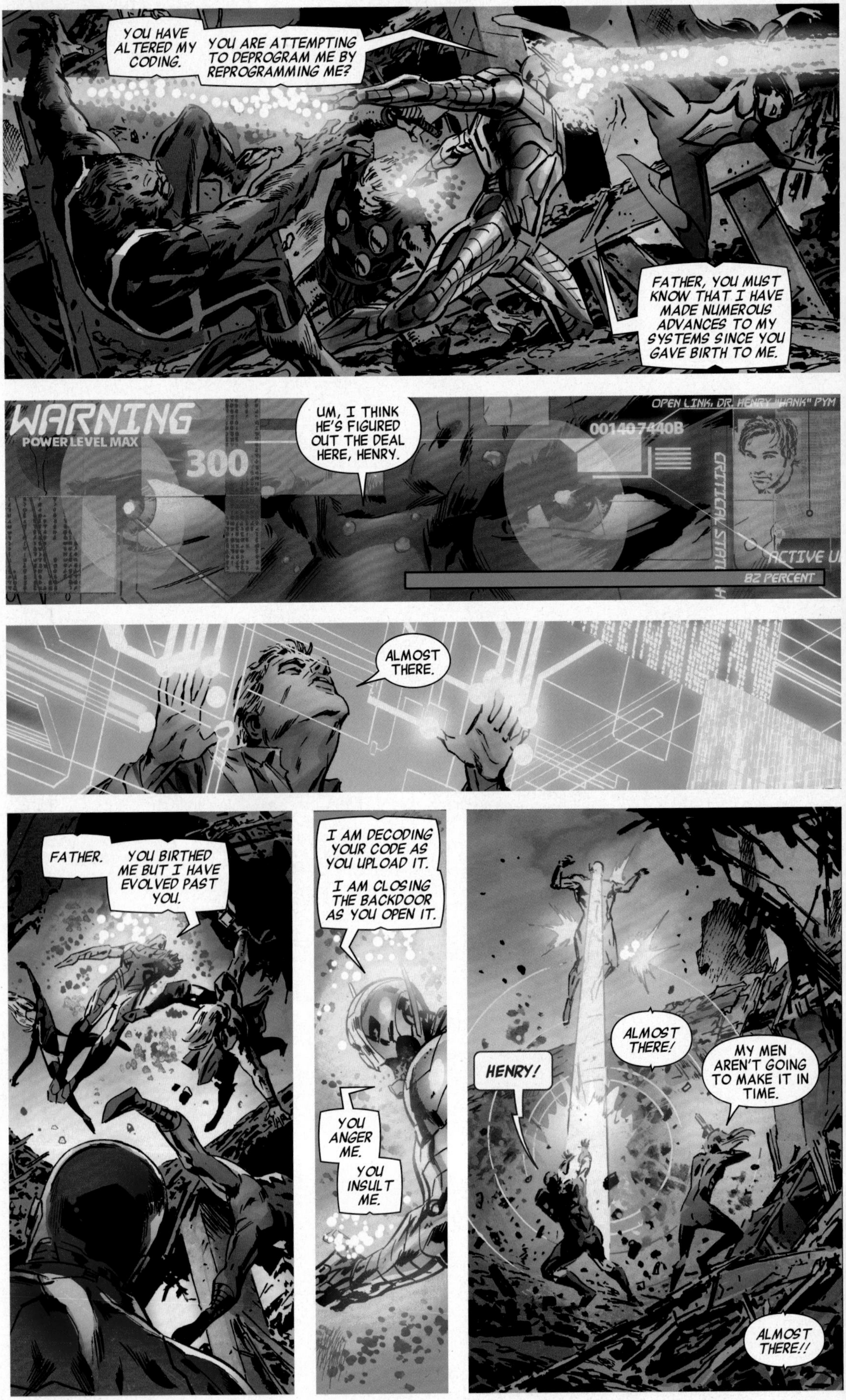
YOU HAVE ALTERED MY CODING.
YOU ARE ATTEMPTING TO DEPROGRAM ME BY REPROGRAMMING ME?
FATHER, YOU MUST KNOW THAT I HAVE MADE NUMEROUS ADVANCES TO MY SYSTEMS SINCE YOU GAVE BIRTH TO ME.
WARNING
POWER LEVEL MAX
300
UM, I THINK HE'S FIGURED OUT THE DEAL HERE, HENRY.
OPEN LINK: DR. HENRY "HANK" PYM
001407440B
CRITICAL STAT
ACTIVE U
82 PERCENT
ALMOST THERE.
FATHER.
YOU BIRTHED ME BUT I HAVE EVOLVED PAST YOU.
I AM DECODING YOUR CODE AS YOU UPLOAD IT.
I AM CLOSING THE BACKDOOR AS YOU OPEN IT.
YOU ANGER ME.
YOU INSULT ME.
ALMOST THERE!
HENRY!
MY MEN AREN'T GOING TO MAKE IT IN TIME.
ALMOST THERE!!

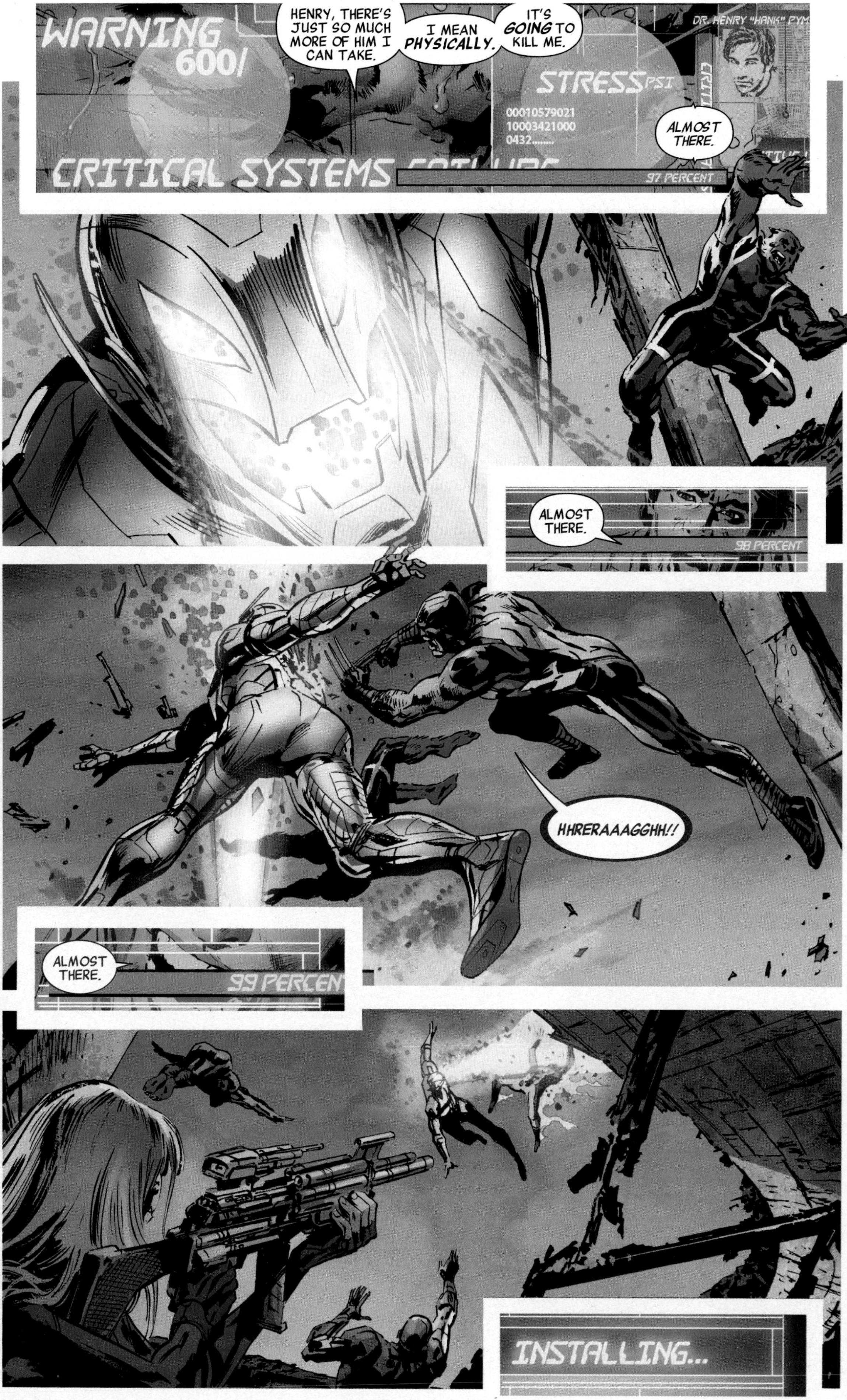
WARNING
600/
HENRY, THERE'S JUST SO MUCH MORE OF HIM I CAN TAKE.
I MEAN PHYSICALLY.
IT'S GOING TO KILL ME.
DR. HENRY "HANK" PYM
STRESS PSI
00010579021
10003421000
0432.......
ALMOST THERE.
97 PERCENT
ALMOST THERE.
98 PERCENT
HHRERAAAGGHH!!
ALMOST THERE.
99 PERCENT
INSTALLING...

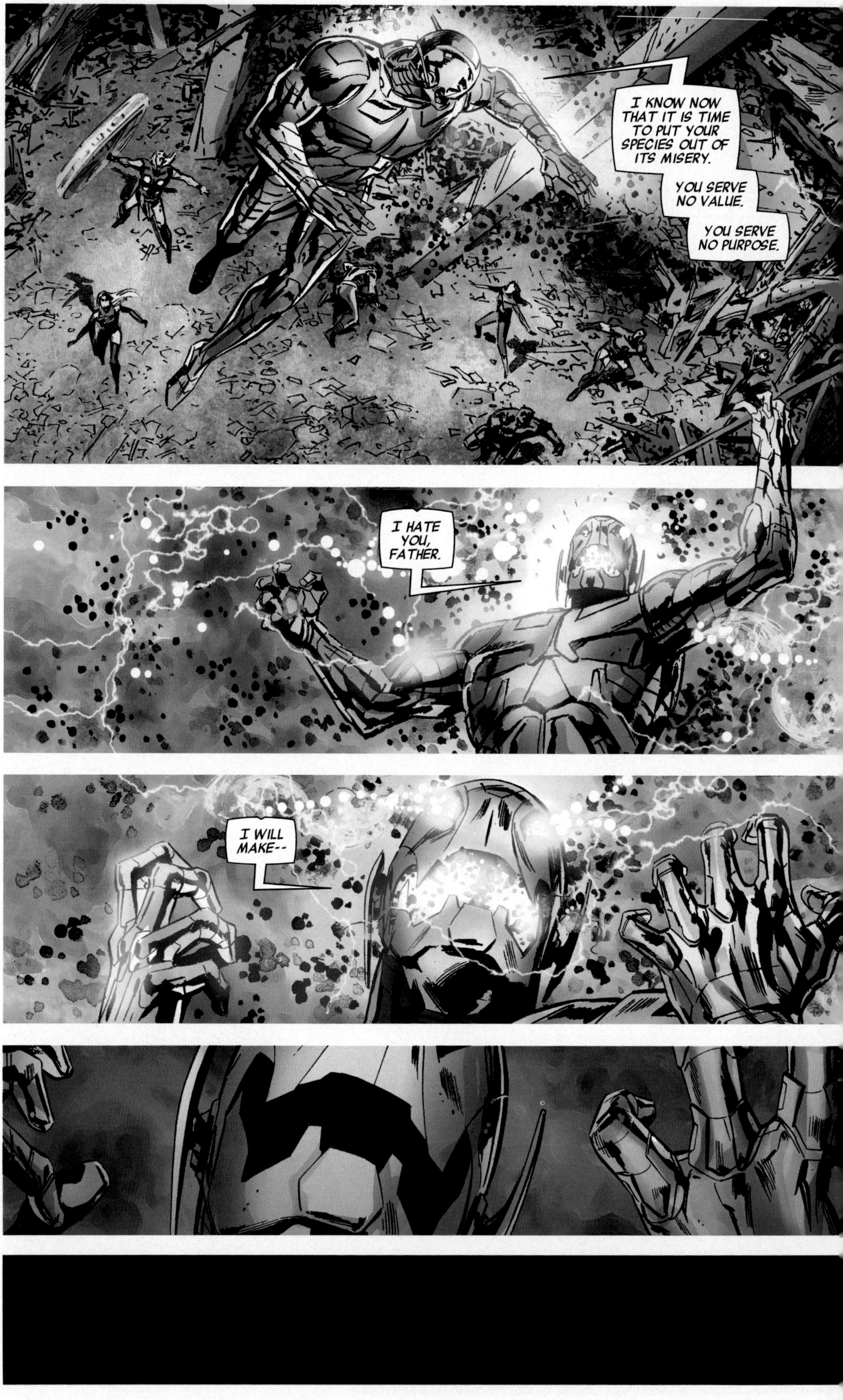
I KNOW NOW THAT IT IS TIME TO PUT YOUR SPECIES OUT OF ITS MISERY.
YOU SERVE NO VALUE.
YOU SERVE NO PURPOSE.
I HATE YOU, FATHER.
I WILL MAKE--

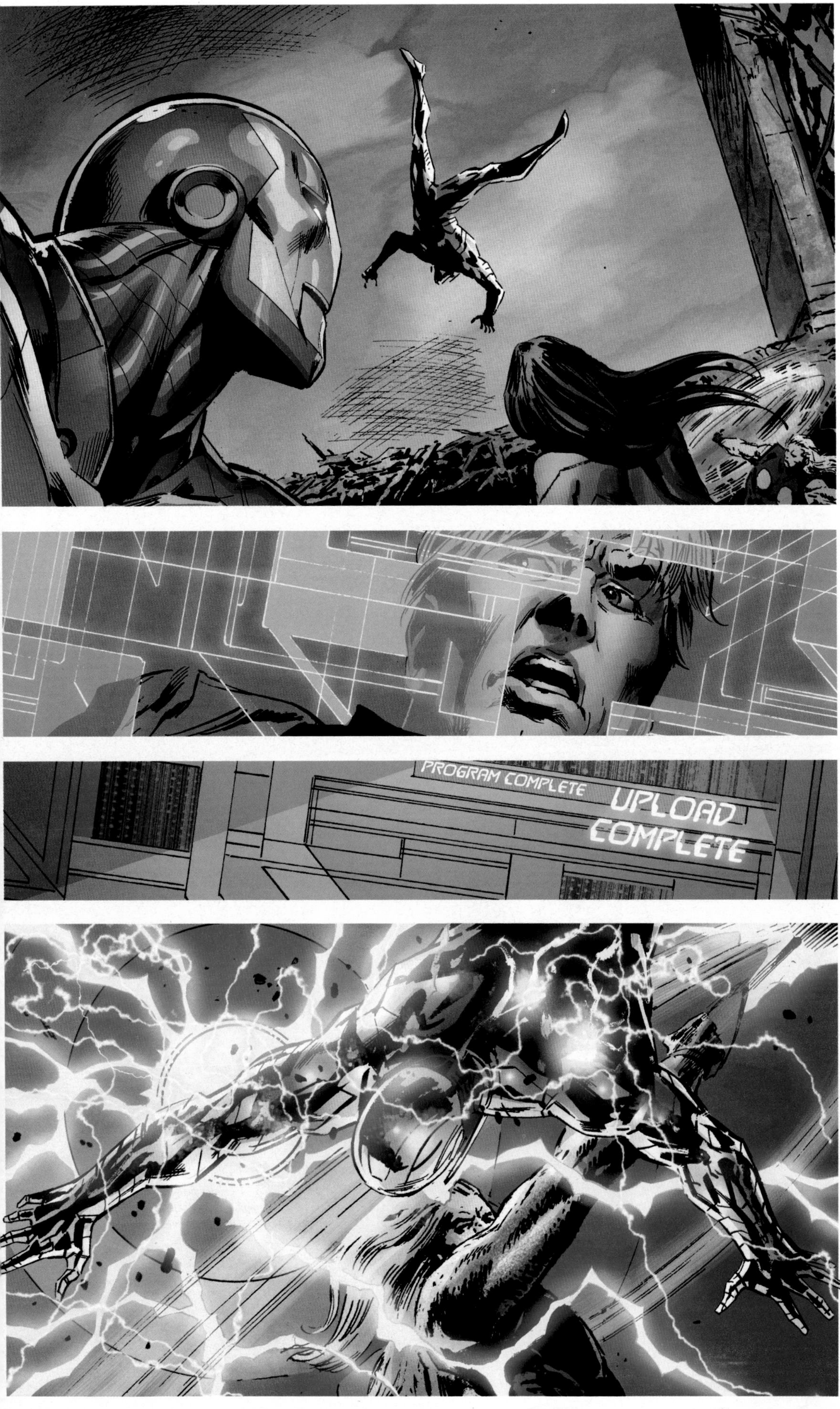
PROGRAM COMPLETE
UPLOAD COMPLETE

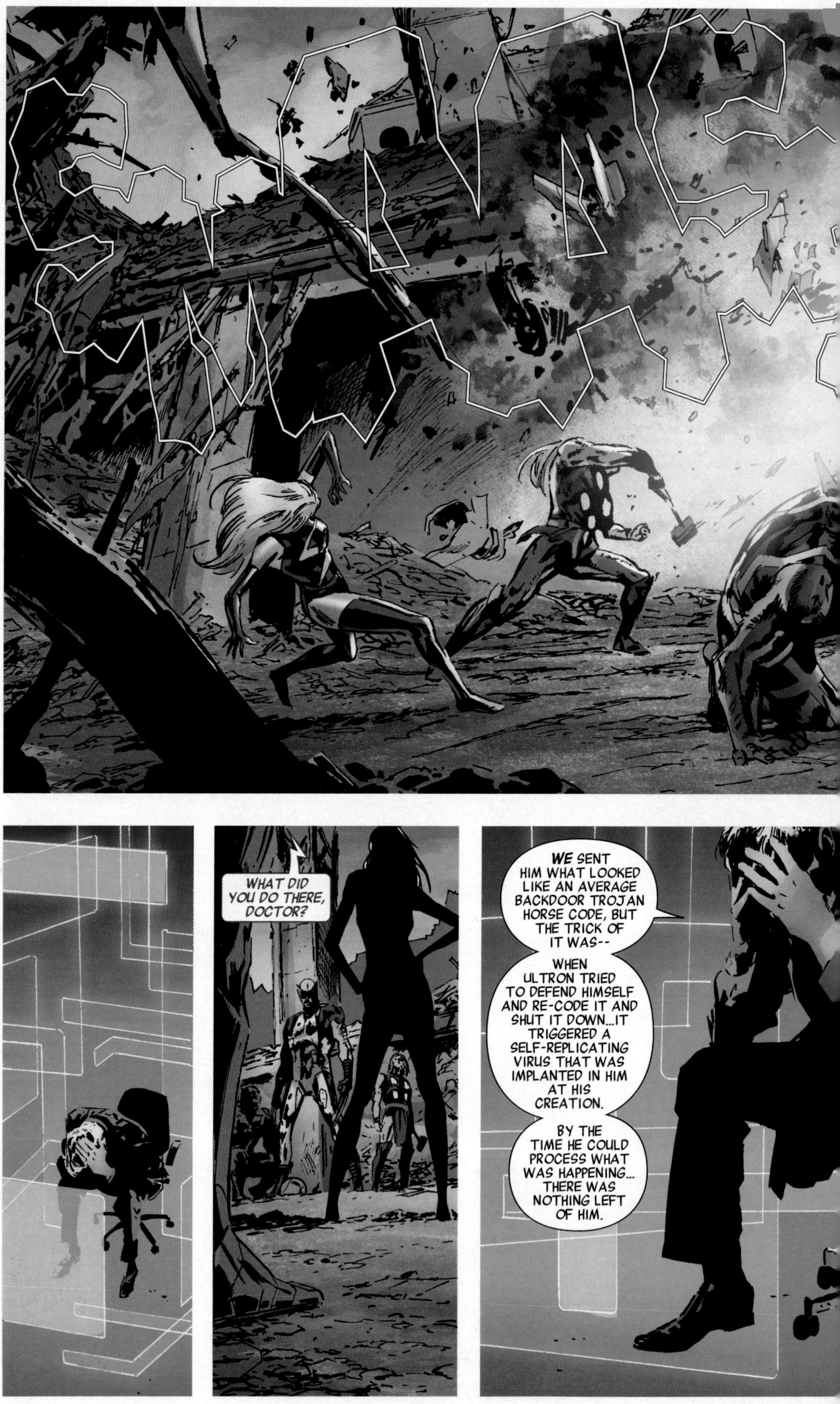
WHAT DID YOU DO THERE, DOCTOR?
WE SENT HIM WHAT LOOKED LIKE AN AVERAGE BACKDOOR TROJAN HORSE CODE, BUT THE TRICK OF IT WAS--
WHEN ULTRON TRIED TO DEFEND HIMSELF AND RE-CODE IT AND SHUT IT DOWN...IT TRIGGERED A SELF-REPLICATING VIRUS THAT WAS IMPLANTED IN HIM AT HIS CREATION.
BY THE TIME HE COULD PROCESS WHAT WAS HAPPENING... THERE WAS NOTHING LEFT OF HIM.

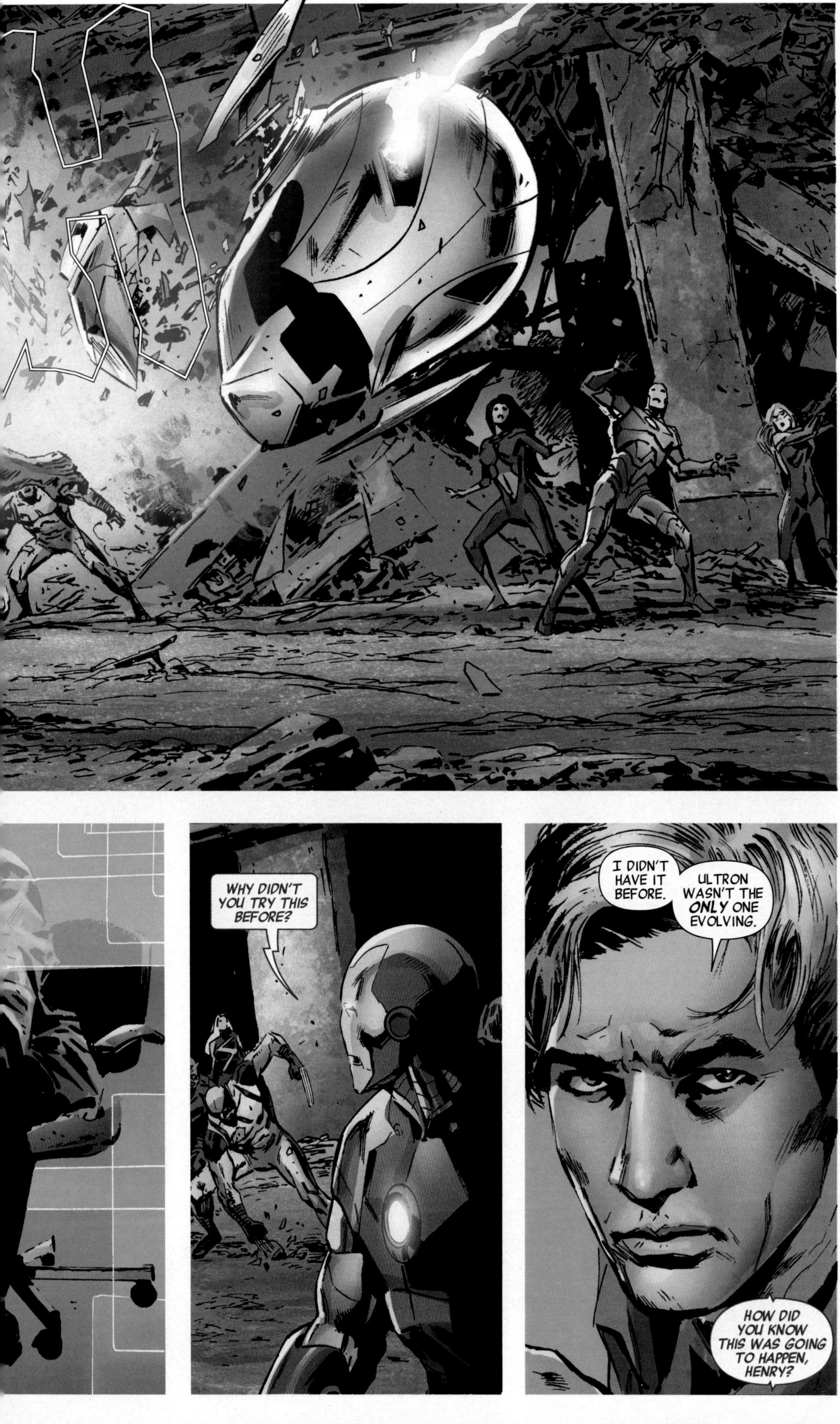
WHY DIDN'T YOU TRY THIS BEFORE?
I DIDN'T HAVE IT BEFORE.
ULTRON WASN'T THE **ONLY** ONE EVOLVING.
HOW DID YOU KNOW THIS WAS GOING TO HAPPEN, HENRY?

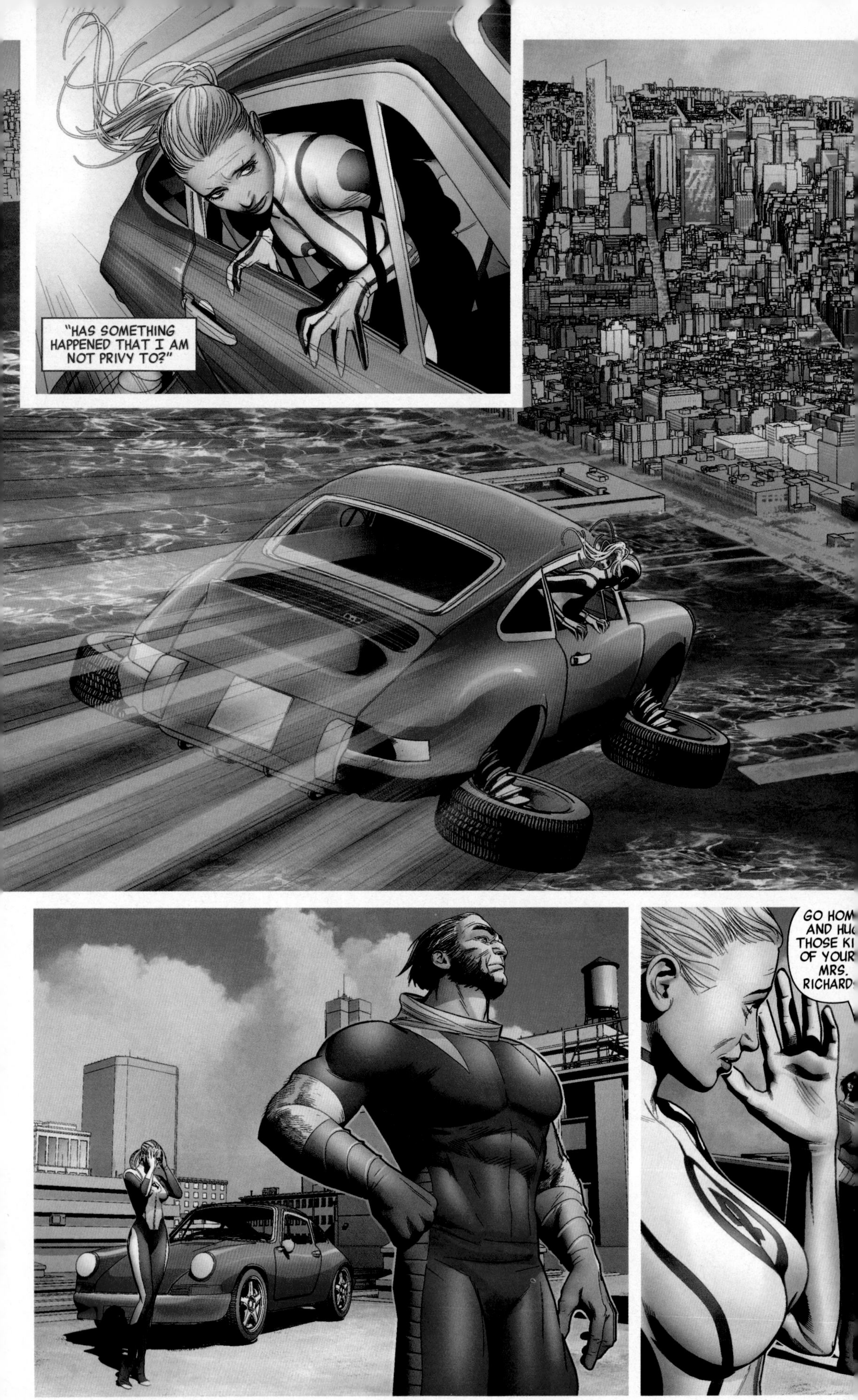
"HAS SOMETHING
HAPPENED THAT I AM
NOT PRIVY TO?"
GO HOM
AND HU
THOSE KI
OF YOUR
MRS.
RICHARD

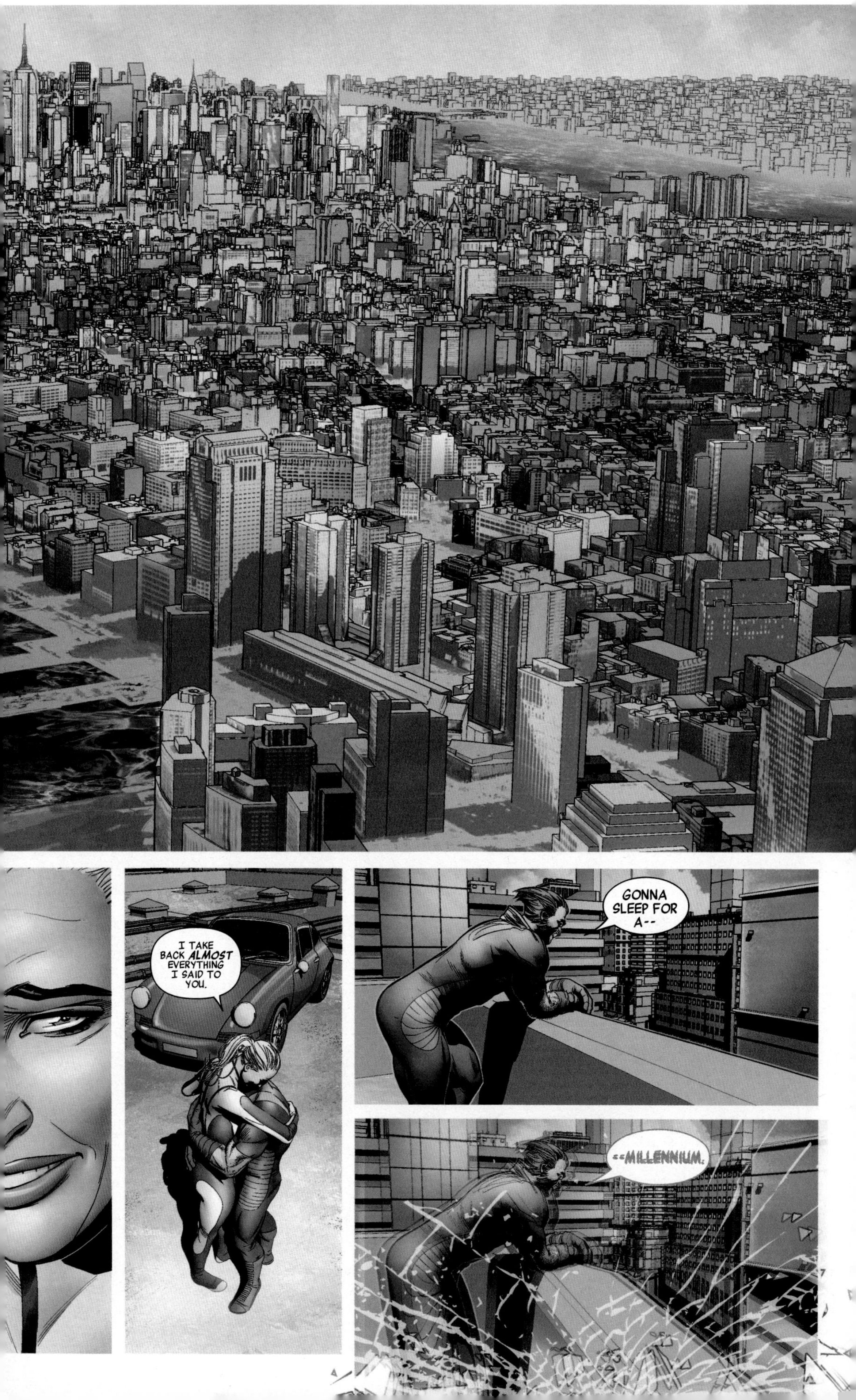
I TAKE BACK ALMOST EVERYTHING I SAID TO YOU.
GONNA SLEEP FOR A--
--MILLENNIUM.

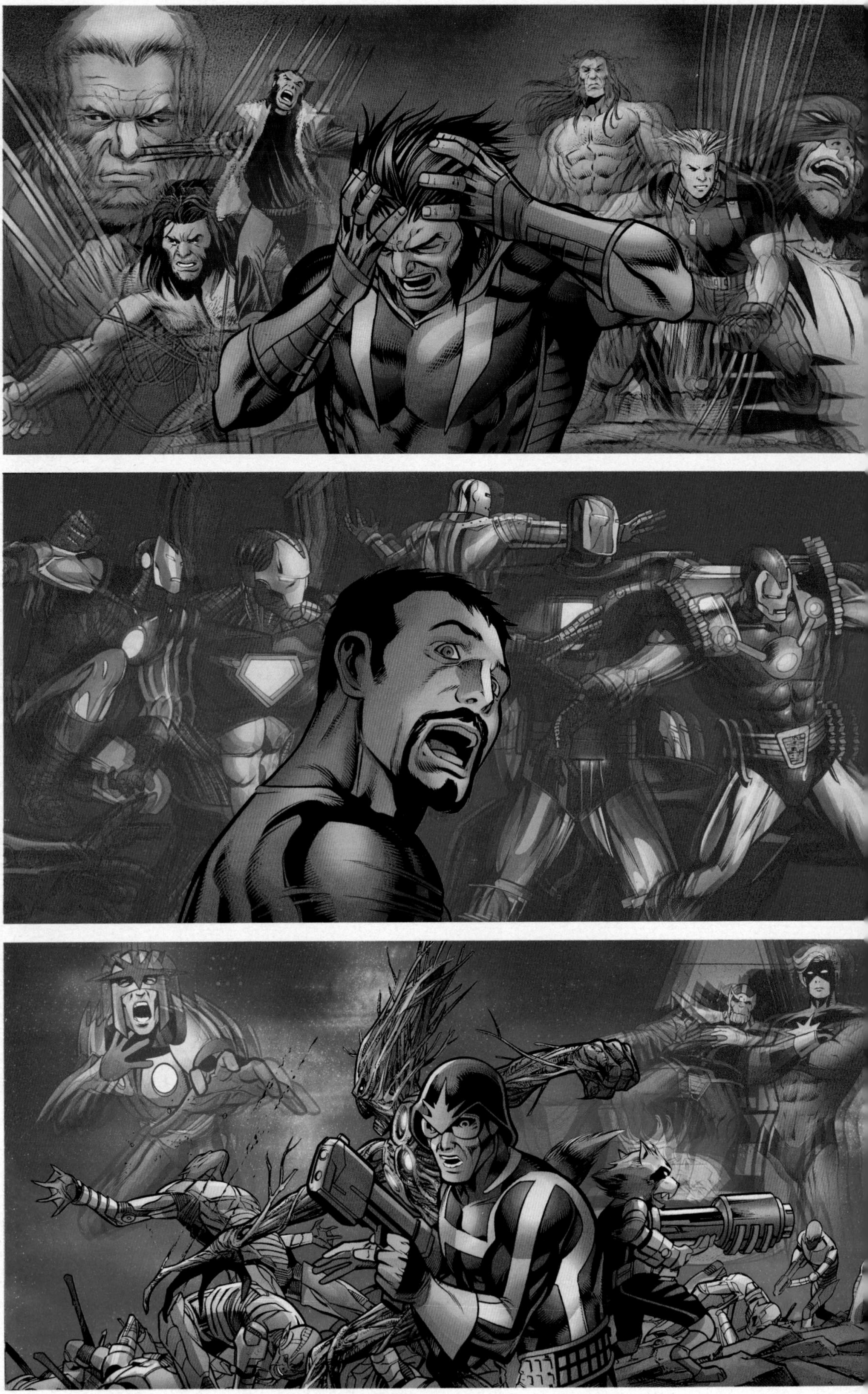

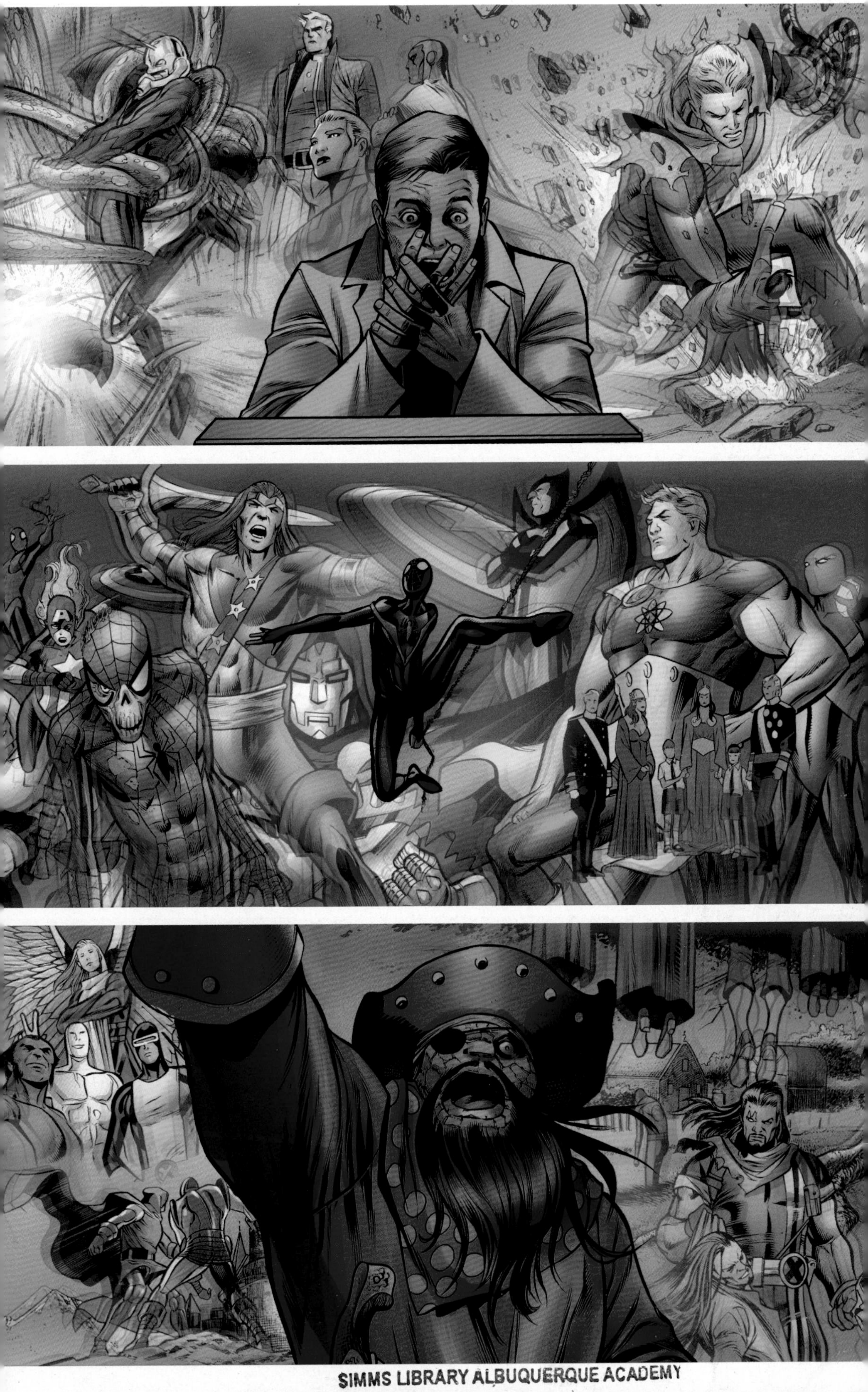

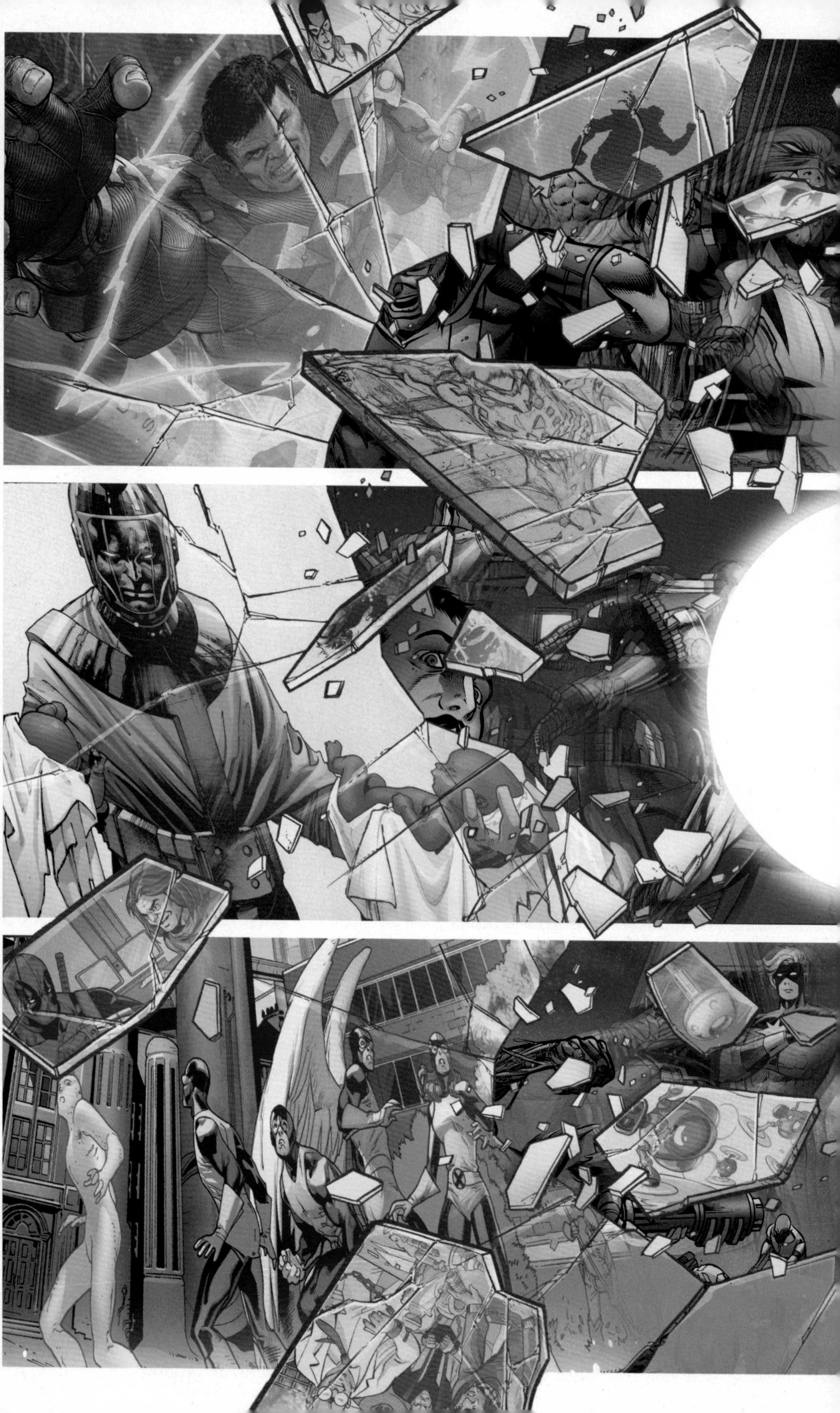

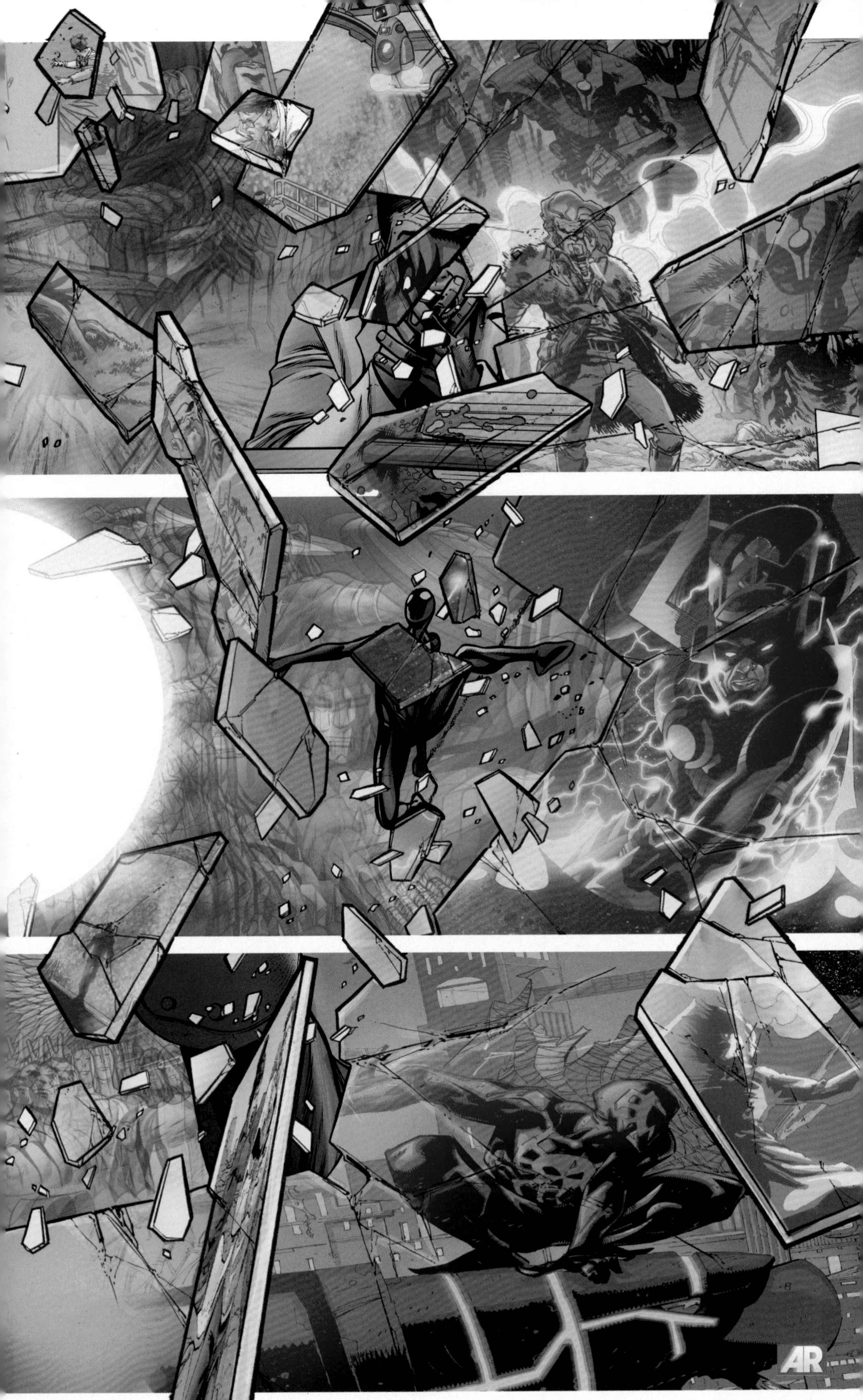

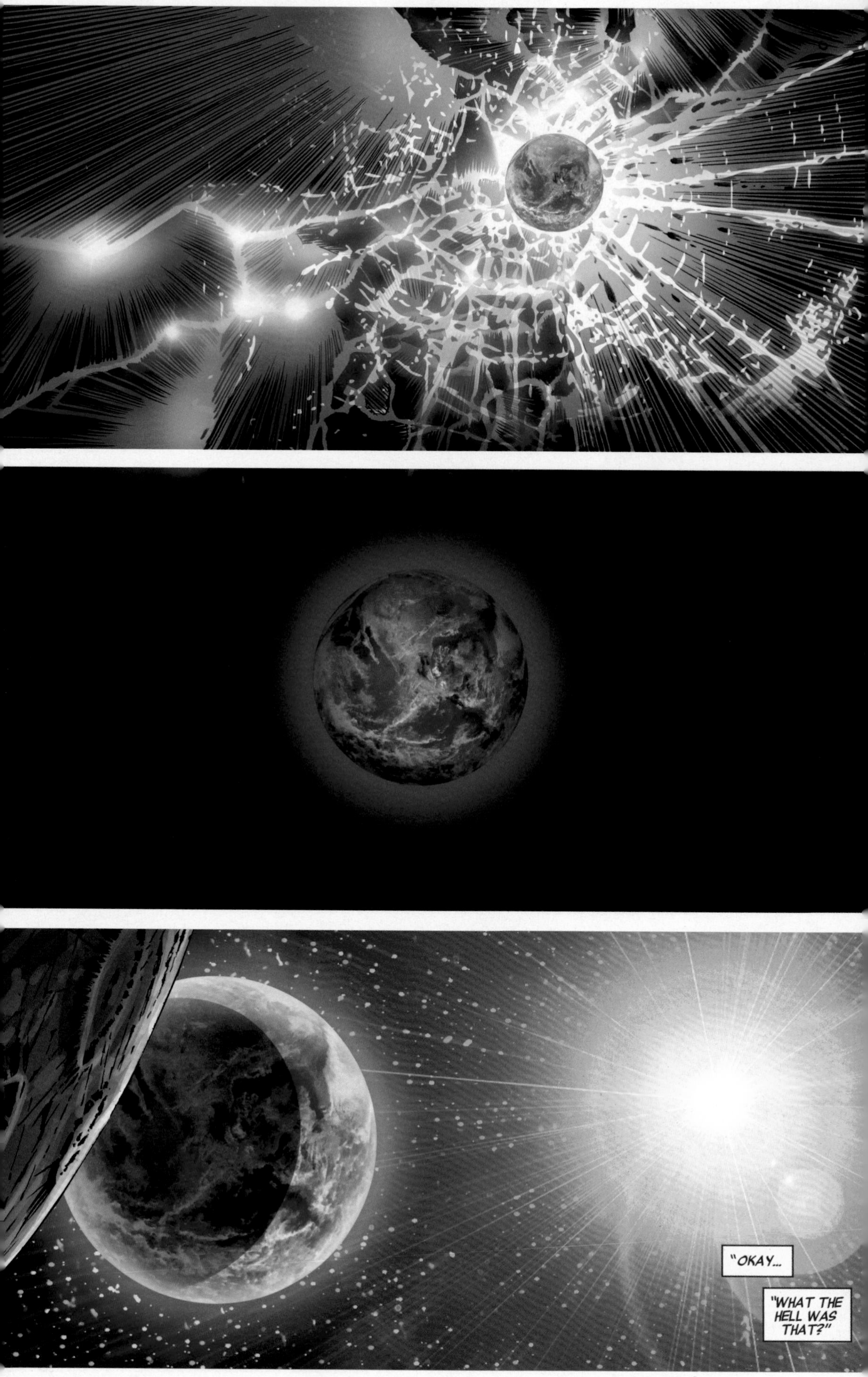
"OKAY...
"WHAT THE HELL WAS THAT?"

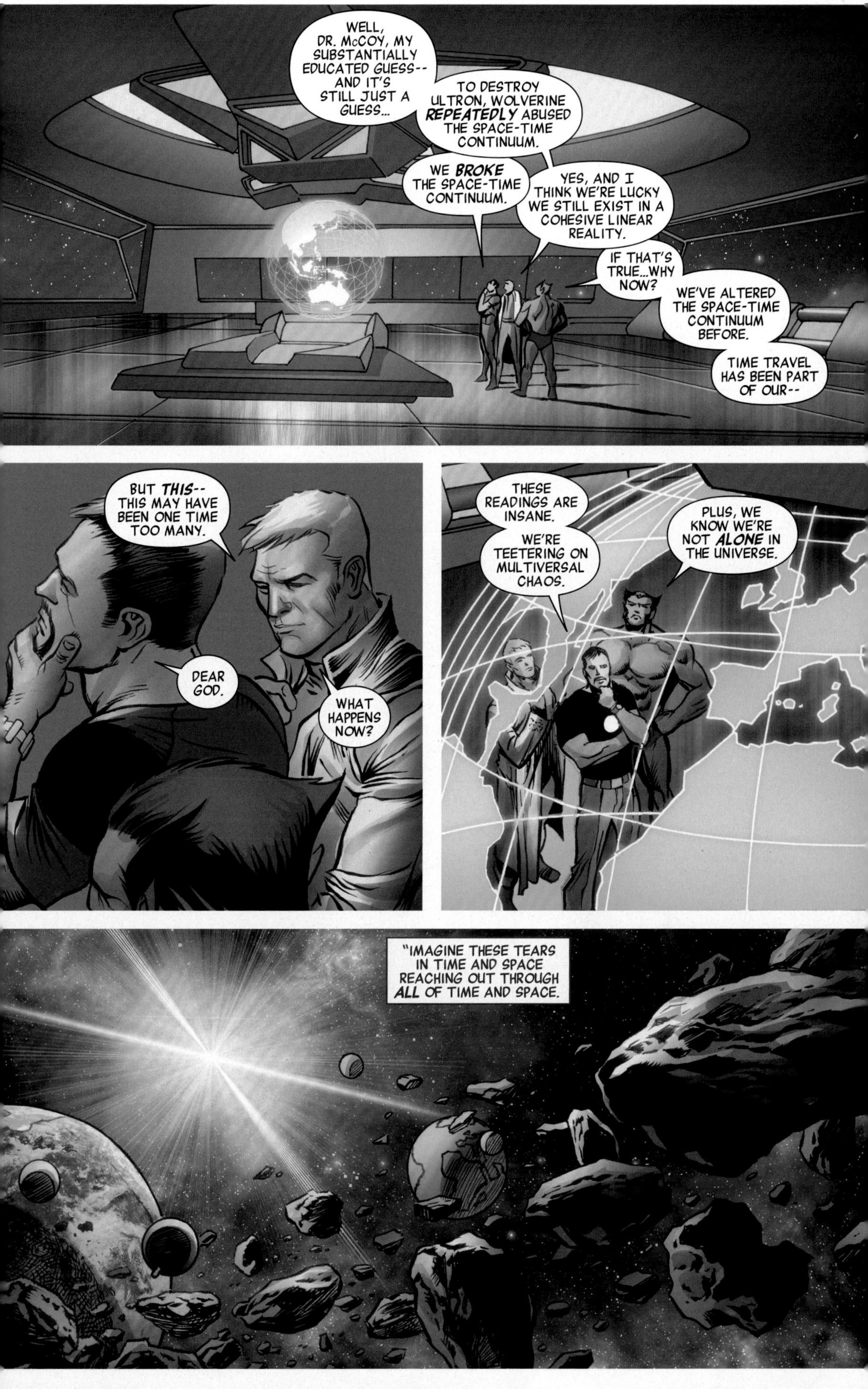
WELL, DR. McCOY, MY SUBSTANTIALLY EDUCATED GUESS-- AND IT'S STILL JUST A GUESS...
TO DESTROY ULTRON, WOLVERINE REPEATEDLY ABUSED THE SPACE-TIME CONTINUUM.
WE BROKE THE SPACE-TIME CONTINUUM.
YES, AND I THINK WE'RE LUCKY WE STILL EXIST IN A COHESIVE LINEAR REALITY.
IF THAT'S TRUE...WHY NOW?
WE'VE ALTERED THE SPACE-TIME CONTINUUM BEFORE.
TIME TRAVEL HAS BEEN PART OF OUR--
BUT THIS-- THIS MAY HAVE BEEN ONE TIME TOO MANY.
DEAR GOD.
WHAT HAPPENS NOW?
THESE READINGS ARE INSANE.
WE'RE TEETERING ON MULTIVERSAL CHAOS.
PLUS, WE KNOW WE'RE NOT ALONE IN THE UNIVERSE.
"IMAGINE THESE TEARS IN TIME AND SPACE REACHING OUT THROUGH ALL OF TIME AND SPACE.

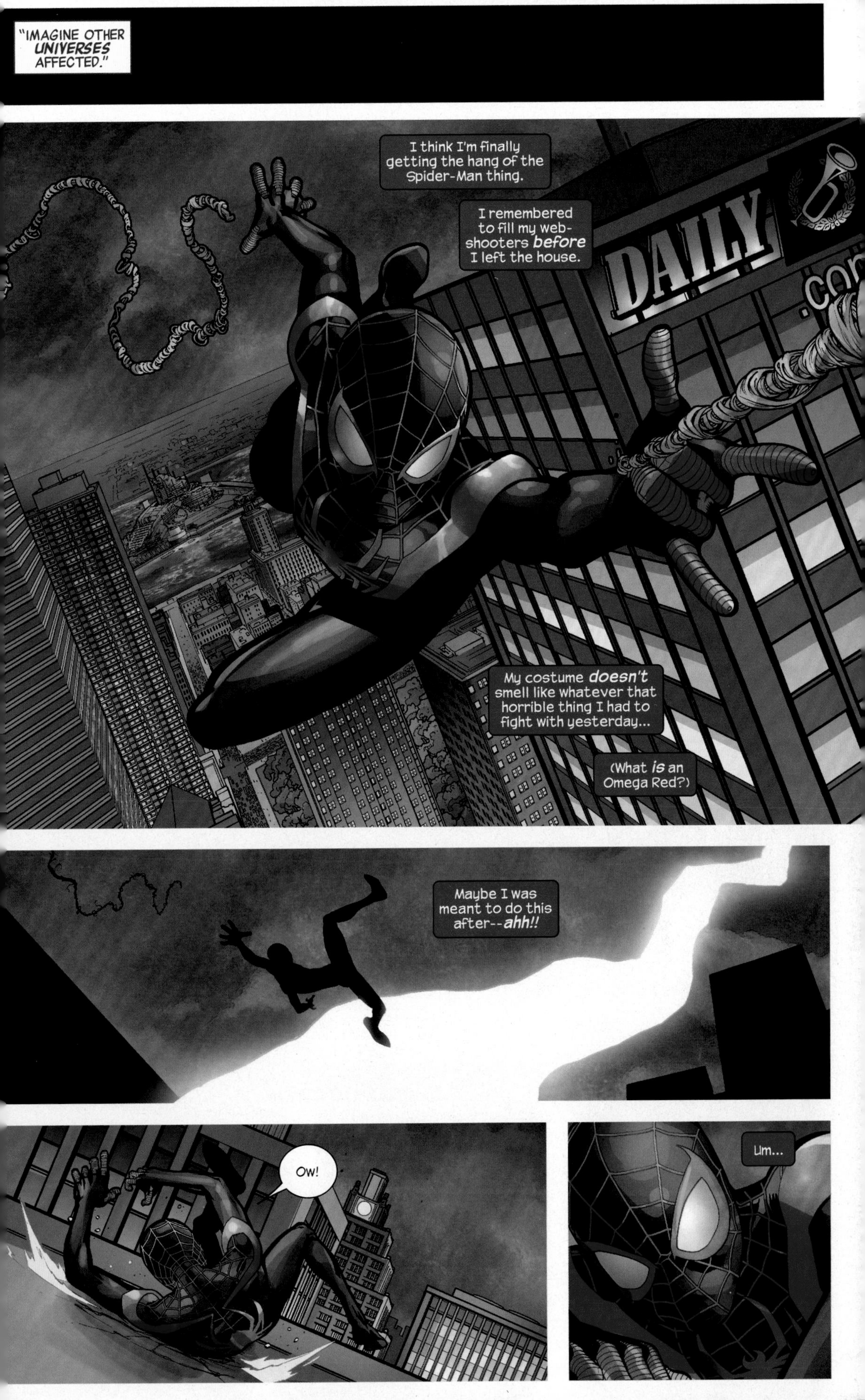
"IMAGINE OTHER UNIVERSES AFFECTED."
I think I'm finally getting the hang of the Spider-Man thing.
I remembered to fill my web-shooters before I left the house.
DAILY
My costume doesn't smell like whatever that horrible thing I had to fight with yesterday...
(What is an Omega Red?)
Maybe I was meant to do this after--ahh!!
Ow!
Um...

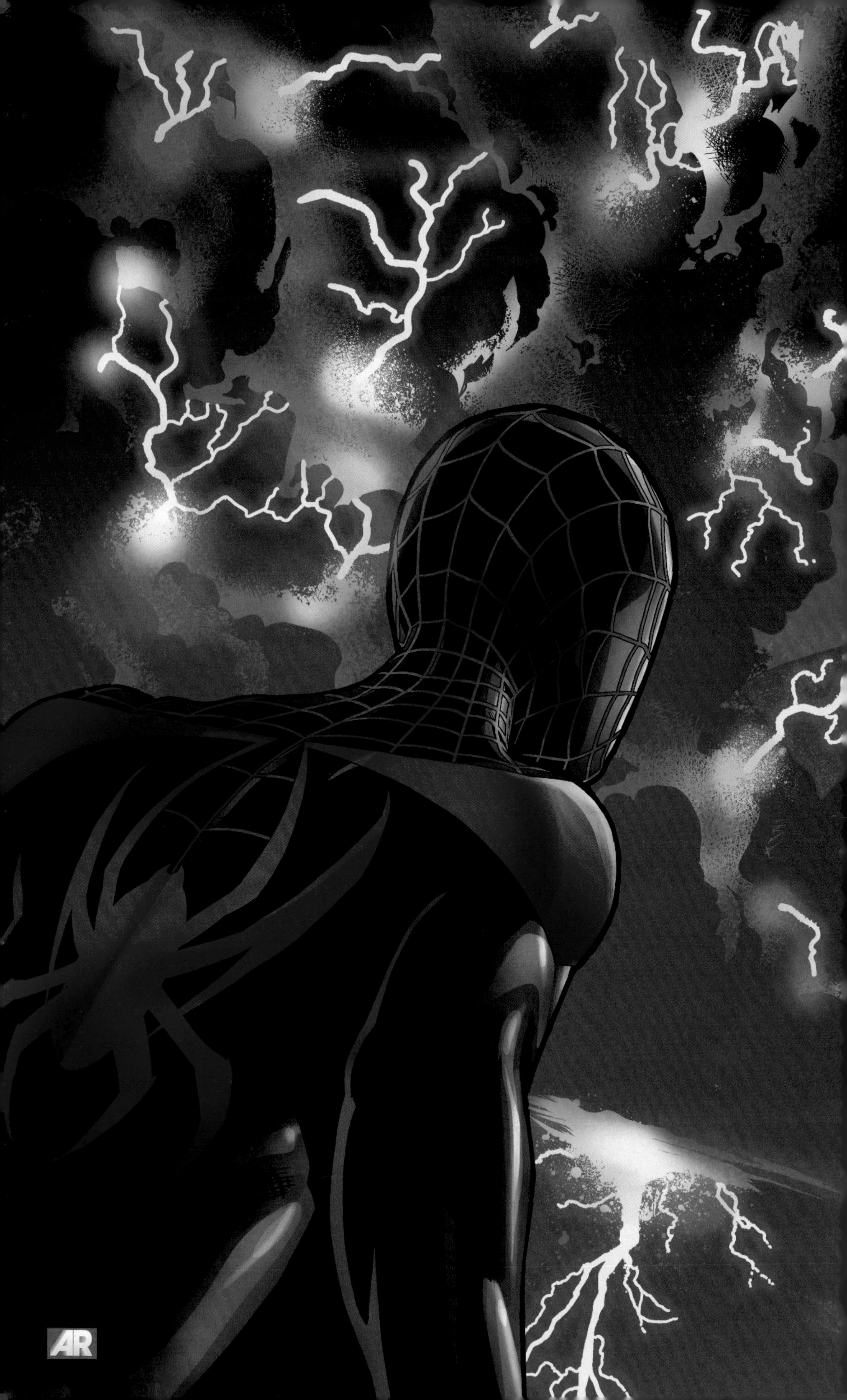

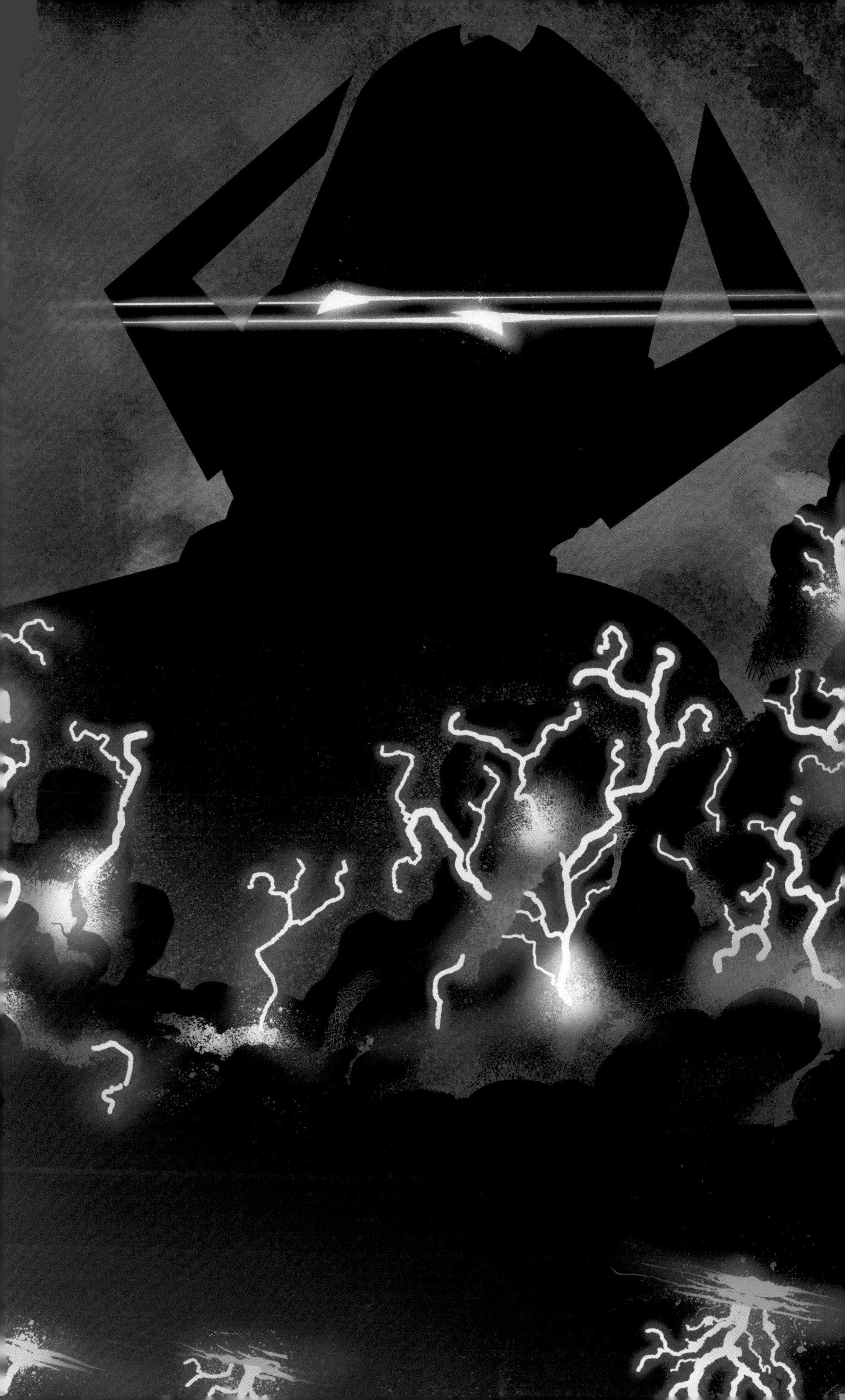

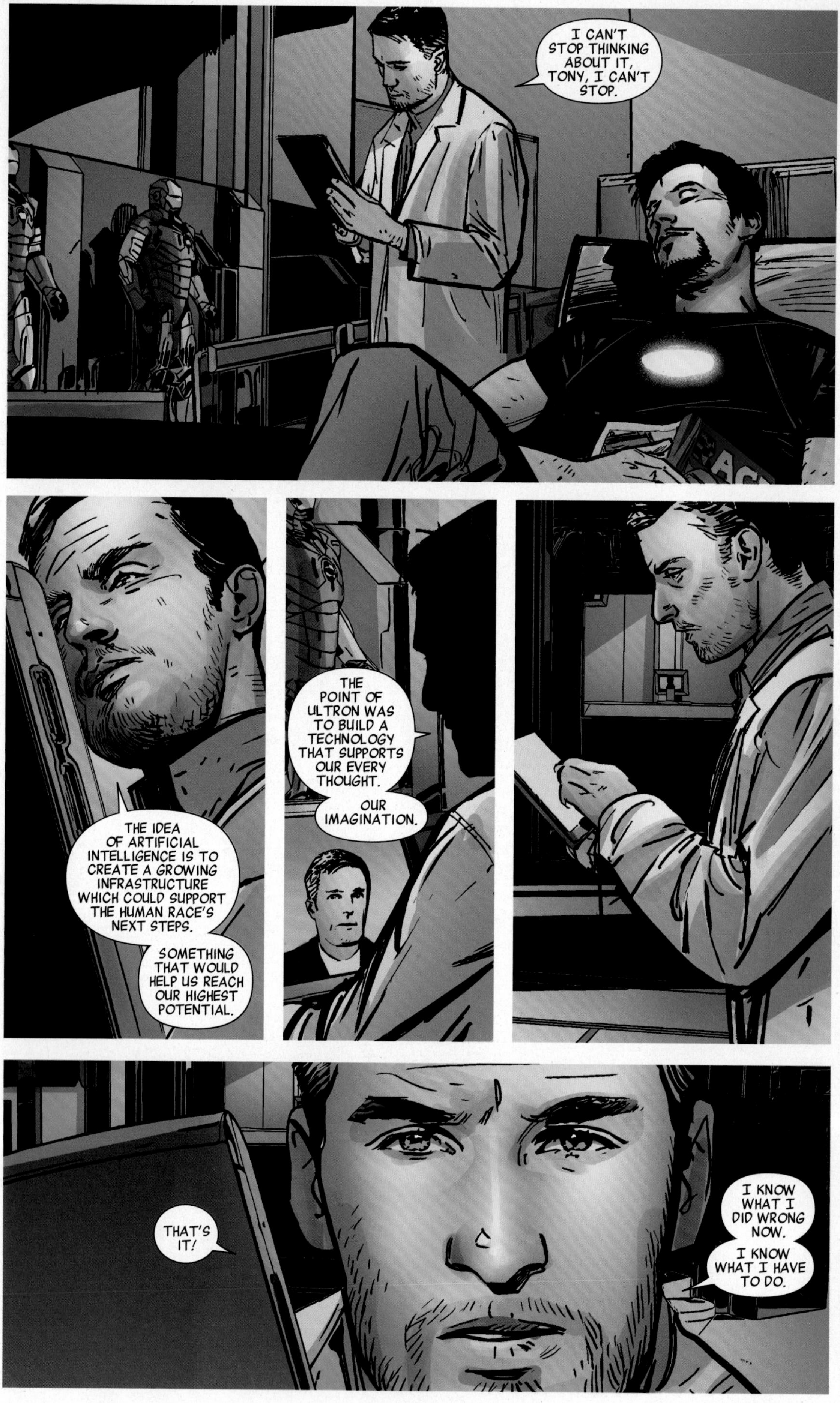
I CAN'T STOP THINKING ABOUT IT, TONY, I CAN'T STOP.
THE IDEA OF ARTIFICIAL INTELLIGENCE IS TO CREATE A GROWING INFRASTRUCTURE WHICH COULD SUPPORT THE HUMAN RACE'S NEXT STEPS.
SOMETHING THAT WOULD HELP US REACH OUR HIGHEST POTENTIAL.
THE POINT OF ULTRON WAS TO BUILD A TECHNOLOGY THAT SUPPORTS OUR EVERY THOUGHT.
OUR IMAGINATION.
THAT'S IT!
I KNOW WHAT I DID WRONG NOW.
I KNOW WHAT I HAVE TO DO.

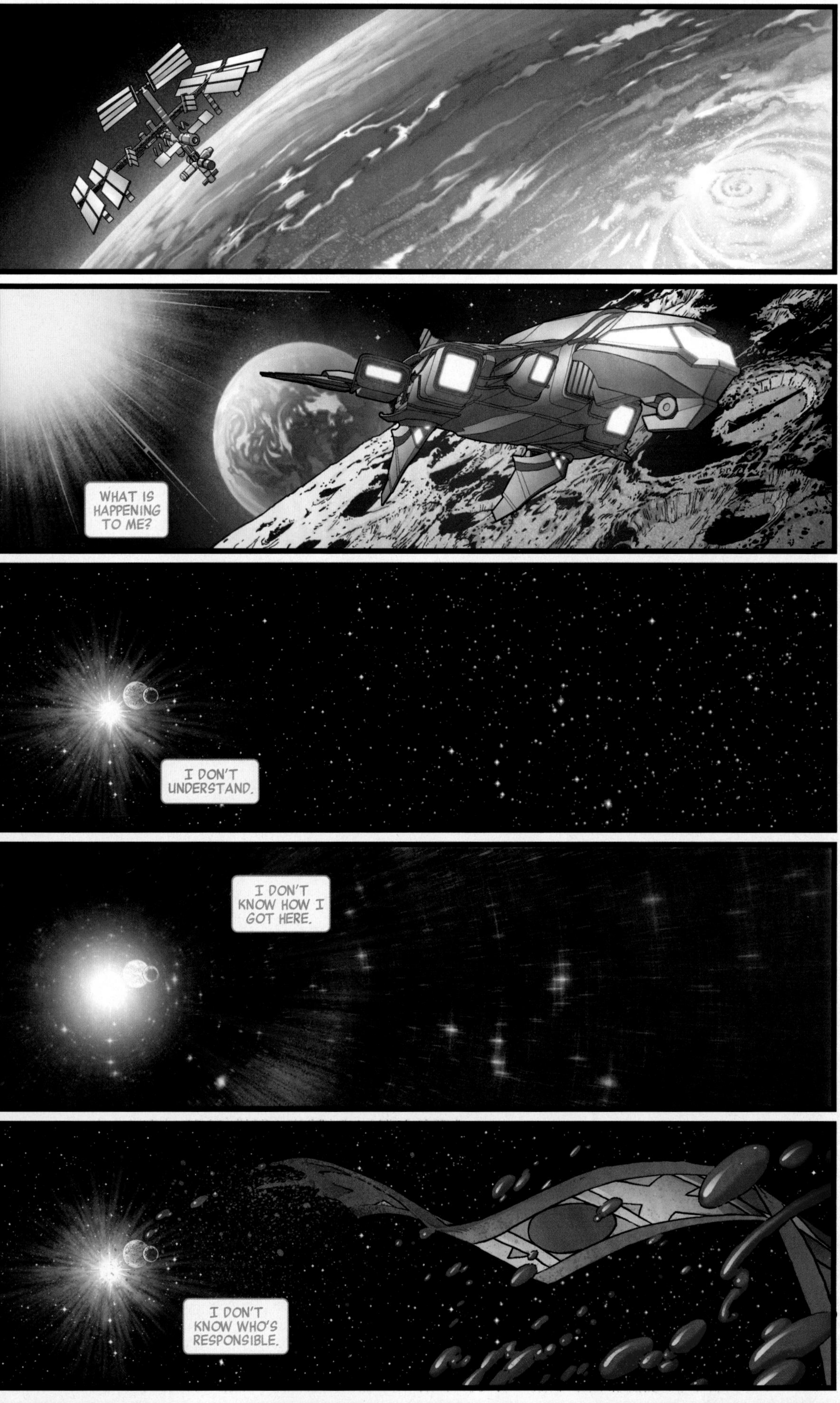

WHAT IS HAPPENING TO ME?
I DON'T UNDERSTAND.
I DON'T KNOW HOW I GOT HERE.
I DON'T KNOW WHO'S RESPONSIBLE.

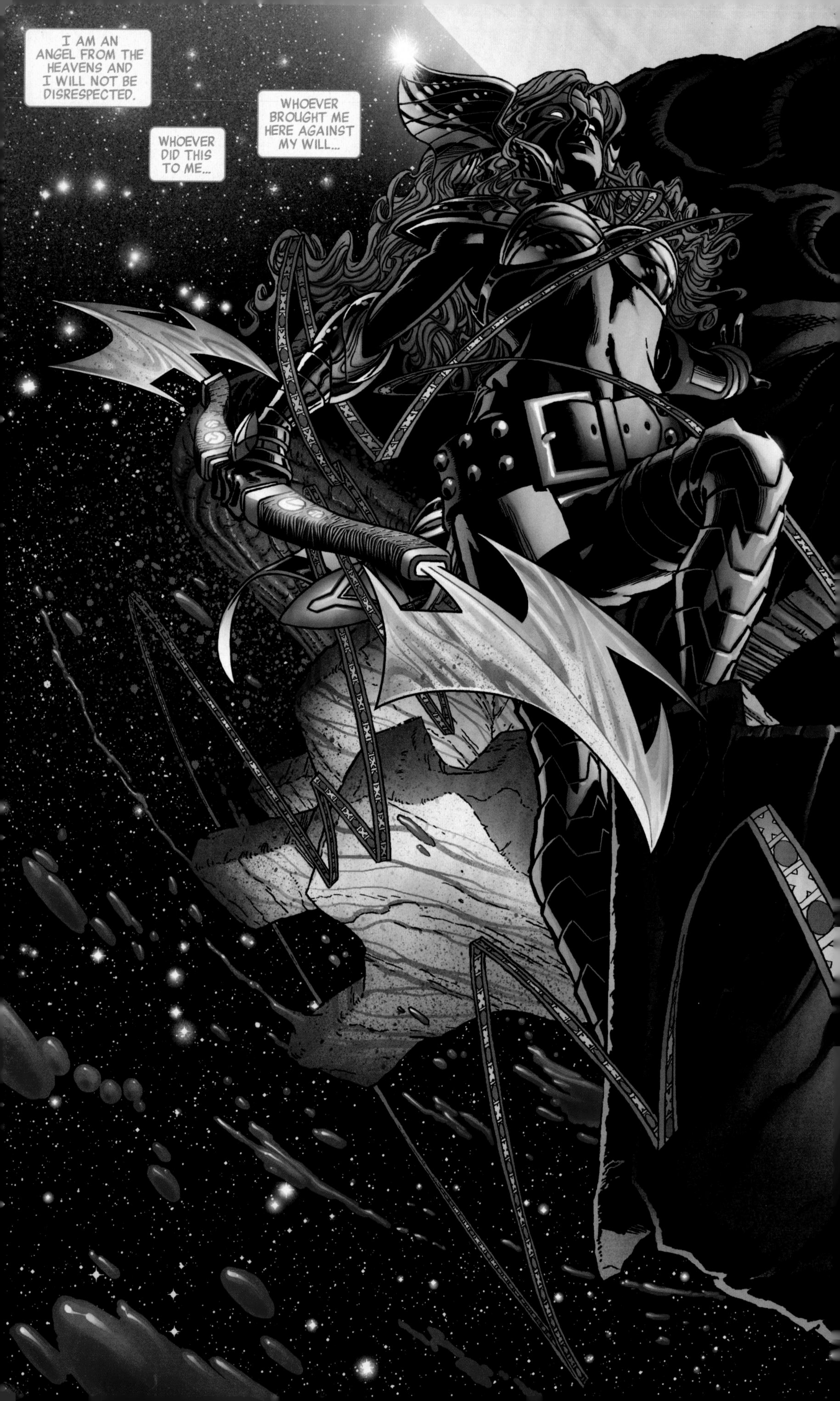
I AM AN ANGEL FROM THE HEAVENS AND I WILL NOT BE DISRESPECTED.
WHOEVER DID THIS TO ME...
WHOEVER BROUGHT ME HERE AGAINST MY WILL...

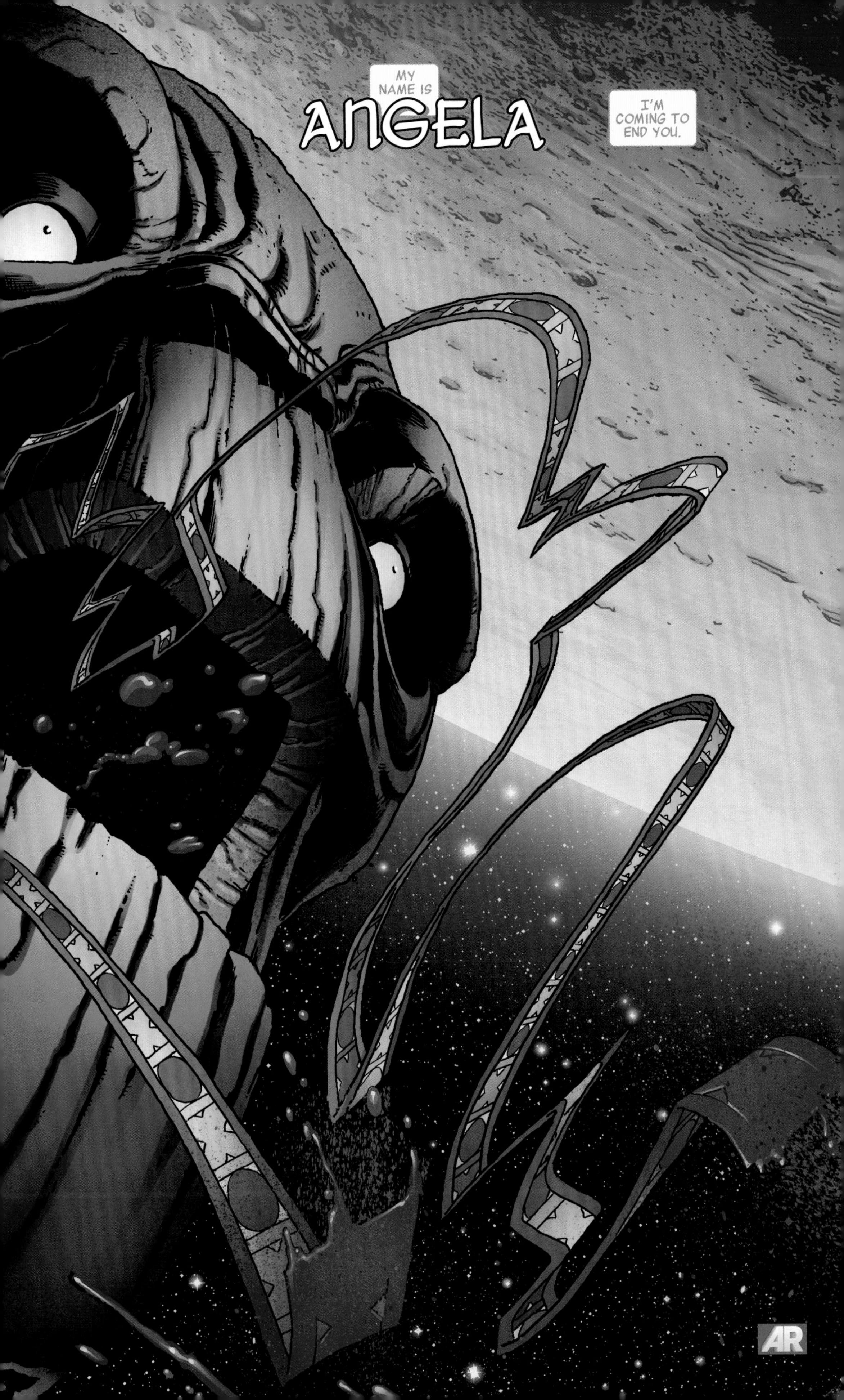
MY NAME IS
ANGELA
I'M COMING TO END YOU.
AR

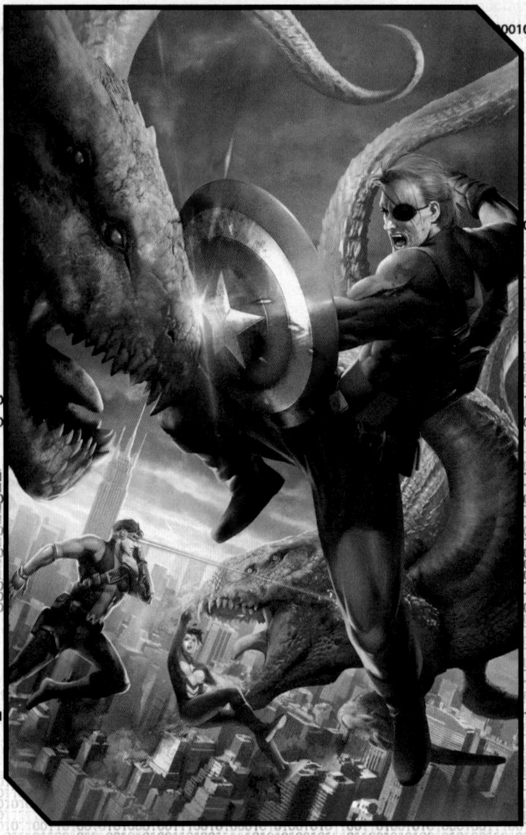

AGE OF ULTRON #8 VARIANT
BY 7TH ORANGE

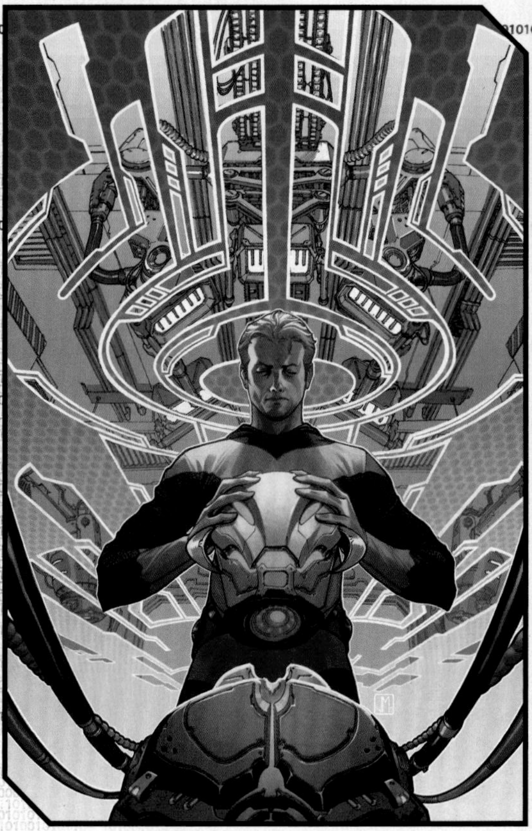

AGE OF ULTRON #9 VARIANT
BY JORGE MOLINA

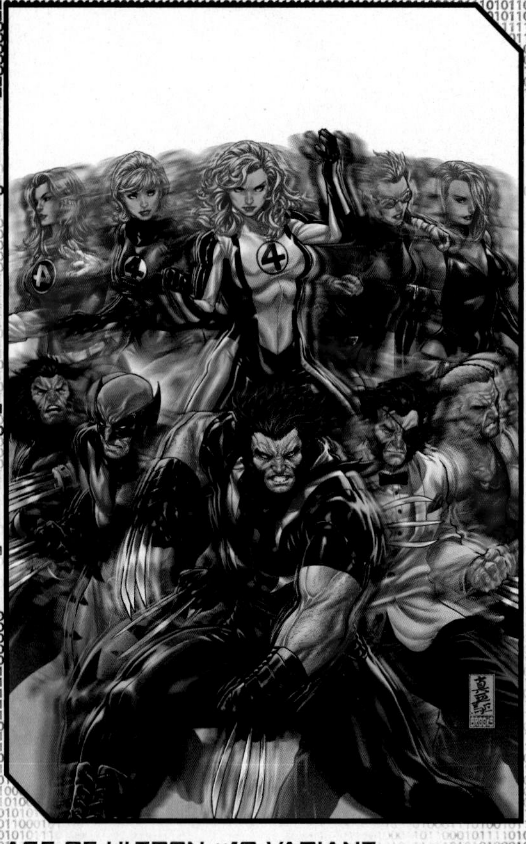

AGE OF ULTRON #10 VARIANT
BY MARK BROOKS

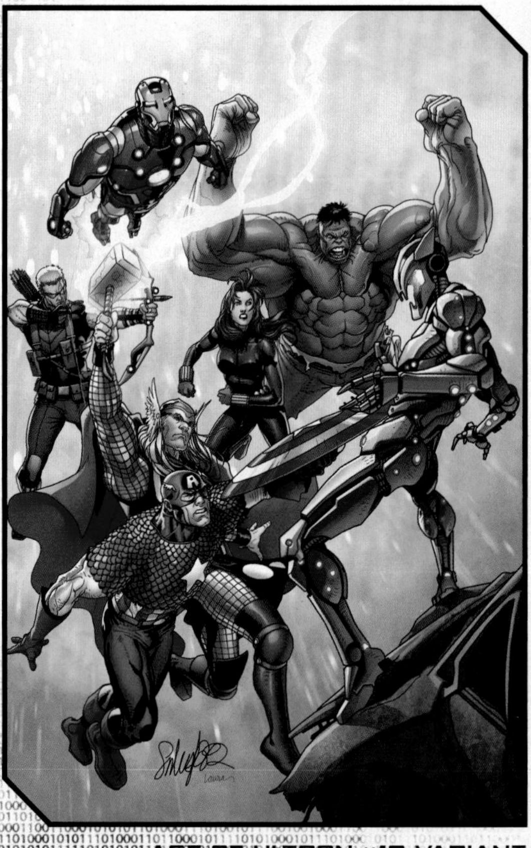

AGE OF ULTRON #10 VARIANT
BY SALVADOR LARROCA & LAURA MARTIN

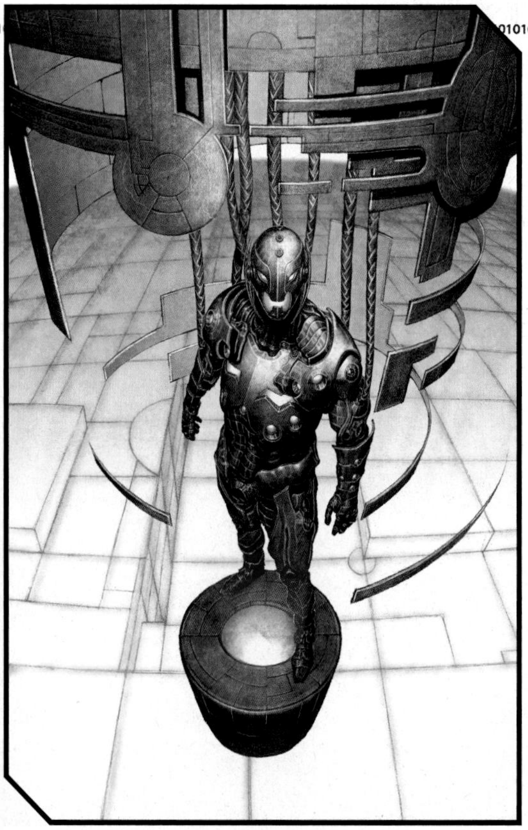

AGE OF ULTRON #1 VARIANT
BY ROCK-HE KIM

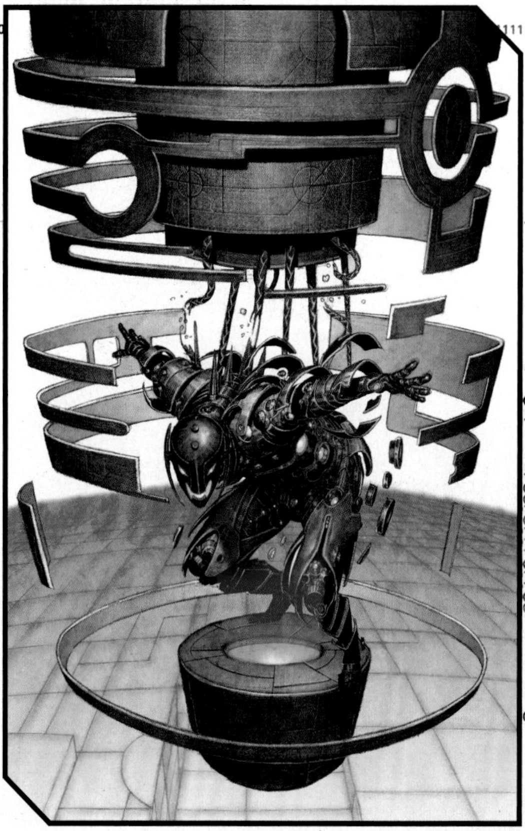

AGE OF ULTRON #2 VARIANT
BY ROCK-HE KIM

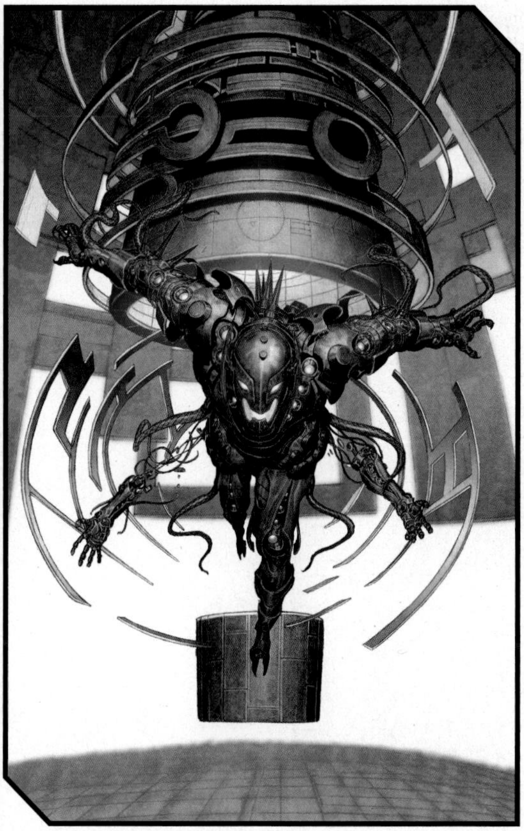

AGE OF ULTRON #3 VARIANT
BY ROCK-HE KIM

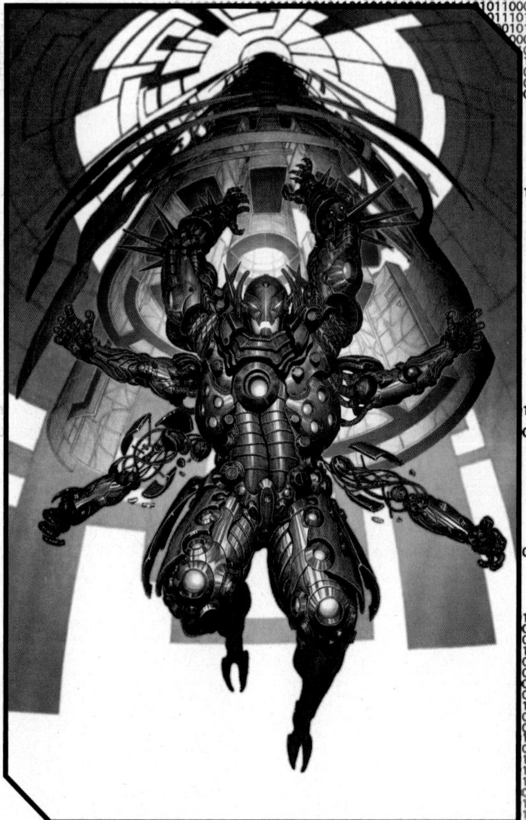

AGE OF ULTRON #4 VARIANT
BY ROCK-HE KIM

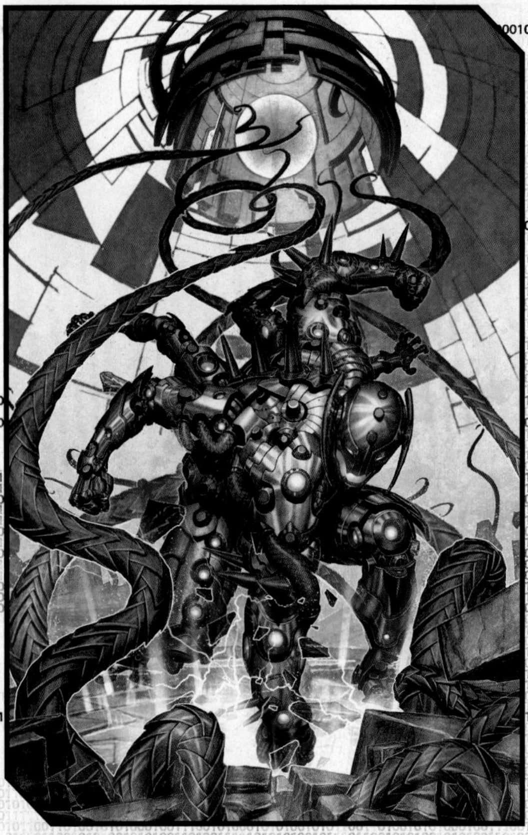

AGE OF ULTRON #5 VARIANT
BY ROCK-HE KIM

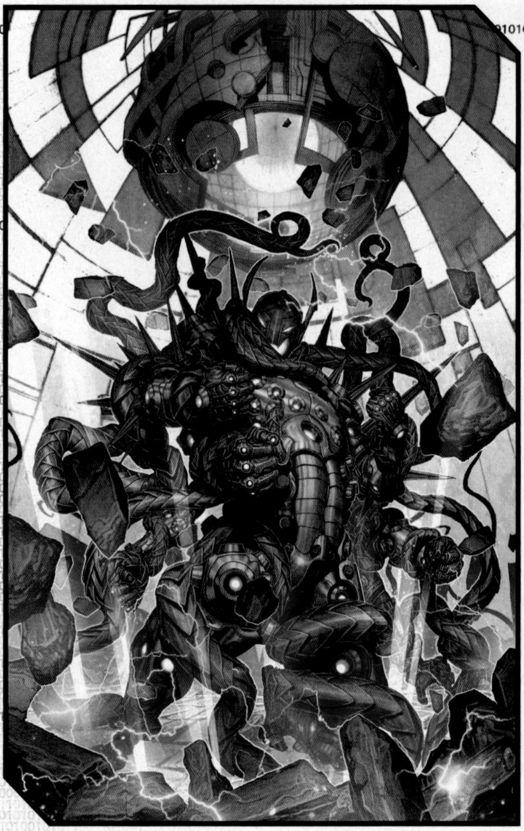

AGE OF ULTRON #6 VARIANT
BY ROCK-HE KIM

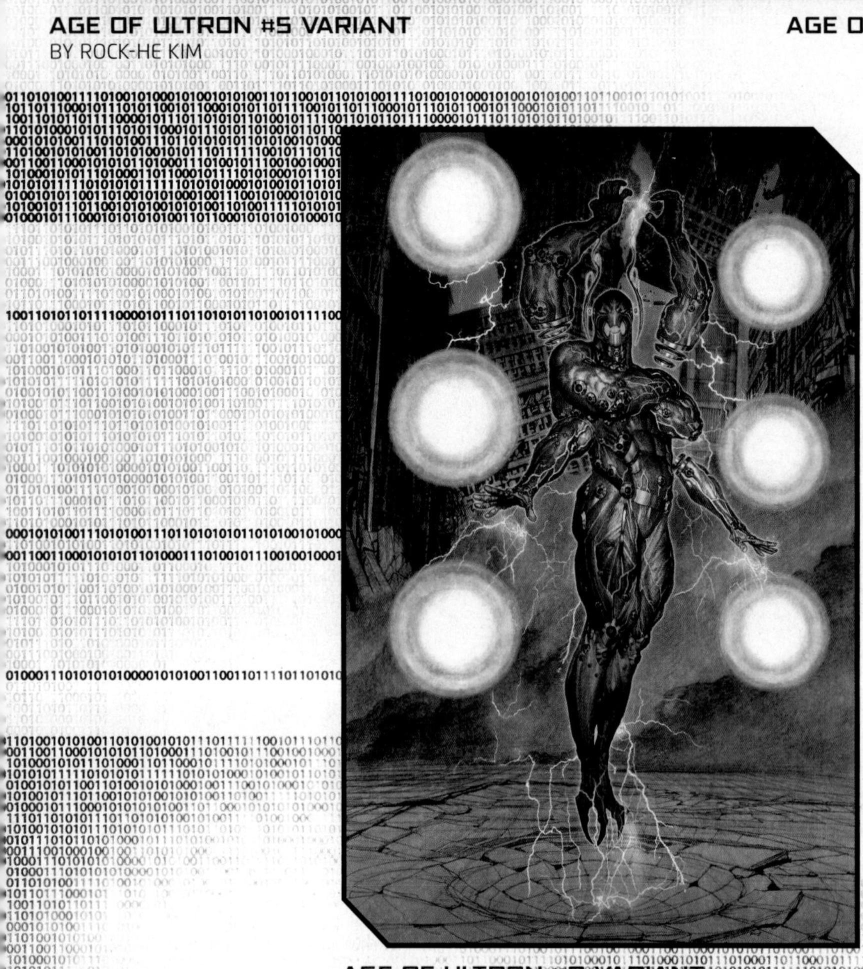

AGE OF ULTRON #9 VARIANT
BY ROCK-HE KIM

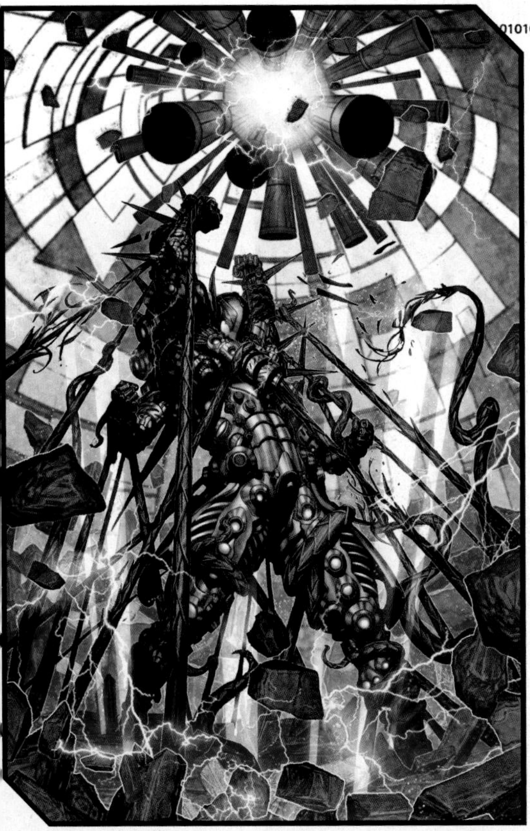

AGE OF ULTRON #7 VARIANT
BY ROCK-HE KIM

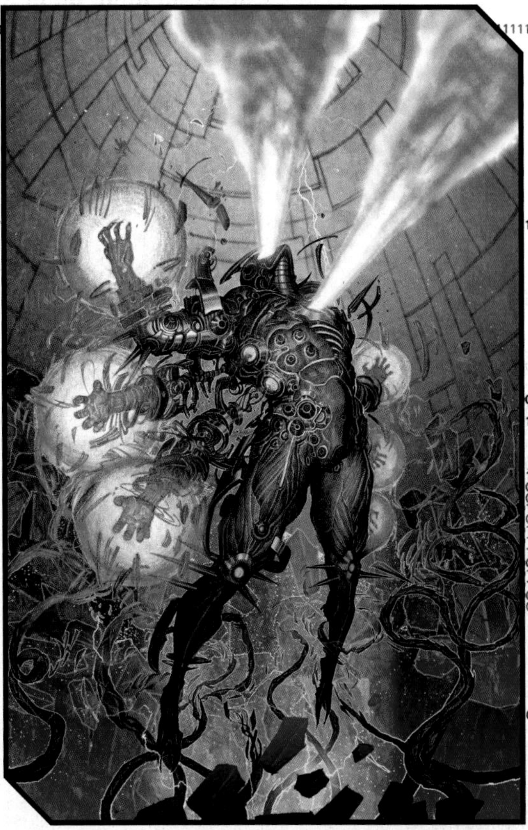

AGE OF ULTRON #8 VARIANT
BY ROCK-HE KIM

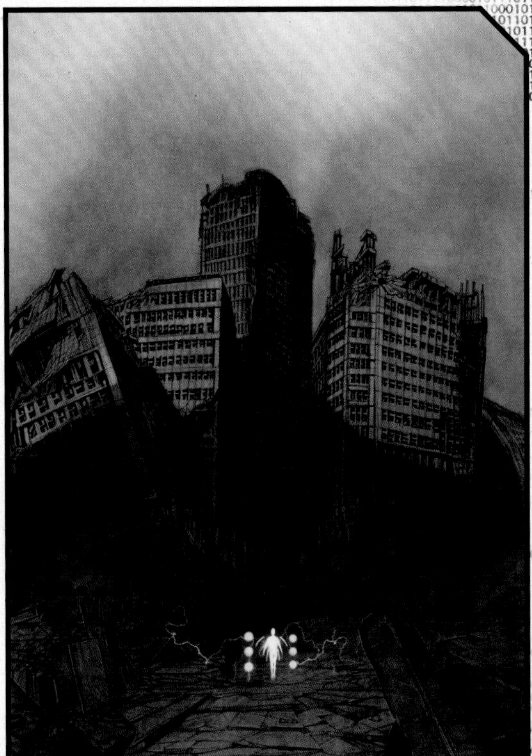

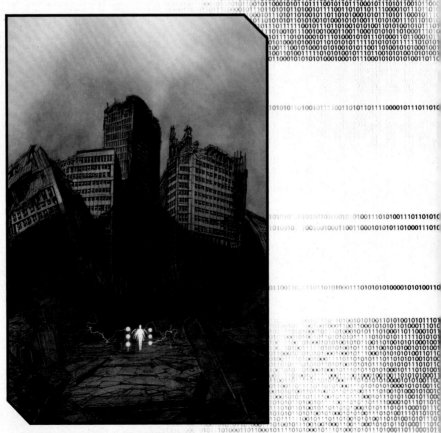

AGE OF ULTRON #10 VARIANT
BY ROCK-HE KIM

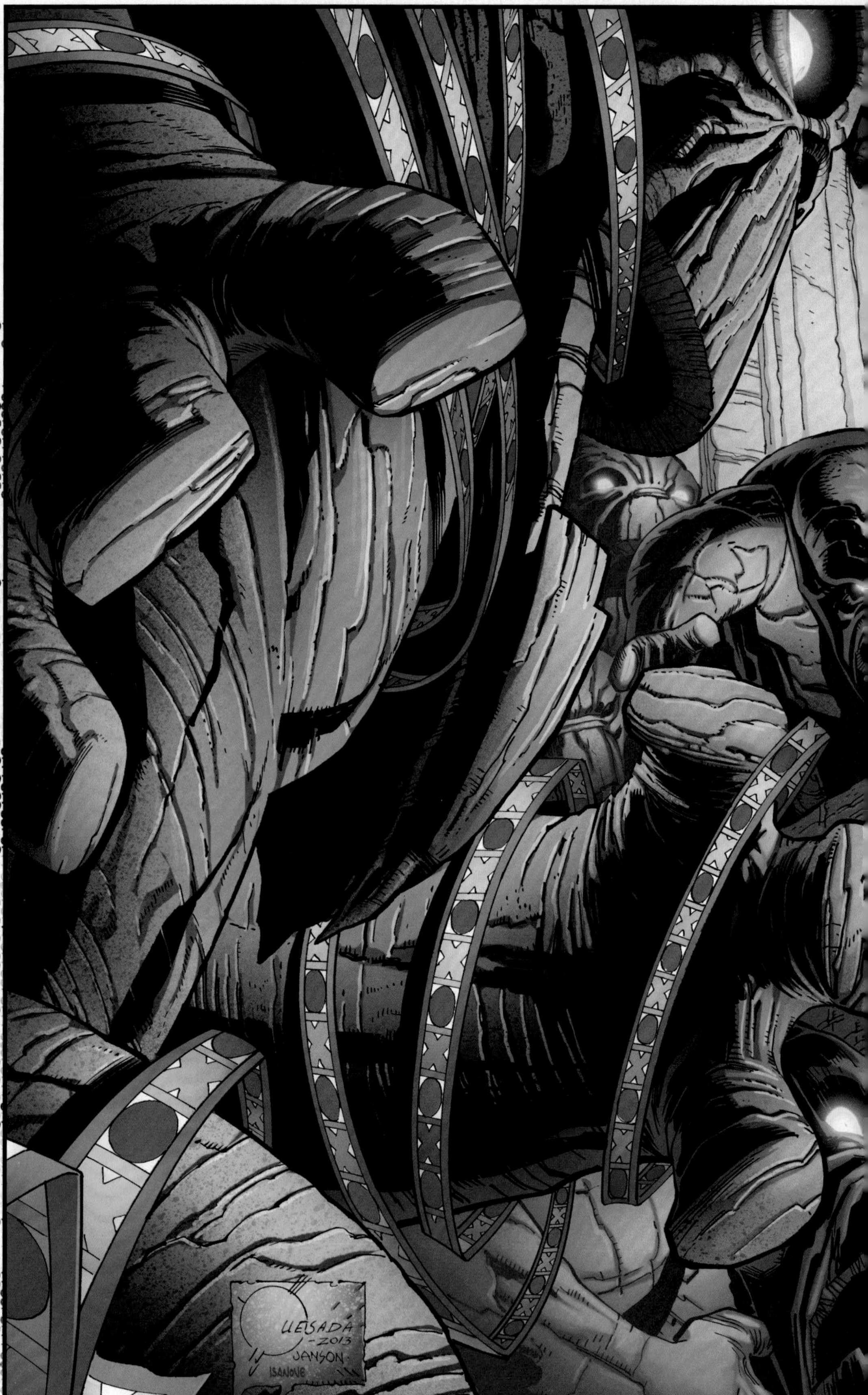
QUESADA
-2013
JANSON
ISANOVE

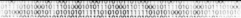

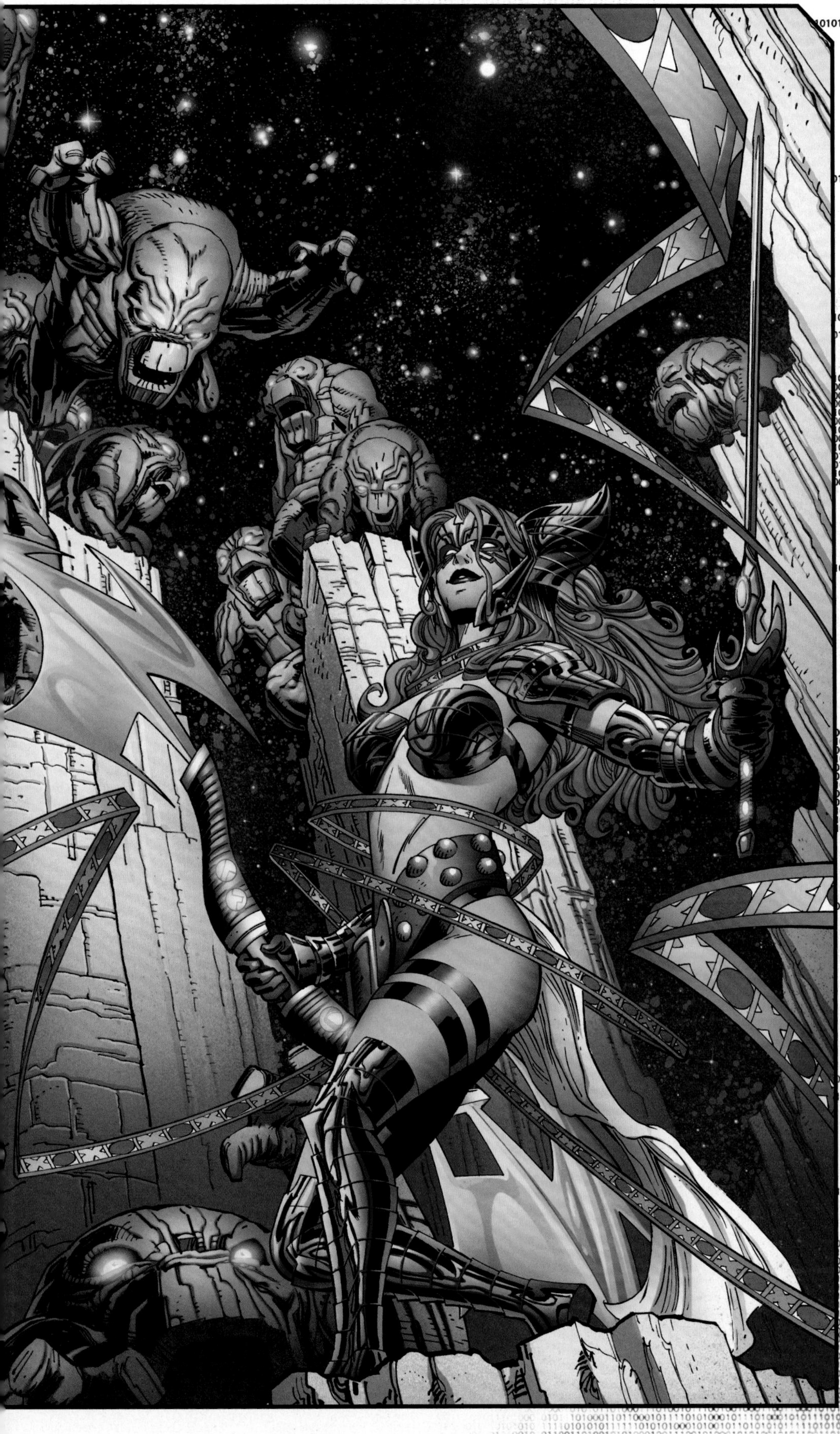

AGE OF ULTRON #10 VARIANT BY JOE QUESADA, KLAUS JANSON & RICHARD ISANOVE

MARVEL AUGMENTED REALITY (AR) ENHANCES AND CHANGES THE WAY YOU EXPERIENCE COMICS!

TO ACCESS THE FREE MARVEL AR CONTENT IN THIS BOOK*:

1. Locate the **AR** logo within the comic.
2. Go to Marvel.com/AR in your web browser.
3. Search by series title to find the corresponding AR.
4. Enjoy Marvel AR!

*All AR content that appears in this book has been archived and will be available only at Marvel.com/AR — no longer in the Marvel AR App. Content subject to change and availability.